KT-431-749

Greenwich Readers: 9

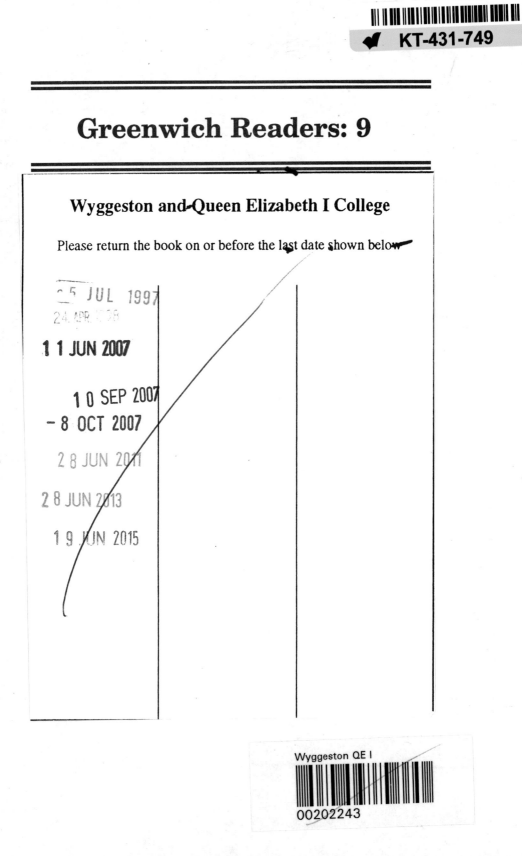

Wyggeston and Queen Elizabeth I College

Please return the book on or before the last date shown below

25 JUL 1997

24 APR 28

1 1 JUN 2007

1 0 SEP 2007

- 8 OCT 2007

2 8 JUN 2011

2 8 JUN 2013

1 9 JUN 2015

Wyggeston QE I

00202243

The Making of Modern Japan

A Reader

edited and introduced
by

TIM MEGARRY

 **Greenwich University Press**

Wyggeston QEI College

Selection, arrangement, introduction and linking passages are
© Greenwich University Press 1995

All rights reserved. No part of this publication may be reproduced, stored in a retrieval system, or transmitted in any form or by any means, electronic, mechanical, photocopying, recording, or otherwise without the prior permission of the publisher.

First published in 1995 by
Greenwich University Press
Unit 42
Dartford Trade Park
Hawley Road
Dartford
Kent DA1 1PF
United Kingdom

British Library Cataloguing-in-Publication Data
A CIP catalogue record for this book is available from the British Library

ISBN 1 874529 35 3

Designed and produced for Greenwich University Press by
Angela Allwright and Kirsten Brown.

Printed in Great Britain by The Bath Press, Avon.

Every effort has been made to trace all the copyright holders, but if any have been inadvertently overlooked the publishers will be pleased to make the necessary arrangements at the earliest opportunity.

Acc. No.
00202243

Class No.
952
MEG

Contents

Introduction

Japanese Society and History: Some Questions for Social Scientists

Japan's extraordinary rise to world prominence, and the extensive social and economic change that it has experienced in the past century and a half, provoke a range of important questions for social scientists. In considering this dramatic change and new-found eminence we are confronted by a country which has been transformed more rapidly and decisively than any Western counterpart. A closed society ruled by a feudal warrior caste, which for several centuries had been separated from the world by self-enforced isolation, emerged as a successful industrial power in little more than two generations. Japan, consequently, presents us with an absorbing set of problems that call for the investigative skills of the sociologist, economist and historian, who are best advised to join forces to achieve a comprehensive understanding of Japanese society and culture.

This book of readings seeks to present and describe some of the key themes and issues which are encountered in the study of contemporary Japan and its path to modernity. The purpose of this introduction, however, is to provide an outline of the scope of inquiry that lies behind the choice of the extracts contained in this anthology. A historical, political and economic perspective has been adopted as a means of understanding the forces and constraints that have moulded society since Japan began on its road to modernity. A brief review of some of the historical circumstances from which modern Japan emerged is needed if some of the principle questions that arise in the analysis of modern Japanese society are to be approached in their full context.

Perhaps the most frequently posed question concerns Japan's spectacular economic success in recent times. Why and how was it possible for an isolated, defeated, second-rate industrial power, which in the late 1940s had the GNP per capita of a Third World country, to become a leading economic giant by the 1980s?

The facts of Japan's economic might — the rate of growth and the speed of ascent to superpower status — are impressive by any standard and are without precedent: they have also met with considerable surprise in the West. In 1993 Japan's GDP was valued at $4,190.3 billion, which was 65 per cent of the size of the world's largest economy, the USA, with a GDP of $6,377.9 billion. Japanese GDP was also more than four times as large as that of the UK, which stood at $939.4 billion. Yet thirty years ago all other industrial countries had economies that were larger than that of Japan. The Japanese economy has been growing at more than twice the rate of America and Britain for over four decades. In the twenty-six years from 1965 to 1991 the average annual growth rate of Japan's GDP was 5.4 per cent against 2.6 per cent for both the USA and UK. Real GDP per capita rose more than six and a half times between 1960 and 1990 in Japan while in the UK it increased less than two and a half times and barely doubled in America. Japan's high growth rate has meant that its economy has benefited from a marked increase in capital. It now has the highest GDP per capita of all industrial countries with large populations and is only just exceeded by Switzerland. In 1993 Japan's GDP per capita stood at $33,701, while the USA had $25,009 and the UK $16,239. Britain and the leading European economies were overtaken by Japan during the 1970s and 1980s in terms of GDP per capita. It is predicted that in terms of gross size Japan's economy will draw level with America's by the year 2000, and will become the world's largest economy by 2005.

Japan's rate of economic growth is all the more extraordinary for a country that is only one and a half times the size of Britain, has a population half the size of the USA and which forty years ago had Third World status. This rapid reversal in global economic fortunes is best illustrated by the fact that in 1950 Japan had the GDP per capita of an average Latin American country, almost the same as Mexico in fact, but well below the levels of GDP found in Brazil, Argentina and even Peru. At least one clue to Japan's soaring ascent lies in its wholesale commitment to economic growth which is seen in its savings and investment performance. Japan's gross national savings represented 34 per cent of national output in 1994 compared with 13 per cent in Britain. In 1990 Japan spent $702 billion on direct economic investment, exceeding America's $544 billion in absolute terms by close to one third. In relative terms, however, this difference is seen even more starkly: Japan invested 25 per cent of GDP in its economy in 1990 compared with 11 per cent for America and a declining 10 per cent for Britain.

When the first glimmerings of the Japanese economic miracle became evident in the late 1950s few people in Europe or America realised that economic ascendancy, which would take Japan close to world supremacy by the 1990s, was a serious prospect. Even with the appearance of the first Nikon cameras and Honda motorcycles on the European market in the 1960s there was little awareness of rapidly impending industrial rivalry. Japan's products were then seen as little more than interesting curiosities made by a plagiarising nation of manufacturing upstarts. For several generations 'Made in Japan' had been synonymous with shoddy goods produced by cheap labour in a backward economy. This image was to change only in the 1970s with the arrival of high quality products designed and priced to capture mass markets across the world. By then the Western impression of industrial precocity had to give way to one of an emerging economic leviathan growing at a rate unparalleled in economic history.

Japan's success has come as a shock to the West which was psychologically unprepared for any challenge to its domination of manufacturing. No Lancashire mill operative and no car worker in the West Midlands or Detroit before the mid-1970s would have been able to imagine a time when British and American textiles and vehicles would be all but ousted from both domestic and world markets by the products of Japan. The idea of direct investment by Japanese corporations in these original industrial heartlands, or the production of Japanese goods by British and American workers would have seemed even less conceivable. Yet this has in fact happened. Strong, and at times lethal competition, in the case of motor cycles and cars, has caused a radical restructuring of these traditional home industries within the space of a generation. Japanese electronic goods and cameras have gained a near complete monopoly in world mass markets and there are now few sectors of any modern economy that are unaffected by the challenge of Japanese competition.

The evidence for this global shift in manufacturing and trade is now found in every home and high street in the form of Japanese-made consumer products and our primary question why has Japan succeeded?, is a popular issue at the forefront of Western consciousness. For a social scientist, however, there are more fundamental questions which demand that this recent success is related to the full context of Japanese history. What aspects of Japan's social and economic past contributed to its ascent to industrial superpower status? The rise to world eminence is certainly connected to immediate post-war circumstances but it is also intimately joined to a more long-term historical tradition. The present Japanese economic miracle is in fact part of both a modern wave of economic change, which is currently transforming East Asia and parts of the Third World, but is also a product of the primary indigenous industrialisation which began to transform Japan during the 1870s alongside the industrial revolutions of Europe and America. Seen in this context the need for a close scrutiny of Japanese history becomes obvious. But as the historical record is unrolled in further detail two other primary questions are revealed which are crucial for a sociological understanding of Japan and its route to the twentieth century.

The first of these questions revolves around the problem of why Japan alone among all societies beyond the cultural orbit of Europe made an autonomous decision to abandon its 'feudal-like' social order and whole-heartedly commit itself to full-scale capitalist industrialisation. The Japanese made a deliberate and decisive break with their two thousand year historical tradition following the Meiji Restoration in 1868 and within fifty years they had created an industrial economy. The full authority of the emperor, who since the ninth century had ruled only as a figure head, was restored and the hereditary feudal office of *shogun* — the locus of real power — was abolished. At the beginning of this revolutionary era the power of the feudal nobility, the *samurai,* was to be conclusively ended as elements within this ruling class abolished all the rights and privileges associated with the old order. The Meiji leaders, who were themselves members of the samurai class, fully dismantled the near sacred social status and charismatic authority of this élite caste which had dominated Japan for more than a millennium. Japanese feudalism was therefore formally terminated by the feudal ruling class itself in an extraordinary act of apparent self-destruction. This move was unique and unprecedented among all of the pre-capitalist societies that were in contact with expansionist European powers from the sixteenth to the twentieth centuries and calls for close investigation.

Japan's first contact with the West was with Portugal, whose traders and missionaries arrived on its Western coasts in 1543. The Portuguese were soon joined by the Spanish, Dutch and English who established trading stations, and a period of intense interest and mutual communication between Japan and Europe followed for nearly a century. From their arrival until 1616, when exclusion policies began, foreigners moved through the country freely. Simultaneously, Japanese travellers reached Mexico and Europe. Diplomatic channels of a sort were established with England, whose King James I received a suit of samurai armour from the Governor of Edo (Tokyo) in 1613. Italian princes and nobles received their Japanese counterparts, and in one instance in Venice in 1585 publicly celebrated their conversion to Catholicism at an elaborate high mass with music specially composed by Andrea Gabrieli.

Cultural diffusion between the West and Japan began to inculcate intense curiosity about European science and ideas among the samurai which was to be retained and embellished during the centuries of seclusion. Both firearms and Christianity were introduced to Japan during this era which coincided with the end of a turbulent period of civil war among factions of the ruling class. Once Japan had been reunified by the Tokugawa clan under its leader, Ieyasu, following the decisive battle of Sekigahara in 1600, the struggle for central control and officially sanctioned cultural exchange came to an end. The new centralising military government of the shogun — the supreme overlord whose temporal power paralleled the spiritual authority of the emperor — perceived Christianity to be a direct threat to its jurisdiction. Japan, like the rest of East Asia, had long been syncretic: Buddhist, Confucian and Shinto beliefs coexisted harmoniously in both society and the individual, and no dogmatic objections were raised toward Christianity. The fierce intolerance and persecution which was about to be unleashed on this new religion were products of official anxiety over the integrity of its sovereignty rather than a clash of rival theologies.

Catholic missionaries had successfully converted half a million new believers by 1615. It was, however, the conversion of many *daimyo*, the great lords, with substantial domains in south-west Japan which most perturbed the shogun. The proximity of this region to foreign traders and the association of Japanese Christians with foreign missionary priests was politically unsettling to a bureaucratically inclined government intent upon stamping its new hard-won authority upon the whole country. Some of the south-western daimyo had been the opponents of the Tokugawa regime at the battle of Sekigahara while others were too powerful to be easily subordinated to Tokugawa authority. These daimyo had accordingly been given the special hereditary status of *tozama* or 'outside lord'. A successful rebellion by these disgruntled Christian forces based on the illicit importation of guns was therefore a realistic fear. It was these pragmatic and strategic reasons which motivated the shogunate to end foreign contact rather than doctrinal objections. Foreigners were accordingly excluded and the country was finally sealed from the outside world in 1639. Apart from the minimal presence of the Dutch at an isolated trading post, which was rigorously segregated from ordinary society, the Japanese islands remained hermetically sealed from the outside world. Thereafter Japan fell away from European consciousness and by the early nineteenth century had become a bi-word for remoteness.

United States' interest in the Pacific region came only in the middle of the last century when expansion within North America led to development of the West Coast. In this new context Japan was perceived to be vital to American trade routes with Asia. Accordingly, a US naval mission arrived at Uraga, at the entrance to Yokahama Bay, in July 1853 to demand that Japan be opened. Acquiesence was the only practical option for the shogun, who ended nearly two and a half centuries of isolation in March 1854.

Fourteen years of foreign contact followed which were marked by all the manifestations of social and economic disintegration that the Treaty Port system had introduced to the rest of nineteenth-century Asia. Western contact might have been cataclysmic as it was in China and could well have heralded the final demise of Japan's political autonomy. But Japan did not collapse or retreat like India and China. Though massively vulnerable to the military might of the Great Powers and economically defenceless against their imports, it did not succumb to Western contact as all other non-capitalist societies beyond Europe had. Japan was not destined for long-term semi-colonial status and neither was a protracted period of disunity, civil war, dismemberment or partial loss of sovereignty to follow the enforced opening to the world. Japan's older neighbour, China, which was recognised as a source of cultural identity and had long been venerated by the Japanese as a moral superior, was to endure all of these misfortunes.

The avoidance of any of these consequences must be attributed largely to Japan's highly unusual reaction to the West. It is, of course, true that in the latter half of the nineteenth century the impact of imperialism on Asian societies had become predictable and some elements of the Japanese response could be interpreted as a correct perception of this threat. But the recognition of this potential outcome by Japan's leaders is not an explanation of the positive measures which they took to protect national interests. After 1868 the new innovative rulers were to administer Japanese society with a self-inoculatory dose of Western technology linked to a Western capitalist system. Rather than react as China had by launching what would have been ineffective armed resistance to Western encroachment or by refusing to acknowledge the need for change, which was manifested by China's withdrawal and immersion in delusions of cultural superiority, Japan responded with planned economic and social change comprising a blueprint for industrial construction. Full-scale capitalist transformation of both economy and society by government-led business corporations and an active interventionist state was inaugurated as a means to compete with the West.

The nature of this original and most profound social metamorphosis should never be forgotten. Understanding the transition to capitalism in Japan simultaneously implies gaining an understanding of the context and means in which modern social institutions were forged. It was in this era, for instance, that many elements of Japanese society which were to be responsible for the post-war economic miracle first emerged. The role of the state in economic life, the form of industrial discipline and the pattern of social class interaction are all examples that are also closely interrelated with Japan's recent economic ascension.

A second question that arises from a study of Japanese history, which is of equal importance in the analysis of modern society, concerns the nature of Japan's frequently termed 'feudal' past immediately before the Meiji era began in 1868. The issue here is the correct identification of this form of society and its influence upon subsequent historical development.

It has long been customary in the West to describe Japanese society before industrialisation as feudal. In making this designation the idea that both Japan and Europe at some time in their separate histories exemplified a similar type of society is also suggested. This resemblance is based upon comparative analysis which, it is often claimed, reveals a set of corresponding social institutions in both locations. It is further proposed that if broadly similar modes of social organisation can be readily identified, then it is also likely that both Japan and Europe may have been driven by a similar form of historical dynamic. What is at stake here is the extent to which feudalism in both Japan and Europe served as an effective instrument in the transition to industrial capitalism.

But to what extent was Japan ever really feudal? If a feudal society is defined simply as one comprising a land-based economy grounded on the labour of a subservient peasantry, whose subordination was exemplified by legally binding ties to the soil; by weak and shifting monarchical government with frequent lapses in central control which necessitated strong social bonds between lords and their armed retainers; and by the granting of landed estates for this military service, then both Japan and Europe do at times exemplify two different varieties of feudalism. Common features are easy to identify and describe. In the sixteenth century the first European visitors to Japan often experienced a recognition shock. Having arrived in Japan by way of India, South-East Asia and China — societies which contained centralised state systems ruled by court officials and meritocratically-recruited bureaucrats — Europeans were struck by their meeting with what they took to be genuine aristocrats. The samurai were observed to be economically independent gentlemen in the service of a daimyo, or liege lord, but they were also the master and controller of their own estates. On this basis a lord–vassal complex is easily identified with the European knight as a military class comparable with the samurai. Fiefs, or *shoen* as they were called in Japan, may also be claimed as equivalents. Prolonged periods of civil war and insurrection produced perennial insecurity for the masses and endlessly shifting political authority among the élites in both places. The utter servility and total compliance demanded of the Japanese peasantry was also reflected in serfdom and in later serf-like conditions of peasants in Europe.

If these similarities can serve as the basis for identifying different varieties of the same form of social system, it is also important to be aware of some of the vital differences between the historical contexts of Europe and Japan before industrialisation. After 1600 a strong centralised state system developed in Japan and within a few decades the samurai were removed from their rural estates, and henceforth were paid an annual stipend in rice. At no time did the social contract between daimyo and samurai include a fully reciprocal agreement for protection and aid. No obligation to protect a vassal existed in Japan as it did in Europe, nor was there direct labour service by the Japanese peasant or administration by the clergy. There is no space to provide an adequate survey of these dissimilarities or to discuss fully the proposal that Japanese feudalism possessed potentialities for social change which were not present in other Asian societies: both of these issues are given attention in the section on *Feudal Japan*. Despite their apparently matching social elements the contentions that Japanese feudalism was really comparable with that found in Europe, that Japan alone in nineteenth-century Asia had a feudal society, or that Japan was favoured by its feudal system in coming to terms with the need for major economic and social change are by no means secure. This last contention, that feudalism in Japan had the effect of inducing industrial capitalism, has now become less popular. The rise of new dynamic industrial economies, which are currently transforming China and other Asian societies, has made this last idea much less tenable.

There is one important dissimilarity between the West and Japan, however, that demands attention. This difference relates to Japan's industrialisation in the absence of a bourgeois class. In Europe the slow decay of feudal authority was accompanied by a growth of commercial activity for several centuries before the rise of industrial capitalism. The increase in trade and the business of producing specially for trade, which this mercantilism increasingly involved, simultaneously created new social classes. A rising middle class and urban artisan class with new social values and aspirations developed in Europe long before the economy and society were transformed by the factories and cities of a new economic order. The constituents of the new 'culture of capitalism' were diverse but at the most general level they included demands for lifting any restraint on trade, political representation, particularly on matters such as taxation, and quite new philosophical ideas concerning liberty and individualism. New cultural forms also accompanied the emergence of this social class and the impact of new values was clearly evident in literature, painting and music. Above all it was the manifestation of new conceptions of politics and culture in the revolutionary challenges to autocracy in Europe — that were to be followed by social and economic development in bourgeois interests — which distinguishes the pattern of industrialisation in the West from Japan.

There was no equivalent of a bourgeois class in nineteenth-century Japan or any challenge to the feudal social order. The construction of a capitalist economy was not left, as in Europe, to evolution by the market mechanism: it was undertaken by the state. At the outset of this economic transformation only state initiative could be relied upon in the absence of a true bourgeois class to mobilise capital for modern industry. Real entrepreneurial activity, including large-scale investment in production and infrastructure, could only be performed by the government in lieu of even an incipient capitalist class within the feudal order. Despite extraordinary commercial expansion and urban growth during a long economic boom in the eighteenth century, the large merchant class never won even a degree of political autonomy and remained passive during the process of transition to industrial capitalism.

Throughout the eighteenth century Japan experienced a rapid increase in urban population as a result of an unprecedented growth in commercial activity and handicraft production, but this occurred entirely within the constraints of the feudal economy. In 1780 Japan had the world's largest cities: Edo had more than a million inhabitants, Osaka and Kyoto over 400,000, making them greater than either London or Paris. But Japan, with a closed society and economy, provided no opportunity for the merchant class to transform itself into a bourgeoisie — a class able to realise its own political interests. Merchants and craftsmen remained compliant and subservient to feudal lords whose patronage they depended upon. At least some of this political timidity was due to economic insecurity. There was no legal framework to protect the rights of capital or any legitimate form of defence from arbitrary authority. No distinction between economic rationality and moral conduct existed in the minds of the shogun's officials, who confiscated merchant capital with impunity and gave no thought to the damage they inflicted on the economy. Since the complete expropriation of commercial property might follow relatively minor infringements of edicts which stipulated details of pious conduct toward the samurai, the form of dress that was appropriate to the station of a merchant, or even what dishes he might serve at dinner, submissiveness was the safest option.

New departures in culture did arise in these times. The kabuki theatre, colour print-making and the novel were all the innovative products of new creative urban classes. Some of Japan's greatest dramatists and artists such as Chikamatsu, Utamaro, Hokusai and Kuniyoshi worked in this era. But despite the experimentation found in these new art forms they usually remained well within the traditional value system and presented no more than the mildest ideological challenge to the social order. The feudal authority of the Tokugawa shoguns was absolute and pervasive, and offered no respite or any means of avoiding the full force of its domination. In Japan there was no equivalent to regions where the power of a feudal noble was ambivalent or compromised by rival claims. There were no free cities governed by guildsmen, nor was there international trade and travel or diplomacy which merchants in Europe exploited to reduce the impact of feudal controls.

With no bourgeois class industrialisation could occur only on the back of an aristocratic revolution, and the absence of a bourgeois value system was to characterise the pattern of social change that led Japan into the twentieth century. The full gravity of this historical factor is still forcefully apparent today and remains as an important influence on ordinary social life. A potent reminder of this lies in the political dimension of Japanese society.

Only late in the Meiji era did the aging ex-samurai rulers begin to think about the need for constitutional government, and then only because they feared rebellion by newly arising social classes. The Meiji state system was at first unashamedly constructed on an authoritarian model which was still tied to expectations of feudal compliance. A Prussian constitution, the antithesis of liberalism, was adopted two decades later and the franchise, at first granted to less than half a million taxpayers, was only then grudgingly extended to other males in the years up to 1925. But more important than this was the fact that parliamentary institutions, or any form of consultative assembly, had no social foundation in Japan. Some form of national assembly seemed appropriate if both society and economy were to be fully modernised, and the Meiji leaders' aspirations of gaining acceptance by the Western powers as their equals were to be achieved. But when the Diet first met in 1890 its deliberations did not include debate or the questioning of government policy. From then until 1945 government in Japan could be said to have been constitutional but not parliamentary. The foreign idea of an official parliamentary opposition was incomprehensible and could only be translated as 'a party of rebellion'. Effective political opposition by liberals, let alone any party that genuinely attempted to represent the interests of the masses, was banned for most of this period and their adherents persecuted. Political power then, as now, was held narrowly by élites within the cabinet, civil service and business hierarchy. Real parliamentary democracy did not accompany industrialisation and has yet to take a firm root in Japan.

The results of this tradition are that modern Japanese society has developed in the absence of a liberal value system and that various forms of authoritarian control remain embedded in political practice at many social levels. The overt denial of ordinary civil rights and universal repression of liberals, trade unionists and socialists, which was present on a massive scale until the American occupation at the end of the war, has now been replaced by new constitutional protection. Yet the tight hold on power by the modern conservative élite, and a lack of real political dialogue which their monopoly of government entailed, has led to continual right-wing rule since 1952. From 1955 until its first electoral defeat in 1993 the Liberal Democratic Party represented conservative forces. It is as yet unclear if the current series of political realignments will really end the corruption and gerrymandering on which conservative rule by the LDP was based but there is no doubt that right-wing forces still hold considerable power in Japan.

However, Japanese conservatism has not evolved in contact with a liberal value system and cannot be compared in a simple sense with the ideology of its Western equivalent: it differs in at least two important respects. The first difference concerns relations between the state and the economy which in Japan has always been close and direct. No government in Japan has ever been content to allow free market forces alone to determine economic activity. The state initiated and nurtured a genuinely capitalist business class in the late nineteenth century, and the first industrial corporations were established by the state only to be sold to the private sector once they and the new entrepreneurs they had created became economically viable. Large-scale industrial and financial monopolies were given pride of place in the economy until 1945 and the political power of these combines was directly incorporated within the state. In the post-war era state control has led to the transformation of these firms into a series of gigantic competing oligopolies, for which government agencies provide constant nurture and consciously plan every aspect of their production and marketing strategies in the interests of the national economy. This current relationship between the state and business and the lack of any inhibition by the government about directing the economy is one of the principle reasons for Japan's economic miracle. Japan has a planned industrial economy directed by conservatives whose ideology has never been compatible with the *laissez-faire* economics of their Western counterparts.

A second difference concerns the role of power and authority in personal life and the boundaries which Japanese culture has drawn between these two facets of society. Concepts of liberty and individualism, which are inseparable aspects of Western liberalism, are not values with which Japanese conservatism has developed. Accordingly, the degree to which it is thought legitimate for external forms of authority to intervene in ordinary social life differs markedly in Japan from that found in Europe or America. What would be taken in the West as invasive forms of intervention in the personal life of the citizen are common in Japan.

The presence of the police in each urban ward is represented today as it was in the Tokugawa era by a neighbourhood box, a mini-police station, which serves the area. Within the police box are records of the local inhabitants who are visited regularly and questioned informally on security issues, minor regulations and irregular occurrences. Any form of unconventional activity or visitors to the ward are routinely noted. Street life in Japan is safe, vandalism rare, the crime rate low and the proportion of prison inmates in the population insignificant compared with either Britain or America. However, these positive gains rely upon a high degree of official surveillance of personal life and the acceptance and compliance with this by the citizen.

Intervention is just as common in the workplace and the social distinction between priorities for work and home life is left ambiguous. An employee is expected to show loyalty and devotion to the employing firm to the same extent as to his family. Job changing is difficult and normally stigmatised as betrayal. Social life is oriented more toward colleagues than partners and the six day working week, overtime and commuting will invariably mean only a minimal amount of time spent in the home. The work hierarchy dominates almost every aspect of social life. Company foremen visit the homes of errant workers to inquire about the domestic circumstances underlying their lack of commitment and a section chief may be given a courtesy visit at New Year ahead of an employee's parents. Marriages may be arranged through the firm's marriage broker, housing and medicine provided as part of the job and a woman dismissed at 30 or on marriage if this comes first.

It would be wrong to leave the impression that Japanese society does not contain growing social forces which have questioned these manifestations of conservatism or that viable political alternatives are not present in Japan. The twentieth century is full of examples of radical challenges to entrenched conservatism that have come from a variety of directions including established political parties within the Diet, trade unions and pressure groups representing peasants, environmental interests, repressed ethnic minorities, students and women. But conservatism remains as the dominant ideological force in modern Japanese politics and its decisive influence on society has proved unassailable throughout the post-war era. Like the officials of the Tokugawa shogun, the present conservative political and economic establishment have attempted to prevent social change. They have refurbished, embellished or maintained a range of archaic or recently invented social practices, often against considerable social opposition, which under the normal processes of social decay would be expected to have disappeared in an advanced industrial society. The justification for preserving these 'beautiful customs', such as the life-time employment system which began early in this century, is backed by appeals to patriotism and cultural chauvinism. The demands for social consensus in the workplace, as in other areas of social life, serve only to obscure the facts of monolithic forms of power-holding by government and corporations whose authority has yet to be displaced by truly democratic and pluralist institutions.

The refusal of the conservative élite to share its power and privilege with wider groups in Japanese society has had a variety of social consequences. The power of genuine trade unions, for instance, remains minimal and Japanese workers have the longest hours, shortest holidays and smallest share of the national product of any workforce in the industrialised world. Priorities for economic growth and industrial expansion have far outweighed due attention to the domestic environment which has been grossly abused in the past fifty years. Compared with any other advanced industrial country Japan has an acute lack of investment in urban infrastructure, housing and social amenities. Most homes are very small by Western standards and many are still not connected to sewers. Parks, public services and social spaces are limited, and taken as a whole this deficiency of social capital and provision has led critics to identify Japan as a country with a rich state and a poor society.

Where does all of this leave Japan? The Japanese economy, like the economic systems of Britain or America, has evolved to become a variant of modern industrial capitalism.

In some minor instances Japanese society has also developed social features which are common in Western society. The movement toward a nuclear family and less emphasis on extended kinship relations are examples. Yet as a whole Japanese society remains unlike Western societies at many levels. These differences demonstrate the futility of arguments which propose that industrialisation leads inexorably to convergence as similar forms of society and social life arise from a supposed logic imposed by the industrial economy. In Japan, as elsewhere, the weight of historical and cultural tradition, and its continual regeneration and development in the present, provide the means of maintaining a persisting and distinctive social identity.

Tim Megarry
July 1995

Publisher's note

The contents of the readings in this anthology have been reproduced as they appear in the publications from which they are taken. In the majority of cases footnotes and bibliographic material are included, the exceptions being where they are of excessive length.

A Chronological Overview of Modern Japanese History

(Key events and dates are in bold)

16th Century	an era of civil wars by competing clans to gain the supreme authority held by the shogun.
1543	Arrival of Portuguese merchants and missionaries.
1600	**Battle of Sekigahara**, the final battle of the civil wars.
1603–1868	Tokugawa Shogunate based at Kyoto.
1638	Japanese Christians defeated in the Shimabara Rebellion.
1638–1640	Anti-Christian legislation and final exclusion edicts close Japan to foreigners and prohibit Japanese from travelling abroad.
1853	Arrival of US Navy 'Black Ships' at Uraga, Yokahama Bay, Edo.
1854	US Commodore Perry demands the shogun open Japan to foreign trade.
1857	Shogun's government signs commercial treaties with Western powers. Treaty ports open to the West.
1868	**Meiji Restoration** after a coup which removed the last Tokugawa shogun. **Meiji era begins**.
1871–1872	Abolition of feudal domains and formal samurai status.
1873	Conscription begins and a modern army established.
1876	Prohibition on wearing swords.
1877	Satsuma Rebellion. Armed opposition to the new Meiji state, motivated by a desire to return to traditional values which privileged the samurai ethos, was defeated, leading to the suicide of its leader, Saigo Takamori.
1889	Meiji Constitution. Elementary education widespread.
1890	First general election and meeting of the Diet.
1894–1895	Sino–Japanese War: Japan gains Taiwan and Korea as satellite states.
1900	Japanese army sent to China as part of an international force to suppress the Boxer Rebellion.
1902	Anglo–Japanese Alliance.
1904–1905	Russo–Japanese War.

1906	Japan Socialist Party formed.
1910	Korea annexed.
1912	Death of the **Meiji Emperor Mutsuhito**. **Taisho era begins**.
1918	Japanese forces sent to Siberia to check Soviet armies.
1919	Japan gains former German held concessions in China.
1923	Kanto earthquake causing the deaths of 150,000 and the devastation of large areas of the Tokyo–Yokohama region. Socialists murdered in prison. Koreans massacred by rioting mobs.
1926	Death of the **Taisho Emperor Yoshihito**. **Showa era begins**.
1930	London Naval Conference forces Japan to restrict the size of its navy causing resentment among the armed forces.
1931	Manchurian Incident: Japanese advance into China begins. Failure of coup by right-wing ultra-nationalist officers.
1933	Japan leaves the League of Nations after its aggression in Manchuria is internationally condemned.
1936	Army officers coup in Tokyo fails after assassination of leading politicians. Closer links with Nazi Germany and beginnings of a war economy.
1937	Full-scale Japanese invasion of China.
1939	Japanese forces defeated by Soviet army at Nomonhan.
1940	Rome–Berlin–Tokyo Axis established. Imperial Rule Assistance Association dissolves political parties and abolishes trade unions. Emperor and military rule Japan. Rapid advance by Japanese forces into South East Asia.
1941	Japanese forces attack Pearl Harbour.
1942	Battle of Midway lost by Japanese navy; the Pacific War turns against Japan despite its occupation of vast areas of China and South East Asia.
1944	Intensive incendiary bombing of Japanese cities by America begins, killing 668,000 civilians by the end of the war.
1945	Fire storm in Tokyo kills 125,000 on 9–10 March alone. Atomic bombs destroy Hiroshima and Nagasaki on 6 and 9 August with the loss of 210,000 lives by the end of 1945. Japan is forced into unconditional surrender and is occupied by US forces in the name of the Supreme Command Allied Powers (SCAP).

1946	Japan ruled by SCAP in theory but by America and General MacArthur in practice. Major reform programme affecting politics, society and economy including land reform. Emperor Hirohito renounces his divinity. Trials of war criminals begin.
1947	New constitution. Brief period of socialists in government in coalition with the Democratic Party.
1948	Era of post-war conservative government begins.
1949	Ministry of International Trade and Industry (MITI) established.
1950	Korean War. SCAP purge of left-wing from politics and media.
1951	Japan and US sign a peace treaty.
1952	End of SCAP occupation.
1954	US–Japanese agreement on Mutual Defense.
1955	Liberal Democratic Party formed from merger of conservative parties.
1956	Japan admitted to the United Nations.
1959	Mass political unrest and protest at the renewal of US–Japan defence treaty increases with widespread rioting.
1961	Income Doubling Plan commits Japan to rapid economic growth.
1964	Tokyo Olympics restores Japan's international standing.
1966	Vietnam War escalates and Japan becomes a major arms supplier to US. Economy booms; GNP annual growth rate of 13% from 1965–1970.
1968	Militant demonstrations and mass college occupations by students at Japan–American relations.
1970	World's Fair, Expo 70, held in Osaka. Widespread opposition to the building of Tokyo's new airport on confiscated agricultural land leads to battles between peasants and police.
1973	Middle East War: Japan suffers an oil crisis and inflation. Courts find Minamata mercury poisoning and pollution to have been perpetrated by the Chisso Co.
1975	Hirohito visits America.
1976	Lockheed Scandal: corruption among top politicians and business leaders, including ex-prime minister Tanaka.
1982	International and domestic protests over the content of official government approved history textbooks which understate Japanese war crimes in Asia.
1989	Death of the **Showa Emperor Hirohito**. **Heisei era begins**.

1993	End of LDP political dominance. New conservative forces form a government.
1994	Verbal admission of Japan's war guilt in Asia by Prime Minister Hosokawa but rejection of compensation for war-time sex slaves.
1995	Kobe earthquake. Over 5,000 killed and 300,000 made homeless. Government criticised for poor relief work. Poison gas attack on Tokyo underground. A Diet resolution, which expresses remorse for Japan's conduct in World War II but does not include an apology, is passed because of abstention by the LDP. On the 50th anniversary of the Japanese surrender Prime Minister Murayama issued a personal apology for Japan's wartime conduct in Asia and the Pacific. This, however, appears to fall short of an unequivocal official apology on behalf of the Japanese government.

Japanese Emperors of the Modern Era

Reign Name		Emperor Name	Date
Meiji	'Enlightened Rule'	Mutsuhito	1868–1912
Taisho	'Great Righteousness'	Yoshihito	1912–1926
Showa	'Enlightened Peace'	Hirohito	1926–1989
Heisei	'Attained Peace'	Akihito	1989–

In Japan everyday events like births, deaths and marriages are commonly marked by the year of the Emperor's reign. A person is more likely to be referred to as having been born in Meiji 40 than in 1908. The same person might have graduated from high school in Taisho 13 (1925), got married in Showa 10 (1936), had a first child in Showa 15 (1941), and grandchildren born in Showa 55 (1981) and Heisei 1 (1990).

A Glossary of Japanese Terms

Amaterasu: The shinto sun goddess and ancestress of Japan's emperors.

Bakufu: Literally 'tent government'. The central administration of the shogun.

Burakumin: Modern name for the outcast group replacing the vulgar and insulting term 'eta'.

Bushi: The samurai or warrior class.

Bushido: The code of the warrior.

Ching Dynasty: The last Imperial dynasty which ruled China from 1644 to 1911 and comprised a line of foreign Manchu emperors.

Cho: A land measurement equivalent to 2.45 acres.

Chonin: Townspeople in the Tokugawa era.

Choshu: An important Tozama clan which played a significant part in the Meiji Restoration with territory in south-west Honshu and northern Kyushu.

Chu: Loyalty.

Confucianism: A religion or set of ethical principles that stress the virtues of harmony, loyalty and filial piety which were first espoused by the Chinese sage, K'ung-fu-tzu (551–479 B.C.)

Daimyo: A great lord of the Tokugawa era and often also the leader of a feudal clan who held a domain with an estimated annual equivalent of ten thousand koku of rice.

Edo (Yedo): Renamed Tokyo or Eastern Capital in 1868. Edo was the location of Shogun's Bakufu in the Tokugawa era.

Fudai: Feudal lords who were hereditary vassals of the Tokugawa Shogun.

Fukoku-hinmin: 'Enrich the country – impoverish the people'. A slogan current in recent decades that is intended as a criticism of the post-war economic miracle.

Fukoku-Kyohei: A slogan of the early Meiji era meaning 'rich country – strong army'.

Gagaku: 'Elegant Music' played at the Imperial Japanese court.

Gaijin: 'Outside person', a Western foreigner.

Geisha: Literally 'performer' or 'artist', a highly accomplished courtesan.

Genyosha:	The Black Ocean Society. Founded in 1881, this earliest ultra-nationalist group advocated military expansion by Japan into Asia.
Genro:	Elder statesmen who, together with military cliques before 1945, formed an extra-constitutional advisory body. Major political decisions were made by this unelected power-base.
Gokenin:	A houseman or vassal.
Giri:	Duty or social obligation.
Habatsu:	Factions found within firms and in political parties, criminal gangs, the army and artistic movements.
Haiku:	A poem of seventeen syllables.
Han:	A domain, the fief or clan of a daimyo.
Heisei:	The name given to the era of the present emperor Akihito, who has reigned since 1989.
Hizen:	An important Tozama clan which played a significant part in the Meiji Restoration with territory in north-west Kyushu.
Ie:	The traditional form of kinship unit and Japanese 'family system'.
Imperial Way Faction and Control Faction:	In the 1930s ultra-nationalist groups within the armed forces (the Imperial Way Faction) sought a radical transformation of Japan and imperialistic expansion. They were opposed by other nationalist groups who comprised the Control Faction.
Juku:	Evening schools or crammers to which secondary school students frequently resort in the hope of passing university entrance examinations.
Kabuki:	Popular theatre of the urban masses since the seventeenth century.
Kaikoku:	An anti-Tokugawa slogan meaning 'open the country'.
Kaisha:	A company or business corporation.
Kamikaze:	Literally 'divine wind'; organised suicide tactics used in the final phase of the Pacific War.
Kendo:	A martial art in which heavily armoured opponents fight with wooden sword substitutes.
Keiretsu:	Literally 'Enterprise Group'. As reformed zaibatsu, these vast groups of independent but co-operating companies have formed the basis of the 'economic miracle'.
Kodo Ha:	(Imperial Way Faction). See Imperial Way and Control Factions.
Kokutai no Hongi:	The cardinal principles of the national polity.

Koku: A measurement of capacity used for rice equivalent to 4.69 English bushels.

Kuge: The imperial court aristocracy.

Kyoto: The Imperial capital of Japan until 1868.

Mama-san: The female owner of a bar or night-club who mothers regular male customers.

Manga: Comic books which frequently depict violent and sado-masochistic occurrences.

Meiji: The name given to the era of the emperor Mutsuhito who reigned from 1868 to 1912.

Miai: A formal meeting arranged by a go-between at which two families involved in an arranged marriage come together to appraise each other and the prospects for the proposed union.

Miso: Fermented bean paste, often used in soup.

Namban: Literally 'southern barbarian'. Applied to the first European visitors and their culture in the 16th and 17th centuries.

MITI: Japan's highly influential Ministry of International Trade and Industry.

Nenko: The wage seniority system found in modern Japanese industry in which pay automatically rises with length of service.

No: Classical theatre of the aristocratic élite.

Nohon sugi: A conservative social philosophy current among ultra-nationalists before 1945 which held a profound dislike of urban-capitalism. Nohon sugi was marked by belief in the natural virtues of rural life which were seen as a model for society.

On: Indebtedness.

Oyabun-kobun: Literally a 'parent–child' relationship which is used to apply to a patron-client or mentor-pupil attachment. This common relationship is frequently encountered both at work and in other social contexts which, besides mutual respect, involves the exchange of benefits and services.

Ronin: Literally 'wave man'; a masterless samurai without land or attachment to a lord.

Ryo: Gold coin of the Tokugawa era which until 1850 was equivalent in value to one koku of rice.

Sake: Rice wine.

Sakurakai: The 'Cherry Blossom Society'. An organisation of radical right-wing Army officers which during the 1930s organised a series of coup d'états in its attempt to 'reform the Army and the Nation'.

Samurai: Literally 'one who serves', a member of the warrior class and thus an aristocrat usually in the service of a daimyo.

Sankin-Kotai: Alternate residence of the daimyo at the shogun's court at Edo.

Satori: The Zen form of enlightenment.

Satsuma: An important Tozama clan which played a significant part in the Meiji Restoration with territory in southern Kyushu.

SCAP: Supreme Command Allied Powers, in effect the American administration which ruled Japan from 1945 to 1952.

Shagaiko: Literally 'extra workers'. The casual or temporary labour force, i.e., the majority of Japanese workers employed on short-term contracts by large companies or by sub-contractors.

Shiki: Literally 'offices' or the rights to income from feudal estates.

Shimpan: Feudal lords who were related to the Tokugawa family.

Shinto: The most ancient and indigenous religion of Japan.

Shoen: A feudal estate or fief in which a lord was autonomous and exempt from imperial taxes.

Showa: The name given to the era of the emperor Hirohito who reigned from 1926 to 1989.

Shogun: Literally 'barbarian-subduing generalissimo'. The office of supreme leader and general of the army, the military and political ruler who since the ninth century held real power. In theory the shogun was appointed by the Emperor but in practice this was a hereditary office.

Shunga: Erotic art which since the seventeenth century has been a notable aspect in the work of the great masters of the ukiyo-e printmakers.

Shunto: Literally 'Spring Offensive'. A pre-emptive strike by trade unions which occurs *before* pay negotiations.

Shushin Koyo: Lifetime employment.

Sohyo: General Council of Labour Unions.

Sonno-joi: Slogan current in the 1860s used by enemies of the Tokugawa Bakufu in the last days of the shogunate meaning 'Honour the Emperor, Expel the Barbarian'.

Taisho: The name given to the era of the emperor Yoshihito who reigned from 1912 to 1926.

Tatami:	A traditional floor mat of standard dimensions. Rooms in Japanese houses are specified in tatami units.
Tenno:	Emperor or lord, until 1868 a religious and moral figure-head without political power, resident at Kyoto, the Imperial capital.
Tennoism:	'Lordism' or excessive subservience to authority.
Tokugawa Era:	Rule of Japan by a line of hereditary shoguns from the Tokugawa clan from 1600 to 1868 after the decisive victory at Sekigahara by Tokugawa Ieyasu.
Torii:	An archway at a Shinto shrine.
Tosa:	An important Tozama clan which played a significant part in the Meiji Restoration with territory in southern Shikoku.
Tosei Ha:	(Control Faction). See Imperial Way and Control Factions.
Tozama:	Literally 'outside lords' designated as such by the Tokugawa Bakufu as nominal vassals because of their power and opposition to the Shogunate. The fall of the Tokugawa Bakufu was largely instigated by these daimyo.
Ukiyo:	The 'floating world' in urban areas devoted to entertainment, the arts and sex.
Ukiyo-e:	Literally 'floating world picture'. The wood block print.
Yakuza:	Japan's mafia. These groups of organised criminal fraternities, whose main activities include loan-sharking, prostitution and drugs, have been frequently shown to have ultra-nationalist sympathies and connections with the extreme right.
Yen:	Monetary unit of modern Japan.
Yome:	A daughter-in-law within an ie.
Yoshiwara:	The area of Edo which from the eighteenth century was associated with the ukiyo or floating world.
Yoshi:	A son-in-law who, in the absence of male heirs within his wife's ie, is adopted by them. The Yoshi thereby becomes a successor to his wife's ie and provides continuity for her lineage.
Zaibatsu:	Literally 'financial clique', the oligarchy of great firms controlled by single families such as Mitsubishi, Mitsui, Yasuda and Sumitomo that arose from the 1880s. Until their transformation into keiretsu after 1945 the zaibatsu dominated the Japanese economy.
Zaikai:	A clique of business leaders who direct and control Japan's economy through direct and regular links with government.
Zen:	A form taken by Buddhism peculiar to Japan.

Feudal Japan

The need of Western readers to locate modern Japan within a historical framework was argued for in the Introduction. A similar requirement, to recognise Japan's cultural distinctiveness, is also necessary. After all Japan is part of the East Asian cultural orbit and has evolved with Confucian and Buddhist ethics as well as with an indigenous Shinto value system. Taken as a single entity these disparate but frequently merged and coexisting religious systems form very different cultural foundations from those found in Europe with its strong links to Antiquity. Just as the ideological aspects of East Asia's ancient civilizations like indebtedness to one's ancestors, sacred forms of social propriety and filial piety play little part in European culture, Japan's cultural tradition did not mature in contact with Greek logic, Roman law or Hebrew prophecy. It should also be remembered that while concepts of virtue and morality are fully developed in Japanese culture, the Western compulsion, associated with the Judaic–Christian tradition, to connect sin and guilt with sexual behaviour, is also absent.

A comparative approach to Japan's historical tradition is helpful. Japanese and European forms of feudalism may be contrasted at a variety of levels. Anderson does this in the first extract which presents an overview of feudal society in its two main forms before and after 1600. It becomes clear that feudalism in Japan, as in the West, was neither static or without the structural antagonisms inherent in the social relations between classes. An exposition of the growth and diversification of agriculture — the most significant sector of the Tokugawa economy — is provided in the first of T.C. Smith's contributions. Smith shows that a movement toward greater agricultural productivity and a dynamic and diversified agrarian system, which are both prerequisites for industrialisation, were present in the late Tokugawa era. His second contribution provides a fascinating contrast between the pattern of pre-modern economic growth found in Japan and Europe. His agrarian theme continues with the revelation that in Japan immediately before industrialisation, unlike Europe, it was the countryside not the towns that was responsible for economic change. Urban population actually declined in nineteenth-century Japan — the reverse pattern of pre-industrial Europe — while it was the villages that produced key elements in the process of early industrialisation such as technical innovation, new skills and attitudes.

Knowledge of Japan before the Meiji era is a necessary part of understanding modern Japanese society and the brief examination of feudalism presented here is intended as more than a mere historical background. Direct and immediate connections exist between Japan's feudal past and modern society that have no real precedent in the West. These connections are not represented only by quaint survivals of archaic rituals or aspects of an artistic tradition, they constitute a significant influence on contemporary social life.

One example worth exploring is the influence of the samurai which goes far beyond the constant depiction of this warrior caste on film, in television soaps and manga comic books. Although samurai status was abolished formally in 1872, and no social division

1

between aristocrats and commoners recognised formally after this — despite the existence of a parliamentary peerage from 1884 to 1946 — a strong samurai ethos remains. The prevalence of the martial arts or the militant behaviour of the extreme right-wing in Japanese politics show direct lines of contact between the present and the past. But from the late 1920s until the end of the World War II, Japan as a whole was dominated by a reconstituted version of the samurai spirit which became widely inculcated. The mounting tide of Japanese aggression in Asia in these times and the reversion to dictatorship, which eventually led to the Pacific War with America in December 1941, together with the appalling destructive consequences and tragic aftermath of this conflict cannot be understood properly without an examination of the samurai tradition.

By the opening decades of the twentieth century rapid modernisation had produced a wave of social change that included an influx of foreign ideas along with imported Western technology. An era of pro-Western enthusiasm before 1920 led to widespread disenchantment among right-wing conservatives and the officer corps which was largely recruited from old samurai families. A true samurai, 'one who served' a single master with loyalty and faith to the point of ultimate self-sacrifice, disdained any form of materialism and, in theory, would not even recognise the value of a coin. Western values, including democratic liberalism, embodying ideals enshrined as civil rights and an implicit denial of any ascribed form of social ranking, were resented by this social group who foresaw the destruction of Japanese virtues through these alien principles. Both capitalism and socialism were rejected as materialistic and egalitarian forms of moral pollution that were antithetical to the samurai spirit of the officer élite. Their remedy, a vague political programme which called for the restoration of a Japanese essence through Imperial virtue, became linked with a series of violent attempted coups and the assassination of politicians which pushed Japan toward increasingly dictatorial government and foreign aggression. Groups of ultra-nationalists in the army were motivated by an arcane ideology which stemmed from a set of nostalgic and élitist principles implicit in the samurai code. Their radical activities culminated in an army mutiny and the murders of cabinet members in the centre of Tokyo in 1936.

Echoes of these times occurred in 1970 with the comic tragedy surrounding a minor insurrection and the ritual suicide of its leader, a samurai descendent and internationally acclaimed novelist, Yukio Mishima. Mishima denounced a mounting tide of Westernisation and affluence which he claimed was prostituting Japan's soul and called for a rebellion by the armed forces. He was ignored and opened his stomach with a sword before being beheaded by his second. The news was greeted with more derision than sympathy within Japan but it would be wrong to imagine that this episode of semi-farce marked the end of the samurai as a potent social influence.

Another aspect of the impact of samurai culture on modern society derives from the long Tokugawa peace during which this expensive warrior élite became largely redundant. Provincial daimyo, together with the shogun's government, could no longer afford to maintain such a large body of fighting men and their families, who by the late eighteenth century numbered close to two million or six per cent of a national population of thirty million. Many retainers were dismissed by daimyo and became ronin, masterless samurai who lost all material support from a lord but kept their social status. During these times the samurai became transformed: the uncouth gut-ripping provincial warrior of the sixteenth-century civil wars gave way to the educated Confucian gentleman. With their social prestige and charisma still intact — and their martial skills continually maintained — this group became an able administrator/official/scholar élite which survived the passage to modern industrialisation. Samurai control over society was widened and strengthened and the form of social deference which this élite commanded remained underpinned by semi-sacred forms of legitimation. Unconditional obedience to superior authority and the honour and esteem with which this form of dominance is accorded is known in Japanese as *tennoism* or 'lordism'. This crushing form of hierarchical and authoritarian control thoroughly imbues Japanese working practices and politics today and, despite vigourous critical opposition from a wide social constituency, still remains as a contemporary manifestation of the samurai ethos.

1.

Japanese Feudalism

Perry Anderson

In the 7th century A.D., a centralized imperial polity was formed in Japan under strong Sinic influence: the Taika reform of 646 abolished the previous loose congeries of noble lineage-groups and dependent cultivators, and installed a unitary state system for the first time. Administratively modelled on the T'ang Empire in contemporary China, the new Japanese State, which came to be regulated by the Taihō Codes issued in the early 8th century (702), was based on an imperial monopoly of landownership. Soil was allocated in small allotments, which were periodically redistributed, to tenant cultivators who owed taxes in kind or corvée duties to the State: initially applied to the house domains of the imperial line itself, the allotment system was gradually extended throughout the country over the next century or so. An extensive central bureaucracy composed of a civilian aristocratic class, recruited to office by heredity rather than examination, maintained unified political control of the country. The realm was systematically divided into circuits, provinces, districts and villages, all under tight governmental supervision. A permanent conscript army was also created, if somewhat insecurely. Symmetrically planned imperial cities were built, along Chinese lines. Buddhism, syncretically mixed with indigenous Shinto cults, became an official religion, formally integrated into the apparatus of the State itself.[1] From 800 or so onwards, however, this Sinicized Empire started to dissolve under centrifugal pressures.

The lack of anything like a mandarinate proper within the bureaucracy rendered it prone to noble privatization from the start. The Buddhist religious orders preserved special privileges on the lands donated to them. Conscription was effectively abandoned in 792; redistribution of allotments in 844 or so. Semi-private estates or *shōen* increasingly sprang up in the provinces, the proprietary domains of nobles or monasteries: initially subtracted from State ownership of land, they eventually gained fiscal immunity and finally exemption from cadastral inspection by the central government altogether. The larger such estates — often originating from newly reclaimed land — covered several hundred acres. The peasants tilling the *shōen* now paid dues directly to their lords, while within this emergent manorial system superimposed rights of access to the produce (mainly, of course, rice) were acquired by intermediate layers of managers or bailiffs. The internal organization of Japanese manors was greatly influenced by the nature of riziculture, the basic branch of agriculture. There was no three-field system of the European type, and commons were comparatively unimportant, given the lack of livestock. Peasant strips were much smaller than in Europe, and village-clusters fewer, amidst a considerable density of rural population and shortage of land. Above all, there was no real demesne system within the farm: the *shiki*, or divisible rights of appropriation of the product, were collected uniformly from the whole output of the *shōen*.[2] Meanwhile, within the

Perry Anderson: 'Japanese Feudalism' from *LINEAGES OF THE ABSOLUTIST STATE* (New Left Books, 1974), pp. 435–461. Reproduced by permission of Verso.

5

political system, the court aristocracy, or *kuge* developed a refined civilian culture in the capital, where the house of Fujiwara gained a prolonged ascendancy over the imperial dynasty itself. But outside Kyōtō, the imperial administration was increasingly allowed to lapse. At the same time, once conscription disappeared, armed force in the provinces gradually came to be the appurtenance of a new military nobility of samurai warriors or *bushi* who first became prominent in the course of the 11th century.[3] Both public officials in the central government and local *shōen* proprietors gathered personal bands of such warriors about them, for purposes of defense and aggression. Civil strife escalated together with the privatization of coercive power, as provincial *bushi* troops intervened in the struggles of court cliques for control of the imperial capital and administrative framework.

The breakdown of the old Taihō system culminated with the victorious foundation of the Kamakura Shogunate by Minamoto-no-Yoritomo in the late 12th century. The Imperial dynasty and court in Kyōtō, and the traditional civil administration were preserved by the new ruler, who was Kyōtō-bred and showed great respect for their legacy.[4] But side by side with them a new military apparatus of rule was created under the command of the Shogun or 'generalissimo', manned by the *bushi* class and centred in a separate capital at Kamakura. Real power in Japan was henceforward exercised by this para-imperial authority. The Shogunate, which came to be referred to as the *Bakufu* ('tent' or military headquarters), at the outset controlled the loyalty of some 2,000 *gokenin* 'housemen' or personal vassals of Yoritomo, and appropriated or confiscated many *shōen* for its use. In the provinces, it appointed military governors or *shugo*, and land stewards or *jitō*, drawn from its retainers. The former in practice became the dominant local power in their regions, while beneath them the latter were charged with tax-collection from the *shōen* manors, over which they gradually came to acquire increasing *shiki* rights themselves, at the expense of their former proprietors.[5] The new *shugo-jitō* network, created by and responsible to the Shogunate, represented a preliminary form of benefice system: repressive and fiscal functions were delegated to *bushi* followers by it, in exchange for titles to income from land. Formal 'letters of confirmation' granted local vassal rights to both land-revenues and men-at-arms.[6] Imperial legality and bureaucracy, however, still subsisted: the Shogun was technically appointed by the Emperor, the *shōen* remained subject to public law, and the bulk of the land and population stayed under the old civil administration.

Financially and militarily weakened by the Mongol attacks in the late 13th century, Kamakura rule eventually collapsed in civil strife. It was during the Ashikaga Shogunate which succeeded it, that the next decisive step towards a full feudalization of Japanese society and polity occurred, in the course of the 14th century. The Shogunate was now transferred to Kyōtō itself, and the lingering autonomy of the imperial court abolished: the sacred dynasty and *kuge* aristocracy were deprived of most of their lands and wealth, and relegated to purely ceremonial roles. Civilian administration in the provinces was completely eclipsed by the military *shugo* governorships. But at the same time, the Ashikaga Shogunate itself was much weaker than its Kamakura predecessor: consequently the *shugo* themselves became increasingly unbridled regional lords, absorbing the *jitō*, levying their own corvées, and annexing half the proceeds of the local *shōen* on a province-wide scale; sometimes even 'receiving' the whole *shōen* outright from their absentee owners.[7] By now a true fief or *chigyō* system had developed, which for the first time represented a direct fusion of vassalage and benefice, military service and conditional landholding: the *shugo* themselves both possessed such fiefs and distributed them to their followers. The adoption of primogeniture within the aristocratic class consolidated the new feudal hierarchy within the countryside.[8] The peasantry below underwent a corresponding degradation, as their mobility was restricted, and their prestations were increased: the petty rural warriors of the *bushi* stratum were in a better position to squeeze the surplus from the direct producers than the absentee *kuge* nobles had been. There was a spread of commodity production in the countryside, especially in the central regions round Kyōtō where *sake* brewing was concentrated, and the volume of monetary circulation increased. Rural productivity improved with better farm tools and increased use of animal traction, and agrarian output rose steeply in many areas.[9] Foreign trade expanded, while artisan and merchant guilds of a type similar to those of mediaeval Europe developed in the towns. But the archaic imperial framework still persisted, although now honeycombed by new feudal hierarchies, under a comparatively weak central Shogunate. The gubernatorial jurisdictions of the *shugo* continued to be much wider than their enfeoffed land, and by no means all the *bushi* within them were their personal vassals.

It was the eventual collapse of the Ashikaga Shogunate after the outbreak of the Ōnin Wars (1467–77), which finally dissolved the last vestiges of the Taihō administrative legacy, and completed the process of country-wide feudalization. Amidst a wave of anarchy in which 'lower ruled higher', the regional *shugo* were overthrown from below by usurper vassals — often their ex-deputies, and the *shōen* clusters and provincial jurisdictions over which they had presided disappeared altogether. The war-born adventurers of the new Sengoku epoch carved out their own principalities, which they henceforward organized and ruled as purely feudal territories, while any real central power disintegrated in Japan. The *daimyō* or magnates of the late 15th or early 16th centuries controlled compact domains, in which all warriors were their vassals or rear-vassals, and all land was their suzerain property. Divisible *shiki* rights were concentrated into single *chigyō* units. Feudalization was territorially more complete than in mediaeval Europe, for allodial plots were unknown in the countryside. Samurai retainers swore oaths of military loyalty to their lords, and received full fiefs — grants of land together with rights of jurisdiction — from them.[10] Enfeoffment was calculated in terms of 'villages' (*mura* — administrative units more than actual hamlets), and the tenantry submitted to direct *bushi* supervision. Castle-towns and subinfeudation developed in the *daimyō* domains, which were regulated by new feudal 'house laws' codifying the prerogatives of their overlord and the hierarchy of personal dependences beneath him. The bond between lord and vassal in Japanese feudalism remained marked by two peculiarities. The personal link between seigneur and retainer was stronger than the economic link of the retainer to the land: vassalage tended to predominate over benefice within the fief nexus itself.[11] At the same time, the relationship between lord and vassal was more asymmetrical than that in Europe. The contractual component of homage was much weaker; vassalage had a semi-familial and sacred character, rather than a legal one. The notion of seigneurial 'felony' or breakage of the bond by the lord was unknown: nor did multiple lordship exist. The intra-feudal relationship proper was thus more unilaterally hierarchical; its terminology was borrowed from that of paternal authority and the kinship system. European feudalism was always rife with inter-familial quarrels, and was characterized by an extreme litigiousness; Japanese feudalism however, not only lacked any legalistic bent, but its quasi-patriarchal cast was rendered the more authoritarian by extensive paternal rights of adoption and disinheritance, which effectively deterred filial insubordination of the type common in Europe.[12] On the other hand, the coefficient of feudal warfare, with its premium on the valour and skill of armoured knights, was fully as great as in late mediaeval Europe during this epoch. Fierce fighting was constant between contending *daimyō* principalities. Moreover, in the gaps left by the political fragmentation of Japan, autonomous merchant towns reminiscent of those of mediaeval Europe — Sakai, Hakata, Ōtsu, Ujiyamada and others — were able to flourish: the port of Sakai was to be termed an oriental 'Venice' by Jesuit travellers.[13] Religious sects created their own armed enclaves in Kaga and Noto on the Japan Sea. Even insurrectionary rural communes, led by disaffected gentry and based on a rebellious peasantry, briefly appeared: the most notable being established in the central Yamashiro region itself, where commercialization had created acute indebtedness among the rural population.[14] The turmoil of the times was further increased by the impact of European fire-arms, techniques and ideas after the arrival of the Portuguese in Japan in 1543.

In the second half of the 16th century, a series of massive civil wars between the major *daimyō* potentates led to the victorious reunification of the country by successive military commanders — Nobunaga, Hideyoshi and Ieyasu. Odo Nobunaga forged the first regional coalition to establish control of central Japan. He liquidated Buddhist militarism, broke the independence of the merchant towns, and gained mastery of a third of the country. The formidable work of conquest was completed by Toyotomi Hideyoshi, leading huge armies equipped with muskets and cannons, and composed of a block of allied *daimyō* forces grouped under him.[15] The result of Hideyoshi's subjection of all other magnates to his own authority was not, however, a restoration of the vanished centralized state of the Taihō tradition. It was rather a reintegration of the mosaic of regional lordships into a unitary feudal system for the first time. The *daimyō* were not dispossessed of their domains, but were vassalized in their turn to the new ruler, from whom they henceforward held their territories as fiefs and to whom they granted kin as hostages for their fealty. The imperial dynasty was retained as a religious symbol of legitimacy, above and apart from the operational system of feudal suzerainty. A new cadastral survey stabilized the landowning system, consolidating the reorganized pyramid of lordships over it. The population was divided into four closed orders — nobles, peasants, artisans and merchants. *Bushi* were separated from the villages and congregrated in the castle-towns of their *daimyō*, as disciplined men-at-arms ready for immediate military deployment. Their numbers were officially registered, and the size of the samurai class was henceforward fixed at some 5–7 per cent of the population, a comparatively large sword-bearing stratum. Peasants were by the same token deprived of all arms, bound to the soil and juridically forced to deliver two-thirds of their product to their masters.[16] The autonomous cities of the Ashikaga and Sengoku epochs were suppressed, and the merchant class forbidden to purchase land (just as the samurai were excluded from commerce). On the other hand, the castle-towns of the feudal magnates themselves grew prodigiously in this period. Trade developed rapidly, under the protection of the *daimyō* whose castellar headquarters provided the central nodes of a greatly enlarged network of cities in Japan. At Hideyoshi's death, supreme power was won by Tokugawa Ieyasu, a *daimyō* from the original Toyotomi bloc, who mobilized a new coalition of lords to defeat his rivals at the battle of Sekigahara in 1600 and become Shogun in 1603. Ieyasu founded the Tokugawa state which was to last two hundred and fifty years, down to the epoch of the industrial revolution in Europe. The stability and longevity of the new regime was greatly reinforced by the formal closure of Japan to virtually all contact with the outside world: a device initially inspired by Ieyasu's well-founded fear that the Catholic missions which had become established in Japan were an ideological spear-head for European political and military infiltration. The effect of the rigorous seclusion of the country was, of course, to insulate it from any external shocks or disturbances for the next two centuries, and petrify the structures established by Ieyasu after Sekigahara.

The Tokugawa Shogunate imposed unity on Japan, without centralism. It in effect stabilized a kind of condominium between the suzerain shogunal regime, based on the Tokugawa capital of Edo, and the autonomous *daimyō* governments in their provincial fiefs. Japanese historians have consequently designated the epoch of its dominance as the *Bakū-han* period, or combination of rule by the *Bakufu* — the Tokugawa governing complex — and the *han* or baronial houses in their own domains. This hybrid system was integrated by the dual foundations of Shogunal power itself. On the one hand, the Shogunate possessed its own Tokugawa domains, the so-called *tenryō* lands which amounted to some 20–25% of the country — a far larger block than that possessed by any other feudal lineage — and strategically commanding the central plains and coasts of Eastern Japan. Just over half of these were administered directly by the *Bakufu* apparatus itself; the rest were granted as minor fiefs to the *hatamoto* or 'banner-men' of the Tokugawa house, of which there were some 5,000 in all.[17] In addition, the Shogunate could rely, firstly on the 20 or so large Tokugawa collateral lines or *shimpan* lords, who were entitled to provide successors to the Shogunate, and secondly on the numerous smaller lords who had been loyal regional vassals of Ieyasu, prior to his rise to supreme power. These latter composed the so-called *fudai* or 'house' *daimyō*: there were about 145 of them by the 18th century, and their lands covered another 25% of the surface of Japan. The *fudai* provided the bulk of the higher officialdom of the *Bakufu* administration, whose lower echelons were recruited from the *hatamoto*, whereas the major collateral houses were excluded from the Shogunal government itself, as potentially overmighty in their own right, although they could act as advisors to it. The Shogunate itself gradually underwent a process of 'symbolization' comparable to that of the Imperial line itself. Tokugawa Ieyasu had not displaced the Imperial dynasty any more than had his predecessors Nobunaga and Hideyoshi: if anything, he had carefully restored much of the religious aura surrounding it, while segregating both the Emperor and the *kuge* court nobility more completely than ever from any secular power. The monarch was a divine authority, relegated to spiritual functions in Kyōtō which were wholly divorced from the conduct of political affairs. The residual duality of Imperial and Shogunal systems in one respect provided a kind of attenuated correlate of the separation of Church and State within European feudalism, because of the religious aura of the former; there were always potentially two sources of legitimacy within Japan in the Tokugawa epoch. In other ways, however, since the Emperor was also a political symbol, this duality reproduced the fissured sovereignty characteristic of any secular feudalism as a whole. The Shogun ruled in the name of the Emperor, as his delegate, by an official fiction which institutionalized 'government from behind the screen'. The Tokugawa dynasty which provided the successive Shoguns who formally controlled the *Bakufu* state apparatus, however, eventually ceased to exercise personal authority within it themselves: after several generations, substantive political power receded to the Shogunal Council of *rōjū*, composed of nobles recruited from the medium *fudai* lineages — in a second degree of 'government from behind the screen'.[18] The Shogunal bureaucracy was extensive and amorphous, with widespread confusion of functions and plurality of tenures within it. Tenebrous vertical cliques manoeuvred for office and patronage within its shrouded machinery. About half of the bureaucracy was civilian and half military in duties.

The *Bakufu* government could theoretically call on a feudal levy of 80,000 mounted warriors, composed of 20,000 or so banner-men and house-men, plus their rear-vassals: in practice, its real armed potential was much smaller, and relied on the strength of loyal *fudai* and *shimpan* contingents. The peace-time strength of its permanent guard-units was some 12,200.[19] The revenues of the Shogunate were basically derived from the rice-yields of its own domains (initially some two-thirds of its total income),[20] supplemented by its monopoly of gold and silver mines, from which it minted coinage (a declining asset from the 18th century onwards); later, when it ran into increasing financial difficulties, it resorted to frequent debasements of currency and forced loans or confiscations of merchant wealth. The extent of both its army and treasury was thus set by the limits of the domanial territory of the Tokugawa house itself. At the same time, however, the Shogunate exercised formally tight external controls over the *daimyō* outside the boundaries of its own direct jurisdiction. All the lords of the *han* domains were, in fact, its tenants-in-chief: they were invested in their fiefs by the Shogun, as his vassals. Their territories could in principle be revoked or transferred, although this practice died out in the later phases of the Tokugawa epoch, when *han* domains were effectively hereditary.[21] Shogunal marriage policy at the same time sought to tie the major baronial lines to the Tokugawa dynasty. The *daimyō* were, moreover, obliged to maintain an alternate residence in the *Bakufu* capital of Edo, where they had to displace themselves every other year or six months, and leave family hostages behind when they returned to their fiefs. This so-called *sankin-kōtai* system was designed to ensure a permanent watch over the conduct of regional magnates, and to hamper independent actions by them in their strongholds. It was backed by an extensive system of informers and inspectors, who provided an intelligence service for the Shogunate. Movements along the main highways were tightly policed by use of internal passports and road-blocks; while marine transport was subject to government regulations which forbade the construction of craft above a certain size. The *daimyō* were permitted to keep one castle-complex only, and ceilings on their armed retinues were fixed in the official rolls of the Shogunate. There was no economic taxation of the *han* domains, but irregular contributions could be requested from them by the *Bakufu*, for extraordinary expenditure.

10

This imposing and inquisitorial set of controls appeared to give the Tokugawa Shogunate complete political paramountcy in Japan. In fact, its real power was always less than its nominal sovereignty, and the actual gap between the two increased over time. The founder of the dynasty, Ieyasu, had defeated the rival lords of the South-West at Sekigahara: he had not destroyed them. The *daimyō* numbered some 250–300 under the Tokugawa Shogunate. Of these, about 90 represented *tozama* or 'outside' houses, whom had not been early vassals of the Tokugawa, and many of which had fought against Ieyasu. The *tozama* houses were regarded as potentially or traditionally hostile to the Shogunate, and were rigorously excluded from participation in the machinery of the *Bakufu*. They included the great majority of the largest and richest domains: of the 16 biggest *han*, no less than 11 were *tozama*.[22] These were located in the peripheral regions of the country, the South-West or North-East. The *tozama* houses together accounted for some 40 per cent of the land in Japan. However, in practice, their wealth and power became more formidable than their official listings on the *Bakufu* registers revealed. Towards the end of the Tokugawa epoch, the Satsuma *han* controlled 28,000 armed samurai, or twice the official rating permitted it; the Chōshū *han* mustered 11,000, again more than it was supposed to possess; while the loyal *fudai* houses were generally under their nominal strength, and the Shogunate itself could in practice field only some 30,000 or so warriors by the early 18th century — less than half its theoretical levy.[23] At the same time, the newer lands in the outlying *tozama* domains contained more unreclaimed surface for conversion to riziculture than the older *tenryō* house-lands of the Shogunate itself in the centre of the country. The rich Kantō plain, the most developed zone in Japan, was controlled by the *Bakufu*; but precisely the new commercialized crops which characterized it tended to elude traditional Tokugawa fiscal collection, based on rice units. Certain of the *tozama* tax-yields thus eventually came to be higher than those of the Shogunal domains.[24] Although aware of the discrepancy between the nominal rice-assessment for the *tozama*-fiefs and their real output, which in some cases existed from the outset of the *Bakū-han* period, the cessation of Shogunal authority at *han* borders prevented Edo from redressing the situation. Moreover, when commercialized agriculture reached the outlying regions of Japan, the more compact and vigorous *han* governments were able to establish lucrative local monopolies in cash crops (such as sugar or paper), increasing *tozama* revenues while *Bakufu* income from mining was falling. The economic and military strength of any daimiate were closely linked, since samurai warriors had to be supported from rice-revenues. The material position of the great *tozama* houses was thus much more powerful than it readily appeared, and grew more so with the passage of time.

Within their domains, moreover, all the *daimyō* — whether *tozama*, *shimpan* or *fudai* — commanded an untempered authority: the direct writ of the Shogunate stopped at the frontiers of their fiefs. They issued laws, administered justice, raised taxes, and maintained troops. The political centralism of the *daimyō* was actually greater within their *han* than that of the Shogunate in its *tenryō* lands, because it was no longer mediatized by subinfeudation. Initially, the *han* territories were divided into *daimyō* house-lands and vassal fiefs granted to their armed retainers. However, in the course of the Tokugawa epoch, there was a steady increase in the number of samurai within every *han* who were simply paid stipends in rice, rather than enfeoffed with land as such. By the end of the 18th century, virtually all *bushi* retainers outside the Shogunal territory itself received rice salaries from the domain granaries, and most resided in the castle-towns of their lords. This shift was facilitated by the traditional tilt within the intra-feudal relationship towards the pole of vassalage rather than benefice. The divorce of the samurai class from agrarian production was accompanied, in both the *Bakufu* and *han* sectors of Japan, by its entry into bureaucratic administration. For the Shogunal State apparatus, with its proliferating posts and uncertain departments, was reproduced in the territories of the provincial lords. Each *daimyō* house came to acquire its own bureaucracy, staffed by vassal samurai, and directed by a council of higher retainers or *kashindan*, which like the *rōjū* board within the Shogunate often exercised effective power in the name of the *han* lord himself, who frequently became a figure-head.[25] The class of *bushi* was now itself stratified into a complex hereditary ranking system, only the top grades of which provided the senior officials of the *han* governments. A further result of the bureaucratization of the samurai was to make it an educated class, with an increasingly impersonal loyalty to the *han* as a whole, rather than to the person of the *daimyō* — although revolts against the latter were virtually unknown.

At the base of the whole feudal system, the peasantry were juridically tied to the soil and forbidden to migrate or exchange their holdings. Statistically, the average peasant plot was extremely small — some 2 to 3 acres — and dues on it owed to the lord amounted to some 40–60 per cent of the product in the early Tokugawa epoch; this declined to 30–40 per cent towards the end of the Shogunate.[26] Villages were collectively responsible for their dues, which were generally paid in kind (although cash conversions were to increase) and collected by the *daimyō*'s fiscal officials. Since the samurai no longer performed any manorial functions, all direct relationship between knights and peasants on the land was eliminated, apart from rural administration by the *han* magistrates. The long peace of the Tokugawa epoch, and the fixed assessment methods of surplus extraction established under it, permitted an impressive advance of agrarian output and productivity in the first century after the installation of the Shogunate. Major reclamations of land were undertaken, with the official encouragement of the *Bakufu*, and there was an increased diffusion of iron field-implements. Irrigation was intensified and the area of paddy-fields extended; fertilizers were more widely used; and crop variants multiplied. The official estimates for rice acreage increased by some 40 per cent in the 17th century: in fact, these assessments always undercalculated the real situation because of concealments, and total cereal production probably nearly doubled in this epoch.[27] Population increased by 50 per cent to some 30 million in 1721. Thereafter, however, it levelled off as bad harvests and famines henceforward struck down excess labour, and villages started to practise malthusian controls to fend off these dangers. Thus in the 18th century, demographic increase was minimal. At the same time, the growth in gross output seems to have slowed down considerably: land under cultivation increased by less than 30 per cent according to official reckoning.[28] On the other hand, the later Tokugawa period was characterized by much more intensive commercialization of agriculture. Riziculture continued to make up two-thirds of rural production down to the end of the Shogunate, benefiting from the introduction of improved threshing-machines.[29] The rice surplus siphoned off by seigneurial dues was ultimately monetized by the feudal class in the towns. At the same time, regional specialization developed rapidly in the course of the 18th century: cash crops such as sugar, cotton, tea, indigo and tobacco were produced directly for the market, their cultivation often promoted by *han* monopoly ventures in specific commodities. By the end of the Shogunate, it is clear that a remarkably high proportion of total agricultural output was commercialized,[30] either directly by peasant production for the market, or indirectly via the sale of feudal rice revenues from the tax-system.

The invasion of a money economy into the villages and the sharp conjunctural fluctuations of rice prices inevitably accelerated social differentiation among the peasantry. From the very outset of the Tokugawa epoch, land tenure within the Japanese villages had always been very unequal. Rich peasant families typically possessed larger than average holdings, which they worked with the aid of dependent labour masked in various forms of pseudo-kin or customary relationships with poorer peasants, while they dominated village councils as a traditional commoner elite.[31] The spread of commercial agriculture greatly enhanced the power and wealth of this social group. Although sale or purchase of land by them was technically illegal, in practice poor peasants were widely driven in desperation to mortgage their plots to village usurers when harvests were poor and prices were high, during the 18th century. There thus emerged within the rural economy a second exploiting stratum, intermediary between the seigneurial officialdom and the immediate producer: the *jinushi* or usurer-landlords, who were usually by origin the richest peasants or headmen (*shōya*) within the village, and who often increased their wealth by financing new cultivation, undertaken by dependent sub-tenants or wage-labour. The pattern of land-holding within the *mura* thus became steadily more concentrated, and kin fictions were abandoned for cash relationships between villagers. Thus while *per capita* income probably increased during the later Tokugawa period with the halt in demographic growth,[32] and the *jinushi* stratum expanded and prospered, the net result of the same process was also to undermine the pitiful livelihood of the poorer peasantry. Punctuated by ruinous dearths, the 18th and 19th centuries saw increasing numbers of popular rebellions in the countryside. Initially local in character, these tended as time went on to acquire a regional and finally quasi-national incidence, to the alarm of both *han* and *Bakufu* authorities.[33] The peasant revolts of the Tokugawa epoch were still too random and unorganized to be a serious political threat to the *Bakū-han* system: they were, however, symptoms of a gathering economic crisis within the old feudal order.

Meanwhile, within this agrarian economy, as in feudal Europe, there had developed important urban centres, engaged in mercantile operations and manufactures. The municipal autonomy of the trading towns of the Ashikaga and Sengoku epochs had been durably suppressed at the end of the 16th century. The Tokugawa Shogunate permitted no urban self-government: at most, honorific merchant councils were allowed in Ōsaka and Edo, under the firm control of the *Bakufu* magistrates charged with the administration of the cities.[34] The *han* castle-towns naturally afforded no space for municipal institutions either. On the other hand, the pacification of the country and the establishment of the *sankin-kōtai* system gave an unprecedented commercial impetus to the urban sector of the Japanese economy. The consumption of luxury goods by the higher aristocracy developed rapidly, while the conversion of the knight class into salaried officials augmented the demand for comforts beneath it (both Shogunal and *han* bureaucracies were congenitally overmanned because of the size of the samurai class). There was an overwhelming drainage of *daimyō* wealth to Edo and Ōsaka, caused by the costly construction and ostentatious itineraries attendant on the serial residence of the major feudal lords in the Tokugawa capital. It is estimated that up to 60–80 per cent of *han* cash outlays were accounted for by *sankin-kōtai* expenditure.[35] There were over 600 official residences or *yashiki* maintained by the *daimyō* in Edo (most major lords had more than three each). These residences were in fact sprawling estate-compounds, the largest of which would be up to 400 acres in extent, including mansions, offices, barracks, schools, stables, gymnasia, gardens and even prisons. Perhaps a sixth of the *han* retinues were permanently stationed in them. The great urban agglomeration of Edo was dominated by a concentric system of such *daimyō* residences, carefully distributed about the vast Chiyoda fortress-palace of the Shogunate itself in the centre of city. In all, half of the population of Edo lived in samurai households, and no less than two-thirds of the entire area of the city was the property of the military class.[36] To sustain the enormous costs of this system of compulsory feudal consumption, the *han* governments were obliged to convert their tax-revenues, extracted for the most part from the peasantry in kind, into cash incomes. Their rice surplus was thus marketed in Ōsaka, which came to be a distribution centre that was the commercial pendant to the consumption centre of Edo: it was there that specialized merchants managed *han* warehouses, advanced credit against taxes or stipends to lords or their vassals, and speculated in commodity futures. The enforced monetization of feudal revenues thus prepared the conditions for a rapid expansion of mercantile capital in the cities. At the same time, the *chōnin* class of town-dwellers was legally forbidden to acquire agricultural land: the Japanese merchants of the Tokugawa epoch were consequently prevented from diverting their capital into rural property, after the manner of their Chinese counterparts.[37] The very rigidity of the class-system created by Hideyoshi thus paradoxically encouraged the steady growth of purely urban fortunes.

There thus developed in the course of the 17th and 18th centuries an extremely prosperous stratum of merchants in the larger towns, who engaged in a wide range of commercial activities. *Chōnin* companies in the cities accumulated capital through marketing of the agricultural surplus (dealing in both rice and newer crops like cotton, silk or indigo), transport services (coastal shipping developed intensively), exchange transactions (there were over thirty major currencies in circulation in this period, since the *han* issued paper notes in addition to the *Bakufu* metallic coinages), manufacture of textiles, porcelain or other commodities (either concentrated in urban workshops or dispersed in the villages via a putting-out system), lumber and construction enterprises (frequent fires necessitated constant rebuilding in the towns), and loans to the *daimyō* or the Shogunate. The largest merchant houses came to control incomes equivalent to those of the most prominent territorial lords, for whom they acted as financial agents and sources of credit. The spreading commercialization of agriculture, accompanied by massive illegal migration to the towns, permitted an enormous expansion of the urban market. By the 18th century, Edo may have had a population of 1,000,000 — larger than contemporary London or Paris; Ōsaka and Kyōtō had perhaps 400,000 inhabitants each; and perhaps a tenth of the total population of Japan lived in towns of over 10,000.[38] This rapid wave of urbanization led to a scissors effect in the prices of manufactured and agricultural goods, given relative supply rigidity in the rural sector from which the nobility derived its income. The result was to create chronic budgetary difficulties for both the *Bakufu* and *han* governments, which became increasingly indebted to the merchants who advanced them loans against their fiscal revenues.

The deepening aristocratic deficits of the later Tokugawa epoch, however, did not betoken any corresponding ascent of the *chōnin* community within the social order as a whole. The Shogunate and the *daimyō* reacted to the crisis in their incomes by cancelling their debts, coercively extracting large 'gifts' from the merchant class, and cutting the rice stipends of their samurai retainers. For the *chōnin* were juridically at the mercy of the nobility whom they supplied with credit, and their gains could arbitrarily be erased by obligatory benevolences and special levies on them. Tokugawa law was 'socially shallow and territorially limited': it covered only the *tenryō* domains themselves, lacked any real judiciary and was mainly concerned with repression of crime. Civil law was rudimentary, grudgingly administered as 'a matter of grace' in litigation between private parties by the *Bakufu* authorities.[39] Legal security for capital transactions was thus always precarious, although the large Shogunal cities afforded merchants protection against *daimyō*, if not *Bakufu*, pressures. On the other hand, the preservation of the *Bakū-han* system blocked the emergence of a unified domestic market and hampered the growth of mercantile capital on a national scale, once the limits of *sankin-kōtai* expenditures had been reached. *Han* checkpoints and border guards impeded free passage of goods and persons, while many of the major *daimyō* houses followed protectionist policies of import restriction. Most decisive of all for the fate of the *chōnin* class in Japan, however, was Tokugawa isolationism. From the 1630's onwards, Japan was closed to foreigners, except for a Dutch–Chinese enclave off Nagasaki, and no Japanese was permitted to leave the country. These sealed frontiers were henceforward a permanent noose on the development of merchant capital in Japan. One of the fundamental preconditions of primitive accumulation in early modern Europe was the dramatic internationalization of commodity exchange and exploitation from the epoch of the Discoveries onwards. Lenin repeatedly and rightly emphasized that: 'It is impossible to conceive a capitalist nation without foreign trade, nor is there any such nation.'[40] The Shogunal policy of seclusion, in effect, precluded any possibility of a transition to the capitalist mode of production proper within the Tokugawa framework. Deprived of foreign trade, commercial capital in Japan was constantly reined in and re-routed towards parasitic dependence on the feudal nobility and its political systems. Its remarkable growth, despite this insurmountable limit to its expansion, was only possible because of the density and scale of the domestic markets, despite their division — with 30 million inhabitants, Japan in the mid-18th century was more populous than France. But there could be no 'capitalism in one country'. Tokugawa isolationism condemned the *chōnin* to a fundamentally subaltern existence.

The great metropolitan boom caused by the *sankin-kōtai* system came to an end in the early 18th century, together with the tapering off of population growth as a whole.

Restrictive official monopolies were licensed by the Shogunate in 1721. From about 1735, construction and expansion ceased in the large *Bakufu* cities.[41] Commercial vitality had, in fact, by then already shifted from the Ōsaka bankers and merchants to smaller inter-regional wholesalers. These in turn acquired monopolistic privileges towards the end of the 18th century, and entrepreneurial initiative moved further outwards into the provinces. In the early 19th century, it was the rural landlord-trader stratum of *jinushi* who proved the most dynamic business group, profiting from the lack of guild restrictions in the countryside to implant village industries such as *sake* brewing or silk manufacture (which migrated from the towns in this epoch).[42] There was thus a progressive diffusion of commerce outwards which was transforming the countryside at the close of the Tokugawa epoch, rather than revolutionizing the towns. For manufacturing activity itself remained extremely primitive: there was little division of labour in either urban or rural enterprises, no major technical inventions, and relatively few concentrations of wage-labour. Japanese industry, in fact, was overwhelmingly artisanal in character, and exiguous in equipment. The extensive development of organized commerce was never matched by an intensive advance in methods of production. Industrial technology was archaic, its improvement foreign to *chōnin* traditions. The prosperity and vitality of the Japanese merchant class had produced a distinctive urban culture of great artistic sophistication, above all in painting and literature. But it had not generated any growth in scientific knowledge or innovation in political thought. *Chōnin* creativity within the *Bakū-han* order was confined to the domains of imagination and diversion; it never extended to enquiry or criticism. The merchant community as a class lacked intellectual autonomy or corporate dignity: it was circumscribed to the end by the historical conditions of existence imposed on it by the feudal autarky of the Shogunate.

The immobility of the *Bakufu* itself in turn perpetuated the structural paradox of the State and society to which the Shogunate had given birth. For unlike any variant of feudalism in Europe, Tokugawa Japan combined a notably rigid and static parcellization of sovereignty with an extremely high velocity and volume of commodity circulation. The social and political framework of the country remained comparable to that of 14th century France, in the judgement of one of its major modern historians,[43] yet the economic magnitude of Edo was greater than that of 18th century London. Culturally, too, overall educational levels in Japan were remarkable: perhaps 30 per cent of the adult population, and 40–50 per cent of men, were literate by the mid-19th century.[44] No other region in the world, outside Europe and North America, contained such integrated financial mechanisms, such advanced commerce or such high literacy. The ultimate compatibility between the Japanese polity and economy in the Tokugawa epoch fundamentally rested on the disproportion between commodity *exchange* and *production* within the country: for, as we have seen, the monetization of the seigneurial surplus which was the basic motor of urban growth did not correspond to the real scale of commercial agriculture by the peasantry as such. It was an 'artificial' conversion of feudal deliveries in kind, superimposed on a primary production that was still predominantly subsistence, despite an increasing market orientation of its own in the later phases of the Shogunate. It was this objective disjuncture at the base of the economic system which *internally* permitted the conservation of the original juridical and territorial fragmentation of Japan, dating from the settlement after Sekigahara.

The *external* precondition of Tokugawa stability — fully as vital — was the sedulous insulation of Japan from the outside world, which sealed it off from ideological infections, economic disruptions, diplomatic disputes or military contests of any kind. Nevertheless, even within the airless world of the Chiyoda keep, the strains of maintaining an antiquated 'mediaeval' machinery of government in a dynamic 'early modern' economy were becoming increasingly evident by the early 19th century.

For the *Bakufu* was gradually gripped, just as much as the provincial daimiates, by a creeping revenue crisis: at the material intersection of sovereignty and productivity, its fiscal system was logically the most vulnerable link of the Shogunate. The Tokugawa government itself did not, of course, have to bear the expenses of the *sankin-kōtai* system which it imposed on the *han*. But since the whole social rationale of the ostentatory consumption involved in it was to demonstrate grades of rank and prestige within the aristocratic class, the Shogunate's own voluntary costs of display were necessarily even greater than those of the *daimyō*: the palatine household alone, composed of the women of the court, absorbed a larger share of the budget in the 18th century than the combined defense establishment of Ōsaka and Kyōtō.[45] Moreover, the *Bakufu* had to perform certain quasi-national functions as the unitary apex of the pyramid of feudal sovereignty in Japan, while itself disposing of only about one-fifth of the land-resources of the country: there was thus always a potential imbalance between its responsibilities and its tax capacity. Its extensive bureaucracy of *bushi* retainers was naturally far larger than that of any *han*, and was extremely expensive to maintain. The total cost of the rank and office stipends of its liege vassals covered about half its annual budget; while official corruption within the *Bakufu* eventually became widespread.[46] At the same time, the fiscal yield of its house-lands tended to decline in real terms, because it could not prevent increasing cash commutation of rice taxes, which depleted its treasury because the conversion rate was usually below market prices and coinage values were themselves steadily depreciating.[47] In the early phase of the Tokugawa epoch, the bullion monopoly of the Shogunate had been a hugely profitable asset: Japanese silver output at the turn of the 17th century, for example, was about half the volume of total American exports to Europe, at the height of the Spanish convoys.[48] But by the 18th century, the mines were suffering from flooding and production declined greatly. The *Bakufu* responded by resorting to systematic debasements of the existing coinage: between 1700 and 1854, the volume of nominal currency in circulation issued by the Shogunate increased by 400 per cent.[49] These devaluations eventually came to supply something between a quarter and a half of its annual income: since no competing specie was entering the country and demand was expanding within the economy as a whole, there was relatively little long-term price inflation. No regular taxation of commerce existed, but periodic and major confiscations were made from the merchant class from the early 18th century onwards, when the Shogunate so decided. Repeated budgetary shortfalls and financial emergencies nevertheless continued to harass the *Bakufu*, whose annual deficits were well over half a million gold ryō by 1837–41;[50] while short-term price oscillations during bad harvests could precipitate crises in countryside and capital alike. After nearly a decade of crop failures, much of Japan was haunted by famine in the 1830's, while the incumbent *rōjū* clique vainly strove to beat down prices and consolidate house income. In 1837, Ōsaka was the scene of a desperate attempt at plebeian insurrection, which revealed how charged the political climate of the country was becoming. At the same time, the armed apparatus of the Shogunate had — after over two centuries of domestic peace — been drastically corroded: the outmoded and incompetent guard units of the *tenryō* were to prove incapable of assuring security within Edo itself in a civil crisis;[51] while the *Bakufu* no longer had any operative superiority over the forces that could be mustered in the *tozama han* of the South-West. The military evolution of Tokugawa feudalism was the antithesis of that of European Absolutism: a progressive diminution and dilapidation of its troop-strength occurred.

The Japanese feudal order was thus already in the throes of a slow internal crisis by the early 19th century: but if the commodity economy had eroded the stability of the old social and institutional instructure, it had not yet generated the elements for a political solution to supersede it. The Tokugawa peace was still intact at mid-century. It was the exogenous impact of Western imperialism, with the arrival of Commodore Perry's squadron in 1853, which suddenly condensed the multiple latent contradictions of the Shogunal state, and set off a revolutionary explosion against it. For the aggressive intrusion of American, Russian, British, French and other warships into Japanese waters, demanding the establishment of diplomatic and trade relations at gun-point, posed an ominous dilemma for the *Bakufu*. For two centuries, it had systematically instilled xenophobia into all classes in Japan, as one of the most sacred themes of official ideology: the total exclusion of foreigners had, indeed, been one of the sociological lynch-pins of its rule. Yet it now confronted a military menace whose technological power — embodied in the iron-clad steam-ships hovering in the Bay of Yokohama — it immediately became aware was easily capable of crushing its own armies. It therefore had to temporize and concede the Western demand for the 'opening up' of Japan, to preserve its own survival. By doing so, however, it immediately rendered itself vulnerable to xenophobic attacks from within. Important collateral lineages of the Tokugawa house itself were rabidly hostile to the presence of foreign missions in Japan: the first assassinations of Westerners in their enclave at Yokohama were often the work of samurai from the fief of Mito, one of the three main cadet branches of the Tokugawa dynasty. The Emperor in Kyōtō, guardian and symbol of traditional cultural values, was also ferociously opposed to dealing with the intruders. With the onset of what all sections of the Japanese feudal class felt to be a national emergency, the imperial court was suddenly reactivated as an effective secondary pole of power, and the *kuge* aristocracy in Kyōtō soon became a constant focus of intrigue against the Shogunal bureaucracy in Edo. The Tokugawa regime was, in effect, now in an impossible situation. Politically, it could only justify its progressive retreats and concessions before Western demands by explaining to the *daimyō* the military inferiority which necessitated them. But to do so was to admit its own weakness and thereby invite armed subversion and revolt against itself. Pinned down by the external danger, it became increasingly unable to cope with the internal unrest that its delaying tactics provoked.

Economically, moreover, the abrupt end of Japanese seclusion upset the whole viability of the Shogunal monetary system: for since the Tokugawa coinages were essentially fiat issues, with far less bullion content that their denominational value, foreign merchants refused to accept them at parity with Western currencies based on real silver weightages. The advent of foreign trade on a large scale thus forced the *Bakufu* to devalue steeply to the actual bullion content of its coinage, and to issue paper money, while external demand for key local products — silk, tea and cotton — soared. The result was a catastrophic domestic inflation: the price of rice quintupled between 1853 and 1869,[52] causing acute popular unrest in towns and countryside. The Shogunal bureaucracy, convoluted and divided, was unable to react with any clear or decisive policy to the dangers now pressing in upon it. The lamentable state of its security apparatus was revealed when the one resolute leader produced by the *Bakufu* in its last phase, Ii Naosuke, was assassinated by xenophobic samurai in Edo in 1860;[53] two years later, another *attentat* forced his successor to resign. The *tozama* fiefs of the South-West — Satsuma, Chōshū, Tosa and Saga — by their structural position always antagonists of the *Bakufu*, were now emboldened to pass over to the offensive and conspire for its overthrow. Their own military and economic resources, husbanded by regimes more compact and efficacious than the Edo government, were put on a war footing. *Han* troops were modernized, enlarged and reequipped with Western armaments; while Satsuma already possessed the largest samurai cadre in Japan, Chōshū commanders recruited and drilled rich peasants to, create a commoner force capable of use against the Shogunate. Popular expectations of great changes were now spreading in superstitious forms among the crowds of Nagoya, Ōsaka and Edo, while the tacit support of certain *chōnin* bankers was won to provide the necessary financial reserves for a civil war. Constant liaison with the *kuge* malcontents in Kyōtō ensured the *tozama* leaders of crucial ideological coverage for the projected operation: it was to be nothing less than a revolution whose formal aim was to restore the Imperial authority that had been usurped by the Shogunate. The Emperor thus supplied a transcendental symbol to which all classes could in theory be rallied. A swift coup delivered Kyōtō to Satsuma troops in 1867. With the city under military control, the Emperor Meiji read a proclamation drafted by his court formally ending the Shogunate. The *Bakufu*, subverted and demoralized, proved incapable of any determined resistance within a few weeks, the whole of Japan had been seized by the insurgent *tozama* armies, and the unitary Meiji State had been founded. The fall of the Shogunate spelt the end of Japanese feudalism.

Economically and diplomatically undermined from abroad, once the safety of its seclusion had gone, the Tokugawa State was politically and militarily undone from within by the very parcellization of sovereignty that it had always preserved: its lack of any monopoly of armed force, and its failure to suppress imperial legitimacy, eventually rendered it impotent before a well-organized insurrection in the name of the Emperor. The Meiji State that succeeded it promptly proceeded to a sweeping arc of measures to abolish feudalism from above — the most radical such programme ever to be enacted. The fief system was liquidated, the four-estate order destroyed, the equality of every citizen before the law proclaimed, calendar and dress reformed, a unified market and single currency created, and industrialization and military expansion systematically promoted. A capitalist economy and polity emerged directly from the elimination of the Shogunate. The complex historical mechanisms of the revolutionary transformation accomplished by the Meiji Restoration remain to be examined. Here it is only necessary to stress that, contrary to the supposition of some

Japanese historians,[54] the Meiji State was not in any categorical sense an Absolutism. Initially an emergency dictatorship of the new ruling bloc, it soon proved itself a peremptory capitalist state, whose mettle was within a few decades to be fittingly tested in action against a genuine Absolutism. In 1905, the Russian debacles at Tsushima and Mukden revealed to the world the difference between the two. The passage from feudalism to capitalism was effected, to a unique extent, without political interlude in Japan.

Notes

1. For a lucid account of the Taihō State, see J.W. Hall, *Japan from Prehistory to Modern Times*, London 1970, pp. 43–60.

2. For a comparative analysis of the *shōen*, see Joüon des Longrais, *L'Est et l'Ouest, Institutions du Japon et de l'Occident Comparées*, Paris, 1958, pp. 92–103.

3. The origins of the *bushi* are sketched in J.W. Hall, *Government and Local Power in Japan 500–1700*, Princeton 1966, pp. 131–3.

4. M. Shinoda, *The Founding of the Kamakura Shogunate 1180–1185*, New York 1960, pp. 112–13, 141–4.

5. See the extensive discussion of the *jitō* in Hall, *Government and Local Power in Japan*, pp. 157–8, 182–90.

6. Shinoda, *The Founding of the Kamakura Shogunate*, p. 140.

7   H.P. Varley, *The Ōnin War*, New York 1967, pp. 38–43.

8. *Ibid.*, pp. 76–7.

9. Hall, *Japan from Prehistory to Modern Times*, p. 121.

10. For the textual wording of a vassal oath and land grant of this epoch, see Hall, *Government and Local Power in Japan*, pp. 253–4: Sengoku feudal orgainzation generally is depicted, pp. 246–56.

11. This characteristic is much stressed by Joüon: *L'Est et l'Ouest*, pp. 119–20, 164.

12. See the acute comments by Joüon, *L'Est et l'Ouest*, pp. 145–7, 395–6. It should be noted, however, that despite the terminological bias of Japanese feudalism towards pseudo-kin relationships, in practice vassalage was considered a more secure bond of loyalty than consanguinity by baronial lords of the epoch: significantly, branch families of a magnate line were typically assimilated to vassal status. See Hall, *Government and Local Power in Japan*, p. 251.

13. For an account of Sakai, see G. Sansom, *A History of Japan 1334–1615*, London 1961, pp. 189, 272–3, 304–5.

14. The circumstances which produced the Yamashiro commune are sketched in Varley, *The Ōnin War*, pp. 192–204.

15. 'Hideyoshi's victory represented not a true unification but the conquest of Japan by one *daimyō* league over the entire country': Hall, *Government and Local Power in Japan*, p. 284.

16. Sansom comments that the actual proportion collected was nearer two-fifths, because of widespread evasion: *A History of Japan 1334–1615*, p. 319.

17. A Craig, *Chōshū in the Meiji Restoration*, Cambridge USA, 1961, p. 15. Land in Japan was officially assessed from Hideyoshi onwards by its rice-yield, in *koku* (about 5 bushels)

18. The successive phases of this process within the Shogunate are carefully traced in C. Totman, *Politics in the Tokugawa Bakufu 1600–1843*, Cambridge USA, 1967, pp. 204–33.

19. Totman, *Politics in the Tokugawa Bakufu 1600–1843*, pp. 45, 50.

20. P. Akamatsu, *Meiji 1868: Révolution et Contre-Révolution au Japon*, Paris 1968, p.30.

21. Hall, *Japan from Prehistory to Modern Times*, p. 169.

22. Craig, *Chōshū in the Meiji Restoration*, p. 11.

23. Craig, *Chōshū in the Meiji Restoration*, pp. 15–16; Totman, *Politics in the Tokugawa Bakufu*, pp. 49–50. The origin of the exceptionally high samurai ratios in the South-Western *tozama* fiefs lay in the post-Sekigahara settlement, when Ieyasu drastically reduced the domains of his enemies. The result was to concentrate their retainers into much smaller areas. The *tozama* lords, for their part, concealed the real output of their lands in order to minimize the scale of the reductions ordered by the *Bakufu*.

24. See the tentative calculations in W.G. Beasley, 'Feudal Revenues in Japan at the Time of the Meiji Restoration'. *Journal of Asian Studies*, XIX, No. 3, May 1960, pp. 255–72.

25. The role of the *daimyō* varied greatly, however: in the *Bakumatsu* period, for example, while the Chōshū lord was a cipher, the Satsuma or Tosa lords were politically active.

26. Kohachiro Takahashi, 'La Place del la Révolution de Meiji dans L'Historie Agraire du Japon', *Revue Historique*, October–December 1953, pp. 235–6.

27. Hall, *Japan from Prehistory to Modern Times*, p. 201.

28. Hall, *Japan from Prehistory to Modern Times*, pp. 201–2. Reclamations of new land had in some cases, as in feudal Europe or mediaeval China, led to deterioration of older lands, and over-extended riparian works had resulted in disastrous floods. See J.W. Hall, *Tanuma Okitsugu, 1719–1788*, Cambridge USA, 1955, pp. 63–5.

29. The new threshing-machines of the 18th century seem to have been the only major technical invention in Japanese agriculture during this period: T.C. Smith, *The Agrarian Origins of Modern Japan*, Stanford 1959, p. 102.

30. The exact extent of this commercialization is a matter of considerable dispute. Crawcour asserts that 'it is safe to say' that over one half and perhaps nearer two-thirds of gross production was marketed in one form or another by the mid-nineteenth century: E.S. Crawcour, 'The Tokugawa Heritage', in W. Lockwood (ed.), *The State and Economic Enterprise in Japan*, Princeton 1965, pp. 39–41. Ohkawa and Rozovsky, on the other hand, discount any such high estimate, stressing that even in the early 1960's, only some 60 per cent of Japanese agrarian output reached the market: they reckon that, excluding tax-rice, the index of real (peasant) commercialization was probably not more than 20 per cent in the 1860's: 'A Century of Japanese Economic Growth', in Lockwood, *The State and Economic Enterprise in Japan*, p. 57. It should be emphasized that the structural distinction between noble and peasant forms of commercialization is crucial to an understanding of both the dynamic and limits of Tokugawa agriculture.

31. Smith, *The Agrarian Origins of Modern Japan*, pp. 5–64, presents a comprehensive account of this traditional pattern.

32. The overall performance of the later Tokugawa agrarian economy is still a focus of

controversy. In his important study, revising official rice-estimates at the start of the Meiji epoch upwards, Nakamura develops a set of hypotheses which indicate an increase in *per capita* product of some 23 per cent over the period 1680–1870: see J. Nakamura, *Agricultural Production and the Economic Development of Japan 1873–1922*, Princeton 1966, pp. 75–8, 90, 137. Vigorous objections to his assumptions, however, have been made by Rozovsky, who argues that the yield-ratios imputed to Tokugawa riziculture by Nakamura must be too high, since they exceed those of all other countries of monsoon Asia in the 20th century: H. Rozovsky, 'Rumbles in the Rice-Fields: Professor Nakamura versus the Official Statistics', *Journal of Asian Studies*, XXVII, No. 2, February 1968, p. 355. Two recent articles give euphoric but impressonistic accounts of *Baku-han* agriculture, without any attempt at quantification: S.B. Hanley and K. Yamamura, 'A Quiet Transformation in Tokugawa Economic History', *Journal of Asian Studies*, XXX, No. 2, February 1971, pp. 373–84, and Kee Il Choi, 'Technological Diffusion in Agriculture under the *Baku-han* System', *Journal of Asian Studies*, XXX, No. 4, August 1971, pp. 749–59.

33. Between 1590 and 1867, modern research has so far identified some 2,800 peasant riots; another 1,000 popular outbreaks occurred in the towns: Kohachiro Takahashi, 'La Restauration de Meiji au Japon at la Révolution Français', *Recherches Internationales*, No. 62, 1970, p. 78. In the 19th century, the number of inter-peasant (as opposed to anti-seigneurial) riots increased: Akamatsu, *Meiji 1868*, pp. 44–5.

34. C.D. Sheldon, *The Rise of the Merchant Class in Tokugawa Japan 1600–1868*, Locust Valley 1958, pp. 33–6, who comments that peasant headmen exercised more power in the villages than merchants in the towns.

35. T.G. Tsukahira, *Feudal Control in Tokugawa Japan: The Sankin-Kōtai System*, Cambridge USA 1966, pp. 96–102. For a graphic account of the new urban life-styles affected by nobles and merchants in Edo, see Hall, *Tanuma Okitsugu*, pp. 107–17.

36. After the Restoration, the Meiji government released the following figures for urban property in Edo: 68.6 per cent was 'military land', 15.6 per cent belonged to 'temples and shrines', and only 15.8 per cent was the property of townspeople or *chōnin* themselves: Tsukahira, *Feudal Control in Tokugawa Japan*, pp. 91, 196. Totman reckons the size of the whole Chiyoda castle at one square mile, and the administrative complex of the Main Enceinte alone at 9 acres: *Politics in the Tokugawa Bakufu*, pp. 92, 95.

37. The *chōnin* class technically included both merchants (*shōnin*) and artisans (*kōnin*). Subsequent discussion of them here refers essentially to merchants.

38. Hall, *Japan from Prehistory to Modern Times*, p. 210.

39. D.F. Henderson, 'The Evolution of Tokugawa Law', in J. Hall and M. Jansen, *Studies in the Institutional History of Early Modern Japan*, Princeton 1968, pp. 207, 214, 225–8.

40. Lenin, *Collected Works*, Vol. 3, p. 65; see also 1, pp. 102–3, 2, pp. 164–5.

41. Sheldon, *The Rise of the Merchant Class in Tokugawa Japan*, p. 100.

42. For these successive shifts in the centre of commercial gravity under the Shogunate, see E.S. Crawcour, 'Changes in Japanese Commerce in the Tokugawa Period', in Hall and Jansen, *Studies in the Institutional History of Early Modern Japan*, pp. 193–201.

43. Craig, *Chōshū in the Meiji Restoration*, p. 33.

44. R.P. Dore, *Education in Tokugawa Japan*, Berkeley 1965, pp. 254, 321.

45. Totman, *Politics in the Tokugawa Bakufu*, p. 287

46. For salary costs, see Totman, *Politics in the Tokugawa Bakufu*, p. 82. For corruption and purchase of office, see the engaging candour of Tanuma Okitsugu, Grand Chamberlain in the Bakufu in the late 18th century: 'Gold and silver are treasures more precious than life itself. If a person brings this treasure with an expression of his desire to serve in some public capacity, I can be assured that he is serious in his desire. A man's strength of desire will be apparent in the size of his gift.' Hall, *Tanuma Okitsugu*, p. 55.

47. Totman, *Politics in the Tokugawa Bakufu*, pp. 78–80. The legal limit for cash conversion was 1/3 of the tax, but the average actually came to be over 2/5.

48. Vilar, *Oro y Moneda en la Historia*, p. 103.

49. P. Frost, *The Bakumatsu Currency Crisis*, Cambridge USA 1970, p. 9.

50. W.G. Beasley, *The Meiji Restoration*, London 1973, p. 51.

51. A striking sign of the military archaism of the Shogunate was the continued official precedence given to swords over muskets, despite all the experience of the Sengoku epoch in the superiority of fire-arms: Totman, *Politics in the Tokugawa Bakufu*, pp. 47–8.

52. Frost, *The Bakumatsu Currency Crisis*, p. 41.

53. For this critical episode, see Akamatsu, *Meiji 1868*, pp. 165–7.

54. See, for example, the classic Marxist study of the Restoration, available outside Japan only in Russian: Shigeki Toyama, *Meidzi Isin, Krushenie Feodalizma v Yaponii*, Moscow 1959, pp. 183, 217–18, 241, 295. There is no space here to do more than make the bald assertion above: a full discussion of the historical character of the Meiji Restoration must be reserved for a later study. Lenin's view of the nature of the victor in the Russo–Japanese War may, however, be noted. He believed that 'the Japanese bourgeoisie' had inflicted 'a crushing defeat' on the 'feudal autocracy' of Tsarism: 'autocratic Russia has been defeated by constitutional Japan'. Lenin, *Collected Works*, Vol. 8, pp. 52, 53, 28.

2. The Agrarian Origins of Modern Japan
Thomas C. Smith

If a backward country, such as Japan was in 1850, is to modernize as rapidly as Japan did, it seems necessary that it satisfy a minimum of four conditions. First, it must have a leadership with a vision of a future radically different from the past. Second, the leadership must have control over a government with a high degree of authority and stability for decades; otherwise it will be unable to channel income into investment on the necessary scale, to overhaul or abolish traditional institutions that impede change, and to bring the people to the pitch of effort required to become something they are not. Third, the economy must afford the means of investing on a significant scale. Last, industry must have a satisfactory supply of labor. That these conditions could be satisfied in Japan in the second half of the nineteenth century was in no small part due to the agrarian changes of the preceding century and a half. Let us consider each condition in turn.

Japanese modernization as a rapid and deliberate movement began in 1868 with the Meiji Restoration. This event brought to power new men who used the authority of the state to drive the nation swiftly toward goals of industrial strength and military competence; the transformation of the country in the next few decades was largely their deliberate work. No one would deny that there were certain long-term trends in Japanese society and economy favorable to this work, but without a political revolution they might have come to nothing. How, then, did the revolution itself come about?

We know that many of the revolutionary leaders were warriors of relatively low rank who used their lords' fiefs (in which they had already won considerable power) as political and military bases to destroy the Shogunate and create a new government around their Emperor. But why did they choose to use power as they did, for sweeping reform rather than to restore the feudal system along lines more to their advantage? And how did lowly and often impecunious warriors gain such power in the first place? We shall probably never know in satisfactory detail, since many of the critical episodes of the drama were backstage maneuvers in an atmosphere of conspiracy and suspicion. Although the agrarian background of politics of that period throws no direct light on these confused events, it helps us understand their outcome. But first something must be said of the place of the village in the political system.

The 250-odd fiefs in existence at the end of the Tokugawa period were similarly organized. Each was a more or less extensive territory held by a lord (*daimyō*) who lived in a castle town surrounded by armed retainers through whom he administered his lands. The administration consisted essentially of two echelons of officials: those who manned the central bureaus located in the castle or nearby in the town, and the district magistrates who were scattered about the fief. Each of the latter had an area

Reprinted from *THE AGRARIAN ORIGINS OF MODERN JAPAN* by Thomas C. Smith with the permission of the publishers, Stanford University Press. Copyright © 1959 by the Board of Trustees of the Leland Stanford Junior University.

in which he collected taxes, administered justice, maintained public order, carried out the orders of higher organs of government; in short, where he represented the lord in all of his manifold functions.

There were fewer of these district officials than seems possible today when we recall their heavy responsibilities. Although each had a staff of runners, secretaries, copyists, and servants, he was the only official between the village and the castle town, which in some cases was scores or, in the case of detached territories, even hundreds of miles away. Most surprising, perhaps, he usually had no military force at his command except a handful of armed men for guard duty. Nor were there warriors scattered through the villages who could rally quickly to his support with retainers, horses, and arms. Three hundred years earlier, in all but a few localities, the warriors had been removed from the countryside to the castle town in order to eliminate the danger to the lord of armed retainers directly in control of land and subjects. Thus the district magistrate, stationed in some tiny town or village surrounded by thickly settled hamlets stretching as far as the eye could see and well beyond, was charged with governing thousands of peasant families, with no immediate source of support more substantial than his insignia of office.

What made possible this extraordinary economy of force and officialdom was the competence and reliability of local government. Nowhere, for instance, did the lord undertake to levy taxes on individual peasants; rather, he laid taxes on villages as units, leaving each to allocate and collect its own, and to make up any deficit that might occur in the payments of individual families. This was but one of many administrative functions performed by villages in all parts of the country. Villages maintained their own roads and irrigation works, policed their territories, administered common land and irrigation rights; validated legal transactions among members, mediated disputes, and passed sentence and imposed punishment in petty criminal cases; enforced the lord's law and their own, stood responsible as a whole for a crime by any of their members, borrowed money, made contracts, sued and were sued. Aside from transmitting the lord's instructions to the villages, the magistrate normally did little more than help assess villages for taxes and receive their payments and hear the more serious civil and criminal cases they referred to him. Indeed, when local government was working well, he might even absent himself from his district for considerable periods, merely leaving an assistant in charge.

This administrative system was by no means merely a contrivance of the warrior class for its convenience; it had been evolving since pre-historic times. From the beginning of agriculture the village had a strong corporate life. The pattern of compact settlements testifies to the fact, as do the character of the tutelary deities and the ritual surrounding them. Even without these indications, however, one might guess at the character of the village from the authority the village exercised over its members and the need for continuous cooperation in farming.

As villages grew through immigration and the proliferation of families, a hierarchy of lineage, wealth, and political rights formed naturally in each, through the operation of the inheritance system and discrimination against immigrants. Cooperation in farming and the distributive system both were organized around these hierarchies; the villages were governed by them insofar as villages governed themselves. The evolving structure within the village was not radically modified until it was finally disrupted by the market, but the relations of the village to outside authority underwent many changes. The problem of government for successive military rulers was to make full administrative use of, without being menaced by, these stable local systems of power, typically headed by warrior families. By far the most successful attempt to solve this problem was the last, under the Tokugawa. It gave the village an extraordinary degree of autonomy *after* removing the warriors from it: an arrangement that brought the country two and a half centuries of peace, together with an unprecedented measure of popular welfare and justice.

But no balance between local government and higher authority could be final, and the sources of strength in the Tokugawa system were potentially sources of weakness. Power had been delegated downward so far, and on such a scale, that it could no longer be easily recovered. The system worked amazingly well; but everything depended on the continuing loyalty and discipline of the peasants. No breakdown of these supports of government was likely to occur — and none did, in fact — so long as the economic and social systems of the traditional village remained undisturbed. But what if these structures were violently upset: if the hierarchy of lineage, wealth, and political rights were disrupted from the outside?

No one in 1600 could have foreseen any such development. Yet the very success of the Tokugawa system created conditions favorable to change; cities grew, communications improved, productivity in agriculture increased, industry spread from town to countryside. Government did its best to isolate the village from the effects of these and other changes. But, as we have seen, the best efforts were unavailing and what was most feared happened: the stable structure of power in the village was upset.

Instability in the villages must have affected warrior politics within fiefs and nationally; for by 1860 the warrior class was deeply divided over foreign policy and the position of the Emperor. The contending parties would not have overlooked the opportunity to use village factions to their advantage since to control the villages of a fief was already to control half of its government. Besides, agrarian issues — posed by the spread of tenancy, the movement of population to towns and cities, and official trade monopolies — themselves contributed to the growing political crisis, forcing warrior parties to take positions on reform legislation certain to arouse intense interest — whether hostile or approving — in the villages.

It is not surprising, therefore, to find evidence of peasants taking part in the Restoration movement. Not only were loyalist sympathies common among the educated class of the village; a surprising number of peasants were given court honors for their part in the Restoration, and there must have been many more whose help was never so dramatically acknowledged. It is impossible to say with certainty how important peasant support was to the success of the Restoration; but it seems to have been of some consequence, and it was perhaps also important in turning the new government away from the temptation, undoubtedly present, to use victory merely to redistribute power within the warrior class.

That a backward nation's leaders are enlightened is not enough to guarantee success in modernizing; the leaders must have continuing support from the nation. Japan's new leaders commanded such support — despite what they demanded of the nation: nothing less than that it become an industrial society within a generation. One need only think what that overriding goal implied — in social dislocations, psychological strain, the disturbance of vested interests — to understand how difficult was the problem of organizing support.

To mobilize and hold support it was clearly necessary to formulate goals the nation could understand. But how state goals compellingly when they far transcend the experience of the community? How talk about national power, industrialization, or the march of science to a still agrarian people just emerging from feudalism? Japan's new leaders found the answer to this problem in translating these goals into a traditional language of loyalty and obligation. This was the language of feudal and family ethics expressing ideals central to the experience of nearly all Japanese. With suitable interpretation to make all little loyalties lead up to one great loyalty to the Emperor, these ideals called up prodigies of effort and self-sacrifice. No government could ask for more.

But, in thus using tradition on behalf of change, the new government soon found itself in a painful dilemma. Old values might sanction the building of a new society, but the new society could never be as hospitable to them as the old had been. In fact as an industrial society came into being, traditional values became increasingly irrelevant or obstructive, and steadily lost the power to command belief. Let me cite a few examples.

Rationalist thought, which an educational system dedicated to the advancement of science and technology was bound to promote, gradually called into question central elements of the political myth — imperial divinity and the family state. Modern industry gave rise to new and harsher class antagonisms that made the ideals of solidarity and duty to superiors harder to cherish. The authority of the family and the power of its symbols declined as the family lost economic functions to the market, and as the difference in outlook between generations widened. Nevertheless, the primary old values of loyalty and obedience did not collapse: they were continuously reinforced by stronger, more efficient measures of indoctrination and thought control by the state.

The groups in control of the state had no choice but to sustain orthodoxy as best they could. Without it there was no sanction for their monopoly of power, or for the wrenching changes of the forced march to industry and empire. If that effort should collapse, so must Japan's precarious international position, bringing loss of foreign markets, unemployment, perhaps social revolution. These were unthinkable alternatives. There was no way to go but ahead; but that way lay a further weakening of tradition which, the weaker it became, was the more needed to give stability and command effort. So leaders pushed ahead at any cost with supreme nerve or blind faith — it mattered little which. The ultimate price the nation paid was to be led without enthusiasm into a war that could not be won.

Long before this, however, the nation was paying in malaise for industrial success. Japanese life was wracked by the mounting tension of trying to live by the values of another age. Tensions did not take the form of ideological or political struggle between the parties who stood by tradition and those who would overthrow it. Such overt struggle might have been easier, or in any case would have put the stress between groups and parties rather than inside individuals. Except for Marxist intellectuals, however, no notable segment of the Japanese population openly disfavored the official ideology; no one could, without becoming an enemy of the state and in some real sense ceasing to be Japanese. But as time passed fewer and fewer people bore the weight of tradition comfortably; despite nearly universal protestations of loyalty and belief there was secret or unconscious alienation.

It is easier to guess than prove the existence of inner conflict deep beneath the surface of conduct. Still, testifying to it there were unwitting — and even some witting — flashes of candor. Take this passage from the novel *Sore kara*, by Natsume Soseki, in which a young man reflects on his father.[1]

> His father had received the moral upbringing usual for samurai before the Restoration. This upbringing taught a code of conduct utterly removed from the realities of day-to-day living, yet his father believed in it implicitly — and this despite the fact that he was forever being driven by the fierce demands of business life. Over the long years he had changed with these demands, and now he bore little resemblance to what he once was, though he was quite unaware of this. Indeed, he was always boasting that it was his strict warrior education that accounted for his success! But Daisuke thought differently. How could one fulfill the hourly demands of modern life and live by a feudal ethic! Even to try, one must wage war against oneself.

Or consider the case of Ishikawa Takuboku, one of Japan's most famous poets. Takuboku wrote a novel (*Kumo wa tensai dearu*) in which the hero, who is surely Takuboku himself, thinks existing society utterly corrupt and worthy only of destruction. While writing this novel, Takuboku wrote to a friend that he badly needed the money from its publication to discharge a long-neglected duty to his elder brother. What this duty was he did not say, but the term he used for it was *giri* — one of the central concepts of the ethics taught in the schools; and Takuboku was at this time a village school teacher, and his story's hero was the principal of a village elementary school. Conflicts like that of Takuboku, who seems a rebel against society's conventions while a slave to them, were not uncommon, and few aspects of modern Japanese culture would not reveal some evidence of them to careful analysis. Let me cite a few other examples.

Except on the far left, which did not count in the parliamentary struggle, no political party openly challenged the theory that all political authority derived from the Emperor. For parliamentary parties this theory had serious disadvantages since it placed governments beyond their control — cabinet ministers being responsible only to the Emperor. To overcome this inconvenience, almost continuously from 1880 to about 1935 one party or another advanced the view — strongly resisted by the military and the bureaucracy — that cabinet ministers should be responsible to parliament: the Emperor would still appoint ministers, but from the majority party in the lower house only. Those who held this view disclaimed any intention of encroaching on the power of the Emperor; they proved it (to their own satisfaction) by giving the doctrine of the Emperor as father of the people an ingenious if unconvincing twist. Since the Emperor was a wise and benevolent father who desired nothing but the welfare of his loving and filial subjects, there could be no conflict between throne and people; and to make the government responsible to parliament would merely bring the two closer together, thus making more effective the single will of both — now sometimes frustrated by selfish (and presumably unfilial) ministers! This argument was advanced by parties representing modern businessmen who, though aware of the stabilizing uses of the throne, were from time to time embarrassed and bullied by the governments that manipulated the throne's occult powers. The argument was, in essence, a radical attack on authoritarian government, hidden in a statement of the purest orthodoxy. There was no dishonesty in this — just divided minds and hearts.

Other examples come to mind: the drive to rationalize operations in business firms organized on the family principle; indoctrination in the values of the hierarchical family in an egalitarian educational system; the emperor cult and class struggle in the labor movement. But let us consider an important problem our argument raises. How was it that the old values continued to be strong enough to serve the purposes of the state and to create tension in men's minds? Why did the values rather not quickly lose their emotional power? The answer cannot merely be that the government sustained them through the educational system, military training, and public information media: for then what sustained the resolution of the government as its social base was transformed?

This brings us back to the character of agrarian change, which was determined as much by what did *not* change about farming as by what did. As was noted in the [Introduction], change occurred within relatively narrow technical limits; and of the relatively unchanging elements of farming, the most important were the small size of the units, family organization of production, and the unsparing use of hand labor.[2] Whatever the reasons for these extraordinary continuities — and they are hotly debated, they had the effect of perpetuating the peasant family as an economic unit, thus allowing little change in its social character. The family's welfare continued to be of transcendent value, its authority immense. Solidarity and obedience were taught to the young as conditions of survival, and these traditional values carried over to behavior outside the family.

Another repository of tradition was the village. In many countries industry broke up the peasant village and dispersed its population, or greatly weakened its solidarity by creating deep class divisions. Neither development occurred in Japan, at least not on a comparable scale. Family farming remained the almost invariable rule, preserving the pattern of compact settlements and blocking the growth of large capitalist farms. Landownership did tend to concentrate, but large owners turned their land over to families of tenants or part-tenants rather than work it themselves. Despite increasing differences of income and the growth of by-employments, therefore, the village remained predominantly a community of small peasants faced with similar problems of small-scale cultivation and marketing. Sentimental and organizational ties from an earlier period persisted with special force, and the authority of the village over its members remained exceedingly strong.

30

Rice culture also contributed to this result. Rice was cultivated wherever soil, climate and terrain permitted, which is to say on at least part of most holdings. Because rice must be made to stand in water much of the growing season to get maximum yields, there was need in nearly every village for an extensive system of ditches, dams, dikes, ponds, tunnels, and water gates. Since these could be constructed and maintained only by community effort, their use was subject to community control. A rice farmer never owned or controlled all of the essential means of production himself, and he could not individually make all of the critical decisions of farming. He might wish, for instance, to turn an unirrigated field into paddy, but he would not be allowed to do so if this would impair the water supply of others. And, if this was the case, he would refrain from insisting on his wish since he had been taught he must and village opinion would be ranged solidly against him if he did not. The habit of obedience to community opinion where water was concerned likewise carried over to other community affairs (including the preservation of tradition), since any serious breach of solidarity directly threatened the communal foundations of farming.

Family farming and the emphasis on rice as a crop tended to preserve tradition among the peasantry in another way. These two factors kept farming less commercial than one might think in a country with as large an urban market as Japan. Most peasant families supplied all or nearly all of their own food, and food took a relatively large share of individual output. Hence, about one-third of the total agricultural income of the average peasant family in 1935 was received in kind, which is to say was consumed without marketing. Thus the Japanese peasant's involvement in the market was far from complete; commercial values did not penetrate a very large area of economic relations, which remained embedded in custom-bound social groups.[3]

Despite some weakening, the peasant family and village remained enormously powerful, conservative institutions. And it must be remembered that agriculture was not changing — or these institutions weakening — at the same rate in all parts of the country. There were great variations in this respect. In some places, for example, individual agriculture was a reality by the end of the Tokugawa period; in others it had just begun to appear. So the world of traditional values was not dead even in the early part of this century, but was full of life over large parts of Thōku, Hokuriku, and Kyūshū, and in some other areas.

Thus, although modernization generated in towns and cities new attitudes destructive of tradition, and greatly affected some important aspects of agriculture, the countryside remained a vast and populous hinterland of conservation. Nor did the demographic ratio between town and country alter with the growth of industry as rapidly as in some countries. Owing to the intensive nature of farming, the agricultural population was almost perfectly stable from 1868 to 1940. As a result, persons employed in agriculture in Japan in 1930 accounted for 50.3 percent of the total labor force — as compared with 18.8 percent in the United States in 1940, 16.3 percent in Germany in 1933, and 6.2 percent in England in 1938! Here, then, was one of the most important reasons the state was able to sustain tradition even in the face of breathless change.

This brings us to a third condition for late but rapid modernization. Even though a government is strong and has the will to modernize, it must still find the means to invest on a grand scale in schools, factories, roads, harbors, railways, and so on, or its ambitions will come to nothing. If funds cannot be had from foreign sources, they must be taken from the domestic economy — which in most cases means from agriculture: thus the ability to modernize comes to depend largely on the productivity of agriculture and the willingness of the peasantry to part with current income for distant and half-understood goals.

This was Japan's predicament during the second half of the nineteenth century. Being fearful of the political consequences of foreign borrowing, the government financed investment almost entirely from domestic sources — mainly agriculture. The land tax accounted for 78 percent of ordinary revenues (the bulk of total revenues) from 1868 to 1881, and although the figure tended to fall after that it still stood at 50 percent in 1890. High as the rate of tax on land was, however, it did not represent an increase over the Tokugawa period. Already at the end of that period the take from agriculture by the warrior class was immense, and the Meiji government merely redirected it into new channels. Modernization was achieved, therefore, without reducing rural living standards or even taking the increase in productivity that occurred.

This bespeaks a very high level of productivity in agriculture by the end of the Tokugawa period, and it could not have been achieved except for the changes that had taken place in farming since 1600. These had freed the peasant of the goals of subsistence farming, concentrating his attention on raising crop yields, and they had given him new fertilizers, crops, and plant strains. At the same time they had loosened the control of the social group over his methods and routine, leaving him, within certain broad limits, free to farm as he would whatever others might do. This is but half of the story, however. Changes in farming had created a "surplus": but the traditional features of agrarian society made it possible for the government to continue to take the surplus over many generations. Had the rural population been moving away from tradition as rapidly as some other elements of the population, it is at least doubtful that so large a rate of investment or so fast a rate of modernization could have been sustained.

Finally, let us briefly consider the need for fit human materials for modernization. Industry clearly can develop no faster than the quantity and the quality of the labor force allow, which in practice usually means no faster than the character of agriculture permits, since workers must be recruited mainly from the farm population.[4] The offer of high wages (assuming such wages are feasible) does not alone assure a sufficient flow of labor, sufficiently trained. Market incentives may be too weak because they meet with a nearly universal aversion to factory employment or dislike of separating from a family. Or there may be no difficulty in attracting labor but no quick or economical way of overcoming its ineptitude and psychological unfitness. (Throughout this argument I am assuming that force may not be used wholesale in place of incentives.)

It is easy to overlook the significance of labor in Japanese industrialization because it posed no major problem. For upward of two hundred years the agricultural labor force had been unwittingly preparing for the transition to factory employment. Commercial farming and the experience of working for wages had taught peasants to respond with alacrity to monetary incentives, and had given them a certain tolerance of impersonal relationships in pursuing monetary goals; but at the same time agriculture had not changed so much as to destroy the habit of loyalty and obedience. Another factor of importance was that wage labor had already begun to make the individual worker to some extent as economic unit. Wages after all were paid to him; and even if he turned them over to the family head, they were often saved in part to finance his marriage later on. In any case, working for wages had taught him that it was possible, and might also be advantageous, to cut family ties and make his way alone. This essential psychological preparation made it relatively easy to draw the peasant away from the village to the city. He came to the city already half-trained, too. Rural industry had given him a certain quickness of hand and eye, a respect for tools and materials, an adaptability to the cadences and confusion of moving parts; and city industry (or backward sectors of it where he could begin) was not technically so far advanced as to make his skills irrelevant. Few countries have embarked on industry with a superior labor force at hand.

But it was not only labor that rural Japan contributed to the city. Through the public schools and universities, many men (and some women) who were country-born rose to important positions in banking, industry, politics, education, letters, government, and so on. Indeed, an astonishing proportion of Japan's leaders in the past century have been men who reached adolescence in village environments. This bespeaks a high level of cultural achievement and aspiration in the countryside but also a narrowness of opportunity. Migration in Japan was a selective social movement. Men left their homes because they were restless and ambitious: because they saw elsewhere an avenue of advancement but barriers blocking it where they were.

For the past century therefore the villages have been exporting much of their best human material, or rather those best fitted for the relentless competitive struggle of urban life. Part of the dynamism of Japanese modernization must be found in this continuous flow of talented, aggressive, ambitious people. What was there in village life to produce such people in great number from the end of the Tokugawa period on? What social alchemy made of peasant boys men who could found international banks and trading companies? I do not know, but beyond question part of the answer is to be found somewhere in the history of change in rural Japan before 1868.

Notes

1. *Sōseki zenshū*, compiled by Iwanami Shigeo, 1936, V, 532.

2. The continuing importance of the family in farming is revealed by the following figures, which show, on holdings of different size, the average percentage of labor that came from each of various sources in 1954: Ōuchi Tsutomu, *Nōka keizai*, Tokyo, 1957, p. 163.

Size of Holding (in *tan*)	Family	Hired by Year	Hired for Short Periods	Labor Received Through Various Forms of Social Obligation
Under 5	94.9	0.0	2.5	2.6
5–10	95.7	0.2	1.9	2.2
10–15	94.8	0.6	2.5	2.1
15–20	92.3	1.8	3.9	2.0
Over 20	88.2	4.2	5.4	2.2

3. Nor has the situation changed radically since the war. In 1954, the percentage of total agricultural income received in money by various classes of holders was as follows:

Percentage of Size of Holding (in *tan*)	Total Agricultural Income in Cash
Less than 5	42.8
5–10	58.0
10–15	64.8
15–20	68.5
Over 20	72.6

These figures bring out very clearly that the degree of commercialization is especially low on small holdings. (*Ibid.*, pp. 85, 170)

4. Alexander Gerschenkron points out that "... industrial labor in the sense of a stable, reliable, and disciplined group that has cut the umbilical cord connecting it with the land and has become suitable for utilization in factories is not abundant but extremely scarce in a backward country. Creation of an industrial labor force that really deserves its name is a most difficult and protracted process." ("Economic Backwardness in Historical Perspective," Bert F. Hoselitz (ed.), *The Progress of Underdeveloped Areas*, Chicago, 1952, p. 7.)

Transition and Transformation in Early Modern Japan

Two major sociological issues are posed in this section. One question — why Japan alone among non-Western societies in the nineteenth century made a commitment to social and economic change — is pursued in extracts from the work of Smith, Moulder and Norman. Smith presents a sociological rarity: a revolutionary aristocracy or rather a section of the aristocratic class which in 1868 overthrew feudalism. He examines the motivations of this class and some of the long-term sociological consequences of their rebellion. Moulder sets the problem within a comparative approach in which both the social structures of Ching dynasty China and Tokugawa Japan are examined. She also provides a much needed critical review of the theories which have attempted to explain why these two culturally related East Asian countries were to follow such diverse historical paths into the twentieth century. Excerpts from E.H. Norman's classic work, *Japan's Emergence as a Modern State*, provide a superb analysis of the social forces at work within the Meiji Restoration and the earliest phases of modern economic change. The effects of this transformation upon the peasantry, agriculture and new political formations are also considered. Norman's task is to explain the pattern of social relations which developed in Japan during the process of early industrialisation. He examines the interaction of the evolving mosaic of old and emerging social classes in the context of the Meiji transformation and its aftermath.

A related problem of equal importance to the first issue presented in this section, the nature of the Meiji state and its impact on contemporary Japanese society, is pursued through differing perspectives by Jansen and Halliday. While the feudal state system of the Tokugawa shoguns was replaced by the Meiji leaders, their new form of centralised control over society was no less absolutist. The authority and person of the newly restored Emperor was to be central to the new state system as Ito Hirobumi, a leading oligarch and statesman in the new regime, makes clear in his *Commentary* on the Emperor's constitutional position. The divinity of Mutsuhito, the Meiji Emperor, his charisma and omnipotence are revealed in the *Imperial Rescript on Education* which was issued in his name in 1890.

Japanese social scientists have likened the condition of society and economy in the Meiji era to a forced march toward the goal of industrialisation. This formative phase of modern Japan's early development cast long shadows into the future which can be detected in everyday behaviour and values today. Frugality, sacrifice and repression was the price paid by the common people for the benefits of an efficient Western style army and navy founded on an industrial base. While the infrastructure of a new society was being laid down in this forty year period there were few social groups beneath the dominant classes that really gained from economic growth and diversification. The phases of modern economic growth that are implied here — Japan's progress toward full-scale industrialisation — are well described by Ohkawa and Rosovsky. This process of catching-up with the West is seen in comparative perspective by Landes, who reviews Japan's early stages of industrial growth against European experience.

The Meiji era marked the end of feudalism and the instigation of rapid social change, but it was itself marked by continuity with the absolutism of the old regime. Peasant repression was to continue under the linked domination of new capitalist landlords and the state which combined to extract high levels of rent and tax from agriculture. The autocracy typical of the shoguns was eased only slightly and civil rights remained undefined. Compared with their feudal predecessors the Meiji rulers appear innovative and far-sighted. However, the state and society which they created was shaped by the Tokugawa regime as much as by their own progressive goals. Rather than indicting feudal Japan's failure to evolve new economic and social institutions, we should examine the lines of continuity which link the Tokugawa state with Meiji capitalism.

The representation of the Tokugawa regime as an embodiment of xenophobic reaction which pulverised all creative forms of adaptation to social change is not entirely fair. In the early nineteenth century as European encroachment grew closer, the shoguns, in what were to be their last years, initiated a civil service department which, unlike any other in an Asian society, was to undertake extensive studies of foreign learning, albeit under the cloak of supposed total seclusion. The extraordinary degree of curiosity about the outside world which was manifested by the Japanese in these times, which again was without precedent in the rest of Asia, was to become a feature that has been retained in the national culture. Even before this government initiative Japanese scholars had investigated European science. Working entirely from written sources, samurai engineers had assembled a working model of a steam engine and artists like Kuniyoshi experimented with Western perspective.

The Tokugawa shoguns had unwittingly left Japan a legacy of order and social deference that might have been envied by any modernising élite. Japan was administered as a single nationally unified country, albeit with a degree of autonomy permitted within the domains of provincial daimyo. Peace had prevailed for centuries and no major social divisions based on language, race or ethnicity disturbed the tranquillity of society. No serious political challenge which could present a viable social alternative to feudalism had emerged prior to the coming of the Americans in 1853, and the integrity of central authority remained intact and unquestioned. The Tokugawa state directly controlled large sections of the economy. Over a quarter of all lands in addition to mines and seaports, coinage, policing, and a civil service bureaucracy with voluminously prolific records were in government hands. State economic control and direction, which was to become a highly significant role for government in post-war Japan, was a properly instituted feature of society well before the Meiji era.

A greater part of their legacy was perhaps the ability of the Tokugawa shoguns to preside over a long-term growth in agricultural output and productivity. Neat, ordered villages with a gradually rising standard of living marked by sufficiency, if not prosperity, had replaced the famine stricken condition of the peasantry in the early seventeenth century. National food supply was adequate and with yet further rises in productivity a growing urban labour force could be supported. But the villages of Japan were also the centre of two other ingredients that were to be vital for the process of social and economic development. One factor lay within peasant social life itself. Rural society, which had evolved symbiotically with rice cultivation, demanded very high levels of labour co-operation. In a society depending upon public works for water conservation social consensus had a premium value and the peasantry's traditional subordination in the Confucian social hierarchy, together with a history of perpetual repression, served to ingrain a thoroughly servile and obedient demeanour. Little effective social opposition, no peasant rebellion for instance, was to come from the agricultural masses despite their ruthless exploitation in the Meiji era.

Secondly, peasants were by no means only food producers. A large concentration of labour in the cities would have prejudiced national food supply which meant that manufacturing could only be located in villages. The Japanese countryside contained a large handicraft sector as part of the village economy. Production of textiles, building materials, paper, metal and most manufacturing, including food-processing, was not located in urban areas: it was rural-based and used the available labour of agricultural communities in the non-growing season whenever a relief from cultivation was possible. Village workshops employed surplus members of the rural labour force in a range of industries but by far the most numerous of these were young female labourers in silk production. Many of these operatives were recruited by a gang labour boss who paid a girl's wages directly to her parents. A reservoir of skilled and docile labour was available in the countryside for the Meiji leaders' new economic policies which could be syphoned into new urban factories whenever this was convenient. Japan's first industrial workers, like those in England, were young women and girls. Schooled in an ethos of compliance and loyalty, and frequently employed in a live-in compound factory, this new workforce, like its immediate peasant forebears, was not to be a real source of political resistance in the first forty years of industrial capitalism.

The issues and problems which are addressed in this section comprise a number of fundamental questions about the nature and impetus of economic growth and social change. The authors whose work is represented here correctly place Meiji Japan within an expansive and comparative historical background and do not retreat from the difficulties presented by the analysis of such large-scale questions.

3. Pre-modern Economic Growth: Japan and the West

Thomas C. Smith

I begin with a definition of the term "Pre-modern Growth", which is used here in a very restricted sense to mean economic growth only during the century or so immediately before industrialization. There was such growth in England and France and some other Western countries; and it was apparently an important factor in their subsequent industrialization. If Professor Kuznets's estimates are approximately correct, presently advanced countries, which are nearly all European or derive from Europe, enjoyed *per capita* incomes on the eve of industrialization several times those of underdeveloped countries today.[1] Surely this astonishing advantage was crucial to their early industrialization, and "pre-modern growth" important in achieving the advantage.

This inference is strengthened by the case of Japan, the earliest non-Western industrializer, which also experienced "pre-modern growth". From the early eighteenth century until the middle of the nineteenth, approximately the last half of the Tokugawa period, the output of the country grew more or less steadily, though of course very slowly, while the population remained nearly unchanged. The growth of output is indicated by a variety of indirect evidence: rising crop yields, increased by-employments among farmers, a very large number of minor technical innovations, the spectacular growth of manufacturers catering for mass consumption (especially textiles), and a spate of books stressing the efficient use of land and labour. About population we have more precise, if not essentially better, evidence. Between the first and last country-wide "census" of the period, in 1721 and 1746, which Japanese historians regard as approximately accurate, the total number of commoners increased barely three per cent. What combination of factors held population in check for this long in the face of expanding output — especially after previous rapid growth — is one of the more important and mysterious secrets of Japanese social history. Whatever it was, however, the effect was to make every percentage gain in output for over a century an equivalent percentage gain in *per capita* income. It is perhaps unnecessary to insist that the resulting benefits were not very evenly distributed and that large numbers of Japanese were not better off.

It seems unlikely that by 1860 Japan had attained anything approaching the pre-industrial level of *per capita* income of nations like England, the Netherlands or Sweden. But there can be no doubt that the country was far better prepared for industrialization than a century before. Commercial institutions were larger and more specialized, business men more numerous and more widely spread geographically and socially; labour was more mobile, literacy much commoner, agriculture more productive and capital more plentiful. This is not to mention a changed political

Thomas C. Smith: Extracts from 'Pre-modern Economic Growth: Japan and the West', in *PAST AND PRESENT* (1973), Vol. 60, pp. 127–160. Reproduced by permission of Oxford University Press.

climate, perhaps the most important new element of all. If we imagine away even some of these changes, the transformation of the economy following the overthrow of the Tokugawa in the late 1860s becomes unthinkable.

So there is a seeming parallel between widely separated countries: "pre-modern growth" followed by industrialization; and, to the best of my knowledge, the second term of the sequence did not occur anywhere in the world without the first during the nineteenth century. But the first itself was strikingly different in Japan and the West. "Pre-modern growth" in the West was accompanied by marked urban growth; towns and cities grew in size and number, and probably also their inhabitants as a percentage of total population.[2] But in Japan during the eighteenth century and the first half of the nineteenth towns generally stagnated or lost population. Moreover the heaviest losses were suffered by the largest towns or towns located in regions with growing economies; on the other hand, rare instances of town growth occurred only in backward and economically stagnant parts of the country.

By towns I mean places of five thousand inhabitants or more, or places legally designated "towns" regardless of size. The more important such places were castle-towns, most of which had grown from small beginnings during the century and a half before 1700. There were about two hundred of them scattered over the country, roughly as population was distributed, ranging in size from dusty little places of several thousand up to Edo (modern Tokyo) with about a million inhabitants in the 1720s.

In view of the subsequent loss of urban population, it is pertinent to ask in passing what may account for the dramatic growth of castle-towns before 1700, though this is much too complex a question to answer in a few words. (1) Most important was the forced removal of almost the entire warrior (*samurai*) class, with their families, retainers and servants, from the land to compact residential quarters laid out around the lord's (*daimyō's*) castle. This measure aimed at firmer control by the great lords over their vassals and the vassals' fiefs. (2) Warrior removal in turn resulted in the gathering of merchants and artisans in the growing castle-towns to provide goods and services. (3) This tendency was reinforced by legislation drastically restricting the practice of crafts and trade outside legally designated towns, including castle-towns. (4) Rapid population increase during apparently the whole of the seventeenth century, perhaps at a rate approaching one per cent a year, permitted both the growth of towns and, simultaneously, a sufficient expansion of arable land and agricultural population to feed the enlarging urban population. (5) The achievement through the Tokugawa hegemony of peace and order and a substantial degree of political centralization after a long period of civil war, made everything else possible.

The decline of town population during the latter half of the Tokugawa period was offset to an unknown extent by the growth of a multitude of places in the country which were small and not legally designated as "towns", but which contained a considerable number of artisans and merchants. However, by any conceivable standard — size, residential density, occupational diversity, culture — these places were far less urban than the declining towns. It must be kept in mind, too, that Japan remained a conspicuously urban country for its time, with towns everywhere and several cities of great size. We are remarking a trend, not an absolute level. Nothing perhaps bespeaks the trend so poignantly as the sad decline of urban culture, which reached a peak of creativity at the end of the seventeenth century and gradually lost life and originality thereafter.

The decline of towns in the course of "pre-modern growth" calls for an explanation. I will argue that the decline was neither a statistical illusion (as I first thought), nor an inexplicable aberration, but a function of growth itself. Without a considerable degree of de-urbanization no growth could have taken place. This mode of "pre-modern growth", so different from the Western type, will be seen to have had ramifications throughout the society, and to have influenced powerfully the character of Japan's subsequent industrialization. But let us try now to get some notion of the magnitude of town decline.

I have assembled all the figures available at scattered dates [between 1700 and 1850] in the Tokugawa period for 37 castle-towns . . .

Twenty five towns declined by 10 per cent or more: 9 or these declined severely or by more than 30 per cent; 16 declined at a more moderate rate. Six others, with a population change of less than 10 per cent, may be regarded as stable and 4 with gains of 10 per cent or more as growing . . . When the [data] are aggregated, despite somewhat different observation dates, the overall loss of population is 18 per cent.

Edo and Osaka were omitted from the table in order to avoid overweighting with two places far larger than the others, since each had a commoner population approaching half a million in the early eighteenth century. But their inclusion would not have changed the results significantly. Edo was nearly static from the early eighteenth century to the mid-nineteenth; Osaka continued to grow until 1763, somewhat later than most castle-towns, then lost population steadily until 1868, when the number of inhabitants stood at 67 per cent of the figure of a century before.

No systematic sampling of other towns has been attempted. The number of such towns is great and population data for them scarce and difficult to come by. Such figures as are at hand give an impression of a decline similar to the castle-towns; but the sample is small and geographically skewed, coming mainly from the central, Kinki district, and no conclusion is warranted. The most one can say is that complaints of urban decline came from all over the country and made no distinction between castle and other towns. On the other hand, as noted before, there were a large number of growing places which, though usually legally designated as "country" (zaikata), were socially partly urban, some even approaching town size. We refer to these settlements ambiguously (for lack of a better term) as "country places".

The distribution over the landscape of castle-towns in different stages of growth and decline is suggestive, and three features especially stand out. First, severely declining castle-towns were concentrated in the Kinki and the Inland Sea regions, economically the most advanced parts of the country; but growing towns were without exception located in remote and economically backward districts. Secondly, severely declining castle-towns tended to be ports and hence to have access to relatively cheap, fast and long-ranging transport. But stable and growing towns were located inland, where transport was mainly overland and so relatively expensive, slow and short-range. This is, of course, the opposite of what one would expect; taken in conjunction with the first point it strangely suggests that town decline was somehow associated with economic development and superior communications, and stability or growth with their opposites.

Thirdly, castle-town and regional population change often ran strongly counter to one another. Of twenty-five declining and severely declining castle-towns, it will be noted that fifteen were located in provinces with some population increase, and in many cases the divergence was striking. Hiroshima, for example, a castle-town and port with a magnificent location on the Inland Sea, sustained a population loss of 33 per cent while the population of its province, Aki, increased by 69 per cent — a divergence of 102 per cent. This was an unusual case; but Kokura, Ueda, Kochi, Takada, Karatsu, Hakata, Tottori, Himeji, Akita, Matsuyama, Kofu and Fukuyama were other declining castle-towns which were sharply at odds with the demographic trend of their provinces . . .

But these are all cases from neighbouring fiefs on the Inland Sea, a region of extreme castle-town decline, and may therefore be unrepresentative of the country as a whole. Yet our impression is strengthened that castle-town decline was somehow associated with surrounding economic growth.

Each declining castle-town lost population for a somewhat different set of reasons, but the commonest cause cited by contemporaries was the development of trade and industry in the surrounding countryside. Government attempted to block this development, which it regarded as likely to divert labour from farming and make the peasants lazy, quarrelsome and greedy. Also, it sought to confine trade and industry to the towns in order to assure their provisioning, and to facilitate price control and the taxation of non-agricultural income.

Complex legislation designed to achieve these ends, however, was largely ineffectual. For the putting-out system spread in nearly every part of the country, and in many rural places as large a number of different, non-agricultural occupations could be found by the early nineteenth century within a radius of a few miles as in fair-sized towns. Whole districts came to earn a major part of their living from by-employments, and the production of commodities to be shipped directly from country places to remote towns and to other country places without passing, as the law stipulated, through nearby towns. The determination of the government to stop these circumventions gradually weakened so that by the end of the Tokugawa period much of the restrictive legislation on behalf of towns had become a dead letter.

The growth of rural trade and industry might have redounded to the benefit of castle-towns by expanding their markets in the countryside, but in fact it was apparently achieved at some net cost to their prosperity. From the early eighteenth century the towns complained loudly that their merchants and artisans were being ruined by country competition. In 1789 a city magistrate in Okayama, a severely declining castle-town with a commoner population of over twenty thousand, alleged that ships were putting in, in growing numbers, at country ports in order to avoid selling their cargoes at less favourable prices in the town. Ships entering the town had consequently fallen to one-third of the number for the period 1736–1750; and a statute of about the same time describes what this loss meant to the inhabitants:

> Commerce in this city has steadily declined and many small merchants find themselves in great difficulty. On the other hand, ships from other provinces stopping at places such as Shimoshii village and Saidaiji village have steadily increased, bringing trade in the country (*zaikata*) into a flourishing condition. People used to come into the castle-town from the surrounding area to shop or to take goods on consignment in order to sell them in the country. But now people from the castle-town go to the country to shop and town shopkeepers send agents to the country to arrange to receive goods on consignment Thus the distinction between front and back, town and country, has been lost; farmer and tradesmen have exchanged positions. Naturally this has resulted in the impoverishing of many people in the town.

Nor was it only merchants who suffered from country competition; the brewers of the town alleged in 1802 that their number had been reduced from sixty-seven to forty-four by business failures in the past thirty years. This, they said, was because country rivals enjoyed the advantage of lower production costs and freedom from guild and municipal restriction, and hence were able to make and sell "just as they please". Characteristically, the town brewers asked not for equal freedom for themselves but the suppression of country brewers.

Complaints of this kind came from nearly all castle-towns; only the details are different, as one illustration must suffice to suggest. A petition of 1819 from the rice merchants of Mito, a backward district, charged that the rice brought by peasants into the town for sale was only about half the amount of former times, since country merchants were buying up rice and other products for shipment and sale elsewhere — presumably because this brought a higher return. The village of Aoyagi, located near the castle-town, had become a prosperous port through this illegal trade, it was said. A related difficulty was that the brewing industry, once concentrated in the castle-town, had spread through the rice-growing region in the southern part of the fief, adversely affecting the castle-town brewers and the town rice merchants who supplied them. Remedies were suggested but proved difficult to enforce. Two years after this petition, for example, the headmen of the wards of Mito town complained about retail shops in the country although, except for a few items of daily use, the sale of manufactured goods within a prescribed radius of the town had been strictly prohibited in 1636 and the prohibition repeated many times since. Yet:[3]

> year after year the retail trade in country districts increases. *Saké*, dyes, dry goods, toilet articles, hardware, lacquerware — everything you can think of — are sold in villages. Moreover, recently [village shops] have begun to buy directly from Edo [rather than from the castle-town]. And as for rice, wheat and other cereals, it is well known that they are bought up in the country and that the amount coming into the castle-town has been greatly reduced. The result of all this is that the castle-town declines more and more, and every year the number of vacant stores and houses increases.

One finds fragmentary and scattered evidence indirectly supporting such complaints. A list of 197 "men of wealth" in the Mito fief drawn up in 1804 showed that less than one-quarter were residents of the castle-town. When the lord of Miyazu, a rich textile region opposite Kyoto on the Japan Sea, called on the wealthy merchants and manufacturers of his domain for financial contributions in 1860, more large contributions and more contributors in all came from outside than inside the castle-town. In the textile district around Hachioji more middlemen buyers (*nakagai*) of cocoons, silk yarn and cloth lived in villages than in the fifteen towns of the district.

But the most impressive evidence of the country's hurting the towns is the growth of scores — perhaps hundreds — of country places through the expansion of industry, trade and transport. Contemporaries often alluded to such places. I have made no systematic effort to collect population figures on growing country places but there were undoubtedly a great many. A list of twenty-nine compiled haphazardly, excluding those thought to be growing through the expansion of arable land and hence of the agricultural population, presents several features worth noting.

First, most of the places were small compared to the average castle-town; all but eight were under three thousand and most were under one thousand. Secondly, the majority, as far as can be determined, were legally villages rather than towns. Thirdly, all grew fairly rapidly through a major part of the century and a half after 1700, several doubling or tripling in that time. Although the irregular and wide spacing of observations makes generalization difficult, there seems to have been more growth in the group after 1750 than before; and a number of places show a distinct acceleration of growth after 1800. Fourthly, in nearly all cases growth was accompanied by the local expansion of trade or industry, and it is not surprising therefore that eighteen of the twenty-nine were ports. This included a number on the Inland Sea, a location that in castle-towns almost guaranteed decline; and some of these Inland Sea ports were, in fact, located near severely declining castle-towns. For example, Mitarai and Kofurue were near Hiroshima, and Fukiage and Shimoshii near Okayama.

Little is known about the demographic mechanisms of castle-town decline and country-place growth, but migration was clearly among them. Castle-towns were probably like contemporary European towns in normally recording an excess of deaths over births, hence in depending on immigration for the maintenance or increase of population. In the latter half of the Tokugawa period when Edo's population was static, a quarter of the commoners in the city were found to have been born elsewhere, and a high ratio of immigrants also appears in other towns.

Many immigrants were live-in "servants" (*genin*) who came into town from the country on yearly or seasonal employment contracts. As employment opportunities expanded in the country, the flow of rural labour to the towns evidently slowed. For example, live-in servants in two wards of Tennōji, a town on the outskirts of Osaka, declined from eighty-four in 1806 to a mere five in 1858, during which time the ward population fell from 755 to 451 or 40 per cent. There was also a decline of 24 per cent in the number of households in these wards, which was especially severe among families renting houses in contrast to house-owning families. Some of the regular residents of the town were obviously leaving in hope of bettering their luck elsewhere.

It would be surprising if migrants went in large number directly from declining castle-towns to growing country places. Patterns of migration were more complex and diffuse than this. Every town and village annually registered people moving to and from many other places for marriage, adoption and employment, or as a result of the termination of these arrangements. When towns or villages gained or lost population over the long term through migration, it would seem to have been the outcome of small and wavering changes in net flows between many points on a grid, rather than of large transfers between a few.

In any case, growing places were augmented by migration as declining towns were diminished. Kiryū, a textile town or village — significantly, documents use both designations — in Kōzuke province, tripled in size between 1757 and 1855. A document of 1835 tells how: "Weavers came to make a living hiring women operatives to spin and weave, and people came crowding into the town from other provinces, renting houses there and even in surrounding hamlets". Nor was Kiryū unique in this respect, for in 1846 we find the village (or town) complaining of a local labour shortage and blaming it on the neighbouring village of Ashikaga, which was said to be tempting Kiryū workers away at "exorbitant" wages. Some Ashikaga weavers were allegedly employing as many as "thirty, forty, fifty or a hundred or more" operatives each. The figures ought not to be taken too seriously, but the competitive hiring was real enough.

Servants appear in the population registers of growing country places in large numbers, often coming from surprising distances, suggesting a shortage of labour not only locally but also in the surrounding district. Twenty of twenty-three workers employed by a silkworm egg producer in a Fukushima village in 1815 came from outside the province. The large servant population in the rapidly growing commercial and salt-making town of Takehara-shimo'ichi came mainly from Iyo province across the Inland Sea. A record of the servants in a Settsu village near Osaka showed a total of 221 servants employed from outside the village between 1707 and 1810 — 180 of these from other provinces. The records of a master weaver in Kiryū show him employing 132 operatives between 1788 and 1817, nearly half of whom came from outside the province.

The ability of country places to attract and hold labour in competition with castle-towns bespeaks comparative economic advantages, five of which were mentioned by contemporaries or can be read between the lines. (1) Nearness to raw materials and water power; (2) closeness to the growing rural market for goods and services; (3) tighter and more reliable networks of face-to-face relations at a time when, in the absence of a developed commercial law, such relations, rather than contract, were the principal basis of security in commercial transactions; (4) the ability of workers in the country to shift back and forth between farming and other employments; and (5) greater freedom from taxation and guild restrictions. These advantages require no special comment since, with the possible exception of the third, all were widespread in Europe before the nineteenth century. But another advantage that contemporaries did not see clearly, and the ineffectiveness of economic legislation on behalf of the towns which they did see, need some explanation.

After the mid-eighteenth century, the government increasingly attempted to confine the sale of certain staples in each region to licensed wholesalers in towns who paid for their monopolies handsomely in financial "contributions", "thank-money" (*reikin*) and taxes. These monopolies were the government's chief device for taxing trade and industry, the most vigorously growing sectors of the economy; and the government's need of additional revenue, already pressing in the eighteenth century, became more acute with time. The establishment of the monopolies, however, inevitably created incentives for producers and buyers to circumvent them in order to avoid rigged prices, taxes and the high transport charges consequent upon circuitous shipping. Despite this, monopolies were relatively well enforced in towns, where guild organization could be harnessed for the purpose and the surveillance area was limited in extent and swarming with *samurai* officials and police. Enforcement was far more difficult in the country. Few guilds existed there and the obstacles to surveillance presented by space and terrain were great. Moreover, enforcement was largely in the hands of village authorities; except for a sprinkling of district magistrates, who were rarely long enough in a locality to know its people intimately. *Samurai* had for a century or more been removed from most of the countryside and concentrated in castle-towns to give the lord (*daimyō*) security against his vassals. No serious thought was ever given to undoing this achievement. But the result of the concentration of the *samurai* in towns was the need to delegate the day-to-day enforcement of the law in the countryside to solidary communities whose members, in this and some other matters, had a strong interest in non-compliance. This interest was often especially marked on the part of village officials, who were likely to be merchants as well as landholders.

There were, of course, offsetting advantages on the side of the castle-towns; the most important was the degree of occupational specialization they permitted. Nevertheless the overall advantage in many expanding branches of industry probably lay with the country. It is suggestive of this that scattered wage data show that real daily wages (money wages converted to rice at local prices) were higher in villages around Osaka, a region of exceptional rural economic development, than in Kyoto, a city of about four hundred thousand, thirty miles away. Carpenters' wages were approximately the same in the two places in 1810 but distinctly higher in the country by 1846; plasterers' wages were higher in the country at the three dates (1814, 1835 and 1846) at which comparisons can be made; and most significant perhaps, day-labourers' wages were over 50 per cent higher in the country at the only two observation dates we have (1810 and 1814). Nor was this a unique situation, though it is impossible to say how common it was, for, as early as 1762, the Sasayama regional government set identical money wages for male and female servants in the castle-town and country, which almost certainly meant higher real wages in the latter.[4]

* * *

Yet, when one looks at Europe, it is clear that the comparative advantages of country places alone cannot account for the decline of castle-towns. These same advantages were present in Europe with different results. Much of the history of European industry before the factory is the story of its spread in the countryside, which leads David Landes to term the characteristic locational pattern of pre-industrial manufacturing, "rural settlement".[5] As a consequence of rural competition, it is true,

46

towns declined in parts of Europe for long periods, but this was never the overall pattern. Roger Mols states that, except perhaps for the period 1350–1450, the major cities of Europe as a whole grew in number and size in every century from 1300 to 1800. In any case, however, our comparison is with the period of "pre-modern growth", when, despite rural settlement, the growth of urban population in Western Europe is not in doubt.

Contemporary explanations of the decline of castle-towns suffice only within the system of which they were a part; similar factors in England and on the continent led to rather different results. We need therefore to look to differences in the larger environment, and those in respect to foreign trade and overall population growth attract particular attention. Limitations of knowledge and space rule out detailed treatment of the interplay of these factors with urban growth and decline, and I have consequently had recourse to two crude models to suggest their working.

In both models foreign trade, urban growth and population increase are interdependent. It is assumed that the increase of foreign trade — which has already reached an inter-continental scale and on one continent embraces a dozen countries with a combined population of over a hundred million — encourages population growth.[6] It makes possible food imports in bad years, especially in towns; and it widens employment.[7] The resulting demand for labour encourages immigration, earlier marriage and a higher marriage rate. Towns — and above all, port towns — are the chief places of settlement of the new population.[8] Excellent harbours are scarce, as are the complex capital and specialized skills necessary for overseas trade, with its long voyages and precious cargoes; and accordingly docks and warehouses, bankers and lawyers, shipwrights and drayers concentrate there. The demand for labour cannot be continuously met short of significant labour-saving innovations, unless population grows. Should this growth fail, foreign trade must cease to grow directly — or, what comes to much the same thing, labour be withdrawn from farming, bringing on food and raw material shortages with consequent price rises that wipe out comparative advantages in foreign trade.[9]

The difference between the two models is that foreign trade and population are both growing in the European model, sketched above, whereas foreign trade is non-existent and population static in the Japanese. The absence of foreign trade in the latter is the result of a political decision made possible by hemispheric location amidst countries not making up an international state system and not each avidly seeking trade. Coastal shipping is growing but this is hardly equivalent to foreign trade; its overall dimensions in a single country of about thirty million people are of an entirely different order. Already short shipping distances are made still shorter by frequent stops along the way at night and in bad weather. Ships and cargoes, though numerous, are individually insignificant in size and value. Shipping may be dispersed through a multitude of small ports rather than being forced to gather in a few great ones; it therefore stimulates the growth of "country places", where other occupations are typically combined with farming, instead of the towns, where such combination is rare.

A new factor must now be introduced to account for the decline of towns in the Japanese model. This is that, despite everything, the economy is slowly expanding by virtue of a host of mouse-trap innovations, a positive investment rate and progressive relaxation of government control over the economy. The expansion of the economy in the absence of foreign trade and population growth induces the decline of towns. For, as *per capita* income rises, so invevitably does the demand for the products of secondary industry and services, which therefore require more labour. Labour cannot be withdrawn from farming for obvious reasons, including the danger of widespread starvation. It can nonetheless be found in ample supply and good quality and in a stable social environment in the form of peasant family members, who can rarely be kept busy full-time in farming. As industry and trade spread in the country, therefore, by-employments on the farms begin to reduce the annual flow of migrants to the towns, and the towns, unable to sustain themselves by natural increase, lose population. The loss is most marked in the economically more advanced parts of the country, where rural trade and industry are growing, and is less noticeable or not to be found at all in the backward districts, where such development is slight.

It will now be convenient to relax the assumption that population is static overall and ask why, with increased employment in the country, population does not begin to grow. I believe the reason is that non-agricultural occupations continue to be carried on mainly in conjunction with family farming. They do not create many independent new livings, many new slots for new families. Parents still cannot provide for "surplus" children (in excess of replacements for themselves) without parcelling already small holdings and so endangering family continuity. Rather than this they do as they have done for generations whenever arable land is not expanding sufficiently to allow for additional families; that is, as the Jesuits observed in the seventeenth century, through abortion and infanticide and perhaps other means, they limit the number of children to be raised. This practice increases the chance of dying or reaching old age without a natural male heir, a prospect which anthropologists tell us peasants abhor; but in this case the culture offers a happy evasion. It has always been possible in Japan to adopt a male heir, even of adult age, as a husband for a daughter or outright, so long as there is property to inherit. If only property is not dispersed, the heir will not be a problem. Moreover, he is in every sense but sentimentally, and perhaps not always with that exception — legally, socially, religiously, even genealogically — the exact equal of a natural heir; and he has the bonus advantage that if he works out badly, he can be disinherited and replaced.

Family priorities, which keep population in check, would presumably change if the country were opened to foreign trade, thus accelerating economic expansion and making a limited number of ports the focal points of growth. Then better prospects for children off the farm would reduce the incentive to limit families. And in fact when foreign trade was commenced in the 1850s both national and town populations, after more than a century of stagnation, began to grow rapidly.

It is not to be hoped that these models will constitute a satisfactory explanation of the difference in "pre-modern growth" between Japan and the West, but only that they may be suggestive. But whether they are or not, my point is the same: we are not dealing with chance divergences but rather different modes of growth, one urban-centred and the other (if such a phrase may be used) rural-centred, which seem to colour a great many other things of importance. Let me cite a single illustration. Consider certain changes in the relations of social classes accompanying "pre-modern growth" in Japan that would have struck a contemporary European of almost any nationality as extremely odd.

For one thing, though "pre-modern growth" brought gains to the Western bourgeoisie, it unquestionably imposed losses on the urban class in Japan, which was smaller and less prosperous in 1850 than in 1700, and also less spirited. Castle-towns, of course, continued to perform vital economic functions. But by 1850 their merchants had been suffering for several generations from country competition on the one hand and oppressive taxation and regulation on the other. One might expect urban merchants to help themselves in such circumstances by political means, at least in time, but they seem to have been quite unable to do so, and no lapse of time was likely to have changed that. Living in the shadow of the lord's castle and in the midst of his soldiers, without corporate freedoms and representative assemblies, townsmen could not conceive of a change in government brought about by themselves. Indeed, the more difficult their economic plight became, the more they clung to government. All over the country, as towns declined, townsmen asked for more laws, more strictly enforced, against country trade and industry, and their pleas were anything but demanding. The authors asked government to give them relief not as a matter of right or justice but out of sympathy for their sufferings and in consideration of past loyalty, obedience and payment of taxes.

Secondly, the decline of castle-town merchants was more than matched by the rise of rural entrepreneurs, who were consequently not only more important to their society than their counterparts in England and France but, I believe, a rather different breed. The history of this class, unfortunately for us, has yet to be written. It sprang from diverse origins: at one extreme from large holders who had once worked land with unfree labour and who descended remotely from warriors left on the land; and at the other extreme from new men, coming from no one knew where, who made their way up through petty trade and money-lending. The origins of capital were similarly mixed. Some capital came from commercial farming, some from the exploitation of unfree labour, some from the profits of money-lending and some also from loans by city capitalists. Contemporaries who wrote of this class, being generally Confucian and nearly always disapproving, may have exaggerated its wealth and power to alarm readers. Yet there was undoubtedly truth in their accounts. Surviving business records show cases of country merchants trading across greater distances, with larger amounts of capital at risk, than many town merchants. They can be seen in local documents amassing land, entertaining famous scholars, building fine houses, sending sons off to town to school, writing poetry, collecting ceramics, wearing swords and celebrating masses to the dead in *samurai* style. Such men were far from being peasants with an abacus.

It is impossible to go beyond impressions; and we know little about variations in the class from one line of business and locality to others. Sometimes country merchants faintly resemble a business class as it is supposed to behave in feudal societies. At these times they are at odds with government over taxation and commercial legislation, opposing openly, sabotaging and evading. We also find them in conflict with government over its intervention in local affairs, in matters concerning village common land, irrigation rights and the selection of headmen, since such intervention was sometimes against the powerful of the village on behalf of the weak. Country merchants were also inclined to be restive, hankering after honours reserved to the *samurai* and access to office and influence in the higher levels of government. Judging from opinions expressed in the books on agriculture and rural industries they wrote — and read — some, dissenting from the orthodox ideal of a hierarchical society of stable ranks, thought that men with enough intelligence, education and enterprise to alter their social position by their own efforts ought to be able to do so; and if there were enough such men, society would be changed for the better.

But if some members of this class favoured a more open system above, nearly all opposed any such thing below. There was a certain logic in this position. Almost without exception they were large landowners by local standards, exploiting their holdings through tenants and hired labour. Partly for this reason, but also by virtue of their commercial activities and often the claims of old family, they were powerful men in their villages and consequently in their districts. The man who spoke for his village, with its autonomous administration and solidarity towards the outside, was inevitably an important man in the district. This circumstance had obvious commercial and social uses, and also gave rise to large political ambitions.[10] Hence the desire for openness above. But the whole structure of influence that made this desire understandable depended on the continued solidarity of the village, which was increasingly in doubt. As trade and industry spread to the countryside there was an increase in rural disorder, and threats of violence, even occasional acts of violence, against the rural rich, and chilling millenarian slogans about "remaking the world" (*yo naoshi*). This was the first challenge for many centuries to the existing order of rural society; and as often happens when things long taken for granted are threatened, the chief beneficiaries of that order became its passionate defenders and in doing so transformed the wonted solidarity and structure of rural villages into an ideology of *community*.

Thirdly, the *samurai* class, which might be compared to the European aristocracies, came on the hardest of times for reasons linked to the decline of towns. Government revenues, nearly the sole source of *samurai* income and coming in large part from the land tax, remained approximately the same in real terms after 1700, while government expenditure rose. Thus, government became poorer as the country grew richer. The reason for this was not chiefly the incompetence or extravagance of government, as usually alleged, but the removal of the *samurai* from the land in the seventeenth century and the consequent investiture of the village with the functions of local government, including that of collecting taxes and reporting the creation of new arable land and changes in the productivity of old arable.

Unable in these circumstances to increase income from the land tax, the government sought to reduce expenditure, and the readiest way was to cut the payments to the *samurai*, which in most fiefs amounted to half or more of all government expenditure. This was accomplished in ways too many and too devious to list. The most straightforward was to withhold a portion of *samurai* pensions as a "contribution" to the lord's treasury. In many domains this withholding tax took 30 or 40 per cent of nominal *samurai* income.[11] Contributions and other exploitive measures impoverished large numbers of *samurai*, especially in the middle and lower pay-grades, demoralizing and embittering them, and driving them to degrading expedients such as domestic industry, taking in lodgers, house-breaking, cheating retainers, selling rank, pimping and pawning armour. It also turned loyalty to the lord into anger, which was among the most powerful internal causes of the overthrow of the Tokugawa.

The reduction of *samurai* stipends would seemingly have contributed to the decline of castle-towns since it reduced consumer demand there. But what was taken from the *samurai* by the government was then spent by it on other goods and services in the town; so the net effect was about nil. A more important income factor would seem to have been a secular decline in the price of rice relative to other commodity prices. A large part of government and *samurai* income was received in rice, while a large and growing share of other commodities, manufactured as well as agricultural, came from the countryside. Yet the government might have compensated for this shift in real income towards the countryside and away from itself, the *samurai* and the towns by increased taxes on the country people. It tried desperately to do just this, and failed; and it seems to have failed fundamentally because, having removed the *samurai* from the land, although it could keep the peace and suppress uprisings readily enough, it could no longer enforce its will in the countryside in the details of daily life, except through the co-operation of self-governing villages run by those it would tax. One might almost argue that while in the West towns often enjoyed "liberties" not normally found in the country, the situation was just the reverse in late Tokugawa Japan — except, of course, that the liberty enjoyed by Japanese villages had no legal basis. It was the practical result of institutional weakness on the part of the government, albeit of a kind not to be overcome without a revolutionary political and administrative change.

Perhaps the preceding sketch of class change will be enough to suggest how widespread were the effects of "pre-modern growth" in Japan, and how different from those in Europe. It is arguable that these differences account in part for the distinctive features of Japanese industrialization, which may be brought out by comparison with the Gerschenkron model of European industrialization before 1914.[12]

According to Gerschenkron, the major differences in the speed, methods and other characteristics of industrialization among European countries before that date arose mainly from the different levels of economic backwardness at which industrialization began. The more backward the country, the greater the gap between the possibilities offered by the most advanced technology and that country's actual condition; and the greater too, therefore, were the obstacles to be overcome. In bridging the gap between present and promise, backward countries typically borrowed technology most aggressively from the most advanced industries of advanced countries for two reasons. This was where the greatest benefits from borrowing could be realized; and the industries concerned were capital-intensive, hence their technologies would compensate to an extent for one of the severest barriers of backwardness to development, namely the scarcity of industrial labour in the sense of a disciplined and stable force of workers cut off definitively from the land. From this choice came the main characteristics of European industrialization outside England, a country which was never backward in the Gerschenkron sense. These characteristics — varying "in

51

direct relation to the *degree* [my italics] of backwardness" — were in part dependence on technological borrowing, the speed of industrial growth, the stress on the bigness of plant and enterprise, and the role of banks and government in capital formation and the co-ordination of effort.

If the Gerschenkron model may be taken as a fair approximation of what happened in fact, Japanese industrialization differed from the European on several counts. These have been pointed out at some length by Henry Rosovsky in his excellent book on capital formation in Japan.[13] The most important is the only one we need note here, however, since it goes to the heart of the model. Until the 1930s, the leading sector of modern industry in Japan was not heavy industry but textiles, where labour was a relatively important factor, units of production rather small, private capital predominant, and the rôle of government and banks modest and mostly indirect. Rosovsky accounts for this radical divergence from the Gerschenkron model by emphasizing the surprising ability of the Japanese, despite backwardness, to create a disciplined and reliable labour force. This ability made highly profitable industries based on relatively labour-intensive technologies that would otherwise have been unprofitable.

Rosovsky seems to say that this ability turned on the astuteness of Japanese entrepreneurs in building a factory system around pre-industrial values, which eased the problem of recruiting and training an industrial labour force. It avoided the costly resistances and inefficiencies this task typically met with in backward countries. Here Rosovsky's analysis stops; but it begs for an answer to the further question: How did it happen that pre-industrial values were adaptable to modern industry in Japan and that Japanese entrepreneurs were sensitive to them?

My answer to this question brings us back to rural-centred "pre-modern growth", though I can do no more here than list some of the connections with industrialization. (1) At the end of this growth a very large proportion of Japanese farm families, approaching 100 per cent in some places, had behind them a generation or more of experience in working part-time at non-agricultural occupations, often off the farm and for an employer. (2) Handicraft, artisan and commercial skills of all kinds were accordingly widespread among them. So was the habit of moving for work; and the custom of depending on an employer in some degree for housing and social credentials in a strange community. (3) No industry gave so much non-farm employment to peasant families as textiles; but other industries such as paper, ceramics, metals, mining, brewing, wood products, transport and food processing were not far behind. (4) Networks of commercial institutions covered the countryside linking rural districts to towns and to one another. Given the technical limitations on transport and communication, these institutions were effective in integrating different processes of manufacture, disseminating price information, mediating transactions at a distance, signalling investment opportunities and distributing labour where it seemed most needed.

My argument, it will be perceived, is that the growth of the modern textile industry was made possible by the specific skills, attitudes, rôles, capital accumulations and commercial practices brought into being mainly during the period of "pre-modern growth". Without these "building blocks", the stimulus of foreign technology and foreign markets would not have resulted in the rapid expansion of the textile industry under private auspices after 1880. It is impossible to prove this. But the conclusion is strongly supported by the following considerations: the modern textile industry grew mainly in districts of traditional manufacture; much of the growth occurred in villages and former "country places"; entrepreneurs, plant managers, buyers, shippers and labour contractors came from these same districts; and the labour came overwhelmingly from farm families.

The pre-industrial values incorporated in the emergent factory system were not immemorial. In so far as they included willingness to work for long periods off the farm for wages and were associated with industrially useful skills, they were mainly the product of the Tokugawa period, and of its last century especially. Modern Japanese industry took over these *new* pre-industrial values, changing them in the process, though as many observers have noticed less than one would think. In the early decades the changes may have consisted largely of a self-conscious codification.

This was a natural and efficient development. Workers, foremen and entrepreneurs, many of whom were "carry-overs" from traditional industry, were all sensitive to those values. It is probable, indeed, that many individual personal relationships in traditional industry were transferred intact to the new era. No one thought that any radical change in the modes, customs and spirit of relations between persons in authority and those under them was necessary or desirable; no such proposal for change was made except by union organizers, who were ignored until they learned to adapt their unions to these very values. The carry-over of skills and values was easiest in light industry. It was more difficult in heavy industry, where technology created a gap between past experience and new requirements. But even here traditional skills and attitudes, conditioned by "pre-modern growth", were immensely useful. There is evidence of this in the fact that in 1880, only eight years after British engineers had built the first railroad in the country between Yokohama and Tokyo, Japanese "engineers" and workers laid a more difficult line, over about the same distance through the broken country between Kyoto and Otsu, entirely without foreign engineers. They had learned from the British, of course. But to have learnt so quickly they must have brought useful experience and relevant motives, as well as raw aptitude, to their study.

To summarize, Japanese industrialization differed radically from the Gerschenkron model of European in that textiles were the leading sector (and traditional light industry generally important) during the first four or five decades. This peculiarity, which gave the whole process a distinctive look, was a consequence of rural-centred "pre-modern growth". Such growth spread the skills, attitudes and rôles adaptable to modern industry more widely among the rural population than the country's relative degree of economic backwardness, which was certainly great, would suggest.

In this (and some other respects) the crucial influence would seem to have been not the degree, but a particular cultural variant, of backwardness. This variant, as we have seen, was deeply rooted in the historical circumstances of Japan's "pre-modern growth", closed economy, a nearly unchanging population and isolation from war —

surely a rare combination for long. Although clearly associated with backwardness in a very general way, it would be difficult to argue that this variant (de-urbanization) was associated with a particular degree of backwardness, especially as it became more rather than less marked with the growth of the economy in the last century of the Tokugawa period. This is not intended as a criticism of the Gerschenkron model, which concerns the *degree* of backwardness and is explicitly limited to Europe before 1914. But it does make one wonder about the argument for the model from the experience of European history in which Professor Gerschenkron relies heavily on cultural and institutional factors to explain national differences in industrialization. Are such factors uniquely associated (at least conceptually) with particular degrees of backwardness? If not, then in so far as the argument relies on them rather than degrees of backwardness, to that extent the empirical verification of the model is weakened, and seems to reduce to a statement that backward countries are different in many ways and hence the modes of industrialization are also many.

Notes

1. Simon Kuznets, "Underdeveloped Countries and the Pre-industrial Phase in the Advanced Countries", in A. N. Agarwala (ed.), *The Economics of Underdevelopment* (New York, 1963), pp. 143–4; also David Landes, *The Unbound Prometheus* (Cambridge, 1969), p. 13.

2. In the century 1650–1750, London grew from 7 to 11 per cent of English population: E. A. Wrigley, "A Simple Model of London's Importance in Changing English Society and Economy 1650–1750", *Past and Present*, no. 37 (July 1967), pp. 44–5. Phyllis Deane and W. A. Cole (*British Economic Growth 1688–1959* [Cambridge, 1962], p. 7), estimate that the proportion of the British population living in towns of over 5,000 rose from about 13 to 25 per cent in the course of the eighteenth century. See also, Roger Mols, *Introduction à la démographie historiques de villes d'Europe du XLVe au XVIIe siècle* (Louvain, 1955) iii, p. 526; and T.S. Ashton, *An Economic History of England — The Eighteenth Century* (London, 1955), pp. 8, 95–6. Mols lists the population of 34 large French towns at five dates between 1726 and 1801. These figures give a picture of vigorous growth: only 7 of the 34 towns lost population and many of the others grew dramatically; overall growth of the 34 between 1726 and 1801 was 40 per cent. According to census figures, the 25 largest French cities grew from an aggregate 1,949, 574 in 1801 to 2,725,452 in 1846, another 40 per cent increase. Paris at these dates was 547,736 and 1,053,897. French towns of 50,000 or more grew at an annual rate of 1.18 per cent between 1801 and 1851. Mols, *op. cit.*, ii, pp. 513–6; Charles H. Pouthas, *La population française pendant la premiére motié du XIXe siècle* (Paris, 1956), p. 98; Marczewski, *op. cit.*, p. 130.

3. Kidota Shiro, *Meiji ishin no nōgyō kōzō* [Agriculture in the Meiji Restoration] (Tokyo, 1960), p. 45.

4. This is not inconsistent with the earlier statement to the effect that low wages were normally one of the advantages of the country over the town. Higher real wages in the country were confined to districts where agriculture, trade and industry had created an intense local demand for labour; industry could always find cheaper labour by moving deeper into the countryside, though at some cost in higher transport charges.

5. Landes, *The Unbound Prometheus*, pp. 188, 554.

6. The population of England and Wales probably increased slowly in the century 1650–1750 and then more rapidly in the next half century: Deane and Cole, *British Economic Growth*, pp. 5–6. Wrigley ("London's Importance", p. 48) stresses the slowness of population growth

in the century 1650–1750. French population is estimated to have increased from 21–22 millions in 1700 to 29.5 in 1806: L. Henry, "The Population of France in the Eighteenth Century", in D. V. Glass and D. E. C. Eversley (eds.), *Population in History* (London, 1965), p. 440. For other European countries, H. Gille, "The Demographic History of the Northern Countries in the Eighteenth Century", *Population Studies*, iii, no. I (June 1949), p. 19; Michael Drake, *Population and Society in Norway*, 1735–1865 (Cambridge, 1969), pp. 42, 43; Carlo Cipolla, "Four Centuries of Italian Demographic Development", in Glass and Eversley, *op. cit.*, p. 573.

7. "The growth of overseas trade enabled a national deficiency to be overcome by drawing grain from overseas. And better facilities for storage led to the holding of large reserves. Such a run of wet seasons [a commentator wrote in 1773] as we have had in the last ten or twelve years would have produced a famine a century or more ago": cited in Ashton, *An Economic History of England: The Eighteenth Century*, p. 8. For the seventeenth century, see B. E. Supple, *Commercial Crisis and Change in England 1600–1642* (Cambridge, 1959), pp. 14–19. Goubert notes that the important trading countries like England and Holland did not suffer severe loss of life from starvation; nor did southern Mediterranean countries, presumably owing to the ease of importing food: "Historical Demography", p. 41.

8. London, Bristol, Liverpool, King's Lynn, Yarmouth, Exeter and Hull in England; Marseille, Bordeaux, Dunkerque, Le Havre, Brest, Cherbourg and Rochefort in the eighteenth century in France. Patterns of urban growth shifted in the early nineteenth century in France, but ports continued to be well represented among the fast-growing places.

9. The new agricultural practices associated with enclosure created new demand for labour and the population of agricultural villages grew about as rapidly as the population of industrial areas. The decline in agricultural population in England did not begin until the mid-nineteenth century.

10. An extraordinary example was Kikuchi Yasusada, a member of the rural élite, who memorialized his lord in 1858 suggesting, in effect, that *samurai* be done away with and replaced in their functions by rural gentry who would be attached to the lord by direct bonds of loyalty. He argued that *samurai* were hated, feared and incompetent, whereas rural leaders had powerful, local followings and were greatly respected by the people of their districts generally.

11. Dazai Shundai in 1744 claimed that all *daimyō* large and small had become impoverished and "borrowed" from their vassals' stipends. He went on to say that the "borrowings" often took up to 50–60 per cent of stipends; hence the term *hanchi* or "halfing" stipends came into use. The Matsuyama fief "borrowed" from stipends every year but once in the 160 years 1709–1869; the lowest rate of "borrowing" (as a percentage of the stipend withheld) was 10 per cent and the highest 60 per cent. In 87 per cent of the years of record the rate was 30 per cent or more. Tanaka Toshio, 'Forced Contributions in the Matsuyama Fief', *Jl. of Aichi University*, December 1955, pp. 233–46; Tsuruoka City History, i, pp. 321 ff.

12. Alexander Gerschenkron, *Economic Backwardness in Historical Perspective* (Harvard, 1962), pp. 1–52.

13. Henry Rosovsky, *Capital Formation in Japan 1868–1940* (Glencoe, 1961), pp. 55–104.

4.   Japan's Aristocratic Revolution
Thomas C. Smith

"An aristocracy," Alexis de Tocqueville wrote, "seldom yields [its privileges] without a protracted struggle, in the course of which implacable animosities are kindled between the different classes of society." Despite our democratic partialities, most of us would add, "And why should it?" To know the exalted pleasures of power, and the grace of refined taste with the means of satisfying it; to believe oneself superior on the only evidence that gives conviction — the behavior of others; and to enjoy all this as birthright, with no vitiating struggle, nor any doubt that one's privileges are for God, King, country, and the good of one's fellow man — what happier human condition, for a few, have men devised?

Yet, not all aristocracies have behaved as one fancies they must. Japan's warrior class, a feudal aristocracy though it differed from European aristocracies in crucial respects, did not merely surrender its privileges. It abolished them. There was no democratic revolution in Japan because none was necessary: the aristocracy itself was revolutionary.

Consider the bare outlines of the case. Until 1868, Japan was ruled by a class of knights who alone had the right to hold public office and bear arms and whose cultural superiority the rest of the population acknowledged. A party within this aristocracy of the sword (and swagger) took power in 1868 and embarked on a series of extraordinary reforms. Where there had before been little more than a league of great nobles, they created an immensely powerful central government: they abolished all estate distinctions, doing away with warrior privileges and throwing office open to anyone with the education, and ability to hold it; they instituted a system of compulsory military service, although commoners had previously been forbidden on pain of death to possess arms; they established a system of universal public education; and much else. The result was a generation of sweeping and breathless change such as history had rarely seen until this century. I believe, though of course I cannot prove, that these decades brought greater changes to Japan than did the Great Revolution of 1789 to France.

Why was the Japanese aristocracy — or part of it — revolutionary? Why did it abandon the shelter of its historic privileges for the rigors of free competition, which, incidentally, many warriors did not survive? Its behavior, like that of a man who takes cold baths in the morning, requires a special explanation.

Two general lines of explanation have been offered; though no bald summary can do them justice, even on fuller account they leave much unexplained.

One might be called the prescient patriot theory. That is, the foreign crisis — to be quite specific, the unamiable Yankee, Commodore Perry, and the Americans, English, and Russians who followed him — stimulated the patriotism of the warriors and

Thomas C. Smith: 'Japan's Aristocratic Revolution', in *THE YALE REVIEW* (1961) Vol. 50, pp. 370–383.

demonstrated to them the inadequacy of existing institutions, prompting them to make revolutionary innovations in the name of national salvation. This I believe is quite true in a way. But it takes for granted what most needs explaining. Communities in danger do not necessarily seek safety in innovation; commonly they reaffirm tradition and cling to it the more resolutely. Such was the first response to the challenge of the modern West in China and Korea; it also had intelligent and patriotic spokesmen in Japan.

The other explanation may be called the Western analogue theory. It emphasizes (in the century before Perry's arrival) the improvement of transport, the growth of towns, the development of trade, and the rise of a wealthy merchant class — all important developments which add much to our knowledge of pre-modern Japan. But, suggestive as they are, these developments would better explain, keeping the Western analogy in mind, an aristocracy being overthrown or reluctantly forced to share power with a rising new class, than an aristocracy conducting a social revolution.

Differences, rather than analogies, would seem more to the point. The man who takes cold baths is made of different stuff from most of us; and the Japanese warrior differed from the European aristocrat in ways that throw light on his seemingly odd class behavior. I wish to discuss three such ways that any satisfactory explanation of the aristocratic revolution, as I shall call it, would have to take into account. One has to do with the relations of the warrior to the merchant class; another with social and economic distinctions within the warrior class; and the third with the relations of the warrior class to land and political power.

My earlier statement that there was no democratic revolution in Japan because the aristocracy was revolutionary has an important corollary: had there been a democratic revolution, the aristocracy would not have been revolutionary. Nothing unites an aristocracy so quickly and firmly in defense of its privileges as an attack from below, by classes in which it can perceive neither distinction nor virtue.

Unlike the Western bourgeoisie, townsmen in Japan never challenged aristocratic privileges, either in practice or theory. They were seemingly content with a secondary political role, finding apparent satisfaction in money-making, family life, and the delights of a racy and exuberant city culture. This political passivity is puzzling. It is not to be explained by numerical weakness (Tokyo was a city of a million people in the late eighteenth century, and Osaka was only slightly smaller); nor by poverty, nor illiteracy, nor political innocence. Least of all is it to be understood as reflecting an absence of resentment at the warrior's smug and strutting pretensions. There was resentment aplenty and there were many instances of private revenge; but for some reason resentment never reached the pitch of ideology, never raised petty private hurts to a great principle of struggle between right and wrong. For whatever reasons, townsmen acknowledged the political primacy of the warrior, leaving him free to experiment without fear that to change anything would endanger everything.

But, one may suppose, no ruling group ever launches on a career of radical reform merely because it is free to do so; there must be positive incentives as well. In the Japanese case these incentives were in part born of differences within the aristocracy.

Such differences were not unique to Japan, of course, but they can rarely have been more pronounced anywhere.

On the one hand were a few thousand families of superior lineage and very large incomes, with imposing retinues and magnificent houses, who in practice, though not in law, monopolized the important offices of government; some offices in effect became hereditary. On the other hand was the bulk of the warrior class, numbering several hundred thousand families, who were cut off from high office and lived on very modest incomes; many in real poverty, pawning their armor and family heirlooms, doing industrial piecework at home to eke out small stipends, and resorting to such pitiful tricks as sewing strips of white cloth to the undersides of their collars so people might take them to be wearing proper undergarments. As warrior mothers proudly taught their children, a samurai might have an empty belly but he used a toothpick all the same.

But it was not so much the contrast between his own and the style of life of his superior that moved the ordinary warrior to fury. It was, rather, the impropriety of the merchant's wealth. Surely it was a perversion of social justice, that the warrior, who gave his life to public service, should live in want and squalor, while men who devoted themselves to money-making lived in ease and elegance, treated him with condescension and even rudeness, and in the end not infrequently found favor with the lord.

The merchant himself was not to blame since he merely followed his nature. Though he was feared and hated for that, ultimate responsibility lay with the effeminate high aristocrats who, through idleness or incompetence, failed to use their inherited power for the proper ends of government. No secret was made of the failure either. Political writings were full of charges of the incompetence and corruption of government, of the fecklessness and indifference of princes; and the only remedy, it was said, lay in giving power to new men — men of lower rank, who were close to the people and whose characters had been formed by hardship. This was no revolutionary doctrine. It called for a change of men, not institutions; but the men it helped to power were in fact radical innovators.

This brings me to the final difference — or rather to two differences — between the Japanese warrior class and European aristocrats. Japanese warriors did not own land, and their political power was to a greater extent bureaucratic. I want to say more on these points, but first it will be helpful to see how a once feudal aristocracy had come to be without private economic or political power.

We must go back to the late sixteenth century. At that time warriors were scattered over the land in villages where they were overlords, levying taxes, administering justice, and keeping the peace. To defend their territories and lessen the hazards of life, they had long since banded together into regional military organizations consisting of a lord and his vassals. The normal state among such groups was war or preparation for war, that being the most direct means of increasing territory and territory of increasing strength and security.

59

Then, about the turn of the century, Tokugawa Ieyasu, a man of authentic genius, who had the remarkable good fortune of having two predecessors who had already half done what he intended, succeeded in conquering the country. Instead of destroying the feudal leagues or groups, however, he chose to use them to govern, taking care only to establish his own firm control over them. Seemingly a compromise between order and chaos, the resulting political structure, surprisingly, kept the peace for two and a half centuries.

These long years of orderly government, which favored economic growth and urban development, brought profound changes to the warrior class, altering not so much, however, the fact of warrior power (which remained uncontested) as the nature of it. I would like to mention three such changes in particular.

First was a change in the relation of warriors to the land. The lord, in order better to control his vassals and to achieve greater uniformity of administration within the territory he dominated, gradually restricted his vassals' power over their fiefs. He forbade them to administer local justice; he moved them from the land into a town which now grew up around his castle; he decreed what taxes they might collect and at what rates, then decided to collect the taxes himself and in return to pay them stipends in money or kind from his treasury.

There were local exceptions to the rule, but taking the country as a whole, fiefs in land disappeared. Land and the seignorial rights associated with it, once widely dispersed through the warrior class, were now consolidated in the hands of a few hundred noble families. The typical warrior had become a townsman living on a salary paid him by the lord, with the townsman's disdain for the country and country people. Both his juridical and social ties with the land were gone. If his fief was still an identifiable piece of land at all, it was rarely more than a unit of account, with other land, under the lord's common administration.

Second was the resulting bureaucratization of government. The lord, having taken into his hands his vassals, political and judicial functions, now governed an average population of about 100,000. To police so large a population, to collect its taxes and regulate its trade, to give it justice and maintain its roads and irrigation works, required a small army of officials and clerks. The lord, or course, used his vassals to perform these functions, to man the expanding and differentiating bureaucracy under him. The warriors who manned the bureaucracy exercised far more power over the rest of the population than warriors ever had before; but it was a new kind of power. Formerly power was personal and territorial: it pertained to a piece of land and belonged to a man as inherited right. Now it was impersonal and bureaucratic: it pertained to a specialized office to which one must be appointed and from which he might be removed.

There is unmistakable evidence of the increasingly bureaucratic nature of power in the more and more impersonal criteria for selecting officials. However writers on government might differ on other matters, by the late eighteenth century they were in astonishingly unanimous agreement that ability and specialized knowledge should take precedence over lineage and family rank in the appointment and promotion of officials. To this end they devised tests for office, job descriptions, fitness reports, official allowances, salary schedules, and pensions.

It was only in lower ranks of officials that the ideal of impersonality came close to realization. Nevertheless, men of low rank were sometimes promoted to high office; merchants and occasionally even peasants with specialized qualifications were ennobled that they might hold office; and promotion in the bureaucracy became for warriors an important means of improving status. If the highest offices usually went to certain well-placed families, this was looked on as an abuse rather than proper recognition of rank, and an abuse that struck at the very foundations of good government. Moreover, many families of high rank were without office, and office rather than rank or wealth gave power.

Thus a group of young samurai who met on the morrow of Perry's first alarming visit to Japan, to consider what they might do for their country, were exhorted by their leader to do what they could *even though none held office*. One cried out: "But what *can* we do without office!" No one, it seems, complained of the lack of age, wealth, or high rank in the group.

The third change I would like to mention followed very largely from the second. The relationship between vassal and lord was slowly, silently, and profoundly transformed. It had been an intimate, intensely emotional relationship, based in no small part on the personal qualities of the lord, a relationship which existed between men who had fought side by side, grieved together at the loss of comrades, whose safety and families' safety depended on their keeping faith. During the centuries of peace of urban living, however, the relationship lost much of its emotional significance. It became distant and formal; it was hedged about by ceremonies and taboos; the vassal came to look on his lord less as a leader in war (for there was no war) than as an administrative head.

One sees this change in the changing concept of the ideal warrior. Once a strong, stout-hearted fellow, quick and warm in his sympathies, generous to the weak and unyielding to the strong, he becomes a man whose native intelligence has been disciplined in the classroom, who gets on harmoniously with his colleagues, who deals with matters within his jurisdiction without fear or favor. Loyalty is still the highest virtue for him; but where once it had meant willingness to follow the lord to death, now it meant giving the lord disinterested advice and conducting oneself in a way reflecting credit on his administration. Qualities of the ideal bureaucrat had come to be viewed as the very essence of the warrior.

Moreover, the power of the lord as administrative head increasingly became merely symbolic; actual power passed to lower echelons of officials. Partly this was a result of the growing complexity of government, but in greater measure it was because the lord's position was hereditary and as time passed fewer and fewer of his breed were men of force and intelligence, fit for the top job. Vassals who still looked on the lord with awe were likely to be men who regarded him from a distance; those who saw him closer, despite all outward deference, could often scarcely conceal their contempt.

Indeed some hardly tried. An anonymous author, writing about 1860, calls the lords of his day time-servers; men brought up by women deep in the interior of palaces where no sound of the outside world penetrated; surrounded from childhood by luxury and indulged in every whim, they were physically weak and innocent of both learning and practical experience. But it was not revolution that was called for, only better education for rulers, that they might choose better officials. "The secret of good government," the writer confidently declared, "lies in each official discharging his particular office properly, which in turn depends on choosing the right man for the right job."

To summarize up to this point: the two and a half centuries of peace after 1600 brought great changes to the warrior class. They brought a change in the warrior's relationship with the land, which became purely administrative; in his relationship to political power, which became bureaucratic; and in his relationship to his lord, which became distant and impersonal.

I should like now to show, as concretely as I can, the connection between the changes and some aspects of the economic and social transformation of the country after 1868 — my so-called aristocratic revolution.

Consider the creation in the years immediately after 1868 of a highly centralized government. This was a brilliant achievement which permitted the new leaders who came to power to formulate for the first time a national purpose and to call up energies that did not before exist. Political power had lain scattered in fragments over the map, each lord collecting his own taxes, maintaining his own army and navy, even following an independent foreign policy. Then, with astonishing speed the fragments were pulled together; a central government created; the entire country subjected to a single will. Feudal lords and their miniature kingdoms were swept away and one bureaucratic empire emerged in their place.

This change was possible in part because warriors had long since been removed from the land and stripped of seignorial rights. Had these interests remained, the warrior must first have been dispossessed of them — the base of his power and source of his pride. Whoever might eventually have succeeded in this would not likely himself have been a warrior, nor have accomplished the feat without a long and bitter struggle. As it was, only the great lords had to be deprived of their power, and the deed was sooner done because their powers had come to be exercised, in fact, by officials who might trade them for similar powers within a vastly larger organization.

But what of the vaunted loyalty of the samurai? One would think this must have prevented liquidation of the great territorial lords by their own vassals. The unconditional loyalty to the lord as war leader, however, had shrunk to the conditional loyalty of the administrative subordinate to his chief — a loyalty valid only so long as the chief performed his duties efficiently. That the great lords had long ceased to do this was known to all. Meanwhile a new and higher loyalty emerged, sanctioning — indeed, those who prevailed thought, demanding — the transfer of all power to a central government. This was loyalty to the Emperor, in whose name the aristocratic revolution was carried out. Nor was the emergence of this new loyalty unconnected with the decline of the older one: one suspects that men brought up in the cult of loyalty to the lord, as an absolute obligation and the noblest of human ideals, needed some escape from the disloyalty they felt in their hearts.

Second, consider how the new central government used its power to liquidate the four estates of which society was legally composed. Each estate — warrior, peasant, artisan, and merchant — was theoretically closed, and subject to detailed restrictions concerning occupation, residence, food, and dress peculiar to itself. The new government swept away such restrictions, and endowed men with extensive civic, though not political, rights. Henceforth anything that was legally permissible or obligatory for one, was permissible or obligatory for all; moreover, a system of free public schools very soon gave this new legal dispensation concrete social meaning. The warrior lost his privileges and immunities and was forced to compete in school and out with the sons of tradesmen and peasants. Even his economic privileges were done away with. Warrior stipends were commuted into national bonds redeemable in twenty years, after which time warriors, as such, had no claim on the national income.

Now, how is one to explain a ruling class thus liquidating its privileges, and not by a series of forced retreats but at a single willing stroke? Surely part of the answer lies in warrior privileges not being bound up with the ownership of land. To restrict or even abolish them, therefore, did not arouse fears for the safety of property, or stir those complicated emotions that seem to attach peculiarly to land as a symbol of family continuity and an assurance of the continuing deference of neighbors. Few ruling classes have ever been so free of economic bias against change. Warrior power was based almost exclusively on office-holding, and this monopoly was not immediately in danger because no other class had yet the experience, education, and confidence to displace warriors in administration. The striking down of barriers between estates, on the other hand, opened up to warriors occupational opportunities formerly denied them, a not insignificant gain in view of the large number of warriors who, with more than normal pride but neither property nor important office, were nearly indigent.

This brings me to a third aspect of the revolutionary transformation of Japanese society after 1868: the explosion of individual energies that followed the sudden abolition of status distinctions. Until then opportunity was very limited; men looked forward to following the occupations of their fathers, and even to living out their lives in their same villages and towns and houses. After it, everything seemed suddenly changed, and young men strove with leaping hope and fearful determination to improve their characters, to rise in the world, to become something different from their fathers.

For warriors the abolition of status restrictions meant finding new occupations and new roles in society. Few had enough property after the commutation of stipends to live without work, and not all could continue in the traditional occupations of soldier, official, policeman, and teacher. A very large number were forced either to suffer social eclipse or become merchants, industrialists, lawyers, engineers, scientists; or they saw in these occupations exciting new opportunities for wealth and fame.

In any case, there was a grand redirection of warrior talent and ambition. Despite the traditional warrior aversion to money-making and the merchant's love of it, for example, most of the first generation of modern entrepreneurs, above all the earliest and most daring, came from the warrior class. Nor is this to be explained merely by the occupational displacement of the warrior. Part of the explanation lies in the warrior's aristocratic background — his educational preferment under the old regime, his cult of action, and (at his best) his intense social idealism.

Okano Kitaro, a man born in a warrior family of low rank, who founded an important provincial bank, illustrates the point. He writes in his autobiography:

> "I lost my wife and third daughter in the earthquake of 1923. They were on their way to a resort hotel when the great quake struck, and their train plunged into the sea. When news of the accident reached me my courage failed, but after a while my sense of responsibility returned and I thought to myself, 'You are head of the Suruga Bank! You must discharge your duty as a banker in this time of trouble! Compared to that, your personal loss is a trifling matter!' My whole body trembled."

Other classes were scarcely less affected than warriors. Finding themselves suddenly free to become whatever wishes, effort, and ability could make them, with not even the highest positions in society closed to competition, they responded with an heroic effort at self-transcendence. Freedom of this kind must always be heady; but one wonders if it is not especially so when it comes suddenly, in societies with a strong sense of status differences, where the social rewards of success are more finely graded and seem sweeter than in societies less schooled to such distinctions.

In a charming little anecdote in his autobiography, Ito Chubei, the son of a peasant who became a leading industrialist, gives some hint of the poignancy of the hopes for success he shared with other peasant boys of his generation. Upon graduating from elementary school not long after 1868, the first boy in his village to do so, Ito called on the headmaster to take leave. He was not surprised to meet with an angry scolding, since he had been far from the model boy. After the master finished his scolding, however, he spoke glowingly of Ito's future and predicted that, despite his rebelliousness, he would be a success. "You will make your mark in the world, I know it!" he exclaimed. And at this the young boy, unable to hold back his tears, wept aloud. Years later, in recounting this incident to a reunion of his classmates, Ito was so affected that he wept again, and his gratitude to his former teacher was no less when, after the meeting, he discovered that all of his classmates had been sent off with exactly the same exhortation!

Such hopes were real because, although not everyone was equal in the competition for wealth and honor, the privileged estate under the old regime had no prohibitive or enduring advantage. In respect to income, for example, warriors were at no advantage over the rest of the population, and though they were the most literate class in society, literacy was very widespread among other classes as well, and it rapidly became more so through the new schools. But most important, perhaps, warriors could not for long claim a cultural superiority, compounded of superior education, elegance, and taste, to act as a bar to the achievement of others, or to divert others from achievement in the pursuit of aristocratic culture. Indeed, by the twentieth century, one can scarcely speak of an aristocratic culture in Japan, despite the peerage created by the government in 1885. Whether a young man came of warrior family could no longer be reliably told from his speech, manners, or social ideas; moreover, his origins were far less important to his self-esteem and the good opinion of others than whether he had a university diploma and where he was employed. I want to return to this point.

In hope of making its revolutionary behavior less puzzling than must otherwise appear, I have discussed three ways the Japanese warrior class differed from Western aristocracies — its relation to other classes, its internal divisions, and its relation to economic and political power. I should like now to suggest, very briefly, some of the ways in which Japanese society seems to be different because its modern revolution was aristocratic rather than democratic.

First, a point so obvious it need only be mentioned in passing: the aristocratic revolution, despite the civil equality and economic progress it brought, has not made for a strong democratic political tradition — but the contrary.

Second, more than any other single factor, perhaps, that revolution helps to explain Japan's rapid transition from an agrarian to an industrial society. How different the story must have been had the warriors behaved as one would expect of an aristocracy, if they had used their monopoly of political and military power to defend rather than change the existing order.

Third, as there was no aristocratic defense of the old regime, there was no struggle over its survival; no class or party war in which the skirmish line was drawn between new and old, revolutionaries and conservatives. There was, of course, tension between traditional and modern, Japanese and Western, but not a radical cleavage of the two by ideology. All parties were more or less reformist, more or less traditional, and more or less modern; excepting perhaps the Communists, whose numbers were insignificant, no pre-war party thought of the past, as such, as a barrier to progress. It was a barrier in some respects, in others a positive aid. Modernization therefore appeared to most Japanese who thought about it at all, not as a process in which a life-or-death confrontation of traditional and modern took place, but as a dynamic blending of the two. I wonder if this does not account in large part for what has seemed to many people the uncommon strength of tradition in the midst of change in modern Japan.

Fourth, status-consciousness is relatively strong in Japan in part because there was no revolutionary struggle against inequality, but for that reason class-consciousness is relatively weak. These attitudes are by no means contradictory. The nervous concern of Japanese for status is quite consonant with their relatively weak feeling about classes — higher-ups to some extent being looked on as superior extensions of the self. This is an attitude familiar to us elsewhere. It is illustrated in Jane Austen by the servant who fairly bursts with pride when his master is made a baronet; and by Fielding's story of Nell Gwynn. Stepping one day from a house where she had made a short visit, the famous actress saw a great mob assembled, and her footman all bloody and dirty. The fellow, being asked by his mistress what happened, answered, "I have been fighting, madam, with an impudent rascal who called your ladyship a whore." "You block-head," replied Mrs. Gwynn, "at this rate you must fight every day of your life; why, you fool, all the world knows it." "Do they?" the footman said in a muttering voice; "They shan't call me a whore's footman for all that."

Finally, and this brings me back to an earlier point about the absence of an aristocratic culture in modern Japan, since warriors were never thrown on the defensive by the hostility of other classes, they never felt the need to make a cult of their peculiar style of life, either as evidence of virtues justifying their privileges or as compensation for loss of them. One wonders if Western aristocracies did not put exceptional value on leisure, gambling, dueling, and love-making, as aspects of the aristocratic way of life, in good part because they were a dramatic repudiation of bourgeois values.

In any case the warrior did not have the means of supporting a leisurely and aesthetic style of life. The revolution found him separated from the land, living on a government salary rather than on income from property; he therefore carried no capital inheritance from his privileged past into the modern age. He had no country estates, no rich town properties, no consols to spare unbecoming compromises with the crass new world of business. On the contrary, warriors were the chief makers of this world and they scrambled for success in it to escape social and economic oblivion.

Then too, this new world was irrevocable bound up with Western culture, whence it came (with whatever modifications) much of its technology and many of its conventions. Success in it had very little to do with traditional skills and tastes, and much to do with double-entry book-keeping, commercial law, English conversation, German music, French painting, and Scotch whiskey. Traditional arts were not forgotten, but they were never identified with a particular social class, least of all perhaps the upper class. It is significant, for example, that the pre-war Peer's Club in Tokyo, located within easy walking distance of the Foreign Office and the Ministry of Finance, was a great ugly stone building with marble stairways, thick carpets, mahogany bar, wallpaper, glass chandeliers, and French cuisine. In respect to such things all classes of Japanese, during the first generation or two after 1868, were born cultural equals. One could not learn of these things at home, any more than one could learn there a foreign language or the calculus. Such subjects were taught only in the schools, and the schools were open to anyone.

5. The Meiji State: 1868–1912

Marius B. Jansen

In January 1868 an imperial rescript announced that "the Shogun Tokugawa Keiki has abdicated his administrative power. Henceforth all administration will be carried out under Our direct control, and all public affairs will be executed under the name of Emperor, instead of Taikun, as it has been hitherto. Further, special officials will be appointed for intercourse with foreign countries." A few weeks later the shogun, charging that the court had been manipulated by his enemies into a breach of the understandings under which he had resigned his powers, made an unsuccessful attempt to regain military ascendancy at the imperial capital. After his efforts failed, he himself made no great effort to defend his patrimony, but sporadic resistance from his closest vassals led to a civil war with the new "imperial government" that extended into the early summer of 1869.

In April 1868, long before the issue was decided, the imperial government made an important bid for national support with a five-point pledge. This Charter Oath promised that the government would provide the opportunity for "all classes" to achieve their "just aspirations," give attention to the general will by establishing a council chamber, conduct a search for wisdom "throughout the world," and abolish "absurd customs of the past," in order to establish firmly "the foundations of the Empire."

This combination of military force and political and psychological appeal brought the new government steady gains over its less united opponents, and by the fall of 1868 it was ready for a symbolic act that inaugurated the Meiji period. On October 23 the young emperor Mutsuhito, in a Shinto ceremony, selected a slip of paper that bore the Chinese characters "bright" and "rule," pieced together from a quotation in the *Book of Changes*. The combined characters read "Meiji," thus designating the era that would extend until the emperor's death in 1912. The announcement of the era of "enlightened rule" was joined with the statement that henceforth there would be only one era name per sovereign. History was to unfold in emperor-sized units, instead of being divided into eras at the discretion of the government in accordance with numerological wisdom. Thus, a development that had begun in China with the Ming dynasty in 1368, one that signified the final stage of imperial absolutism there, came to Japan at the beginning of the modern era.

A few weeks earlier the court had renamed Edo, the shogun's capital as Tokyo, or "Eastern Capital." And in November, the boy emperor set out on a visit to his new city. A procession of three thousand men surrounded his great palanquin, which was topped by a phoenix and carried by a host of yellow-robed bearers. Having watched the approach of the strange conveyance, which was carried a full six feet above the ground, a reporter wrote that

'The Meiji State, 1868–1912' by Marius B. Jansen from *MODERN EAST ASIA: ESSAYS IN INTERPRETATION*, edited by James B. Crowley. Copyright © 1970 by Harcourt Brace & Company. Reprinted by permission of the publisher.

a great silence fell upon the people. Far as the eye could see on either side, the roadsides were densely packed with the crouching populace. And as the phoenix car with its halo of glittering attendants came on ... the people without order or signal turned their faces to the earth. No man moved or spoke for a space, and all seemed to hold their breath for very awe, as the mysterious presence, on whom few are privileged to look and live, was passing by.[1]

Thus the symbolism of a hallowed past, one recently revived by the fervor of the leaders of the national cult, was utilized to sanctify the changes that the discovery of Japan's inability to deal with the outside world had shown to be necessary. And the children of the uncomprehending commoners who crouched in the dust by the roadside as the procession passed were to learn as schoolboys that their rise to equality within Japanese society, like Japan's rise to equality in the world at large, had its origins in the will and virtue of the silent occupant of that Phoenix-topped palanquin.

The Meiji Restoration

The Meiji Restoration represents a remarkable combination of fact and fiction that puts it in a special category among the turning points in the history of the modern world. Viewed as a symbol of Japan's rise to modernity, it can be seen as the product of the interaction of external pressures with the long-range development of Tokugawa thought and society. The economic strains within the Tokugawa system had produced increasingly difficult problems for shogunal administrators and reformers, and the intellectual currents of the eighteenth century had substituted for the neat, hierarchical structure of official Confucianism a dynamic mixture of voluntarism and practicality, emotive national affirmation, and curiosity about the learning of the West. The arrival of the West in the middle of the nineteenth century made impossible a preservation of the delicate balance of centralization and decentralization, custom and reason, status and ambition, that had characterized late feudal society. And the discovery of the inadequacy of their society and political system in safeguarding the national integrity against the threat of the West, the sudden realization of Japan's weakness and inferiority, led a generation of Japanese to remarkable efforts to correct these failings. The Restoration was thus nothing less than the opening of a political system that had been closed for more than two centuries. Though the Restoration began as a movement within a small sector of the old elite, and though it was later surrounded with emperor-centered mystique, the need of the Japanese government to attract a broad response in the face of national danger and disunity led it to make the restoration a national renovation.

The opening of the country had been prepared for by an opening of minds. Late Tokugawa Japan had seen a growing interest in the knowledge of the West. In the early decades of the nineteenth century the shogunate, as well as a number of important domains, made efforts to encourage and also to control, channel, and utilize the information about medicine, war, and technology that could be found in Western books. By the late 1830's some conservatives were beginning to doubt the advisability and safety of such potential subversion of the traditional wisdom, but the shattering intelligence of Britain's defeat of China in the Opium War made it a matter of urgent necessity to intensify efforts to learn about the West. Shortly after the coming of Commodore Perry, the shogunate responded affirmatively to memoranda proposing the establishment of centers for instruction, training, and translation, and in 1857 the Bansho Shirabesho, an "Institute for the Investigation of Barbarian Books," was opened near Edo Castle with a staff that had been selected in a national search for qualified specialists.

It was in good measure the Japanese awareness of the impossibility of resisting the West, an awareness prepared through Nagasaki and underscored by the failure of China's resistance, that produced the opening of ports to Westerners in the half-decade between the Treaty of Kanagawa, negotiated by Perry in March 1854, and the arrival of consuls and merchants in 1859 under terms of the treaty that Townsend Harris had worked out the previous year. With this beginning, a pattern of unequal treaties, like those worked out earlier with China, began to take form. Treaty ports were set for Nagasaki, Hakodate, and Yokohama, then Niigato and Kobe. More important still, Osaka and Edo were to be opened in 1862 and 1863. Foreign ministers and consuls were given legal jurisdiction over their countrymen, customs duties were fixed, and the "most favored nation" clause made the system operate to the perpetual and increasing advantage of the outside powers. This was the more certain as a virulent antiforeignism, the product of samurai extremism and economic hardships exacerbated by foreign trade, began to take its toll of foreign lives — and tempers. Outrage led to indemnity and, in two instances, reprisal, in the course of which Japanese inability to withstand the guns of Western ships was made apparent.

The pressures connected with the opening of the ports also produced openings in Japanese politics. The shogunate's first reaction to the problem of Perry's request for a treaty had been to issue a request for the opinion of its vassals; and, since its options were limited by its strength, the shogunate inevitably went on to alienate and antagonize its supporters in the course of accommodating its rivals.

The agreement with Townsend Harris had been made in haste, in fear of new foreign dangers, and in confidence of ability to secure the approval of the imperial court. But this approval proved elusive in fact, and efforts by the shogunate to secure it showed that events of the 1850's had served to activate court nobles as well as daimyō to a new interest in national policies. Conservative Tokugawa collaterals, who disapproved of the agreement with Harris, seized the opportunity to intrigue with Kyoto nobles. They tried to tie reform of the bakufu with approval of the treaty. Since the reforms they proposed included innovation in succession procedures to ensure the choice of a mature and "able" shogun, they provided startling evidence of the way the outside threat had produced reverberations in the center of what had always been the private concerns of Tokugawa house policy. For a brief period the emergence of a strong-willed Tokugawa vassal, Ii Naosuke, as chief administrator in the Edo councils produced reaffirmation of shogunal prerogatives. The succession issue was dealt with according to tradition to thwart the hopes of innovators. The innovators, who included collateral Tokugawa vassals as well as reform-minded outside lords, were dealt with firmly to discourage further efforts at interference. Their retainers were dismissed, and in some cases executed, to emphasize the arbitrariness of bakufu power. From carrying out this "Ansei purge," as it became known, Ii Naosuke then turned to wringing approval of the Harris treaty from a now reluctant imperial court. It was granted in February 1859.

These Tokugawa "victories" proved expensive. Foreign policy and accommodation to the West's demands had now been lodged at the center of Japanese feudal rivalry and politics. Thereafter they were to be associated with Tokugawa policy, while the leadership of the antiforeign cause would be out of Tokugawa hands and outside its domains–although it did not pass there without a final drama in which Ii himself lost his life. On a snowy day late in March 1860, at the very gate of the shogun's castle, he was cut down by a small party of samurai, most of them from the vassal domain of Mito (whose daimyō he had disciplined). Their manifesto associated resistance to foreigners with the Imperial Will and invoked the sanction of the Sun Goddess to rebuke the bakufu's first minister. The murder of the regent in 1860 revealed the strength and intensity of opposition to the new diplomatic moves and inaugurated years of loyalist energy that marked the border between Tokugawa and Meiji Japan.

The political issues of the 1860's in Japan defy neat categorization. The Western world, to the degree that it was not consumed with its own problems, was fortunately engrossed by the tumultuous upheavals of the Taiping insurrection in China. The result was that Japan had the better part of the decade to work out the greatest crisis and disunity it had experienced since the sixteenth century.

The alternatives were not a simple acceptance or repulsion of the West, although this is the way they were phrased by the catch-slogan of the day, *kaikoku/jōi* ("Open the country/ Drive out the barbarians"). These alternatives were complicated by advocacy of reconciliation between court and shogun (*kōbu gattai*) and simply phrased insistence on reverence for the emperor (*sonnō*). In these amuletic phrases political and philosophical discourse was structured to produce, or as often to conceal, a steadily growing emphasis on the prerogatives of the imperial court at the expense of the Edo bakufu.

The logical sponsors of the court in national politics were the great domains of southwestern Japan. Satsuma and Choshu had known defeat by the Tokugawa armies in 1600, and both came through the Tokugawa centuries reduced in land and wealth as a result. Cut off from office or influence in the bakufu, they were nevertheless more autonomous, more proud, and more military in their internal structure than most of central Japan. They were remote from the great Tokugawa cities and less involved in their problems. More integrated and sizable as domains, they were also more capable of internal, local reform and economic controls than were the great majority of fiefs. In both Satsuma and Choshu resentment of Tokugawa dominance had survived. They were sufficiently remote from Tokugawa control to be able to import Western small arms by way of the newly opened ports, and both areas experimented with military resistance to the West — Choshu in the shelling of foreign ships in the straits of Shimonoseki, and Satsuma in the effort to resist British demands for punishment of an antiforeign outrage. Neither effort succeeded; the British shelled Kagoshima in 1863, and a Western flotilla shelled Shimonoseki in 1864. Both areas also sponsored efforts to learn directly of the West — Satsuma through the education of students sent to London in the 1860's and Choshu through the experiences of Itō Hirobumi and

Inoue Kaoru, two of the Meiji leaders, in Europe. By the second half of the decade, many Japanese were looking to these baronies. As a contemporary loyalist put it, "Satsuma and Choshu are the two han that will be able to stir the realm in the future; ... anyone can see that we will all be following the orders of these two domains."2

Cooperation between them, however, was hindered by a jealousy and distrust that were as great as the suspicion they both bore the bakufu. During the early 1860's they competed in posing as sponsors of the court in advancing a series of plans for restructuring the bakufu-court relationship. These efforts were not without result, and in 1863 a new and reformist group in the bakufu came to the forefront. But revolutionary discontent among the samurai outran the concessions made to them, and each concession was inadequate by the time it was made. What was necessary constantly turned out to be more than what was politically possible. Gradually the "reformist" schemes began to hide intentions of overthrow.

These developments came gradually and at different speeds for different groups and areas, but within this process two developments were of critical importance. The first was the politicization of large numbers of samurai. The conviction of imminent crisis from foreign danger, domestic treachery, and personal distress as foreign trade altered long-standing patterns of distribution and resources affected the warrior elite profoundly. Significant numbers of young men left their homes and their immediate loyalties in the name of a higher, national loyalty. The excitement or participation in the political maelstrom of antiforeignism resulted in a wave of terrorist violence that brought home to many more the instability and crisis of the times.

A second development was the readiness of groups of men in several domains, but especially in Choshu, to stand sponsor to zealots from other areas and to challenge their regular authorities for control of the direction of han policy. The extremist stand taken by Choshu leaders led to their being driven out of Kyoto in 1863 through the cooperation of Tokugawa and Satsuma units, and to their defeat by a Tokugawa-led coalition in 1864. But shortly afterward the Choshu loyalists rose again, deposed their samurai superiors, and manipulated their daimyō in a flagrant rejection of Tokugawa authority.

The bakufu had alarmed many of its erstwhile supporters by a vigorous reform program. A new group of able leaders seemed bent on increasing traditional Tokugawa dominance and utilizing French support to create a centralized Tokugawa state. They first tried to crush Choshu. In February 1866 Satsuma and Choshu reached an agreement to cooperate. The bakufu's effort to chastise Choshu in battle failed miserably.

When it seemed that Japan was slipping into full-scale violence and international danger, moderates who had ties to Satsuma and Choshu as well as to the bakufu introduced ideas of compromise. The daimyō of Tosa proposed to the shogun that he resign his powers and agree to stand as but one, though still the greatest, feudal lord in a new national structure headed by the emperor. The present disunity, he argued, was "a great disaster to us and of great happiness to the foreigners. This is exactly what they have been hoping for." What was needed was a government "for which no shame need be felt before future generations of foreign countries." This proposal was

71

agreed to by the shogun, who petitioned the court to accept the return of his political powers on November 9, 1867.

The court, however, was soon in the hands of Satsuma and Choshu leaders, who secured an edict directing the shogun to surrender his lands as well. The Tokugawa, as has been noted, resisted, but not to the death. The outcome had indeed been foreshadowed by a document the shogun had addressed to the foreign representatives in January. "As to who is the sovereign of Japan," he admitted, "it is a question on which no one in Japan can entertain a doubt. The Mikado is the Sovereign."[3] As a result, the former Tokugawa head, despite his protests, accepted deposition from his rule over country and house and retired to Shizuoka, while his vassals to the north were still resisting the Satsuma, Choshu, and Tosa (now officially termed the "Imperial") armies.

As of 1868, the year of the Charter Oath and the emperor's procession to Tokyo, the Meiji Restoration had not gone beyond a coup within the ruling class. The appearance of the West had shown the need for drastic changes in Japan's state structure. It was clear that greater unity was the country's most immediate need and equally clear that unity could best be achieved under the aegis of the emperor. But the way this should be done was still to be worked out.

Yet the events of the restoration did change Japan permanently. They produced a clean break in Japan's political continuity and offered the opportunity for equally striking institutional innovations. Scarcely less important, the Restoration achieved symbolic importance as a breakthrough made possible through the individual commitment of its leaders. One of the most interesting and colorful aspects of the Restoration struggle was its legacy of national heroes. The "men of high purpose" (*shishi*), the young activists who had put the national purpose ahead of traditional family and feudal claims, gave the decade much of its color and its life. They became the ethical ideals for later times and models for later revolutionaries of both left and right, men who saw in their courage, individualism, and determination examples of what times of crisis demanded of committed youth.

The Meiji Revolution

Tokugawa resistance ended with the surrender of the shogunate's naval units to the national government in the early summer of 1869. Political power was now in the hands of the Satsuma–Choshu forces and their allies in the fief of Tosa. The court nobles who had worked with them and the young emperor they served held promise of legitimacy of rule. But these forces held chiefly their own domains and those of the Tokugawa lords whose armies they had defeated or outmaneuvered. Few thought they had seen an end to the fighting. The Tosa leaders, who expected a new war between Satsuma and Choshu, worked out an alliance with their Shikoku neighbors and made plans for a quick dash to rescue the emperor once fighting broke out. Yet somehow things held together. By the time the new leaders were seriously challenged a few years later they were ready for the contest, and by then their plans for fundamental reform were already well underway.

How was this possible? Clearly, the patterns of Tokugawa decentralization helped the new leaders at first. Their limited geographical control also limited the political and economic responsibilities they inherited. Moreover, their strongest foes, the Tokugawa vassals, had just accepted defeat and imperial admonition. Most of the other lords maintained a cautious inaction. Samurai in the southwestern fiefs like Satsuma and Choshu still had heroic expectations of importance in the new order. The Satsuma–Choshu–Tosa leaders recruited further support from the domain of Saga (or Hizen), thereby tapping the considerable knowledge of Western technology that that domain, with its access to Nagasaki, had built up. The four-way partnership of power, Satsuma–Choshu–Hizen–Tosa, that would characterize the Meiji political picture was now in being.[4]

Perhaps most important for the early Meiji transition, the leaders of the new regime had time to experiment and plan because there was no revolution from below. The peasants who crouched with foreheads to the ground as the imperial procession passed in 1868 were seldom a problem. Since, as Thomas Smith has pointed out,[5] there was so little pressure from below, since administration went on as before in so many parts of the country, those at the center had an invaluable period of time in which they could think about problems and priorities and consolidate their power.

The most important consensus of Restoration days was that Japan needed more unity. Feudal decentralization was badly out of place in the international society of the nineteenth century, and Japanese leaders were determined to build a political order for which their descendants would "know no shame," one that could stand up to external pressure. Their anxiety to end every cause of shameful weakness was conspicuous throughout the memorializing of 1868. The Charter Oath of that year spoke of ending "uncivilized customs" of the past. It soon became clear that these customs included the divisions of feudalism that had made so difficult any effective response to the threat of Western imperialism. Like their Tokugawa predecessors, the Meiji leaders realized that new provisions had to be made for external defense and internal security, but unlike their predecessors, they no longer had to keep the stability of the existing political structure in mind in planning their steps. The Tokugawa fall had already interrupted political continuity. Not only were the existing feudal principalities a limitation on the power of government to lead, but as individuals the principal architects of the Meiji state were themselves in a position of inferiority to higher feudal authority and dependent on personal and factional favor for political opportunity. Thus they had as much interest in ending the feudal structure in Satsuma and Choshu as in Japan at large.

Although their personal situation was different from that of the Meiji leaders, the great majority of daimyō do not seem to have seen things very differently. The routine and ritual of daimyō life produced few figures of ability and initiative in the 1860's. Also, in the hectic politics of pre-Restoration decades the daimyō had been the object of constant pressure and criticism from their underlings, for whom the domain had long ago come to outweigh the person as primary focus of consideration. Moreover, few daimyō had realms that were in any sense profitable or economically viable. Repeated economic crises and attempted solutions had found them unable to adapt an archaic tax structure based upon subsistence agriculture to the expenses of rearmament and reform of their times. Nor, in any event, were their realms truly their own personal property. According to Tokugawa feudal theory, founded on the memory of an overwhelmingly powerful bakufu that had moved daimyō almost at will during the seventeenth century, domains were merely held in trust from the shogunate and administered in accordance with broadly phrased directives that came from it. And, as will be recalled, daimyō life in Edo, like samurai life in castle towns, had long tended to separate the fief-holder from his land. All these factors combined to suggest retrocession of the fiefs. The first petition from a daimyō to the new government requesting permission to return his lands, in fact, cited financial difficulties as the reason.

The new government had already established its control over the Tokugawa realms, which included the economic heartland of the country, in the Restoration wars. The baronies of the southwest, which had led in the Restoration, were the second most powerful group, after the Tokugawa core. When the daimyō of these baronies, at the behest of their young advisers, petitioned the imperial government to accept the return of their land registers in 1869, the remainder of the feudal lords were sure to follow, lest, as laggards, they seem less loyal.

In March 1869, before the surrender of the last Tokugawa holdouts, the lords of Satsuma, Choshu, Tosa, and Saga petitioned the court:

> Now that a new regime is being sought, the great Polity and the great Authority should not be delegated. The abode where we dwell is the Sovereign's land; the people over whom we rule are his people. Why should we privately own them? Now, therefore, we respectfully restore our domains to the Sovereign.

They went on to ask that

> the domains of all the han be reorganized, and also that all the regulations, from the ordering of laws, institutions, and military affairs, even to the fashioning of uniforms and instruments, issue from the Imperial Government, [and that the] conduct of all the affairs of the realm, whether great or small, be placed under unified control. Then only, name and reality complementing each other, the Empire can stand beside the foreign powers.

The court accepted the petition. It bridged the transition by appointing the former daimyō as governors of their realms. Within the year orders were issued simplifying the numerous degrees of status. Court nobles and daimyō were now one rank, upper samurai a second, ordinary samurai a third, and everybody else was "commoner," including the former pariah class. Now the government leaders began to give meaning to their talk of bringing society and customs into line with world standards. Some of the new leaders returned to Choshu, Satsuma, and Tosa and set in motion sweeping changes that struck at the system of official and social status that earlier had hampered their own rise to power. These reforms proceeded in tandem with plans for national change. In August 1871 the new government announced that abolition of feudalism and the assumption of central control over the former han, which were now redivided into larger, more rationally structured prefectures. Successive changes reduced the two hundred and fifty or so han into some seventy-five prefectural units of administration, a number that was later reduced by another third.

These jurisdictional changes were accompanied by sweeping instructions from the center to abolish legal distinctions between classes. Restrictions on occupation, cropping, and residence were removed, and commoners received the long-desired dignity of family names. Now that it finally had responsibility for administration and power to tax, the new government inaugurated land surveys in 1873 to prepare for a predictable tax income that would permit budgetary planning. The new land tax was set at three percent of the assessed value of the land, and with it came certificates of land ownership for farmers. The removal of feudal restrictions on peasant farmers represents the abandonment of the old efforts to increase revenue by extracting a greater yield from subsistence agriculture. It was a process that had begun in late Tokugawa times, as the shogunate and han struggled to find bases for taxation in money instead of in kind. With the Meiji changes, commercial agriculture had become the basis of the government's income and, by extension, the basis of Japan's emerging capitalist economy.

It was now necessary to educate and activate the commoners to serve their country. The task could no longer be left to the privileged classes of Tokugawa feudalism. Here also, changes represented in part a continuation of developments in the Tokugawa period. The Tokugawa emphasis on education had brought Japan into the Meiji period with one of the highest literacy rates of any nonindustrial society. What was needed was the utilization of this education for national purposes. Nothing more impressed Japanese travellers to the West than what they learned about popular patriotism, the more so in view of the contrast it offered to the relative indifference of the Japanese masses. For just as the commoners had bowed, impassive, as the imperial procession passed in 1868, they had watched, unparticipating, as English gunners dismantled Shimonoseki fortifications and Tosa armies stormed the defenses of Tokugawa vassals in northern Japan. Thus, education of the masses, in the arts of peace and of war, seemed essential to national safety. Japanese returned from Europe convinced, as one put it, that public education was the essential "foundation for a strong army," and a leading educational bureaucrat argued that the way to bring Japan to "the leading position among all countries of the world" was to "lay the foundations of elementary education." Few were prepared to dispute the contention of the Fundamental Law of Education, which appeared in 1872, that "education is the key to success in life, and no man can afford to neglect it." The goal announced by the law was that there should be "no community with an illiterate family, and no family with an illiterate person."[6]

The military extension of this attitude was the conscription law of 1873. The decision to abandon Japan's long-standing reliance upon the warrior class was not made without difficulty, but the combination of Western example and recent performance of the nonsamurai units in the Restoration fighting settled the issue. In addition, of course, the disestablishment of the samurai provided the most obvious source for government savings. If the samurai were no longer to rule the land, it made no sense to support them in idleness. And so their privileges disappeared. They were first permitted, and then ordered, to give up their swords; their distinctions of dress and their special status under law disappeared, and with these their incomes. Sharply reduced salaries gave way to pensions and those in turn to interest-bearing bonds. No doubt most of the leading figures in most walks of life were former samurai, but the number of those who could be accommodated with dignity in the new structure was limited. Far larger was the number of those who soon were in difficult straits, their pensions and bonds squandered or swallowed by inflation. Yet in some sense even these steps were only a continuation of the progressive attenuation of samurai income that had accompanied their separation from the land and their conversion into salaried bureaucrats during late Tokugawa times. The impoverished samurai had long been a stock figure of Tokugawa storytelling. In the Meiji Period, with his special airs, dress, and punctilio his pension slipping through his fingers, he became the perfect example of waste and human and material resources in an age of efficient, businesslike reconstruction. The former daimyō were in time absorbed into the new nobility that was set up in 1884 and retired to moderate affluence and prestige. Having long been symbols rather than wielders of power, they were well suited to lives of ceremonial inactivity. Life was harder for the samurai.

Changes of these dimensions could hardly be announced without stirring opposition. The substitution of new for familiar forms of rule produced sporadic distress and nearly two hundred local rebellions or protests within the first ten years of the Meiji period. Some were the result of groundless fears, some were based on resistance to change, and some were responses to specific local outrages. By and large, however, the commoners forebore; their expectations were modest, and the changes they experienced were sufficiently gradual to provide at least some appearance of continuity. The practical applications of decrees for conscription and education and taxation were some time in coming home to farmers, and they did so at different times in different parts of the country.

Revolution and dissent came from the samurai whose expectations had been highest, especially from those within the leading southwestern fiefs, whose military force had won the Restoration wars. The discovery that the freewheeling activism in which they had gloried in the 1860's was at an end must have come as a shock to many. Now that all policies were to come from the center, said a government statement ostensibly designed to praise them for their valor, "it is hoped that those who had previously left their han will return to their original prefectures, properly registered, abide with faith and justice, mind their conduct, and cooperate with and assist the Government." That took care of the individualists. But the problem came with members of the leadership who took strong exception to the priorities that had been set.

An inviting issue that presented itself concerned policy toward Korea. The peninsula state, most conservative of the East Asian respondents to the Western challenge, rejected Japanese attempts to modernize and regularize the traditional, tribute-style trade that had gone on between the two during the Tokugawa period and scornfully grouped the Meiji Japanese with the Western barbarians as beyond the pale of civilization. Meiji samurai, smarting from their inability to avenge Western insult, desired a solution that would combine domestic and foreign objectives; an expedition to "punish Korea," they held, would occupy and reward the increasingly impoverished samurai class. When these counsels were rejected by those who held that an adventurous foreign policy would benefit only the waiting European imperialists, important members of the leadership left the government. A compensatory agreement made in 1874 to punish aboriginal tribes in Taiwan for the murder of Okinawan sailors satisfied no one. Rebellions broke out in Choshu, then in Saga, and in 1877, in Satsuma, where the new government met its severest test in a rebellion led by the Restoration hero Saigō Takamori. After the failure of this uprising, the Meiji government had for the first time complete freedom of action at home. It also had a new leadership, for the suicide of Saigō was preceded by the death of the Choshu leader Kido Kōin and followed by the murder of the Satsuma figure Ōkubo Toshimichi. The three leading figures of the first decade of the Meiji state were gone.

Despite the flurry of edicts, the chief accomplishment of the first ten years of the Meiji period had been the demolition of the old order. Much of the work required for the creation of a new infrastructure for modernization still lay ahead. The significance of what had happened, it can now be seen, was that a modernizing elite had emerged, a group firmly committed to making their backward country a modern nation-state. Their goals were expressed in terms of the models of which they had knowledge: the capitalist, representative, dynamic, industrial, and maritime powers of the Atlantic world. Those goals were further fixed by the misfortunes of their immediate neighbors in China, where resistance to change had brought humiliation and defeat. And, since a new idea is always easier to explain in terms of an old one, their thoughts of strength and unity had instinctively formed around the imperial symbol.

As the Meiji period went on, the surviving members of this leadership group, who were of restricted numbers all had common origins and much shared experience, had also developed an unusual ability to work, and disagree, and nevertheless cooperate, with one another. Many of them had gone abroad for eighteen months in 1871–73 and had returned to find their jobs waiting for them. They respected one another's feelings in defeat and concealed their own exultation in success. Having shared goals, they tended also to share power. In the more visible posts there was and continued to be a good deal of rotation to bring balance between factions, which helped to institutionalize and smooth the rivalry inevitable among them. Perhaps most important and remarkable, the modernizing oligarchy — which is what it became — made no attempt to perpetuate itself or to seat its heirs in posts of power. This is worth noting, for the men sprang from a patriarchal, hereditary class. It is true that the modern world of which they had knowledge was moving in the opposite direction (though perhaps most slowly in the Germany they admired); but the Meiji leaders performed a great service by failing to provide powerful progeny, and the abolition of the peerage after World War II ended even ceremonial honors for a group that was already past its service for the country. The development of the Meiji state was thus dominated by concerns for succession and legitimacy, problems that centered around the court and for which solutions were sought through the preparation of the Meiji Constitution.

The Meiji State

Not all who broke with the leadership over the issue of Korea were conservative in inclination, and not all had recourse to arms. A group led by Itagaki Taisuke from Tosa, which included most of the Tosa men in the central government, resigned and issued a statement (in which they were joined by a group of Saga men who later rose in revolt) calling for an elected assembly in order to avoid further violations of "public opinion." Future decisions, they argued, would then reflect the will of the people, and national unity could be perfected. The Itagaki document showed the influence of recent Japanese familiarization with European constitutional thought, but it also related to the assumptions put forth in the original 1867 Tosa petition to the shogun asking him to resign his powers. The Tosa men saw representative government as the only possible alternative to domination by the Satsuma–Choshu clique. Initially their ideas of popular will were undoubtedly restricted to the consultation of samurai elite like themselves; but the points they made and their own subsequent descent from office, gave their arguments a broader significance and application. The government needed all the support it could get in the years of crisis that followed 1874 and Itagaki was briefly persuaded to return to office in 1875; but he soon returned to the task of organizing his followers, first in Tosa and then nationally. By 1881 he had made the beginnings of a national structure for the Liberal party (Jiyūtō), the ancestor of Japan's presently ruling conservative party. Widespread enthusiasm resulted in rapid growth of the organization. Initially a group of ex-samurai, it soon extended its influence to rural leaders, and by the mid-1880's, years of deflation and agricultural depression, the Jiyūtō was becoming an important and vocal force in politics.

The Meiji government had in fact become committed to the idea of a representative structure even before Itagaki's demand. The Charter Oath of 1868 had promised the creation of public councils. Experimentation with crudely representative bodies had been incorporated in the political structures of 1868 and then given up. First-hand experience with the West had helped convince the Meiji leaders of the advantages of broadening the base of popular support for government, and their own recent discontent with the Tokugawa despotism was fresh in mind. Gaining support greater than that evoked by their old institutions clearly would require some sort of popular participation. The large party of government leaders that toured the Western world under the leadership of Prince Iwakura between 1871 and 1878 returned convinced by the lessons they had learned. Kido Kōin of Choshu used the tragic fate of Poland to argue that "laws and constitutions" that prevented arbitrary action by governments in the pursuit of selfish ends were the only guarantee of national survival. In addition to these truths, it was painfully evident that Japanese ability to escape from the humiliations and handicaps of the unequal treaties — an escape equally essential to economic development and to national independence — would depend on a measure of conformity to what the West considered adequate guarantees for regularity of administration. As Ōkuma Shigenobu put it years later,

> It was perceived that in order to attain an equal footing with the Powers, it was necessary to change the national institutions, learning and education. Hence the replacement of clans by prefectures took place as well as coinage reform, enforcement of the conscription law, revisions of various other laws and promulgation of new ones, establishment of local assemblies, and the granting of local self-government — a step that led at length to the promulgation of the Constitution.[7]

In the 1870's an early, unsuccessful "senate" was charged with preparation of a draft constitution. The government felt that the proposals of this constitution would lead to the establishment of a parliament with excessive powers, and thus called for individual drafts from all government leaders by the end of that decade. These varied widely in degree of liberality, but the process was speeded by Ōkuma, a Saga man, who had remained with the government after the departure of many of his fellow provincials in 1874. His draft, which he submitted directly to the emperor in 1881, proposed a basically English system of government by political parties and suggested that an elected parliament be convened the following year. The Satsuma–Choshu leaders, together with Iwakura, now forced Ōkuma's resignation from the government and simultaneously had the Meiji emperor promise that a parliament would be convened in 1890. Gradualism had now been accepted as government policy, and a clear commitment to constitutionalism had been made.

Ōkuma, in private life, now organized a "Reform party," which became, with Itagaki's, the progenitor of modern Japanese bourgeois politics. For the next few years the two political parties battled each other as vigorously as they did the government, which was able to hamper their activities through restrictive press and association laws. They disbanded for several years and re-formed at the end of the decade to resume work in the new parliamentary structure. Throughout the 1880's newspapers, magazines, and political novels were full of speculation and debate about the kind of state structure that Japan should develop.

The adoption of a Western-, especially Prussian-style, constitution was by no means the simple operation that some who write of Japan's "Westernization" have suggested. The "West" was, after all, a complex cultural phenomenon. For a time the Meiji Japanese saw it as a unit in which the railroads, guns, and Bibles were all interrelated, but by the late 1880's greater familiarity with the West made it clear to them that distinctions were possible and in fact necessary. Okakura Kakuzō (who worked out his own equally misleading characterization of "Asia is one") put it well on a return to Japan in 1887:

> Where is the essence of the West in the countries of Europe and America? All these countries have different systems; what is right in one country is wrong in the next; religion, customs, morals — there is no common agreement on any of these. Europe is discussed in a general way; and this sounds splendid. The question remains, however, where in reality does what is called Europe exist?[8]

The debate over constitutional structure was carried on in terms of Western theory and example, with arguments drawn from Anglo–French and German sources, but it was essentially concerned with traditional predispositions, each of which could be clothed in Western dress. The advocates of popular sovereignty and political party responsibility found Rousseau and English practice, respectively, congenial to them; but their advocacy of these preferences was full of Confucian overtones phrased in terms of Mencius' emphasis on the importance of the people. Nakae Chōmin's evocation of Rousseau owes as great a debt to Mencius as to Rousseau, and the same can be said of his disciple (and pioneer anarchist) Kōtoku Shūsui. A generation later the Taisho political philosopher Yoshino Sakuzō used some of these same themes in his elaboration of democracy under imperial aegis, which he defined as "people based" (*mimponshugi*). The Meiji "radicals" moreover shared with their opponents a belief in the importance of national unity, and they often reached instinctively to the totalist implications of Rousseau's "general will." "How is the government to be made strong?" Itagaki's document had asked in 1874, and it had answered, "It is by the people of the empire becoming of one mind." And a council chamber was the means for having government and people "mutually unite into one body. Then and only then will the country become strong."[9] The goal, in other words, was still a truly perfect unity in which groups would find no need to organize.

The government leaders, for their part, saw theories of natural rights as dangerous to national unity, and they were convinced that the nation could best be built through reliance upon the authority of the imperial institution. In this they inevitably made contact with the currents of historicism that underlay the thinking of their German constitutional advisers, who thought of the state as a historic, living entity. Party cabinets, they thought, would be divisive. In the absence of an agreed-upon code of religion with political utility like Christianity, Japan should instead make the most of its indigenous cult of a sacred emperor. "The one institution in our country which can become the cornerstone of our constitution is the Imperial House," Itō Hirobumi argued. "Because the imperial sovereignty is the cornerstone of our constitution, our system is not based on European ideas of separation of powers or on the principle . . . of joint rule of king and people."[10] The constitutional debate thus became an important vehicle for the articulation of views of national consciousness and identity, and its solutions channelled and gave form to what was permissible in that debate until midway into the twentieth century.

Itō Hirobumi played the principal public role in the creation of the constitution. He returned from a study mission to Europe in 1883; created a European-style peerage (with an upper house in the Diet in mind) the following year; headed the first modern cabinet in 1885, its seats evenly divided between Satsuma and Choshu men; submitted his draft of the constitution in 1888; and then chaired the Privy Council that considered the document before it was approved. After its promulgation in 1889, he showed his relief upon hearing of Western approbation of the document: "Now for the first time," he wrote, "I feel relieved... There was doubt in my mind whether Europe and America would accept Japan, with a constitution conforming to Japanese National polity and history and yet containing substantial constitutional elements, as a member of the family of Western constitutional states."[11]

The Meiji Constitution took the form of a gracious grant by the emperor and began with an affirmation of the unbroken imperial line. The imperial oath that was prepared for the promulgation put it clearly:

> In view of the progressive tendency of human affairs and the advance of civilization, it has been incumbent upon Us . . . to establish fundamental laws and clearly explain their provisions . . . the Imperial House Law and the Constitution . . . We solemnly regard as merely *a reiteration in Our own day of the grand precepts of government that have been handed down*

80

by the Imperial Founder of Our House and by Our other Imperial Ancestors to their descendants.[12]

The constitution's provisions were couched in general terms. Effective power lay with the executive, which was not closely defined lest it obscure the emperor's majesty. The emperor was "sacred and inviolable"; he commanded the armed services (which consequently had separate access to him), he made war and peace, and he dissolved the lower house at will. Yet the constitution also represented very solid gains. Private property was inviolate, and the freedoms the constitutions granted, even though most were qualified by the phrase "within the limits of the law," were greater than any the Japanese had known before. The lower house had the power to initiate legislation. The Diet had to approve the annual budget, but in the event it refused to do so the previous year's could be followed. Yet even the budgetary arrangements meant the Diet had to approve budget increases, the perennial needs of any administration. And, while the initial voting laws, which set a fifteen-yen direct-tax restriction, limited the electorate to less than five hundred thousand voters, that tax qualification was lowered in 1900 and again in 1920 and finally removed altogether in 1925. Government leaders began with the hope that they could, as representatives of the emperor, stay above all factional disputes, but within a decade their difficulties in getting the cooperation of the lower house were sufficiently great to stir Itō Hirobumi himself to organize his own political party. The constitution thus allowed for steady growth in political participation. But because it, and its sacred emperor, were inviolate, the gains scored under it in practice were never consolidated institutionally or admitted in theory. In consequence they could, in the 1930's, be modified again, still without alteration in the durable Meiji Constitution.

The year 1890, in which the constitution went into effect, was also important for the issuance of the Imperial Rescript on Education. That document, the product of a long dispute between conservatives and modernizers in the oligarchy, represented an attempt to lay down a code of behavior and belief for the newly participating citizenry. Experiments with a "National Teaching" had been carried on very early in the Meiji period, but during the apogee of institutional reform and enthusiasm for Westernization in the 1880's the idea of Japanese national essence or individuality seemed to some conservatives to be in danger. The builders of the educational system also became concerned about the need to inculcate patriotism in the commoners, who would man the new instruments of state power, and by the late 1880's a course in public morality had become the center of the compulsory education curriculum. With the Rescript on Education the pattern for citizens' beliefs was deemed complete. Schoolchildren memorized and recited the rescript's praise of "loyalty and filial piety" as "the glory of the fundamental character of Our Empire, and . . . the source of Our Education." They were to be filial, harmonious, and true and were told to "advance public good and promote common interests; always respect the Constitution and observe the laws; should emergency arise, offer yourselves courageously to the State, and thus guard and maintain the prosperity of Our Imperial Throne coeval with heaven and earth."

The emperor system, which seemed to the Meiji leaders their best hope for channeling patriotism and loyalty in a largely secular society, became in time the focus of a mystic faith for the commoners. In the 1880's newspapers still felt called upon to explain Japan's good fortune in having an emperor and chided their readers for not knowing more about him. Within little more than a decade the diffusion of the ideology of the modern state made this quite unnecessary. The emperor-idea thus began as a force for modernization in the early Meiji period; in later years, its application began to seem a block to further enlightenment. As with symbol, so with presence; the Meiji Emperor himself was a participant in the power circle made up of his trusted ministers; his immediate successors, without that shared experience or personal ascendancy, became more mysterious and distant, more spoken for than speaking.

The 1880's, so important in the shaping of political and educational institutions, were equally definitive for the development of other important supports of the modern state. Tokyo University became the training ground for the modern bureaucracy, and its graduates quickly became the central figures in the new, specialized ministries. Yamagata Aritomo organized both bureaucracy and military, introduced the German general-staff system, and secured imperial rescripts to soldiers and sailors that provided the core of their indoctrination. Perhaps more important still was the series of careful steps whereby Matsukata Masayoshi, finance minister for more than sixteen years, turned back the inflation that the Satsuma rebellion had generated and instituted a reliable, convertible currency. Despite the outcries caused by his policies of austerity and deflation, he managed, by cutting government expenses to the bone, to save more than one-quarter of the current revenue, thereby providing a solid beginning for capital accumulation and the industrial growth that followed. During his years at the helm, earlier government ventures in pilot plants and mines were discontinued. The bulk of these earlier enterprises ended up in the hands of a few great family combines that later came to be denounced as "money cliques" (zaibatsu). The truly significant economic growth of the Meiji period, economists suggest, began after 1886; Matsukata had provided the setting for it.

Through all this the slogans — Meiji Japan, like modernizing China, was urged on by slogans — continued to point toward economic strength as a corollary to military strength. *Fukoku-kyōhei* ("rich country–strong military") were paired. Institutional reform was prerequisite to the willingness of Western imperialist powers to loosen their hold on Japanese tariffs, trade, and jurisdiction; and changes in those sectors were prerequisite to effective economic nationalism. It was clear to the leaders that Japan had to be patient, avoid adventurism, and concentrate on the main business at hand. Foreign Minister Inoue Kaoru put it succinctly in 1887: "What we have to do," he wrote, "is to transform our empire and our people, and make the empire like the countries of Europe and our people like the people of Europe. To put it differently, we have to establish a new, European-style empire on the edge of Asia."[13] For him and his contemporaries, affiliation with the West necessarily meant taking care to keep the West from mistaking Japan for her less progressive neighbors. As the educator-publicist Fukuzawa Yukichi put it:

> When judgements of China and Korea are applied to our country it hurts our foreign policy. We do not have time to wait for neighboring countries to develop and then to join them in the revival of Asia. We ought instead to get away from them and join the company of Western, civilized nations. If we keep bad company we will only get a bad name.[14]

In the setting of the nineteenth century these judgements were shrewd, and the policies to which they led were successful. The implementation of a constitution and codes of modern law made it possible in 1894 to renegotiate the unequal treaties. Although full tariff autonomy would come only in 1911, Japan was now a full member of the family of nations. The following year a victory over Manchu China enabled the Meiji government to join the circle of China's uninvited guests by exacting both the usual concessions and some additional ones from the prostrate Manchus, to claim Taiwan, and, for a fleeting moment, to gain a foothold in South Manchuria as well. Territory for expansion, indemnity for investment, and gratification in achievement all rewarded the end of a caution that had lasted a quarter-century. The road to power, empire, and prestige in the international order was now open.

Some Meiji values

No recital of policies in Meiji times should end without some indication of the color and the motivations of Japan in this striking period of world history. Meiji Japan was, after all, the first, and in some respects is still the only, latecomer to modernization to make a successful bridge between indigenous institutions and values and imported technology and techniques.The resulting combination of old and new, native and import, was of particular interest for the marks it left on a generation that experienced a rapid erosion and virtual overturn of its views of self and world. China, so long the source of civilization, was for a time decried as a symbol of backwardness. In 1868 the Japanese government still found it useful to remind its people that foreigners were not, as some had it, to be grouped with "wild barbarians, dogs, and sheep"; instead, it warned, "we must work out arrangements to show that they are to be considered on the same level as Chinese." But by the end of the Meiji period those same foreigners were well above the Chinese in the scale of Japanese esteem and treatment. Because it seemed somehow feudal and backward, Buddhism, so long the creed of Japan, was the object of a furious assault in the early Meiji years that resulted in the destruction of many temples and much art. Confucianism, however basic to the code of most educated Japanese, was also roundly attacked as unprogressive. During its first years in power the Meiji government continued the Tokugawa persecution of Christians, but the Iwakura Mission's view of the West changed all that, and soon skeptics like Fukuzawa seriously proposed declaring Japan a Christian country so that it could qualify for the related boons of modernization. But then, in the 1890's, the currents once again ran differently. A suitably nationalized blend of Confucianism and Shinto was seen as basic to the national polity (*kokutai*). Confucian studies again found sponsors, and Christianity, no longer essential to the modern state, became the object of discrimination in education out of fear that its converts would deny support to the national cult and hence weaken patriotism.

These judgements about the outside world were instrumental rather than basic to the values of the Meiji Japanese. Their first and strongest urge was certainly that of nationalism. Throughout most of the Meiji period the leadership in most walks of life, and certainly the tone of public life and discourse, were provided by members of the samurai class. A self-confident, committed group, educated to lead and schooled in the primacy of the collectivity of the political unit, the samurai provided Japan with single-minded, nation-directed leadership. The phrase *kuni no tame* ("for the sake of the country") was a constant in political discussions, but it is more striking to find authors using it as a rationale in their determination to build a modern literature, create an epic poetry, and develop new schools of painting and areas of scholarship. Here, no less than in the state structure, there was agreement that something should be built for which "future generations would feel no shame."

The main current of youthful ambition was political, although those who lacked contents were likely to find their ambitions frustrated. For the Meiji generation the Restoration activists had set the style, and any red-blooded young man was expected to want to be a minister of state. Even those who rejected this goal as old-fashioned subservience to authority — Fukuzawa Yukichi, with his call for independence and autonomy, or Shibusawa Eiichi, with his determination to build a private banking system — formed their objections within this community of discourse; the argument was not whether the nation needed building, but how it could be built most rapidly and effectively.

These things are reflected with particular clarity in the values of the business class. Its leading representatives contrasted the patriotic role of industrialist, to which they aspired, with the selfish, nonproductive role of the traditional merchant, and they did their best to wrap themselves in the borrowed garb of samurai values. Adam Smith's "invisible hand," which pictured the common good as being advanced by private ambition, went quite the other way in Meiji thinking; here entrepreneurs accumulated great wealth by accident while working for the national interest. Shibusawa Eiichi, who built one of the great Meiji fortunes (and incidentally became a patron of Confucian studies), assured his countrymen the "never for a moment did I aim at my own profit." In turn, one writer had it that "just as the samurai gathered behind Minamoto to follow him into the battle of war, so now the younger generation gathers around Shibusawa to follow him into the battle of enterprise."[15] Some of this logic was of course self-serving and disingenuous. But the public posture, and the assumption of its necessity, remain significant.

Closely related to the goal of national service were themes of ambition and achievement. *Risshin shusse* ("Make something of yourself!") was a slogan that typified the tone of much of the Meiji period until at least the 1890's, when government conservatives began to fear that private goals were beginning to infringe on public ones. Samuel Smiles' *Self-Help*, first translated in 1871, set the style for journals and novels in which the ideals of ambition and success were lauded. Itagaki's first political organization, formed when he left the government in 1874, was called the Self-Help Society (Risshisha). And it was typical of Meiji times that many of these ideas, conceived for the individual, were applied to national purposes and needs. It seems clear that many readers of Smiles came to view Japan as a poor apprentice in the family of nations, a country that would have to scrimp and sacrifice with a view to future affluence and power. Much of the literature of economic individualism of the nineteenth-century West could with little adjustment be translated to conform to the political priorities of Meiji Japan. At the same time, of course, the intense striving for success and honor that distinguished official and popular culture in Tokugawa Japan provided a strong basis for this further reinforcement from the nineteenth-century West.

84

The slogan "Civilization and enlightenment!" (*bummei kaika*) expressed in terms of inevitable progress the requirements of cultural advancement for a Japan in the process of change. At home, it could be involved in applying for a bank charter, as when Osaka merchants petitioned that:

> As we live presently in the era of civilization and enlightenment, we feel ashamed to follow the old foolish practices of each one considering nothing but his own profit . . . We have been cherishing . . . the desire to shoulder our share, as far as our weakness permits, of the burden to promote the progress of civilization . . . enlightenment by the banking act, we shall immediately work for the establishment of a bank . . .[16]

Abroad it merged smoothly with the traditional tendency to erect a hierarchic ranking of nations, one that was now justified in terms of Herbert Spencer's science. For Fukuzawa Yukichi, aborigines, nomads, undeveloped (Asian) states, and civilized (Western) states indicated a smooth progression that would lead in time to equality with Europe and America. Mori Arinori, minister of education, could hold out the even higher hope that through effort, education, and perseverance Japan could come to hold the leading position among all countries. Every urge of patriotic effort or personal ambition, and every thought of history or international affairs, seemed to contribute to a congruent view of Japan's goals and problems.

Meiji successes owed much to the stability of leadership, which provided the time in which to work things out. The time it took was greater than it seems. Returns for the effort expended began to come only in the 1890's, and a recent authority notes that "in a number of important respects the amount of time required for the political modernization of Japan has not been much shorter than that required in the classic Western cases."[17] Yet without the consensus on goals, without the agreement on the urgency of addressing all efforts to attaining equality with the West, that same stability of leadership would not have been possible.

By the 1890's there were signs that the consensus was beginning to weaken. A new generation was coming to the fore — one that had not personally experienced the weaknesses and fears of Restoration disunity, that was less securely rooted in Confucian values than its fathers had been, and that was impatient with the frustrations of Meiji nation-building. No longer satisfied with catching up, it sought areas in which to excel. What was Japan, and what could it do supremely well? In a world increasingly dominated by the maritime imperialist powers and the civilizations of the Atlantic world, where could Japan still find a mission? The late 1880's saw a new affirmation of nationalism: Journals like *Nihonjin* and newspapers like *Nihon* examined the questions of national essence and goals and wondered how Japan could be kept Japanese. In the arts the native styles, temporarily threatened by the wave of Westernization, were being restored to favor, and in religion Christianity, briefly on the rise in the early 1880's, never again seemed a viable candidate for a national faith.

It was in this mixed setting of doubt and affirmation, in this search for definition and destiny, that the constitution and Rescript on Education had their meaning and effect. Within a few years after they were issued, the opportunity to take assertive steps at last made Japan the victor over Manchu China. Fukuzawa spoke for millions when he editorialized in his newspaper that "we intend only to develop world civilization and to defeat those who obstruct it... Therefore this is not a war between people and people, and country and country, but a kind of religious war." And Tokutomi Sohō, a popular journalist, rhapsodized that at last "the true nature of our country, our national character, will emerge like the sun breaking through a dense fog."[18]

The new day was to bring new problems, frustrations, and burdens. Imperialism would dismay a few and tax the many. New military burdens and strategic responsibilities would also lead to heavy industry and to the great industrial development of twentieth-century Japan. The Meiji Restoration and revolution were at an end, and imperial Japan was ready to join the circle of the Great Powers it had learned to emulate.

Notes

1. Cited in F.V. Dickens and Stanley Lane-Poole, *The Life of Sir Harry Parkes* (London: Macmillan, 1894), Vol. 2, p. 98.

2. Cited in Marius B. Jansen, *Sakamoto Ryōma and the Meiji Restoration* (Princeton, N.J.: Princeton University Press, 1961), p. 210.

3. U.S. Minister R.B. van Valkenburgh to Secretary of State William Seward, enclosure in dispatch of January 16, 1868.

4. It would return, at least in memory, as late as the 1930's, when an anti-Choshu faction in the Imperial Army sought to build a factional alternative by promoting men from Tosa and Saga.

5. "Japan's Aristocratic Revolution," *Yale Review*, Vol. 50 (Spring 1961), pp. 370–83.

6. Cited in Herbert Passin, ed., *Society and Education in Japan* (New York: Teachers College Press, 1965), p. 69.

7. Cited in Joseph Pittau, S.J., *Political Thought in Early Meiji Japan, 1868–1889* (Cambridge, Mass.: Harvard University Press, 1967), p. 39.

8. *Ibid.*, p. 128; quoted from Masaaki Kosaka, *Japanese Thought in the Meiji Period*, trans. D. Abosch (Baltimore: Johns Hopkins Press, 1958), p. 220.

9. Cited in Nobutaka Ike, *The Beginnings of Political Democracy in Japan* (Baltimore: Johns Hopkins Press, 1950), p. 57.

10. Cited in Pittau, *Political Thought in Early Meiji Japan*, p. 178.

11. Cited in George Akita, *Foundations of Constitutional Government in Modern Japan, 1868–1900* (Cambridge, Mass.: Harvard University Press, 1967), p. 13.

12. Cited in R. Ishii, *Japanese Legislation in the Meiji Era*, translated by W.J. Chambliss (Tokyo: 1958), p. 386.

13. Cited in Marius B. Jansen, "Modernization and Foreign Policy in Mejij Japan," in Robert E. Ward, ed., *Political Development in Modern Japan* (Princeton, N.J.: Princeton University Press, 1968), p. 174.

14. Marius B. Jansen, "Japanese Views of China During the Meiji Period," in Albert Feuerwerker, Rhodes Murphy, and Mary C. Wright, eds., *Approaches to Modern Chinese History* (Berkeley, Calif.: University of California Press, 1967), pp. 172–73. See also Kimitada Miwa, "Fukuzawa Yukichi's 'Departure from Asia': A Prelude to the

Sino–Japanese War," in E. Skrzypezak, ed., *Japan's Modern Century* (Tokyo: Sophia University and Charles E. Tuttle, 1968), p. 17.

15. Byron K. Marshall, *Capitalism and Nationalism in Prewar Japan: The Ideology of the Business Elite, 1868–1941* (Stanford, Calif.: Stanford University Press, 1967), p. 47.

16. Johannes Hirschmeier, S.V.D., *The Origins of Entrepreneurship in Meiji Japan* (Cambridge, Mass.: Harvard University Press, 1964), p. 37.

17. Ward, *Political Development in Modern Japan*, p. 589.

18. Cited in Kenneth B. Pyle, *The New Generation in Meiji Japan: Problems of Cultural Identity, 1885–1895* (Stanford, Calif.: Stanford University Press, 1969), p. 173.

6. Japan and China in Theories of Development and Underdevelopment

Frances Moulder

One cannot but be struck by the great differences among the various countries of East Asia in the speed and nature of their responses to the West in the past century. . . . These variations in response must be attributed mainly to the differences in the traditional societies of the countries of East Asia. Only such differences can explain why a basically similar impact could have brought such varied initial results . . . why relatively small Japan, for example, soon become a world power, while China sunk to the status of an international problem.

(Reischauer and Fairbank, *East Asia: The Great Tradition*, p. 670)

What was it that enabled Japan to take a course so radically different from that of all the other countries in the now underdeveloped world? . . . The answer to this question . . . comes down to the fact that Japan is the only country in Asia (and in Africa and in Latin America) that escaped being turned into a colony or dependency of Western European or American capitalism, that had a chance of independent national development.

(Baran, *The Political Economy of Growth*, p. 158)

Japan in theories of underdevelopment: "the exception that proves the rule"

The case of Japan is of great importance to theories of economic change. Japan was the first non-Western nation to become a major industrial power. Japan's industrialization also occurred early; it began in the latter part of the nineteenth century and was well under way by World War I. Thus Japan's industrialization occurred only somewhat later than that of more advanced Western nations, such as the United States, Germany, or France.

Today, over half a century later, Japan is *still* the only non-Western advanced industrial power. Although considerable economic progress has been made in several other non-Western nations since World War II (for instance, in the capitalist world, Brazil, and in the socialist world North Korea and China), none is highly industrialized and only China can be regarded as a world power, playing a significant, independent role in international power politics.

Japan was also the first "Third World" nation to become a major industrial power. The term *Third World* refers to those countries of Asia, Africa, and Latin America that have been economically and politically dominated by the industrial capitalist nations. It is often forgotten (as least outside Japan) that Japan was partially controlled by the Western capitalist nations during the nineteenth century. Although Japan never

Frances Moulder: 'Introduction: Japan and China in Theories of Development and Underdevelopment' from *JAPAN, CHINA AND THE MODERN WORLD ECONOMY* (Cambridge University Press, 1977), pp. 1–23 became a formal colony, the country was forced to trade with the capitalist nations under a set of treaties that reduced national autonomy and set up obstacles to industrial development. Western observers during the nineteenth century were just as confident of their sway over Japan as over the other areas of Asia, Africa, and Latin America. "The Japanese are a happy race, and being content with little, are not likely to achieve much," wrote the *Japan Herald* in 1881.

What accounts for Japan's unique transformation? Why do the other nations of the Third World remain underdeveloped? These two questions are intimately linked, and there is little agreement on the answers. There are currently two major theories of Third World underdevelopment, which I will term *traditional society* theories and *world economy* theories. These theories are contradictory, and the case of Japan has been utilized by theorists in each camp as "the exception that proves the rule."

Since World War II, the study of economic development in America and Western Europe has been dominated by a concern with how "traditional" social, cultural, and personality factors influence economic development or underdevelopment. Traditional society theories stem from the concerns established by Max Weber in his famous comparative studies of the "ethics" of the Chinese, Indian, Hebrew, and Protestant civilizations. Poverty in the Third World countries is attributed primarily to their social characteristics rather than to their relations with imperialist powers. To traditional society theorists, Japan is the exception — the only Third World nation that had a change-promoting indigenous social system.

Traditional society theories of Third World underdevelopment have been challenged in recent years by a perspective that emphasizes the relationship of Third World societies to the world political economy. World economy theories, which stem from the studies of Marx, Engels, and Lenin, attribute underdevelopment to the "satellite" or "dependent" position of the Third World nations in a world economy that is constructed to benefit the Western industrial nations. To world economy theorists, Japan is again the exception that proves the rule — the only Third World nation that escaped becoming a satellite of the Western powers.

Let us examine the traditional society and world economy theories more closely.

Traditional society theories

In traditional society theories, the influence of the industrial nations on the nonindustrial nations is seen as basically development promoting, and underdevelopment is analyzed as a function of native social, cultural, and personality factors that block development. The argument of such theories could be summarized as follows:

The industrial nations have historically provided a "stimulus" to economic growth in the non-Western world. First, they have supplied *economic* preconditions for development that were absent or insufficiently present in the Third World prior to contact with the industrial world. For instance, the "diffusion" of capital and modern technology from the West, the creation of new markets for traditional products, and the establishment of an "infrastructure" of economic development, such as railroads, public utilities, and modern banking, have created a potential for development that was hitherto lacking.

Second, the industrial nations have supplied *social* preconditions for industrialization. For example, Eisenstadt speaks of "modernizing elites" that emerge to promote development in imitation of Western entrepreneurs and statesmen.[1] Rostow speaks of a "reactive nationalism," appearing under the threat of control by the more advanced nations, that leads political and military elites to "take the steps necessary to unhinge and transform the traditional society in such ways as to permit growth to become its normal condition."[2]

Underdevelopment persists despite all this because Third World societies are unable, due to their very nature, to "respond" adequately to the "stimulus" to industrialization. This is because they are basically "traditional"; they fail to encourage change and innovation. For example, they lack such value orientations and qualities of personality which promote industrialization as "universalism," "specificity," "achievement motivation," and the capacity to "empathize."

Aspects of their social structure also block economic development. For example, caste, clan, guild, or village loyalties may hamper economic growth by restricting the efficient utilization of labor and blocking geographic and social mobility. Or powerful and corrupt official bureaucracies may hamper the operation of business enterprise by their irrational and unpredictable administrative policies and by heavy taxes on commerce. In Rostow's words, traditional societies lack "the existence or quick emergence of a political, social and institutional framework which exploits the impulses to expansion in the modern sector."[3]

In sum, traditional society theories argue that Third World societies are by their very nature insufficiently "open" to the development-promoting world economy created by the industrial nations.

World economy theories make precisely the opposite argument. They see underdevelopment as a result of a too-great openness to the world economy.

World economy theories

In world economy theories, the influence of the industrial capitalist nations on the nonindustrial nations is seen as basically development blocking, not development promoting. Underdevelopment is analyzed as a function of the subordinate or satellite position of the underdeveloped nations in a world economy that provides disproportionate benefits to the industrial nations. The argument of such theories might be summarized as follows:

The Western nations have forcibly turned the non-Western nations into their economic dependencies. In the earliest stages of this process the non-Western nations became primary-producing satellites, outposts supplying the industrial nations with raw materials and consuming the output of their industries. The industrial countries failed to promote industrial development in their satellites, which would have seriously competed with metropolitan industry: foreign investment concentrated in primary production — agricultural and mineral produce for export — rather than in industry.

At the same time, the industrial countries set up obstacles to indigenous efforts to promote industrialization. Native handicraft industries were ruined and the development of modern industries was hampered by the competition of manufactures from the metropole. This was accomplished through the elimination of tariff barriers in the satellites on imports from the metropole and through the establishment of tariff barriers in the metropole on manufactured imports from the satellites. Industrialization was also hampered by the consequences of the economy's becoming "skewed" toward production of one or a few primary products for export. The fluctuation of prices of primary products on the world market deprives the satellite countries of a steady flow of funds for industrial development. The nation also becomes subject to *declining terms of trade*, that is, the trend toward declining prices of raw materials relative to manufactures, which makes it more and more difficult for the satellite countries to purchase necessary producers' goods.

According to world economy theorists, the infrastructures that were established in satellite nations did not promote industrialization but merely furthered the development of the export-oriented primary-producing sector. For instance, railway systems were constructed to link primary-producing areas to the seaports, rather than to form a national network that would promote the development of a national market. Banking systems were created to provide short-term credit for agricultural export purchases, not long-term loans that would have been suitable for industrial development. And so forth.

In the later stages of the process, metropolitan capitalists also invested in modern industry in the satellite countries and native capitalists and/or governments succeeded in establishing modern industries, particularly during periods when imperialist controls were weakened, as during and between the two world wars. However, it is argued that this has not led to full-scale industrialization but is simply a "new dependency." For example, a large part of the profits from foreign-owned industrial enterprises is repatriated to the metropoles rather than invested in the expansion of industry within the satellite. Capital must also be exported to the metropoles to pay for access to modern technology, which is controlled through patents. A large part of the necessary supplies for the enterprises is also imported from the metropole, rather than sought within the satellite economy. Many industrial enterprises in Third World countries consist of processing plants' putting together commodities whose parts have been manufactured elsewhere and utilizing machinery (often obsolete) imported from abroad; thus development-promoting "backward and forward linkages" to the rest of the economy are prevented. Moreover, the types of industries established are often not geared to the needs of the local masses; rather, they supply luxuries and durable consumer goods of an affluent minority.

Thus world economy theorists regard satellite nations as essentially depleted and impoverished. Although some industrialization occurs, it is inevitably a backward, externally oriented industrialization that remains many steps behind, and dependent upon, the advanced metropolitan countries and that fails to advance the living standard of the masses of the population. "Economic growth," for the majority of the population, is a step backward. Agricultural output grows, in the form of commercial crops exported to the metropolitan nations, yet the local population lives under threat of starvation. Industrial output also grows, yet millions live in urban slums without employment or the means to buy the output of industry.

The society of this kind of depleted satellite nation cannot be thought of as traditional, according to world economy theorists. The very notion of "traditional society," they argue, must be criticized on two counts. First, it conceives of the satellite society as an entity in and of itself, rather than as a unit that is an integral part of a worldwide system or totality. Second, it conceives of the satellite society as a static, ahistorical phenomenon, rather than a society that is constantly changing within the world system. For example, traditional society theorists overlook major changes that have occurred in societies of the Third World due to the process of satellitization. New political structures, ranging from direct colonization to indirect rule through native-led regimes, have been created to serve Western interests. New classes have arisen (bourgeois classes, participating in the export sector and dependent industrialization), and new regimes have risen to power, while others have lost. If these new classes and new regimes hamper industrialization, it is not because they are "traditional" but because their fate is linked to the new, dependent economy, which can develop only if full-scale national industrialization is prevented. At their most radical, the best the new classes and elites can do is "negotiate the conditions of dependence."[4]

Changes in the direction of greater inequality are also over-looked. With satellitization, the class structure grows increasingly unequal. Peasants and urban workers are increasingly impoverished relative to the unprecedentedly affluent urban and rural bourgeoisie. Again, if the new upper class consumes or invests its profits in ways detrimental to national industrialization, or in the face of mass hunger and unemployment, it is not because it is "traditional" but because it is constrained within a worldwide system, which can develop only if national industrialization in the satellites is avoided.

As noted above, world economy and traditional society theorists regard Japan as the exception that proves the rule. In the logic of traditional society theories, if Japan industrialized it must be because Japan is the only Third World nation that had a culture and social structure favorable (rather than unfavorable) to economic development. For instance, Marion Levy remarks in his comparison of "traditional" China and Japan: "It was not differences in the new forces introduced to China and Japan that accounted for their different experiences in industrialization. It was rather differences in the social structures into which the new forces were introduced."[5]

In the logic of world economy theories, if Japan industrialized it must be because Japan is the only Third World nation that remained relatively insulated from pressures to become a satellite within the world system. For instance, Paul Baran remarks in a comparison of India, Japan, and China:

> It should not be overlooked that India, if left to herself, might have found in the course of time a shorter and surely less torturous road toward a better and richer society. . . . It would have been . . . an entirely different India (and an entirely different world) had she been allowed — as some more fortunate countries were — to realize her destiny in her own way, to employ her resources for her own benefit, and to harness her energies and

93

abilities for the advancement of her own people. This is speculation to be sure, but a legitimate one. For the alternative to the massive removal of their accumulated wealth and current output, to the ruthless suppression and distortion of all indigenous economic growth, to the systematic corruption of their social, political, and cultural life that were inflicted by Western capitalism upon all of the now underdeveloped countries is by no means purely hypothetical. This can be clearly seen in the history of the only Asian country that succeeded in escaping its neighbors' fate and attaining a relatively high degree of economic advancement. For in the period under consideration — when Western capitalism was ruining India, establishing its grip over Africa, subjugating Latin America, and opening up China — conditions in Japan were as conducive, or rather as unfavorable, to economic development as anywhere else in Asia.[6]

Japan is thus a critical case for demonstrating the validity of either of these two major theories of underdevelopment. Their contradictory propositions about Japan's development, and about underdevelopment elsewhere in the Third World, need to be tested through comparative study. Unfortunately, there is not a body of empirical studies that has compared Japan systematically to one or several other non-Western societies. The only exception is a number of studies that compared Japan with Imperial China. Do the results demonstrate the validity of either interpretation of underdevelopment? The answer, I will conclude in the following pages, is no. Although considerable attention has been directed to Japan and China, the studies must be regarded as inconclusive.

Comparing Japan and China: world economy theories

There are very few comparisons of Japan and China by world economy theorists. I will take Paul Baran's statement in *The Political Economy of Growth* as an example, since it has probably been most widely read in the West. Baran argued that Japan's industrialization was possible because Japan was the only Third World nation to escape becoming a "colony" of the capitalist industrial nations. Why did Japan escape?

There are essentially two reasons, according to Baran. First, during the early nineteenth century, when merchants from the capitalist countries first appeared in East Asia, they became preoccupied with exploiting China, India, and other areas. By the time they got to Japan, the European nations had become burdened with intra-European wars. They were therefore not in a position to turn their full attention to Japan. Second, by the time Japan came under Western influence, after the 1850s, fierce competition had developed among the Western nations in Asia. Because of this, Japan escaped becoming a colony of any single power, as had India, and China during the greater part of the nineteenth century (China having relations predominantly with Great Britain).

Because Japan did not become a colony, Baran argued, this permitted the establishment of a capitalist-dominated regime that promoted the interests of industrialization. The country's economic surplus remained in Japanese hands and was utilized by the state and the capitalists to industrialize the country. Moreover, there was no large influx of Western traders, adventurers, and missionaries, and the

Japanese were not stirred to xenophobic reactions against everything Western, which might have hampered industrialization, as were the Chinese and other peoples.

Baran indicated the possibility of differences in the internal social structures of China and Japan, but denied their analytic significance. His argument is made within the context of a Marxist stage theory of the development of societies from feudalism to capitalism. Baran argued that all preindustrial societies, both Western and non-Western, were feudal and all were undergoing, more or less rapidly, a series of transformations in the direction of capitalism. These transformations included increases in agricultural output, deepening class divisions in the countryside, the emergence of a potential industrial labor force made up of the poorest peasants, the growth of towns and a class of merchants and artisans, and the accumulation of capital by wealthy merchants and rich peasants. The structure of feudalism was not everywhere the same, however. There were "far-reaching divergences" between the different feudal systems; feudal Japan was quite different from feudal China, India, and other places. The significant difference between Japan and the other nations, however, was not Japan's special social structure but its greater independence from nineteenth-century imperialism. The lesson of Japan is that development can occur only if a nation is able to escape colonial status.

This interpretation raises several problems. First, though Japan was not a colony, neither, of course, was China, if by *colony* we mean a country that is under the full and direct political control of another country. Mao Tse-tung had characterized China before 1949 as a "semi-colony," that is, not directly and completely ruled by an outside power, yet lacking political and economic autonomy. Was not Japan in a similar situation? For example, as traditional society theorists have pointed out, both Japan and China were subjected to the "treaty port system." Under this system, a number of ports were opened to Western trade and residence; import and export tariffs were set in such a way as to benefit Western trade; "extraterritoriality" was established, removing Westerners from the jurisdiction of native courts; and Western diplomatic corps were installed in the capitals and major ports. Did this not put Japan and China in a similar position with regard to the industrial capitalist countries?

Second, the traditional society studies have amassed considerable evidence that Japan and China were in fact quite dissimilar. In the face of this, is it appropriate to characterize both systems as feudal? And if the social systems were divergent, are we to believe that this had little impact on how the two countries changed as they were integrated into the world system?

Comparing Japan and China: traditional society theories

The most striking characteristic of comparative studies within the traditional society perspective is that they simply exclude the question whether there might be differences in the relationship of China and Japan to the world political economy. For some authors, such as Moore, Holt and Turner, Jacobs, and Sheldon, the exclusion is a matter of emphasis. Others have excluded the question explicitly; for instance, Marion Levy: "In both China and Japan *the external sources were virtually identical. They were the factors involved in modern industrialization.*" (emphasis added) Or Reischauer and Fairbank, in the statement also cited at the beginning of this chapter:

> One cannot but be struck by the great differences among the various countries of East Asia in the speed and nature of their responses to the West in the past century. . . . These variations in response must be attributed mainly to the differences in the traditional societies of the countries of East Asia. Only such differences can explain why a basically similar impact could have brought such varied initial results . . . why relatively small Japan, for example, soon became a world power, while China sunk to the status of an international problem.[7]

Just as Baran pointed out differences between Japan and other Third World societies, yet denied their analytic significance, traditional society authors occasionally point out that the Western impact on Japan was much smaller than that on China, but deny that this has any analytic significance. To Fairbank, Reischauer, and Craig, for example, it is a "startling paradox" that Japan's "greater response" followed a "less violent impact" than in China:

> As compared with the Chinese experience, the initial impact of the West on Japan in the middle of the 19th century was gentle. No wars were fought, no smuggling trade developed, no territory was forfeited. . . . And yet, Japan's response was far quicker and greater than that of China. . . . This startling paradox — that Japan's greater response followed a less violent impact than in China — has posed difficult questions of historical interpretation. What forces at work in Japan produced so great a ferment? Obviously, Japan in the mid-nineteenth century, even though it had derived a large part of its higher culture from China, was a very different country, capable of very different responses to the Western challenge.[8]

Alvan Obelsky has translated this approach into a Parsonian framework. He proposes three sets of "conditions" for economic development: "necessary," "initial," and "sufficient." Necessary conditions are "cultural" conditions (in the Parsonian sense of the term) that provide the most general, but latent, conditions for development. They do not themselves initiate development, yet are necessary for its ultimate emergence. Initial conditions are *social-structural* conditions, such as political and economic institutions. The sufficient conditions "activate the potential implied in the first two sets of conditions . . . they are the effective 'challenge'" that unleashes development. Obelsky suggests that these conditions are interrelated in the following way. "Given the minimum *necessary* conditions for development, the outcome will depend on the strengths of the remaining two sets of conditions. The more favorable the *initial* conditions, in this case, the *less insistent* need to be the *external stimulus* in order to qualify as the *sufficient* condition." This, of course, stands the world economy thesis on its head.

The traditional society studies of Chinese and Japanese development may be divided into two categories, which I will term *factor theories* and *ideal-type theories*.

Factor theories are "particularistic," as Koya Azumi has put it; they search out and describe any and all differences between the two societies, and make little effort to analyze the consequences of the various factors in terms of a general theory of social change. The assumption seems to be that any aspect of Japan's social structure, geography, population, or culture that differed from China's is relevant to an analysis of why Japan was able to industrialize.

For example, Fairbank, Reischauer, and Craig attribute Japan's development, versus China's underdevelopment, to the following miscellaneous factors: insularity; feudal loyalty, religion, "goal-orientation," "diversity and pragmatism of thought"; the military character of the ruling class; the small size of the country; diversity of the social structure; nationalism; relative advancement of the traditional economy; breakdown of traditional class structure; and the existence of an "imperial institution."[9] Another factor theorist, Jacobs, has attributed Japan's development, compared to China's, to differences in their traditional institutions of exchange and property, authority, occupation, stratification, kinship and descent, religion, and "integration and stability."[10]

The factor theorists are especially responsible for strewing confusion in the study of Japan and China. Because a theoretical focus is lacking, factors that have been singled out as the causes of development in Japan are often identified as the causes of underdevelopment in China or elsewhere, sometimes even by the same author. Thus Fairbank, Reischauer, and Craig see Japan's "imperial institution" as a factor in development, while simultaneously arguing that China's imperial government was an obstacle to development. Or Japan's industrialization is sometimes inexplicably attributed to a set of factors that are completely divergent from those identified by other authors to explain industrialization elsewhere. For example (as noted above), Fairbank, Reischauer, and Craig have proposed that Japan's development was related to the small size of the country, its insularity, and so on, whereas China's underdevelopment was related to its larger size, continentality, etc. Theorists of United States development, in contrast, have often attributed America's growth to the large size of the country, the possibility of continental expansion, and so forth.

Ideal type theories make a greater effort to relate the comparisons of China and Japan to a general theory of development. They link several contrasting features of the "traditional societies" into two societal "types," then analyze the consequences of these typical features for industrialization and underdevelopment. A theory of industrialization is implied in the construction of the ideal types and in the analysis of their consequences.

No two "traditional society" ideal-type conceptions of China and Japan are exactly alike. Various theoretical perspectives have been utilized, ranging from the Parsonian AGIL scheme (Holt and Turner) to Weber (e.g., Jacobs) and/or Marx (e.g., Wittfogel, Moore). However, there is a convergence around one theme, which recurs in almost every study. This is a theory of industrialization that I will term the *class theory*. The class theory of industrialization is a simplistic argument that reduces the rise of industrial capitalism — whether in Japan, China, Europe, or elsewhere — to the growth of commerce and the rise of a bourgeois class. This theory is widely popular, and has deep roots in Western intellectual history. Thus it is worth devoting some attention to it.

97

The simplistic class theory of industrialization

A synthesis of this theme, as presented in the various traditional society comparisons of Japan and China, might be as follows. Japan developed during the nineteenth century because it had a "feudal" tradition similar to the societies of Europe. China remained underdeveloped because it had a "bureaucratic" (or "centralized" or "despotic" or "Asiatic") tradition, radically different from the Western or Japanese experience.

Japan was a feudal state, a conglomerate of domains ruled by a warrior nobility, or *daimyo*, and hegemony was exercised by the most powerful *Tokugawa* domain. Under the daimyo were the *samurai*, an upper class of warriors who were dependent for their livelihood on stipends of rice allocated by the daimyo. Below the daimyo and samurai were the merchant, artisan, and peasant classes. The importance of the feudal state is that it is weak vis-à-vis the nobility and bourgeoisie. The Tokugawa rulers were unable to prevent the rise of commerce and the development of an increasingly powerful and wealthy bourgeois class in town and countryside. "Commercialization" began to erode the feudal social order in several important ways.

First, as the new bourgeoisie increased in wealth, it was increasingly discontent with restraints placed on commerce by the Tokugawa rulers and with the general subordination of merchants and rich peasants to the samurai and daimyo. Second, commercialization created a fiscal crisis within the domains, to which the daimyo responded by cutting the stipends of lower-ranking samurai, causing their deep disaffection with the feudal order. Third, the loose hegemony exercised by the Tokugawa over the other domains began to collapse as commercial development enabled the latter to increase their wealth relative to the Tokugawa. After Japan was significantly affected by the arrival of the Europeans, the two disaffected classes (bourgeoisie and lower-ranking samurai) in several of the wealthier domains united to overthrow the Tokugawa government and establish a new state (the Meiji Restoration).

The new Meiji government abolished Tokugawa restraints on commerce and industry and undertook many reforms that furthered industrialization. Although the new Meiji rulers were from the old samurai class, they acted in the interests of industrialization because they were allied with the rising bourgeoisie.

In contrast, the Chinese imperial state was a strong or bureaucratic state. China was ruled by the Manchu conquerors through a centralized officialdom. This officialdom was drawn from the Chinese landed upper class, but power in China was based on officeholding rather than (as in Japan) domain ownership. The Chinese bureaucracy was opposed to the rise of commerce, and because the state was strong it was able to contain the rise of commerce and the growth of a powerful bourgeoisie. Because there was no bourgeoisie in China with which a segment of the ruling class might ally, China's rulers remained conservative; no Chinese equivalent of the Meiji Restoration could occur after the arrival of the Europeans. China was thus compelled to remain underdeveloped.

Note the assumptions behind the class theory. First, industrialization is primarily the inevitable result of the appearance of a class that supports it. In capitalist industrialization, this is normally the bourgeoisie (the large mercantile bourgeoisie and/or bourgeois newcomers arising from the ranks of artisans or small farmers), which has appeared within the feudal society with the growth of commerce.

Second, a state policy of promoting industrialization is also necessary. Such state policies appear only after the state apparatus has come under control of the rising bourgeoisie.

The class theory of industrialization has its origins in nineteenth-century European social thought. It rose and flourished during the industrial revolution, and was invoked to explain the enormous transformations in Europe at the time and to justify (or criticize) the establishment of bourgeois rule. Europe's social and economic progress became equated with industrialization and the "rise of the bourgeoisie."

The class theory of European industrialization was frequently buttressed by comparing Europe with China, and was just undergoing its spectacular decline into subordination and underdevelopment. (Japan was hardly noticed in the literature of the time.) Prior to the nineteenth century, China had not been regarded as a bureaucratic state that was dedicated to the smashing of commerce and the suppression of all change. China was regarded as *different* from Europe, but frequently in a favorable light, and even as a model to which Europe might aspire. The Physiocrats, for example, wrote approvingly of the beneficial effects of Chinese economic policy on agriculture. All this changed in the nineteenth century. If European progress was the work of the bourgeoisie, it followed that Chinese backwardness must have been due to the absence of a bourgeoisie.

As noted above, many traditional society theorists of China and Japan have been influenced by Karl Marx and Max Weber. Both of these major nineteenth-century social theorists of European modernization used China (also India and other Eastern societies) as a foil, against which they displayed their conceptions of Western social and economic progress. And although Marx and Weber interpreted the nature of Western progress differently, both touched on certain class-theory arguments about the nature of Europe versus China.

Marx and Engels, at various points in their work, elaborated the conception of a special *"asiatic" mode of production* that diverged from that of feudalism. This concept, which Marx and Engels never fully integrated into a systematic statement on comparative history, has greatly influenced subsequent theorists, who have utilized it in a simplistic way that I doubt Marx and Engels intended.

Marx and Engels mentioned five characteristics that distinguished "asiatic" societies from "feudal" Europe:

1. Agriculture, because of geographic and climatic conditions, was based on large-scale irrigation and flood-control works that were managed by the state. Marx wrote in the *New York Daily Tribune* in 1853:

> Climate and territorial conditions, especially the vast tracts of desert extending from the Sahara, through Arabia, Persia, India and Tartary, to the most elevated Asiatic highlands, constituted artificial irrigation by canals and waterworks the basis of Oriental agriculture. . . . This prime necessity of an economical and common use of water, which in the Occident drove private enterprise to voluntary association, as in Flanders and Italy, necessitated in the Orient where civilization was too low and the territorial extent too vast to call into life voluntary association, the interference of the centralizing power of government.[11]

2. Unlike feudal Europe, property was undeveloped in Asia. There was no nobility, no bourgeoisie. On the one hand, the state was the "real landlord," that is, all property was legally owned by the state; village communities possessed land only as a grant from the state. This constituted the rationale for tribute or labor services extracted from the villagers by the state. On the other hand, land was in fact the communal or common property of the villagers who tilled it.

3. Unlike feudal Europe, the division of labor was little developed in Asia. Production was organized through a multitude of tiny, similar, self-sufficient village communities. Cities were not autonomous centers of industry and commerce but administrative outposts of the state, superimposed on the fundamental, village economic structure.

    The village communities united agriculture and domestic manufacturing, "that peculiar combination of hand-weaving, hand-spinning and land-tilling agriculture which gave them self-supporting power." That is, the villagers owned the means of production and produced for their own use; thus both the market and the laborers for capitalist production were lacking.

4. The combination of centralized control over the water supply and the isolation of peasants within self-sufficient villages provided a solid foundation for a highly despotic form of government, "asiatic" or "oriental despotism."

5. Finally, as a result of the above, "asiatic" society was "stagnant" or "stationary." Marx commented on India: "India has no history at all, at least no known history. What we call its history, is but the history of the successive intruders who founded their empires on the passive basis of that unresisting and unchanging society." It was only with the extension of capitalism to Asia by the British and others that real social and economic change began to occur:

    > English interference, having placed the spinner in Lancashire and the weaver in Bengal, or sweeping away both Hindoo spinner and weaver, dissolved these small, semi-barbarian, semi-civilized communities by blowing up their economical basis and thus produced the greatest, and to speak the truth, the only social revolution ever heard of in Asia . . . England, it is true, in causing a social revolution in Hindostan, was actuated by the vilest interests, and was stupid in her manner of enforcing them. But that is not the question. The question is, can mankind fulfill its destiny without a fundamental revolution in the social state of Asia? If

not, whatever may have been the crimes of England, she was the unconscious tool of history in bringing about the revolution.

Thus the concept of the asiatic mode of production emphasizes the absence of a property-owning class in Asia that might have furnished an impetus to economic transformation. The economy was controlled by the state, on the one hand, and by isolated peasant villages on the other. No bourgeoisie existed to develop the productive forces to a higher level.

To Weber, the content of modern progress also was closely connected with the rise of the bourgeoisie. Weber also noted the function of the Chinese state in the management of water-control works, the administrative character of Chinese cities, and the lack of development of private property. However, the emphasis of his argument lies elsewhere. He was less interested in the processes of capital accumulation, the division of labor, and industrial investment than in the extension of "rationality" into social life. Industrial capitalism, Weber argued, depended on the development of a class with a "rational" spirit, which in turn has extraeconomic origins.

Weber argued that "from a purely economic point of view, a genuinely bourgeois, industrial capitalism might have developed from. . . petty capitalist beginnings" in China.[12] The reason why it did not was, in part, the nature of the Chinese state and in part the nature of the Chinese ethic. The state, which he characterized as a "patrimonial' or "prebendal bureaucracy," failed to create a rational, calculable structure of law and administration within which a class of capitalists might be motivated to operate. Justice was substantive, not formal; arbitrary, not consistent. Private property was not "guaranteed." There were no civil liberties. "Capital investment in industry is far too sensitive to such irrational rule and too dependent upon the possibility of calculating the steady and rational operation of the state machinery to emerge under an administration of this type."[13]

Above all, however, the failure to develop industrial capitalism stemmed from the Confucian ethic of the "literati" stratum that staffed the Chinese patrimonial bureaucracy. The literati failed to promote industrial capitalism, or to encourage other classes to do so, because of the goals emphasized in Confucianism. Confucianism contrasted sharply with the Puritan or Protestant ethic of the Western European countries, which Weber regarded as significant in the rise of capitalism in the West. The Confucian ethic stresses the prime goal of self-perfection through a literary education. Confucian training rejected practical and specialized expertise in worldly affairs; the Confucian gentleman possessed the "ways of thought suitable to a cultural man" and was "thoroughly steeped in literature."[14] Proof of one's status as an educated gentleman was passing the state's official examinations. "The typical Confucian used his own and his family's savings to acquire a literary education." The Puritan ethic, in contrast, stressed personal salvation through hard work, sobriety, and thriftiness. "The typical Puritan earned plenty, spent little, and reinvested his income as capital in rational capitalist enterprise out of an aesceticist compulsion to save."[15]

Thus, Weber argued, capitalism failed to emerge originally in China, as in Europe, because the dominant class in China pursued the goal of education and office-holding rather than the rational accumulation of capital.

In this century, major China scholars have continued to support a class theory to explain why industrial capitalism emerged first in Europe, rather than in China. Etienne Balasz, for example, has popularized a view of China as the "mirror image in reverse" of Europe, drawing on many points mentioned by Weber and Marx. The geographic and climatic foundations of "oriental" governments and the power of the "bureaucracy" to smash private property have been greatly elaborated in the works of Karl Wittfogel.

Wittfogel's main contribution to the discussion was to extend the concept of the asiatic mode of production (Wittfogel's term is *"hydraulic" economy or society*) to account for something that Marx and Engels omitted: the widespread existence of private property in land, commerce, and industry in China and other Asian societies. Wittfogel argued that although there were large amounts of private property in China and elsewhere, it was kept "weak" by the powerful despotic or bureaucratic state. The state prevented private property owners from building enough private wealth and from organizing politically on a national level in such a way as seriously to challenge state power. The state had decisive "acquisitive power" over private wealth in (1) heavy taxation of landlord, merchant, and industrial profits, (2) outright confiscation of private wealth, and (3) "fragmenting" inheritance laws (i.e., inheritance laws that dispersed property among all heirs rather than concentrated it in the hands of one). The state also possessed decisive "organizational power" over private property owners, especially through a national postal and intelligence network, and the ability to mobilize and supply vast masses of peasants for military service or other central purposes. These methods led to a "state stronger than society," a state that thoroughly controlled and stifled all opposition, all class conflict, and all change.

It is probably safe to say that a rough class theory is still *the* theory of why European development diverged from the development pattern in other parts of the world. Versions of it appear everywhere. Lichtheim's formation, in his *Imperialism*, is typical:

> A fairly typical alignment during the Medieval epoch enlisted the urban agglomeration, the *bourg*, on the king's side against rebellious nobles. Alternatively, the city fought for freedom from feudal and monarchical oppression. These medieval class conflicts gave rise to the city-state, perhaps Europe's most distinctive contribution to political history. The East never saw anything like it, for there theocratic monarchies strangled civic autonomy along with security of private property. For the same reason, the Orient never developed a genuine capitalism.[16]

Traditional society theorists have simply adopted this theory (designed to explain why capitalism developed originally in Europe, not in China) and used it to explain why industrial capitalism developed in Japan, but not in China, *during the nineteenth century*. Another quote from Lichtheim shows the logic of the jump from the original question to the situation in the nineteenth century:

102

This statement (as to the failure of capitalism to develop in the Orient) applies to India and to the Islamic world with greater exactitude than to China and Japan, *the last mentioned country at least having developed a genuine feudalism and the notion of private property in land that commonly goes with it.* In China, and still more in India and the Middle East, this development was strangled at birth by the system of government usually described as Oriental Despotism. *The realization that capitalism could sprout from feudalism in Europe (and subsequently in Japan) forms the connecting link between Marx's and Max Weber's theorizing.*[17]

It is probably a mistake to attribute such thinking either to Max Weber or to Karl Marx. Although Weber believed that the pre-European rise of industrial capitalism was hampered in China by the Chinese state and the Confucian ethic, it is unclear, as far as I can tell, what view he held of the Tokugawa state. Moreover, he did not transfer this theory wholesale to the nineteenth century; otherwise it would be hard to understand the comment he made in his work on China: "The Chinese in all probability would be quite capable, probably more capable than the Japanese of assimilating capitalism which has technically and economically been fully developed in the modern culture area."

It seems abundantly clear that Marx regarded *imperialism* as a primary factor in China's nineteenth-century underdevelopment, rather than the asiatic mode of production. What Marx and Engels intended to say on why industrial capitalism emerged *originally* in Europe, rather than in Asia, may be more open to debate. Did Marx and Engels, as Mandel claims, intend the contrast between the asiatic mode of production and feudalism to be an explanation of this question? This seems doubtful to me.

Marx and Engels did not write a systematic historical and comparative study attempting to answer the question of why industrial capitalism originally emerged in Western Europe rather than elsewhere. Marx's major concern appears to have been to understand the nature of the capitalist mode of production, with a view, above all, toward understanding its contradictions and eventual revolutionary transformation toward socialism. He seems to have been concerned with non-capitalist modes of production primarily in order to describe how they *differed* from the capitalist and as a method of understanding the latter. His theories were oriented toward influencing practical action in his time, and a pedantic concern with the origins of industrial capitalism has been left to his followers.

Much of what Marx wrote on the asiatic mode of production is contained in the *Grundrisse*, which was prepared in 1857–1858 for the subsequently published *Critique of Political Economy and Capital.* (The *Grundrisse* was not published in Marx and Engels' lifetimes.) It is difficult to believe that what Marx wrote in the *Grundrisse* was intended to be such a comparative historical study. As Hobsbawm has pointed out, Marx's discussion of various "pre-capitalist" modes of production in the *Grundrisse* (asiatic, ancient, feudal) is "not 'history' in the strict sense." For example, the propertyless society with an undeveloped division of labor, described under the asiatic mode of production in the *Grundrisse*, is not that of complex eighteenth- or nineteenth- (or even twelfth-) century China. Marx surely had more information on the real, historical China than is evidenced in the *Grundrisse*, yet it was not used.

What Marx and Engels deemed worthy of publication contains little about the asiatic mode of production. Engels, in *Origins of the Family, Private Property and the State*, the latest and most developed historical work, omitted the asiatic mode of production altogether. The *Critique* says little about it, commenting (in passing) in the Preface: "In broad outlines we can designate the asiatic, the ancient, the feudal and the modern bourgeois modes of production as so many epochs in the progress of the economic formation of society."

In *Capital*, comments on asiatic societies are not introduced in the context of asking why capitalism originated in Europe rather than Asia. Rather, they are used as cursory illustrations for basic concepts and arguments. For example, in Volume I Asian public works projects are used as examples of "simple cooperation"; the undeveloped division of labor within Indian communities, *along with the European medieval guild system*, are used as examples of hindrances to the establishment of the division of labor within capitalist workshops. In Volume III, Asian forms of agricultural production and land tenure are used, along with the "ancient world" and feudal Europe, as examples of precapitalist forms, in the context of analysis of the structure and dynamics of capitalist agriculture. Moreover, what Marx *does* say in *Capital* about the rise of capitalism in Europe suggests a far more complex argument than the "asiatic" versus "feudal" contrast. Marx saw the rise of capitalism in Europe in terms of a twofold process: the accumulation of capital in the hands of a bourgeoisie and its investment in the means of industrial production, and the emergence of a "free" proletariat, dispossessed of means of production and forced to work for the bourgeoisie in return for wages.

Marx did not see the emergence of these two contradictory classes as a simple outcome of the "rise of commerce"; rather, it involved a variety of forces, including, for example, European colonial expansion, the establishment of state debts, national policies of protectionism, the impact of rising wool prices on enclosures of farmland, and repressive labor legislation. (The contradiction is "overdetermined," in Louis Althusser's terms. See *For Marx* [New York, 1970], pp 200ff.) This suggests that had Marx or Engels in fact written a systematic comparative historical study of why industrial capitalism originally emerged in Europe, they would not have stopped with a contrast between asiatic and feudal modes of production.

A number of facts about European, Chinese, and Japanese history are not consistent with a simple class theory of industrialization.

First, there does not seem to have been a straight line leading from the autonomous towns and the "rise of commerce" in medieval Europe to the capitalist industrialization that occurred in the eighteenth and nineteenth centuries. Medieval England had the least-independent towns, yet England was the first European nation to industrialize. Medieval Germany had some of the most powerful, autonomous towns in Europe, yet nineteenth-century Germany was a latecomer to industrialization. The same is of course true of Italy, which experienced urban progress in the Middle Ages, followed by relative industrial backwardness in the nineteenth century. Poland had many flourishing towns in the Middle Ages, yet moved to agrarian status after the sixteenth century. In some cases the very commercial success of a nation seems to have contributed to its failure to industrialize rapidly. For example, in Holland, a powerful commercial bourgeoisie successfully opposed the institution of protective tariffs that elsewhere encouraged industrialization.

Second, the commercial bourgeoisie has repeatedly shown itself reluctant to invest in modern industry without government prodding and encouragement. In Japan after the Restoration, there was little interest by bourgeois investors in investing in large-scale modern industry. Industrial investment was forthcoming only after vigorous state efforts to prove its potential profitability and to eliminate risk. It appears that Japan's bourgeoisie would have remained commercially oriented in the absence of government intervention and would have doomed the nation to industrial backwardness. This is true, however, not only of non-democratic, industrial latecomers but also of states with the most impeccable bourgeois democratic credentials. For example, the U.S. bourgeoisie invested in railway development only when it was encouraged by large state subsidies in the form of land giveaways.

Third, there does not seem to have been a simple relationship between bourgeois control of the state in Europe and state policies that furthered capitalist industrial development. Many Western European rulers, prior to bourgeois control of the state, and in pursuit of their own goals (such as increasing state power vis-à-vis other European states), engaged in policies that promoted national commerce and industry, such as colonial expansion, subsidies to industry, and unification of tolls and tariffs. Policies were probably more systematically carried out and more successful once the state was strongly influenced by the bourgeoisie, but this active character of the European governments, I believe, distinguishes them from both the Chinese and the Japanese governments prior to the Western impact.

Finally, the class theory does not explain why declining feudalism in one place (Europe) gave way to original industrialization, whereas declining feudalism elsewhere (Japan) did not, until the latter was "stimulated" by external factors. The view that feudalism per se promotes the rise of commerce, and eventually industry, founders on the massive facts of slow economic growth during Tokugawa times in Japan, compared to early modern Europe. No one seriously contends that Tokugawa Japan was undergoing a commercial or industrial revolution comparable to what happened in Europe. Yet the class theory of industrialization does not account systematically for why this was not so.

The problem

The comparative studies of Japan and China are thus not very conclusive. The world economy studies suggest differences between the social structures of Japan and China but deny that these differences were of consequence for Japan's nineteenth-century development and China's underdevelopment. The traditional society studies point out differences in the relationship of Japan and China to the Western industrial powers but deny that they were of consequence. And many of the traditional society studies make highly problematic assumptions about the relationships among feudalism, bureaucracy, commercialization, and industrialization.

The purpose of this study is to re-explore the cases of Japan and China with the aim of clarifying the several questions that have been raised by the comparative studies but not adequately answered:

1. What was the nature of Japanese society, compared to Chinese society, "on the eve of the Western impact"? Were they really radically different? Do the terms *feudal* and *bureaucratic* adequately characterize the two societies? Can Tokugawa Japan be usefully compared with the nations of Europe? Why had industrial capitalism failed to emerge in *both* Japan and China by the time of the European expansion into Asia?

2. Did different relations evolve during the nineteenth century between the industrial powers and China and between these powers and Japan? Did Japan enjoy substantially greater autonomy in its relationship to the industrial capitalist nations than China? Or was the nature of the "Western impact" on the two countries basically similar?

3. If differences existed — if Japan enjoyed greater autonomy — did these differences affect the two countries' internal political–economic structures and processes, so that Japan had achieved "development" or "national industrialization" by the early twentieth century whereas China was "underdeveloped"?

Notes

1. S.N. Eisenstadt, *Modernization: Protest and Change* (Englewood Cliffs, N.J., 1966), pp. 55ff.

2. W.W. Rostow, *The Process of Economic Growth* (New York, 1962), pp. 314-316.

3. Rostow, *The Process of Economic Growth*, p. 284.

4. Johnson, *The Sociology of Change and Reaction in Latin America*, p. 46.

5. Levy, "Contrasting Factors in the Modernization of China and Japan," p. 496.

6. Paul A. Baran, *The Political Economy of Growth* (New York, 1957), pp. 150-151.

7. Reischauer and Fairbank, *East Asia: The Great Tradition*, p. 670.

8. Fairbank, Reischauer, and Craig, *East Asia: The Modern Transformation*, p. 180.

9. Fairbank, Reischauer, and Craig, *East Asia: The Modern Transformation*, pp. 179ff.

10. Jacobs, *The Origin of Modern Capitalism and Eastern Asia*.

11. Shlomo Avineri, ed., *Karl Marx on Colonialism and Modernization* (New York, 1976), p. 85.

12. Weber, *The Religion of China*, (New York, 1964), p. 100.

13. Ibid., p. 103.

14. Ibid., p. 121.

15. Ibid., p. 247.

16. George Lichtheim, *Imperialism* (New York, 1971), p. 44.

17. Ibid., p. 59, n. 1 (italics mine).

7. Economy and Social Classes in Ch'ing China and Tokugawa Japan

Frances Moulder

What was the nature of Chinese and Japanese society on the eve of nineteenth-century Western capitalist intrusion into Asia? This section argues that traditional society theorists have exaggerated the differences between Ch'ing China and Tokugawa Japan on the one hand and the similarities between Tokugawa Japan and the societies of early modern Europe on the other. Although there were certain similarities in *political* structure between Japan and early modern Europe ("feudalism"), the process of Japan's political–economic–social development, taken as a whole, was more similar to that of China than that of Europe.

European industrialization occurred within a different *total* developmental context from that of China and Japan. In Europe there was an ever greater centralization of state power; European governments developed from feudal to what I call "imperial," into centralized, "national" states. National economic policies of mercantilism emerged aimed at strengthening, unifying, and expanding the national economy, and contributed to the industrialization and "intense" commercialization of Europe during the eighteenth and nineteenth centuries. Accelerating military expenditures and growth of the state apparatus led to the establishment of large national debts in Europe, which greatly furthered capital accumulation and thus contributed to industrialization.

In neither China nor Japan was there a comparable trend toward ever greater centralization of state power. Japan remained feudal, China remained imperial, and neither showed signs of developing toward a centralized national state. In neither China nor Japan did governments have a comparably active mercantilist relationship to the national economy which would have strongly encouraged national industrialization and "intensive" commercialization. In neither country did accelerating military expenditures and a rapidly growing state apparatus, on a scale comparable to Europe's, give impetus to capital accumulation. Whatever differences there were between feudal Japan and Imperial China were encompassed within a dynamic of development that was distinct from the dynamic of development in Europe.

In consequence, on the eve of the Western intrusion, as Baran put it, "conditions in Japan were as conducive, or rather as unfavorable, to economic development as anywhere in Asia."

*　　　　*　　　　*

Frances Moulder: Part I; Chapter I, 'Economy and Social Classes in Ch'ing China and Tokugawa Japan' from *JAPAN, CHINA AND THE MODERN WORLD ECONOMY* (Cambridge University Press, 1977), pp. 25–44.

Similarities in agricultural and industrial foundations

Traditional society theorists have overlooked enormous similarities in the economic foundations of Ch'ing China and Tokugawa Japan in their rush to find traditional institutional divergences that might have caused China and Japan to take different paths during the nineteenth century. Above all, both China and Japan were fundamentally agrarian. Agriculture accounted for about 70 percent of the national income in each country. The vast majority of the population, perhaps 80 to 85 percent in both countries were peasants; working directly in agriculture production. Moreover, although economic growth was occurring in both Japan and China, the rate of growth was quite slow compared with that of developing countries today.

Peasants in Ch'ing China and Tokugawa Japan produced largely the same things and by largely the same methods. Food production was paramount, and grain, especially rice, constituted the bulk of agricultural production. (Even in 1877, after the Meiji Restoration, rice still accounted for 60 percent of all farm products in the Kinai, one of Japan's most advanced areas.) In addition to grain and lesser food crops, peasants in China and Japan cultivated a variety of similar crops that went into handicraft industry, for example , silkworm eggs and cocoons, mulberry leaves, cotton and tea.

Both China and Japan were, of course, "pre-industrial": draft animals, and especially human beings, provided the energy for planting, harvesting and transporting crops . Similar kinds of agricultural technology prevailed in both countries. Intensive rice cultivation , based on the construction of irrigation, drainage, and flood-control works, was a key feature of both economies. Other basic farming techniques, practiced in both countries, included multiple cropping, seed selection, and the use of commercial fertilizers, such as night soil, mud from sewers and ponds, oil cake or dried fish. A wide variety of farm implements was used in China and Japan during the Ch'ing and Tokugawa periods (e.g., hoes, water pumps, and plows), yet few new mechanical implements were developed in either society.

Peasants and urban artisans carried on flourishing industries in both countries. The textile industry (cotton and silk) was perhaps the most important industry in both countries. Other major industries included tea processing, oil pressing, grain milling, pottery, rice wine production, paper and ink. Industry, however, remained on a handicraft basis in both Ch'ing China and Tokugawa Japan. Needham has argued that China's and Europe's industrial technologies were at a roughly similar level up to 1450, after which Europe moved ahead. Japan's seems to have remained close to China's.

Processes of change

Although change was occurring slowly, neither the Chinese nor the Japanese economy was standing still, and both, in general, were changing in the same ways. Several important economic and social transformations in both societies prior to the nineteenth century will be considered here: growing agricultural productivity; increasing population; improvements in transportation; a process that will be termed *"extensive" commercialization*; expansion, then relative closure, to foreign trade; and social changes accompanying commercialization, including the monetization of tax structures, the growth of an increasingly broad-based and powerful merchant class, and changes in rural stratification from "status" to "class".

The major difference between China and Japan seems to be that these changes began much *later* and occurred more *rapidly* in Japan. Traditional society theorists may have confused this greater rapidity of change in Japan with a higher level of development. Another difference is that certain processes of growth seem to have halted or slowed markedly in Japan during the eighteenth century, but not in China. (In this chapter I will simply take note of these differences. Their causes will be taken up [subsequently], after discussion of the relationship of state and economy in China and Japan.)

It must first be noted that it is highly artificial to draw a line at the Ch'ing period in a discussion of changes in Chinese economy and society. As Mark Elvin recently emphasized, China underwent a process of marked economic growth during the eighth to thirteenth centuries (T'ang and Sung dynasties), a process that, although broken during the subsequent Mongol or Yüan dynasty and slowed in its intensity, continued into the following Ming and Ch'ing times. From the eighth to the thirteenth century, Elvin argues, China underwent what amounted to an "economic revolution." Agricultural productivity increased notably as the population shifted from the dry North to the Southern irrigated rice areas; land transport was improved and a nationwide water transport network was established; credit devices were developed and the amount of money in circulation increased; commercialization occurred, and a network of urban centers was established that reached from tiny rural periodic markets to the largest cities; foreign trade flourished; the urban population grew, as did the proportion of the urban population in the largest cities; and there were technological innovations in the textile and other industries as well as progress in mathematics and medicine. After the thirteenth century, however, according to Elvin, technological innovation halted and foreign trade was curtailed. However, economic growth continued at a slower pace and social transformations continued, for example, in class relations and in the organization of the urban marketing network. The Ch'ing period constituted no sharp break in this process of slow-paced growth.

The Tokugawa period seems to mark a more distinct period in Japan's economic history than does the Ch'ing in China's. Although some of the transformations (to be considered below) had begun earlier in Japan — such as the growth of commerce and the formation of an urban network — it seems that they reached their fullest development only after 1600. For these reasons it will be possible to limit the discussion of Japan primarily to the Tokugawa period, but it will be necessary to reach further back into Chinese history.

Population was growing in both China and Japan. Both countries had a very high population density compared to the nations of Europe. China's population had reached the 100 million mark in the eleventh century, during the Sung dynasty. The rise and fall of the Mongol dynasty was accompanied by great loss of life through killings, disease, and starvation caused by crop destruction. However, population began to grow thereafter, rising more or less steadily from an estimated 65 to 80 million around 1400 to 120 to 200 million in 1600, to about 270 million in 1770 and about 400 million during the nineteenth century. Japan's population also grew about 50 percent from

1600 to 1721; thereafter, however, it grew at a slower rate, and by the mid-1700s growth had halted, in contrast to the continued expansion in China. (China of course, was much larger in terms of population, about ten times the size of Japan; in fact China had about 30 percent of the world's population at the time.)

As population grew, grain production increased in both China and Japan. Japan's rice production grew at a rapid rate, probably doubling during the years from 1600 to 1730. The rate of growth seems to have slowed, however, beginning in the eighteenth century. Grain production in China, as noted above, had increased markedly during the Sung period, and it continued to increase steadily during the Ming and Ch'ing periods, more or less keeping pace with population growth and slowing down only in the nineteenth century.

Largely similar factors seem to account for rising grain production in China and Japan. First, there was an increase in the amount of land under cultivation. Second, there was an increase in yields per unit of land. An important factor behind increasing yields in both countries was the expansion of acreage under high-yielding irrigated rice cultivation. Japanese peasants devoted increased efforts to irrigated rice cultivation during the Tokugawa period, both on new lands and by converting dry fields to paddies. The Chinese had been expanding their rice cultivation frontier for many centuries. As noted above, a major population movement from the North into the Southern rice growing area had occurred from the eighth to the thirteenth centuries. During the Ming and Ch'ing dynasties, the peasants continued to move onto new lands and open them to rice cultivation. There was also an extension of rice cultivation northward and increased double cropping of rice with other grains.

Other factors underlying increased yields in both China and Japan included the introduction of the techniques mentioned above: improved seeds, increased double cropping, and the application of purchased fertilizers. In China these techniques had been introduced prior to the Ch'ing period; in Japan they appear to have been introduced primarily during the Tokugawa period. Fertilizer use, for example, appears to have undergone three stages in both China and Japan. In the first stage the fertilizers were grasses cut by the peasants. In the second stage, fertilizers were purchased, such as night soil and oil cake. The third stage is the use of modern chemical fertilizers, industrially produced. The Chinese peasants probably shifted from the first to the second stage during the Sung, Mongol, and the Ming periods, whereas the Japanese made the shift during Tokugawa times.

Transport was greatly improved in China from the eighth to the thirteenth century. There was a continual expansion of the main road networks, spurred by the government's desire for a nationwide postal network. Water transport, above all was improved. "Ways were found to pass through or around previously unpassable difficult places in rivers" and river and canal shipping expanded as "a number of hitherto separate waterway systems were now linked into an integrated whole." Sea transport also increased as ships were improved and safety was increased by use of the compass. The Grand Canal, linking North and South China, was built during the Sui dynasty (581–617) and was extended to the vicinity of Peking during the Mongol dynasty, becoming one of Ming-Ch'ing China's major shipping arteries. Elvin has argued that by Ch'ing times, China's water transport system was probably as developed as it could have been without a major leap forward into the technology of steamships. Transport in Japan was greatly improved during the Tokugawa period. Despite barriers to travel erected by the daimyo domains, five main roads, radiating from the capital, tied the nation together and imposed a hitherto lacking centralization on the road network. Because it was an island, more of Japan was accessible to water transport than China. China's dry North and Northwest were restricted to land transport, but all parts of Japanese territory, and most of the major cities, were linked by ocean routes during the Tokugawa period.

Population increase, greater agricultural productivity, changing agricultural techniques, and improvements in transportation were accompanied in both countries by a growth in commerce and attendant changes in class structure. Was Japan's economy more "commercialized" than China's?

The question of "commercialization"

Commerce, commercialization, and related terms such as *national market*, which are frequently applied to the economic development of Europe, China, and Japan, are in great need of clarification.

Commercialization seems to have two aspects, as it is commonly used. First it refers to a decline in *regional* self-sufficiency. That is, each region no longer produces all the food and manufactured goods it needs. Second, it refers to a decline in *local* self-sufficiency, or the growth of interchanges between town and countryside. That is, peasants no longer produce simply for their own consumption and no longer consume only what they have themselves produced; they are part of a trading network or hierarchy of urban centers, producing goods that are shipped "upward" to even higher urban levels and consuming goods that are produced in or channelled through large urban centers.

The process of commercialization, in either of these two aspects, may be "extensive" or "intensive," depending on the extent to which self-sufficiency is lost and exchange relations come to dominate production. An increase in commerce occurs in an extensive way when increasing regions or people that had hitherto been self-sufficient become involved in exchange relationships, but only to a minor degree. It occurs in an intensive way when these regions or people begin to specialize in production of one or another commodity to such a degree that they are highly dependent on exchange relationships for their livelihood.

Extensive commercialization occurs, for instance, when region A, earlier self-sufficient, begins to consume the cotton produced in region B but remains self-sufficient in the production of other goods. Or, again, when peasant A, who had hitherto been self-sufficient , begins to sell beans and to purchase oil at market, but continues to produce his own grain, vegetables, yarn, cloth, and the like.

Intensive commercialization occurs when region A begins to specialize in producing cotton, sugar, silk, etc., and begins to depend on other places for most or all of the other necessary articles of livelihood. Or, again, when peasant A specializes in sugar or mulberry production and depends on the market for most or all other goods. That is,

111

intensive commercialization implies the destruction of peasant industry primarily oriented toward producing items for the peasants' own consumption.

The term *market* is frequently used in two ways, which are not synonymous. First, it refers to market*place*: a place or site where goods are exchanged. Second, it refers to a market: the situation in which the prices of goods being exchanged are influenced by the interaction of supply and demand.

On the one hand, goods may be sold and bought in a "marketplace" at prices determined by fiat, as by decision of a government authority — as well as by the interaction of supply and demand. On the other hand, "markets" for commodities may exist without being located in a specific place.

In a *national market* the prices of goods are determined by the interaction of supply and demand on a nationwide scale (and thus the price that a commodity fetches in one city greatly affects its price in other urban centers in different regions of the nation). A *national marketplace*, on the other hand, is simply a central place into which goods are channelled for exchange, whether by means of barter, purchase, and sale at market prices or at prices determined by government or guild decree.

The conception of a national market assumes that regional and local self-sufficiency have broken down, that producers and distributors will channel goods where they will receive the highest price. This is not the case with a national marketplace, which may exist with the most extreme variations of prices in various regions, reflecting regional barriers to trade.

The economies of Western Europe passed through two phases in relation to commercialization and market formation. The first phase, which lasted until the late eighteenth and early nineteenth century, was one of extensive commercialization and the emergence of national marketplaces. After the decline of the Roman Empire, commerce again began to expand significantly in the tenth and eleventh centuries. Rural areas increasingly exchanged goods with the towns, the regions of Europe exchanged a variety of goods with one another, and European commerce with the rest of the world increased (especially, of course, after the sixteenth century).

During the first phase, the interaction of region and region and town and country was slight. In the eighteenth century, the situation in most of Europe was still similar to what an English observer reported of northern England: "Almost every article of dress worn by farmers, mechanics and labourers is manufactured at home, shoes and hats excepted....There are many respectable persons at this day who never wore a bought pair of stockings, coat or waistcoat in their lives." National marketplaces also appeared during this period: cities such as London and Paris came to be centers into which goods flowed from all over the country. However, national markets for most commodities hardly existed.

Intensive commercialization began only in the late eighteenth and early nineteenth centuries. It was associated with the industrial revolution — the enormous advances in output achieved through the use of mechanical energy — and with the revolution in transport: with the rapid expansion of canal and, especially, rail networks, which accelerated the circulation of goods from town to country and region to region. As

Marx noted, "Modern industry alone, and finally, supplies in machinery the lasting basis of capitalistic agriculture, expropriates radically the enormous majority of the agricultural population, and completes the separation between agriculture and rural domestic industry."[1] And as the self-sufficiency of localities and regions dwindled rapidly, national markets for a wide variety of commodities began to emerge.

Was Japan more commercialized than China? It will be argued here that (1) *intensive* commercialization was not occurring in either Japan or China; (2) although both economies were becoming increasingly commercialized in an *extensive* way, the level of extensive commercialization was not greatly different in Japan and China during the Tokugawa and Ch'ing periods; and (3) a national market did not yet exist in either country.

Commerce and markets in China

Chinese peasants were hardly self-sufficient. Since the Sung dynasty, at least, many of them had come to purchase such goods as oil, fertilizers and metals, which they did not themselves produce. They also produced goods beyond their personal needs, which were sold. These exchanges were made in local periodic marketplaces, which proliferated in China with the growth of population and the increasing numbers of people involved in exchange relations. These local marketplaces were linked into a hierarchy of urban places that functioned as centers for ever larger areas of exchange.

Peasant dependence on the outside was not great, however. For most peasants, cash crops and handicraft items were sold to supplement their subsistence production. Only a small percentage of the peasantry was so specialized that it depended upon purchases for its survival. Only a small percentage of total farm production went into exchange. Perkins has estimated that perhaps 20 to 30 percent of China's farm produce was exchanged within local areas in the nineteenth century; 5 to 7 percent went into long-distance trade; and another 1 or 2 percent was marketed abroad. Balasz estimated that 20 to 30 percent of farm output was exchanged during the Sung period. Thus China may have been no more intensively commercialized in the nineteenth century than during the Sung dynasty.

Nor were the regions of China self-sufficient. For centuries there had been a great deal of regional specialization in China. This was founded primarily on the unequal distribution of climatic and soil conditions necessary for producing certain goods. For example, sugar cane could best be grown in Kwangtung, Fukien, Szechwan, and Taiwan. Tea and mulberry leaves for silkworm production could best be grown in Chekiang and southern Kiangsu. Cotton was most easily grown in the Kiangsu area and the North. Copper, which served as the basis of the empire's coinage, was found mainly in Yunnan. Manchuria and the Northwest supplied timber, wool, fur, and various products of the forests. All these goods were transported from their places of origin to the other regions of China. Regions that were favorably situated for producing raw materials usually came to specialize in the manufacture of goods made from them. Thus, for example, peasants of the Kiangnan area produced silk and cotton yarn and cloth, which were shipped throughout the empire.

113

The interregional transactions in China can be regarded as taking place between more or less industrially developed areas. The provinces of Kiangsu, Chekiang, Anhwei, Kiansi, Fukien, Kwangtung, Shansi, Chihli, and Honan produced manufactured goods and exported them to Manchuria, Shensi, Kansu, Hupei, Hunan, Kwangsi, Szechwan, Yunnan, Kweichow, Taiwan, Mongolia, Sinkiang, Tsinghai, and Tibet, from which they imported primary products. As commerce and industry developed, even grain began to enter interregional commerce on a large scale. During the Ch'ing period the manufacturing provinces of Kiangsu and Chekiang imported rice from Anhwei, Hunan, Kiangsi, and even Szechwan. Interestingly, there do not seem to have been insurmountable political or economic barriers preventing the more backward regions from "catching up." For example, Northern China, once dependent upon the Kiangnan region for cotton textiles, became a center for the production of such goods after the sixteenth century.

Regional commercialization was not intensive in China, however. Only a small variety of goods entered interregional trade: primarily cotton and silk, tea, sugar, salt, drugs, and grain. These were usually goods that could be produced only in certain areas due to climatic conditions and/or luxury goods that were consumed by the upper classes and thus could bring high profits, despite the high transport costs in China's premodern economy.

There were a number of important national marketplaces in China, such as Peking, Canton, Nanking, Wuban, Foochow, Chungking, Chengtu, Soochow, Hangchow, and Sian. Did a true national market exist in Ch'ing times, prior to the Western expansion? Data are lacking, but it seems doubtful, due to the country's strong regional and local self-sufficiency and the importance of such factors as high transport costs.

Commerce and markets in Japan

Japanese peasants of the Tokugawa period were also losing their self-sufficiency — purchasing fertilizers and other commodities in exchange for food and handicraft items. As in China, commercialization was accompanied by a proliferation of rural periodic markets that served the needs of the peasants and were linked into a network of ever larger urban centers. It might be noted that these rural markets spread throughout Japan despite efforts of the daimyo to curtail their growth in order to centralize all commerce in the domain capitals. Their rate of growth seems to have slowed after 1700, however, in contrast to China's where local markets continued to multiply into the twentieth century.

There was also a good deal of regional specialization and exchange in Japan. For example, cotton production was concentrated in the Kinai area and silkworm production and silk reeling in the three prefectures of Fukushima, Yamanashi, and Gumma. Certain domains produced more porcelain, lacquer, paper, silk, or wax than others. Satsuma produced sugar on a large scale and exported it throughout Japan. As in China, there were interchanges between more and less developed areas of the country, some of the domains exporting manufactured goods, others primarily agricultural products.

The process of commercialization in Tokugawa Japan is frequently described as though it were intensive. Smith comments:

> In the late Tokugawa period one still found villages with the characteristic subsistence pattern of cropping. But by the beginning of the nineteenth century, this stage was long past. Except in notably backward places — wild and remote valleys, isolated promontories, areas cut off by poor soil from the main stream of economic development — peasants by then typically grew what soil, climate and price favored, regardless of what they themselves happened to need. If a family were short of food or critical raw materials as a result, it made no difference since nearly anything was available in the local market, supplied with commodities from places scores, or even hundreds of miles away.[2]

And Crawcour:

> In contrast to the subsistence agriculture of the Early Tokugawa period, by the 1860's agriculture over most of Japan was basically commercial agriculture, that is to say that the bulk of farm produce was grown for a market rather than for consumption by the cultivator.[3]

However, when such authors begin to cite figures the extensive character is striking, and the figures are not very different from those cited by authors on commercialization in China. As noted above, Perkins estimates that 20 to 30 percent of the farm output in China went into local trade, 5 to 7 percent into interregional trade, and another 1 to 2 percent into foreign trade. Smith cites figures from a work by Furushima on the percentage of "total agricultural production" in Japan that was accounted for by "cash crops" in several regions. They vary from 10 to 27 percent, the median being 12 percent. Unfortunately, Smith does not say exactly what is meant by "cash crops." However, if these figures are at all comparable, the difference between China and Japan was not very great.

The conceptions of commerce and market, as used in this context, must also be clarified. Crawcour later qualifies the comment (quoted above) that in Japan the "bulk of farm produce was grown for a market" by saying that "in the part of agricultural produce grown for a market we must include the significant proportion of staple crops used to pay taxes in kind and marketed by the federal (i.e., the domain) authorities."[4] (Domain taxes, mainly rice, were largely collected in kind; perhaps one-third of what was collected was shipped to the city for sale.) According to Rozman, grain taxes marketed in the city constituted 2 million koku, or about 10 percent of the total rice output of the domains, compared to around 7 million koku, or some 30 percent of the rice output, that was marketed directly by peasants or other private persons. It is this 30 percent figure that should be compared to Perkins' estimate for China, because estimates of marketed grain in China do not normally include grain taken in taxes by state authorities. (Grain taxes taken in kind in China, however, amounted to less than 1 percent of farm output, according to Perkins [*Agricultural Development in China*, p.150].)

It is frequently stated that a national market was emerging in Tokugawa Japan. It seems to me that this results from a confusion between *market* and *marketplace*. It is true that there were two cities with strong central or national marketplace functions: the cities of Osaka and Edo. However, was there a true national market in Tokugawa Japan? The price of rice throughout the land is said to have been strongly affected by prices prevailing at Osaka. But was this true of most other commodities? Again, it seems doubtful, given the high level of local and regional self-sufficiency in Japan.

Foreign commerce

Consideration should also be given to foreign trade in a discussion of commerce. Both Ch'ing China and Tokugawa Japan conducted a slowly growing commerce with other nations. Yet in both countries this commerce contracted after an earlier period of expansion. China had long traded with other parts of the Asian world. Prior to the Sung period, this trade was generally carried by Southeast Asian, Persian, and Arab ships. During and after the Sung period, however, Chinese ships became involved, and both Chinese merchants and the government undertook lengthy trading expeditions to Southern Asia, the Arab world, and even East Africa. This trade was generally controlled by the government, but to varying degrees: the policies of the earlier dynasties were less restrictive than those of the later dynasties.

For example, during Sung times there was a government monopoly in specified import goods, but private merchants could trade in them after the government's business was done. The government also taxed imports, and licensed Chinese merchants who wanted to go overseas, but did not prohibit other Chinese from going abroad or foreigners from coming to China. China's coastal cities in that period came to be filled with foreign residents. The Ming dynasty witnessed the famous official trading expeditions led by the eunuch admiral, Cheng Ho. However, these expeditions were soon halted and increasing restrictions were placed on foreign trade. Chinese were prohibited from going abroad and ships from abroad were allowed to trade only as part of an official "tributary mission" from another state to the Chinese government. The ban on Chinese going overseas had a checkered career, being lifted in the 1560s, reimposed in the last years of the Ming and the early years of the Ch'ing dynasties, then lifted in 1684 and reimposed in 1717.

The Ch'ing period generally continued the restrictive Ming policies. Chinese were prohibited from going overseas, with the exception of an officially approved copper trade with Japan. Foreign traders were restricted to the frontiers of the country — for example, to the seaports of Canton and Macao and the "landports" of Kiakhta and Nerchinsk on the Russian frontiers. Only Chinese merchants who had official approval were permitted to trade with them. The institution of the tributary mission also was maintained, with a certain amount of trade accompanying missions to Peking and such ports as Foochow.

In Japan, the Tokugawa period marked a retreat from earlier, less restrictive policies. Prior to this period, the Japanese had engaged in a flourishing trade with other parts of Asia, and numerous foreign merchants came to Japan. However, during the early seventeenth century the Tokugawa rulers forbade Japanese to go abroad and drove foreigners out of the country, with the exception of a certain number of Dutch and

Chinese traders. The Dutch and Chinese were restricted to a particular number of ships per year and, while in Japan, were not permitted to leave the town of Nagasaki. (This trade was essentially an exchange of Japanese and Chinese goods, with the Dutch and Chinese acting as middlemen: there was little trade between Japan and Holland.) There was also some trade with China, carried on by the Satsuma domain through the Ryukyu Islands.

The Ryukyu Islands trade provides a fascinating glimpse into Asian interstate relations. The Ryukyus, like a number of other small Asian kingdoms, were involved in a tributary relationship with Ch'ing China. In 1609, however, the Ryukyus had been conquered by Satsuma, reduced to a dependency, and deprived of fiscal and military autonomy. However, the Satsuma daimyo permitted the Ryukyu king to retain his title and continue to receive investiture from the Chinese throne as he had in the past, so that tribute missions might continue to be sent from the Ryukyus to China. These missions, carefully controlled by Satsuma, came to be vehicles of a regular Japanese–Chinese commerce.

Social transformations

The development of commerce in Japan and China was accompanied by major yet, again, quite parallel changes in class structure and political structure. First, relations between peasants and local overlords changed from "status" relations to monetized "class" relations. Second, taxes came to be paid in money rather than in kind. Third, merchants grew wealthy and increased in power vis-à-vis those who controlled the land.

The upper-class population in both China and Japan was composed of merchants, on the one hand, and a leisure class of those whose position was primarily based on ownership or control of the land and its surplus. The controllers of the land were divided into two levels in each country, which I will term the *tax-dependent* and the *mercantile* strata. The upper level, or tax dependents, was the stratum of the population that lived off taxes or tribute extracted from the peasants by the coercive and/or ideological powers of the state. The lower-level stratum enjoyed what Eric Wolf calls a "mercantile" relationship to the peasantry: income was derived from ownership of alienable private property.

The upper level of the landed class in Ch'ing China consisted of several groups, amounting to no more than 1 or 2 percent of the population. The first group comprised members of the conquering Manchu nobility and their troops (the bannermen) — some 200,000 households, or around a million people — who lived on tax-derived stipends on state-granted lands that were worked by peasant tenants. The second group was some 27,000 Manchu and Chinese civil and military officials and their families (altogether some 135,000 people), who were paid tax-derived stipends or salaries. The third group was made up of some million Chinese "quasi-official activists" and their families (altogether about 5.5 million people); the vast bulk were men who had passed only the lowest level of civil service examinations, thus held only the lowest academic title, and were not eligible to hold office. These activists utilized state connections to extract income from the peasantry, charging the peasants for services rendered in organizing

117

water-control projects, local or clan charity operations, crop preservation associations, teaching, and the like.

The lower level of the landed upper class in China was the Chinese "landlords." By the Ch'ing period they were a highly urbanized group of absentees who often used bursars to collect the rents from their noncontiguous and far-flung landholdings. Landlords also profited from lending money to the peasants and engaging in commerce and industry. (The Chinese landlords and the tax-dependents must not be regarded as two completely distinct groups since, in fact, the landlords, together with the merchants, provided most of the candidates for the official examinations. Although the majority of landlords probably were not officials or quasi-official activists, many of the officials and activists were landlords.)

The daimyo and the samurai constituted the upper level of Japan's landed upper class, amounting to 5.5 to 7.5 percent of the population. Japan was divided into some 200 domains, or han, ruled by hereditary daimyo to whom the samurai owned allegiance. The Tokugawa house, essentially the largest domain, exercised hegemony over the rest of the daimyo. The daimyo and the Tokugawa rulers collected taxes from the peasants and paid stipends to the samurai. The lower level of the landed upper class was an emerging stratum of landlords. They were an upper level of the rural peasantry who, like the Chinese landlords, lived off rents, moneylending, and profits from commerce and industry.

The development of commerce in China was accompanied by a transformation in the way taxes were collected, from taxes in kind to money payments. During the late sixteenth and early seventeenth centuries the so-called single-whip reform was extended throughout the land. Before this, land taxes had been owed in kind and in the form of labor services, and they were assessed primarily in terms of the households (i.e., people) in rural areas rather than in terms of land. The single-whip reform merged these taxes into a single tax (thus "single whip") that fell primarily on land, rather than on people, and commuted them into a money payment. Thus China's tax dependents came to stand in an increasingly monetary relationship to the peasantry.

A similar process occurred in Japan. In most domains in Tokugawa Japan, only about one-third of the land tax had been commuted. However, in the Tokugawa realm the share of money payments came to average 45 percent of the total toward the end of the period.

The mercantile lower stratum of the landed upper class also developed an increasingly monetary relationship to the peasants. Chinese peasants of the Sung period had lived on manors and were bound in serflike fashion to manorial lords, to whom they had labor obligations. During the next centuries, and with the growth of exchange, these lords transformed themselves from a rural status group, living off the peasants' obligatory labor, into the urban landlord class described above. They moved into the towns and cities and lived off rents extracted from peasant tenants, interest on loans they made to the peasants and others, profits from commerce and industry, and income from office-holding or quasi-official services.

118

At the beginning of the Tokugawa period most of the Japanese peasants had also been bound to local overlords in various ways. These overlords were also categorized as peasants, and were subordinate to the ruling samurai class, but were raised above the rest of the peasantry by their control of the village offices, through which the domain tax collectors communicated with the peasants, and by various status privileges given them by the daimyo. For example, they had the power to allocate the tax burden among the villagers (which the tax collectors imposed on the village as a unit) and they were sometimes permitted to wear swords, a privilege normally confined to the samurai. The peasants performed services for these lords and were dependent upon them for farm animals and tools. The peasants and lords were often bound by kinship ties as well, the lords being the "main family" of the extended family and the peasants the "branch families."

As the Tokugawa period progressed, these local overlords began to transform themselves into a landlord class, renting out the land they claimed instead of asking for labor services. They also began to lend money to peasants at interest and to engage in commerce and industry. Thus, as in China, relationships in the countryside changed from status to class relationships.

The merchant population also changed in China and Japan with the growth of commerce. In both societies it became an increasingly broad-based group and gained in power vis-à-vis the landed sector of the upper class. The broadening of the merchant class in China is evidenced by the proliferation of merchant associations, the *hui-kuan*. These associations were formed by merchants in one region or locality in order to further their economic interests when they were trading far from home. In 1560 there were hui-kuan only in the capital city. By the late sixteenth and early seventeenth century there were hui-kuan in most major cities. By the late Ch'ing period there were 400 hui-kuan in Peking alone, and others in all provincial capitals, major and minor ports, and in some smaller towns.

Commercialization in China also increased the merchants' wealth, prestige, and power. In the early dynasties Chinese merchants had been restricted by various sumptuary laws. They were also prohibited from holding office and were the objects of government persecution. Although these restraints were often evaded in practice, they were nontheless there, a social fact to be contended with. However, by the Ming period the merchants had become sufficiently forceful to get the government to permit them to take the civil service examinations and enter the officialdom. Sumptuary laws were dropped and, as will be discussed later, persecutions became rare. Thus the Chinese upper class became a highly fluid group: landlords and officials engaged in commerce and merchants bought land, obtained degrees, and became officials. Although social distinctions still remained, dividing the upper class in China into a landed and a commercial sector, these distinctions were increasingly eradicated with the growth of commerce, and it would be a mistake to depict the interests of China's tax dependents and landlords as inexorably opposed to those of merchants.

The same is true of Japan, albeit to a lesser extent, because the changes occurred later. As in China, Japanese merchants began to make their influence increasingly felt vis-à-vis the landed upper class. For example, they began to purchase samurai rank from impoverished samurai families. However, they had yet to cast aside as many barriers as in China. Japanese merchants were still largely excluded from holding political office, which was reserved for members of samurai families. Thus the Japanese upper class remained divided into two sectors with more distinct interests.

One major difference between China and Japan has been emphasized here: the lateness and rapidity with which change occurred in Japan. Japan came late to many changes that occurred earlier in China. Transformations that began centuries earlier in China began in Japan during the Tokugawa period. Yet once they began, they happened quickly, so that Japan was rapidly "catching up" with China. China's extensive commercialization pattern had been established centuries prior to the Ch'ing period; in Japan it was completed during the Tokugawa period. Chinese peasants had been using purchased fertilizers at least since the Ming dynasty, Japanese peasants primarily since the Tokugawa. Relations between Chinese peasants and their mercantile overlords had changed from those of status to increasingly monetary class relations long before the Ch'ing period; this transformation began in Japan primarily during the Tokugawa. Chinese taxes were commuted to money payments prior to the Ch'ing; this was under way in Japan during the Tokugawa period. Much earlier, Chinese merchants had become powerful enough to break the barriers between themselves and the landholding class, whereas Japanese merchants began this process only during the Tokugawa period.

Another major difference is that some of these changes appear to have halted or slowed in Japan, but not in China. For example, population growth ceased in Japan after a certain point but it continued in China; the growth rate of agricultural production appears to have declined earlier in Japan than in China; the rate of addition of local periodic markets slowed in Japan but not in China.

Why did changes occur more rapidly in Japan than in China? Why did some of them slow, or halt? Was the pattern of change in Japan a manifestation of a different kind of social order, similar to the societies of early modern Europe? Is it likely that the kind of change in Tokugawa Japan would have led to industrialization? And, in contrast, is it likely that such a transformation was inevitably stifled in China?

Notes

1. *Capital*, I: 820-821.

2. Smith: *The Agrarian Origins of Modern Japan*, pp. 68-69.

3. Sydney Crawcour, "The Japanese Economy on the Eve of Modernization," *Journal of the Oriental Society of Australia* 2 (1963) : 35.

4. Crawcour, "The Japanese Economy on the Eve of Modernization," p. 35.

8. Japan's Emergence as a Modern State
E. H. Norman

1. The Restoration

To understand the Restoration, one must realize that the continual degradation of the warrior class, the conversion of loyal *samurai* into indigent embittered *ronin*, was a major factor in shifting the loyalty of this class from the clan or Shogunate to those forces working for the overthrow of the *Bakufu*.

The feudal–merchant alliance and the Meiji Restoration

We see then a twofold and mutually interrelated process accompanying the decay of feudal society: (1) the *chōnin* by their economic power gain admission to the warrior class through adoption or purchase, and from that vantage point some of them become the most clear-sighted pilots who as *yonin* (or chamberlains) steer the anti-*Bakufu* forces through the troubled waters at the end of the Tokugawa period; and (2) the feudal rulers (both *Bakufu* and clan), always on the brink of bankruptcy and anxious to increase their income, chiefly for military purposes, adopt capitalist methods of production and to a considerable degree they become tinged with the capitalist outlook. *Samurai* frequently sought shelter in *chōnin* families and were among the first organizers of industry in post-Restoration Japan. Already, before the Restoration one notes a blurring and breaking down of the old class lines, the uneven fusion of one wing of the feudal ruling class, the anti-*Bakufu* leaders, with the more powerful merchants, and the absorption of *chōnin* into high official positions as symbolized by their newly assumed badge of authority, the *samurai's* two swords. This was a portent even in Tokugawa times of that union of the "yen and the sword" which has characterized not only Meiji but contemporary Japan. This amalgamation of classes at the end of the *Bakufu* period clearly foreshadowed the breakdown of the rigid caste-hierarchy so elaborately erected by the Tokugawa administrators, yet it would be an exaggeration to say that this fusion was consciously anti-feudal. It was most assuredly anti-*Bakufu* and it represented a concerted political movement directed against the Tokugawa hegemony, but it probably did not imply any conscious desire to uproot the feudal system. On the contrary it was to a great extent a movement designed to shake off the dead hand of conservatism and lethargy so characteristic of later Tokugawa rule, and to accomplish the vitally necessary reforms without precipitating any cataclysmic changes in the social structure. Thus one might say that the Meiji Restoration does not connote so much a complete reversal of pre-Restoration policy in trade, industry and diplomacy as a thorough house-cleaning which permitted the more rapid and effective working-out of tendencies already visible in the closing, decades of the Tokugawa era.[1] The rubbish cluttering up the house was the ornate but fusty feudal trappings of the Tokugawa caste system which had to be thrown away, and in the process of renovation

Copyright © University of British Columbia 1960. Reprinted with permission of the publisher from *Japan's Emergence as a Modern State: Political and Economic Problems of the Meiji Period. I.P.R. Inquiry Series* by E. Herbert Norman (Institute of Pacific Relations: New York 1940).

the windows were thrown wide open, allowing the air of Western science and culture to blow in and revivify the atmosphere of age-old exclusion. The revolutionary aspect of the late *Bakufu* period was typified by the incessant *jacquerie*[2] which might be said to have been the *motive* power behind the anti-feudal movement. True, it lacked consciousness of its goal but it so shook the foundations of the old structure that, combined with the threat from abroad and the political activity of lower *samurai* and *ronin*, these revolts of ever widening extent underlined the crying need for a new regime capable of winning the loyalty of all classes and of solving the chronic agrarian problem, if society was not to descend into worse decay and anarchy. The lower *samurai* — often *chōnin* in the position of *samurai* — were the most conscious leaders in the movement to overthrow the *Bakufu*, and they, together with the younger *kuge*[3], were the most consistent champions of Restoration.

Origin of the modern bureaucrat in the movement for clan reform: example of Choshu

It now becomes germane to an analysis of the Meiji Restoration to illustrate the political aspect of this fusion of *chōnin* with one section of the feudal ruling class in which the leadership of the lower *samurai* can be most clearly seen. Those *samurai* who were not blinded by caste-prejudice were often the most active spirits in steering clan policy toward mercantilism. This entailed a monopoly over trade with a view to the accumulation of specie in order to begin manufacturing, especially of armaments in a word, to shift the economic basis of the daimiate to merchant capitalism.[4] The clan bureaucrats, whether of pure *samurai* or *chōnin* origin, virtually took over clan affairs, and by serious economic rather than moral methods attempted to increase the depleted clan treasury and to raise money for the struggle against the *Bakufu*. The most advanced among this group went so far as to promote the adoption of Western military science, meeting of course the blind opposition of clan authorities steeped in the old, time-honored military usage. We can understand the unique position held by the bureaucracy and the military clique in modern Japan if we examine this trend in Choshu, the clan most adamant in its hostility to the *Bakufu* and one of the highest in the councils of the Meiji Government.

Admirably situated in respect to trade and foreign intercourse, Choshu was one of the most "advanced" of the various anti-*Bakufu* clans in its policy and administration. The nominal leaders of the clan at the end of the *Bakufu*, were the two Mori, Motonori (1839–96) and his adoptive father Yoshichika (died 1871). They were driven into temporary retirement as expiation for the riotous turbulence of Choshu men in Kyoto which reached its climax in the bloody *émeute* in the summer of 1863. On this occasion, Choshu *ronin* and *samurai* had tried to seize the person of the Emperor to extricate him, as they would say, from the clutches of traitors, the Tokugawa politicians. Without going into the complexities of clan politics, suffice it to say that the clan was split into two factions — the party of the Vulgar View (*Zokuronto*) which was conservative, and the party of the Enlightened View (*Kaimeito*) which was radical. After first experiencing defeat, the latter party finally emerged victorious from this clan feud and annihilated the leaders of the conservative party. It then immediately acted as the *de facto* leader of the clan, determined its policy toward Shogunate and Court, and re-organized the military system against the punitive expedition which the

Shogun was preparing to launch in 1864. Just prior to that however, Choshu, which had been the most vocal in its demand to expel the barbarian, suffered a severe bombardment at Shimonoseki from the combined fleets of England, France, Holland and America. This proved a turning-point in Choshu policy and even in Japanese history. The party in power, the party of the Enlightened View, quickly made its peace with the foreign powers toward which they bore no grudge for such a rough lesson in *realpolitik*, and now concentrated all their resources in opposing the *Bakufu*.[5]

At this critical juncture a young *samurai* came to the fore in clan affairs, Takasugi Shinsaku (1839–67), probably the outstanding Japanese military genius of his day. Although he died prematurely from consumption on the eve of the Restoration, those closely associated with him were among the great names of the Meiji era: Omura Masujiro (1869) and Hirozawa Sanetomi (1871), both ministers in the Meiji Government who were assassinated, Shinagawa Yajiro, Kido Takayoshi (1878), Ito Hirobumi, Inouye Kaoru, Yamada Akiyoshi and Yamagata Kyosuke (later Prince Yamagata Aritomo).

Takasugi brilliantly outmaneuvered the Shogun's forces, and in the campaigns of 1864–65, punctured what little remained of the *Bakufu*'s prestige. His instrument in this was the *Kiheitai* (literally, shock or surprise troops), a band of volunteer soldiers recruited and trained by Takasugi and his lieutenants. The revolutionary element in this *Kiheitai* lay in the fact that many of the rank and file and lower officers were drawn from the non-military classes, well-to-do peasants, small townsmen, and of course *ronin* of all shades . . .

By routing the feudal levies of the Shogun, the *Kiheitai* first demonstrated that the *samurai* was not the only man of fighting caliber in Japan, a concept which cut at the root of preceding history and tradition. In this sense the *Kiheitai* was the precursor of general conscription enacted in 1873. Secondly, the *Kiheitai* gave scope to men of talent from the ranks of commoners, whether merchant or rich peasant, enlisting their loyalty and above all their financial support so necessary for the purchase of modern weapons.[6] The *Kiheitai* also produced the first example of the modern Japanese military bureaucrat. The effectiveness of the military reforms instituted by the Choshu *Kiheitai*, makes it easier to understand the function and history of the military bureaucracy in Japan. This Choshu plebeian army, composed of poor *samurai, ronin,* peasants and townsmen backed by good burgher gold, led by a young *samurai* from the lower strata of the warrior class, presents a microcosmic replica of the similar social intertwining and interrelationship which characterized government and society in Meiji Japan. In fact we might say that the struggle which went on within Choshu on the eve of the Restoration — the struggle of the Enlightened View Party against the Vulgar View Party — was a rehearsal *in parvis* of that nation-wide struggle fought out at the time of the Restoration, between the emergent forces of Westernization and modernization on the one hand and of conservatism and isolation on the other. The victory of the Enlightened View Party in Choshu was an earnest of the triumph of those same forces on the national stage in 1867–68 and the years following. The great clans which joined together for the overthrow of the *Bakufu* were precisely those which were marked by the greatest development in commerce and staple industries as organized under the clan monopoly system where Western capital was most deeply implanted. Of these clans, Satsuma, Choshu, Tosa and Hizen were most conspicuous for their economic strength based upon the new mercantilist policy described above. Staple industries included handicrafts, sugar-refining, tobacco and rice monopoly. In Satsuma there were a comparatively profitable mining industry, textile mills and trade monopoly. In Tosa, where *ryogaeya* or money changers abounded, money economy had penetrated deeply into the feudal interstices; moreover it was famous for its production of paper and for such diversified agrarian products as indigo, the wax tree (*rhus succedanea* or *haze*, Japanese) as well as for its rigid trade monopoly. Choshu, situated astride the straits of Shimonoseki through which all marine transport between Korea, China and Osaka had to pass, was able by means of trade and transport monopoly to accumulate considerable wealth. The Saga clan in Hizen was the center of the Arita porcelain industry, and also one of the pioneers in the manufacture of guns under Dutch instruction (1842) and also in the use of the reverberatory furnace (1850).[7]

In these clans the *Kinno* or Loyalist party, the clearest expression of anti-*Bakufu* feeling, had been making steady headway until it finally dominated clan policy. This political trend was accompanied by a radical reform in clan organization, roughly on the model of Choshu, carried out by the younger *samurai* and clan *goyonin* (financial assistants and advisers) who became the clan bureaucrats, able, disinterested, domineering, devoted to the Imperial House and with a deep-dyed military psychology. This clan reform which signalized the defeat of the old clan leadership, traditionalist and parochial to the core, drawing together the other clans of a similar tendency, represented the first stage in the process of centralization which was one of the greatest accomplishments of the Meiji Government.

In the economic sphere these reforms, while rescuing the clan finances from bankruptcy, strengthened rather than weakened the monopoly system, and so placed heavier burdens on the peasantry and artisan class.[8] These clan reforms, so far from tending to emancipate the peasantry and in this way create an internal market for manufactured goods, kept prices up by the monopoly system and by the practice of commuting rice tribute into money, as well as by levying fresh extortions which aggravated agrarian distress. Thus it is no mere coincidence that the peasant revolts were most bitter and prolonged in the domain of these rich anti-*Bakufu* clans where merchant capital was strong and where factory industry was beginning to take root on a limited scale.[9] To suppress such revolts the *daimyo* had to call on the *samurai* who, accordingly, for all their growing economic distress felt closer to the governing class than to the rebellious peasantry. This *samurai* psychology is apparent also in the turmoil of the early Meiji.[10] It would be wrong to believe that the increase in the fortunes of a few leading *daimyo* by reason of the shift from the earlier agrarian to a mercantile policy turned them either into modern entrepreneurs or their peasants into independent farmers. But this trend illustrates two remarkable phenomena: first, the stunting of the growth of a capitalist class and its consequent dependence on a section of the feudal ruling class, and second, the social transformation from a feudal to a capitalist economy carried out with the minimum of social change in agrarian relations. These clan reforms were accomplished, not through the momentum of popular revolt nor by the participation of the people's deputies in the clan government, but by a handful of military bureaucrats whose political inheritance was autocratic or paternalistic and whose insight taught them the need both for sweeping military and economic changes in the face of the foreign menace and for an absolutist centralized government as the only instrument able to undertake these tasks swiftly and decisively in the face of continued social unrest. The logic of their position dictated to them the creed of "a firm hand at the helm" or in other words an enlightened absolutism. Hence from the first, even during the transitional years, Japan experienced no liberal era. The only magnetic force capable of holding together the centrifugal atoms of feudalism was the Throne, and the only agents in a position to perform the gigantic task of reconstruction were the clan bureaucrats of the four great "outside" clans, men such as Kido Takayoshi (sometimes known as Katsura Kogoro), Inouye Kaoru, Maebara Issei and Hirozawa Saneomi, all of Choshu; Okubo Toshimichi, Saigo Takamori, Kuroda Kiyotaka and Terajima Munemori of Satsuma; Itagaki Taisuke, Goto Shojiro and Sasaki Takayuki of Tosa; Okuma Shigenobu, Eto Shimpei and Oki Takato of Hizen — together with a few *kuge*, notably Iwakura Tomomi and Sanjo Saneyoshi. Here we have returned to the postulate whence we set forth at the beginning of the chapter, that the political leadership in the Meiji revolution was in the hands of the lower *samurai* but that the economic propulsion behind it was the growing money power of the big merchants, such as the Mitsui, Sumitomo, Konoike, Ono and Yasuda.

The agrarian movement in the early Meiji Period (1868–1877)

But, the reader asks, where do the peasantry, the bulk of the population, fit into this picture? Although the Meiji Restoration represents an epoch-making change from feudalism into modern capitalism, it would be an historical misunderstanding to expect the appearance of a full-grown industrialized society on the morrow of this successful political revolution which first and foremost removed the chief obstacle to the sprouting of the seeds of capitalism already germinating within feudalism. In a country so tardily awakened from its isolation and feudal sluggishness, where nature had been niggardly in resources and where capital accumulation was meager, after the establishment of a centralized state a long transitional period was required for the initiation of industry under government auspices, for the setting up of military defenses based on this industry, for tariff revision and above all for the liquidation of such social problems as *samurai* unemployment and peasant discontent. This political revolution cleared away the feudal underbrush and laid the foundation for a modern industrial society. It was not, however, the victorious outcome of a social revolt of city *sans-culottes* and land-hungry peasants, as in France, but a settlement arrived at by one wing of the feudal class, the great *tozama* with their *samurai* and *goyonin*[11] as spokesmen, and allied to the wealthiest city merchants. This is not to minimize the effect of peasant revolt in loosening the shackles of Tokugawa feudalism, but unlike France these revolts did not succeed in cutting through those bonds, and so the peasant was left relatively unaffected on the immediate morrow of the Restoration . . .

The peasantry, bewildered by the rapid succession of dramatic events leading up to the Restoration, enjoyed no substantial benefit from the new regime. In fact they behaved even more riotously than before, possibly because in some instances vague hopes had been raised by the overthrow of the old regime, hopes that their burden of tribute and debt would be lightened. Promises had been held out by the new Government that all state land (except temple lands) would be divided up among the peasants. But they soon discovered that their burden of rice tribute was not to be lessened, nor was there any question of their receiving allotments from state lands. Disappointed in their expectation of release from the yoke of the old regime, suspicious of the purposes and innovations of the new, the peasantry renewed those revolts which had been characteristic of the last decade. Agrarian revolts reached a crescendo of violence and frequency in the year 1873, after which they decreased until by 1877–8 they became small and inconsequential riots. Thus the year 1877 forms a convenient dividing line in analyzing the significance of peasant revolts in the early Meiji era. Professor Kokusho Iwao makes a striking comparison between the intensity of agrarian unrest in the early Meiji and in the Tokugawa period. He gives the number of revolts in the 265 years of Tokugawa rule as somewhat under 600, while the number for the first decade of the Meiji era (1868–78) is well over 190. The most arresting feature of these early Meiji uprisings is that they were precipitated by two contradictory forces — one revolutionary, that is to say anti-feudal, aimed at the final eradication of feudal privilege over the land and those who worked it, and the other reactionary, in the sense that many of these risings arose from the instinctive opposition of a conservative-minded peasantry toward the innovations of the new government.

Indeed at first glance, many of these revolts appear to be merely demonstrations of resentment against the many aspects of modernization. Tumult and rioting only too often greeted decrees announcing the reform of the calendar, the abolition of the queue, the legalization of Christianity, the emancipation of the *Eta*[12] (outcasts), vaccination, the establishment of government schools, conscription, the land survey, numbering of houses and the like. Peasants frequently were excited by wild rumors that the numbering of houses was a preliminary measure to the abduction of their wives and daughters; that the phrase "blood-taxes" in the conscription decree of 1873 was to be taken literally, so that in joining the army their blood would be drawn and shipped abroad to make dye for scarlet blankets; that the telephone and telegraph lines would be used to transmit the blood; that the children herded into the new schools would also have their blood extracted. But if we look closer we notice that while these old wives' tales and naive misunderstandings of the healthy attempt of the government to modernize the nation acted as the *spark* which ignited the uprisings, somehow the *flames* always spread to the quarter of the richest usurer, the land-grabbing village headman, the tyrannous official of the former feudal lord. When the new calendar was introduced, consequent indignation could easily arise from the not unjustifiable fear that money-lenders would take advantage of the reform to juggle accounts to their own advantage. The feeling against the school system arose possibly because government schools might necessitate an increase in the local tax. Conscription meant less hands to help on the farm, and although it flattered the peasant to be told he was fit to bear arms, it also insulted the *samurai* who, as we have seen were often in a position to set themselves at the head of a peasant uprising in order to direct its course against the government which dared to infringe upon their exclusive military prerogative. The objection to the land survey is even more obvious, when we learn that of its total expense of 40,000,000 yen, 35,000,000 yen was paid by the proprietors. The reform whereby local lords yielded political power in their clans and were supplanted by governors appointed by the central government, was, like other reforms, received with mixed feelings by the peasantry. If the local lord had a reputation for benevolence, the peasants strenuously objected to his withdrawal in favor of an unknown appointee; but in those fiefs where the lord was odious to the population, his final departure was a signal for an outburst of joy and relief and even for an assault upon his castle. Other outbreaks such as those directed against the abolition of the outcast *Eta*, against toleration of Christianity and against vaccination, are clearly manifestations of prejudice which centuries of superstition, medieval bigotry and Buddhist indoctrination had burned into the consciousness of the people.

According to Professor Kokusho, the fundamental underlying cause of peasant revolt in this period must be distinguished from the casual or accidental, both of which are so closely intermingled. Even such a cursory survey of agrarian unrest before 1877 shows us of what a strange mixture of reaction and revolution, of superstition and shrewd estimate of class interest it was compounded. Though its weight was in the main thrown against the usurer, the rice-broker, the village headman or the harsh official representing the lord, in short against all personifications of feudal oppression, it had undeniably the other darker side, that feudal side which many *samurai*, chagrined at their failure to receive patronage or official position from the government and dreaming of a return to the old warrior-dominated society, were able to exploit in their own campaign against the government, thanks to their knowledge of peasant psychology.[13] What is common to the peasant movement of these ten years was a stubborn antagonism to rent, usury and exorbitant taxation. The basis for the intrusion of anti-feudal revolts from the pre-Restoration into the post-Restoration period can be summed up in this way; the burden of feudal dues and taxation, even after the surrender of the clan land-registers to the Government in 1869, was still maintained if not actually increased, with the result that peasant protest was intensified until the tax reduction in 1877, when the agrarian movement took another path. As far as the peasant was concerned then, the Meiji Government, although holding out hopes of improvement, actually left him untouched for several years after the Restoration. In fact we might say that whereas under feudalism peasant dues to the lord though high were traditional and thus subject to some flexibility (for in bad years a lord might not collect his full quota of the land revenue), in the early years of the Meiji the extremely high rate of exaction which existed under late feudalism — that is about 60 to 70 per cent of the produce — was legalized, standardized on a national scale, and strictly enforced regardless of all circumstances . . .

*   *   *

2. Early industrialization

Before industrialization on a nation-wide scale can take place, there must exist two prerequisites, an adequate supply both of capital and of labor. In expanded form these fundamental prerequisites can be conveniently summarized as, (1) a sufficiently high level in the production and circulation of commodities and in the division of labor, (2) a certain accumulation of capital in the hands of the producers, and (3) the existence of an adequately large body of free labor — free in the sense of being untrammeled by any ownership of the means of production and hence ready to offer themselves in the labor market. To grasp the distinguishing features of Japanese industrialization we can perhaps do no better than trace these three preconditions for the rise of industrial capitalism as they existed in Japan . . .

Production and circulation of commodities

Although rice was still the *standard* for exchange, money had become predominant as the *means* of exchange, especially in towns and cities. What made this great trading activity possible was production for the market, that is production over and above the needs of the producer which naturally kept pace with the steady rise in the productivity of agriculture and with the advance in the division of labor. The demand for goods was stimulated in turn by the rapid growth of cities attendant upon the concentration of *samurai* in castle towns and the brisk movements of transport and trade activities which were connected with the *sankin-kotai* system. How great this demand for goods must have been can be surmised from the population of Edo, which was, at the turn of the eighteenth century, probably the greatest city in the world, numbering from 1,300,000 to 1,400,000; Osaka, even in 1665, had a population estimated at 268,760; and Kyoto, the busy hive of skilled handicraft trades in Japan, was considered by the observant traveler, Dr. Engelbert Kaempfer in 1691 to be the greatest manufacturing center in Japan with the most diverse trades and industries.

Division of labor

The division of labor, which Adam Smith maintained was the chief cause of increasing its productivity, had advanced far enough in this period for there to be a distinct line of demarcation separating the production of raw materials and the manufacture of commodities. Specialization was noticeable in the crafts so that the builder of a house would have to secure the services of the craft guilds of carpenters, sawyers, painters, plumbers, roof-thatchers, bricklayers, plasterers, masons and mat-layers. In time, of course, the nature of guild exclusiveness became a brake on productivity which thus required their abolition (which was effected once and for all after the Restoration); but what is important for the division of labor in this period was the sharp difference between the producer and the seller of goods, the former organized into craft or workmen's guilds, the latter into the monopolistic wholesalers, the *Tokumi Donya*, and the *Kabu Nakama* or Federation of Guilds.

Together with this went regional specialization, replacing the old clan self-sufficiency, never complete even in remote times. Yamagata Hoshu wrote in 1820, "There are provinces that abound in rice, others in grain, others in cloth, and still others in paper and timber and so forth. Thus, most of the provinces have come to produce one or two kinds of goods in large quantities and do not make other things themselves."

The division of labor, was, however, restricted by the prevalence of widespread household industry dominated by trading capital and including the manufacture of porcelain, lacquer, silk, cotton, brass, and articles of wood and bamboo, straw matting, *sake*, and *shoyu*[14]. The chief commodities produced for the market were largely in the hands of peasant or poor *samurai* households which worked at such tasks to supplement their meager family income. The invasion of cheap foreign commodities, especially cotton yarn, together with the products of Japanese machine manufacture, ruined the household industry of thousands of these primitive hand producers, thus accelerating the division of labor and the creation of the home market.

Accumulation of capital

As to the second condition, the accumulation of capital in the hands of producers, all our evidence points to the conclusion that the chief agents in the accumulation of capital during late feudalism were traders and usurers, and in this connection the role of the Osaka *fudasadhi* (rice brokers and agents) was particularly important. Commercial capital, severely hampered by Tokugawa isolation, had to batten exclusively upon internal trade, which was as highly organized as the restrictions of feudal economy permitted. Chief of these restrictions was the overlapping of agriculture and industry (i.e., household industries) and the consequent narrowing of the home market.

Commercial capital as it existed in Tokugawa Japan was accumulated in the hands of a few great traders and privileged money-lenders, like the Mitsui, Ono and Konoike families, and one can estimate roughly the extent of such accumulation from the inventory of the huge fortune confiscated by the *Bakufu* from Yodoya Saburoyemon, the great rice merchant in Osaka during the Genroku period (1688–1702).[15] We know that a few merchant princes under the protection of the *Bakufu* and powerful feudal lords succeeded in accumulating a respectable pile if we may judge by the size of *goyokin* (forced loans). But barred as they were from any chance to reap profits from overseas adventure, or to feed upon colonial plunder and trade which enriched the great companies and merchants of Western Europe under the mercantile system, Japanese merchants had to be content with working the very limited market for all it was worth in collaboration with the *Bakufu* or clan governments, and with speculating on the rice market, in general, rather modest operations which retarded the rate of accumulation when compared to the great trading nations of Europe. We might say that Tokugawa policy had so constricted Japanese mercantilism as to prevent it from reaching its full-blossomed, most profitable and characteristic stage, namely that period when monopoly trade between an overseas colony and its metropolis is regulated to profit the latter at the cost of the former . . .

European and Japanese mercantilism compared

In pre-Tokugawa Japan foreign trade, piracy, even the beginning of colonization — e.g., Yamada Nagamasa (1578–1633) in Siam — and above all Hideyoshi's Korean expedition pointed to a policy of mercantilism which corresponded to the trading, piratical and colonizing activities of contemporary Europe and England in particular. The long years of seclusion thus did not merely hamper Japanese economic growth; it retarded it both absolutely and relatively so that, as Mr. Orchard justly observes, 18th century Japan ought to be compared, not to 18th century England on the eve of its great industrial revolution, but rather to 16th century Tudor England, overwhelmingly agricultural and possessing widespread domestic handicraft industries. Even so, the comparison is still generous toward Tokugawa Japan, because Tudor England had already laid the foundations of her overseas trade (in the great trading companies of the 16th century), and of her naval expansion under Henry VII; she had even begun to acquire colonies (Newfoundland, discovered and claimed in

1497), and by successfully challenging Spanish naval supremacy she was well on the way to securing control of vital trade routes to the Indies and the Americas. To express it briefly, the Meiji Restoration had to begin where Hideyoshi left off. But since the 250 years of isolation had left deep marks on Japanese economy and society by stunting its national growth, Meiji Japan had to wrestle with those accumulated disabilities inherited from Tokugawa practices. The Restoration was not merely a continuation of Hideyoshi's policy of trade expansion, for the simple reason that in the 19th century Japan was faced with a struggle for existence as an independent power against the menace of foreign capital. It was a race to overtake the advanced Western nations with their machine technology and armaments, and Japanese economic and even political independence were at stake; Japan had to enter the race with the handicap of a tariff fixed by the unequal treaty system which lasted for half a century. Meiji economic policy was a blend of the old mercantilism, with its state protection, and the new style monopoly. This new monopoly was linked organically to the pre-existing mercantile monopoly in Tokugawa Japan so that to a large extent the same favored merchant families with banking interests now became privileged directors of banks and industries . . . In other words, one might say that the mercantile system with its monopoly of trade and reliance on the absolutist state (as in 16th–17th century France and England) was the crutch with which capitalism learned to walk. Grown to full strength, European capitalism discarded the crutch, absolute state power, and finding it a hindrance, turned against it and destroyed it. In Japan the immature capitalist class was unable to dispense with this crutch of absolutist power and relied upon it even more completely in the Meiji era than it had under the *han* or *Bakufu* regimes.

The feverish haste of the Meiji leaders to accomplish in a generation what had taken other nations a century or more to do was now to be checked by the gulf which separated Japanese primitive feudal technique from the industrial technique of the most advanced nations. To leap over this gulf, rather than to plod along the intervening valley road taken by pioneer nations would require time to train a great body of skilled labor and to amass a large store of capital. Japan still lacked the former in the early Meiji era, and as for the latter, only a very few wealthy families had a sufficient accumulation to enter the field as entrepreneurs in factory industries, a condition which incidentally favored monopoly or highly centralized capital right from the beginning of Japanese capitalism. But these few financial magnates who were, as we have seen, very close to the Government, showed hesitation in risking their capital in enterprises which demanded at the very outset such an immense outlay of capital, and before there was any clear indication of the profitability of such undertakings. The lag in distance between primitive Japanese technique and the best Western methods of production created very hard conditions for the genesis and growth of private capital in industry. Although a wide field for industrial investment lay fallow, the merchant princes were reluctant to become pioneers in working this field; so the government with the aid at first of *goyokin* (loans) from these same magnates and together with its limited revenues, chief of which was the land tax, had itself to develop industry. Thus, early Japanese capitalism may be described as a hothouse variety, growing under the shelter of state protection and subsidy. Big private capital preferred to remain in trade, banking and credit operations, particularly in the safe and lucrative field of government loans, while small capital had no inducement to leave the countryside where trade, usury and, above all, high rent — averaging almost sixty per cent of the tenant's[16] crop — prevented capital invested in agriculture from flowing into industrial channels.

Predominance of banking capital in Japan

Banking capital, while growing out of all proportion to industrial capital, by the end of the 19th century gave a striking example of concentration, in this way continuously strengthening the position of the financial oligarchy or *Zaibatsu*. In Japan the concentration of capital, as distinct from its accumulation, was accelerated by the Government's policy of subsidy and artificial encouragement. The speed with which concentration of capital was affected in Japan came from (1) the generally low level of accumulated capital, (2) the need for large amounts of capital to begin industrial enterprises run on the latest Western scale, (3) the adoption of the joint-stock company system in Japan right from the beginning of industrialization (1869, the *Kawase Kaisha*) and (4) competition with advanced foreign countries also favoring a high concentration of capital. In those industries which turned out products to compete either in the home or international markets with the products of other capitalist countries, trusts or cartels were formed in the very course of the industrial revolution, notably in the textiles in the 1880's. Japanese concentration of capital, of course, has not been unique in its tendency to grow through big capital swallowing small especially in times of economic crisis. This is the most characteristic method by which the *Zaibatsu* or financial clique comprising notably the Mitsui, Mitsubishi, Sumitomo and Yasuda companies has strengthened itself in recent times. The absorption in 1927 of the Suzuki Company by the Mitsui is an outstanding example. But as Professor Allen points out, their impregnable position lies, not just in their size or their close government connections, but in their pre-eminence both in finance on the one hand and industry and commerce on the other. Thus this triple aspect gives them an immense competitive advantage. But the citadel of their strength is finance, the foundations of which were firmly laid in the early Meiji period.

In Japan, banking and loan capital, leaning heavily upon the state for support, was used in turn by the government to create those branches of industry requiring a greater capital investment, while at the same time small capital tied to domestic industry had to get along as best it could with under-capitalization and high interest rates. Small companies would use up their capital on hand in building and equipping a factory and then find that to commence operations they had to resort to the banks for a loan. The rate of interest at the end of the 19th century was as high as ten, twelve, fifteen or even eighteen per cent, while interest on deposits was seven to eight per cent. Unable to meet their financial obligations on such terms, these small companies by the end of their first year became mortgaged to the banks. In this way small and middle capitalists were obliged to undertake only those types of enterprise which were left over from the sphere of interest of big capital, such as the small, peculiarly "Japanese" industries, porcelain, silk, lacquer, straw, *sake*, *shoyu* and the like, which require less capital equipment and do not have to compete with foreign production. But in time these small industries have fallen more and more into the power of banking and loan capital, a trend which has continued up to the present day.

In most nations, during the formative stage of capitalism banking capital has usually been distinct from industrial capital, but in Japan industrial capital did not develop independently; the state initiated industrialization, developed it and turned it over at amazingly low rates to a few private enterprises, mostly representatives of the great banking houses. In this process no new class of industrial capitalist was created; what took place was only the strengthening of banking and usury capital (including the more affluent nobility) and its partial transformation into industrial capital. This smothering of the seeds of an independent class of industrialists is a reflection of the immature, hot-house character of capitalism in Japan and of its serious weakness in this respect compared to the strongest capitalist nations. Here again it may be helpful to emphasize the effect of high rent in agriculture acting as a strong inducement to keep private capital tied to the land rather than invested in industrial enterprise with its greater risks and its lower return on the money invested.

Role of foreign capital in early Japanese industrialization

We have noted the foreign menace to Japan during the chaotic years at the close of the *Bakufu*, a danger not so much of military invasion as of the more insidious penetration of foreign capital within the economic strongholds of the nation, which might easily dwarf or strangle its free development as in China. Although future economic development was already jeopardized by the unequal treaties negotiated by the *Bakufu* whereby Japan's tariff autonomy was forfeited for half a century, these leaders did their utmost to avoid further entanglement in the meshes of foreign capital. Therefore in spite of the anemia of domestic capital they resisted the temptation to seek heavy foreign loans which might well have compromised the nation's economic independence.

From the Restoration until the end of the century only two foreign loans were contracted. The first was a loan of £1,000,000 (to be exact, £913,000) at 9 per cent floated in London in 1870 to help in the construction of the first railway, from Yokohama to Tokyo. The second was also floated in London in 1873, a loan of £2,400,000 with interest at 7 per cent, and was intended to help the government meet the cash needs for pension commutation and capitalization. The first loan was redeemed in 1881, the second in 1897, and until a London syndicate purchased in that same year (1897) 43 million yen of bonds through a contract with the Bank of Japan no foreign capital was introduced into the country. In view of the desperate need for working capital in the early Meiji period we cannot but ask why no further efforts were made to secure foreign capital. Perhaps the most authoritative answer was given by Sakatani Yoshiro, writing in 1897 as Director of the Bureau of Computation of the Department of Finance, and later one of the financial leaders in the Government. He gives four reasons. The first was the depreciation of non-convertible notes. Despite the Government's attempt to cancel these non-convertible notes, they kept increasing in volume until they reached dangerous proportions in 1877, when the Government had to increase the issue of notes to meet the huge expenses incurred in suppressing the Satsuma Revolt, with the result that in the next year the notes depreciated and became subject to constant fluctuation. Furthermore, the excess of imports over exports precipitated a heavy efflux of specie. In 1886 the Government began the conversion of

132

notes until the difference between silver and notes disappeared. This situation made Japan an unattractive field for foreign investment.

The second reason was the difference in monetary standards. Foreign nations were on the gold standard — Japan was on a *de jure* silver standard from 1871 to 1878; thereafter, bi-metallic, until October 1899, when it went on the gold standard. Thus the variations in the ratio between gold and silver made foreign capital cautious about investing in Japan.

Thirdly, the unequal treaty system did not allow foreigners to engage in business in the interior, while extraterritoriality made commercial and financial relations between Japanese and foreigners extremely complicated and so acted as a deterrent to the free import of capital.

Fourth and most decisive, was the fear of both government and people of the dangers arising from a late-awakening nation's dependence on foreign capital. Our authority, Sakatani, mentions specifically the unhappy experiences of Egypt and Turkey, which had mismanaged foreign capital introduced into their countries and so had invited foreign intervention. Those keen observers of past and present events, the Meiji statesmen, were determined not to fall into a similar error. By the end of the century none of these four reasons, some of them appreciated by potential foreign investors and the last by Japanese statesmen, was any longer valid, so that the Government had no fear of foreign capital. But by that time (1897) the flotation of 200 million yen worth of railway bonds was largely subscribed by Japanese capitalists who were now strong enough to absorb the lion's share of such gilt-edged securities.

How deeply the national consciousness was stirred over the question of foreign loans can be seen from the words of Viscount Inouye Masaru regarding railway development. "To be more precise, the people generally disliked the railway because of the heavier burden it would throw upon their shoulders by causing additional taxes. Many even of the governmental officials stood on the side of opposition, some of them crying out 'to make (sic) a foreign loan is to sell the country.' They did not understand what a foreign loan was."

The result of the prudence shown by Meiji statesmen in regard to foreign capital was to accentuate certain characteristics of Japanese capitalism: the predominant position of state enterprise supported by the financial oligarchy, the retardation of the tempo of industrialization, and the heavier tax burdens on the population, particularly on the agricultural community.

The history and influence of strategic industries

With the fate of China before its eyes as an ever-present warning of foreign menace, and with the tumultuous years following the war for the Restoration adding considerable danger to the regime from agrarian discontent and *samurai* insurrection, the Meiji Government devoted its energies to the centralization and modernization of the standing army and the police system. These forces for defense against foreign invasion and internal disturbance had begun to be built up haphazardly in the last few years of the *Bakufu*, when under the impact of foreign relations, the Shogunate itself undertook to acquire new military equipment on the French model, Satsuma on the

English, Kii on the German, and other clans again on the Dutch. The armies of the clan-coalition which overthrew the Shogunate were enlarged and reformed on the French model, while the navy with strong Satsuma influence adopted the English system from the first. This army, originally composed exclusively of ex-*samurai* and enlarged by the conscription of 1873, was the core of the future standing army. At the same time, the police system was hurriedly unified and enlarged, being of vital importance in maintaining law and order in the critical transitional years and in serving as the bulwark of absolutism in its struggle against liberalism in later years. The armed forces, reorganized after the Meiji Restoration, were merely a skeleton without flesh and blood and would have been helpless without modern industries and a transportation system. Consequently, since the problem of defense was foremost in the last few years of the *Bakufu* and the first years of the Meiji era, the keenest minds were concerned with such questions as the creation of trade and industry, not for their own sake, but rather to establish those industries which one might conveniently call *strategic*, as the *sine qua non* of a modern army and navy, the creation of which was the central problem of the day. To put the sequence of emphasis in logical order, the Meiji leaders thought somewhat as follows: "What do we most need to save us from the fate of China? A modern army and navy. On what does the creation and maintenance of modern armed forces depend? Chiefly on heavy industries, engineering, mining, shipbuilding, in a word *strategic* industries." Thus the first stage of industrialization in Japan was inextricably interwoven with the military problem, and it fixed the pattern for its later evolution. This pattern was indeed already apparent before the end of the Shogunate.

Western military industries were first introduced by such clans as Satsuma, Hizen, and Choshu. The first reverberatory furnace (used in the making of cannon) was set up by the Saga clan (Hizen) in 1850 and was ready for use in 1852. Cannon had been made by that same clan on the Dutch model as early as 1842. Reverberatory furnaces were built in rapid succession in Satsuma (1853), Mito (1855) and also for the Shogunate (1853), thanks to the labors of its greatest military reformer, Egawa Tarozaemon whose services were not valued at their true worth by the obscurantist *Bakufu*. In Satsuma a factory equipped with machinery for cannon-boring was completed in 1854; two iron-smelters were built in 1852 and six ships equipped with cannon between 1853 and 1856. In Choshu an iron foundry was first built in 1854, and a shipyard where cannon could be mounted on ships was opened in 1857. An iron foundry and gunsmithy were built in 1840 by the Mito clan on the Dutch model under the supervision of Tani Zenshiro at Kanzaki. In 1855, after surmounting great difficulties in securing suitable materials and without having seen any of the models introduced into southern Japan, this clan constructed a reverberatory furnace, following the instructions of Dutch textbooks.

In 1855, the *Bakufu* commenced work on an iron foundry completed in 1861; in 1857 it built a steamboat, and in 1865 established with French help the famous Yokosuka Iron Foundry and dockyards. Thus under the necessity of modernizing military industries, the *Bakufu* introduced machine production on a limited scale in the strategic industries.

The Meiji Government inherited the problems of the Tokugawa regime, and accordingly it had first to perfect its military preparations; hence Japanese machine production was cradled during those days of military urgency in the strategic industries. Technology was still at a pre-capitalist stage; the spirit of enterprise among the capitalist class was still timorous, and capital accumulation on a very low level. For these reasons and on strategic grounds as well, it was necessary for the state to undertake the centralization and further development of these industries. The Meiji Government confiscated the *Bakufu*'s military establishments and came forward as the chief entrepreneur in mining and heavy industrial production. For instance the Tokyo arsenal founded by the *Bakufu* and known as the Sekiguchi arsenal was taken over by the new government in 1870. Foreign instructors were engaged in order to raise the technical level of arsenal workers as rapidly as possible, and such institutions as the *Juho Kyoikujo* were established for training in the manufacture of guns. The Osaka arsenal was opened in 1870 with machinery taken from the Nagasaki Iron Foundry belonging formerly to the Shogunate. Foreign instructors for the Yokosuka shipyard had been used even under the *Bakufu*, but the number was increased when these famous shipyards were confiscated by the Meiji Government, which by 1881 was employing 1,861 persons (Japanese) in one of the largest factories in Japan at the time. Other great shipyards in the country were also taken over by the government; the Nagasaki in 1871, later sold to the Mitsubishi; and the Ishikawajima shipyards, first built by the Mito clan in 1854, acquired by the *Bakufu*, then confiscated by the Meiji Government and later, like the Nagasaki shipyards, put up at public sale by the government. Engineering, technical and naval schools were founded with foreign instructors, while the best students were sent abroad to master the technique required in these key industries.

Mining followed much the same lines. The government confiscated all the mines formerly operated by the *Bakufu* and clan governments and later sold the greater part of them to those financial circles close to it. The government's policy has been concisely stated by a Japanese authority: "At that time (the Restoration) ten important mines namely Sado, Miike, Ikuno, Takashima, Ani, Innai, Kamaishi, Nakakosaka, Okatsura and Kosuka were worked by the Government itself to obtain quick development, but after having been fairly started, they were transferred to the hands of private persons. Nowadays all mines except some few of iron and coal which serve some special objects are in private hands." In order to increase production the government employed some of the best foreign experts they could secure.

Transportation and communication were developed at a rapid pace thanks to the restless energy of the Meiji leaders. These activities were jealously watched to safeguard the interests of the state. The history of railway construction in Japan has been told many times; its task of opening up the home market is of particular importance. Although private capital was used in its development, the first lines were built by government enterprise with a loan of £913,000 from London. Toward the end of the century private capital in railways exceeded government, but in 1906 all but narrow-gauge lines were nationalized. Looking at it from the politico-military view, we must note that the railroads were regarded as one of the most useful instruments in national unification, and their strategic value has never been neglected by the military wing of the government. For instance, in 1892 when the law for railway construction was passed establishing the principle of government ownership, a supervisory council was set up; this was called the *Tetsudo Kaigi*, composed of twenty members, several of whom were military men, and its first president, General Kawakami Soroku, was perhaps the greatest strategist of his day. A most interesting example of military strategic considerations overriding commercial motives appears in the discussion regarding the construction of the Nakasendo line traversing mountainous, thinly populated country. Difficulties and expense seemed so great that the plan was temporarily abandoned, and, in the words of the authority on Japanese railroads, Viscount Inouye, "But this was objected to (i.e. abandoning this route) by military men who insisted upon the advantages of the Nakasendo from a strategical point of view. This consideration loomed large from the first in the task of weaving the web of transportation and communication.

One or two references to government documents will illustrate the attention paid to the strategical aspect of the telegraph and telephone systems. In response to request for private ownership of telegraph lines, a proposal urging rejection of the request came to the *Dajokan* (Council of State) on August 2, 1872, which read in part: "In the West there are countries where private lines are established for the purpose of communication; but *the private lines often bring inconvenience in regard to secrecy of Government.* Besides, communications have a bearing on intercourse with other countries, so henceforth it is desirable to put an end to privately-owned lines and in the future make all lines government undertakings." This proposal was accepted. That the value of the telegraph in modern warfare was so precociously grasped by the Meiji government may be seen in the effective use they made of it to outmaneuver the Satsuma rebels in 1877.

Private ownership of telephonic communications was similarly rejected. "At that time (1889), however, the Government was not in a position to open the service for public use, and an attempt was started to set up a private telephonic service. The Government decided, however, in favor of making it an official undertaking as in the case of the Telegraphs, and in 1890 the Telephone Service Regulations went into force."

These few quotations from official or semi-governmental sources are intended to illustrate, not the main objectives in the modernization of the country through new industry, railway and telegraphic communications, but the special attention paid from the first to their *strategic* importance, which in turn arose from the *political necessity* of throwing up a rampart of defense around Japan to ward off the danger of attack which had been hanging over the country ever since the beginning of the 19th century, while at the same time guarding against internal disturbance which might arise from the excessive burdens laid upon the population in paying for this modernization. This condensed and one-sided account of the fostering of the strategic industries does not imply that there was anything sinister in the industrial policy of the early Meiji Government, nor is it intended to prove that modern Japan was planning from the start to embark on foreign conquest. But it is meant to show how political necessity, whether of foreign or internal origin, inevitably made the founders of new Japan sensitive to the strategic aspect of the industrialization of the country. It is to the credit of these Meiji leaders that, understanding the trend of the times, they resolutely set about reshaping the defenses and economic foundations of the country. In contrast we might note the utter incapacity of the Manchu Dynasty to accomplish a similar task in China. It was no fault of the Chinese themselves that they were unable to prevent the Western powers from penetrating the crumbling defenses of their empire; on the contrary, every patriotic attempt to modernize the country met with ruthless dynastic suppression. It is, however, to the lasting shame of the foreign dynasty then ruling over China, that it preferred to make a deal with foreign powers at the expense of national integrity in order to maintain its own precarious position as ruler of an estranged and sullen people. The unpatriotic policy of the Manchu Dynasty is reflected in the Chinese aphorism, "It is better to make a present to friendly states than to give it to your domestic slaves." The logical end of this policy was strikingly seen when China was defeated by Japan in 1894–5. It was then discovered that the revenues marked for the creation of a modern fleet and for national defense had been used by the Old Buddha, the Empress Dowager, and her representative Prince Ch'un, on her pet project, the Summer Palace near Peking. When this Chinese fleet intended for national defense met the Japanese navy, it had only one round of ammunition per gun. This incident vividly illustrates the gulf which separated the policy of the Ch'ing rulers, who thought more of their dynastic security and comfort than of Chinese independence, from the Meiji program of national reconstruction. This contrast might serve to illustrate a fable entitled, "How can foreign rulers ever be patriots?"

Starting point of Japanese industrialization conditioned by military necessity

One aspect of the preceding major point is that in Japan, because of this concern with strategic industries, the normal order of the starting point and succeeding stages of capitalist production was reversed. In the classical type of capitalist development the starting point is the production of consumers goods, chiefly by light industries such as the great textile mills of Lancashire which began to be important in the first quarter of the 18th century. Only when the light industries are nearing maturity does the production of capital goods become significant. Heavy industries in England did not assume importance comparable to the light branch until the invention of the lathe at the end of the 18th century. This normal order of transition from light to heavy industry was reversed in Japan. Before the first introduction of cotton spinning machines in Japan in 1866, even before the importation of foreign fabrics, engineering works and arsenals had been established. Cannon were cast as early as 1844 in Mito, and engineering works were established, as we have seen, in 1856 for military and naval purposes in southern Japan. Reverberatory furnaces, arsenals, foundries and shipyards were built in Satsuma, Saga, Choshu and also in the *Bakufu* domain in the fifties. The first silk mills to be equipped with modern machinery were not built until 1870 with the filature of Maebashi, on the Italian model, and the French model mill at Tomioka in 1872, with Italian and French technical supervisors.

This reversed order brought about a certain deformity in Japanese technological growth. From the first the strategic military industries were favored by the government, and technologically they were soon on a level with the most advanced Western countries. We have noted how the arsenals in Nagasaki were originally under Dutch supervision, the Yokosuka shipyard arsenal and iron works under French, and other shipyards under English care. These foreign technicians trained the Japanese so that in time native workers were technically as literate as their foreign tutors. In the textile industries foreign managers and assistants were also employed: English in the Kagoshima spinning mill, French in Tomioka and Fukuoka, Swiss or Italian in the Maebashi filatures. For training in engineering, government technical schools were established with foreign instructors, while the best Japanese students were sent abroad to master the most up-to-date technique, to replace foreign advisers on their return.[17] In this way the military key industries were technically advanced while those industries which were not of strategic value, or did not compete against foreign articles in the international or home market were left in their primitive handicraft stage of development.

It was the Meiji policy to bring under government control the arsenals, foundries, shipyards and mines formerly scattered among various *han* or *Bakufu* domains, then to centralize and develop them until they reached a high level of technical efficiency, while at the same time initiating other strategic enterprises such as chemical industries (sulphuric acid works, glass and cement factories); and the last step was to sell a large portion of these industries to the handful of trusted financial oligarchs. But control over the most vitally strategic enterprises, such as arsenals, shipyards and some sectors of mining was kept in government hands.

Change in industrial policy and the law for the transfer of government factories

This peculiarity in early Japanese industrialization — the predominance of state control over industrial enterprise — is reflected in the manner in which the government, while retaining and strengthening its control over the key industries, disposed of the peripheral or less strategic industries by selling them into private hands. This change in government industrial policy from direct control to indirect protection was symbolized in the promulgation of the *Kojo Harai-Sage Gaisoku* (Regulations or Law on the Transfer of Factories) on November 5, 1880. The reason given by the government for the change of policy appears in the preamble. "The factories established for encouraging industries are now well organized and business has become prosperous, so the Government will abandon its ownership (of factories) which ought to be run by the people." Although the preamble expresses the belief that various enterprises created and fostered by the government could now be turned over to private ownership to operate at a profit, it was admitted elsewhere by Matsukata that many projects under direct state control were not at all profitable, but on the contrary threatened to become a drain on the revenue rather than a source of profit for the exchequer. The gradual disposal of government-owned factories, chiefly, as we shall see, of enterprises not strictly military, left the government free to devote its finances and administrative energy more exclusively to the military or strategic industries. Without making this distinction, an American authority has described this change of policy. "There are few modern industries in Japan today that do not owe their existence to government initiative. In most cases the government has endeavored to withdraw from the industries as soon as possible and to turn them over to private companies, but in some cases that has been impossible and the government has continued as an active agent in manufacturing."

138

The general tendency described above should not be interpreted too strictly, as if the new policy ushered in by the law for the sale of factories divided Japanese industries into two sharply defined groupings, the one related to the armament industries where government control was maintained, and the other embracing all the remaining non-strategic industries which were suddenly to be exposed to the vicissitudes of pure *laissez-faire*. The distinction to be made is rather in the *different form* of paternalism adopted by the government after 1880; that is to say, the government retained paternalism as before, both in the military and non-military enterprises after the sale of government factories, but in a form appropriate to each of these two sectors of industry. The *Noshomusho* (Department of Agriculture and Commerce), established in April 1881, was the government organ fashioned to realize its new policy.

As indicated above, the first transfers were made in the non-military industries. The model cotton-spinning mills set up by the government in 1881 in Hiroshima and Aichi with the most up-to-date English machinery were sold to Hiroshima prefecture (1882) and to the Shinoda Company (1886) respectively. The Shinagawa Glass Factory was handed over to the Ishimura Company in 1885, and the Shimmachi Spinning Mill to the Mitsui in 1887 and the Fukuoka filature to the same company in 1883; the Fukagawa Cement Factory was leased to the Asano Company in 1883, and sold outright the following year.

In the sphere of railroad construction, government ownership of lines was partially abandoned in 1880, and the next year the Nippon Railway Company was founded, receiving generous government loans and subsidies during the most active period of railroad construction.

The role of government subsidy is most spectacularly demonstrated in sea transportation. Long before the law for the sale of factories, the government gave *gratis* to Iwasaki Yataro, the founder of the Mitsubishi Company, the thirteen ships used for military transport in the Formosan expedition of 1874; and this was soon followed by another stroke of fortune for the company, the purchase of the Yubin Jokisen Kaisha, a semi-governmental fleet, for 320,000 yen. In the government's desire to build up a strong mercantile marine it favored this company from the beginning by giving it a yearly subsidy of 250,000 yen, starting from 1875 and lasting for fifteen years. To bolster the monopoly position of this company, the government enacted in 1876 the *Gaikokusen Norikomi Kisoku* (Rules regarding the Boarding of Foreign Ships), thus delivering a crushing blow to the P. and O. hopes of obtaining a monopoly in its newly opened Yokohama–Shanghai service. In the period immediately following the promulgation of the law for the sale of factories the government temporarily abandoned its policy of favoring exclusively the Mitsubishi Company, and with a view to stimulating sea-transport through competition, it established a rival line, the Kyodo Un'yu Kaisha, in 1883, thereby precipitating a bitter struggle with the Mitsubishi. Mobilizing all its financial resources, as well as its wide-spread political agents and allies, the Mitsubishi succeeded in effecting amalgamation with the Kyodo Un'yu Kaisha in 1885, forming the world-famous Nippon Yusen Kaisha. The government now threw its full weight behind this great monopoly firm, granting it a yearly subsidy of 880,000 yen.

After disposing of some of its model factories in the non-military industries, the government gradually turned over some of its mining and shipbuilding enterprises to private hands. Among the most notable transfers in this sphere was the lease (in 1884) and sale a few years later of the great Nagasaki shipyards to the Mitsubishi Company. In 1896 the same company acquired the Ikuno silver mine and the Sado gold mine. The Mitsui Company secured a large share in the confiscated *Bakufu* and *han* enterprises, including textile mills and the famous Miike coal mine. The Furukawa Company bought from the government the Ani gold mine in 1880 and the Innai gold mine in 1894.

One could go on describing the process of transfer of large sections of government-controlled industry into the hands of the financial oligarchy. Among Japanese scholars there is considerable controversy regarding the real motivation of the government in its sale of these industries. But there is no doubt that this policy greatly enhanced the power of the financial oligarchy, especially in view of the ridiculously low prices at which the government sold its model factories. But what is most striking in this process is that, from their favored position as financial supporters of the new regime, a few families, such as the Mitsui, Mitsubishi, Sumitomo, Yasuda as well as the lesser Kawasaki, Furukawa, Tanaka and Asano, have continually strengthened their advantage through such measures as the purchase at low rates of the well-organized government industries. But most important is the position of the smaller circle of financial oligarchs, the *Zaibatsu*, made up of the first four companies in the above list, which, through the tremendous leverage given by their interlocking control over banking on the one hand and industry and commerce on the other, have been able to swallow lesser industrial concerns.

As stated above, the government policy of selling some of its enterprises into the hands of the favored financiers left it free to concentrate on purely military industries which were kept strictly under government control as formerly. After the suppression of the Satsuma Revolt, the government resolutely set about expanding its armament industries; despite retrenchment in other state expenditures in this period (1881–7) there was a sharp increase (over 60%) in military expenditures and (1881–91) naval estimates (200%).

These projects required the import of expensive finished and semi-finished military equipment. But in this sphere of enterprise profit or loss was of no account, and strategic consideration was everything. However, this great expansion in the armament industries had the effect of stimulating the drive for self-sufficiency in Japanese industry. The military industries thus became a mold which shaped the pattern of Japanese heavy industry.

The policy of keeping a tight control upon military industries while maintaining paternalism of appropriate sorts over other types of enterprise has continued down to the present and is one of the most distinctive characteristics of the history of Japanese industrialization. It can be traced back beyond the days of the Restoration to the time when feudal lords took a sudden interest in acquiring modern Western military equipment long before they thought of engaging in other forms of industrial enterprise.

Let us for the moment trace very briefly the effect of this unique government control over key industries as it affects the importance of the bureaucracy.

The key industries and the bureaucracy

The scarcity of accumulated capital in the Tokugawa period, the technical backwardness of Japanese industry, Japan's poverty in raw materials and the restriction on the tariff made it exceedingly difficult for private capital to compete with foreign capital on the home market and, at a later date, on the international market unless it received from the start generous state aid in the form of subsidies. This tendency was strengthened toward the end of the century as other nations advanced from *laissez-faire* to monopoly, creating conditions favorable to state intervention and to the interlocking of state and monopoly capital in Japan. The merging of private and state capital, particularly in those branches of industry close to war economy, such as transport, steel, and machine-making, gave new strength to the bureaucracy, placing it politically on an equal if not superior level to its partner, private monopoly capital. It is generally agreed that in the early Meiji period government-controlled enterprise provided wide scope in the employment of the declassed *samurai* who formed part of the new bureaucracy as managers, administrators and departmental officials . . .

In fine, the features conditioning Meiji policy were, first, the insufficient accumulation of capital which necessitated state enterprise and facilitated the centralization of capital and economic control in the hands of the financial oligarchy. Even after state enterprise was partially abandoned, the government policy of subsidy was maintained if not strengthened. This policy was partly the outcome of the treaty system, whereby after the first commercial treaty of 1858 the tariff was restricted to a low rate and still further reduced by the tariff convention of 1866. Tariff autonomy was secured through the general treaty revision of 1899 and went into force in 1910. Second, it was the military aspect of industrialization dictated by the international situation and internal forces which caused those sections of industry most closely connected with defense to remain even to this day under close state supervision. Finally, we note the policy of transference of certain branches of industry to a narrow circle of large banking houses whose position, fortified at the time, has continued to dominate Japanese industrial activity to the present day.

With respect to technical development in Japanese industrialization, two distinct tendencies stand out in bold relief. There is, first, the growth of those branches of national economy most closely linked with military enterprises in a wider sense — engineering, shipbuilding, mining, railways and the like —where the government maintained strict control, backed by politically favored and trusted financial houses. These industries, most highly developed in the technical sense and fashioned after the most up-to-date Western models, were the pride of the state bureaucracy which jealously guarded them even after large parts were acquired by private capital. Secondly, we note the development of "left-over" industries engaged in the manufacture of typically Japanese products both for the home and foreign markets. These industries have been dominated by the capital of small traders and usurers, and have been compelled to remain at a primitive stage technically, employing to a large extent domestic and female labor.

3. The agrarian settlement and its social consequences

The trend toward private ownership in land

Annexation of land by a new landlord class had been going on surreptitiously under the feudal regime; it was legally recognized following the Meiji Restoration. After their emancipation from feudalism the peasants became nominally free-holders, but this process actually opened the way for the dispossession of the peasantry, since the removal of the ban prohibiting the sale and division of land legalized the various mechanisms for the unlimited acquisition of land by forced sale, mortgage and the like. So we can say that the Restoration brought genuine emancipation to the peasant *qua* landholder but not necessarily *qua* cultivator. At the beginning of the Meiji era most of the peasantry were independent cultivators, and although accurate figures do not exist, it has been estimated that shortly after the Restoration tenant land occupied 30 per cent of the area cultivated.

*   *   *

Land Tax Revision of 1873

Since the Land Tax Revision of 1873 fixed once and for all the framework within which modern Japanese agrarian relations are confined, it is perhaps worth spending a few pages on an examination of its form and content.

Before it was possible to establish a uniform land tax assessed according to the value of land and not by the feudal system of sharing the produce between lord and peasant, it was necessary that each piece of land whether worked by tenant or independent cultivator should have a recognized owner. In other words, the proposed land tax entailed the fullest recognition of the private ownership of land. We have seen some of the measures logically leading up to this revision, and these were to be supplemented now by the distribution of certificates of landownership known as *chiken*. The first lot were issued in January 1872, another series in February and finally a third in July of the same year. This system of *chiken* served as an entering wedge in the drive to uproot the old feudal land system and to gain recognition for the concept of private ownership of land, while at the same time it provided the basis for an assessment of the land according to its sale value, before the land survey of the Empire could be carried out (1875–81) . . .

The three basic principles of the land tax were: (1) whereas formerly the norm for tax payment had been the harvest, now it was to be the value of land; (2) the rate of taxation was to be 3 per cent of the land value (reduced in 1876 for a short time to 2½ per cent) with no increase or decrease for good or bad years, an adjustment possible under the paternalistic feudal regime; (3) the tax was to be collected in money, not as formerly in kind. This tax at 3 per cent of the land value actually meant a reduction from the old feudal tax if the local tax at 1 per cent were not included. But it cut deeper than this; it meant a qualitative as well as quantitative change from the feudal tax system. These points of difference can be summarized as follows: first, the diverse forms of levy which were imposed both arbitrarily and by custom under the *Bakufu*

142

and *han* governments were now unified under a national central government. Secondly, in former days the *direct producers*, irrespective of whether they were tenants or independent cultivators, were the tax-payers, but now only the *landowner*, whether independent producer or absentee landlord, paid the land tax. Thirdly, under the *ancien régime* the tax was fixed according to the yield, or according to the type of soil; but after revision it was fixed at the uniform rate of 3 per cent of the land value without regard to bumper or lean years. Finally, the former payment of the tax in kind, principally in rice, was now changed to a money payment.

The Meiji leaders saw the necessity of taking this step in order to get rid of the fluctuations caused by the variations in the harvest as well as in the price of rice or other agricultural products which had been used as payment for a tax in kind. In other words, by providing for a *constant* source of revenue, they were making possible a modern budgetary financial system. In a country still agricultural and lacking tariff autonomy it was natural that the very considerable burden of military expenditures as well as of capital outlay for model industries and the maintenance of a large body of bureaucrats should be made dependent on the land tax, and it was important that this revenue should not fluctuate. We saw how removing the ban against permanent annexation of land — a measure bound to come in time — logically preceded and blazed the way for the new tax system, because it was absolutely essential for the guarantee of the new tax system that revenue from the land should cease to depend on the paying capacity of each landowner; in other words someone legally identifiable as the owner has to be responsible for the tax on every acre of land regardless of who works it. There is another fundamental difference from the old system. Under feudalism the principle governing the amount of tax paid by the peasant was to appropriate as much as possible, leaving the producer enough for only the barest subsistence, or, in the phrase current in that age, "to see that the peasants had just enough to live on and no more." The system of collection was based upon the group responsibility of the village divided for administrative convenience into teams of five men, and by this method peasant privation was at once deepened and universalized. But under the new government the burden of payment shifted from producer to landholder; the peasants were now freed from the oppressive bondage of feudalism and at the same time deprived of the "paternal" consideration of their lord whose problem it was to see "that they neither died nor lived." In the new society they were free to choose their own fate; to live or die, to remain on the land or sell out and go to the city. In this way the majority of the rural population, while released from the tyranny of feudalism, were not at the same time accorded state protection in the same way as were the landlords by the guarantee of the right to private ownership of land. The position of the small landowner working his own piece of land was precarious in the extreme, subject to all the vicissitudes of nature (bad crops, storms, blight) and of society (fluctuations in the price of rice) and yet unable to escape the responsibility of paying a fixed amount of cash every year to the government as tax. To meet this demand the peasant proprietor could give up the struggle to remain on the land, dispose of his tiny plot by sale, or resort to the village usurer and so enter upon the long uphill path of debt payments, which might end at any time in foreclosure. Furthermore, with the low level of capitalist development prevalent in the countryside, the sudden requirement to turn from 25 to 30 per cent of his proceeds into money in order to meet the land tax placed a heavy burden on the small isolated cultivator, living off his pigmy-sized farm, who was not yet swept into the main reaches of the national market. By being thrust from a position of comparative self-sufficiency to one of dependence on the market, the peasant was forced to sell his rice as soon as it was harvested, and thus exposed to all the dangers arising from price fluctuations which did not affect to the same extent the position of the large landlords who could store rice in granaries. Here we are speaking of the small producer who owned his land and accordingly paid the land tax himself. The tenant still paid rent, for the most part in kind, to the landlord who, after deducting the amount to be forwarded to the government as land tax, pocketed the remainder as clear profit.

Comparison of peasant dispossession and its effects in Japan and England

A similar process of peasant expropriation accompanied the change to capitalist relations in the countryside in England during the enclosure movement for grazing in the 16th century and the far more sweeping enclosure movement for cereal crops in the 18th century. The economic forces at work brought about a sharp decrease in the number of small owners who lacked either capital or holdings sufficiently great to keep pace with the new improved scientific agricultural production for the market, whose household industries were ruined by the new machine industries of Lancashire, and who consequently were forced to leave the land and migrate to the city. In England this movement was accompanied not only by the concentration of land in fewer hands, but also by the very considerable increase in the scale of farming. In Japan, however, this process was very complex, and, unlike the English enclosures of the 18th century, it did not precipitate a wholesale exodus of peasants to the cities in the years immediately following the Land Tax Revision. On the contrary there has been no absolute decrease in the number of agricultural *honke* (or households) working the land. The answer to the apparent contradiction of a peasantry which suffered expropriation on the large scale described above, yet which remained on the land as tenants or part tenants, cannot be given merely by pointing to the well-known fact that in the early and middle Meiji years there were as yet no highly developed industries which could absorb a dispossessed peasantry, because even after the industrialization of Japan there still remains a constant or rather steadily increasing number of agricultural households on the land. The answer would seem to lie rather in the Japanese tenant–landlord relations with excessively high rent and consequent atomization of land. The high rent characteristic of Japanese landlordism has made the non-cultivating landowner interested exclusively in collecting rent and has deterred him from using his capital to enter agricultural enterprise as a capitalist. In England the fulfillment of capitalist development in agriculture left the land concentrated in the hands of fewer individuals who, after driving off the old customary tenants through acts of Parliament enforcing enclosure, increased the unit of cultivation and worked the land for profit as a capitalist enterprise. The old semi-feudal customary tenant was forced off the land in England once and for all, and he had to seek employment with all his family in the rapidly growing city industries. In Japan, however, because of the attractively high rent, the landlord or usurer has not been intent on driving off all the old tenants or peasant proprietors for the sake of taking over the enterprise himself; he has preferred to leave the peasant household working its tiny farm in return for an exorbitant rent.

With the ruin of the old time-honored household industries and the increasing pressure of over-population on the countryside following the removal of feudal restrictions on the birthrate, and with the rise of a modern factory industry, younger members of the family, in particular the women, left the countryside for the city in the hope of supplementing the meager family income. What is of particular significance in this city-ward movement is that the overcrowding of the agricultural family, its desperate financial plight aggravated by the ruin of domestic industry, coincided with the rise of the textile industry which was the core of the first Japanese industrial revolution and has remained a vitally important sector of industry, especially for the export trade. This situation made possible the recruiting of female labor from the overcrowded villages and the consequent lowering of labor costs in the textile industry. It has created an industrial working class composed of an unusually high percentage of female labor. The following table will illustrate its extent.

Year	Total Workers	Women Workers	Percentage of Women Workers in Industry
1882	51,189	35,535	69%
1895–99	425,602	252,651	59%
(In five-year averages)			
1900–04	472,955	291,237	62%
1905–09	637,043	391,003	61%
1910–14	828,942	592,320	71%

(These figures cover only factories employing over ten workers and exclude government-owned factories.)

The other important consequence of the agrarian settlement insofar as it affected the migration to the city is that, in contrast to what obtained in England, those members of the peasant household, whether younger brothers or daughters, went to the city only for short periods, returning to the village because of unemployment, or for marriage, or to help out during harvest time. The uprooting of the old self-sufficient customary tenant in English society propelled the whole tenant family city-wards and when a slack season set in, they had to remain idle in the city since their ancient country home had long since disappeared. In Japan, however, they returned to their ancestral village when unemployed. This solution to the problem of unemployment, even though it arose as a natural and not preconceived consequence of the agrarian settlement, is one of the reasons which drives landlords and industrialists together rather than against each other, as occurred, for instance, in England during the agitation for the repeal of the Corn Laws. The reason for this coincidence of landlord and industrialist interest lies in the fact that the burden of the upkeep of the unemployed is largely removed from state and employers, while at the same time the resulting overcrowding of the village bids up the rent rate.

Minute-scale farming in Japan: its cause and effects

Unlike the English experience, the expropriation of the peasantry in Japan did not mean the consolidation or extension of the average unit of land cultivated. On the contrary (despite an infinitesimal increase in the average unit of land cultivated), the extension of tenancy was accompanied by continued atomization of the average unit of land worked by a peasant household. Comparative figures from the early Meiji period are as follows:

In 1874 an examination of the 3 *fu* (i.e., the 3 great urban areas, Tokyo, Osaka and Kyoto) and 27 prefectures (not including Hokkaido) revealed that the average unit of cultivation (both dry and paddy fields taken together) per peasant household was 9 *tan*, 6 *se*, 16 *bu* (2.353 acres), and thirty-five years later this unit, still excluding Hokkaido, was virtually the same, being 9 *tan*, 7 *se*, 10 *bu* (2.384 aces).

The minute parcelation of land characteristic of Japanese agriculture thus remained even after the recognition of the principle of private land ownership and after the rapid increase in tenancy. The reason for this is to be found in the unusually high rent, which, as we saw, was for rice fields as much as 60 per cent of the harvest. This question is so important in Japanese agrarian relations that at the risk of undue repetition we will analyze it further. As long as those who possess capital and land, namely the merchant, usurer or rich peasant, can expect so high a return on capital sunk in the land, they have no incentive to turn themselves from parasitic landlords into agricultural entrepreneurs, working the land for profit on agricultural produce grown for the market and hiring their former tenants or others as wage laborers. As agrarian relations exist in Japan a landlord who is sure of such a high return on his money would be foolish to undertake the risks of enterprise for a profit which might well be at a lower rate than rent. In a word, the exorbitant rent cuts into or discourages the entrepreneur's profit. The result is that land remains as it was in feudal times, parceled into minute lots and worked by a prolific peasantry whose increasing numbers make for competition in leases, thus safeguarding the high rate of rent. This in turn tends to atomize the unit of land cultivated. To this must be added the passionate attachment of the peasant for land which has been consecrated for him by the toil of countless forebears. In his struggle to remain on the land as proprietor or part proprietor, the peasant sells a few *tsubo* of land at a time to cover his tax arrears, to meet his debt to the village usurer or to tide himself over a lean year caused by poor crops, loss of draught animals or some other natural calamity. He surrenders each square yard of land unwillingly, like an outflanked army fighting a hopeless but determined rear-guard action, and the result is that he has to cut down his scale of operations still more on the land that is at his disposal. This is of course only an imaginative case, but it illustrates in part the effects of high rent as a deterrent to the development of pure capitalist relations in agriculture, while the extreme pressure of population on the countryside has the effect of maintaining and in some cases even diminishing the minute scale of operations which existed from feudal times. As a Japanese authority has said: "The farmer himself knows how inconvenient and disadvantageous such an agricultural system is, but substantial improvement is often impossible in a short time on account of the fixed conditions of ownership or tenancy." And again: "On the ruins of feudalism, land-ownership has been divided into small sections; the scale of agriculture management is as small as ever; family labor is still available, no fundamental change has occurred in these old conditions. Japanese agriculture still retains its old form." Thus the peasant, marshaling his whole

146

household to keep on a subsistence level, intensifies agriculture by making the most of every square foot of land at his disposal. This parcelation or atomization of Japanese agriculture is thus an outcome of the land settlement of the early Meiji period and the peculiarities of Japanese topography, and has the effect of intensifying and diversifying agricultural production, but acts as an insurmountable barrier to any attempt at large-scale mechanization or at revolution in agricultural technique. The atomization of land and the peculiar arrangement arising from the Meiji agrarian settlement, whereby an extraordinarily high rent is paid in kind and a heavy tax is paid in money, and above all the effect of high rent which discourages holders of capital from entering agricultural production as entrepreneurs, have left a distinctive mark on Japanese agrarian relations. This can be analyzed best by examining the actual social relations of the Japanese tenant farmer.

Social character of the Japanese tenant farmer

The Japanese tenant farmer is not a capitalist entrepreneur as in other countries, but a cultivator paying a large percentage of his produce in kind to the landlord. Nor is he an agricultural wage laborer receiving a cash wage from a landowner who takes both the risks and profits of the enterprise. The Japanese tenant is a mixture of the two. He resembles the English tenant farmer inasmuch as he shoulders all the risks of agricultural enterprise, but in spite of this the profit from the enterprise is taken by the landowner; so in this respect the Japanese tenant resembles an agricultural day-laborer. The wage of this agricultural semi-proletarian is not a money wage but a payment in kind which depends upon the size of the harvest and subsequent fluctuations in the prices of agricultural products. In a good year the share of the tenant increases somewhat, but since the demand for agricultural products is relatively inelastic, the price of the product falls drastically especially at harvest time. Thus it is possible for the money income of the tenant to decrease despite a good crop. The price of industrial goods on the other hand, which the tenant must buy back, has nothing to do with the harvest but is influenced by other economic forces such as the state of the international market. In a year of poor crops, this price of cereals will rise, but scarcely anything remains of the raw product in the hand of the producing tenant who, especially if he cultivates a very small farm, may actually be compelled to buy back the cereals which he grew. Thus the Japanese tenant-farmer manifests the double nature of capitalist-tenant (who takes the risks of the entrepreneur) and of agricultural proletarian (inasmuch as the landlord, by reason of the high rent, takes a large part of the profits of the enterprise). One aspect is so closely intertwined with the other that it is inaccurate to describe him either as pure tenant or pure proletarian. Here we see again the Janus head of the Japanese peasant, formed by his social relationships. As we noted, this double aspect makes the Japanese peasant at once more conservative and more radical than the French or English farmer. A foreign observer has commented upon this characteristic of the Japanese peasant, as follows: "Yet the 'discontent and radical tendencies' that we usually associate with an urban proletariat are there 'mainly confined to the rural population."

147

The question of a stagnant surplus population and the creation of the labor market

From this analysis it appears that the process of growing landlordism on the one hand, and the divorce of the peasant proprietor from the land on the other cannot be explained as the consequences of capitalist development in agricultural productive relations, which was the driving force behind the English enclosures of the 18th century. This process of peasant expropriation, as well as the separation of industry from agriculture (that is to say, the ruin of domestic industry), moved faster than the development of capitalist enterprise in agriculture or of urban industry. That the process of peasant expropriation described above advanced more rapidly than the development of capitalism both in agriculture and industry is attested by the fact that during the quarter-century following the Land Tax Revision the dispossessed peasantry were not converted to any large extent into an agricultural or industrial proletariat, but became tenants, part-tenants or proprietors of exceedingly small farms, depending for a bare subsistence upon domestic supplementary industries, such as spinning, weaving or sericulture. This vast body of small peasant proprietors, tenants and half-tenants, cultivating in ever larger numbers minutely parceled plots of land, historically forms the reservoir of Japanese stagnant and potential surplus population. The atomized, minute-scale cultivation is quite inadequate to give them a net income sufficient to eke out even a bare subsistence, so their women folk must engage in some form of domestic industry while the men seek part-time employment as coolies working on roads, railway construction and the like. That section of stagnant surplus population which was not afforded the protection of the family system was forced to seek its livelihood in the cities. Those who could not enter the factories became rickshaw-men, longshoremen, coolies, in a word the lowest stratum of unskilled labor. This class includes also those who were driven out of small-scale domestic industry by the introduction of new machine techniques or whose labor became superfluous through the employment of female and child labor. This stagnant surplus population is semi-employed at the best, and its condition of livelihood is marked by irregularity of work, insecurity of employment and, when employed, by extremely long hours of work and very low wages. This stagnant surplus population tends eventually to drift back from the city to the natal village, aggravating the already congested condition of life in the countryside and acting as a depressing factor on the standard of living in the village. The extreme pressure of population on the land prevents many of them from becoming cultivators, so they must seek a living in some form of domestic industry; with the decline of the latter, the unbearable pressure compels them to send their daughters to the textile mills in the city to earn enough — or so they hope — to keep the family debt from reaching ruinous proportions. The population which is expelled from all participation in the process of production in agriculture, and has not succeeded in being enrolled as part of the industrial proletariat, becomes *fluid* as soon as its numbers are sufficient. And just as water tends to seek the lowest level, so this fluid surplus population is compelled to seek the lowest level — that is to say it flows into the most poorly paid types of employment, dragging down with it the general wage level. In a country like Japan, where the development of city industry even though rapid in speed was not widespread, the larger part of the surplus population could not be absorbed by industry. Furthermore, when the overseas labor market, an outlet which helped to solve the surplus population problem in certain European countries at the end of the 19th century, is blocked by immigration exclusion, this surplus population could do nothing but await employment with the further advance in industrialization or seek new opportunities in household manufacture. It is correct to say that the existence of this vast reservoir of stagnant or potential surplus labor has attracted small-scale manufacturers to the countryside. Since the pressure of population in agriculture closes the door of agricultural employment to a great proportion of this stagnant population, the only means of subsistence left to them is industry whether urban or domestic. But large-scale urban industry did not develop to a level sufficient to absorb the reservoir of labor, partly because of factors conditioning the rise of Japanese industry, but to a large extent because of this very pre-existing reservoir of stagnant surplus population. In other words, many Japanese enterprises have been able to dispense with expensive factory equipment simply by distributing piece-work jobs to the households of those living in that limbo lying between agricultural employment, which is closed behind them, and urban industry which has not yet opened before them. In this way Japanese entrepreneurs have gained a certain flexibility in their wage fund, awaiting the sporadic rise and fall of market demands without the risk of deterioration or obsolescence of stock and factory equipment during slack times. This is another instance where mutual interests drive landlords and industrialists together.

Another important consequence of the Meiji agrarian settlement was the creation of a labor market, the third prerequisite for the development of capitalism. The creation of a labor market in Japan was marked by the formation of a reservoir of potential stagnant labor drawn largely from a dispossessed peasantry whose absorption into industries was retarded by the slower pace in the development of large-scale industry. That such absorption took place is not denied, but the extent to which a surplus population was left stagnating in the countryside and in the cities is an important factor limiting the standard of living and the wage level of Japanese labor.

Before leaving the subject we may note the gradual movement of part of the agricultural surplus population into industry, and the slow but steady relative increase in the industrial population. In the period stretching from 1894, when the process of peasant expropriation was almost completed and the first industrial revolution was at its peak, until the eve of the Great War (1913) the total population which can be considered as gainfully employed increased from 24,428,109 to 30,026,403 (i.e., from 100 to 123), while in the same period industrial workers increased from 381,390 to 916,252 (i.e., from 100 to 240). Although the number of agricultural households increased absolutely from 1887 to 1913, it decreased relatively. The proportion of agricultural households in all Japan was 71 per cent in 1887 and only 58 per cent in 1913, while the ratio of agricultural households to industrial workers decreased from 11.1:1 to 6.4:1.

4. Parties and politics

At first sight it might seem incongruous that landowners should form the core of the liberal movement. The word "land owner" at once brings to the mind of the Western reader the English squire and his deep-seated conservatism in all matters relating to society and politics. To explain the Japanese landowner's outlook we must hark back to the analysis of Japanese tenant–landlord relations, as described in the last section.

We saw that the Japanese landlord collects rent while the tenant takes the entrepreneur's risks but not his profits. Thus the landlord is interested primarily in converting the rice or other agricultural produce collected as rent into money at the best possible rate. Hence his only concern is the current price of rice. His interest in turning agricultural products into commodities makes the Japanese landlord a small commercial capitalist who invests his money in land or in local domestic industries connected with the land, such as the making of *miso* (bean paste) and brewing of *sake*, or who becomes a rice-broker or small merchant of artificial fertilizer and the like. A foreigner, who several years ago tramped far and wide over the Japanese countryside, making detailed notes on Japanese rural society, wrote in this connection, "When I drew attention to the fact that there (i.e. a village in Nagano prefecture) the manufacture of *sake* and soy seemed to be frequently in the hands of landowners, it was explained to me that formerly this was their industry exclusively." And in another passage, "Before I left the town I had a chat with a landowner who turned his tenants' rent rice into *sake*. He was of the fifth generation of brewers." And again, "All the shopkeepers seem to own their own houses and all but three have some land." Thus as the collector of an exorbitant rent he is a semi-feudal landlord, but he has also the other side, that of the commercial capitalist. It was this commercial capitalist side which drove the Japanese landlord into politics in the period of which we are speaking. This is seen in the active part played by landlord-manufacturers in forming the Liberal party, the *Jiyuto*. In 1880 a Council of *Sake*-Brewers (*Sakaya Kaigi*) was formed under the leadership of a certain Kojima Minoru and rapidly attracted to it great numbers of *sake*-brewers throughout the country. The government, which was then considering a program of naval expansion requiring increased taxation, proposed among other new methods of revenue increase a tax on *zoseki* (a yeast stone used in brewing). Immediately the *Sakaya Kaigi*, at the first conference of the *Jiyuto* in 1881, opposed this tax and raised the slogan "Freedom of Enterprise," worthy of the purest Manchester Liberal in 19th century England. The great popularity of this organization among village and town gentry alarmed the government, so that in December 1881 the council was dissolved at the order of the governor of Osaka-Fu. Despite the ban the brewers opened their session on a boat in the Yodogawa. The activity of this brewers' council attracted large numbers of landlord-manufacturers and small landlords with commercial interests into the *Jiyuto* and gave it the peculiar coloring described above, that is a Liberal party based on the landlord class. Thus his trading or manufacturing activities made of the Japanese landlord a modest Cobden, but his interests as landlord could make him intensely conservative.

The other concern of the landowning class in general was tax reduction. The government had reduced the land tax from 3 to 2½ per cent to conciliate the landowners and to dampen any sympathy they might entertain for the sporadic *samurai* revolts culminating in the Satsuma Revolt of 1877, which tax-reduction anticipated but did not prevent. Despite this conciliatory gesture, the landowning gentry felt that the weight of taxation was unduly heavy upon them. From 1875 to 1879 the land tax accounted for 80.5 per cent of the revenue, from 1880 to 1884 for 65.6

per cent, and from 1885 to 1889 for 69.4 per cent. Furthermore, the government policy of liquidating inconvertible notes, together with its industrial policy, had caused, so it was believed, a disastrous fall in the price of rice, which was the basic concern of the landlord. At the same time that financial and industrial circles close to the government were receiving subsidies, generous government contracts and trading monopolies, the landowning class saw the price of rice fall steadily from 221 in 1881 (1873 = 100) to 105 in 1888, rising slowly to 154 in 1893. In a word, the agricultural classes felt that the financial and industrial oligarchy enjoyed the exclusive favor and protection of the government while the landowners were paying the bill for industrialization . . .

Accordingly, the landlords participated in the liberal movement, attacking the bureaucratic governing circle and its financial supporters as small commercial capitalists, interested primarily in rice-brokerage, in trading, in usury and in small local investments. It was this side which made them active champions of "Freedom and People's Rights" and "Freedom of Enterprise," and not the pure landlord side with its semi-feudal conservative character. The somber side of the landlord never disappeared even during the hey-day of liberalism, but lay dormant until later years when it completely overshadowed the "liberal" side. The point to note is that Japanese liberalism had its roots in the countryside, unlike English liberalism which was a movement of the cities especially of the city merchants in opposition to the conservative landed gentry.

The theoretical leaders of the liberal movement were ex-*samurai*, chiefly from the former Tosa and Hizen clans which no longer shared equally in the fruits of office with Satsuma and Choshu. That many of these men were inspired by genuinely liberal ideals is not disputed; their later careers and sacrifices are sufficient testimony to their singleness of purpose. Nevertheless, as two Japanese authorities have pointed out, the abolition of the clans had undermined the economic base of feudalism, leaving many discontented *samurai*, while the failure of the advocates for an expedition to Korea (*Seikan Ron*) had embittered others, and so these ex-*samurai* were drawn into the liberal movement merely because it was the *anti-government* movement. Thus individual place-seeking and jealousy of the *Sat-cho* monopoly acted as a stimulus for organizing the first political associations in Japan. It was natural that these ex-*samurai* in opposition to the government should become the acknowledged leaders of the movement which demanded a people's assembly. They enjoyed great prestige as members of the *shizoku* class, and above all as leaders in the Restoration of 1868. On this account some Japanese authorities have called them the heirs of the *Kinno* or *Sonno* Party (loyalists who fought against the *Bakufu*) and the true embodiment of the anti-feudal struggle.

But the impelling force of the liberal movement came from the great mass of small peasants, tenants and city poor who rallied to it urging the reduction of taxes, the establishment of representative institutions, even demanding representation in the liberal movement. It was difficult however for the peasants living in outlying, isolated villages to take active part in politics. It was only natural that the most active element in local politics should be the large landowners, while the national leadership tended to be in the hands of ex-*samurai* or of a few large landlord merchants.

This widespread and loosely connected movement of small landowners and peasants under the leadership of former *samurai* and big landlord merchants took national form in the *Jiyuto* (Liberal Party) organized early in 1881. The quality of its leadership inevitably made the political philosophy of the *Jiyuto* a rather softened, conciliatory liberalism, a liberalism which strove primarily for democracy, for people's rights, for freedom of enterprise — all for the respectable classes . . .

Thus from its start Japanese liberalism as embodied in the *Jiyuto* was of a moderate, temporizing quality and later it was to change into its opposite, uncompromising conservatism, when the *Seiyukai* was formed from the ruins of the *Jiyuto* in 1900. We are not discussing here the extreme left-wing of the *Jiyuto* which later took on almost a revolutionary coloring, but the basic political philosophy of the chief leaders of the *Jiyuto*. Despite any vagueness in its program, the *Jiyuto* before its split into local grouplets with a right and left wing, because of the enthusiastic backing it received from land-hungry tenants and debt-burdened peasant proprietors, had great *élan* and even revolutionary potentialities. For this reason, as we shall see later the Government in its campaign of suppressing political parties launched its fiercest onslaught against the *Jiyuto*.

The government policy toward political parties

The Government's attitude toward the growth of liberal ideas and the organization of political parties was one of misgiving to say the least. When the demand for representative institutions first began to grow clamorous in the years after the defeat of the *Seikan Ron* in 1874, the Government decided to make concessions in that direction without compromising its own autocratic powers, and devised the local or prefectural assemblies (*Fu-Ken-Kai*) established in 1878. These local assemblies were forerunners of the national assembly or Diet not only in point of time but in constitutional powers. Very little public interest was shown in them since all real power still lay in the hands of the ruling bureaucracy. In the opinion of some authorities, the Government's purpose in this was to reduce the growing pressure for representative institutions and at the same time create an organization, the *Fu-Ken-Kai*, as a training center for a local bureaucracy over which the central oligarchy hoped to extend its control. Whatever purpose the Government hoped this local assembly would serve, it revealed a characteristic precautionary policy (which was to be shown again at critical times) of granting a concession with one hand and taking it back with the other. In this instance, however, it reversed this order by first taking a step which to a large extent stultified the concession that followed. Before the creation of the local assemblies with their high property qualifications for electors, the Government in June 1875 had passed a drastic Press Law, which it used unsparingly in the next few years for smothering any effective criticism of the Government policy. Shortly after the creation of these local assemblies, discontent with the Government's high-handed methods again gathered momentum. When the loosely-knit network of local debtors' parties and liberal societies was organized into national parties (particularly the *Jiyuto*), and when agitation for representative institutions became more violent, the Government decided again to make a concession. Accordingly in 1881 it promised the nation a Diet by the year 1889. But the Imperial Edict of October 12, 1881, promising the establishment of the national assembly, did not put an end to the demand for representative institutions, but added fuel to the democratic movement. This movement, as expressed in the growing popularity and power of political parties, was viewed by the Government with the greatest alarm and it took swift action by launching an attack against these two opposition liberal parties, the *Kaishinto*[18] and *Jiyuto*, first by direct repression and secondly by splitting the liberal movement and winning over to its own camp some sections of the opposition. Having promised a Diet within nine years, the Government in 1882 passed new regulations in regard to meeting and association, which were far more severe and more rigorously enforced than the previous regulations.[19] The most stringent repression, however, came only after the Government had succeeded in rendering the political movement ineffective either by winning over some of its leaders or by playing off the *Kaishinto* against the *Jiyuto*, and in this way removing some of the ablest political leaders from successful participation in the democratic movement.

Just at the time when the agitation for people's rights and representative institutions seemed to be sweeping victoriously over the country, indicating a crucial struggle in the near future with the Government, the members of the *Jiyuto* were amazed to learn suddenly late in 1882 that their most experienced leaders, Itagaki Taisuke and Goto Shojiro, were sailing for Europe to study Western political institutions at first hand. Rumors emanating from the *Kaishinto* and aired by the Tokyo–Yokohama *Mainichi Shimbun* insisted that the expenses for this trip were met by the Government. Although many of the *Jiyuto* members stoutly denied the charge that their leaders had been virtually bought off by the Government some of them including Baba Tatsui, Oishi Masami and Taguchi Ukichi shortly withdrew from the party in protest. The truth was that the traveling expenses had been furnished by the Mitsui Company, with Goto and Inouye Kaoru acting as intermediaries. This dubious incident and its repercussions stung the *Jiyuto* into bitter recrimination against the *Kaishinto*. Okuma, the leader of the *Kaishinto*, was accused of acting as the political agent of the Mitsubishi Company and of pouring over-generous subsidies and grants into its coffers. This accusation evoked the cry "*Gito Bokumetsu*" (destroy false parties) and "*Umi-Bozu Taiji*" (subdue the sea monsters, i.e., the Mitsubishi Company). Taking advantage of this attack on the Mitsubishi, the Government established its short-lived Kyodo Un'yu Kaisha under the patronage of Shinagawa Yajiro. The Mitsubishi weathered the storm, amalgamated with the Kyodo Un'yu Kaisha to form the N.Y.K., and drew closer than ever before to the government circles, especially when Okuma or his companions were in office. The upshot of this was that rather than combining to attack their common enemy, the absolutist clan government, the two opposition parties fell into the trap set for them by the Government, wrangled bitterly with each other and dissipated their energies in such a way as to discredit political parties and to strengthen the Government. Following its clever maneuvers in playing off one opposition party against another, the Government capped its campaign against the parties by the severe repression mentioned above. Faced with the alternative of carrying on the struggle by illegal methods or of bowing before the Government's will, most of the leaders of the liberal movement chose the latter course. In October 1884, the *Jiyuto* was voluntarily dissolved, while the *Kaishinto* preceded it by a year, dissolving in September 1883.

New shift of agrarian revolt following dissolution of Jiyuto in 1884

Even before the dissolution of the parties, with the press effectively muzzled and all political activity stringently suppressed, local branches of the political parties had energetically protested against government suppression and had even turned to insurrection as a means of achieving their end — the overthrow of the autocratic government.[20] Many of the lesser leaders in the *Jiyuto*, angered and bewildered by what seemed to them the defection of their chiefs, often supported these ill-starred uprisings. The historical interest of these local incidents arises from the political and economic demands which motivated the rank and file of the liberal movement and the resolution, however misplaced, with which these demands were backed in comparison to the tergiversations of the leaders. One of the shrewdest observers of Japanese national life, Fukuzawa Yukichi foresaw as early as 1881 the tendency for the rank and file in the liberal movement to display a violent impatience with government policy. In writing to Okuma, he says, "The *Minken Ron* (Advocacy of People's Rights) seems to be more and more favoring direct action. If it goes on in that direction, the antagonism between the government and people will become increasingly embittered and in the end I fear it will mean unfortunate bloodshed."

Fukuzawa's forebodings were only too accurate. The first of these revolts broke out in 1882 in Fukushima prefecture . . . An insurrection occurred in Chichibu (Saitama prefecture) in 1884 in which the *Shakkinto* or local debtors' party played a leading role as did also a radical group from the local *Jiyuto*. These political leaders were alleged to have stirred up bad feeling among the peasantry and village poor against the local landlords, and when police arrived on the scene the peasants had resisted them forcibly. What is of interest for our immediate purpose is that this Chichibu uprising symbolizes the great divide in the history of the *Jiyuto* or Liberal Party. We have already seen that leadership in this party was in the hands of landowners who were merchants or manufacturers as well; it was this commercial side of their nature which drew them into politics. However, as government repression became intensified to meet the mounting demand for greater democracy, these local branches, which were often in more radical hands than was the national leadership, stirred up such violent popular sentiment not only in favor of representative institutions but also for rent reduction that it terrified many of the more cautious leaders, bringing out the conservative landlord side of their nature, and thus made party dissolution by no means as unpalatable as it might otherwise have been. As one authority writes, "The *Jiyuto* and *Kaishinto* were more or less directly connected with the exhibition of violence in the provinces, though it is not likely that the leaders of either countenanced the measures adopted. To clear itself of the stigma of inciting to rebellion, the *Jiyuto* at a general meeting held on October 20, 1884, in Osaka, resolved to disband and wait for an opportunity when society will be prepared for its reconstruction."

After the dissolution of the *Jiyuto*, local uprisings such as those just described, usually led by the extremist followers of the *Jiyuto* or its offshoots, took on a most violent and bloody character. Without going into further details, we can merely list the better known uprisings: the Nagoya riots of 1884 in which the local *Jiyuto* played the leading part; the Kabasan (Ibaraki prefecture) insurrection of 1885; the Iida (Aichi prefecture) incident of the same year; and the Shizuoka rising of 1886. Most curious of all the conspiracies and armed revolts of this period was the plot of Oi Kentaro and his confederates, mostly from the *Jiyuto* and all greatly influenced by French revolutionary concepts.[21] Foiled in their political activity by government repression, they planned to go to Korea, spread their political doctrine there, establish a democratic regime in that peninsula and thence conduct liberal agitation in Japan. They were about to sail from Osaka with arms and ammunition when they were seized by police on November 23, 1885.

Thus ends the first chapter in the history of Japanese liberalism. Most instructive in this history is the evidence of the fundamental weakness in a liberalism which stemmed *from the countryside*. In other countries victorious liberalism, whether of the Independents or rather the London Presbyterians during the Cromwellian era or of revolutionary Paris, was essentially an urban movement which could draw on the immense financial power of the city merchant and could be propelled by the highly centralized political organization of the city masses. Above all, English and French liberalism, though led by wealthy merchants, lawyers or even country gentry, was reinforced by the presence in the metropolis of a large and comparatively articulate urban citizenry. This is, of course, equally true of 19th century English liberalism after the Reform Act of 1832, when the Liberal Party drew its strength almost exclusively from the city classes. But in Japan a liberalism based on the countryside with its isolated villages, where local issues often absorbed the attention of the neighboring population to the exclusion of all else and where conditions differed widely from one locality to another, inevitably brought inner clashes and final failure. Furthermore the antagonism between the landlord leadership of the *Jiyuto* and the rank and file peasant following was bound to force a split in the party. We have seen how this leadership of the *Jiyuto* succumbed more easily to the government offensive after the startling incidents described above, when peasants voiced among other cries the demand for rent reduction. Deprived of all central leadership, the local branches of the *Jiyuto* under various names and for various local issues often resorted to violence in order to weaken the grip of government repression. These attempts were too scattered and sporadic, in a word *too local in character* both geographically and politically, to be crowned with even partial success. The government won out all along the line, thanks to the unity of the ruling bureaucracy and its autocratic methods on the one hand, and to the disunity and confusion of the opposition on the other.

The *Jiyuto* was reconstituted again with the opening of the Diet in 1890. But the series of successive splits by which the most radical groups within it had been gradually sloughed off, and the very high property qualifications for the electorate (payment of at least fifteen yen in direct national taxes) made the reformed *Jiyuto* a chastened and moderate party. Its transformation through various intermediate stages into the *Seiyukai* (1900), the party of the landlords, indicates the triumph of that semi-feudal landlord aspect in the leadership of the original *Jiyuto*.

Strengthening of the State: The Constitution of 1889

Liberalism did not die with the dissolution of the political parties in 1883–4. Nevertheless, after that first flush of political enthusiasm and fruitless energy it was to become a still more restrained and compromising movement. We have not the time here to trace the quick shifts and ephemeral coalitions of the various liberal factions led by Itagaki and Okuma; but while these factions intrigued for some share in the rewards of office, the government quietly went on strengthening its defenses against the sort of storm which swept the country from 1880–4. It also effected much needed administrative reforms which gave it greater flexibility and efficiency. The most energetic spirit in this government activity was Ito Hirobumi, who had been sent to Europe in 1882 to study constitutions of Western nations preparatory to drafting the Japanese constitution. His first act after his return in August 1883 was to rehabilitate the nobility (July 1884) by creating the new orders of prince, marquis, count, viscount and baron. The new nobility was made up of the former *kuge* (court nobility), *daimyo* (feudal nobility) and those who had distinguished themselves by conspicuous services during or after the Restoration. This step assured strong support from the aristocratic and official classes for Ito and his policies. His next move was to reform the cabinet system (December 1885) so that in the new cabinet (*Naikaku*) unlike the old Council of State (*Dajokan*) there would be a clear division of departmental work coordinated by the Minister President (*Naikaku Sori Daijin*), who in his powers closely resembles the chancellor of former Imperial Germany. (The office technically termed *Naikaku Sori Daijin* is generally rendered in English as prime minister). The Civil Service was now based upon an examination system, in this way removing official appointments from political favoritism. This reform helped to strengthen the bureaucratic system composed of efficient and usually disinterested civil servants whose loyalty was not attached to any political party or patron but to the bureaucracy as a whole.

At the same time reforms in the educational system had been taking place which were symptomatic of the political philosophy of the government. In 1880 absolute state control of elementary and secondary schools was established. In the following year, the chief center of Japanese higher education, Tokyo University (later Tokyo Imperial University), was reorganized in such fashion as to make it the instrument for training the future bureaucracy. By this reform the entire staff of the University was placed under government control, subject to all the responsibilities and restrictions of government officials, and given places in the bureaucratic hierarchy. The old loose and rather independent departmental organization was now changed to a rigidly centralized control wielded by a President who had to answer only to the Minister of Education who in turn was directly responsible to the Emperor. Thus professors were no longer primarily scholars but government officials, and in this capacity they had to take new oaths to the government. These reforms were undertaken partly under the supervision of that champion of autocracy Kato Hiroyuki, who at this time was re-appointed President. Unquestionably the teaching and intellectual atmosphere at Tokyo University would henceforth adhere closely to the ideals of the ruling oligarchy.[22]

Meanwhile to guard against a threat from political parties which showed signs of reviving, and to prevent any criticism of its attempts to revise the treaty system, the government passed the Peace Preservation Law (*Hoan Jorei*) on December 25, 1887, which some historians have considered to be the most repressive measure since the Restoration.

The greatest single innovation of this period was the creation of the Constitution. Ito had been working on this Constitution since 1884, when the *Seido Torishirabe Kyoku* (Bureau for Investigation of Constitutional Systems) was established with Ito at its head together with Marquis (later Prince) Tokudaiji, Inouye Tsuyoshi, Kaneko Kentaro and Ito Miyoji. This bureau was attached to the Imperial Household Department, thereby becoming sacrosanct and completely removed from any outside influence. One Japanese authority expressed surprise that this department was selected rather than the Senate (*Genro-In*), (which was the chief legislative organ of the government at the time), or the Department of Justice. He answers his own query as follows, "The reason seems to have been to guard the work of framing the Constitution from any contact with public opinion."

In 1888 the Privy Council was created through the initiative of Ito Hirobumi, who was its first president. Its function originally was to pass critical judgment on the Constitution, which was nearing completion. But after the promulgation of the Constitution in 1889, the Privy Council remained as the watchdog of autocratic rule. Its own composition and its power to decide any conflict of opinion which may arise between the different organs of government regarding the interpretation of the Constitution have made it the last stronghold of conservation.

We cannot enter here into an analytical discussion of the Constitution itself. This omission however is not serious in view of the excellent studies devoted to this subject which have already appeared in English. We might note in passing that it was Ito's express opinion, which has been honored ever since, that the Constitution was a gift of the Emperor to his people not a concession to the demand of the people for a Constitution. Only the Emperor can initiate amendments to the Constitution which have to be approved by the Upper and Lower Houses, and its interpretation lies with the courts of the country and, in the last analysis, in the hands of the Privy Council. It was conceived in a spirit of benevolent autocracy and has remained as the inflexible instrument of absolutism.

Since any attempt to amend the Constitution by popular franchise, court decision or vote of either house separately or both together would put the initiator beyond the pale of legality, the greatest constitutional struggles in modern Japan have been fought over the question of suffrage, which was deliberately excluded by Ito from the Constitution and hence left open to legislative change. For this reason many groups and parties sometimes not represented in the Diet, and more often parties associated with the Labor movement, have been active in the campaign to extend the franchise.

A brief account of the franchise in Japan will show the progress made in this direction. Under the original election law of 1890 the vote was restricted to those who paid a direct national tax (land, business or income tax) of not less than fifteen yen for a period of at least one year previous to the time when the electors lists were drawn up. At that time the electorate numbered 460,000. In 1900 the electoral reform lowered property qualifications for the voter to the payment of ten yen in direct national taxes (it was lowered to five yen in 1899 but raised to ten in 1900). The electorate was then increased by approximately three times its original number. This reform could be carried out by the existing political parties because, by extending the electorate in this way, it strengthened parliamentary rule and enhanced the position of political parties. But the further extension of the franchise to the non-propertied members of the community was a step rather too sweeping to be encouraged by any but the more radical members of the Diet or of some labor groups outside the Diet. A pioneer in this movement was Oi Kentaro, one of the early radical members of the *Jiyuto*; as leader of the left-wing split of the Liberal Party, the *Toyo Jiyuto*, he was one of the first spokesmen for universal suffrage. This extra-parliamentary movement for universal suffrage is inextricably associated with the names of those who were most active in the labor and socialist movement, like Nakamura Tahachiro, Kinoshita Naoye, Katayama Sen and Abe Isoh. This agitation became most vocal toward the end of the Meiji period. During Katsura's third and final Government (winter 1912–13) large-scale rioting and police suppression indicated the tension between government and people in regard to this question. It was not until after the Great War, however, and after the famous Rice Riots (1918) had badly shaken the prestige of the Terauchi Cabinet that the stage was set for the next reform in the franchise. In 1920 the property qualifications were reduced from ten to three yen, thus increasing the electorate to something over three millions. It will be seen that the non-propertied classes were still excluded from the vote. The final electoral reform of 1925 (first election, 1928) brought universal manhood suffrage, marking the highest point in parliamentary democracy yet reached in Japan.

Foreign policy and international relations

Despite her scarcity of natural wealth, Meiji Japan had made the most of those few assets she possessed, namely comparative geographic isolation from the Great Powers, the patient industry of her people and the unconquerable will to learn and adapt to her own uses those arts and sciences which were necessary for the fashioning of a modern society. The slogan of the Meiji Reformers *"Sonno Joi"* (Revere the Emperor and expel the barbarian) had served as an excellent rallying-cry in the struggle to shake off the heavy hand of feudal incompetence as well as the grip of foreign capital before it became the constricting vise which was already pressing so heavily upon China. After the downfall of the *Bakufu* that slogan had been discarded in favor of the new cry *"Fukoku Kyohei"* (A rich country and a strong defense). This slogan became a reality through the government policy of state control over industry and rapid industrialization by means of subsidy, together with jealous care for armaments and the strategic industries. Furthermore, the chiefs of the armed forces in new Japan were not laggard in fulfilling their duties to the state. With the historical background of a warrior *élite* class ever present in the minds of the people, and the dangers to which the country had been exposed in the last decades of feudalism still fresh in their memory, it was unthinkable that the ablest leaders of the enlightened bureaucracy recruited from the *samurai* class should neglect the task of creating a modern army and navy.

The Japanese army until 1872 had consisted in a skeleton form of garrisons located in the larger cities and the Imperial Guard stationed at the capital. These troops were made up exclusively of former *han samurai* mostly of the anti-Tokugawa camp. This army was just strong enough to protect the young government from overthrow by *coup d'état* or civil war. Its ability in this direction to suppress peasant or *samurai* revolts was enhanced by the reforms following upon universal conscription first enforced in 1873. This re-invigorated army met its first real test in suppressing the Satsuma Revolt of 1877, a victory for a conscript army of all classes aided by modern arms and equipment (such as the telegraph) over a stubbornly resisting, but outmoded and inevitably doomed, feudal levy of *samurai*. After this revolt no serious internal armed attack against the government was to be expected. Thus the complete re-organization and expansion of the armed forces from 1882 to 1884 and the revision of the conscription law in 1883 were designed to place the army in readiness for some crisis or contingency other than an internal one. This reform of 1882, which went into full effect in 1884, indicates a most remarkable advance in comparison with the strength of the standing army previous to the reform . . .

The quarter in which possible action might arise was suggested in the words of the greatest figure in Japanese military history, Field Marshal Yamagata. "In the meantime the high-handed attitude of the Chinese towards Korea, which was antagonistic to the interests of Japan, showed our officers that a great war was to be expected sooner or later on the continent, and made them eager to acquire military knowledge, for they were as yet quite unfitted for a continental war."

At the same time commenced the period of feverish naval expansion. The naval expansion plan of 1882 provided for the laying of 48 keels in 8 years. But this was considered to be too slow a pace, so in 1886 it was possible by floating naval bonds to increase the number to 54 vessels. These facts show that the Meiji leaders clearly understood the historical situation and the tasks arising from it. For generations Korea had been the constant source of friction between China and Japan. The appearance in 1884 of another contestant for Korean hegemony, namely Russia, which had concluded a commercial treaty with Korea that year, and the still more important "Overland Commercial Treaty" of 1888, heightened Japanese anxiety over the final destiny of the peninsula. The advocates of the Korean expedition in 1872–3 had been defeated in their plan because the men at the helm realized that Japan was not ready for such expansion since she still lacked a modern army and navy and a mature industry capable of supplying a war-machine or of bringing in foreign exchange through a large export trade. When these prerequisites were called into existence, and when the foreign powers, Great Britain in particular, were willing to remain benevolently neutral if not actually giving technical aid, some of those who had opposed the Korean expedition twenty years earlier now saw the possibilities of defeating the effete Ch'ing Dynasty without serious risk. Their calculations proved to be correct, even to the anticipation of some such obstacle as the Three-Power Intervention of 1895 by Germany, Russia and France, when these Powers forced Japan to relinquish the Liaotung Peninsula.

How the struggle for national independence inevitably led to expansion

National consciousness, which had been awakened in the struggle for the Restoration and by the threat of foreign encroachment, gradually permeated all layers of society in the early years of the Meiji and was sharpened by the arduous attempts at revision of the unequal treaties which were finally crowned with success in 1899. In the meantime, Japanese capitalism had passed through its formative stage, deprived from the first of tariff autonomy and hence forced to labor simultaneously on two fronts. *Internally* its task was to hasten industrialization and the development of a home market, and *internationally*, to win recognition as a Great Power — a consummation which would automatically bring treaty revision, better trading privileges, even alliance with some of the Great Powers. These two problems, the internal and external, were so closely interwoven that it does violence to historical science to discuss them independently with no attempt to inter-relate them, as if such and such a foreign policy could have been arbitrarily adopted or discarded according to the fancies or ambitions of statesmen and generals. Actually the evolution of Japan's social organization, together with the constant pressure of international power politics, compelled Japan in the 19th century to expand in search of the foreign markets so desperately needed to realize the profits which could not be obtained from the narrow home market, and in search of cheap essential raw materials which were denied her through the accident of geography. Thus those nations which had compelled Japan during the turbulent years of the Restoration to put her house in order, to look after her defenses first and last as a guarantee of her own independence, and to build up around these defenses industries which were to become the blood and sinews of a modern military system, now had to witness her emergence from incipient colonial subjection to a position of demanding equal status with themselves. Having once entered upon the path of modernization and industrialization, the molders of Japanese policy saw that if they were to escape the fate of China or Egypt, they must adopt the political methods and economic policy of those powers who had been responsible for Japan's rude awakening and for the partial colonization of China. History is a relentless task-master, and all its lessons warned the Meiji statesmen that there was to be no half-way house between the status of a subject nation and that of a growing, victorious empire whose glory, to paraphrase that gloomy realist Clemenceau, is not unmixed with misery.

Consequently the primary task in Japanese foreign policy during the first thirty years of the Meiji period was to abolish that symbol of a nation destined for foreign domination, the unequal treaties. To turn back before they had reached the status of an independent power would spell humiliation, disaster, and possibly submission to foreign rule, while to continue along the course so brilliantly charted by the Meiji leaders meant expansion in the only direction permitted by history and geography, namely the Asiatic mainland where half-awakened peoples were stirring uneasily under the menace of the Western Powers. The leaders of Meiji Japan saw no reason to abstain from the scramble for the partition of China, and if economic pressure, a narrow home market and scarcity of essential raw materials are to be considered as justification, Japan had more of it than the other powers. So through a complex set of motives, including the necessity for foreign markets and raw materials, the fear of the uncomfortable proximity of Russian influence, and the desire to gain status as a Great Power, Japan successfully emerged from this first trial of strength as a modern nation.

That there was no halting place mid-way between a conquering and conquered nation, as far as Japan at any rate was concerned, and that the bitter struggle for national independence logically led to expansionism is strikingly shown by the fact that Japan acquired extraterritorial rights in China before she had shaken herself free of similar foreign privileges on her own land. Viewed from another point of view, this brings into sharp relief another thesis of this study, that the *lateness* of Japan's entry into the comity of Great Powers left indelible marks on her national structure, her society and government, and hence upon her foreign policy. A modern state was established, and industries were started on the foundation of a very narrow home market at a time when other nations, having long reaped the profits of the old mercantile–colonial period, had progressed through the early morning of *laissez-faire* trading capitalism and were now entering the noontide of an imperialist epoch marked by the acquisition of colonies and spheres of influence. We have seen how Japan telescoped a whole century or more of her development as a capitalist power, passing from her restricted type of town-against-country mercantilism to a social organization compounded of monopoly control in private industry and state control of vital industries, thus permitting no economic freedom of the *laissez-faire* variety and consequently very little political freedom. There were circumstances over which the leaders had only partial control; too much had been conditioned by the preceding, complex history of Japan for them to attempt a point of departure parallel to the development, for instance, of the United States or the Scandinavian countries. Entering the race for empire with all the disadvantages of the late comer, Japan had to prove to the Western Powers her own abilities to undertake the responsibilities and tasks expected of Great Powers. Hence the struggle for the revision of treaties was an integral part of the struggle for recognition as a world power and for the fruits which such recognition brings. The Sino–Japanese War of 1894–5 was the first overt step in a direction which had been apparent before then. "In 1894 Japan had gone to war with China ostensibly over Korea, but really as a necessary step in her internal and external development. By this it must not be understood that the Chinese War of 1894–1895 was a war of mere adventure or spoliation; it was a violent movement desired and pushed forward by the whole nation, both as a practical demonstration of power and as an economical necessity."

The national consciousness which had been forced into existence by events surrounding the Restoration, matured in the heated struggle for treaty revision, was to be strengthened a hundred-fold by the famous Triple Intervention, of April 23, 1895 (six days after the signing of the Treaty of Shimonoseki). Although intervention did not come as a complete surprise to the government, it aroused a feeling of national humiliation which was turned into rage by the unnecessary brutality of the German Minister at Tokyo who openly threatened war if Japan did not comply with the *démarche* of the East Asiatic *Dreibund* (Russia, France and Germany). Aside from the immediate sequel to this intervention, which was the retrocession of the Liaotung Peninsula and the imposition of a heavy indemnity in its place, the effect in Japan was to make national sentiment hyper-sensitive to foreign actions. Thus the adoption of a strong foreign policy came to be not only feasible but popular.

The war of 1894–5, therefore, marked a definite turning-point in Japanese foreign policy along the path of expansion, and enormously strengthened the position of the advocates of such a policy. Despite the Three Power Intervention the rewards from the war were such as to strengthen the arguments of these same advocates. The cession of the rich island of Formosa and of the Pescadores, the indemnity of 230 million Kuping taels (about 36 million pounds sterling) which became the basis for introducing the gold standard into Japan, these tangible results together with the diplomatic prestige which Japan gained were rich prizes for a nation which twenty short years earlier had just emerged from feudal isolation. The full recognition of Japan as a power on equal terms with the other nations automatically followed. Thus in 1899 the Anglo–Japanese agreement to abolish consular jurisdiction became the signal for other countries to reach a similar agreement. The participation of Japanese troops with those of the Great Powers in the suppression of the Boxer uprising in 1900 symbolized this entry of Japan into the ranks of the imperialist powers, and the Anglo–Japanese Alliance of 1902 signified that Japan had been singled out by the most experienced Empire builder, Great Britain, as the most effective counter-balance to its rival, Imperialist Russia. It is indisputable that this Anglo–Japanese Alliance, while benefiting England in its attempts to block Russian monopolistic ambitions in Manchuria and North China, was at the same time an invaluable diplomatic weapon in Japan's victory over Russia. Following this victory Japan replaced Russia as the greatest power either actual or potential in Eastern Asia. These rapid steps leading to the recognition of Japan as a world power were a logical outcome of Japan's victory in the war of 1894–5. What twenty years of peaceful negotiation had failed to do was accomplished forcefully almost overnight. This was at least the superficial explanation of success which greatly strengthened the prestige of the expansionist camp.

Notes

1. It is wrong to think of the spirit of pre-Restoration Japan as being wholly unsympathetic to the development of trade and industry. Under the force of circumstances, the *Bakufu* as well as clans adopted, often reluctantly, many reforms so that with the advice of foreigners like Léon Roches the *Bakufu* made considerable progress toward laying the foundation for military industries.

2. *jacquerie*: a rising by peasants [Editor].

3. *kuge*: the Imperial Court aristocracy [Editor].

4. This is clearly brought out in a lengthy quotation from the *Keizai Roku* of Dazai Shundai. It is sufficiently important to merit reproduction here in part. "All high *samurai* and *daimyo* nowadays use money in all transactions, just as merchants do, and so they are bent on possessing themselves of as much gold and silver as they can. They seem to regard the possession of money as the most essential need of the day. The shortest way to get money is to engage in commercial transactions. In some *han* it has been a long-established practice to find the wherewithal to pay the expenses of their *han* by means of such transactions, thereby making up for the smallness of their fiefs. The *daimyō* of Tsushima, for instance, is master of a small province and his fief produces only a little over 20,000 *koku* of rice. He is, however, rich, and is even better-off than a lord with a fief of 200,000 *koku*, because he purchases Korean ginseng and other goods at low prices and sells them at high prices.

5. Despite the presence of strong anti-foreign feeling in Choshu, the party in power (the Enlightened View Party) was represented by radical, younger *samurai* amongst whom were Ito Shunsuke (later Prince Ito Hirobumi) and Inouye Kaoru, who had both just returned from Europe and were staunch advocates of friendly relations with the Western nations. Henceforth, that is after the bombardment of Shimonoseki, the Choshu leaders dropped their program of expulsion of the foreigner and like Satsuma became attentive students of Western science and learning.

6. Some merchants of considerable wealth were active supporters of the *Kiheitai,* and later when Choshu took a commanding position in the Meiji Government, they were drawn very closely into Government circles.

7. Sansom sums up this trend of clan policy. "Deeply involved in debt, the *daimyo* looked round for means of making or saving money. A few encouraged industries in their fiefs, such as cotton-spinning and the production of special kinds of silk textiles, and gradually it became clear to many members of the military class that they could get out of the grip of the merchants only by following the merchants' example."

8. We can deduce this fact from data given us showing the increase or decrease in the taxation by prefectures during the transitional period 1868–73, that is before the revision of the land tax as compared to after the revision. Since the method and rate of taxation was left virtually untouched during this transition period, it is safe to assume that wherever the tax was high in this period it would be correspondingly high in the last years of the Shogunate.

9. Peasant revolts and town riots (uchi-kowashi) aimed at the clan monopoly system are frequently referred to in studies on uprisings in the Tokugawa period.

10. For many generations the peasant felt resentment against the *samurai* who were often called upon to chastise them. Thus the cry "Down with the *Samurai*," was not uncommon in time of peasant revolt.

11. *goyonin*: a financial advisor or chamberlain in the service of a *daimyo* [Editor].

12. *Eta*: now referred to as the *burakumin*, this earlier, more vulgar term, denotes Japan's pariah group who are deemed to be polluted. [Editor].

13. It must not be that all *samurai* were just biding their time to overthrow the new regime. The great majority and the most active of them were loyal adherents of the new government and did the best they could to secure positions for their less fortunate clansmen. Although Professor Kokusho tells us that the *samurai* tried consciously to direct the peasant movement against the government, he states that such a peasant-*samurai* alliance was bound to fail because the interests of these two classes did not run parallel to each other. Actually, a rebellion of disgruntled *samurai* against the government broke out in Saga in 1874, under Eto Shimpei, and in 1875 in Choshu under Maebara Issei, culminating in the great Satsuma Revolt of 1877 under Saigo Takamori, all of them purely reactionary movements and supported almost exclusively by *samurai*. Thus we see that the *samurai* were far from being a homogeneous class; some of them, relatively few in number, became the actual leaders in the new government, others went into trade and finance, where a few succeeded, others found employment as petty officials in the government apparatus, others became police constables, army officers, while a great number became part of the new professional class of teachers, lawyers, publicists, intellectuals. Still another large section of this class became impoverished farmers, artisans and even laborers.

14. *sake* and *shoyu*: rice wine and soy sauce [Editor].

15. The confiscated property included 50 pairs of gold screens, 3 toy ships made of jewelry, 373 carpets, 10,050 *kin* of liquid gold, 275 large precious stones and numberless small stones, 2 chests of gold, 3,000 large gold coins, 120,000 *ryo* of *koban*, 85,000 *kwamme* of silver, 75,000 *kwan* of copper money, 150 boats, 750 storehouses, 17 storehouses for jewelry, 80 granaries, 80 storehouses for beans, 28 houses in Osaka, 64 houses in other places, a rice stipend for one *daimyo* amounting to 332 *koku* and 150 *chobu* of cypress forest.

16. Indeed the condition of tenant farming is far from being satisfactory, for according to investigations made in 1887, out of ten parts of the products of puddy (paddy?) fields

throughout the country the landowners obtain about six and the tenant-farmers only four, while in regard to the upland fields the relative ratio was 4½ parts and 5½ respectively . . . The steady increase in population far beyond that of the tillage of land . . . keeps rent high because tenants have to compete for leases . . . In extreme cases the share of harvest that falls to the lot of the tenant farmers is barely sufficient to pay the cost of the manure applied to the fields." *Japan at the Beginning of the Twentieth Century*, published by the Imperial Japanese Commission to the Louisiana Purchase Exposition, Tokyo, 1904, p. 90.

17. The burning desire of Japanese leaders to overtake Western technique, particularly in the vitally important sectors of industry, is reflected in the words of Okubo when he visited the Kagoshima Spinning Mill in 1869, "I went to see the Iso spinning-machine: the way it operates is marvelously smooth and delicate, and no words can describe it. What a difference there is between the intelligence of foreigners and ours (so that) we must sigh with shame."

18. *Kaishinto*: The Reform or Progressive Party formed in 1882 and the rival *Jiyuto* or Liberal Party [Editor].

19. The severity of these police regulations restricting political association can be seen by examining the full decree. After many annoying but not insuperable obstacles to political association, there comes the regulation which makes it a criminal offense to advertise a meeting or debate, to induce anyone to attend the meeting, to send out invitations by mail, to establish any local branches of a political party or association, to have any communications between different parties or associations, and to hold open-air meetings. The enforcement of this law was if anything more drastic than its provisions.

20. One of the most interesting examples of these left-wing derivatives of the liberal movement was the *Toyo Shakaito* (Eastern Social Party), first organized in May 1882 in a Buddhist temple, the Kotoji at Shimabara in Hizen. (The site of Shimabara is rather interesting since one of the last great uprisings against Tokugawa domination took place there in the early 17th century. The Shimabara Revolt was generally regarded as inspired by Christians who refused to capitulate to the anti-Christian decrees of the regime.) The leaders of this party were Tarui Tokichi and Akamatsu Taisuke. Its program was as follows: (1) Ethical standards were to guide the speech and conduct of the party members. (2) Equality was to be its guiding principle. (3) The greatest happiness of the masses was to be its goal. It was even hoped that its activities would be extended to Korea and China. Its manifesto closed with the words, "We will not make anybody our enemy, but if there are some obstacles in our way, we are even willing to give our lives to achieve our purpose." When this party's existence was brought to the attention of the Home Minister, he ordered its dissolution, but it continued to exercise influence over some of the local parties for some time to come. These details are taken from a memorandum describing the formation of the party in *Meiji Bunka Zenshu*, Vol. II, pp. 434–5.

Professor Abe Isoh considers this effort of Tarui Tokichi to organize a left wing of the *Jiyuto* as the first attempt to introduce socialism into Japan. Its failure postponed the first successful effort until the end of the century, when the rise of great industries gave the basis for a socialist party, the Social Democratic Party of Japan, founded in 1901. See Abe Isoh, "Socialism in Japan," in *Fifty Years of New Japan*, Vol. II. p. 505.

21. The political philosophy of the extremist wing of the *Jiyuto* was greatly influenced by French and Russian revolutionary thought. The *Contrat Social* of Rousseau, popularized by Nakae Chomin, was an important influence in Japanese liberalism. The heady doctrines of Russian nihilism and of the *Narodniki* also found a welcome hearing among the more

intrepid followers of the early *Jiyuto*. Translations of French and Russian revolutionary novels and treatises, particularly the works of Kropotkin, circulated in those times. Such men as Nakae Chomin and Oi Kentaro, whose radicalism stemmed from French revolutionary thought and who were the theoretical guides of the left-wing of the *Jiyuto*, became the spiritual fathers of Japanese socialism. Among their followers was Kotoku Shusui, executed in 1908 on a charge of high treason. See Asari Junshiro, "The Development of the Social Movement and Social Legislation in Japan," in *Western Influences in Modern Japan*, Japanese Council, Institute of Pacific Relations, Tokyo, 1929, Paper Number 4, Volume II, p. 3.

22. In the first clause of the Act of March 1886, establishing the Tokyo Imperial University (before known as Tokyo University), the purpose of the university is stated to be the following: "The purpose of the Imperial university is to teach and investigate those mysteries of science and learning, of arts and crafts, *which are of practical service to State necessity*," (Italics mine E. H. N.).

The changes embodied in the Act of 1886 provided, among other measures, that the President of the University should also act as the Dean of the Faculty of Law. This Faculty was the citadel of conservatism in the University, and especially after the promulgation of the Constitution in 1889 it was deemed essential that the political philosophy of the nation's highest seat of learning should conform closely to the ideas of the prevailing *étatisme*.

9. Social Structure and Change in Tokugawa and Early Modern Japan
[from Chapter 2 — The Meiji State]
Jon Halliday

Japanese capitalism has been the prodigy of the age of imperialism, the only outsider and late starter to join the leaders of world imperialism. It achieved this in spite of a relatively weak and backward economic base and in spite of engaging almost all the other imperialist powers in war at some point. Thus it is necessary to look not only at the advent of the capitalist mode of production and at the transition from feudalism to capitalism, but also at the construction of the new state machinery which formed the *political* bulwark for capitalism at home and imperialism abroad.

Japan's relatively late entrance into the imperialist group allowed the Meiji oligarchs to model the state on the most advanced and repressive examples available elsewhere in the world. The important government mission, headed by Iwakura Tomomi, which was sent abroad in 1871 greatly admired the British economy — but it was the Prussian state which impressed Japanese politicians. Similarly, some ten years later when Itō Hirobumi, probably the most perceptive of all the Meiji leaders of his day, was scouring Europe for ideas for the new Constitution, it was to Prussia and its theorists that he turned for ideas and for material assistance. This determination to construct a certain kind of state took priority over all other ventures. The Meiji oligarchs put politics firmly in command.

The construction of the new system was not a lightning overnight transformation. The actual "Meiji Restoration" itself (the proclamation of a "return to the old monarchy") can be precisely dated: January 3, 1868. But the political revolution was spread out over a long period, some fifty years — from the reforms in the late Tempō period, through the crucial commercial treaties with foreign powers in 1858 to the installation of the Diet in 1890.

The issues involved in the Meiji Restoration are frequently obscured by placing too much emphasis on subjective intentions (how did the Meiji leaders, who came mainly from the aristocracy, play such an important role in a process which largely promoted the rising forces of capitalism?). The changes were not the result of purely autonomous options on the part of the Meiji leaders. They were caused by developments in the relations of production within Japan and by the irruption of the Western capitalist powers. The key internal question concerns the advent to dominance of the capitalist mode of production.

Jon Halliday: 'The Meiji State' from *A POLITICAL HISTORY OF JAPANESE CAPITALISM* (New York: Monthly Review Press, 1975). pp. 3–18. Copyright © 1975 by Jon Halliday. Reprinted by permission of Monthly Review Foundation.

Domestic preconditions: class structure

Tokugawa feudalism

For over two and a half centuries prior to the Restoration of 1868, Japan lived under a regime usually referred to as the Tokugawa shogunate. This regime was formally established in 1603 after the Tokugawa house had led a victorious coalition of feudal lords at the Battle of Sekigahara in 1600. Under the Tokugawa shogunate, the Tokugawa themselves ruled between one fifth and one-quarter of the country directly, mainly in the central part of Japan, with their capital at Edo (later renamed Tokyo). The area directly controlled by the shogunate also included both Kyoto, the imperial capital, where the powerless Emperor resided, and Osaka, which emerged as the main centre of the merchant class. The rest of Japan was ruled by great lords (daimyō), who were semi-autonomous in their fiefs. The Tokugawa regime cannot be characterized as a centralized autocracy, at least in its initial stages. It was more like a nation-wide truce, with a relatively centralized regime ruling about 20 per cent of the country, surrounded by feudal lords of varying degrees of friendliness or hostility to the shogun.

The Tokugawa devised a highly ingenious system for consolidating their grip on the country and ensuring peace. The key elements in the solution were the virtually total isolation of Japan from the outside world and an institutionalized hostage system under which the daimyō had to leave their wives and children permanently in Edo, and also attend the shogun's court there in alternate years (the *sankin kōtai system*).

In certain ways the Tokugawa system can be seen as an attempt to "refeudalize" Japan. Clearly foreign contact was a prime danger, from the point of view both of ideas and of goods such as armaments. By 1638 the shogunate had enacted a strict seclusion policy, which both prevented Japanese travelling abroad and strictly limited foreign traders' activities in Japan. Prior to the exclusion edicts of 1638 Japan had had a developing merchant class, flourishing, like its counterparts in Europe, on foreign trade. Japanese traders and pirates were operating throughout much of Southeast Asia. The "closure" of the country was a political decision connected with security. It both prevented any anti-Tokugawa *han* (fiefs) being able to arm themselves well enough to challenge the shogunate for over two centuries and also blocked off the normal avenues of development for the nascent bourgeoisie.

The shogunate also developed a sophisticated system of internal control, of which the core was the *sankin kōtai*. This hostage system forced obedience from the daimyō and, together with other measures of a similar nature, gave the Tokugawa the power to control political appointments and, to some extent, to regulate economic policy. The Tokugawa project was a wholesale driving back of the bourgeoisie, which covered politics, economics and culture. By the end of the seventeenth-century, after about one hundred years of Tokugawa rule, Japanese society had been formally immobilized. But though the Tokugawa oppressed the merchant class *politically* with considerable success, they never succeeded in destroying it as an economic force. The *sankin kōtai* system, like Louis XIV's Versailles centralization, encouraged luxury and ostentatious expenditure and forced the aristocracy into heavy indebtedness to the bourgeoisie. All of this encouraged the development of a money economy and strengthened the bourgeois class. At the same time changes in agriculture and among the oppressed peasantry further contributed to the weakening and ultimate collapse of the shogunate.

The class structure of Tokugawa Japan

As part of their system of control, the Tokugawa shoguns ritualized and formalized class relations to a very high degree. At the top of the class structure were the Emperor and the shogun, the sovereign and the ruler, respectively. The shoguns sustained the fiction that they ruled because power was delegated to them by the Emperor. In fact the shoguns used the Emperor's spiritual authority, while keeping him virtually powerless for most of the Tokugawa period. Directly beneath the shogun came the great lords or daimyō, of whom there were 266 immediately before the 1868 Restoration.

The rest of the population was formally divided into four classes (the *shi-nō-kō-shō* structure): samurai (or warriors); farmers (or peasants); artisans (or manufacturers), and merchants at the bottom. However, beneath these four groups there were further "sub-human" divisions, people excluded from society to such an extent that they were not even fitted into the formal categorization. These groups included both the *Hinin* (literally "non-people") and outcastes located even lower than the "non-people."

Under the feudal regime *political* power remained firmly in the hands of the shogunate and the aristocracy, while *economic* power moved increasingly into the hands of the bourgeoisie. The formal class system, which placed the merchants below both artisans and peasants, as well as below the samurai, was therefore subjected to growing strains as time went on. Immediately prior to the Restoration of 1868 some fifteen-sixteenths of the country's wealth was reportedly in the hands of the bourgeoisie.

The size of the population during the Tokugawa period is a subject of some dispute. For some time it was widely thought that the population was virtually stagnant for much of the Tokugawa period. Now it seems more probable that it grew, if rather slowly and unevenly, throughout the period. By 1852 the population was between 29.4 and 32 million. The sectoral distribution of the population in the 1860s was roughly as follows:

Primary industry	80%
Secondary industry	4%
Tertiary industry	9%
Samurai	7%

Immediately after the Restoration, in 1872, the distribution of the gainfully employed (total: 17,319,000) was:

Agriculture and forestry	14,100,000
Mining	6,000
Manufacturing	826,000
Fishery	395,000
Communications	118,000
Commerce	948,000
Public service	502,000
Miscellaneous	179,000

The Tokugawa enforced strict class divisions: "Every social class, and every subdivision within it, had its own regulations covering all the minutiae of clothing, ceremony and behavior, which had to be strictly observed on pain of punishment. The criminal code [was] severe even by feudal standards...; in every conceivable way the Tokugawa administration emphasized the difference, the relative degree of superiority or inferiority of one class to another."[1]

The aristocracy

Immediately below the small group of great lords was the class known as the samurai, or warriors. Formally military retainers of the daimyō, they lived on an annual stipend of rice given them by their lord. The imposition of peace by the Tokugawa deprived them of the chance to engage in military activity.

The society was thus encumbered with a huge parasitic class, sitting very close to the apex of the structure. Along with their families, the samurai, on the eve of the Restoration, numbered some two million people, an incomparably larger feudal class than in European feudal societies. Indeed, a single *han* in Japan had a larger number of samurai than the total number of English knights.

The most important feature of the Japanese aristocracy lies in its relationship to the means of production; particularly land. In Japan, unlike Europe, feudal power was based not on direct ownership of the land but on revenue in rice. The daimyō ran his *han* from a castle town, where he and his samurai resided, the samurai accounting for about half the total population of the average castle town. The most important result of this relationship between the feudal class and the land was the commercialization of the economy. The Tokugawa period saw a real "commercial revolution." Thus the ruling class in Japan was fundamentally in a very much *weaker* position than its counterpart in either feudal Europe or China. Whereas in China, the essential class equation of political power and economic wealth held, in Japan, on the whole, it broke down. Samurai status was often extremely out of line with real economic power. This separation of the samurai as a class from the source of wealth, land, made them highly vulnerable.

However, partly as a result of this situation, the aristocracy developed to some extent as a bureaucracy. Feudalism, although essentially *divisive*, also has a strong centralizing tendency in order to try to minimize anarchy. There emerged a distinctive combination of centralization and decentralization, characterized on the one hand by the elaborate bureaucracy of the Tokugawa in Edo and on the other hand by local bureaucracies under the individual daimyō. The latter, emanating from the central castle town in each fief, were sizeable and complex, being responsible for both administration of the entire domain and relations with Edo. This bureaucratization of the aristocracy both contributed to some slight flexibility within the class structure (caused by the need to find competent administrators) and established one of the conditions for the relatively smooth political transition in the latter half of the nineteenth century.

This bureaucratic entrenchment is linked with the position of the samurai as the country's *ruling* class. As a class, the samurai exploited the labour of others and lived off the fruit of their toil. There was no legal redress for the other classes against the samurai, who were frequently cruel and exploitative. "Their social function was chiefly to over-awe the commonalty, to act as the visible agent of the feudal ruling class in its increasingly exploitative policy toward the people and the peasantry in particular."[2] Easy-going samurai were punished if their severity was found lacking.

On the other hand, the samurai set themselves forth as society's cultural leaders. The centuries of peace undermined their martial role. Many of them were not warriors at all. As part of the attempt to preserve feudal rule, the Tokugawa regime discriminated against bourgeois culture: the aristocratic Nō theatre was privileged against the bourgeois Kabuki; Zen culture, integrally associated with militarism and oppression, was turned against the artisans and the merchants. The Japanese ruling class placed a high value on cultural hegemony as can be seen from their success in imposing, to a very large extent (as in England), repressive cultural standards on the bourgeoisie after the end of feudalism.

Recent scholarship, particularly in the United States, argues that the samurai did not form a social class at all. Much of this recent work has been directed against the Marxist interpretations of Japanese authorities, and against the pioneering work of E. H. Norman. The central thrust has been to detail the proliferation of divisions within the samurai. Albert Craig, an eminent exponent of the anti-Marxist school, notes that: "In Chōshū, for example, there were seventeen ranks or strata within the class of *shi* or knights, and twenty-three of *sotsu* or soldiers. Within each of these two divisions there was a certain limited measure of mobility; between them there was almost none."[3] Such detailed analytical work is extremely valuable; it has shown that previously accepted divisions of samurai simply into "upper" and "lower" are untenable. A highly differentiated analysis is required covering status (*shi* and *sotsu* and distinctions within these two groups), regions (distinctions between the southwest and the northeast, for example) and breakdowns between rural and urban aristocracy within a given *han* (for example, the samurai in Kagoshima, the capital of Satsuma, were quite a different group from those in the Satsuma hinterland). But the detailed work of Craig, Jansen and others has shown only that there were refined internal differentiations within the samurai class; it has not demonstrated that the samurai did not form a class in the Marxist sense. Clearly not only did the samurai see themselves as a separate group, but so did the Tokugawa leaders who endowed them with specific political, legal and economic privileges which differentiated them from the classes below them.

The bourgeoisie

Although formally at the bottom of the class ladder, the *chōnin* (bourgeoisie) actually fared better than the peasantry under the Tokugawa. The internal peace which the Tokugawa imposed after Sekigahara was very stimulating for the economy, in spite of the almost total curtailment of foreign trade. The enforced idleness of the large aristocracy, through whom the country's surplus passed, the construction of castle towns, and the vast expansion of Edo, created conditions for the further enrichment of the *chōnin*.

The most obvious specific feature of the Japanese bourgeoisie was its purely domestic character. Cut off since the early seventeenth century from overseas trade, the lifeblood of all other bourgeoisies, the merchant class was deprived of the base which gave it its relative autonomy in Western societies. By driving the bourgeoisie inwards, seclusion reinforced its social and political subordination.

> Unlike the great merchant bourgeoisie of France and England on the eve of the Industrial Revolution, the merchant class of late Tokugawa Japan was closely tied to the existing political order. The power of the French and English merchants, though certainly not independent of their national political systems, was based firmly upon international commerce and thus gained strength from sources outside any one nation's boundaries. Japanese merchants in contrast grew economically strong wholly through the manipulation of an internal economic structure.[4]

By the end of the eighteenth century Edo was the largest city in the world, and there were many other very large towns dotted around the country. These were not classical "bourgeois" cities, but political-military constructs (as in China), administrative centres with large populations of samurai and hangers-on. This was different from the pattern in the West. The samurai were cut off from the land and barred from engaging in commerce, yet they received much of the agricultural surplus. The *sankin kōtai* system both contributed directly to the expansion of Edo and also forced the daimyō and their retainers into colossal expenses to finance the journeys to and from Edo, and to maintain suitable establishments in the capital and in their own fiefs. Vanity and the ostentation of snobbery accelerated expenditure. Merchants became increasingly attracted to the castle towns and to Edo, and thus attached to the centres of feudal authority. After the mid-seventeenth century, merchants were allowed to organize into guilds and many of them prospered, particularly in the earlier period of Tokugawa rule. The centre of bourgeois prosperity was the city.of Osaka, and Osaka merchants came to control about 70 per cent of the entire country's wealth by the time of the Restoration. Osaka's prosperity was largely based on the *sankin kōtai* system: daimyō; converted their rice revenues into money to pay for their *sankin* expenses. Elsewhere, merchants prospered both as middlemen between the growing castle towns and the countryside, and from the commercialization of the rice surplus via the samurai. By the end of the Tokugawa period as much as half "and probably nearer two-thirds of [agricultural] output was marketed in one form or another."[5] The merchants and merchant financiers, who controlled the commercialization of the economic surplus, thus came to perform some of the functions of a central bank. "They controlled the credit system not only of Osaka and its environs, but of all the major centers of Japan."[6] In Crawcour's phrase, they became "quasi-samurai," receiving stipends which could be as much as those of a minor daimyō in some cases. Merchants prospered on the income from interest on loans to the feudal aristocracy.

Politically and legally, Japan remained a feudal society up to the middle of the nineteenth century. The classes below the samurai had no political rights. There were no representative *chōnin* institutions at all, and the classic bourgeois concept of law was totally absent. "Even the most powerful of the merchant houses were without a tradition of legal protection from debt cancellation, forced levies, or even outright confiscation by political authorities."[7] Before the irruption of the West there were no lawyers in Japan at all, an absence indicative of the highly rigid nature of aristocratic rule under the Tokugawa, and the extent to which Tokugawa feudalism succeeded in divorcing political power and "status," on the one hand, from economic power, on the other. Driven inwards into *rural* commerce by the lack of foreign trade, the merchants thus established a position between the oppressed peasantry and the oppressing aristocracy, operating very much as an agent of the latter. Yet even as the more powerful urban merchants were inextricably joined to the feudal regime, rural merchants developed much greater autonomy. The rural merchants were much more aware of, and sympathetic to, peasant discontent. Their objective class interests did not necessarily lie with the preservation of the existing feudal order. In the critical period between the irruption of the West in the 1850s and the Meiji Restoration in 1867–68, a real break became apparent between the urban guild merchants "with their timidity and attachment to the past" and the rural merchants "with their aggressiveness and fresh outlook."[8]

Essentially, the urban bourgeoisie and the aristocracy formed a power bloc well before the Meiji Restoration. "The interests of the feudal ruling class and the big merchants became so closely intertwined that whatever hurt one necessarily injured the other."[9] This imbrication of a large part of the bourgeoisie with the shogunal regime (the Bakufu) and the success of the feudal regime in retaining a monopoly on political and legal power goes a long way towards explaining the general absence of the bourgeoisie, particularly the urban bourgeoisie, from the anti-Bakufu movement.

The Tokugawa period, in short, combined the retention of the feudal mode of production with the rapid expansion of bourgeois control over capital accumulation. It was not a period of struggle between the merchants as a class and the feudal regime. Not only did the bourgeoisie attach itself to the aristocracy, but the shogunate, although officially hostile to the commercialization of the economy, to some degree had to allow commerce to develop, since it was essential to the working of the regime. The shogunate sought only to keep commerce within certain bounds which were *politically* determined by policy considerations relating to internal control.

The system of feudal *political* control directly affected the long-term development of the economy in every aspect. The urban bourgeoisie, almost wholly dependent on domestic trade and finance, and allied with a parasitic aristocracy split from the land, was to play little part in Japan's early and predominantly rural industrialization — a feature which was to mark the whole process of industrialization. At the same time the use by the shoguns and the local daimyō of political power to allocate monopoly contracts to privileged merchants and financiers (the shogunate in the case of the limited foreign trade permitted and the daimyō by manipulating franchises in their own *han*), as Norman stresses, "is of considerable importance in the history of industrialization in Japan since it strengthened the trend toward State subsidy."[10] The calculated restriction of bourgeois activity allowed the state to wield monopolization as an instrument of control throughout the Tokugawa period. This strengthened state-industry ties along monopoly lines; the interests which catered to this monopoly structure also reinforced the ruling bloc in consolidating a system of capital accumulation based on a very high level of exploitation of labour: "perhaps the most significant role which the plateau [i.e., the later Tokugawa] period played was in imprinting the pattern of monopolistic capitalism with its severe income inequality firmly on Japan."[11]

Rural industry in Japan, moreover, unlike that in the countries of Western Europe just before the bourgeois revolutions there, was not strong enough to win independence from the control of commercial capital, because of the burdens imposed by the prevailing Japanese feudal landed property system. "The Japanese rural industrialists," writes Takahashi, "were unable to overwhelm the privileged seigneurial manufacture based on the financial and military requirements of feudal lords (i.e., the coexistence of feudal authority and commercial capital); on the contrary, the country industry was eventually swallowed up by the ruling setup." In other words, the urban bourgeoisie-aristocracy bloc, although impeding the development of industry for political reasons, retained sufficient control over the process of capital accumulation to buy out the more go-ahead rural interests at the time of the political revolution. Behind this lies the crucial fact that the established system of land ownership (the exaction of feudal rent in kind) prevented the growth of free and independent classes of peasants. And it is this feudal agricultural structure which lies behind and beneath the subsequent industrial structure.

Finally, those commercial contacts which did exist during Japan's two and a half centuries of seclusion were in the hands of the aristocracy, an especially important fact in the middle of the nineteenth century when it was the aristocracy in the southwestern *han* who were accumulating foreign techniques and technicians and thus enabling themselves to leap forward in industry after the "opening" of the country as a whole. In Western Europe much of the contact between countries had been in the hands of the bourgeoisie, traders and pirates, which had put that class in the forefront of foreign relations. But in Japan the general absence of commercial relations with foreign nations meant that the process of re-establishing contact was a predominantly political one, and this left the power of discrimination significantly in the hands of the aristocracy

The peasantry

At the time of the Restoration over three-quarters of the population were peasants. Their standard of living, although varying considerably from one area of the country to another, was, on the average, extremely low. Their political power was nil. Their status was far worse than was implied by their formal position in the *shi-nō-kō-shō* four-class structure. The basic agricultural product was rice, a large part of which was handed over by the peasants who farmed it as rent and tax. Many aspects of the peasantry's existence are subjects of controversy, but it seems certain that agricultural output rose quite considerably during the Tokugawa period.

However, the role of the peasantry in the political changes which culminated in the Meiji Restoration is strongly disputed. As Barrington Moore puts it, "For a variety of reasons, the present generation of Western historians tends to minimize the importance of peasant discontent."[12] The classic Western position is simply stated by T. C. Smith, the author of *The Agrarian Origins of Modern Japan*. Smith wishes to refute the view "popular in some academic and journalistic circles in Japan, that members of the ruling class succeeded in turning the 'revolutionary energy' of the peasants to their own ends — so distorting what would otherwise have been a genuine class revolution . . . The Restoration was not a product of class struggle, though its social consequences were nonetheless revolutionary."[13]

There are really two questions here. What was the nature of the peasant struggles which did indisputably occur? And to what extent did they contribute to the political revolution in the nineteenth century, not just to the Restoration of 1868, in the limited sense of the term?

By their very nature, peasant revolts tend to be poorly documented. History is rarely written by poor farmers, particularly under a feudal regime. But the evidence that exists, allowing for ups and downs within the general trend, shows a steady trend upwards in peasant uprisings throughout the Tokugawa period. The curve continues upwards through the Restoration and peaks in 1873.

The original documents assembled by Hugh Borton in his "Peasant Uprisings in Japan of the Tokugawa Period" give a devastating picture of rural life. Time after time groups of peasants rose in revolt against their feudal lords and against the appropriation of their hard-earned "surplus." These revolts occurred in spite of very harsh laws introduced in 1741, what Borton calls an attempt at "tranquilization by intimidation," which included an almost certain death penalty, usually by crucifixion, for the leaders of the revolt irrespective of whether or not the peasants' complaints were acknowledged to be "justified." The documents also show that the feudal ruling class saw the peasantry's opposition as a *general* threat to feudal power. The shogunate was organized on a national level against peasant revolts, and daimyō were enjoined to assist one another where necessary. Borton, too, in stating his opposition to a peasant revolution, strongly implies that the peasantry were viewed *as a class*: "Japan was spared the ordeal of a bloody revolution such as France had endured. It was fortunate, perhaps, that the farmers had been kept subjugated as a class and had never been unified within the whole country ready to forcibly revolt as a mass against the old feudalistic form of government."[14]

The question of whether or not these revolts can be called "anti-feudal" is disputed. Some of the revolts certainly attacked what the feudal administration saw to be *its* power — and *was* its power. Further, a revolt to prevent the alienation of the peasantry's surplus clearly attacked the very base of feudalism as a system. That the uprisings very rarely set about trying to overthrow the *han* administration, much less the shogunate, says more about the shogunate's success in keeping the peasantry in ignorance than about the class *nature* of the uprisings.

In fact, in spite of Borton's disclaimers, his material supports Norman's contention that "the peasant risings of the Tokugawa period . . . played a noteworthy part in overthrowing the Bakufu. Thus the Restoration, to a large degree, can be justly called the harvest of peasant revolt." The peasant uprisings had made it impossible for the feudal administration, depending as it ultimately did on the dominance of the feudal mode of production, to continue.

It was thus the cumulative effect of repeated uprisings, rather than any one single "peasant revolution," which brought about the downfall of the Bakufu. This is hardly surprising, since it was extremely difficult to communicate from one part of the country to another, as movement between *han* was banned, except on special occasions such as a pilgrimage. Poverty and its attendant problems added to the difficulty. The nature of class antagonisms and class alignments under the Tokugawa can perhaps be further elucidated by a glance at the landholding system and the development of a money economy under the Bakufu.

The prevailing system was that of feudal land ownership based on rent in kind. Both before and after the Meiji Restoration, the key distinction in most Japanese villages was between the *jinushi* or large landowners and the *kosaku* or small dependent peasant-farmers who were tied to paying rent in kind (rice). The "classical" division into capitalist farmers and agricultural wage labour did not occur on the same scale as it did in Western Europe, where the polarization into capital and wage labour led to the disintegration of the village "community."

As the money economy expanded, the feudal lords intensified their exactions from the *kosaku*. Many peasants were driven into extreme poverty and were forced, in spite of the legal prohibitions, to raise money on the security of the lands they leased. But, although the larger peasant revolts did bring about some changes in the shogunate's economic policy, there was no change in the mode of production or in production relationships: "the parasitic system formed itself in imitation of, and side by side with, the land ownership sanctioned by the seigneurial system."[15]

The development of a money economy gradually built up new pressures in the countryside, particularly in the southwest where the money economy was most advanced. Many of the revolts in the later Tokugawa period were against both the feudal system of appropriation and against the new, wealthy farmers. As Horie Hideichi argues: "Agrarian revolts which were anti-feudalistic disturbances at first, later became movements against the wealthy farmers who held a strong economic control over the agricultural field. Agrarian revolts developed into 'Yonaoshi ikki' or 'World levelling revolts'." In the more advanced *han* of southwestern Japan the wealthy farmers managed to turn these revolts against feudalism, and under pressure, the feudal class often split, sometimes allowing alliances to be formed between wealthy farmers and "lower-class military." This development was greatly accelerated by the opening of the ports in 1858 under Western pressure, a move which caused prices to rocket upwards "and brought much suffering to the lower classes."[16] In the north of Japan, where a mercantile economy had not yet developed, the military class stood solid behind the feudal regime.

However, the alignments around the time of the Meiji Restoration cannot be explained primarily by reference to the economic level. In fact the major common feature of the three key *han* in the Restoration, Satsuma, Chōshū and Hizen, was their political autonomy as *tozama han*, which enabled them to mobilize their economic forces to the best effect.

Yet the Restoration of 1868 did not by any means satisfy the discontented peasant class. Although the original "causes" of these uprisings varied greatly, "somehow the

176

flames always spread to the quarter of the richest usurer, the land-grabbing village headman, the tyrannous official of the former feudal lord."[17] Though there were different immediate causes behind the revolts, which did not manage to coalesce, yet, once detonated, the revolts continued to demonstrate clear class characteristics. The new regime soon set about demobilizing this rural potential for revolutionary action.

The dialectic of the internal and the external

The most obvious question about Japan's experience in the nineteenth century in the global context is: why did the competing imperialisms not turn Japan into a colony? And how, after the forcible "opening" of the country, could Japan experience a relatively rapid and unusually "autonomous" economic growth? What, therefore, was the international economic context in which Japan "emerged" from seclusion? By first examining the role of the imperialist powers and their expanding economies in forcing Japan out of seclusion, and then describing which forces inside Japan responded to these external pressures, it will be possible to understand the relationship between this "response to the West" and the domestic forces of production and class struggle.

The irruption of the West

> What is the "impact of the West"? It is the effort of the Western bourgeoisie, as Marx and Engels said in the *Manifesto of the Communist Party* of 1848, to remould the world after its own image by means of terror.
>
> Mao Tsetung, 1949

Until 1853 the only official contact between Japan and the West was via a small establishment of Dutch traders who had been permitted to maintain a post on an island called Deshima in Nagasaki Bay. Limited official contact was also permitted with Japan's two main Asian neighbours, China and Korea. Some of the *han* carried on unofficial trade with the Asian continent. Satsuma, for example, one of the key *han* in the overthrow of the Bakufu, controlled trade with the Ryukyu Archipelago, where it had a base for trade with China. Satsuma also had unofficial relations with Britain towards the end of the Tokugawa period. Thus, Japan was not completely isolated from the rest of the world, but its contacts were very limited and, mainly, controlled by the shogunate.

The three Western countries which played the main roles in breaking Japan's seclusion were Russia, Britain and the United States. The only Western power actually with a base in Japan, the Dutch, played a negligible role in this process, although they were the conduit for new ideas in the period leading up to the Restoration. Dutch interest was concentrated further south in the East Indies (now Indonesia).

Russia had had intermittent contact with the Japanese in Sakhalin and the Kuriles since the early eighteenth century. Early Russian interest was evident in the establishment of an Institute of Japanese Studies in St. Petersburg in 1736. In 1804–5 a fruitless attempt was made to open official relations, via a mission which stayed six months in Japan, but was rebuffed. After the 1804–5 failure, Russian activity flagged, reviving in the middle of the century when it was decided to pursue an active policy in the Pacific and try to make friends with Japan in order to check American and British influence in East Asia. In August 1853 a Russian embassy, headed by Rear Admiral E. V. Putiatin, reached Nagasaki — one month after the American, Commodore Perry, arrived at another port, Uraga, near Edo. Russia subsequently signed consular and commercial treaties with Japan in 1855 and 1858.

During the seclusion period, Russia's drive across the great Eurasian land mass was Japan's most acute worry. The shogunate seems never to have been quite sure of Russia's intentions, as probings and minor clashes occurred in Sakhalin, the Kuriles and even on Hokkaido (then called Ezo). In the early part of the nineteenth century the shogunate is recorded trying to put pressure on a group of daimyō to meet the encroachments of Russia. It was against the Russian threat that the first major attempts at a defence system were mooted.

However, by the middle of the nineteenth century, when Putiatin's mission arrived, Russia seemed primarily interested in a diplomatic friendship with Japan to protect its Pacific flank. Russia at the time was engaged in a major land-grab on the Asian mainland, which culminated in the Treaty of Aigun of 1858, under which China, exhausted by fighting against Britain and France, was forced to sign away vast territories to the Tsar. With its position on the Pacific coast of North Asia thus consolidated, Russia became extremely interested in controlling Sakhalin, where there was a strong Japanese presence. In 1875 Russia and Japan signed a treaty under which Japan renounced its claims to any part of Sakhalin in return for possession of the Kurile Islands. As Sansom has pointed out, Western historians tend to underrate the effect Russia's trans-Asian encroachment had on Japan over the years. Russia presented a territorial and military threat, more than a commercial, economic one. Russia remained fairly unimportant in Japan's trade.

In the middle of the nineteenth century Britain was the number one imperialist power in the world; it had a strong economy, the most powerful navy in the world, and large colonial possessions in Asia, of which the most important was India. Britain had paid little attention to Japan, and London had refused support for attempts by the leading British pirate and looter in East Asia, Stamford Raffles, to break the Dutch monopoly in 1813–14. However, the possession of India led directly to attempts to open up China as a market for Indian opium (and thus as a means to finance British colonialism in India) and as a market for Lancashire textiles. British attempts to unload their unwanted colonial merchandise on the Chinese people led to the Opium War of 1840–42 which both greatly weakened the central Chinese government and led to Britain acquiring its first colonial possession in China, Hong Kong (formally "acquired" in 1842).

The combination of China's weakness and British ruthlessness in the Opium War galvanized many Japanese into an acute awareness of their predicament. The Opium War, followed shortly by the Taiping Rebellion (1850–65), a mass peasant uprising aimed at overthrowing the Manchu regime which had capitulated to British imperialism, had a stimulating effect on the Japanese. The idea of resistance to imperialist pressures was further strengthened by the great revolt in India in 1857–59 (the so-called Indian Mutiny).

The Opium War had two wider effects which connect closely with why Japan was not turned into a colony. First, the grab for China tied up most of Britain's energies in the area over the ensuing decades. Second, the forcible opening of China for foreign trade and the concomitant weakening of the Manchu regime put penetration of China right at the top of most imperialists' list of priorities.

The effect of the Opium War was almost as great in America as it was in Japan. And it was immediately followed by important developments involving the consolidation of the Union's power on the Pacific coast: in 1846 Britain ceded Oregon to the Union; California was added in 1848. The California gold rush focussed America's attention on the Pacific, just when China was being "opened up." Japan, up to then thought of mainly as a possible port of call for whalers, became attractive as a refuelling point on the route to Shanghai. Right from the start Japan was seen by the United States as subordinate in interest to China, and more a *strategic* than an economic goal.

The story of Commodore Perry's intrusion into Japan is fairly well known. Perry made his first successful landing in Japan in July 1853. Formal diplomatic contacts followed and a first treaty was signed the next year. Though the treaty did not explicitly mention trade, it did open two ports to the Americans who saw it as a tactical preliminary to a full "opening." Agreements similar to Perry's followed in quick succession with other powers, including Britain. The "opening of the ports" came in 1858, when Japan was obliged to sign unequal economic treaties with the United States (in the person of Townsend Harris, on July 29, 1858), followed in rapid order by Holland (August 18), Russia (August 19), Britain (August 26) and France (October 9). These treaties, which "opened" Japan to foreign trade on very harsh terms, were the subject of fierce controversy within Japan. The treaties accelerated the general economic disintegration of the period. Foreign trade, naturally, soared, with huge profits for foreign traders because of the extraordinarily large amounts of gold in Japan. The government had to debase the coinage; there was serious inflation, and violent fluctuations in the price of rice.

Part of the reason why Japan was not turned into a colony was the organized resistance of the Japanese ruling class. It had a long and uninterrupted tradition of rule behind it and enjoyed a very high level of literacy and education. Japan's population was also unusually well-educated; its culture was relatively homogeneous. The Japanese regime was not completely successful in keeping the Western imperialists away, but it certainly made penetration of Japan appear a daunting, and perhaps unrewarding prospect — an aspect which must not be underestimated, when it seemed there were quick killings to be made elsewhere. Japan just did not look very attractive.

Connected with this was the fact that China was being invaded *simultaneously*. Both Britain and America which, in spite of their great power, did not have limitless resources, were much more interested in China than in Japan. The British interest involved not simply prising open markets, but also fighting; and for some of these years, Britain also had the Indian Rebellion to fight. Britain, like France and Russia, was also much preoccupied with the Turkish question: the Crimean War started in 1854, the year of the first Japanese treaties with the Western powers. France was tied down in Mexico for a lot of the time and then had to prepare for the war with Prussia. Germany had not yet come on the scene, and when it did its main energies were directed further south and towards the China coast. Russia had the Crimean War to worry about and needed Japan as an ally against the British and the French. Russia's poor communications would have made any assault on Japan at this stage impossible. Spain, already in the Philippines for centuries, was a declining power, not keen to get involved any further. Portugal, somnolent in Macao, reacted likewise. The United States, which had led the best-coordinated drive on Japan, was soon plunged into the Civil War, which meant there could be no military follow-up to Perry. There was a short period of expansionism under Seward in the 1860s, when Alaska and the Aleutians were acquired from Russia, but no full-scale drive across the Pacific.

Revolution and counter-revolution

The Restoration Process, 1853–68

Though Japan was not colonized by any of the Western powers, between 1853 and 1868 various Western powers forced the Bakufu to enter into diplomatic relations and to open major ports to trade under unequal treaties and under unequal trading conditions. The Western powers also landed several thousand troops in Japan and engaged in such sizeable military operations as the opening of the Straits of Shimonoseki in 1864.

The Western powers first attempted to break into Japan by suborning the Bakufu, the central government. The Bakufu made a number of major concessions, including the opening of the ports. These concessions infuriated the aristocracy in many of the *han*, not only those who might be adversely affected economically, but also those who objected politically. This anti-Bakufu feeling at first crystallized around the slogan of *sonnō jōi* ("Revere the Emperor, expel the barbarians"), a negative political position which could hardly be implemented. In this early period it was the Bakufu which was the main supporter of foreigners' rights in Japan, while the *tozama han*, especially in the southwest, were opposed to them. For a time, the Bakufu, under the outstandingly able leadership of Abe Masahiro, the shogunal counsellor, manoeuvred to conciliate the survival of the shogunate with the intrusion of imperialist trade, culture and law, but after a few years of stop-gap measures, Abe's policies were bowled over by the huge socio-economic storm unleashed by the unequal treaties.

Dissatisfaction with the performance of the Bakufu was widespread, and was particularly strong in several of the southwestern *han*, especially in Satsuma, Chōshū and Hizen. These were all *tozama han*, which had a degree of political autonomy from the Bakufu. Their relative economic backwardness meant they had been less integrated economically with the central government. Being in the southwest, they were more in touch with news from abroad, which came through the Dutch at Nagasaki, and thus more alert to the dangers exemplified by the Opium War. They were also involved in illegal foreign trade.

With the increase in internal disorder during the Tempō famine, they turned to Western models for advancement, smuggling *samurai* overseas, setting up schools on the fiefs to teach new learning, and creating Western-style armies in preparation for foreign invasion, or possible conflict with the Bakufu. Meanwhile, the Bakufu, facing the same situation of bankruptcy as the *han*, sought to save itself by currency manipulation and cancellation of debts or interest.

In the period 1853–68 the shogunate's control over much of the country weakened. Part of the samurai class in certain *han* stood by the Bakufu; others, especially in the southwest, turned against it. Some of the samurai who turned against the Bakufu were closely connected to the local *han* administrations; others were *rōnin* (masterless samurai), who often operated as free-lance aides to members of the bourgeoisie in activities as varied as fencing teachers and debt collectors. In the Western *han* a new highly educated technical bureaucratic samurai group emerged, brought up with Western military technology and political ideas. This group, while Western-influenced, was also in favour of the *jōi* ("expel the barbarians") policy and can not be easily characterized as "progressive" or "reactionary." Some were interested in improving their economic position, in the face of increasing *chōnin* power and prestige; others were more interested in military reassertion; some in political anti-feudalism; others in samurai reinstatement. As the showdown came nearer, actual military equipment, as well as martial spirit, became important, and here again it was mainly the southwestern *han* which had been active in importing advanced Western technology.

Notes

1. Norman, *Japan's Emergence*, p. 12.

2. Norman, "Andō Shōeki," p. 113.

3. Albert Craig, "The Restoration Movement in Chōshū," *JAS*, Vol. 18, No. 2 (February 1959), p. 189. Chōshū is in southwest Honshu.

4. Thomas O. Wilkinson, *The Urbanization of Japanese Labor, 1868-1955* (Amherst, University of Massachusetts Press, 1965), p. 28.

5. Crawcour, "The Tokugawa Heritage," p. 41. I am very grateful to Ben Brewster for allowing me to consult his paper, "Pre-Restoration Conditions for Economic Growth in Japan" (manuscript, 1967), which elucidated many issues.

6. E.S. Crawcour, "Changes in Japanese Commerce in the Tokugawa Period," *JAS*, Vol. 22, No. 4 (August 1963), reprinted in Hall and Jansen, eds, *Studies in the Institutional History* . . ., p. 196.

7. Wilkinson, *Urbanization of Japanese Labor*, p. 32; Norman, *Japan's Emergence*, p. 82; for some qualification, Toyoda, *History of Pre-Meiji Commerce*, p. 91.

8. Ike, *Beginnings*, p. 17; cf. Crawcour, "Changes in Japanese Commerce in the Tokugawa Period," pp. 199-201.

9. Norman, *Japan's Emergence*, p. 50.

10. Norman, *Japan's Emergence*, p. 19; Sheldon, *Rise of the Merchant Class*, p. 22. On this, and many other matters, see W. Donald Burton, *The Origins of the Modern Japanese Iron and Steel Industry, with Special Reference to Mito and Kamaishi 1853-1901* (Ph.D. thesis, London University, 1972).

11. Spencer, "Japan's Pre-Perry Preparation for Economic Growth," p. 214.

12. Moore, *Social Origins of Dictatorship and Democracy*, p. 255.

13. T.C. Smith review of Craig, *Chōshū in the Meiji Restoration*, and Jansen, *Sakamoto Ryōma JAS*, Vol. 21, No. 2 (February 1962), p. 216. Smith's use of the world "journalistic" helps to cover the fact that such a view is "popular" in *political* circles. His conclusion involves a magical approach to history where there are "revolutionary consequences" which are not the product of class struggle.

14. Borton, "Peasant Uprisings," p. 95.

15. Takashi, "Recent Trends of the Studies in Economic History in Japan," p. 19.

16. Hideichi Horie, "Revolution and Reform in Meiji Restoration," p. 28.

17. Norman, *Japan's Emergence*, p. 73; cf. Norman, *Soldier and Peasant*, on the urgent need for conscription to build up an army to ensure peasant submission to the new state.

10. Commentaries on Constitutional Provisions Relating to Emperor's Position, 1889

Ito Hirobumi

One of the principle Meiji oligarchs, Ito Hirobumi (1841–1909), was also the first Prime Minister of Japan from 1885–8. Ito was to be a leading figure in the transformation of Japan, who was largely responsible for shaping the state and political system in the Meiji era. His influence is seen in the Meiji Constitution of 1889, of which he was the main draughtsman. The authoritarian and hierarchical ethos of this constitution, which was inspired by Bismarck's Prussia, was to become an enduring facet of Japanese society. [Editor]

The Emperor

The Sacred Throne of Japan is inherited from Imperial Ancestors, and is to be bequeathed to posterity; in it resides the power to reign over and govern the State . . .

ARTICLE I. *The Empire of Japan shall be reigned over and governed by a line of Emperors unbroken for ages eternal.*

Since the time when the first Imperial Ancestor opened it, the country has not been free from occasional checks in its prosperity nor from frequent disturbances of its tranquility; but the splendor of the Sacred Throne transmitted through an unbroken line of one and the same dynasty has always remained as immutable as that of the heavens and the earth. At the outset, this Article states the great principle of the Constitution of the country, and declares that the Empire of Japan shall, to the end of time, identify itself with the Imperial dynasty unbroken in lineage, and that the principle has never changed in the past, and will never change in the future, even to all eternity. It is intended thus to make clear forever the relations that shall exist between the Emperor and his subjects.

By "reigned over and governed" is meant that the Emperor on his Throne combines in himself the sovereignty of the State and the government of the country and of his subjects. An ancient record mentions a decree of the first Emperor in which he says:– "The Country of Goodly Grain is a state, over which Our descendants shall become Sovereigns: You, Our descendants, come and govern it." . . . It will thus be seen that the Imperial Ancestors regarded their Heaven-bestowed duties with great reverence. They have shown that the purpose of a monarchical government is to reign over the country and govern the people, and not to minister to the private wants of individuals or of families. Such is the fundamental basis of the present Constitution . . .

Source: Lu, D.J. (ed.). *SOURCES OF JAPANESE HISTORY* (McGraw-Hill, 1974).

ARTICLE III. *The Emperor is sacred and inviolable.*

"The Sacred Throne was established at the time when the heavens and the earth became separated" (*Kojiki*). The Emperor is Heaven-descended, divine and sacred; he is pre-eminent above all his subjects. He must be reverenced and is inviolable. He has indeed to pay due respect to the law, but the law has no power to hold Him accountable to it. Not only shall there be no irreverence for the Emperor's person, but also shall he neither be made a topic of derogatory comment nor one of discussion.

ARTICLE IV. *The Emperor is the head of the Empire, combining in himself the rights of sovereignty, and exercises them, according to the provisions of the present Constitution.*

The sovereign power of reigning over and of governing the State, is inherited by the Emperor from his Ancestors, and by him bequeathed to his posterity. All the different legislative as well as executive powers of State, by means of which he reigns over the country and governs the people, are united in this Most Exalted Personage, who thus holds in his hands, as it were, all the ramifying threads of the political life of the country, just as the brain, in the human body, is the primitive source of all mental activity manifested through the four limbs and the different parts of the body. For unity is just as necessary in the government of a State, as double-mindedness would be ruinous in an individual. His Imperial Majesty has himself determined a Constitution, and has made it a fundamental law to be observed both by the Sovereign and by the people. He has further made it clear that every provision in the said Constitution shall be conformed to without failure or negligence . . .

ARTICLE V. *The Emperor exercises the legislative power with the consent of the Imperial Diet.*

The legislative power belongs to the sovereign power of the Emperor; but this power shall always be exercised with the consent of the Diet. The Emperor will cause the Cabinet to make drafts of laws, or the Diet may initiate projects of laws; and after the concurrence of both Houses of the Diet has been obtained thereto, the Emperor will give them his sanction, and then such drafts or projects shall become law. Thus the Emperor is not only the center of the executive, but also the source and fountainhead of the legislative power . . .

ARTICLE VIII. *The Emperor, in consequence of an urgent necessity to maintain public safety or to avert public calamities, issues, when the Imperial Diet is not sitting, Imperial Ordinances in the place of law. Such Imperial Ordinances are to be laid before the Imperial Diet at its next session, and when the Diet does not approve the said Ordinances, the Government shall declare them to be invalid for the future.*

. . . It will be seen that Article V, providing that the exercise of the legislative power requires the consent of the Diet, regards ordinary cases; while the provisions of the present Article, authorizing the issuing of Imperial Ordinances in the place of laws, refers to exceptional cases in times of emergency. This power mentioned in the present Article, is called the power of issuing "emergency Ordinances." Its legality is recognized by the Constitution, but at the same time abuse of it is strictly guarded against. Thus the Constitution limits the use of this power to the cases of urgent necessity for the maintenance of public safety and for the averting of public calamities, and prohibits its abuse on the ordinary plea of protecting the public interest and of promoting public welfare. Consequently, in issuing an emergency Ordinance, it shall be made the rule to declare that such Ordinance has been issued in accordance with the provisions of the present Article. For, should the Government make use of this power as a pretext for avoiding the public deliberation of the Diet or for destroying any existing law, the provisions of the Constitution would become dead letters having no significance whatever, and would be far from serving as a bulwark for the protection of the people. The right of control over this special power has, therefore, been given to the Diet by the present Article, making it necessary, after due examination thereof at a subsequent date, to obtain its approbation to an emergency Ordinance.

Of all the provisions of the Constitution, those of the present Article present the greatest number of doubtful points. These points will be cleared up one after the other, by presenting them in the form of questions and answers . . . Sixthly: When the Diet has refused its approbation, may it demand the retroactive annulment of the Imperial Ordinance in question? As the Sovereign is authorized by the Constitution to issue emergency Ordinances, in the place of law, it is a matter of course that such Ordinances should have effect as to the period of time they have been in existence. The refusal of approbation by the Diet is consequently to be regarded simply as its refusal to approve the future continued enforcement of the Ordinance as law, and such refusal cannot reach the past. Seventhly: Can the Diet amend such an Imperial Ordinance before giving its approbation to it? According to the express provisions of the present Article, there are only two alternatives open to the Diet; either to give or not to give its approbation; so that it has no power to amend such an Ordinance.

ARTICLE IX. *The Emperor issues or causes to be issued, the Ordinances necessary for the carrying out of the laws, or for the maintenance of the public peace and order, and for the promotion of the welfare of the subjects. But no Ordinance shall in any way alter any of the existing laws.*

The present Article treats of the sovereign power of the Emperor as to administrative ordinances. A law requires the consent of the Diet, while an ordinance holds good solely by decision of the Emperor. There are two occasions for the issuing of an ordinance: the first is, when it is required to regulate measures and details for the carrying out of any particular law; the second, when it is required to meet the necessity of maintaining the public peace and order and of promoting the welfare of the subjects . . .

Emergency Ordinances mentioned in the preceding Article shall take effect within the limits of law, and although they can supply the deficiency of law, yet they shall have no power to either alter any law or to regulate those matters for which a law is required by express provision of the Constitution . . .

ARTICLE XI. *The Emperor has the supreme command of the Army and Navy.*

. . . At the beginning of the great events that achieved the Restoration by the present August Sovereign, his Imperial Majesty issued an Ordinance, proclaiming that he assumed personal military command for the suppression of rebellion, thus manifesting that the sovereign power was centered in him. Since then, great reforms have been introduced into the military system. Innumerable evil customs, that had been long prevailing, were swept away. A General Staff Office has been established for his Imperial Majesty's personal and general direction of the Army and Navy . . . The present Article is intended to show, that paramount authority in military and naval affairs is combined in the Most Exalted Personage as his sovereign power, and that those affairs are in subjection to the commands issued by the Emperor.

ARTICLE XII. *The Emperor determines the organization and peace standing of the Army and Navy.*

The present Article points out, that the organization and the peace standing of the Army and Navy are to be determined by the Emperor. It is true, that this power is to be exercised with the advice of responsible Ministers of State; still like the Imperial military command, it nevertheless belongs to the sovereign power of the Emperor, and no interference in it by the Diet should be allowed. The power of determining the organization of the Army and Navy, when minutely examined, embraces the organization of military divisions and of fleets, and all matters relating to military districts and sub-districts, to the storing up and distribution of arms, to the education of military and naval men, to inspections, to discipline, to modes of salutes, to styles of uniforms, to guards, to fortifications, to naval defenses, to naval ports and to preparations for military and naval expeditions. The determining of the peace standing includes also the fixing of the number of men to be recruited each year.

11.   Imperial Rescript On Education
In the name of Mutsuhito, the Meiji Emperor

The imperial rescript on education was issued by Emperor Meiji on October 30, 1890. It was drafted by Motoda Eifu (1818–1891), a Confucian mentor to Emperor Meiji and Inoue Kowashi (1844–1895) who also participated in the drafting of the constitution. Yamagata Aritomo also took an active part.

It incorporated the neo-Confucian moral precepts in the garb of modern nationalism, and attempted to make them the foundation of education. Children were taught to hark back to "the glory of the fundamental character of Our Empire," and to "render illustrious the best traditions of your forefathers." There was an unmistakable reaction to the rapid pace of Westernization and a desire to return to the purity of "Japanism". It served to indoctrinate generations of school children, through periodic public readings of the rescript and through required memorization, but it was repudiated in 1948 by the second post-war Diet.

Imperial Rescript on Education, 1890

Know ye, Our subjects:

Our Imperial Ancestors have founded Our Empire on a basis broad and everlasting, and have deeply and firmly implanted virtue; Our subjects ever united in loyalty and filial piety have from generation to generation illustrated the beauty thereof. This is the glory of the fundamental character of Our Empire, and herein also lies the source of Our education. Ye, Our subjects, be filial to your parents, affectionate to your brothers and sisters; as husbands and wives be harmonious, as friends true; bear yourselves in modesty and moderation; extend your benevolence to all; pursue learning and cultivate arts, and thereby develop intellectual faculties and perfect moral powers; furthermore advance public good and promote common interests; always respect the Constitution and observe the laws; should emergency arise, offer yourselves courageously to the State; and thus guard and maintain the prosperity of Our Imperial Throne coeval with heaven and earth. So shall ye not only be Our good and faithful subjects, but render illustrious the best traditions of your forefathers.

The Way here set forth is indeed the teaching bequeathed by Our Imperial Ancestors, to be observed alike by Their Descendants and the subjects, infallible for all ages and true in all places. It is Our wish to lay it to heart in all reverence, in common with you, Our subjects, that we may all attain to the same virtue.

Source: Lu, D.J. (ed.). *SOURCES OF JAPANESE HISTORY* (McGraw-Hill, 1974).

12. A Century of Japanese Economic Growth
Kazushi Ohkawa and Henry Rosovsky

Introduction

A century of rapid development is, even for the economic historian, a bit too long for analytical comfort. It must be almost intuitively clear that during this period trends changed from time to time forming identifiable and relatively unified *phases of growth*. The dating, identification, and explanation of these phases are the major tasks which we will attempt in this paper. Our hope is that the suggested phases provide a useful framework within which one can examine the entire experience of modern Japanese economic development.

A growth phase is not an arbitrarily selected period of years; it must conform to certain analytical principles. The following principles have been adopted:

1. The duration of a phase must be long enough to be distinguished from short-term economic movements. By definition it must be of longer duration than the ordinary business cycle, because the distinctive properties of a phase (see below) will transcend the temporary ups and downs of the cycle.

2. The characteristics of a given phase must be distinctive in that, not necessarily singly but in combination, they are unique to that phase.

3. The characteristics of a particular phase must bear an analytical and historical relationship to the preceding and succeeding phases. This involves more than saying that the preceding phase is one of preparation for the given. It involves something less than the claim of an inevitable historical order of phases. In other words, certain properties of one phase will exert influences which bring about the next phase.

4. A phase of modern economic growth must possess certain common and distinctive characteristics within the general analytical scheme. But these characteristics may differ among important groups of units undergoing modern economic growth.

5. Finally, a given phase must display empirically testable characteristics. This does not necessarily confine the analysis to quantification . . . Carefully defined, the range of empirical verification can be quite broad.

Before turning to an exposition of the phases, it may be useful to remind the reader of ten key characteristics which prevailed during the entire century under consideration. These are:

1. A relatively high rate of over-all growth in terms of output and per capita income, with some spurts and some retardations;

Ohkawa, Kazushi and Rosovsky, Henry: Extracts from 'A Century of Japanese Economic Growth,' in *THE STATE AND ECONOMIC ENTERPRISE IN JAPAN: ESSAYS IN THE POLITICAL ECONOMY OF GROWTH*, edited by W.W. Lockwood (Princeton University Press, 1965), pp. 47–92. Copyright © 1965 by Princeton University Press. Reprinted by permission of Princeton University Press.

2. A pattern of population growth which, in terms of rates of natural increase, is reminiscent of the historical experience of Europe rather than that of currently underdeveloped areas, and which did not contain substantial emigration or immigration while retaining a highly flexible labor supply;

3. For the given level of per capita income, a relatively high proportion of domestic investment (and saving) accompanied by several upward movements of the investment (savings) ratio;

4. For the given level of per capita income, a relatively low proportion of personal consumption, accompanied by several downward movements of the consumption ratio;

5. A sustained low capital–output ratio, showing, however, an upward drift in the postwar period;

6. Modern economic growth taking place, in general, in an inflationary setting, the only exception to this being the 1920's;

7. Recurring balance of payments crises such that one may almost speak of a chronic deficit of foreign payments;

8. The general co-existence of traditional and modern economic sectors, this being partly reflected in the bi-modal (large-scale/small-scale) distribution of enterprises;

9. The important role played by government in furthering economic modernization, especially in mobilizing and spending investment funds;

10. A specifically created group of financial institutions which greatly enhanced the supply of capital.

We consider these characteristics to be empirically verified, and will expand on them only as becomes necessary in following the argument concerning the phases. One further point can be made. The enumerated characteristics are not necessarily peculiar to Japan; in large measure they seem to apply also to what are generally referred to as "follower countries" or industrial latecomers."

The phases: short and long

A. The First Phase of Modern Economic Growth, 1868–1905

    I. Transition, 1868–1885

    II. Initial Modern Economic Growth, 1886–1905

B. The Second Phase of Modern Economic Growth, 1906–1952

    III. Differential Structure: Creation, 1906–1930

    IV. Differential Structure: Economic and Political Consequences, 1931–1952

C. The Third Phase of Modern Economic Growth, 1953–present

    V. Postwar Growth, 1953–present

Transition, 1868–1885

The attributes of modern economic growth

The years between 1868 and 1885 form the transition between the time when modern economic growth (hereafter MEG) became the *national* objective and its actual beginnings in 1886. It seems to us that with the Meiji Restoration of 1868 MEG became a national objective for the first time, and we will argue that this type of growth could not really begin in any meaningful sense until the Matsukata deflation had run its full course. Thus, transition examines the lag between the adoption of a national objective and the beginning of its achievement — in Japan, a short period of slightly less than twenty years. An understanding of transition requires two major ways of looking at the data. First, we must examine the *given* conditions, i.e., the state of economy and society at the point where MEG became a national objective. Second, we must see how the given conditions were shaped or changed — by public or private action — to bring about the beginning of MEG.

What is MEG? We define it in terms of the generally accepted Kuznets criteria: (1) the application of modern scientific thought and technology to industry, transport, and agriculture; (2) sustained and rapid rise in real product per capita combined with high rates of population growth; (3) high rates of transformation of the industrial structure; and (4) the presence of international contacts. MEG means the presence to a greater or lesser degree of *all* of these attributes, and we will try to show that one cannot find all of them in Japan until roughly 1886.

We may well begin by asking the following questions: can any of the attributes of MEG be identified in Japan at the precise moment of the Restoration? What were the givens?

To begin with, there is no real evidence to indicate that real product per capita was rising in a rapid or sustained manner in the 1860's. Furthermore, there is no reason to believe that population was increasing rapidly at that time. Let us examine some of the available information. In the late 1870's, 75 to 80 percent of the gainfully occupied population was engaged in agriculture, this proportion may have been slightly higher in the 1860's. When the national income figures begin in the 1870's, the agricultural sector produced about 65 percent of the national product. Per capita product — taking into account all sectors — stood at around ¥20.00 in current prices, or very roughly U.S. $65, using the postwar rate of exchange. This figure could not have been appreciably higher in the 1860's. Whatever one may believe about the level of wealth in pre-industrial Japan, or about the distribution of income, it is pretty clear that the country in 1868 was strongly typified by the small peasant cultivator working only slightly above subsistence levels. And this is an important (if obvious) point, because it implies that raising the growth rate of national per capita product required significant increases in *average national* agricultural practice and the introduction of new industries. In significant amounts all this came only after 1868

Our knowledge about the demographic aspects of early modern Japan is a bit more detailed and reaches back further in time. In 1852 the total population of Japan was roughly between 29.4 and 32 million. A report for 1872 suggests a level of 34.8 million. In the 1870's the rates of increase were of the order of ¾ of 1 percent per year, and no one would be disposed to call this a high rate of population growth. At this time, also, the vital rates were in keeping with those of a backward country. Death rates must have been very high, requiring fertility rates in the neighborhood of 40/1000 to produce slow increases of population.

Let us turn next to the rate of transformation of the industrial structure at the time of the Restoration. In the context of detecting modern economic growth, this must be taken to mean the rapid relative shift from agriculture to manufacturing and perhaps services. The value of manufacturing output amounted to about 30 percent of commodity production. Its structure was as follows:

	Value(%)		Value (%)
1. Textiles	27.7	5. Utensils	7.7
2. Food Products	41.9	6. Paper Products	5.2
3. House Accessories	1.7	7. Capital Equipment	5.9
4. Lamp Oil and Candles	6.3	8. Medicines & Cosmetics	3.6

These figures are subject to a variety of criticisms; nevertheless they clearly reveal certain features of the Japanese economy shortly after the Restoration. We have here a fairly typical pre-modern manufacturing pattern. Textiles and food together account for over 70 percent of the value of all manufacturing output, while what is called "capital equipment" is extremely small. The two most important items manufactured were cloth (15 percent of all manufactures) and the brewing or distillation of alcoholic beverages — mostly sake (16.8 percent of all manufactures). The kinds of cloth which were produced in 1874 are also known. Cotton led by a wide margin (63.3 percent), followed by silk (26.7 percent), mixed cottons and silks (8.0 percent), and linen and others (2.0 percent). However, cotton's dominance does not indicate the presence of the modern factory cotton industry; this did not really begin until the 1880's. In 1874 we are still dealing with the old cotton industry largely processing native raw materials.

In general, it should be obvious that very little of this manufacturing took place in "factories" or even in fairly large-scale enterprises. The typical enterprise was small and worked by domestic methods using little wage labor. Much of the manufacturing took the form of rural by employments. There exist no solid quantitative sources to prove or disprove these propositions, and there may have been some exceptions, but we feel that most students of the subject will agree with this assessment. There is some indirect proof in support of our view in the geographical distribution of manufacturing for the two leading products. Both cloth weaving and sake-brewing were widely distributed throughout the entire country, implying small units of production. The leading six prefectures (out of a total of 63) produced only 29 percent of all alcoholic beverages; the leading 11 prefectures wove 58 percent of all cloth — admittedly a somewhat higher level of concentration.

It would thus be possible to draw a picture of Japan as a fairly typical underdeveloped country: an economy which tended towards being dominated by rice (63 percent of the value of agricultural output), and whose industries were largely of the handicraft type catering to local needs. This need not mean that the industrial structure was static in the 1860's, but it does mean that the pace of progress was slow and the impact of changes was limited. Many students of Japanese economic history may be disposed to object to these characterizations, and there has been much attention paid to the economic changes especially in the first half of the nineteenth century. Although their vocabulary is usually different, a number of factors are commonly cited as evidence for significant changes in the industrial structure: growth of output in agriculture, commercialization of agriculture, diffusion of traditional industries, and the establishment by certain *han* (clans) of some Western industries. We cannot analyze all of these in detail, and instead will simply comment on some of these contentions.

1. First, the growth of output and commercialization of agriculture. Research has demonstrated that agriculture in certain regions became more productive during the late Tokugawa era. It has not — and cannot — show that there were significant increases in the average level of performance. This confusion between regions and aggregate averages is also important in assessments of the degree of commercialization. The statement that Japanese agriculture by the 1860's had become basically commercial is not rare, but it is almost certainly wrong. *At present* (1963) slightly over 60 percent of agricultural output reaches the market. In the 1860's, before the land tax, the ratio probably stood at a level of about 20 percent. There were, it is true, regions where commercial agriculture was dominant (such as the Kinai and Tōsan) but these were more than counterbalanced by areas where the peasant still practiced subsistence farming, as in most of Kyūshū, Shikoku, and Hokuriku.

2. The diffusion of industry during the first half of the nineteenth century — essentially its spread to the towns and villages — is analogous to the undermining of guilds in the West and the rise of cottage industry and the putting-out system. It is evidence of some changes of the industrial structure, mainly in that it must have increased rural by-employments, but it is not a rapid rate of transformation characteristic of MEG.

3. Many scholars have attributed considerable importance to the establishment of certain modern Western industries by a few *han* during the first half of the nineteenth century. Since these were frequently connected with a desire to produce armaments, E. H. Norman[1] went so far as to suggest that the "normal" pattern for an industrial revolution was reversed in Japan, with heavy industry preceding the development of light industry. This is, we believe, a misunderstanding of the implication of an industrial revolution and MEG. One could argue that some of these establishments were useful investments. More to the point, one could stress the technical and managerial experience acquired by a few people. Yet none of this should be exaggerated. Isolated islands of modernity existed and exist in most backward countries, and these should not be confused with the genuine beginnings of an industrial revolution. A few spinning mills and iron foundries cannot be said to change the industrial structure of a country with a population of some 30 million people.

There now remain two other attributes of MEG: the application of modern scientific thought to technology and industry, and the presence of international contacts. Once again we can restrict ourselves to a few brief comments:

1. There existed, in the 1860's, virtually no modern technology or industry, and consequently modern scientific thought could not possibly have been involved in the productive process — except in highly unusual cases. Whatever scientific and technological knowledge was available in pre-modern Japan — and some scholars focusing on *rangaku* (Dutch studies) and the activities of large *han* would conclude that the amounts were not insignificant — must be regarded at this stage as a useful potential for industrialization. If the subject of potentials is to be introduced, there existed one other of much greater eventual importance, and also intimately related to the economic application of science and technology. This was, of course, the stock of education in Japan at the time of the Restoration, As Dore has recently remarked: "Japan, we are frequently told in these days of growing punditry on the course and causes of economic development, is 'different.' And there is by now a growing awareness that one of the ways it differs from most other late-developing countries is in starting its career of forced-pace modernization with a widespread and well-developed tradition of formal institutional education."[2] Briefly, this meant that by the time of the Restoration approximately 50 percent of all Japanese males and 15 percent of all Japanese females were getting some formal education outside of their homes; that total school attendance was over 1,100,000 pupils, mostly in *terakoya* (private elementary schools, primarily for commoners); that the *bushi* (Samurai) class may have been completely literate, and that a large number of merchants and farmers also could read and write; that, in view of all this, the concept of universal elementary education was speedily acceptable. No doubt all of these assets helped in the eventual achievement of MEG. In 1868, however, these were merely potential forces for the most part.

2. The reestablishment of diplomatic and trade relations in the 1850's brought a period of considerable confusion to Japan. To gauge the net effect of these influences at the time of the Restoration is difficult. The amount of foreign trade was still very small, and the situation one of considerable flux. There can be no doubt about the impact of renewed contact with the West — intellectual and economic. Certain segments of the economy benefited, others were hurt. The possibility of economic modernization was uniquely tied up with the expansion of imports and exports. Normalization of foreign political and economic relations, following over 200 years of seclusion was one of the main tasks of the new government. This much can be said: of all the four criteria of MEG, this was the only one in clear evidence at the time of the Restoration; and it was certainly one of the most important forces pushing Japan in the direction of rapid economic change.

How the givens were changed

How the givens were changed to bring about the beginnings of MEG is a story which includes a great many diverse factors. We cannot even list them all, and will have to content ourselves with a highly selective presentation. It seems to us that the government played an especially crucial role in transition, and many of its activities can be subsumed under the general heading of "unification." In this context, unification requires a broad interpretation. It means, for example, the spread of more advanced indigenous agricultural techniques from wealthier to poorer parts of the country, as well as the encouragement of improvements in these techniques. Unification also increased the economic incentives of large groups in the working population. (These aspects will be treated in more detail when we take up Initial Modern Economic Growth, 1886–1905) It can also include some of the major socio-economic institutional changes initiated by the Meiji government: the abolition of the Tokugawa class structure, the freeing of internal and external travel and commercial communications, and the abolition and commutation of *bushi*[3] privileges. Even the most important reform of all — the Meiji land tax — had significant unifying features, in that agricultural taxes were made uniform nationally and farmers were more closely drawn into the national economy. Most of these institutional reforms were accomplished by 1880, and they did much to further the cause of MEG. But by themselves they were not sufficient. MEG also required a new financial base, and since less is known about this episode we will go into somewhat greater detail.

Financial aspects of transition

Let us cast the problems faced by the new Meiji government in the language currently employed in the analysis of economic planning.

1. The long-run objective of the new government was MEG, and the short-run objective was to achieve the conditions which made MEG a realistic possibility. Negatively, this required the abolition of certain pre-modern institutions. Positively, it implied establishing the minimum conditions which would permit MEG to begin.

2. The financial targets of the new government were the creation of a modern public budget system, and a modern currency and banking system.

3. Certain financial and physical resources were available to the government in order to achieve these targets. These were: inherited assets from the pre-Restoration period which could be made available through domestic borrowing (although one must recall that there were also considerable inherited liabilities); foreign borrowing; increases in domestic output; and redistribution of income flows and capital stock. All of these resources were limited.

4. Means of implementation were also limited for the new government because it had to economize its available resources, and also because the range of feasible implementation methods was narrow. In the Meiji period, and thereafter, Japan was never a controlled or planned economy. Consequently, governmental targets had to be achieved by means of an economic, rather than an outright political, mechanism. As a result, implementation brought a variety of economic shocks — such as inflation and deflation.

5. Those factors which limit the ability of a new government to act are called boundary factors, and this necessarily includes factors which are not exclusively economic. The following appear especially relevant to the financial targets of the

transition period. First, the time element was crucial for the new government, because delays in reaching its targets would have magnified internal and external threats. Second, and closely related, was the problem of the power balance between government and anti-government forces. Policies of the Meiji government had to take into account their possible effect on mobilizing forces interested in its overthrow. Third, relations with foreign powers also limited the actions of the new government. These not only restricted foreign borrowing but also gave a set frame to external trade conditions which the government, at that stage, could not change. For example, throughout the period of transition, Japan did not have tariff autonomy, and most exports and imports were in the hands of foreign merchants.

The actual years of transition divide themselves very naturally into two sub-periods. From 1868 to 1876 we find a strangely stable economy in spite of chaotic political and social conditions. The years from 1876 to 1885 produced great shocks, inflation followed by deflation, and were a needed catharsis for the Japanese economy. These events deserve closer examination.

The new central government came into power in September 1868 without a systematic financial program, while carrying heavy inherited burdens from the feudal period. Funds had to be found for vanquishing anti-government forces, for continuing the stipends of the *bushi*, and for assuming the debts of the former *daimyō*. Available budgetary records give a clear quantitative dimension of the difficulties: from September 1868 through December 1872, total public expenditures amounted to ¥148.3 million as against revenues of only ¥50.4 million. This was possible because the government exploited three sources of funds: first and foremost, the issue of inconvertible paper notes, and to a lesser extent loans from big merchants and foreign borrowing. In part, the consequences of these policies were predictable; they also contained some highly unpredictable aspects. Government notes depreciated quickly vis-à-vis specie, but in spite of the considerable increases of money in circulation — from ¥65.4 million in 1868 to ¥102.7 million in 1872 — no substantial inflation is observable. What can be the reasons? We are not at all sure, but the following suggestions may be relevant. During the entire period in question Japan had a large deficit in her international accounts, and this no doubt created anti-inflationary pressure. Furthermore, our speculation is that the velocity of circulation must have been low. At the same time, the transactions demand for money was probably rising as large segments of the population were, for the first time, forced into the money economy. In these terms, the Japanese economy may not have been sufficiently monetized to register the effects of increased note issue. It may have been too early for inflation.

Between 1873 and 1876 the government followed a somewhat more active policy. The land tax was instituted in 1874, national banks were authorized in 1872, inconvertible notes were being retired, and the increases in circulation abated. Governmental fiscal problems, however, remained very serious. The revenue side of the account had been somewhat regularized by means of the land tax, but the expenditure side was still plagued by the size of transfer payments (usually well over 30 percent of expenditures) largely used to meet feudal obligations. These years were not inflationary, and some prices even showed slight declines.

In sum, from 1868 to 1876, from a financial point of view the economic situation was relatively stable. As far as resource utilization and means of implementation were concerned, the government depended heavily on inherited assets and machinery. The issuance of inconvertible notes without the creation of disorder, loans from merchants, the continuing outflow of gold and silver, all depended on pre-Restoration assets — largely the capital stock taken over from the Tokugawa. Foreign borrowing and increases of domestic output cannot, of course, be dismissed even at this time. These too played an important role in resource utilization.

The period of great shocks, 1876–1885, must also be divided: the years of inflation from 1876 to 1881, and the years of deflation from 1881 to 1885. Two historical events are central for an understanding of this period. One was the Seinan Civil War, or Satsuma Rebellion of 1877, which was the last major challenge to the new regime and led directly to an additional note issue of ¥27 million. The other was the compulsory commutation of *bushi* stipends through the issue of bonds amounting to ¥172.9 million. The latter action, especially, led to major changes in the Japanese economy.

To understand the sequence of events connected with compulsory commutation, one must begin by noting that in August 1876, one month before the final action, the government amended the national bank regulations. Accordingly, the recently instituted specie reserve for note issue was abolished, and banks were allowed to issue notes against bonds deposited with the Treasury up to 80 percent of their capital. Relations between bank-note issue regulations and the pension bonds illustrate well the working of boundary conditions. Both schemes were due to a necessary political compromise. On the one hand, the government had to get rid of the heavy transfer payments before it could institute modern budgetary procedures. And it was certainly not powerful enough simply to repudiate the *bushi* stipends; indeed, the government could not afford to antagonize this group too much. On the other hand, the *bushi* did not at all like the pension bonds. When they had been offered on a voluntary basis, only very few takers were found, in part at least because their interest rate was well below market rates. Compulsory commutation was the government stick; amended bank regulations were the carrot. They opened a road for pension bond holders to invest their funds in newly created national banks. In fact, the number of national banks rose between 1876 and 1880 from about 4 to 148, and in the latter year their note issue reached ¥34 million — the legal maximum.

This compromise nearly had disastrous consequences for the Meiji government. It precipitated a rather sharp inflation at a time when the government was least prepared to cope with this type of situation. Total note issue rose from ¥106.9 million in 1876 to ¥164.4 million in 1879, and this time, in contrast to earlier years, the price level responded. It would be interesting to speculate why an injection of money in 1876–1880 created an inflation when it did not have this effect in 1868–1872, but the crucial point is of a quite different nature. The inflation led to distortions in the economy which affected the government — at that time the main agent attempting to initiate MEG — most adversely.

To begin with, the rice price nearly doubled and, taken together with the fixed land tax, created enormous windfalls for the landowners. There is some evidence that these windfalls were not always used productively. For example, *Kōgyōiken* (Survey of Industries, 1884) reported the following concerning the rural industries founded at that time: ". . . most of these (80–90 percent) are luxuries, imitating foreign products and mostly made of imported raw materials. The manufacture of these contributed little to increase the national power." At the same time, the government did not have an easy time in finding private entrepreneurs willing to assume responsibility for modern textile mills.

Most serious, perhaps, were the effects of the inflation on the new land tax. The real purchasing power of government revenue fell drastically, while it did not have the power to siphon off the landowners' windfalls. A public budget crisis was narrowly averted by the introduction of new taxes on sake and tobacco, but expenditures for fostering modern industries and other investments had to be cut down. The targets of the government were in trouble, and optimistic expectations concerning the new national banks were disappointed. These banks, as yet in inexperienced hands, had difficulty in differentiating between commercial and industrial capital, and did little to further MEG. At that time the Japanese economy held slight promise in the eyes of shrewd foreign observers — certainly a bad sign.

In October 1881, Matsukata Masayoshi became Finance Minister. With the installation of this remarkable man, a new era began in Japanese finance, and the targets set in 1868 were safely achieved in 1885. Understanding the corrosions caused by the inflation, Matsukata with great sternness and determination carried out a program of financial orthodoxy: the re-introduction of convertible currency, severe public austerity, and deflation. Public operation of expensive factories and mines was discontinued. Taxes on tobacco and sake were raised, and other indirect taxes were introduced. A redemption program for the public debt, based on government surpluses, was carried out in ten years. Under Matsukata the government succeeded in saving, on the average, 28 percent of its current revenues, and about half of these savings were used for capital formation, the other half being allocated to surplus. Deflation affected government revenues favorably because the land tax was fixed. In sharp contrast to the previous years of inflation, the land tax provided the government with a ready-made vehicle for increasing its real tax revenues. Of course, the disposable income of landowners fell, but this seemed to matter less.

Under Matsukata the quantity of money was reduced by some 20 percent and commodity prices fell sharply. In 1884 the general price level dropped to 75 percent of the 1881 level. Interest rates also declined, and the necessary conditions for convertible currency again came into being. Foreign payments, with the exception of a small deficit in 1881, were also in the black for the first time since the Restoration — and this was not to happen again frequently in the future. Based on these achievements the government could now move toward reform of the banking system. The Bank of Japan was founded in 1885 and took the place of the national banks as the bank of issue. Japan now had a modern currency system and a well-operating public budget structure. It took the government nineteen years to achieve these targets, and now MEG could and did begin.

The Matsukata deflation was the most severe experience of this type in modern Japanese economic history. It was a bold attempt to create the conditions under which MEG could begin — it was a life or death risk. The dangerous inflation which preceded it was the financial result of all the disturbances and hindrances to growth which the Restoration inherited. Private enterprise needed a more rational and elastic currency system, and the government had to have adequate sources of revenue, and both of these came into being largely as a result of the deflation.

Initial modern economic growth, 1886–1905

When MEG begins, in the middle of the 1880's, it becomes convenient to divide the Japanese economy into two sectors: the traditional and modern economy. By traditional economy we mean those sectors which largely preserved pre-modern (indigenous) techniques and organization of production. Agriculture was, of course, the most important sector of the traditional economy, although — in terms of either output or employment — other sectors were not insignificant. The modern economy is largely represented by imported techniques and forms of organization: machinery, factories, corporations, etc. "Modern" and "Western" are almost synonymous. In the real world it is often very difficult to draw a clear line between traditional and modern. We will need a third category, called hybrid, in which traditional and modern elements are combined.

There is little difficulty in applying this classification to Japan. Agriculture, for example, is the clearest case of the traditional economy in operation. In terms of organization of production, there was little change between the end of the Tokugawa era and World War II. The small family farm, land fragmentation, major crops, all these traditional features remained nearly intact. After the Restoration there was important improvement in the general level of agricultural techniques which allowed rapid increases in output and productivity. The most important of these were: (1) more intensive use of fertilizers, and (2) improved irrigation methods, and these improvements applied more widely and intensively the traditional stock of knowledge already available in pre-modern Japan.

Examples of the modern economy are so obvious as to require almost no elaboration. The cotton textile industry, based largely on imported raw materials, imported machinery, and wage labor working in factories, is an outstanding case.

Hybrids become especially numerous in the early years of the twentieth century with the application of the electric motor to small-scale industry. There are also possible examples in the Meiji period — for instance seed improvements. We have stated that irrigation and fertilizers accounted for most of the increases in agricultural productivity. While this is true, improvements in seed selection were also of consequence. These were largely the result of the so-called "salt-water method," perfected by Yokoi Tokiyoshi in 1882, at that time head of the agricultural experimental station at Fukuoka. Yokoi's method involved the principles of modern scientific experimentation and knowledge relating to the varying density of salt water. It was, however, inspired by and based on cruder conventional methods long in use by farmers in Western Japan, and therefore is a perfect hybrid.

199

The mechanism of MEG in its initial phase

We propose to analyze the process of growth during the initial phase in terms of the interrelations between the modern and the traditional economy. The argument an be summarized in the following propositions:

1. In the absence of large capital imports, the initial establishment and subsequent development of the modern economy depended on the accelerated growth of the traditional economy — and also to some extent on the accelerated growth of the hybrid economy.

2. The traditional economy was capable of producing such accelerated growth.

3. However, the growth potential of the traditional economy was limited. When its growth rate begins to decline (1905), the initial phase of MEG comes to an end.

4. By the time the initial phase comes to an end, the dependence of the modern on the traditional economy has greatly decreased — although it has not disappeared.

The validity of the four propositions requires verification. Proposition two requires little argument. A considerable amount of research indicates that the agricultural and nonagricultural traditional sectors of the Japanese economy experienced rising growth rates in the last quarter of the nineteenth century. How to date the beginning of the accelerations is a much more difficult question. We are inclined to believe that they generally started after 1868, and became especially prominent after 1885. Some quickening in these rates may have begun before 1868, but this does not really matter. The major parts of the spurt certainly came after the Restoration

We come now to proposition one which asserts that the development of the modern economy depended on the accelerated growth of the traditional economy. This relationship can be seen most clearly if we ask ourselves what the requirements of the modern economy were, and then examine how they could and were in fact met.

1. Most important, perhaps, were the savings-investment needs of the modern sector. The public and private sectors needed access to a growing pool of savings which could be turned into social overheads and factories. In the case of the government, during these years, the savings came from agriculture, and the land tax was the mechanism by which they were transferred out of agriculture. This transfer of savings from the traditional sector to the modern sector must have also operated on a private basis, although this is much more difficult to document.

2. The modern sector also needed a labor force, and here again the traditional economy was the only real source of supply. A shift from traditional to modern occupations, from agriculture to industry, depended on increased output and productivity in the primary sector. The output of food and other items had to rise in keeping with a growing population, while labor had to be supplied for industry. If agricultural output had not risen in the face of increased needs (i.e., a growing population and rising incomes) the chances for successful MEG would have been greatly diminished.

3. At this time also the development of modern industry was very dependent on Japan's ability to purchase producers' durables and raw materials abroad. Once the Tokugawa hoards of precious metals had been depleted, exports were the only rational means of getting foreign exchange for vital imports. And in this period exports were largely composed of traditional output: tea and silk.

4. Even Japanese capital formation can be examined in the light of the modern-traditional dichotomy. Especially during the initial phase of MEG, the government and to some extent the private sector engaged in a great deal of investment of the traditional type, often facilitating investments for modern industry. Examples are road and bridge building, commercial and to a more limited extent residential construction, riparian works, and natural disaster reconstruction. Thus, the traditional economy once again supplied the needs of its modern infant brother.

5. If there had been no increase in the output of the traditional economy, there could hardly have existed any *domestic* market for the output of modern industry. Throughout the initial phase of MEG, over 65 percent of the gainfully occupied population was engaged in agriculture. The sheer weight of this group made them the only sizable domestic market, and cotton textiles, simple domestic utensils, and other such products of the early modern sector must have been sold primarily to these groups. (The export/output ratio of many modern manufactured items was very low at this time.)

We have attempted to establish that during the initial phase of MEG economic progress was primarily supported by the accelerated growth of the traditional sector. However, the expansion potential of the traditional sector was limited, and its rate of growth began to decline around 1905 — this being the end of the initial phase. This decline, stated in terms of the growth rate, can be attributed to three principal factors: (1) colonial or empire competition, (2) competition from the modern economy, and (3) endogenous reasons for retardation within the traditional economy.

It is convenient to begin with the endogenous reasons for decline in the traditional economy as typified by agriculture. Japan was already in 1868 a densely populated country with a shortage of arable land. As its agriculture grew, using largely traditional methods, it rapidly bumped against this ceiling; and by being forced to use increasingly marginal land faced the steeply rising costs of land reclamation. These conditions were aggravated by the severity of land fragmentation, and the over-all smallness of holdings. In short, given the traditional forms of cultivation, Japanese agriculture had by 1905 reached diminishing returns in terms of the rate of growth.

This leads to an obvious question: why was it not possible to abandon the traditional organization which was now limiting agricultural growth? There were both technical and institutional reasons why this was not possible within the context of early twentieth-century Japan.

Agricultural technology can be conveniently split into two parts — one part relating to improvements of conventional inputs (seeds, fertilizers, nursing, etc.), and the other to improvements of land and capital (irrigation, drainage, machinery, etc.). Between these two parts there exists a complementary relationship: for optimal results,

201

improvements must go hand in hand. Given the character of Japanese agriculture, improvement of inputs was a relatively minor problem. Land and capital improvements, however, became a major problem especially at the beginning of this century. The kinds of investment which were now needed had a "lumpy" character, and due to land fragmentation and the generally small size of holdings were too costly for most landlords.

Institutional limitations were equally severe. Absentee (or, to use the Japanese term, "parasitic") landlordism was on the rise, and the brunt of agricultural difficulties was, to an increasing extent, born by an economically and politically weak peasant class. Consolidation of holdings, one possible method of rationalization, would probably have been resisted by both landlords and tenants, but for quite different reasons. Here one must always keep in mind the factor proportions in Japanese agriculture. Japanese economic growth was very rapid, but it was not rapid enough to modernize the traditional economy. By that we mean that growth was not rapid enough to change the persistently unfavorable man–land ratio. Despite the large exodus of labor to the cities and to modern employment — the pace of this exodus being largely conditioned by the growth rate of the modern economy — the absolute number of workers in agriculture remained nearly the same from 1868 to 1930. Under these circumstances, for the landlords the relative price of capital remained too high (or the relative price of labor was too low) to encourage expensive capital-using modernization. On the other hand, there was always a plentiful supply of people willing, for lack of other opportututies, to assume the burdens of tenancy.

Agricultural competition from the growing empire was another troublesome development, although it became important only after World War I. As Japan experienced increasing difficulties in feeding its growing population, and as rice prices rose alarmingly, the government looked more and more to its colonies for sustenance. Korea and Taiwan became cheap sources of supply, which further increased the difficulties of domestic producers.

Competition from the modern economy as a factor retarding the growth of the traditional economy is an obvious concomitant of MEG in the case of non-agriculture; but its consequences may be quite complicated. In Japan, as modern industry developed, it naturally wiped out numerous traditional crafts. Many examples could be cited. Modern cotton spinning eliminated the native cotton growers because they could not produce raw materials of adequate quality at a competitive price. The modern textile industry in general reduced the levels of home spinning and weaving. In addition, a government system of monopolies and licenses did away with some traditional small-scale production, as was the case with tobacco and sake.

In the non-agricultural sectors of the traditional economy, however, the development of modern industry had both substitution and complementary effects. To some extent, modern small-scale industry — that is to say, modern in some of its techniques and sometimes in its organization — was the heir of traditional non-agricultural industries. As we leave the initial phase of MEG, and especially after World War I, some traditional non-agricultural industries succeeded in integrating themselves into the modern economy. Although their relations with large modern enterprises were nearly always relatively disadvantageous to themselves, they survived and multiplied in their new form. In effect they usually became true hybrids: rather modern in technique (as in their use of electric motors) and rather traditional in their organization (as in the widespread use of non-wage family labor). In this process, the ties between agriculture and traditional (now in good part hybrid) non-agricultural industry became much looser, and in the following phases they must be treated separately.

A slight digression may be helpful at this point. It is an acknowledged fact that in the post-World War II period the rate of growth of Japanese agriculture spurted once again. Does this contradict the assertions made up to now? We do not believe so, for defeat brought many changes and facilitated institutional reform. Land reform became possible, the empire was dissolved, and the government was more active in its support of agriculture. But there was one other very important change, namely, certain advances in technology within the sectors could advantageously be used by agriculture — for example, insecticides, pesticides, vinyl, etc. And this brings to the fore the issue of sectoral reciprocity, a major point. In saying that the traditional economy, during the initial phase, supported the growth of the modern economy, we do not intend to imply that this was exclusively a one-way relationship, although we do say that net support *during the initial phase* flowed from the traditional to the modern economy. After all, what forces can account for the undoubtedly rapid growth of the modern economy from the middle of the 1880's until the Russo–Japanese War? The following appear the weightiest: military expenditures, expanding foreign trade, a slowly developing domestic market, and the competitive strength of modern industry as it innovated and replaced traditional outputs. None of these provided direct support for the traditional economy, and during the initial phase what might be termed modern support was confined to a few technological innovations.

The end of the initial phase of MEG has been defined as the point at which the growth rate of the traditional economy begins to decline, i.e., 1905. This is the end of a phase because from then on the modern economy could no longer count on the same degree of support from the traditional sectors. While the economic relations between the two sectors persisted, the modern economy had to look more to its inner strength or its export capabilities if rapid growth was to be maintained. All this was possible, because, in the twenty years since MEG began, industrialization itself had made considerable progress. Let us briefly review these changes.

1. We had stressed the savings–investment relationship and the role of the agricultural surplus and land tax. By the end of the initial phase, the composition of central government revenues had undergone great changes. Relatively speaking, the role of the land tax had declined, as it was being replaced by excise taxes on consumption, income and business taxes, and customs duties.

2. From the beginnings of MEG until the 1930's the dominant share of the non-agricultural labor force came from agriculture. However, it must also be noted that throughout practically this entire period the rate of growth of the non-agricultural labor force of agricultural origin declines, while that of non-agricultural origin rises. Thus, the natural increases within the modern sectors were beginning to

make themselves felt. This is especially noticeable beginning in about 1910. A qualitative factor may be added. The modern economy must have placed an increasing premium on education, and therefore young people of urban origin may have been more valuable to them.

3. The relative weight of traditional exports and modern durable imports had also been altered. By 1905, tea and raw silk exports were being replaced to a considerable extent by the rapid rise of cotton fabrics, cotton yarn, and silk fabrics — all outputs of modern organization and technology. At the same time, the net import of producers' durables had fallen to about 25 percent of domestic production — from a level of about 200 percent in the 1880's.

4. Another change was in the composition of modern and traditional investments. In 1890 about two-thirds of the investment were traditional in technique. By 1905 the proportion had fallen to one-third. In effect we can say that the modern economy had reached the stage where its facilitating needs could no longer be satisfied by traditional methods.

5. We have also outlined the importance of the domestic market for the development of modern industry, and noted that this largely represented customers in the traditional economy. As the modern economy expanded its output, with the relatively low levels of per capita income of the bulk of its customers, it is clear that the need for other markets increased. Therefore toward the end of the initial phase it is reasonable to find attempts to step up exports in order to tap foreign sources of demand. Statistical evidence for this is available in the rising export/output ratios for many of the products of modern industry. All of these factors yield the same picture — by the end of the initial phase, a modern sector gradually becoming more independent and capable of growing on its own

Differential structure: creation, 1906–1930

Beginning about 1906, and continuing for about a quarter of a century, a new feature entered into Japanese economic development. In essence, this feature was the accelerated growth of the modern economy. In turn, this was based on a number of changes occurring at about the same time: an acceleration of the rate of increase of per worker productivity in the modern economy, and, related to this, a rising proportion of investment and an increase in industrial concentration . . .

Let us, briefly, review some of the major forces in Japanese economic history between 1906 and 1930. We have already commented on the vigorous growth of the modern sector at that time, and now some qualifications must be added. A variety of factors favorable to the development of modern industry appeared shortly after the end of the initial phase. The Russo–Japanese War (1904–1905) greatly stimulated the development of all modern industry directly and indirectly connected with the war effort. This expansion was supported by increased imports, inflation, and rather sizable foreign loans. Government military expenditures during these years were on the increase, and the recently completed nationalization of railroad trunk lines led to further transportation expenditures, We know that the I/GNP proportion begins to rise at about this time, and this must be the reflection of two separate forces. On the one hand, we see here the real beginnings of heavy industry, but it was still tiny and almost exclusively confined to the production of arms. On the other hand, we can also observe the continuing development and modernization of textile production, and especially the substitution of traditional for modern methods (e.g., in raw silk production and weaving). At this time modern industry was also beginning to find an export market in the new empire, while the home market — due to rising per capita incomes — was gradually being strengthened.

And yet all was not well with the Japanese economy — especially with regard to exports and the balance of payments. This can be seen most clearly in the trend of ratios of imports and exports to GNP. Throughout the initial phase, the import ratio shows a sharp increase. During the present phase, it continues to increase though at a somewhat slower pace reaching a level somewhat higher than 20 percent about 1925. After that, the ratio declines until about 1931 and once again rises sharply. The export ratio kept pace with the import ratio during the initial phase of MEG — both expanded at more or less equal rates. But, beginning in the first decade of the twentieth century, the export ratio — with the conspicuous exception of World War I — began to stagnate at an average level of about 15 percent.

In these terms, the specific experience of Japan in World War I becomes especially interesting. Her major economic weakness had been the chronic imbalance of her foreign payments, and now, all of a sudden, this problem was wiped out. Exports expanded even more rapidly than the growing import requirements, and while the bonanza lasted only from about 1914 to 1919, the effects were of lasting duration. During the period of World War I Japanese modern business circles experienced an unprecedented prosperity. Sales of all items were easy, especially to areas where European competition had been temporarily eliminated. Domestic investment boomed, but there were also less beneficial consequences such as a high rate of inflation.

Japan experienced inflation in part as a result of the export boom and in part due to the lack of an adequate government financial policy. The results included a badly distorted wage structure, with many classes of people experiencing a decline in real income. Food prices rose enormously, and the Rice Revolt of 1918 was an ominous warning to the government. Even the entrepreneurial classes faced new and baffling problems as a result of the boom. Perhaps for the first time in Japanese economic history the unlimited supply of labor was interrupted by the unprecedented expansion of the modern sector. There were labor shortages and the real wages of certain groups of workers rose considerably. "Unlimited supply" usually relates to a long-run concept. The experience of World War I is a good illustration of the much lower supply elasticities prevailing in the short run.

We come now to the aftermath of World War I — the difficult and confusing decade of the 1920's — during which the differential structure became solidified. The termination of the war must have come as an unpleasant shock to many Japanese entrepreneurs. Exports fell sharply, terms of trade improved briefly and then declined, and the rapid inflation turned into a prolonged period of falling prices — after the Matsukata Deflation, the second longest such period in post-Restoration economic history. To this gloomy situation the modern sector responded by adopting a rationalization policy. Essentially this meant attempts to increase productivity and to save labor costs through the introduction of more modern techniques. In an indirect sense, the lessons of World War I had much to do with effecting rationalization. Modern industry had realized the inconveniences of skilled labor shortages. Now, facing a highly competitive international market, the leaders of modern industry also realized that they would have to be more efficient in order to survive. All this meant maintaining a higher level of investment, and the adoption of improved technology. It also led to the oligopolization of Japanese industry and to increased power for the *zaibatsu*, (financial cliques or big business).

What did rationalization do to the structure of the Japanese economy? First, it further speeded the increases in product per worker in the modern sector. From 1922 to 1933, product per worker for this group rose by 60 percent — from ¥453 to ¥726 in 1914 prices. At the same time, the real wages of industrial workers rose slowly, even though the unlimited supply of labor had been reestablished. This was not due to the generosity of entrepreneurs. They depended, now, on more modern skills and a higher degree of commitment. Furthermore, productivity increased much faster than wages. And finally, the labor needs for modern industry declined relatively, and labor's relative share once again declined sharply.

While rationalization was proceeding in modern industry, no similar events took place in the traditional economy. Here, productivity and real wages were no longer rising, and the gap between the two sectors widened enormously. This gap — which we call the differential structure — was brought about by long-run forces already identifiable in the early twentieth century. It was, however, considerably intensified by the rationalization of the 1920's. In oversimplified terms, the following statements are true:

1. Before the establishment of the differential structure:

    a. wages in the traditional and modern sectors were more or less the same;

    b. the productivity gap between the modern and traditional sectors was more or less unchanging; and

    c. the share of the traditional economy in output and labor force was dominant.

2. After the establishment of the differential structure:

    a. there existed a growing wage differential;

    b. there existed a rapidly growing productivity gap; and

    c. the share of modern industry, especially in terms of output, becomes much larger.

The widening gap between the traditional and the modern sectors perpetuated a deep cleavage in Japanese economic life. Manifestations of this change can be readily identified.

206

1. Two living standards developed — the higher modern and the lower traditional way of life. This had important political consequences. Especially the dissatisfied rural groups, due to their number, exercised considerable political power. They did much to further power ambitions of the military cliques, and in that sense at least Japanese aggression in the 1930's can be related to the internal economic structure of the country.

2. The differential structure perpetuated the unlimited supply of labor because the labor requirements of modern industry were not growing very rapidly.

3. The continuance of the unlimited supply of labor made available to enterprise a continuing source of relatively cheap labor.

4. Given the differential structure, it was difficult to strengthen the domestic market on a continuing basis. In terms of gainfully occupied workers, the largest segment of the economy was condemned to lower productivity and low incomes.

Differential structure: economic and political consequences, 1931–1952

The demarcation between successive phases of Japanese growth is, as we have seen, reflected in the fluctuations of the annual growth rate of GNP. At the end of the initial phase the growth rate hit a trough, and then shot up with renewed vigor as modern industry expanded. At the end of World War I the growth rate declined, and throughout the 1920's and rationalization the rate stayed at roughly 3 percent — for Japan a somewhat depressed level. A renewed spurt — and a new phase — begins in 1931, and we wish to interpret the next twenty or so years as consequences of the differential structure.

An economic interpretation of the 1930's cannot be one–sided. The Japanese economy grew rapidly partly in response to ordinary economic stimuli. This was especially true of exports. In a world caught in the grips of the great depression, a leading manufacturer of cheap goods (with a recently rationalized industry) had distinct advantages. But this would be a superficial interpretation of the 1930's, because it ignores what might be labeled the "political solution." At the end of the last section we pointed out the grave problems confronting the Japanese economy in the 1920's and indicated our belief that they affected subsequent political action. These actions, more than anything else, explain the brief growth and prosperity of the 1930's.

The political solution which Japan chose ended in disaster. It allowed a few years of relative prosperity, but today few would claim that it was worth the price. In this primarily economic analysis, political judgments may be out of place. We will merely indicate how growth was resumed and how this can be linked with the economic structure of the country.

Once Japan had decided to follow a policy of military expansion, it was a relatively simple matter to step up the growth of the economy, even though the standard of living of the mass of the people did not necessarily maintain the pace. Military expenditures became gigantic in order to fight in Manchuria, Inner Mongolia, China, and in preparation for World War II. The armament industry and associated heavy industries were the leading sector of this growth. (It did not matter at the time that this was a very artificial expansion for heavy industry, largely based on subsidies creating high-cost producers.) This was accompanied by an expansion drive to the colonies. Colonies were made to take exports, native populations were exploited as food producers, and colonial markets were frequently monopolized for the mother country's benefit. Throughout, the government maintained an expansionary monetary policy with the usual consequences.

In the long run, there is nothing especially interesting in these events, even though they do illustrate vividly the economic background of Japanese imperialism and its relation to the differential structure. The policies of the 1930's logically ended in World War II, a conflict which Japan could not possibly win. Japan might have attempted alternative economic solutions — none would have been easy — but this did not become a realistic possibility until after World War II. The war itself, and the rehabilitation period which followed defy normal economic analysis. It is generally conceded that the long chain of events which began with the militarism of the early thirties ended between 1952–1954. By that time, Japan had recovered her independence, and most of the abnormal influences of war and occupation had disappeared Once again the Japanese economy began to spurt, and we must turn to the final historical phase: the years following World War II.[4]

Postwar growth, 1953—

The Japanese *wirtschaftswunder* has attracted an enormous amount of attention in the postwar world. Since 1954 the economy has expanded at an average rate of somewhat more than 9 percent. No other country has matched this record and the Japanese have basked in the warmth of international admiration. One cannot argue that this astounding growth is simply the result of repairing the damage of World War II. After all, the war ended in 1945, and our analysis begins only in 1953 when, hopefully, these influences have disappeared. At the same time, from 1953 to the present is not a complete phase of growth. The historical record is shorter than a decade — we have the beginning of a phase as evidenced by the growth spurt, but the end must remain a matter of conjecture. Nevertheless, the current events must be examined critically because they can contribute immensely to an understanding of Japan's historical pattern of growth. One should not, of course, compare the short-term growth of the postwar economy with prewar trends — even though this has been done all too frequently — but even a comparison of different short-term periods yields valuable insights.

Although the Japanese economy has grown more rapidly during the postwar years than at any other time, there were similar and earlier periods of almost equally rapid growth. For example, the following average annual growth rates apply: 1905–1912, 6.7 percent; 1912–1919, 7.0 percent; 1931–1938, 7.5 percent; 1953–1960, 9.3 percent. The recent average is the highest not so much because peak values have risen (e g., compare 1918–1919 at 18.8 percent with 1958–1959 at 17.9 percent), but because the postwar troughs have been relatively higher. During prewar spurts negative values are not uncommon, while an annual growth rate of 3.3 percent is the bottom of postwar values.

Behind these aggregate measures exist certain rather fundamental changes observable over time. Postwar growth is distinguished by two factors: a rapid increase in the rate of growth of the gainfully employed population, and an equally rapid increase in the rate of growth of productivity per worker *due to* shifts in the industrial structure. These events are related. The natural rate of increase of the Japanese population quickened in the 1920's, maintained comparatively high levels during the 1930's and World War II, and rose to unprecedented heights in the immediate postwar period. (Since 1949 the pace of natural increase has been declining sharply.) This demographic boom has altered the age structure of the population, so that in the postwar period the proportion of the working age population grew rapidly and reached an all-time high. These forces were intensified by the large number of returnees from the empire in the immediate postwar period.

Where did these increased numbers become gainfully occupied? They were not going into agriculture. The rate of growth of the agricultural labor force has never been as sharply negative as at present. Thus, the new increases, and some of the already gainfully employed workers, were shifting out of agriculture and into manufacturing and services. This sort of transfer means movement from lower to higher productivity occupations, and in large measure this combination of increased numbers and transfer explains the higher rate of over-all growth during the 1950's. The growth rate of "productivity proper," by contrast, has changed much less significantly although what is perhaps most interesting is that it has not *declined* in spite of the large inflow of workers.

In trying to understand what factors in the economy made these happenings possible, one's attention immediately turns to the level of investment, and especially the strength of autonomous investment. It is, of course, true that Japan may have had more than her share of economic good luck in the postwar years — favorable terms of trade, the Korean War, no national defense burden — but this cannot explain enough. Investment was a much more sustaining force. In comparing pre- and post-war capital formation, one is immediately aware of some fundamental differences. First of all, the proportion of gross investment to gross domestic expenditure now stands at an unprecedented level. The average proportion for 1953–1960 was 33.2 percent, and in 1960 it reached an almost unbelievable 38.2 percent. In general, the trend of the capital formation proportion has been rising in Japan, but during the earlier phases of rapid growth it never exceeded 23 percent.

What can account for the postwar level? Essentially it is due to a steep rise in the rate of private investment in plant and equipment, especially since 1956. The role of government investment — always an important magnitude — has also been altered, but here the change has been mainly compositional. Before the war, government accounted for 50 percent of all investment if military investment is included, and for 40 percent if it is excluded. By contrast, in 1960 government investment amounted to only 27 percent of the total. This was not the result of an absolute decrease of public investment — in fact, the ratio of government investment to GNP has been rising virtually since the 1880's — but rather the effect of the more rapid growth of private investment. Of course, it must also be stressed that public investment is today much more "productive" because defense expenditures have fallen to very low levels.

While recognizing the advantages of increased productive investment on the part of the government, it is still clear that what really needs to be explained is the unprecedented vigor of the private sector. The figures indicate great private investment spurts, especially following the rather mild recessions, reaching annual rates of increase in the neighborhood of 55–60 percent during 1956–1957. It must be recognized at the outset that the postwar years were especially suitable for rapid technological progress. Japanese industry, due to the war, had been isolated for more than a decade, and great opportunities existed to reduce rapidly a technological gap. Sometimes this has been called the "catching-up" effect, and some may feel that it is still the best explanation of the current investment wave. This is, however, a much too narrow view. Japanese entrepreneurs have been concerned about trade liberalization and relations with the Common Market. This has quickened the introduction of new techniques and is unrelated to wartime isolation.

Catching-up makes much more sense if we understand the concept in broad historical terms. Then it means the transformation of a semideveloped economy into a mature one, and this is what has been happening in Japan. Underlying this transformation is a shift in the industrial structure from light to heavy industry. Productive investment by the private sector has tended to concentrate increasingly on basic heavy industries, and the dominant proportion of the technical innovations came in these sectors. For example, in 1960 the level of plant and equipment investment was 3.25 times higher than in 1955 for all production, but it was 10.5 times higher for the non-ferrous metals industry, 9 times higher for the iron and steel and metals manufacturing industry, and approximately 7 times higher for the machinery, electrical machinery, and transportation equipment industry.

Quite clearly, the entrepreneur did not lack incentives to promote these heavy investments. In the short run, ordinary private profit considerations can adequately explain the desire to introduce new and better techniques. Private profits were high because domestic and foreign demand was strong, productivity was rising, and wages were lagging behind productivity. The entrepreneur was merely maximizing profits. In the longer run, the government did much to bolster expectations of continued rapid growth. It compiled several long-range growth plans as guideposts for private business, and all of these anticipated a rate of expansion maintained at very high levels. Our best guess is that Japan will not be able to sustain the postwar average pace of some 9 percent per year for a long time. Some of the things which have stimulated the economy in recent years may lose their force. This is certainly true of the demographic push. It is also hard to visualize investment kept at present levels. The capital-output ratio has been rising, and this could change entrepreneurial incentives; and once the heavy-industry complex is well established, future technological change may proceed at a more deliberate pace. Catching-up — in the short-term sense — will have been accomplished.

We should remember, however, that catching-up does have a long-term meaning, and because of this there are good reasons for believing that Japan will continue to grow, perhaps at a more rapid pace than the 4 percent prewar long-run average. In many ways, Japan is still a semi-developed country. Per capita income levels are still low, the proportion of workers in agriculture is still high, and a dual economy is still very much in evidence. We think that Japan has now entered a second industrial revolution. The first established a modern enclave and a dual economy. The task of the more recent industrial revolution is to abolish the dual economy and to bring about advanced standards of income, consumption, and industrial structure. Our analysis of the postwar years has identified some signs of the process: shifts in the industrial structure, technological progress, and the importance of productivity gains due to transfer. We believe that this is only the beginning; Japan's path to economic maturity still contains many years of rapid growth.

The longer phases

Shorter or intermediate-range phases average about twenty years in length, and derive their unity and identifiability from the fact that they represent successive spurts of gross output and a subsequent adjustment mechanism to this phenomenon. At the beginning of each phase — in 1868 (more by induction than by measurement), 1886, 1906, 1931, and 1953 — the rate of growth begins to quicken, eventually reaches a kind of peak, and then levels off, until the next phase begins. Within these demarcations we have tried to set forth the major forces accounting for growth. It is also possible to adopt a somewhat wider perspective by combining several phases into one. This sacrifices precision, but it does achieve a clearer historical perspective.

Let us examine first the properties of the so-called first, second, and third phases of MEG. The first phase, 1868–1905, represents the years when the traditional economy is paramount, and when its development is vital to the establishment of the modern economy. A fundamental change takes place with the second phase, 1906–1953, when the modern economy grows on its own base, and securely establishes an up-to-date light (and semi-heavy) industry complex. Finally, the third phase of which we have seen only the bare beginnings, will complete the process of industrialization through the propagation of heavy industries, automation, development of modern services, etc.

Historical phasing is always a hazardous and debatable process, and a degree of overlapping cannot be avoided. Taking an even broader perspective, it may make sense to speak of two industrial revolutions in Japan. The first, lasting from 1868 to 1930, created a semi-developed country possessing a considerable industrial complex, but still characterized by dualism and low per capita incomes. The second industrial revolution, which began abortively in the 1930's and more promisingly after World War II, will transform Japan into a truly mature economy.

Notes

1. *Japan's Emergence as a Modern State* (New York, 1940)., 125–26.

2. "The Legacy of Tokugawa Education," in Marius B. Jansen, ed., *Changing Japanese Attitudes Toward Modernization* (Princeton, 1964).

3. Bushi: The Samurai class. [Editor].

4. We would not wish to imply, of course, that the war and ensuing rehabilitation left the Japanese economy unchanged.

13.   Japan and Europe: Contrasts in Industrialization

David S. Landes

Challenge and response

For the student of European economic history, the story of Japanese industrialization has a special interest. Not only is Japan the only example of a non-Western society to effect an industrial revolution, she accomplished the feat with unprecedented rapidity, and even today her economy continues to advance faster probably than any other in the world. This achievement, moreover, is the more remarkable in that Japan had a far longer path to travel than her predecessors — and this without natural resources for economic prowess. Japan is not a land of wide fields and intrinsically fertile soil; nor is it "a land whose stones are iron and out of whose hills thou mayest dig brass." In particular, Japan has nothing like the great coal deposits that provided the fuel for British, American, and German economic expansion.

What is more, Japan accomplished these gains largely on her own; certainly she relied far less on outside help than did the follower countries of Continental Europe. The government did borrow on occasion from Western businessmen and capitalists — small amounts in the difficult years following the Restoration, a succession of much larger sums from 1899 on. It was not long, moreover, before private companies — railways and then industrial corporations — followed suit and began selling their own bonds and debentures in Western markets. The practice, still exceptional before the war, gained considerably in popularity in the twenties, only to be abandoned in the stringency of the Great Depression. To this formal import of capital should be added the support afforded Japanese foreign trade by Western merchant houses and banks by means of revolving short-term credits. These were particularly important in the early Meiji period, before the privileged Yokohama Specie Bank came to dominate the field. Also, one can find here and there examples of direct Western holdings in Japanese trade and industry. These were few and far between in the nineteenth century: tea-curing factories, a rice-straw rug enterprise, a toothbrush plant; and there was the Takashima coal mine, the most important in Japan, which was owned and operated by an English company until its sale to the government in 1874. In the years before and after the First World War, however, the number and importance of these foreign enterprises increased significantly. Joint Japanese–Western ventures were established, most of them in the engineering and electrical trades, while General Electric, Ford, General Motors, and other Western giants set up fully owned subsidiaries, often with an eye to getting behind newly raised tariff walls.

Landes, David S.: Extracts from 'Japan and Europe: Contrasts in Industrialization' in *THE STATE AND ECONOMY IN JAPAN: ESSAYS IN THE POLITICAL ECONOMY OF GROWTH*, edited by W.W. Lockwood (Princeton University Press, 1965), pp. 93–183. Copyright © 1965 by Princeton University Press. Reprinted with permission of Princeton University Press

Yet foreign capital represented a small fraction of Japanese investment. The early Meiji loans were redeemed quickly; and total government indebtedness abroad, never more than about 30 million yen, fell to a negligible amount in the nineties. It then rose to 195 millions in 1903 and leaped to almost 2,000 millions in 1914 — the equivalent of perhaps two or three years of national savings; to which should be added the comparatively small sum of 70 millions in direct foreign holdings. These debits were offset in part, however, by Japanese claims abroad: liquid assets of 246 million yen and long-term investments estimated at 536 millions. Moreover, thanks to the fat earnings of the years from 1914 to 1918, this was the high point for the period before the Second World War. In 1934 foreigners held perhaps 2,200–2,250 million gold yen in long-term claims on Japan: 1,408 million in bonds of the central government, 583 million in municipals and in the securities of private enterprises, 50 millions of miscellaneous domestic issues, 150–200 million in direct holdings — the whole equal to less than one year's savings. However, at least a third of Japanese securities floated abroad had been repatriated by that date, so that gross indebtedness was probably about 1,500 million yen ($750 million). The total was more than offset by Japanese investments abroad, largely in China and Manchuria, which Lockwood estimates at about 3,000 million yen.

A comparison with the experience of the countries of Continental Europe requires some careful distinctions. All of the European countries drew heavily on foreign capital during the early decades of their industrial development. France placed the bulk of her post-Napoleonic liberation loans abroad, and, until the crisis of 1845–1847 frightened foreign investors into dumping their holdings, from one-third to one-half of her railway shares were held in Britain. Belgium built its industrial boom of the 1830's on French support of her new joint-stock investment banks. And Western Germany owed some of its most progressive enterprises of the 1840's and 1850's — in nonferrous metals and textiles particularly — to French, Belgian, and Swiss initiative and money.

It is impossible, unfortunately, to aggregate these investments and compare them with rates of saving or total capital. One can, however, say something about the balance of capital movements. All of these countries early arrived at a point where exports of capital exceeded imports. The French performance is the most striking here: from the 1820's on, the balance of payments was almost always favorable, until cumulated holdings abroad amounted to over 50 billion gold francs in 1913 (more than a year's net national product); only Britain, with 3.8 billion pounds, had larger foreign investments. Even rapidly growing Germany, whose perennially higher interest rates reflected her appetite for capital, bought up most outside holdings in the fifties and sixties and went on to export large amounts in subsequent decades; by 1913 her investments abroad amounted to some 23.5 billion marks (half a year's income). In quantitative terms, the Japanese experience seems closest to the German pattern: a shift to net creditor status after about forty years of industrial development.

Qualitatively, however, the picture is different. One can find nothing in Japanese history comparable to the kind of strategic investments in major industries cited above — at least not until the development of heavy engineering, automobiles, and electrical engineering in the years before and after the First World War. The initial Japanese advances — in textiles, metallurgy, even railways — were accomplished with domestic savings almost exclusively.

214

Moreover, the proper comparison for our purposes is not with countries such as Britain, France, or Germany, but rather with Russia — Europe's late industrializer *par excellence.* From its first hesitant steps on the path to modernity, the Russian economy leaned heavily on outside support: in 1890, about a third of the country's joint-stock capital was in foreign hands, plus extensive direct holdings and short-term credits. At this point there began a period of exceptionally rapid growth, thanks in large part to an unprecedented influx of west European enterprise and money; by 1900, half the joint-stock capital was held abroad, most of it in France, Belgium, and Germany. And this says nothing of the huge public debt, much of it for railway construction, much of it for armaments, pomp and circumstance, and interest on old loans; half of this was owing to foreigners in 1914. French holdings alone amounted to more than 10 billion francs of public or officially guaranteed bonds — more than the entire annual income of Japan in this period.

By the same token, Japan relied far less than European countries on the skills, knowledge, and enterprise of foreigners. Technicians were brought in when required to build railways, construct and break in new plants, operate ships, above all to teach Japanese how to replace their teachers. We have no over-all count of these imported experts, but we do know that in the Meiji period a good many of them worked for the government and that these were more numerous in the early years than later: 127 in 1872, 213 in 1874, 103 in 1880, 29 in 1883, 56 in 1887. (The numbers would be very slightly larger if one added the skilled workers similarly engaged.) In similar fashion although the aggregate number of foreign technicians employed by private enterprise may well have increased over time, reaching a peak in the 1920's, the pattern in individual branches seems to have been an early rise followed by a drastic decline as the Japanese learned their lessons. When the *Nippon yusen kaisha* (Japan Steamship Company) was formed in 1884, it employed 174 foreigners, whose number increased to 224 during the Sino–Japanese War. By 1920, however, there was not one foreign officer in the Japanese merchant marine.

Incomplete as these figures are, they are far better than anything we have for Europe, where the great majority of migrant technicians hired out as private persons to private enterprises. The British parliamentary inquiry of 1825 into the emigration of skilled artisans — then illegal — heard an estimate of some two thousand Britons active in Continental industry. The number errs, if anything, on the low side, for it does not include the large number of emigrants who had left years before and had been assimilated into their country of settlement. And to this flow from the heartland of the Industrial Revolution must be added a growing stream of French, Belgian, and eventually Swiss and German technicians moving to more backward countries to the east and south. There developed in effect a number of secondary and tertiary centers of technological diffusion, and by the second third of the century skills were moving about Europe as freely as capital.

Moreover, the difference between the European and Japanese patterns was greater than mere numbers would indicate. Few Westerners remained long in Japan, and fewer still founded firms of their own to act as bellwethers to indigenous enterprise. Rather, outsiders were brought in for specific purposes — Rathgen speaks of "a few experts, 'rented' (as the characteristic and vivid saying has it) today here, tomorrow

215

there"—kept only as long as necessary, and sent away. For one thing, they cost five to ten times as much as roughly equivalent Japanese talent; for another, they neither wanted to nor were allowed to settle and melt into the society. This was in sharp contrast to Europe, where most countries encouraged the immigration of skilled artisans and potential entrepreneurs by all manner of inducements— gifts of land, money, and housing, exemption from taxes and military obligations, monopoly rights and similar economic privileges. Independent European enterprise became a significant force in Japan only after 1900, and then often in partnership with Japanese ventures. Its role, as we have seen, was concentrated in the new industries of the so-called "second industrial revolution": electrical engineering, internal combustion motors, automobiles, rubber. The older branches that were at the heart of the breakthrough to modern technology — textiles, metallurgy, railway transport — remained as always in indigenous hands. Above all, one finds nothing in Japan like the situation of the Russian iron industry, in which only one of seventeen works that constituted the modern smelting sector in 1898 was entirely Russian.

This largely independent achievement is the more surprising because one would have expected just the reverse. The usual experience has been that, the poorer an economy and the more backward its technology, the greater its dependence on outside aid. The only significant exception seems to have been Soviet Russia, whose repudiation of pre-revolutionary debts more or less cut it off from the international money and capital markets; though even Russia relied heavily on foreign engineers and technicians during the first revolutionary generation. Moreover, insofar as the Soviet Union did do without capital imports, she was able to do so only because she had inherited a substantial industrial plant from the previous regime — extensive railways, modern smelting mills, coal and iron mines, numerous textile factories — much of it paid for, built, or managed by foreigners. It is therefore less of an exception to the rule than appears at first glance.

All follower countries have done their best, however, to limit their dependence on outside capital and skill. In the first place, they have feared that political dependence would follow economic dependence — as it often has. Secondly, foreign aid is often expensive; technicians and engineers in particular will live abroad, in a strange and often less comfortable environment, only for generous remuneration. Finally, this very gap between the emoluments of domestic and imported labor produces friction that is usually aggravated by differences of manner and temperament. The more ambitious and chauvinistic the client country, moreover, the more acutely these differences are perceived and felt. The very hopes and drives that impel a nation to bring in teachers from abroad and listen to them make it quick to take umbrage and resentful of pupillary status.

Government enterprise in industry

The ability of industrializing economies to achieve independence without sacrificing growth unduly has always depended on their success in mobilizing their initially meager domestic resources, material and human . . . European countries used a combination of a financial innovation, the investment bank and what we would call today the development bank— and government promotion to generate capital for growth . . . The examples of Germany and Russia show that the more backward the economy, the more the reliance on the state rather than on private enterprise.

Japan seems to fit this model well. The government was responsible for an important share of gross domestic fixed capital formation— generally about 30 percent, though rising to about 40 in a few years — for the period 1887–1936. And while we do not have similar data for Europe, it seems unlikely that government share of total investment was so high as in Japan, though it was probably not much lower. On the other hand, a comparison of state investment in isolation is misleading; the model is incomplete. In promoting economic growth, government spending is just one of several devices for mobilizing and allocating resources. For backward countries especially, it is linked closely, as we have seen, to imports of capital from abroad, the one complementing the other. When one examines the Japanese experience in this light, one is less impressed by the contribution of the state; one would expect it to have been higher to compensate for the lack of funds from outside. And one is struck instead by the high proportion of investment accounted for by private enterprise.

Once again, to be sure, one must distinguish between quantitative and qualitative effects. Often a relatively small investment by the state yielded a large harvest of technological progress and increased output. One thinks, for example, of the construction of modern cotton mills which showed the way to private enterprise, and of the purchase of modern British spinning machinery which was then resold to private industry at low prices and on easy terms. "It seem clear," Smith remarks, "that without government help of both kinds, private capital would have been no more successful in developing machine cotton spinning in the decade after 1880 than it had been in the decade before; in short, in this field as in all others except silk reeling, the government was responsible for overcoming the initial difficulties of industrialization."[1]

The value of easy credit in a country still poor and lacking in a resourceful, responsive capital market is undeniable. The role of official entrepreneurship, as expressed in these early "model" plants, is less obvious. These plants no doubt did much to overcome the initial ignorance of machine technology and factory organization, and in so doing to train Japanese cadres for private enterprise. They were also usually fitted out with the latest equipment. Partly for this very reason, however, they were usually inefficient: relative factor costs hardly warranted the choice of such capital-intensive methods. Most of them seem to have lost money regularly, and when an impecunious government sold them off in the 1880's, it received far less than the amount of its investment. Most of these properties subsequently earned substantial profits, so much indeed that some historians have been inclined to see the whole operation as a dilapidation of the public treasury for the benefit of a few insiders. This is not the place to examine such allegations. The important fact for our purposes is the contrast between losses before and profits after, a contrast that throws doubt on the usual assumption of the incapacity of private enterprise to develop successful modern industries without the lesson and example of prior government initiative. To be sure, it may well be that these private profits were simply a consequence of the favorable terms of acquisition. We simply do not know. In the meantime, the burden of proof would seem to lie on those who have taken for granted the superiority of government enterprise. Certainly one may well ask whether development would not have been cheaper and more rapid had the state confined its role to that of honest broker and banker, introducing its citizens to the opportunities of the new technology and assisting their ventures with money and information.

In any event, it is worth noting that Japanese experience in this regard closely paralleled that of the countries of Continental Europe. In France, Prussia, Austria, and the smaller German states, the paternalistic regimes of the eighteenth and early nineteenth centuries invested large sums in selected pilot plants. Many of these were entirely government-owned and were managed by crown officials. Others were operated by private businessmen who received outright subsidies or low-cost loans or took in the state as a partner. As in the case of Japan, it is usually impossible to state categorically whether or not these enterprises made money; the officials charged with their surveillance tended to be reticent about their accounts. All the evidence, however, points to mediocre results.

To be sure, government promotion of industry, whether or not commercially profitable, yielded some beneficial by-products. Even those works that failed could often serve again, and many came to yield a return under more efficient management. A few eventually provided the basis for industrial giants.

This parallel between the Japanese and the European experience suggests not only that the contribution of government enterprise to Japanese economic development has been overrated but that it is best understood in a different context. Japanese scholars are wont to distinguish, I believe, between the industrial ventures of various *han* (feudal domains) in the late Tokugawa period and those of the central government after *bakumatsu* (collapse of the Tokugawa regime): the former were clearly abortive, perhaps misguided, and in any event of minor significance; the latter were serious and an indispensable prodrome to subsequent industrial advance.

Mobilization of human capital

The Gerschenkron model of the historical conditions of economic backwardness[2] concerns itself primarily with the mobilization of material resources; but it can and should be extended to the development of human resources as well. In the course of the nineteenth century, the governments of Continental Europe devoted considerable money and the energies of some of their most capable civil servants to the creation of complete, integrated systems of public education, ranging from grammar schools to universities and scientific research institutes. Much of this program reflected the conviction that only literate people could be moral, effective citizens of a modern society; much of it, particularly the establishment of scientific, technological, and vocational institutions, had the express purpose of freeing the economy from dependence on imported skills and providing a firm cognitive basis for autonomous growth. The extent of these efforts varied considerably from place to place; but all of these follower countries did far more along these lines than Britain; and the industrial gains of several of these economies — e.g., Germany, Switzerland, eventually Denmark — seem to have been closely tied to their successful development of what is now sometimes called "human capital."

The Japanese government also laid great stress on education as a means of forming the citizenry of a modern society. One thinks of the Imperial Rescript of 1872: "The acquirement of knowledge is essential to a successful life . . . It is intended, henceforth, that education shall be so widespread that there shall be no house in any village, no person in any house without learning." And the 1963 white paper of the Ministry of Education, *Nihon no seichō to kyōiku* (Growth and Education in Japan), remarks "that one common factor in the development of the rapidly growing societies of the twentieth century — Japan, Canada, Western Germany, Israel, Russia, and America — has been the great attention paid to education, and particularly a conscious awareness of the importance of technological education."

Yet intention is a long way from realization. The Japan of the 1870's was poor, and in those early days the total annual budget of the Ministry of Education was less than a million yen. The burden was therefore thrown on the local districts, each of which was required to establish at least one primary school. In spite of considerable prodding, it took decades to approximate this minimal standard. In the meantime, the monthly tuition fee was a serious deterrent to attendance, especially in rural areas; and not until its abolition in 1898 did universal elementary education become a realistic goal.

This long delay in generalizing primary instruction was characteristic of many European nations as well. France did not see free public schools until 1881, at which date 17 percent of her army conscripts and 25 percent of her brides could not read or write. In Great Britain, attendance in primary school was not made compulsory until 1880; by then it was more urgent to civilize the wild offspring of an industrial society than to impart the ability to read and write. Germany, however, was an exception. There the duty of parents to send their children to school had been proclaimed by Luther in 1524, and the more progressive states had taken steps to satisfy this obligation long before industrialization began. In Prussia, the General Landschulreglement of Frederick the Great (1763) had made primary schooling obligatory, though not free, and while it took decades to generalize the habit of compliance, attendance was just about universal by the second third of the nineteenth century. Even so, there were backward states— generally those whose economies were overwhelmingly agricultural — and abolition of fees did not become general until 1888. In all these countries, as in Japan, the rural areas were slow in sending their children to school, not only because of the charges and inconvenience but even more because the children could be used for farm chores. Conversely, the main reason why attendance in the cities and towns picked up earlier is that social legislation increasingly curtailed the ability of parents to turn their children into breadwinners.

What is different about Japan, however, is a certain neglect of scientific and technical education; and this is the more surprising in view of the lateness of the Japanese industrial revolution. To be sure, one can cite a number of important advances in this area: the early establishment of the *Kōgakkō*, later the Imperial College of Engineering; of the College of Agriculture; of several higher technical schools and some tens of specialized secondary and "quasi-secondary" schools in the 1870's and 1880's; and of scientific research institutes. Yet all of these together trained a small minority of Japanese students. As late as 1930, only 4 percent of the boys in secondary schools were studying "engineering"; and the vocational and apprentice training schools,

219

enrolled only 7 percent of the boys of secondary-school age in 1900. Moreover in the ordinary middle schools, the time and resources devoted to science were less than one would expect. By contrast, many of the European countries made a special effort in this sphere: Switzerland, Sweden, above all Prussia, where about 30–35 percent of the high school students attended *Realschulen* in the 1850's and 1860's.

One might argue, perhaps, that Japanese students were the better for not concentrating early, that well-trained generalists make better engineers than premature specialists. Yet university training had long focused on the humanities and was directed primarily to preparing bureaucrats. This, after all, was the quickest path to security and position; for as in today's new nations, "there were so few college graduates that those who did finish were virtually assured of a decent place in the government."[3] Science received some attention but nothing like the devotion it received in the *polytechniques* and *technische Hochschulen* of Europe. Higher technical instruction made headway only after 1900, and then mainly in agriculture and commerce. Not until the 1930's did college-level engineering grow substantially, increasing its share from 9 to 16 percent of the degrees awarded.

All of this raises the question how, in view of her limited employment of foreign experts, Japan developed the skills and techniques required to effect an industrial revolution. Some of the answer, no doubt, lies in the manual address and imitative quickness of the labor force — qualities already developed by the indigenous industrial crafts; some lies in the knowledge and experience brought back by Japanese students assigned to study and work abroad. The most important consideration, however, was undoubtedly the composition of Japan's economic activity in these early decades of growth. For one thing, much of the increase of manufacturing output derived simply from the pursuit of traditional trades more efficiently and on a larger scale. For another, the modern sector consisted largely of textile manufacture, crude metallurgy, railway construction and shipbuilding — the mainstays of the classical industrial revolution — which even in Europe continued to rest heavily on on-the-job training and intelligent empiricism. It is no accident that the multiplication after 1900 of licensing agreements and partnerships with foreign firms and the creation of foreign-owned enterprises on Japanese soil are linked to the more complex, science-oriented branches of technology: heavy engineering (including internal combustion motors), electrical engineering, and organic chemicals (including rubber).

By then, however, the decisive breakthrough to industrialization had been made; and within another generation the Japanese were able to establish their independence in these areas as well. All of which raises the most important question of all: how, with this limited recourse to the usual remedies for backwardness, did this latecomer accomplish these gains so quickly?

The rapidity of Japanese growth

The answer, it seems to me, lies paradoxically in the severity of the challenge that confronted Japan in the middle of the last century. The steady aggrandizement of Western commercial and political power in the Far East threatened nothing less than the dissolution of the Japanese polity and the reduction of the society to colonial status. All efforts, therefore, had to be applied to enhancing the country's national power, so that Japan could treat with the "barbarians" on equal terms; and this required the adoption of modern military technology and the establishment of a centralized government that could effectively promote and focus the strength of the nation.

These were the immediate objectives. They constituted the irreducible minimum of the reform program in the last years of Tokugawa and received support from reactionaries and progressives alike. The small group that led the overthrow of the shogunate apparently looked no farther at first. It was soon obvious, however, that political and military changes could not be effected in a vacuum and that, if Japan were to match strength with the great Western powers, she would have to accomplish a metamorphosis. Modern armed forces could be equipped and sustained only by a modern economy, and this in turn required an educated, mobile, motivated population. By the same token, a professional warrior class would no longer suffice for the defense of the nation's interests; only a nation in arms could meet the demands of modern war, and this implied a society of citizens rather than of servile subjects. All the pieces hung together, and the men of the Restoration soon found that they were inexorably engaged on a path whose destination few if any had foreseen. Some of them disapproved and gave up their posts. In the long run, they were replaced by men who accepted the still fuzzy but ever-clearer vision of a new Japan. *Sonnō-jōi* (Revere the Emperor — Expel the barbarians) and *kaikoku* (Opening the country) merged in a national consensus: under the aegis of the Emperor, Japan would take from the foreigner what she needed to maintain her independence and rise to new heights of power.

The integration of economic development in a general program of national enhancement had important consequences for the course and rate of growth. It stimulated and sanctioned productive efforts by all classes, for it conferred a patriotic nimbus on the everyday virtues of diligence, thrift, perseverance, and the like, while making a virtue of acquisitiveness. The evidence concerning the respectability of trade in Tokugawa times is ambiguous: the measures designed to limit the activities and curtail the influence and pretensions of merchants are imbued with scorn and moral disapproval; yet many samurai engaged in business, and numerous businessmen succeeded in attaining samurai status. In any event, insofar as a stigma was attached to moneymaking in the marketplace, it was subsequently erased by the identification of business success with national aggrandizement.

At the same time, the sanction of patriotism apparently facilitated rapid change by dampening the kinds of conflict that usually accompany industrialization. In general, it promoted a sense of duty and a docile acceptance of the burdens of life and responsibilities of citizenship. In particular, it helped dissuade labor from making an issue of the distribution of the social product and thereby fostered a high rate of profit and saving. It may also have done something to reconcile the rural population to their heavy share of the fiscal burdens of reform. In all this, patriotism was seconded by the traditional morality. As Dore has put it:[4]

> "The Confucian ethic of personal relations was reformulated as the uniquely *Japanese* family system. It served to preserve an image of society

221

as properly hierarchical and based on personal loyalties, and thus to strengthen authoritarian tendencies in general, enhance the docility of the labor force, and hold in check the erosion of the government's traditionally sanctioned authority."

Finally, the hostility between state officials and private entrepreneurs that afflicted the economies of Continental Europe seems to have been largely absent in Japan — at least until expansion in Manchuria and China in the 1930's led to a sharp cleavage between the military and the more responsible elements of civilian society within and without the government.

Severity of challenge is never enough in itself, however, to account for response. For one thing, stimulus clearly does not increase indefinitely with severity of adversity; there is such a thing as too much pressure. For another, response varies from one society to another: the same pressure that crushes one will elicit a vigorous reaction from another. China, after all, was also confronted by the threat of Western domination in the nineteenth century and failed the test. The secret of Japanese success, therefore, must also lie in the internal endowment of the nation — which, in view of the relative penury of raw materials, means individual and social resources.

Here, it seems to me, the position of scholars like Thomas C. Smith and E. Sydney Crawcour is unexceptionable. Tokugawa growth may not have been "modern economic growth" by the criteria of Simon Kuznets, as adopted by Ohkawa and Rosovsky. It was certainly not an industrial revolution. But it was a self-sustaining advance that rested on attitudes and values favorable to material development, and as such it provided a basis for a creative and effective response to new opportunities. It was very similar, in this respect, to the gradual development of the economies of Western Europe in the centuries preceding the great inventions of the eighteenth century. There, too, one has the impression of a fundamental contrast between the growth and change of the Industrial Revolution and the immobility of the earlier agrarian society. Yet a closer scrutiny reveals that the first breakthrough to industrialization — in Britain — derived directly from this preliminary development; that the countries of Continental Europe had already proceeded a long way toward a breakthrough when the British achievement thrust upon them the necessity of abridging the process; and that the subsequent success of these responsive revolutions owed much to the autonomous movement that preceded them. The significance of this demonstrated capacity to generate growth and change from within is not to be underestimated. As much as anything, it is this that sets Meiji Japan apart from the underdeveloped countries of the present day.

In the Japanese case, a number of symptoms of progress seem to me deserving of special notice. The first, is the commercialization and industrialization of the countryside, at least in the more advanced areas. The resemblance to "pre-industrial"' England is striking. There the spread of manufacture out of towns into the land had begun very early, so that by the end of the sixteenth century at least half of the output of woollen cloth came from rural cottages. From a by-occupation in times of slack, spinning, weaving, and other industrial activities had become the main support of tens of thousands, whose specialization made them increasingly dependent on markets, peddlers, and shops for their needs. The result was not only an ever-growing output of cheap manufactures that could undersell the better but dearer products of urban guildsmen, both at home and abroad, but an ever-growing national market for more or less standardized products. Supply and demand stimulated each other and made possible, in conjunction with growing markets overseas, a spiral of growth that eventually exceeded the productive capacity of dispersed hand manufacture and gave rise to the decisive technological changes that we denominate the Industrial Revolution.

The Japanese economy, closed as it was to outside trade and handicapped by political decentralization, did not proceed this far. But the commercialization and industrialization of rural areas were both a sign and source of expansion, which called forth a technological response on the appropriate scale. This took the form of devices to save labor: the use of the spinning wheel in cotton manufacture, the occasional application of water power in such branches as oil pressing, above all an increasing division of labor and occupational specialization. Most of this seems small by comparison with European innovations at a similar stage or even earlier — fulling mills, blast furnaces, industrial use of coal. Yet it looms large against the technological stagnation of most non-Western societies, which were content to spin with the distaff and made no use of inanimate power.

The significance of these advances, then, lies not in the gains they yielded in productivity, but in the evidence they offer of a rational, economizing mind at work. This was probably the greatest achievement and legacy of the late Tokugawa period: the rise and spread of attitudes conducive to adaptation and growth. The basic ingredients were there to begin with — diligence, thrift, a sense of responsibility; what these decades added was a leaven that made possible a new kind of economic cake.

Quality and cost of Japanese labor

The basic virtues should not he underestimated. Once Japan found herself on the path of industrialization, her most valuable resource was her supply of cheap, intelligent, hardworking labor. This, more than anything else, it seems to me— more than fiscal measures, more than a high rate of private saving — accounts for Japan's ability to multiply her initially meager wealth so rapidly.

A comparison of the Japanese and European adaptations of technology to relative factor costs is instructive. In Europe, the follower countries made the most of their cheap manpower by building more rudimentary but less expensive equipment, buying second-hand machines whenever possible, and concentrating on the more labor-intensive branches or stages of manufacture. Not until the last third of the century did the Continental economies conform to the usual theoretical model and avail themselves of the opportunity to adopt the latest techniques; and even then they maintained a larger working force per unit of production (spindle, loom, blast furnace) than Britain or the United States. In addition, they tended to be prodigal in their use of labor to manipulate or move materials and goods; for these were activities that were external to those processes of transformation that had been the foci of technical advance (spinning, weaving, smelting, rolling), and methods and equipment were thus not dictated by the requirements of an integrated procedure. Finally, the Continental mills, like the early British factories, worked their equipment as long and hard as possible, into the night even on the Sabbath eve. Sunday morning was set aside for cleaning and oiling the machinery. In time of expansion, the manufacturer added to his capital only as a last resort; it was easier to lengthen the working day; in the of crisis, he did the reverse. Only the introduction of social legislation to protect the health of women and children imposed an upper limit to the demands of the employer — the effort of the worker. Even then, the hands were expected to work overtime in periods of lively demand.

Japanese industry operated along similar lines. The best discussion is provided by Gustav Ranis, who emphasizes the "survival of old-fashioned production functions": cottage-based weaving in silk and cotton, dispersion of preparatory and finishing processes in domestic shops, "the retention of traditional, relatively primitive machinery in many areas." In some branches, of course, modern equipment was so far superior to the old as to make factory production profitable and home manufacture unviable; cotton spinning is the best example. In such fields, the Japanese did adopt modern machines and methods, but adapted them to the pattern of relative factor costs by running the equipment for longer periods and at higher speeds, throwing in additional manpower as required to maintain the machines and repair the more frequent breaks in the yarn. Moreover, as in Europe, resources were channeled toward the more labor-intensive branches of manufacture; the processing of raw silk, which financed almost a third of Japanese imports in the period before 1900, was perhaps the most advantageous instance of such specialization.

To be sure, one can have too much of a good thing, and there is considerable evidence that capital saving was pushed too far on occasion in both the West and Japan. In both France and Germany textile manufacturers often adopted techniques less remunerative than the best available, either because they were reluctant to scrap old equipment that was still working or because they were unable or unwilling to venture larger outlays on new machinery. In areas such as Normandy and Saxony, chronic technological backwardness was made possible only by natural and artificial protection from the competition of more efficient producers. It was the shift away from prohibition to freer trade in the 1860's that broke the resistance to the self-acting mule and power loom in French cotton and wool, and to coke-blast smelting in iron-making; and, by the same token, it was the construction of a national rail network, which brought Rhenish and Westphalian manufactures to Berlin and eastern Germany, that forced the rationalization of Silesian metallurgy and the Silesian and Saxon textile industries.

There is evidence, of a similar miscombination of factors in Japan, at similar expense. Orchard argues, for example, that Japanese enterprises used too much labor, without regard to productivity or costs; that the consequent inefficiency was in effect contagious and "snowballed"; and that cheap labor was thus "a most important weakness of the Japanese industrial system.[5] "Looking from the vantage point of the European experience, however, I am inclined to disagree. I have no doubt that Japanese entrepreneurs often overdid the substitution of labor for capital; American producers often sinned in the opposite direction; indeed, few businessmen anywhere calculate this sort of thing accurately. Probably the Japanese also lost certain byproducts of skill and efficiency (as opposed to productivity) in the process. Yet the absence of prohibitive tariffs prevented to some degree misallocation of resources; and on balance the Japanese undoubtedly gained, achieving a far higher rate of growth than they would have, had they adopted the "best," that is, the most capital-intensive practice.

The process of reform

Prime movers of change

In both Japan and Germany, unification came about through the efforts and under the leadership of only a part of the nation. In Japan, the key role was played by Satsuma and Chōshū; in Germany by Prussia, in particular the eastern heartland of the kingdom. In both countries, these were paradoxically among the most hierarchical and conservative of states; and their leaders stood to lose the most in the long run from a fundamental political and social revolution. That they behaved as they did is testimony to their limited immediate objectives and, for some, to a misestimate of the ultimate consequences of reform. In Japan, numerous officials resigned when they found the Restoration going beyond what they had anticipated; and some went home to mount rebellions against the Restoration betrayed. In Germany, the differences between reaction and reform-from-above never led to armed conflict; unlike the *han*, the Prussian provinces were long dead as autonomous entities and foci of loyalty. Instead, the two parties fought each other within the government . . .

Yet one should not lay everything at the door of unanticipated consequences. In both countries, loyalties to the polity overrode at critical points the prejudices and personal interests of beneficiaries of the old order. In Japan, what we may call the technique of the contagious sacrifice precipitated acceptance of several particularly painful reforms: the most spectacular instance is the surrender by the daimyo of Satsuma, Chōshū, Tosa, and Hizen of their fiefs as a prelude to the transformation of the *han* into prefectures. Nothing like this can be found in the German record to my knowledge; but it is significant that the reformers there were drawn in large measure from the same landed aristocracy that produced their most vehement opponents.

In neither country did reform proceed from the economically advanced regions. In Japan, it was the sea-level plains of central Honshū — the Osaka–Kyoto basin, the Nagoya area, the great Kantō plain around Edo — that had adopted new techniques of cultivation, commercialized much of their crops, developed sophisticated mercantile and banking methods, strewn the countryside with industry. And in Germany it was in the Rhineland, Westphalia, and Hesse that manufacturing and trade were flourishing in the eighteenth century and building up the kind of pressures that had led in Britain to an industrial revolution. Chōshū and Satsuma in Japan, Brandenburg–Prussia in Germany were the Spartas, not the Athens of their respective countries.

This pattern is not surprising. Reform, however much it may have worked to the advantage of the economically progressive areas, was a political response to a political problem. The initiative lay with the toughest, most powerful units, not with "small fry," however prosperous. Indeed, one might argue that, given the nature and knowledge of government in these pre-industrial societies, strong authority and an innovating, progressive economy were incompatible. In Satsuma, the "Prussia of Japan," free enterprise was sacrificed to a cameralist policy[6] of official monopolies and government factories; while the repudiation of the *han* debts wiped out a good part of the assets of the merchant class. In Chōshū, where the government alternated between the establishment of official monopolies and the granting of monopoly privileges to the guilds, the merchants were looked upon as a necessary evil: their "rightful scope" lay in "serving the *han* without procuring great profits for themselves." As for Germany, it was precisely the fragmentation of the Rhineland into weak political units that enabled industry to develop there along new, free lines and to grow faster than in the mercantilist economies to the East.

Revolutions are never made by the masses. They are made by revolutionaries who see and use the opportunities of public weakness and popular discontent to seize power and effect change. In both Germany and Japan, modernization was the work of a small number of statesmen, advised and seconded by a somewhat larger group of dedicated, hard-working civil servants. In both cases, it was the bureaucracy that actually worked out and then carried out the program of reform — a bureaucracy that had long since won its autonomy from the dictates and whims of the overlord and developed an *esprit de corps* and an impersonal loyalty to the polity. At all levels of Japanese government under Tokugawa, the nominal ruler was essentially a figurehead: the Emperor, of course; but the shogun also and the great majority of daimyo. All of them had long been accustomed to leave the business of administering such affairs as came within their domain to their officials; and if they occasionally were able to take advantage of power struggles among their vassals to intervene in politics, they were more often the creatures of vassals who influenced the succession to their own advantage. By contrast, Brandenburg–Prussia was ruled by a series of intelligent and active autocrats from the Great Elector to Frederick II, all of whom tended to treat their civil servants as just that — servants. Their successors, however, were far less capable and decisive — such is the biological penalty of inherited rank. So that well before the end of the eighteenth century, "the Prussian bureaucracy, as a body, gained a considerable amount of executive discretion and irresponsible political influence in detachment from, and veiled opposition to, personalized monarchical autocracy."

Diversity and consensus

We have noted that in both Germany (early 1800's) and Japan (1850's and 1860's) the achievement of consensus on the necessity of change was the result of an enduring commitment and an immediate challenge: of a common loyalty to a national ideal transcending private and local interests, and of the necessity to fight off foreign domination and protect the polity from dissolution. Yet when all is said and done, this was a very meager common denominator, and at that, not common to all. Throughout Germany and even in Prussia, there were those who were content, or pleased, to collaborate with the French. And the advocates of resistance were split along lines very similar to the opposition between *kaikoku* and *sonno-joi*:[7] there were those who called for reform after the British and French models; and those, like Marwitz, who argued that these Western innovations were the negation of the best and noblest in Prussian society, and that what was needed was a return to antique virtues and selfless loyalty to the King.

"The Discontented"

In one way ideas did directly influence events — by suggesting new standards of social selection and thereby exacerbating class conflict within the traditional order.

In both Germany and Japan, the confrontation with an outside system encouraged introspection that fostered in its turn dissatisfaction with the status quo. The Japanese were faced by an immediate menace. The Germans of the eighteenth century were under less pressure, but the comparison with richer, freer societies was disturbing and thought-provoking. In both cases, once thoughts came, they fed on themselves and developed a force of their own. This discontent might, of course, have led to unbridgeable cleavages and class conflict, as indeed it was to do in Germany in 1848 and 1918. Under the wider menace to the polity, however, horizontal lines became vertical, drawn between institutional systems rather than class groups. Smith suggests that for Japan, it was partly this very "leaven of class discontent which made possible, within these [vertical] guidelines, new political combinations capable of revolutionary acts."[8] The same was, if anything, even more true in Germany, where over the course of the nineteenth century the bourgeoisie — and eventually even the working class — sublimated their ambitions and assuaged their frustrations in the drive to national unity and aggrandizement.

Agrarian reform and economic progress

In Japan the system of land ownership and tenure seems to have conduced to other values. The Tokugawa had made it a point to separate the samurai from the soil, thereby depriving them of autonomous control over revenues and manpower. The motives and direct consequences of this policy are well known. After a long period of civil conflict, Japan had come to appreciate the disadvantages of an independent and inevitably insubordinate aristocracy; and under the Shogunate there were to be no Junkers or great barons to exercise local sovereignty and challenge the authority of the central government. But for our purposes, it is the indirect and unintended consequences that are of interest: land ownership never became the symbol of social eminence and prestige, the hallmark of quality, and hence did not have the attraction for new wealth that it had in the West. So that when Japan entered on the path of industrialization, the successful businessman, whatever his social origin, did not feel it necessary to put the seal on his economic ascent by placing a good part or all of his fortune into estates. To be sure, the farmers themselves were not exempt from the characteristically immoderate peasant appetite for soil; and in Japan, as in the West, the wealthier residents of the village often coveted land for the political influence it brought with it. But at least the non-rational flow of entrepreneurial funds out of the modern sector was less than it would otherwise have been; and insofar as there are social differences in the efficiency of capital, this was undoubtedly a major gain.

Further similarities and contrasts

One could cite other substantial differences between the patterns of German and Japanese economic growth. One of the most obvious is the contrast between their respective natural endowments: Germany, rich in coal and ores, inherited a tradition of skillful metallurgy and metal-working and raised these branches to international preeminence in the course of her industrial revolution. Japan perforce made considerable progress in these areas; her goal of economic independence and parity required it, and one of the strongest motives for her penetration of the Asian continent was the acquisition of the raw materials she lacked at home. Yet the strength of her modern sector lay in light industry, while the heavy branches never showed the same competitive strength on the world market. Significantly, Japan's recent successes in exporting metal products have been concentrated in those branches where labor constitutes the most important input and material costs are relatively low: light machinery, electrical and optical equipment, small vehicles.

Another difference between the two countries lay in their technological roles. Germany, thanks to the precocious development of scientific and technical education, was a major innovator even before she was an industrial nation. She was in the forefront of steel technology in the 1840's and pioneered in electrical engineering, chemicals, optics, agronomy — to name only a few areas — from the middle of the century on. Japan, though she could boast of important innovations in the period before the Second World War — the Toyota loom is the one most frequently cited — was much more the imitator. Insofar as she did invent new methods and devices, they were more adaptive than revolutionary; that is, they rendered borrowed techniques more suitable to the circumstances of Japanese production. Much of her skill went to copying the wares of more advanced countries. As a result, she was often accused of lacking originality, and hard-pressed competitors fulminated against the immorality of economic plagiarism. This pattern of technological development reflected in large part the inadequacies of the educational system. Equally important, however, was the structure of factor costs: an economy endowed with cheap, skilled manpower is less likely to seek for improvements in methods or equipment, while the labor-intensive techniques it does employ will throw off less opportunities for or stimuli to innovation.

Yet in the last analysis, the similarities between the courses of development in the two countries are even more striking and more significant than the differences. One of the most obvious is the cleavage in both between the modern and traditional sectors, a cleavage wide enough to warrant the use of term "dualism . . ."

The dualism of rapid growth is very different. Essentially it is nothing more than the gap implicit in uneven development; since economic development is never even, all industrializing countries have known some degree of dualism. Productivity gains are inevitably greater in some branches than others, and capital flows are correspondingly selective. Institutional arrangements play a role: some parts of the economy are freer than others to change and grow, because less subject to political or collusive restraints; while competition is never perfect, and pressures to rational allocation of resources are weakened accordingly. And there is always the human factor: peasants, for example, are far more traditional in their outlook and slower to change than businessmen. It would therefore be a mistake to look upon dualism as something that sets Japan apart from European countries.

On the other hand, the size of the gap between modern and traditional in Japan is not to be ignored. Rather, it is important as a particularly good example of a larger phenomenon, which one may almost state as a law: dualism is inversely proportional to the length of preparation for industrialization and directly proportional to the rate of growth in the course of industrialization. The German experience was essentially similar. Nor is it a coincidence that in both countries, industrialization was so closely tied to political aims. In each case the decision to develop the economy as a means of national aggrandizement implied extensive state intervention, for better or for worse; and intervention in turn meant a certain distortion of capital flows and a preferential development of some branches rather than others. Moreover, these tendencies toward unevenness were accentuated by a natural channeling of talent and effort toward those activities most closely related to the national cause. It was not only that this is where the money was, here lay also prestige and honor.

The same considerations go far to explain the structure of big business in the two countries. I am not thinking here only of the size of the largest German and Japanese firms or even of their vertical and horizontal integration. Similar giants could be found in other countries, including some, like Holland, where the role of the state has always been extremely small and the question of national aggrandizement has never arisen.

The penalties of ambition

The ultimate consequences of politicized economic development in Germany and Japan were enormous. Growth was more uneven than in other industrializing countries and more uneven than it need have been. Economic power was formalized and concentrated to a greater degree than in any other free enterprise system. Private interests were protected and coddled; yet in the last analysis political and military considerations had precedence. The economy was an instrument in the service of the nation, rather than the reverse.

Notes

1. Thomas C. Smith, *Political Change and Industrial Development in Japan: Government Enterprise, 1868–1880* (Stanford, 1955), p. 63. Cf. John E. Orchard, *Japan's Economic Position: The Progress of Industrialization* (N.Y., 1930), p. 90: "There are few modern industries in Japan today that do not owe their existence to government initiative." And again: "The part played by the government cannot be overemphasized. Japanese industry of the present day owes its state of development primarily to the efforts of a highly paternalistic central government."

2. See Alexander Gerschenkron (1962), *Economic Backwardness in Historical Perspective.* Cambridge, Mass.

3. Shibusawa Keizō, *Japanese Life and Culture in the Meiji Era* (Tokyo, 1958), p. 299. "In 1885 Tsuboichi Shōyō described typical student-houseboys swaggering down a Kanda street as though they owned it and reminding people that despite their ragged clothes and worn-out hats they would some day be great men. Students liked to point out that the national councilors of the day had all been students once." *Ibid.*, 300–01.

4. Ronald Dore, "Some Comparisons of Latin America and Asian Studies, with Special Reference to Research on Japan," S.S.R.C. *Items*, XVII, no. 2, (June 1963), 18.

5. Orchard, *Japan's Economic Position*, p. 362, (N.Y., 1930).

6. Cameralist policy denotes economic activity directed by a state bureau that is controlled by an aristocracy. [Editor]

7. See above [page 221] and glossary. [Editor]

8. T.C. Smith (1962), *Journal of Asian Studies*, Vol. 22, p. 219.

Militarism, Fascism and the Pacific War

The attainment of an industrially-based economy by European countries was frequently accompanied by a desire for Great Power status. The lesson that these aspirations could be realised by imperialist expansion was rapidly assimilated by the Japanese modernisers who swiftly learned that in the late nineteenth century force paid dividends. An aggressive imperialist tradition, which sent Japanese forces to the Asian mainland, was to begin in Japan almost from the inception of the Meiji era. China's island province of Taiwan was attacked in 1872 and an indemnity later demanded from China. Plans made to invade Korea in 1873 were cancelled but Korea was briefly attacked and forced to open ports to Japanese trade only three years later. The Kurile and Ryukyu Islands were acquired from Russia and China in 1875 and 1879 respectively. The Sino–Japanese War of 1894–5, which had been provoked by Japan, ended with the defeat of China and the occupation of Taiwan, the Pescadores Islands and part of Manchuria as Japanese colonies. Japanese troops took part in suppressing the Boxer Rebellion in North China in 1900, and Japan was rewarded with a degree of international equality from Britain manifested in the Anglo–Japanese Alliance of 1902. However, it was Japan's defeat of Russia in a brief war in Manchuria from 1904 to 1905 which marked the achievement of full status as a world power. Thereafter Japanese control of the Korean peninsula and South Manchuria increased steadily providing opportunities for colonial settlement and economic expansion. Further expansion on the Asian mainland came with the acquisition of new territories in China in 1919. The province of Shantung and a vastly enlarged Manchuria were annexed by Japan after World War I, and an invasion of Siberia in 1918 tested the possibility of taking Russian territory.

Japan's part in World War II and aggression in China from 1931 represent the culmination of this tradition which was to lead to the brief control of several hundred million Asian peoples from 1942–1945. Asia was to suffer many millions of civilian and military deaths in armed conflict and numerous barbarous atrocities committed by Japanese forces, and through large-scale economic disruption. In 1937 Nanking fell to the Japanese army which embarked on several weeks of murder, rape and looting which ended in the massacre of 300,000 Chinese civilians and troops, and the exodus of more than a million refugees from North China. Many thousands of young Korean and Chinese women, including the mothers of young children, were abducted and forced to work in military brothels throughout the war. European and American servicemen received appalling treatment from their Japanese captors. The building of the Bataan railway alone cost the lives of over 100,000 allied POWs while torture and starvation were routine in Japanese prison camps. There were medical units in the Japanese army that were guilty of performing experiments on at least 3,000 living prisoners. In their quest to produce bacteriological weapons army Unit 731 deliberately infected Chinese, Russian, Korean and Mongolian prisoners with gangrene and equally virulent pathogens while others died in vivisection experiments.

The callousness of Japan's wartime regime was also seen in the appalling indifference to the suffering of its own soldiers and civilians. The Japanese soldier's manual was clear that live captives were the object of universal disgrace. Soldiers were informed officially that when faced with defeat they should, 'always save the last bullet' for themselves. Japanese troops were obliged to hold their positions with fanatical determination, even in the face of overwhelming odds, and civilians were forced to share in this sacrifice. In June 1945, with the war all but over, the defence of Okinawa cost the lives of over 200,000 Japanese, more than half of whom were civilians. The use of suicide missions on land and at sea, as much as the famous *kamikaze* pilots, who attacked American ships in the last ten months of the war with only a three per cent success rate, illustrates official disinterest in the welfare of ordinary citizens.

The Pacific and Asian wars led to 3,500,000 military casualties for Japan. Civilian losses in air raids in 1944 and 1945 numbered 668,000 in a year of saturation bombing. The loss of 125,000 people in a single raid on 9 March 1945 was more than twice the losses suffered by bombing in Britain during the entire war. American raids involved the dropping of an unprecedented tonnage of incendiary bombs by a massive fleet of aircraft. Fire storms caused gale force winds to spread conflagrations across vast urban swathes and, in place of the oxygen consumed, created poisonous gases which indiscriminately slaughtered whole communities. But the deaths of 210,000 people from the atomic bombs dropped on Hiroshima and Nagasaki in August 1945, and the prolonged aftermath of radiation sickness and genetic damage which persists to this day, has come to overshadow conventional bombing in modern consciousness.

Well before the intensity of bombing raids precipitated surrender, the economy was near to collapse. The war had brought many people close to starvation, few Japanese consumed more than 1500 calories per day and many were forced to scavenge for food in the countryside. An enormous expanse of urban area had been decimated by bombing causing the population of Tokyo to fall from six and a half to three million people. Whole districts within cities were obliterated. Twenty five per cent of all homes were destroyed and a further fifty per cent of buildings were damaged. A quarter of Japan's entire physical capital stock was annihilated in the Pacific War. In what must be considered as one of the greatest understatements of all time Emperor Hirohito concluded, in his surrender broadcast of 14 August 1945, that: "the war situation has developed not necessarily to Japan's advantage".

Halliday chronicles the years leading to Japan's defeat and Morris provides a flavour of the desperation and psychological pressures which led to the instigation of suicide in strategic planning by the Japanese high command. What kind of social system would both perpetrate and endure such extreme forms of aggression? Since 1868 Japan had developed with an unreformed agrarian system and a new capitalist class without the liberalism or political experience of a European bourgeoisie. The emperor system and resurgent forms of feudal ideology manifested as ultra-nationalism were at the heart of Japanese politics. The rise of sinister extreme right-wing factions within the army in the 1930s and their effects on Japanese society are provided by Storry, while the details of the Pacific War for which these forces were largely responsible is described by Beasley. The philosophy of ultra-nationalism and its radical programme for the social transformation of Japan is revealed in the writings of Kita who, until his execution in 1937, was the chief ideologue and mentor of the Imperial Way Faction within the army and was frequently taken in the West as Japan's only real fascist. A sensitive and insightful analysis of the psychology of ultra-nationalism is presented by

Maruyama, who provides a valuable explanation of the barbaric conduct of the Japanese forces in war time. The affinity of this form of ideology — and the politics with which it was associated — with that of the European fascist movements with whom Japan was to become allied is examined by Radek, who compares Japan's social structure with that of contemporary Germany and Italy. Despite having gained an advanced industrial base by the 1940s, Japan still held a vast rural population living in social conditions that closely resembled those of the Tokugawa era. The connection between these conditions and militarism is outlined by Dore, while Fukutake describes in detail the appalling plight of the peasantry during the 'forced march' dictated by industrial capitalism.

It is necessary to enter the debate on whether or not Japan was ruled by a fascist political system in these times. The differences between European forms of fascism and what may have been their equivalent in East Asia are marked. No demagogue like Hitler or Mussolini arose in Japan and neither was there a mass movement or popular political party. If fascism did arise in Japan it is difficult to be precise about the historical moment when it became dominant. Equally there was no new or distinctive fascist ideology or a declaration of intent like *Mein Kampf*. On the other hand, Japan had become an ally of Nazi Germany and fascist Italy in the Axis pact of 1940 and internal social developments suggest the existence of a fascistic state system which had penetrated almost all parts of society. Nationalism and militarism had become fused together as a single entity in the half century preceding Japan's defeat. The power of the extreme right-wing grew steadily and the far from liberal Diet voluntarily dissolved itself in 1940, giving way to the Imperial Rule Assistance League which established a corporate state and gave concrete expression to ultra-nationalist ideology. But do these developments denote fascism? There are cogent arguments against this thesis. Japan was doing no more than develop along lines set down in the nineteenth century and this continuity with the past fully explains the totalitarian nature of Japan's state system, its aggression and ideology.

By way of an afterthought it is perhaps worth briefly considering the behaviour and attitudes of the post-war Japanese élite in relation to the war. Ruling conservative forces in both the state and business have failed to come to terms with Japan's undoubted war guilt. By not facing up to the facts of Japanese aggression and to the many atrocities committed in Asia and the Pacific, an important responsibility to post-war generations has been evaded by the élite. Children today learn little about the war and, in the case of even well-documented massacres, the officially sanctioned school textbooks refer only to 'unfortunate incidents'. The result has been that several post-war generations manifest a dangerous form of collective amnesia. Japan is seen only as a victim of Western power politics and as the recipient of two atomic bombs — the greatest crime against humanity — and the reality of both the causes and horrible events of the war remain unavailable for active consideration. Recent apologies by Japanese politicians for Japan's part in the war have come only after years of agitation by other Asian countries and by the left in Japan itself. But the refusal of successive governments to consider compensation for the surviving victims of Japanese aggression — maimed ex-service men, and women who endured enforced prostitution — even at a distance of fifty years forces us to return to the point that the élite still maintains an ostrich-like stance to Japan's war guilt.

14. The Dark Valley
Richard Storry

I

The Japanese often give the name, *kurai tanima* — 'dark valley' — to the period between 1931 and 1941, the decade immediately preceding the outbreak of the Pacific War. For during those years the still delicate plant of liberalism and personal freedom that had sprouted during the twenties was effectively killed. To change the metaphor again, liberal-minded men in politics, the services, education, literature, and art found themselves, after 1931, treading a path increasingly beset with dangers from the twin forces of reaction and revolution, expressed in violence none the less menacing for being intermittent and on occasions haphazard. This violence had two aspects — unchecked aggression abroad and murderous conspiracy at home.

It may be that only a minority of the nation saw the situation, at the time, in these terms. But this minority consisted of the Japanese intellectual élite, headed by the emperor himself. Why then was it unable to put up a stronger fight against the rising surge of ultra-nationalism, embracing both traditionalist and revolutionary national socialist elements, of which the army was the spear-head?

The answer lies in the nature of the structure of the Japanese state in those years. According to the Constitution, the emperor stood at the apex of power, vested with immense prestige of at least a semi-religious character. In theory he was the ultimate arbiter of all questions, those relating to military and naval strategy as well as to law and politics. In reality, of course, his powers were exercised only on the advice of specific persons representing such entities as the cabinet, the Army and Navy General Staffs, and the Privy Council; and these often cherished conflicting opinions, and therefore they struggled against each other. Unhappily there was no supreme coordinating body. In the past this had been supplied, very efficiently, by the group comprising the *Genro*. After 1924, however, Saionji was the sole surviving member of this august and once most powerful body; and Saionji hoped to see Japan progress slowly but certainly towards something resembling a state under a constitutional monarchy and a parliamentary form of government. Therefore on the whole he deliberately refrained from interfering in political affairs, except to recommend a new premier after a cabinet resignation and to insist on being kept well informed as to what was going on. Saionji was not in favour of the emperor himself filling the role of coordinator of policy, in the manner of a German kaiser or a Russian tsar. On the contrary, his great concern was to keep the Throne aloof from any responsibility for making decisions of high policy. He was afraid that the emperor would become embroiled in controversy if he were to take a stand on any issue, however right and sensible it might be. Saionji feared that in the perilous context of the thirties this

Richard Storry: 'The Dark Valley' from *A HISTORY OF MODERN JAPAN* (Penguin Books, 1960; 4th revised edition, 1982), pp. 182–213. Copyright © Richard Storry 1960, 1961, 1968. Reproduced by permission of Penguin Books Ltd.

might endanger the prestige of the emperor or even shake the position of the imperial house. It is too facile to dismiss Saionji's view as over-timid, to point out that because the emperor's words were obeyed in 1945 they would have been obeyed with docility in 1931 or 1932 if the emperor, speaking *ex cathedra*, had called upon the army to retire in Manchuria. The risk of disobedience seemed very real. All we can claim, with the advantage of hind-sight, is that it would have been better for Japan and for the world if this risk had been taken in the thirties. Only an imperial rescript could have reversed the course of armed expansion across the Yellow Sea. One can say that the emperor's inclination was to take action of this kind, had he received firm encouragement from Saionji.

It may be asked whether in fact there was any real risk that ultra-nationalists, more especially army officers, would have ignored a specific order from the emperor. After all they claimed to be passionately loyal to the emperor, more loyal than any other group of Japanese subjects. But here we have to remember the essentially emotional, illogical psychology of such fanatics. Just as Saigo in 1877 never regarded himself as a rebel, so inevitably some right-wing 'patriots' would not necessarily have considered themselves disloyal in opposing an imperial rescript that they held to be inspired by 'evil counsellors'. In August 1945 there were to be a few who would not accept, in a sense, the evidence of their own ears, who defied the Surrender broadcast. Japanese ultra-nationalists were loyal to their conception of what the emperor ought to be. To the emperor as he was they were grossly disloyal — and a few of the more sophisticated among them were well aware of this fact.

When all this has been said, however, the balance of probability — on the showing of the overwhelming response to the Surrender broadcast of 1945 — suggests that an imperial rescript restraining the army in Manchuria or, later, in China would have been obeyed by the great majority of officers, although no doubt there would have been armed insubordination by the minority; and this would have led to short-lived confusion, even a kind of brief civil war. It was precisely this prospect that horrified senior officers and cabinet ministers, causing them to shrink from the really firm action that was required. Senior officers thus found themselves in a position of being in effect blackmailed by the threats of a lunatic fringe of 'Young Turks', very few of whom held a rank higher than that of colonel. The stage was quickly reached when senior officers in their turn could blackmail successive cabinets. A minister of war, for example, when opposing or proposing some measure in the cabinet would assert that, unless his views prevailed, it would be impossible to maintain order and discipline in the army.

We shall see in this chapter that the emperor more than once took a firm line with the army leaders; but he could do this only, as it were, on a personal level, behind the closed doors of the palace. This had at times some effect, but it was not enough. Court advisers and cabinet ministers could not agree, when it came to the point, to advise open and official action by the emperor to curb the army.

An unusually determined prime minister, of the Hamaguchi mould, might have been able, overcoming the *Genro's* hesitation, to make such action possible. Premier Inukai appears in 1932 to have planned imperial intervention of this kind; and this was the probable reason for his assassination. A few years later Konoye, as Premier, hoped to play the part of coordinator of high policy, believing that he could control the army. He deceived himself. His temperament unfitted him for the task.

On the side of the army a man of the calibre of Yamagata might well have succeeded in putting a stop to what the Japanese call *gekokujo*, or 'the overpowering of seniors by juniors'; although in fairness to the generals of the Showa period we must bear in mind that in Yamagata's heyday Choshu completely dominated the army, and *samurai* clan obligations served to strengthen Yamagata's authority. By the thirties many officers, including three or four of high rank, had no connexion with Choshu. An increasing number did not even come from families of *samurai* stock. All the same, the army leaders of the Showa period were unworthy heirs of Yamagata and Nogi. Their efforts to restore unity and discipline were spasmodic, however sincere; and there was all too often an unreadiness to accept individual responsibility.[1] Even collectively they took the line of least resistance. So in the end they brought their country to the critical impasse of 1941, when it was presented with three brutal alternatives — massive loss of face, economic suicide, or war. This downhill course must now be described, beginning with the 'Manchurian Incident'.

II

For many months before September 1931, when the Mukden *coup* occurred, there was serious friction between the Japanese, in their leased territory and along the zone of the South Manchurian Railway, and the Chinese authorities in Manchuria headed by Chang Tso-lin's son, the 'Young Marshal', Chang Hsueh-liang. For the latter, having associated himself with the Kuomintang regime, had begun to wage economic warfare against the Japanese by the construction of lines competing with the Japanese-owned South Manchurian Railway system. This was a very natural course for Chang to have adopted; and in view of Shidehara's declared policy of friendship, Chang may have felt that there was little risk of the Japanese resorting to the kind of retaliation that he provoked from the Russians in 1929, when he tried to take over their controlling interests in the Chinese Eastern Railway. On that occasion Soviet forces lost no time in intervening, and Chang had to give way to Russian demands. Certainly it was Chinese policy to squeeze out, little by little, Japanese interests in Manchuria. This general Sino–Japanese quarrel in Manchuria was aggravated in the summer of 1931 by some minor incidents which confirmed certain Japanese officers on the spot in their determination to gain control of all Manchuria before it was too late. These officers had friends and supporters in Tokyo, notably in General Staff Headquarters — the same men who had planned the abortive 'March Incident'.[2] So in the summer of 1931 a plan was worked out by these officers, in Tokyo and at Kwantung Army Headquarters, for the sudden occupation of Mukden, to be followed by the seizure of other towns in Manchuria. To what extent those in high military command were aware of this plan cannot be assessed with any certainty. What can be said is that army leaders were exasperated with Shidehara's 'weak diplomacy' and were eager for Japan to adopt a very firm stand in Manchuria. Indeed in August 1931 the Minister of War, now General Minami, called a conference of divisional commanders and other important senior officers, and in addressing them he openly attacked the China policy of his cabinet colleague, the Foreign Minister.

The Japanese generals were also perturbed by insistent pressure from the Minister of Finance, Inouye Junnosuke, for a reduction in the army budget; and there also loomed ahead the prospect of a World Disarmament Conference at Geneva early in the following year. The government was already asking the army to nominate its delegates.

Early in September, if not before, Shidehara began to receive reports from Japanese consular officers in Manchuria that some kind of 'direct action' was being planned by the Kwantung Army against the Chinese. These reports were sufficiently specific and reliable to alarm both Shidehara and the Premier, Wakatsuki. They protested vigorously to General Minami, the Minister of War. They must have underlined the ominous significance of these reports when reporting their substance to the emperor; for the latter saw Minami and told him to his face that the army in Manchuria must be restrained.

In response to those admonitions Minami adopted a curious course of action. He wrote an urgent and confidential letter to the Commander-in-Chief, Kwantung Army, advising him to cancel any plans that might have been made for military action against the Chinese. Then he gave the letter to a major-general in Tokyo and told him to take it to Manchuria. This major-general had been heavily involved in the 'March Incident', and even if he was not equally implicated in the plot to seize Mukden, he was known to favour 'direct action', and to be intimately associated with ultra-nationalist junior officers. The War Minister's letter could hardly have been entrusted to a less suitable courier; and what happened was not very surprising. The major-general, instead of flying at once to Port Arthur, travelled by train through Korea to Mukden. He arrived in the Japanese zone at Mukden in the evening of 18 September. He met the colonel who was in fact one of the principal architects of the *coup d'état* that was to be carried out a few hours later and then proceeded to a geisha-house. Later that night, while he was regaling himself — his letter still undelivered — the first shots were fired in what became known as the 'Manchurian Incident'.

The Japanese claimed that Chinese soldiers tried to sabotage the South Manchurian Railway just north of Mukden. To this day the precise truth of this allegation remains unknown. At any rate it gave to the Japanese officers on the spot the pretext they needed for an attack on Chinese troops in Mukden, and fighting on a noisy and considerable scale was soon in progress. The local Japanese Consulate remonstrated with the colonel directing operations but was told to mind its own business; and when a member of the Consulate (in later years a Socialist representative in the Diet) visited this colonel's headquarters he had a rough reception, one officer threatening him with a drawn sword. Meanwhile the Commander-in-Chief, at Port Arthur, was asked to put his seal to orders already prepared for the movement of more troops into Mukden, and he approved an immediate signal to the Commander-in-Chief, Korea, appealing for reinforcements.

On 19 September, then, the cabinet in Tokyo was presented with the *fait accompli* of the Japanese military occupation of Mukden and, later on the same day, of Changchun many miles to the north. That night, in Mukden, General Minami's courier at last handed over the urgent letter from Tokyo.

There now followed weeks of public embarrassment and secret humiliation for the Wakatsuki government. While the army in the field boldly extended the scope of its operations, Japanese representatives at the League of Nations in Geneva, and at London, Washington, and other capitals, declared that these military measures were only temporary and would soon cease. Indeed, on 30 September Japan accepted a resolution by the Council of the League calling for the withdrawal of Japanese troops to the South Manchurian Railway zone. So far from any withdrawal taking place, further advances were made and Chang Hsueh-liang's provisional capital was bombed from the air.

This blatant contrast between Japanese promises and the action of Japanese troops spreading fan-like through Manchuria led the world to suppose that the cabinet in Tokyo had adopted a policy of deliberate chicanery and deceit. This was not so. What was happening was the breakdown of coordination between the civil and military wings of the Japanese structure of state power. The position of the Wakatsuki administration is best summed up in the words of Saionji's secretary, who in a private talk at the time to members of the House of Peers declared: 'From the beginning to end the government has been utterly fooled by the army.'

As military operations went forward, overcoming Chinese resistance everywhere, and as almost all Manchuria passed under Kwantung Army control — Chang Hsueh-liang retired south of the Great Wall at the end of the year — there arose in Japan a wave of nationalist emotion; and the climate of the day soon made it seem treasonable for anyone publicly to oppose what was happening. There was in any case, for the Japanese, an almost mystical significance about south Manchuria, where so many lives had been lost in the struggle against the Russians. There was now, thanks to the depression, a very practical interest in the open spaces of Manchuria, which it was thought might help to solve Japan's population problem. World disapproval, symbolized by the hardening of the attitude of the League of Nations, merely cemented instinctive patriotic feeling.

The government's anxieties were not lessened by the discovery in October of another officers' plot in Tokyo. This conspiracy, which was exposed thanks to a change of heart among some of the ringleaders, envisaged the annihilation of the cabinet, while in session, by air bombardment and the establishment of a military junta in control of affairs. A day or two under arrest, a reprimand, and posting outside Tokyo were the only punishment meted out to those involved. This so-called 'October Incident' was of course carefully hushed up, and no hint of it was allowed to leak out to the public. The Premier now began to talk of resigning; but he struggled on until December, when the refusal of the Home Minister to attend meetings of the cabinet effectively sabotaged the government.[3]

The Wakatsuki cabinet was followed by a *Seiyukai* administration under Inukai Tsuyoshi. It was the last party cabinet in Japan until after the Pacific War. Just as there were close affiliations between the *Minseito* cabinet of Wakatsuki and the Mitsubishi *zaibatsu*, so there existed similar contacts between the *Seiyukai* cabinet and Mitsui. Almost the first act of the new government was to reverse the financial policy of its predecessor and take Japan off the gold standard. There was much to be said for this, but the merits of the action attracted less public attention than the fact that it happened to be immensely profitable at that moment to certain segments of the Mitsui empire.

Inukai was seventy-five when he became Premier. He was something of a chauvinist; but in the past he had opposed clan oligarchy and he did not look with any favour on military usurpation of political power. He was determined, being a very loyal as well as a courageous old man, to heed the message passed to him from the emperor when he was asked to form a cabinet. The emperor's bidding included the following sentence:

> The army's interference in domestic and foreign politics, and its wilfulness, is a state of affairs which, for the good of the nation, we must view with apprehension.

So, using channels of his own, Inukai tried to open negotiations with the Chinese. A trusted friend was sent on a secret mission to China, and arrangements were made for him to communicate directly with the Prime Minister in a code unknown to the army. At the same time, if we can accept his son's evidence, Inukai set about preparing for the emperor to issue a rescript commanding the army to cease all operations in Manchuria. But the chief cabinet secretary, an ambitious *Seiyukai* politician unwisely confided in by Inukai, was on intimate terms with extreme nationalists in the army and outside. They were informed by him, so it seems, of Inukai's plans.

Meanwhile, early in 1932 fighting broke out in Shanghai between the Chinese 19th Route Army and the Japanese naval landing party stationed in the city. A world not yet entirely hardened to the spectacle of repeated air attacks on densely populated towns was shocked by the vigorous bombing, by Japanese naval airplanes, of Chinese positions in the Chapei district of Shanghai. The naval force had to be rescued from defeat by the army, which in the end committed no less than four divisions to a battle that raged with great ferocity for about six weeks before the resolute Chinese withdrew.

The Shanghai fighting was dying down when it was announced from Manchuria that an independent government had been set up there under Pu Yi, the last of the Chinese emperors. This young man had been escorted in the previous autumn from Tientsin to south Manchuria by Kwantung Army officers. He was made chief executive of the new state of Manchukuo, and later he was made emperor of this Japanese creation. Tremendous efforts were made — their disingenuous character was almost engaging — to convince world opinion that Manchukuo was a truly independent state. In particular it was hoped that the Lytton Commission, sent to the Far East on behalf of the League of Nations, would be bamboozled by the fiction of this new Manchurian nation established by the will of the inhabitants of the country with some benevolent help from the Kwantung Army.

It was during the Shanghai fighting and while the Kwantung Army was acting as midwife to the birth of Manchukuo that two notable murders took place in Japan within the space of four weeks. The victims were Inouye Junnosuke, the former Minister of Finance, and Baron Dan, chief director of the Mitsui holding company. They were killed by members of a secret association of young ultra-nationalist fanatics known as the 'League of Blood'. This group had made ready a list of some twenty people, famous in politics and business, who were to be assassinated, individually as opportunity offered. Premier Inukai was among those on the list.

However, he was to meet his death at the hands of another, though related, gang of assassins. On 15 May 1932 his official residence was invaded by nine young men, naval officers and army cadets. They sought out and shot down the old man who had received them with composure and suggested that they talk things over before using their weapons. While this was going on, another detachment, made up of young farmers, attempted to sabotage the Tokyo power stations.

This affair, known as the '15 May Incident' effectively put an end to party cabinets in Japan for the next thirteen years; henceforth the army would not supply a minister of war to a government headed by a party leader. Furthermore, although people in Tokyo were undoubtedly shocked by the murder of Inukai and by the two assassinations carried out by the 'League of Blood', at their trial there was much public sympathy with the murderers, for their motives were regarded as purely unselfish. None received a capital sentence, and most of them emerged from prison well before the Pacific War.

Inukai's successor was Admiral Saito. He held office until July 1934, when his cabinet resigned in consequence of allegations, totally unproven, that certain ministers had been concerned in a notorious bribery scandal. Admiral Saito, who had been a rather enlightened Governor-General of Korea in the previous decade, was conservative, high-minded, realistic, moderately liberal, but over-cautious no doubt and inclined to be too sanguine about the way events were shaping. 'Everything will be all right', he remarked privately, in the summer of 1932, 'so long as we old men are here to put on the brakes.'

But the most powerful man in the cabinet was General Araki, the Minister of War. He and his friend General Mazaki, soon to be made Inspector-General of Military Training, were regarded as leaders of a faction in the army known as the *Kodo-ha*, or 'Imperial Way School'. Its great rival was a faction usually called the *Tosei-ha*, or 'Control School'. The *Koda-ha* was the more influential from about 1932 until the end of 1934, when its supremacy started to wane very rapidly. The years 1932–6 can be interpreted in terms of a struggle for power between these two dominant factions in the army. Both factions embraced ultra-nationalist elements, with civilian hangers-on. The *Kodo-ha* was the more radical of the two, for it contained most of the young officers who were active in the cause of 'the Showa Restoration'. But the leaders of the *Kodo-ha*, although they sympathized with the naïve aspirations of their juniors, were not necessarily in favour of changing the system of government by *coup d'état*. They were obsessed by the prospect of war with the Soviet Union. In their view the occupation of Manchuria was the requisite first step in the direction of a struggle with the Russians, and they were not very interested in plans for a Japanese advance south of the Great Wall into China. On the other hand, the *Tosei-ha* thought it wise to maintain friendly relations with the Soviet Union and to make China the main target of Japanese expansion once Manchuria had been secured.

These internal stresses within the Japanese army were of course hidden from the contemporary world. What was undeniable was that Japan appeared to be firmly committed to a programme of aggression on the continent of Asia; within a year of the

241

creation of Manchukuo Japanese troops advanced into Inner Mongolia and soon compelled the Chinese to accept a very large demilitarized zone between Peking and the Manchurian border. Within this zone, and in fact in north China generally, Japanese political and commercial penetration increased at a remarkable pace.

Inevitably the Lytton Report on the Manchurian affair was a condemnation, none the less clear for being tactfully phrased, of Japan's action. It was adopted by the League of Nations. Whereupon Japan, much to the private anguish of the emperor, flounced out of the League.

Diplomatically the country was now as isolated as it had been in 1895, after the Triple Intervention. Economically it was hard pressed. In terms of armed strength alone it was undoubtedly formidable. Liberal-minded people in Europe and America began to place Japan in the same camp as Fascist Italy and the new Nazi Germany. To those who relied on the League of Nations to keep the peace Japan appeared as an outlaw among the nations; for she had defied the League with impunity.

Nationalism scored a notable triumph in Japan when, soon after the occupation of Manchuria, the barely tolerated left-wing social democratic movement split between those who adhered to the ideals of international socialism and those who succumbed to patriotic sentiment, or to the fear of intensified police surveillance, and came out in support of the army's action; and there was unquestionably a sincere conviction among many socialists who climbed on to the nationalist band-wagon that the army had a real sympathy, not very noticeable among most *Minseito* and *Seiyukai* politicians, with those oppressed by capitalism. Indeed, the Kwantung Army boasted that it would not allow the established *zaibatsu* in Japan, such as Mitsui and Mitsubishi, to exploit the wealth of Manchukuo. This country, it was said, would be run on national socialist lines, as a kind of pilot project for the later 'Showa Restoration' in Japan.[4]

Government action against Marxist thought was much intensified, being symbolized by the death in police custody of the young left-wing writer, Kobayashi Takiji. But life became progressively more difficult for all who were in any way out of tune with the superheated atmosphere of the day. The teaching profession from top to bottom was forced to give more time in the school curriculum to the propagation of Shinto mythology, to ethnocentric ideas generally, and to military training. It is then no wonder that in the years after 1945 the Japan Teachers' Union should have acquired a reputation for being very Left in its complexion. In the universities conformist pressure, though in some ways less directly overpowering, made it increasingly hazardous for academic staff to retain the self-respect that comes from intellectual integrity. Between 1933 and 1937 several scholars were forced to resign from their university posts, and some of them saw their publications banned. One professor at Kyoto, a Marxist economist with a national reputation in the academic world, was arrested and spent some years in prison. But perhaps the most publicized case was that of Professor Minobe, a very distinguished *savant* and a member of the House of Peers. In a speech that electrified the country he was violently attacked early in 1935 by a fellow member of the House, for having dared to discuss the emperor's position in the state in terms of conventional political science rather than in those of divinity. The book in which this had been done had already been out for years, but the general fuss was exploited by extreme nationalists, the more sophisticated of whom used the agitation for ulterior ends to discredit not only the cabinet but also the emperor's personal advisers, who were considered to be disgracefully liberal in their convictions. In consequence of what was known as his 'organ theory', Minobe was driven out of public and academic life; but he was fortunate at least in escaping imprisonment or assassination — though a personal assault was made on him. The emperor's comment on the affair bears quotation:

> Much is being said about Minobe; but I do not believe he is disloyal. Just how many men of Minobe's calibre are there in Japan today? It is a pity to consign such a scholar to oblivion.

Barely two years later the emperor himself was to be an object of criticism, in nationalist circles in Tokyo, for spending too much time on the scientific study, marine biology, to which he was devoted. The shadows of *kurai tanima*, 'the dark valley', were deepening on every side.

III

The Saito cabinet, before it resigned in the summer of 1934, had survived a murderous conspiracy as sensational as any that had been known before. The plot, like the 'October Incident' of 1931, included preparations for the liquidation of the government at one blow by bombing from the air. The military cabinet to be established by the *coup d'état* was to be headed by a prince of the imperial house. However, on this occasion the army, in the persons of politically active junior officers, was not involved in the conspiracy. The ringleaders were civilian extremists. It was only by a lucky chance that the police were able to discover the plot in the nick of time.

No mention at all was made of the affair until 1935, two years after it had occurred. The trial of the accused did not begin until 1937 and was not completed until 1941, when a judgement was given that (in the words of the *Japan Times*) was 'a triumph of law in Japan and a brilliant piece of political adjustment'. The accused received short terms of imprisonment, with immediate remission of sentence. However, this particular plot, since it came to nothing, was a minor affair compared with the famous outbreak, or mutiny, of February 1936, which terminated the life of the next cabinet, that of Admiral Okada.

The military eruption of February 1936 was to some extent heralded by premonitory rumbles caused by that factional struggle within the army to which reference has already been made. From the end of 1934 the *Kodo-ha*, the so-called 'Imperial Way School', began to lose ground very rapidly to its rival, the *Tosei-ha* or 'Control School'. Early in that year General Araki, the Minister of War, resigned due to ill-health. This was a blow to the *Kodo-ha*, for Araki and his friend General Mazaki held two of the three supposedly most important positions in the army — Araki as Minister of War, Mazaki as Inspector-General of Military Training. The third post, that of Chief of the General Staff, was occupied by Prince Kanin, who as a member of the imperial house could not properly be identified with any faction. His Vice-Chief, however, belonged to the *Tosei-ha*; and so did an officer, Major-General Nagata, who held an appointment of great significance in the Ministry of War, that of Chief of the General Affairs Bureau, in control of military postings and promotions as well as of army administration generally. Araki's successor as Minister of War was General Hayashi Senjuro, and he soon came under the influence of his subordinate at the Ministry, Major-General Nagata, who was determined if possible to remove known members of the *Kodo-ha* from key commands and staff appointments in the army. This could not be done, of course, while Araki was Minister. From the point of view of Nagata and the *Tosei-ha* it was desirable to secure the removal of Mazaki from his post of Inspector-General. Nagata claimed that the retention of Mazaki in this appointment was bad for discipline, that Mazaki was idolized by the radical young officers whose agitation must be checked at all costs. Nagata strengthened his case in the eyes of the Minister of War and the Chief of the General Staff by uncovering, in November 1934, a good deal of dangerous political activity, aimed at securing 'the Showa Restoration', among officers at the Staff College and cadets at the Military Academy. Nagata, however, was in a vulnerable position when he talked of enforcing military discipline, for he himself had been intimately involved in the 'March Incident' of 1931. Nevertheless, he insisted on the dismissal from the service of the officers concerned in the alleged Staff College conspiracy; and he then began to make plans for the removal of Mazaki.

Eventually, after a good deal of intrigue and much debate, Mazaki's resignation was effected, greatly to his chagrin. A few weeks later, in August 1935, an obscure lieutenant-colonel, excited and angered (like many other officers) at the manner of Mazaki's virtual dismissal, travelled up to Tokyo, walked into the Ministry of War, entered Nagata's room, and cut him down with a drawn sword.

There was almost hysterical support for the murderer from the wilder elements of the *Kodo-ha*, who tried to turn his court-martial into a sounding-board for their views. The defendant, through his military lawyer, summoned a number of prominent men as witnesses. Great play was made of the evils of favouritism in army administration, and this was a veiled but unmistakable attack on the *Tosei-ha*.

While this trial continued, Tokyo was alive with rumours that there would be further violence, on a much greater scale. It was said, quite correctly, that the First Division, stationed in the city, contained some unusually determined supporters of the 'Showa Restoration', that they were in close touch with the officers whom Nagata had purged and with the fanatical writer and agitator, Kita Ikki. To prevent trouble this division was ordered to proceed to Manchukuo. The advocates of 'direct action' realized that they would have to strike at once, albeit without sufficient preparation.

During the early hours of 26 February 1936, in a severe snowstorm, detachments from two infantry regiments of the First Division, together with some sympathizers from the Guards Division, left their barracks. They split into a number of parties. Some of these made attacks on the homes of the Prime Minister and other public men; and before daylight there were some terrible scenes as doors were forced and the victims, nearly all old men, shot down. Admiral Okada escaped death, his brother-in-law being mistaken for him. Two former Premiers, Saito and Takahashi, and Mazaki's successor as Inspector-General were killed. The Grand Chamberlain, Admiral Suzuki, was dangerously wounded and was left to die. (He recovered, and he was to become Japan's last war-time premier nine years later.) An effort was made to catch the aged Saionji at his country villa; but he got word in advance and was not at home. Other groups occupied various important buildings near the palace. The insurgents numbered about fifteen hundred officers and men. There was no officer above the rank of captain.

Having accomplished their attacks and set up a kind of occupied zone in the centre of Tokyo, these young captains and lieutenants did nothing more, except to issue a manifesto declaring that Japan's ills were due to such persons as the *Genro*, the *zaibatsu*, and political parties, and that those responsible had to be killed. The young officers went on to say that in taking direct action they were performing their duty as subjects of the emperor.

The latter, however, did not see the affair in this light. He told the Ministry of War that this was a mutiny, and that the rebels must be crushed within an hour. If the leading figures of the *Kodo-ha* had plans for stepping in and taking over the reins of government — which was what the rebels expected and hoped would happen — the emperor's immediate and unhesitating stand gave them second thoughts. Martial law was declared; troops were brought into Tokyo from outside; naval ratings were put ashore in the port area of the city. There was some parley with the rebels at first, Mazaki himself making great efforts to persuade them to hand in their arms. This they refused to do. But appeals to the rank and file, couched in emotional language and dropped from aircraft or suspended from captive advertisement balloons, were more effective. After four eerie days, in which two bodies of troops gazed silently at each other from their barricades across the snow, the mutineers gave in. There was no point in further resistance, as the generals of the *Kodo-ha* on whom, misled no doubt by hints and nods and sympathetic grunts, the mutinous officers had relied did not play their part. One rebel captain shot himself. The other officers gave themselves up, in the expectation of a public trial at which they could expound their views. But in the event they were tried by secret court-martial. Thirteen of them were executed; so were Kita Ikki (the ideological sponsor of the 'Showa Restoration') and the fanatical lieutenant-colonel who had killed Nagata.

The mutiny did great harm to the *Kodo-ha*, which was believed to be responsible, indirectly at any rate, for the whole affair. At the same time, rather paradoxically, it strengthened immensely the political power of the army as a whole, as well as that of the *Tosei-ha*. The ordinary people of Japan were rather disgusted at the idea of their capital city becoming the focus of world attention thanks to the mutinous behaviour of regular officers and men; and one consequence was a mild but fairly general popular revulsion against the army. This made it all the more essential for the military leaders, the *Tosei-ha* generals, to tighten their grip upon the state machine; and in fact they had little difficulty in dictating policy to the new cabinet of Hirota that was formed soon after the mutiny collapsed. Hirota was a professional diplomat; as Foreign Minister in the outgoing cabinet he had done well in completing negotiations for the Japanese purchase of the Russian-controlled Chinese Eastern Railway in Manchuria. When he began forming his cabinet he found that the Minister of War, General Terauchi (son of the earlier Prime Minister), had the final say in the choice of his government colleagues.

The *Tosei-ha* was now firmly in power, the Hirota cabinet being little more than its tool. Preparations were rushed forward to make Japan fully equipped for war. The proportion of the budget devoted to the armed services rose to nearly fifty per cent, and the development of heavy industry was stimulated by increased orders for munitions. The navy had abrogated the Washington and London Disarmament Treaties at the end of 1934 and had withdrawn from the London Naval Conference of the following year. It was free, therefore, to engage on expansion limited only by the country's resources.

In the field of foreign policy Japan signed the Anti-Comintern Pact with Germany in December 1936 — the negotiations had been carried out by the army, not by the Foreign Ministry — and this agreement protected Japan's north-western flank in the event of a military advance south into China.

On the home front the Ministry of Education prepared a new book on the basic principles of the *Kokutai*, of 'national polity', for distribution to all schools and colleges. The army insisted that all aspects of policy should be subordinated to national strategic needs. By the latter half of 1936 the Minister of Finance was using the phrase, 'quasi-wartime economy', to describe a situation in which military requirements were supreme.

In January 1937 a member of the *Seiyukai* had the temerity to attack the army in the Diet for its usurpation of power, and he became involved in an angry battle of words with Terauchi, the Minister of War. Terauchi told the Premier that the House of Representatives must be dissolved. The political parties seemed to be raising their heads again; and this was not at all to the liking of the army. But Hirota would not agree to a dissolution, so Terauchi resigned, bringing the cabinet down with him. The venerable Saionji recommended General Ugaki as the new Premier; but Ugaki could find no soldier to serve as Minister of War, for his rather uncertain connexion with the 'March Incident' was remembered against him. The choice then fell on General Hayashi. He was Prime Minister for only four months. He was better fitted for the barrack square than the committee rooms of the Diet. At the General Election of April 1937 his supporters were defeated, and the *Minseito* and *Seiyukai* joined forces in opposition to his Cromwellian behaviour. For the first time since 1931 the army seemed to be almost on the defensive. But it was determined not to lose any of the power that it had seized. At the same time Hayashi could not act like Yamagata and ignore the Diet altogether. So after some weeks he recognized the decision of this Election and resigned. It was the last, rather feeble, success for the Diet parties until after the Japanese Surrender nine years later.

The new Prime Minister was Prince Konoye, of the ancient and famous Fujiwara line. He had been President of the House of Peers since 1933. Even so he was much younger than the run of Japanese premiers, being forty-six years of age when he took office. He was liked and respected by nearly everyone, and he could have been premier after the February mutiny had he wished, for the army, among whom he had many friends, thought he would make a splendid figurehead. This was not so much because the generals imagined that he would be their complacent puppet, but rather because they perceived that his mind was somewhat in tune with the nationalist movement, in spite of the fact that his political mentor had been Saionji. It is also true that his character was uneven. The elements of weakness often seemed dominant; and this impression was enhanced by the fact that, like many very refined persons, he was something of a hypochondriac. Konoye was an excellent listener. This was part of his weakness, but it endeared him to most of those who called on him, since he usually agreed, far beyond the requirements of Japanese courtesy, with what his visitors had to say. His range of acquaintances was extremely wide, and few premiers have taken office in an atmosphere of greater goodwill. Above all, it was felt that Konoye would have an entirely impartial approach to state affairs; that therefore his appointment would have a unifying effect on the political life of the nation. For his part, Konoye was not at all eager to be premier, but he thought that he would be able in his own way to exercise some control over the army.

He lost his first and perhaps vital battle within six weeks of forming his cabinet. Early in July fighting broke out near Peking between Japanese and Chinese troops. The situation deteriorated, and the Minister of War — a tough-minded *Tosei-ha* general named Sugiyama — proposed to make it worse by the dispatch of reinforcements from Manchukuo and Korea. Konoye, backed by the Navy and Foreign Ministers, tried to resist this demand. Sugiyama was adamant; so, dreading the political crisis that would occur if the War Minister resigned, Konoye gave way.

Thus the clash near Peking was allowed to widen into what became in fact an invasion of China. Undoubtedly this accorded with the plans of the *Tosei-ha*. While there is no convincing evidence, as in the case of the Mukden *coup*, that hostilities in north China in July 1937 originated from an incident planned by Japanese officers on the spot, there is reason to believe that at General Staff Headquarters in Tokyo there was a feeling, especially among colonels and below, that the time had come to settle accounts with Chiang Kai-shek. For it was realized that China's national unity in face of Japanese pressure had been greatly strengthened by the understanding that had been reached some months earlier between Chiang and the Chinese Communists. Konoye and the navy and, in the army, the *Kodo-ha* wanted to halt operations in north China as soon as possible. But even Araki, the paladin of the *Kodo-ha*, had accepted the consequences of Japanese penetration in the Peking–Tientsin region. A year before the Sino–Japanese hostilities of 1937 broke out he remarked that talk of Japanese non-interference in north China was 'like telling a man not to get involved with a woman when she is already pregnant by him'. Chances of localizing the fighting were made more difficult at the end of July when Chinese militia, formally under Japanese control, at Tungchow — between Peking and Tientsin — killed their Japanese officers and then massacred over two hundred Japanese and Korean civilians of both sexes. A local settlement would have been, in any case, very difficult to achieve without unprecedented moderation on the part of the Japanese forces; and there was a new spirit of patriotism among the Chinese that made them determined not to make any concessions.

In August 1937 fighting began in Shanghai. As in 1932, the navy was the first to be involved; and again the army had to come to its help. Troops were poured into Shanghai, and it was not without a severe struggle, lasting for about three months, that the Japanese prevailed. By the autumn, then, undeclared war raged on two fronts, in the north and in the region of Shanghai. China appealed to the League. The latter condemned Japan for having violated the Nine-Power Treaty signed at Washington and the Kellogg Peace Pact of 1928, and proposed a meeting of the signatories of the

Nine-Power Treaty to discuss the situation. The meeting was duly held, at Brussels. Japan refused to attend; and the Brussels Conference achieved nothing.

In December, after an advance up the Yangtze valley, the Japanese captured Nanking. Excesses were committed against the inhabitants of a kind that would not have been tolerated by the generals of the Meiji era. News of the atrocities was not allowed to leak into the Japanese press; but those held responsible — the Commander-in-Chief of the forces in Central China and two divisional commanders were recalled to Japan, as were many of the reservists, summoned to the colours in the late summer of 1937, who had been given a free hand in Nanking for some days after its capture. It was indicative of the partial breakdown of military discipline that just before the fall of Nanking Japanese naval aircraft bombed and sank the U.S.S. *Panay* in the Yangtze, and an artillery unit, commanded by a notorious ultra-nationalist firebrand, shelled the British river gunboat, H.M.S. *Ladybird*. The Chamberlain Government in London felt unready to take a strong line with Japan while its appeasement policy towards Germany had yet to show results. But the *Panay* affair seemed for a moment to bring Japan and the United States to the brink of war. Sincere and prompt apologies by Japan, together with an offer of compensation and the recall of the naval air officers concerned, eased a tense situation that, on the face of it, appeared to be critical. Isolationism was still the dominant factor in popular American thinking on foreign affairs, but this incident, followed very soon by the excesses at Nanking, did fatal harm to what remained of American goodwill towards Japan.

It was generally believed in Japan that once he had lost his capital, Nanking, Chiang Kai-shek would be willing to come to terms. Indeed during the autumn approaches had been made to Chiang by Tokyo, through the good offices of the German Ambassador in China. But Chiang refused to accept the fairly drastic conditions offered to him; and in January 1938 Japan announced that there would be no further dealings of any kind with the official Kuomintang government. Nevertheless, despite this announcement, some efforts were made in 1938 to reach an agreement with Chiang; but these failed, partly because Japan's terms were too severe, but also because the army leaders in Tokyo, under varying pressures from their subordinates, could not make up their minds on the China question. It was known that in the highest circles of the Kuomintang there was a minority, led by Wang Ching-wei, that favoured acceptance of Japanese conditions, including an indemnity. So some Japanese senior officers believed, rightly as it turned out, that Wang Ching-wei could be enticed from Chiang's side. Meanwhile the war went on. After a success in Shantung in April 1938, the Chinese extricated their forces with difficulty, and with heavy losses, from a battle of encirclement mounted on an ambitious scale by the Japanese in the area of Hsuchow on the Peking–Nanking railway.

In early summer of 1938 Konoye, who was almost wistfully eager to wind up the China war, if only to curb the political arrogance of the army, reshuffled his cabinet. Araki was brought back into public life, as Minister of Education, and the rather overbearing Sugiyama was succeeded as Minister of War by a younger man, Itagaki. There was also a new Vice-Minister of War, a lieutenant-general with a Manchurian background: Tojo. General Ugaki became Foreign Minister. Konoye hoped to be able to resuscitate the *Kodo-ha* and thus make it easier for him to exercise some control over the army. In fact

248

he was entirely unsuccessful. It was only with great difficulty that he was persuaded to remain as Premier through 1938.

In the summer of that year Japanese and Soviet troops in some strength fought a serious battle for possession of a hill known as Changkufeng, where the borders of Korea, Manchukuo, and the Russian Far East met in a conjunction not clearly defined. Neither Moscow nor Tokyo wanted war at that moment; but there were certainly influential officers of the Japanese Ministry of War and General Staff who were prepared to fight China and the Soviet Union simultaneously. Japanese forces seemed invincible, and the self-confidence of the army had reached an almost hysterical level. At this juncture the emperor spoke his mind, at a joint audience, to his kinsman, the Chief of the Army General Staff, and to the Minister of War, Itagaki. He told them that in the past the actions of the army had often been 'abominable'. 'From now on', he declared, 'you may not move one soldier without my command.' These angry words had some effect. The Changkufeng affair was settled fairly soon, although it was to be followed within a year by much more bloody and prolonged Soviet–Japanese hostilities at Nomonhan, in the wastes of Outer Mongolia.

In the autumn the Japanese captured Hankow; and from a landing at Bias Bay in south China they advanced at great speed and took Canton. Once again it was believed that Chiang Kai-shek would throw in his hand. Konoye issued a declaration that Japan's 'immutable policy' was the establishment of a New Order in East Asia — meaning a political, economic, and cultural union of Japan, Manchukuo, and China; and soon afterwards Japan's peace terms were announced. The call for a Chinese indemnity was dropped, but in other respects the terms were as onerous as those contained in the most extreme of the Twenty-One Demands. Chiang publicly rejected the offer, and from his new capital in Chungking he announced that he would carry on the struggle. On his part this was a courageous gamble. For although the Japanese did not yet control those areas that they had occupied — they held the cities and railways but not the countryside — it was not true that they were 'bogged down' in China. Provided only that Japan avoided war with the United States and Great Britain, or with the Soviet Union, there was no reason why the Japanese, given time, should fail to impose their will on China in the end. Wang Ching-wei, a powerful member of the Kuomintang, saw the situation in these terms. Having failed to persuade Chiang to consider Japan's terms he escaped to Indo-China, and in 1939, with Japanese cooperation, he made his way to Shanghai. He became the most impressive of Japan's various Chinese puppets, and in due course he set up in Nanking a regime that the Japanese claimed to be the only official government of China.

Konoye, who had wanted to resign much earlier, finally insisted on surrendering his office in the opening days of 1939. The next cabinet, under Baron Hiranuma, lasted for about seven months. It was riven by the struggle between those who advocated a full-scale military alliance with Germany and those who stubbornly resisted this proposal. In view of Germany's overwhelming diplomatic victories in Europe in 1938, Berlin's proposal for a military alliance seemed very attractive. But the Foreign Minister, Arita, and the Navy Minister, Yonai, were suspicious of commitments that might embroil Japan with Great Britain and, perhaps, with the United States also. On the whole the army strongly favoured an alliance of the kind proposed by Ribbentrop, but the opposition was sufficiently firm to delay a decision on the matter. Then came the German–Soviet Pact in August 1939. This was regarded by the Japanese as a slap in the face, for at this very moment their forces were being severely mauled by the Russians, commanded by Zhukov, at Nomonhan on the borders of Manchukuo and Outer Mongolia. The fighting at Nomonhan had begun at the end of May, and was not terminated until September. Under the terms of a secret annexe to the Anti-Comintern Pact Japan might have asked for German support against the Russians. Thus Ribbentrop's flight to Moscow and his diplomatic *coup*, the Non-Aggression Pact with the Soviet Union, were looked upon as acts of betrayal, and there was a sudden revulsion against the Germans. It was generally recognized, except by the most rabidly pro-German elements in the army, that the best policy for Japan during the forthcoming war in Europe would be one of strict neutrality. Hiranuma and his cabinet resigned, and a new administration was formed under a temperate and cautious retired general called Abe, who announced that Japan would adhere to a 'middle course', in other words non-involvement in the European struggle.

IV

So long as the war in Europe remained relatively static and inconclusive it was possible for Abe and his successor, Admiral Yonai, to keep Japan in the position of a disinterested spectator. Although the *Blitzkrieg* in Poland created an impression of German competence, the apparent stalemate on the Western Front made it look as though Germany was not strong enough to challenge Great Britain and France on land.

But the situation was drastically altered once Norway, Denmark, and the Low Countries were overrun, and by the collapse of France. By mid-summer 1940 it argued either staunch pro-British feelings or remarkable prescience in even the wisest Japanese for him to imagine that Germany would lose the war.[5]

Hitler's success had two immediate results so far as Japan was concerned. The first was the official extinction of the existing political parties. They went into voluntary liquidation, after Prince Konoye had agreed to organize a mass national party 'to assist the Imperial Throne'. Thus a form of totalitarianism was grafted on to the Constitution. It differed greatly from the German and Italian varieties, for Japan did not have a single *Führer* or *Duce*. Konoye's so-called 'New Structure' did not in fact do much to change the *status quo*, for the political parties were already virtually impotent. The second result of Germany's victories was the conclusion of the Tripartite Axis Pact of September 1940. By this time Konoye was once again Prime Minister; he succeeded Yonai in July. Japan's alliance with Germany and Italy bound her to the fortunes of these countries. In the eyes of its supporters the great virtue of the pact was that it seemed to place an effective check on any strong action by the United States, either in the Atlantic or the Pacific; for only the United States appeared to stand between Japan and the eventual consummation of the 'New Order in East Asia'. Great Britain seemed to be in no position to resist Japan. In September 1940 Great Britain had agreed to close the Burma Road for six months, as a result of Japanese pressure. As for France, she had been forced to admit Japanese troops into northern Indo-China, nominally in order to close supply routes to Chungking. The position of the Dutch East Indies, a source of oil and many other commodities required by Japan, was obviously very critical. Only America was capable of mustering a fleet strong enough to prevent a Japanese seizure by force of the rich European colonies in south-east Asia.

Konoye's Foreign Minister was a headstrong, voluble nationalist, Matsuoka Yosuke, who seems to have been bewitched by the military might of Nazi Germany. In the early part of 1941 he visited Rome and Berlin, where Ribbentrop urged him to commit Japan to an immediate assault on Singapore. On his way back through the Soviet Union he concluded a Neutrality Pact with Stalin and he returned to Japan satisfied that he was the most dynamic Foreign Minister his country had ever known. But he had not been home long when the news arrived of Germany's attack on Russia; whereupon Matsuoka insisted that Japan should seize the chance of attacking the Russians from the east. This was too much for Konoye, who, in July 1941, got rid of him by resigning together with the cabinet, and then reconstructing the cabinet without including Matsuoka. By now Japan had spent some four years in preparing for war on a large scale. These preparations had not been greatly weakened by the campaigns in China. On the contrary, the war in China stimulated munitions production and gave the authorities an excellent reason for controlling imports and for shaping the economy of the nation generally in accordance with long-term strategic needs. Only a portion of the national resources in munitions and manpower was committed to the China war, which in any case was a valuable proving-ground or dress rehearsal for a future struggle against some more powerful country. Even the Nomonhan disaster — the defeat by the Russians in 1939 — taught the army some lessons, especially the necessity of expanding the size of its armoured forces. Stocks of oil and other strategic products had been built up. But here there was reason for great anxiety. If access to oil supplies in south-east Asia and elsewhere was denied to Japan, then, in the event of war, her own stocks would suffice for no more than two years at the most.

Yet in July 1941 the army embarked on a further territorial advance that produced in retaliation economic sanctions that could have crippled Japan. In that month Japanese forces occupied bases in southern Indo-China. This was a clear threat to Siam, Malaya, and the Dutch East Indies. There is some reason to think that Konoye agreed to this move as the least of various possible evils. Germany's attack on the Soviet Union had produced among Japanese military leaders a wave of interest and excitement. There were some who, like Matsuoka, believed that Japan ought to join her ally in attacking the Russians. There were others who advocated an immediate assault on Hong Kong and Malaya. At all events there was a demand for action of some kind. The move into the Saigon area seemed to Konoye on the whole the least dangerous. Certainly he did not foresee the almost immediate reaction of America, Great Britain, and Holland.

These countries, in response to the Japanese move south, imposed an economic embargo on Japan; at the same time they hastened their military preparations in Asia and the Pacific. Japan now faced her moment of decision. Talks had been going on in Washington for many weeks between the Japanese Ambassador, Admiral Nomura, and the American Secretary of State, Cordell Hull. They had made little progress, for the aims of the two parties were almost diametrically opposed. Japan wanted America to abandon all support of the Chinesc government in Chungking, to recognize Japan's hegemony in east Asia; in return, Japan would consider withdrawing in fact, if not in name, from the Tripartite Axis Pact. America distrusted Japanese motives in Asia and

251

wanted Japan to withdraw from both China and French Indo-China. The Japanese were prepared, in the last resort, to evacuate French Indo-China, but not China proper. When the American–British–Dutch economic embargo was imposed it became urgent for Japan to reach some agreement with America. Otherwise, unless the Japanese were content to suffer slow economic strangulation, war with Great Britain and Holland, and probably the United States also, was inevitable.

In the Washington talks America spoke for Great Britain and Holland as well as for herself. By an act of curious diplomatic self-abnegation Churchill and his cabinet seemed quite ready to leave negotiations with Japan, in a matter affecting Australia and New Zealand as much as Malaya and Hong Kong, to the good sense of the Americans. Indeed at this time there was a tendency to underrate Japan's striking power. It was thought in London, as well as Washington, that the economic sanctions would force Japan to give ground, but that, if this were not so, then by the close of 1941 Japan would find it difficult to overcome the forces that had been built up in the Philippines and Malaya. America and Great Britain, then, faced Japan with a confidence that would have been wholly admirable if it had been based on a true evaluation of strategic realities in south-east Asia.

Among Japanese leaders, on the other hand, only the army felt confident; for it considered that the United States, though rich in material wealth, lacked the fighting spirit of Japan. Both the navy and the civilian members of the cabinet felt very uncertain of the outcome of a struggle with America. To Konoye the prospect of war in the Pacific was a nightmare. But against the intransigence of his Minister of War, Tojo, no arguments seemed to prevail. He might consent, in return for a lifting of the embargo, to an evacuation of French Indo-China; there could be no question, in Tojo's view, of any retreat from the Chinese mainland.

It may be that the Atlantic meeting between Roosevelt and Churchill gave Konoye the idea of seeking direct personal contact with the President. At any rate Konoye approached the American ambassador in Tokyo and asked as a matter of great urgency to meet Roosevelt, so that the Japanese–American deadlock might be broken before the worst occurred. Konoye said that he would take with him, to meet Roosevelt, powerful senior army and navy officers who could be guaranteed to enforce upon their juniors the terms of a settlement reached between Japan and the United States. There seemed for a while a chance that Konoye and the President would meet, either in Hawaii or Alaska. But not without good reason Washington feared the possibility of being deceived by the Japanese army. The word 'Munich' still had power to alarm American officials when they examined the idea of a Konoye–Roosevelt meeting; so the Japanese were told that some solid preliminary agreement ought to be reached before a 'summit' meeting took place.

In September an Imperial Conference — a gathering of cabinet ministers and chiefs of staff and other important officials in the presence of the emperor — formally agreed that Japan would have to be ready to fight America and Great Britain should the talks in Washington fail to make progress by mid-October. Meanwhile exercises in preparation for the attack on Pearl Harbour had already taken place very secretly at Kagoshima. Yet even now the navy was reluctant to engage in war with the United

252

States. In fact, if the Navy Minister and the Chief of the Naval General Staff had possessed the courage of their inner convictions and had openly resisted Tojo, the Minister of War, it is possible, even probable, that with the backing both of the emperor and of Konoye they might have saved Japan at the eleventh hour by advising acceptance of the American demands regarding China. This would have been a diplomatic defeat for Japan, a loss of face; but it would have done no fundamental harm to the nation's vital interests. The navy, however, shifted its responsibilities on to Konoye. Through its representative in the cabinet, the Navy Minister, it refused to declare openly that in its view war with America should be avoided at almost any cost. As Konoye reported to the emperor:

> The navy does not want war, but cannot say so in view of the decision of the Imperial Conference.

When mid-October came Konoye felt that the Washington talks must go on. A formidable crisis developed in Tokyo, since the army believed that the moment had come for Japan to decide definitely in favour of a sudden blow at both America and Great Britain. The crisis was resolved by the resignation of Konoye and the appointment of Tojo in his place, on the understanding that the deadline for the talks would be advanced by some weeks.

The Americans had broken the code in use between Tokyo and the Japanese Embassy in Washington; and therefore they knew that the Ambassador, Nomura, was instructed to obtain some agreement by the end of November. In the middle of that month Nomura was joined by a special envoy, Kurusu, who had been Ambassador in Germany. After Pearl Harbour the world believed that Kurusu's mission was merely a device by Japan to gain time and to lull the Americans into a sense of false security. There is in fact no truth in this supposition. Admiral Nomura was a sailor, not a trained diplomatist. In the critical autumn of 1941 he felt overwhelmed by the difficulties facing him and he asked for an experienced diplomatist of ambassadorial rank to be sent to help him.

Proposals and counter proposals passed between Washington and Tokyo; but neither side would give way to the extent thought satisfactory to the other. Meanwhile naval vessels took up their war stations and at ports in the Inland Sea troopships and freighters were loaded for the south. A fleet of carriers and escorting battleships and cruisers assembled in the lonely Kuriles, and on 26 November set course for the North Pacific. The commander of this fleet was told that in response to a certain signal, although not otherwise, the plan, known to very few, to attack the American fleet must be carried out. Four days after the Japanese carriers had sailed the emperor heard that the navy still wanted to avoid war. So he summoned to audience the Navy Minister and the Chief of the Naval General Staff. Were they confident of success, he asked them. They assured him that they were.

Seven days later the Japanese attacked Hawaii, Hong Kong, Malaya, Singapore, and the Philippines. The Pacific War had begun.

Notes

1. Whatever else may be said of General Tojo it must be recognized that he accepted full responsibility for leading Japan into war. In order to coordinate policy at the highest level he was Minister of War and Home Minister as well as Premier, and in 1944 he assumed the additional office of Chief of the Army General Staff. Yet he declared after the war, and we may believe him, that he was never informed of the details of the plan to attack Pearl Harbour. This was a naval affair, and could not be entirely revealed in advance to an army officer, even if he happened to be Prime Minister. The fact remains that the *decision* to make war rested in the final analysis with General Tojo and the army. The navy leaders for their part prepared a battle plan — the attack on Pearl Harbour — for a contingency, namely war with America, that they hoped would not arise.

2. The 'March Incident' marked the beginning of attempts by extreme right-wing elements within the armed forces to gain power in the name of the Emperor. Under the leadership of the ultra-nationalist Cherry Blossom Society (*Sakurakai*) a group of officers plotted to overthrow the civilian government in a violent *coup d'état* and establish military rule. The plot was abandoned because of opposition by leading army officers; news of the incident was officially repressed and no punitive steps taken against the conspirators. [Editor]

3. The Home Minister, Adachi, advocated a coalition with the *Seiyukai*. He may have been impressed by the creation of the MacDonald 'National Government' in Great Britain. When Wakatsuki objected to his negotiations with the *Seiyukai*, Adachi refused either to attend cabinet meetings or to resign.

4. None of this was put into practice; but the economic development of Manchukuo was largely kept out of the hands of the existing *zaibatsu*. At first the South Manchurian Railway Company dominated the field. After 1937, when the development of Manchukuo was accelerated following the outbreak of the Sino–Japanese war, new business groups, notably the Nissan firm, became very powerful in Manchukuo. These new groups, encouraged by the army, were known as *shinko-zaibatsu*, or 'new zaibatsu'.

5. There were, however, a few thoughtful Japanese who predicted Germany's defeat. Shigemitsu, the ambassador in London, always believed that Great Britain would win. And Saionji, in his ninety-first year, remarked: 'In the end I believe Great Britain will be victorious.' He said this shortly before he died, in the autumn of 1940.

15. From the Washington Conference to the Pacific War (1922–41)
Jon Halliday

This chapter has two theses. First, that in the 1920s and 1930s Japan did not undergo a basic change of political regime, much less degenerate from "democracy" to "fascism," as some would have it. Second, that there was fundamental agreement between business and the military on an imperialist policy — although there were conflicting viewpoints within both groups. In general, the chapter attempts to explain the breakdown of the world imperialist system in Asia by synthesizing the specific internal features of Japanese society (the depression, the ambivalent nature of the army) and the main elements of the clash between the group of Western powers and Japan's more backward imperialist system.

The breakdown of the Washington arrangement

The imperialist powers who gathered at Washington all agreed on one thing: that they should continue to plunder China and exploit the Chinese people. In Saitō's words, the arrangement "which emerged from the Washington Conference could be said to be based on a new form of suppressing China."[1]

This arrangement, while apparently coherent, was rather shortsighted, as it left out of consideration a number of important factors: above all, the Chinese masses, aroused to new heights of political activism by the May 4 Movement. It also ignored the dynamism of the Comintern. The powers which met at Washington refused to accord full sovereign status to China. They insisted on their "rights" to intervene, but left a whole number of issues vague. They wanted to keep China as a preserve, but failed to define their own interests among themselves and their interests as a group against China. As a result, they were soon confronted with new Chinese initiatives, the Northern Expedition by the Nationalists in the summer of 1926 and the drive for treaty revision, which upset the internal balance of power. The unilateral Japanese moves which soon followed led to renewed contradictions among the imperialist powers. The Peking Tariff Conference (1925–26) was "the last occasion where the Washington powers tried, unsuccessfully, to give concrete content to their definition of a new order."

The Washington settlement was exploded by Chiang's anti-communist coup in 1927, which caused the Western imperialists to break ranks and swing from the straightforward old policy of opposing all Chinese forces to backing Chiang and the Chinese bourgeoisie. The Western powers, economically more advanced and self-confident, decided to combat the Chinese Revolution by allying with Chiang and the comprador bourgeoisie. Japan, more backward, poorer and immediately threatened by the loss of exclusive control over Manchuria and North China, and by expanding Chinese textile production, felt obliged to fight not only the Chinese Revolution as

Jon Halliday: 'From the Washington Conference to the Pacific War (1922–41)' from *A POLITICAL HISTORY OF JAPANESE CAPITALISM* (New York: Monthly Review Press, 1975). pp. 116–140. Copyright © 1975 by Jon Halliday. Reprinted by permission of Monthly Review Foundation.

such, but even the Kuomintang (KMT). It was Japan's war with the Kuomintang that caused Tokyo to be exiled from the Washington group.

To a large extent this was inherent in the Washington settlement, which was constructed to favour the Western powers in China. In Crowley's words, Japan

> alone of the Washington Treaty powers . . . had continental possessions in Northeast Asia (Korea); alone of these powers, it had "semicolonial" rights in China (South Manchuria) that were the key to its overseas investments; of these powers, only Japan was non-Caucasian; and only Japan was singled out by the other sea powers as a potential threat to their economic interests in China.[2]

Initially, it appeared Japan might be able to cope with the combined hostility of the Chinese people and the pressures from the Western powers. Japan's "semicolonial" position in Manchuria was generally tolerated by the West. And Japan continued to take part in the exploitation of the rest of China alongside the Western imperialists. Shanghai was the centre of foreign capital in China; indeed, Japanese investments increased faster, proportionately, in Shanghai between 1914 and 1930 than in Manchuria.

The Japanese rulers disagreed about how to deal with the "China problem." A number of proposals were put forth at various stages, including the possibility of supporting a *strong* Chinese government — for example, under Chang Tso-lin and Wu P'ei-fu in 1926. The "positive policy" of Premier Baron General Tanaka Giichi in 1927–28 involved supporting both Chang Tso-lin and Chiang Kai-shek and playing one off against the other. Most Japanese governmental opinion at this time was for maintaining the status quo, with forceful measures to be used only as a last resort "and then only to protect Japan's rights in Manchuria and not to bring about a drastic change in its political status."[3] In May 1928 the situation got temporarily out of hand when Japanese troops, at the instigation of Japanese army officers, against the advice of Tanaka's government, clashed with Chiang Kai-shek's forces at the town of Tsinan (the "Tsinan Incident"). But the clash was brief. Since 1928 brought an end to a shortlived Sino–Japanese amity, the murder of Chang Tso-lin by Kwantung Army officers, and the Kwantung Army's initial preparations for possible conflict with Chinese forces, it is important to ask why there was no "Manchurian Incident" or complete take-over of Manchuria until 1931.

After the Tsinan Incident and the assassination of Chang Tso-lin, the Tanaka (Seiyūkai) cabinet fell and was replaced by a Minseitō party government with a so-called "soft-line" China policy.

The army was still in some public disrepute over Japan's first undeclared war, and a public consensus had not been developed on the necessity of taking over Manchuria by force, given the international and local complications that were likely to ensure from such action. Nor was Japan's actual domination in Manchuria yet fundamentally threatened. This "soft-line" dampened down militant feeling to some extent until the London Naval Conference in 1930, the aftermath of which toppled the Minseitō cabinet.

The events of the late 1920s, however, were extremely important, particularly in building up resentment in the Japanese army, and a combination of this and other elements produced the Mukden Incident in late 1931 and the take-over of Manchuria. The Tokyo regime successfully silenced left and liberal opposition criticism on China policy. The military involved itself more effectively in the political process, not only in the government, but also in the area of political propaganda and "opinion moulding." The London Conference and its aftermath caused a major political crisis. And the depression built up explosive potential in both Japan and its colonies, which became linked in the economic crisis.

Domestic political changes after the First World War

Premier Hara's period in office (1918–21) was distinguished by two features: the consolidation of bureaucratic rule and failure to deal with the basic economic and political structural contradictions of the society.

The bureaucracy had changed considerably since the early Meiji period, and grown enormously bloated. By 1922 it had five and a half times more members than in 1890 when the Diet was first convened. Within it, the biggest change was the growing preponderance of Tokyo University graduates in key positions. A study of the situation in eight prefectures shows that fifty-eight of the seventy-one Governors of these prefectures from 1905 to 1925 were Tokyo University graduates. These graduates, more-over, represented a much more diversified class and geographical body than in 1890 when 90 per cent of Tokyo University had come from the samurai class, especially from Chōshū and Satsuma. This proliferation of bureaucrats did not promote democracy or even parliamentarism, but the consolidation of a governmental apparatus with close links to business and the military. Working behind the scenes, its only immutable characteristic was isolation from and hostility to the masses.

Hara had been lifted into office as the representative of the industrial bourgeoisie to cope with the problems which were drastically revealed by the 1918 uprisings. He responded to the pressure of the masses by marginally easing the franchise law and allowing greater freedom of expression. But he failed to deal with the key structural problems, particularly the bottlenecks in agriculture. He promoted a policy for increasing rice production in Korea and Taiwan which later had a catastrophic effect on rural Japan itself. He thus failed to eliminate the *internal* contradiction which subsequently underlay many of the autonomous initiatives of the reforming elements in the army.

After Hara was assassinated in 1921, these internal problems became even more acute. His party, the Seiyūkai, started pushing repressive legislation in 1922 to undermine the left. This trend culminated in the enactment of the 1925 Peace Preservation Law ("the law against dangerous ideas.") which, along with the new tenant laws, made the new suffrage bill safe and acceptable. Once again repression and "liberalization" went hand in hand. Indeed the so-called Universal Suffrage Law not only excluded all women outright, but also those who "received public or private relief or help for a living on account of poverty." The bill raised the number of those who could vote from about 3 million to 12.5 million. "Home Minister Wakatsuki felt obliged to assure the Diet that the suffrage bill was not designed to promote democracy."[4]

The government which put through the set of measures in 1925 was headed by Count Katō Takaaki. Katō Takaaki and his successor, Wakatsuki Reijirō, represent a synthesis of old and new bourgeoisie, encompassing the successful second-generation samurai plus the war profiteers from both the Russo–Japanese War and the World War, the bankers who rode high through the 1920 bank failures, and the construction millionaires from the aftermath of the 1923 earthquake (soon to be joined by some spectacular winners from the 1927 financial crisis). The Katō (Takaaki) cabinet was a bourgeois government in the sense that Mitsubishi men held the key positions of power, but the *system* of government remained the same as before. The bourgeoisie had had a great boost from imperialism and a couple of easy wars; but it continued to support the existing forms of oligarchic and autocratic rule (the bureaucracy, rather than absolutism). Although it often differed about the leaders best suited to execute policy, and sometimes about which tactics were correct, the aims of the bourgeoisie coincided very closely with those of the old Meiji ruling class. Katō and Wakatsuki were most successful in promoting the political integration of old and new bourgeoisie and the Meiji aristocracy, while integrating and demobilizing working class pressure. However, their failure to deal with renewed pressure from the Western imperialists abroad, and with the severe contradictions in the land-holding system at home, brought about some violent reactions among the military. In 1927, on the crest of a financial crisis, General Tanaka became premier.

The way in which the Wakatsuki cabinet fell and Tanaka came to power is symbolic of the state of Japanese politics at the time. The system itself was so constructed as to be virtually irresponsive to any outside control, and Tanaka did not even have to stage a putsch to get into power. He simply bribed his way in as the leader of one of the two major established parties, the Seiyūkai, and became premier via the Diet and its traditional procedures.

The instruments of power, while at one level highly functional to the ruling strata, at another level were still to an extraordinary extent unintegrated — hence the widespread existence of bribery, which is functional mainly at a certain point in the development of a capitalist state. Just as Tanaka became premier via the Diet and one of the major parties, using bribery, so Wakatsuki fell after a conflict with the Privy Council over granting government aid to the bankrupt Bank of Taiwan, a typical new imperial operation (though his position was already weakened by a more traditional scandal involving brothel concessions and land in Osaka).

The industrial bourgeoisie, in short, did not stake out a new political position for itself. As a class, it both repressed the left and failed to undertake any basic reform of the political system. This failure can not be reduced to a preference for undercover dealings and behind-the-scenes operations, for Japanese politics in the age of industrial capitalism hewed very close to the lines laid down in the nineteenth century. The bourgeoisie had a structural interest in behaving as it did; because of its historical imbrication with other groups arising out of the Meiji compromise, its interests coincided largely with those of the previous ruling strata. And it is this historical compromise-cum-imbrication which explains the relationship between bourgeoisie and military in the years up to 1945.

The army and the Depression

Since Tanaka's assumption of the premiership in 1927 can fairly be taken as marking the advance of the military, it is important to set out a few of the latter's salient characteristics. The army and the navy were relatively distinct and autonomous forces. The original clan division of Meiji times had been considerably broken down by the late 1920s, but the different traditions of Chōshū (army) and Satsuma (navy) lingered on. As is the case virtually everywhere, the navy was less involved in politics than the army. Indeed, the various admirals who rotated as premiers (Yamamoto, Katō Tomosaburō, Saitō, Okada Keisuke and Yonai Mitsumasa) were more in the nature of compromise candidates between the army and the civil bureaucracy than representatives of the military. Yet it was to be the navy which was affected most by the international agreements of Washington and London. Between 1914 and 1921 the naval budget had risen from ¥83 million to ¥483.5 million, but the pace was greatly slowed down by the Washington agreements. Similarly, the 1930 London Naval Conference, which was signed by the Hamaguchi Yūkō government, hit hardest at the navy. There was no separate air force.

In very general terms, the most important distinction between the army and the navy was their different estimate of the optimum imperialist strategy. The army saw Russia as the number one enemy and fought for expansion on the continent of Asia. The navy, more concerned with the United States of America as the number one enemy, wanted to secure Japan's oil supplies, and argued for a southern strategy.

Because of the wartime experience, the Japanese army has usually been written off in the West as an undifferentiated mass of cruel automata. But a more scientific analysis is needed of its composition and objectives.

The Japanese army was overwhelmingly of rural origin. While overall a profoundly counter-revolutionary force, in the conditions of the great depression which hit hardest at the rural areas, it was domestically partly a reforming force. Many of its actions in the later 1920s and 1930s were directed against both the Chinese Revolution *and* a corrupt and sectarian regime at home. Unless this double and simultaneous thrust is grasped, much of the army's activity remains unintelligible. It was both a classic imperialist army (led by the country's élite, scornful of the interests of the peoples whose territory it might be in — particularly in Korea, Russia and China — and counter-revolutionary at home) and rather similar to a reforming army in some of the Third World countries today (bureaucratic, granted, but with genuine links to the rural masses, and containing elements hostile to big business and particularly to foreign big business).

Moreover, the army leadership itself was not of one mind. Two main groups have to be distinguished: those from the Military Academy and those from the War College. The chain of assassinations in the 1930s which became the most spectacular feature of Japanese politics was the work of the first group (from the Academy). These assassinations were not an integral part of the army authorities' attempt to impose their views on the government, and were only indirectly related to the Manchurian problem. They were mainly connected to the depression and to internal social and economic conditions. The real policy-makers in the army were invariably from the War

College, did not engage in assassination, and imposed their views by working successfully within the existing political system. This is the crucial distinction, although it was criss-crossed through with several other distinctive contradictions. Yet while there were important differences of opinion within the Japanese ruling strata, these differences cannot be broken down into a civil/military split. At perhaps the most critical juncture of all, in late 1937, it was the government in Tokyo which pushed for an "ultra" policy towards Chiang against the advice and wishes of General Tada Shun and other army leaders.

The Great Depression and its political effects

Though Japanese agriculture had been languishing in something of a crisis since shortly after the First World War, the full blast of depression hit Japan only in 1927. The crisis which engulfed the country then can be compared to that which hit the United States several years later. This internal depression coincided with Japan's increased problems in China and with General Tanaka's advent to power.

Tanaka's two years in office, from April 1927 to the midsummer of 1929, were ones of considerable chaos at home and incompetence abroad. Japan landed troops in China at Tsingtao, pressured Chang Tso-lin into a railway deal, and had to withdraw from Shangtung. The domestic economy underwent extensive concentration. Business profits rose, real wages (as well as employment) fell; banks and businesses went through a spate of mergers. This irritated the strata who had recently been accorded the vote, and although some of the aggrieved sentiment of the petit bourgeoisie could be deflected against the West, a good deal of it rebounded onto the government. It is as much in the catastrophic effects of the depression as in the more visible and spectacular activities in China that the real degeneration in Japan's political life in the 1930s must be sought. Indeed, the events in China largely reflect the domestic effects of the crisis. Western accounts of Japan's behaviour at the time tend to concentrate on the military and on Japan's moves in China. But by so doing they usually ignore or underestimate how Japan, from a decidedly disadvantageous position, was to deal with the negative effects of the world capitalist system in a time of crisis. Participation in the Western-dominated system set up intolerable contradictions for Japan and accounted for much of the violent oscillation in Japanese economic and monetary policy between 1929 and 1931. After futile attempts at conciliation, Japan accepted the contradiction as antagonistic and launched an assault first on many of the West's private markets, and subsequently on sources of vital raw materials.

In this highly contradictory and chaotic setting, Japan moved into the thirties and eventually war with the West. Hamaguchi, who replaced Tanaka as premier in July 1929, got off to a disastrous start, since his Finance Minister, Inoue Junnosuke decided to return Japan to the gold standard on the eve of the collapse of the system. On top of this came the London Naval Conference (1930) which was a further attempt by the Western powers, particularly the United States, to upset the relatively acceptable naval balance established by the earlier Washington Conference. Controversy over the government signing the agreement led to a critical clash in Tokyo: the cabinet found itself to a large extent isolated, with the parties and popular opinion supporting the navy in its opposition to Hamaguchi. In the depths of the depression, Hamaguchi and the civilian politicians round him seemed to public opinion to have betrayed Japan's vital interests — and, incidentally, to have infringed the Constitution. Hamaguchi was shot in Tokyo station on November 14, 1930. His successor was Wakatsuki, premier in 1926–27.

Japan was also dealt a heavy economic blow by the introduction of the Smoot–Hawley Tariff in June 1930 which raised the import duty on Japanese goods entering the United States by an average of 23 per cent. Japan's exports to China also suffered at the same time and in 1931 the United States overtook Japan to become the leading exporter to China. Japan made a vain effort to get an international agreement to settle China's debt problem in order to get credit going again, but London's unwillingness to see debts owed Britain by China treated on an equal footing with debts owned by China to other countries stoked up ill feeling in Japan. The Mukden Incident in September 1931, which started Japan's main drive to take over the whole of China, was executed at the precise moment when the West was most preoccupied with the British financial crisis.

The Mukden Incident and the attack on China

The famous Incident at Mukden (now Shenyang) was arranged by a group in the Kwangtung Army in Manchuria to provide an excuse for the army to take over Manchuria. In fact, the Kwangtung Army was not able to seize all of Manchuria immediately after the Mukden Incident. While it took South Manchuria, the Tokyo government under Wakatsuki blocked its attempts to move into North Manchuria as well. The move up to the Great Wall went ahead only after the Wakatsuki cabinet had fallen in December 1931 and been replaced by one under Seiyūkai leader Inukai Tsuyoshi. The Kwantung Army entered Harbin on February 5, 1932. The state of "Manchukuo" was formally set up in March 1932.

Shortly afterwards the Japanese began encroaching further on North China; they moved into Jehol once it was clear that the League of Nations Lytton Commission would recommend non-recognition of "Manchukuo." By the terms of the Tangku Truce of May 1933 between the Kwantung Army and local Chinese officials, Manchukuo's borders were extended up to the Great Wall. In December 1934, after the decision to abrogate both the Washington and London naval agreements, Tokyo sanctioned a policy of fostering regional governments in North China as "buffers" between Manchukuo and the Nationalists. In June 1935, two Chinese provinces — Hopei and Chahar — became client regimes (by the so-called Ho-Umezu and Ching-Doihara agreements, respectively). These regimes, the East Hopei Autonomous Council and the Hopei-Chahar Political Council, excluded the Kuomintang and the Nationalist Army from their territories.

Until 1931 Japan refrained from a direct political clash with the Western imperialists. As at the Washington and London conferences, it had always compromised under pressure. The take-over of Manchuria was the first time Japan refused to accept the West's definition of what imperialism should be in East Asia. The events in Manchuria, coming on top of other things, irritated the Western powers sufficiently for them to mobilize the League of Nations against Japan's new moves. This did not mean that the West was pro-Chinese or fundamentally anti-Japanese. All the Western powers were hostile to the Chinese people. But there were important differences, especially between Britain and the United States, as regards the Kuomintang. The United States had close ties with Chiang and the Kuomintang and wanted to strengthen this regime; Washington did not feel that Japan's case in China should be supported. London, on the other hand, was still pro-Japanese (in spite of the economic threat from Japan), was not close to Chiang, and pressured the Nationalist regime to accept Tokyo's terms. Both Britain and the United States wanted Japan to have a place in China, but they both wanted to use the League "to keep Japan in her place."

The West's mobilization of the league had important effects inside Japan. The government was toppled partly because of this, and the unpopularity of the Western powers increased greatly. Tokyo eventually withdrew from the League. In China the mobilization of the League was clearly perceived as part of inter-imperialist machinations against the Chinese people. The Report of the 1932 Lytton Commission made clear the basic complicity among the imperialist powers over the dismemberment of China. As the Chinese saw, the Manchurian crisis did not definitively rupture the West's solidarity with Japan. None of the Western powers went to war with Japan over events in China. Japan was allowed to advance all the way from Mukden to Indochina over a period of ten years with hardly a finger being lifted by the West. It was only when Japan attacked the colonies of Europe and the United States, and Hawaii, that the Pacific War started.

Internally the political changes were towards *decentralization*.

> Beginning in 1932, Japan witnessed a style of cabinet politics and policy-making in which the ministers of state were little more than spokesmen for their respective ministries. The premier became, in the process, an arbitrator between the competing demands of his ministers . . . Parallel with this development, there appeared the embryonic forms of most of the administrative and policy-making agencies and procedures which eventually matured in the late 1930's . . . Essentially, with the "whole nation" cabinet of Admiral Saitō, there occurred a shift to a highly bureaucratic system which was characterized by a remarkable decentralization of power among the respective ministers of state. This pattern of policy-making, not the programs and actions of the ultra-nationalistic groups, the political parties, and army factionalism would determine the foreign policies of the Japanese government after 1932.[5]

The widespread belief in the West that the Japanese regime became more centralized and "totalitarian" in the thirties is false. What is true is that the existing bureaucratic structure both allowed a definite "militarization" of the regime and provided the conditions whereby a decentralized regime could survive. The government became a conglomeration of relatively autonomous bureaucracies among which the premier attempted to operate as arbitrator. The statutory independence of the military as enshrined in the autonomy of the army and navy ministers in the cabinet provided *carte blanche* for increased decentralization.

The extent to which civil and military authorities agreed on imperialist policy in China and to which the main conflicts within the military were in Tokyo rather than between

Tokyo and Manchuria is apparent both in the case of Nagata and the sequel to the Marco Polo Bridge Incident. Major General Nagata Tetsuzan was an army officer who had spent ten years in Europe (1913–23) and had been appointed chief of the bureau of Military Affairs by General Hayashi Senjurō after the resignation of General Araki Sadao. His specific task was to reorganize the top echelons of the army with War College graduates, accelerate the introduction of advanced military technology, and institute economic planning. Nagata's appointment marked a general shift to a wholesale professionalization of the army via the War College, eliminating the more traditional products of the Military Academy, and causing widespread friction among the old-style military leaders. It was in reaction to this trend that Lieutenant Colonel Aizawa Saburō murdered Nagata on August 12, 1935. The supporters of Aizawa's action, led by General Yanagawa Heisuke, decided to use the trial of Aizawa to stir up opinion in their favour. They chose the judges, the procurator and the location of the trial, as well as making the decision that the trial be held in public and "be conducted in a manner that would enable the public to understand the complex motives underlying the assassination of General Nagata."[6] At the melodramatic trial, Aizawa's defence team, which included Dr. Uzawa, the president of Meiji University, was allowed to present Aizawa's motives and the proceedings were turned into an assault on the government. The trial was accompanied by further steps towards military reorganization, and it was out of this atmosphere of tension that there came the rebellion of February 26, 1936 (the "February Incident") — the nearest thing to a real military coup d'état. Even here there was no coup d'état, for when the Emperor ordered the rebellious troops to surrender after a three-day stand-off in central Tokyo, his order was obeyed. Not even the wildest elements dared oppose the Emperor, although they would squabble among themselves about policy.

Shortly after the February Incident, there is some indication that a more moderate North China policy was developing within the ruling circles in Japan, one which aimed to avoid friction with the Kuomintang, Britain, the United States and the Soviet Union, but not the Chinese Communists. The corollary of this new consensus was to shift priority towards the South Seas.

However, this consensus did not last long. On the night of July 7, 1937, came the Marco Polo Bridge (Lukou Ch'iao) Incident. The proposals put forward by the Tokyo government were rejected by Chiang Kai-shek, and on August 14 Nationalist planes bombed Japanese naval installations at Shanghai. Japan wavered. The vice-chief of the general staff, General Tada backed a policy of caution, but this was decisively repudiated on December 1, 1937, by the Tokyo government and the Emperor, with their decision to march on Nanking and apply the "Policy of Annihilation." Thereafter came the Rape of Nanking and all-out war against both the Communists and the Kuomintang, more or less.

Particularly after events like the Asian and Pacific Wars, it is not easy to review history and realize that although there were elements in Japan, such as the right-wing ideologue Kita Ikki, who were planning for war from way back, this was not true of the leadership of the state as a whole. Although the objectives of the leadership were reprehensible, many of the leaders were also confused. Some were against war; others saw events overtake them (often at least in part due to their own complicity). Until

1931 Japan's leaders, both civil and military, followed a general policy of working together and compromising with the Western imperialists. The combination of army moves in Manchuria and the effects of the economic depression, however, caused Japan to articulate a new, autonomous set of policies, in which the commitment to build the state of Manchukuo was central. The new policy, defined as "an Asiatic Monroe Doctrine," involved three basic characteristics: enlarging the army to protect Manchukuo against both the Soviet Union and Nationalist China as well as the people of "Manchukuo" itself; strengthening the navy to guarantee the security of the empire against the U.S. and the British fleets; getting Nationalist China to recognize "Manchukuo," cut its dependence on the Western powers and cooperate with Japan.

This policy was supported by almost all the Japanese leaders in the mid-1930s, although it was opposed by fringe groups in the military and certain sectors of "public opinion." Until 1937 this policy was backed by both the Foreign Ministry and the General Staff. But after the Sian Incident in December 1936, the Chinese Nationalists could no longer tolerate Japanese imperialism in North China, and with the minor incident at the Marco Polo Bridge the accumulated momentum for a more aggressive policy towards China came into its own in Japan. As in 1931, the support for the two policies was rather evenly balanced and the struggle for supremacy in Tokyo raged until mid-January 1938, when the Konoe government announced it would annihilate the Kuomintang regime. It is important to stress that the General Staff of planners and strategists in Tokyo, among whom the key figure was General Tada, were hostile to this new war with China. The field commanders argued that they could wipe out the Kuomintang armies. But Tada and the strategists at the center saw a China war as a deviation into a swamp: China was not the main enemy; the Soviet Union was building up its strength in the Far East. A China war was the wrong war in the wrong place at the wrong time.

Economic factors

The depression greatly promoted concentration in the domestic economy through bankruptcies, take-overs and mergers. The structure of the Japanese economy, with its proliferation of "small and medium enterprises," was a big obstacle to the efficiency needed in time of war. From 1932 onwards, in the wake of the depression concentrations, the state laid out heavy subsidies for further mergers. Car firms had to stop taking private orders in 1933. Export guilds (*yūshutsu kumiai*) were promoted to accelerate a process of concentration which in some sectors was already fairly well advanced. Centralization of control in the crucial area of banking and credit increased, especially after 1937 when the war with China forced big rises in military expenditure.

The military also increased its role within the economy. The military's role in Manchukuo and Korea, as well as the growing importance of munitions and other military hardware in industrial production, naturally helped this trend along. The aggravated contradiction between big spending on "security" and the neglect of domestic welfare and social services led some elements in the military to voice criticisms of big business. A number of new companies emerged during this period which were particularly closely linked to the military, the "new" zaibatsu (*shinkō zaibatsu*). Though some of these undoubtedly made quick killings in the colonies or in arms production, on the whole the big contracts connected with Japan's expansion went to the old zaibatsu, headed by the big four (Mitsubishi, Mitsui, Sumitomo and Yasuda).

The government also moved to restrict foreign capital in Japan, which was quite powerful in some sectors. In 1936 Ford and General Motors together accounted for about three-quarters of the total output of motor vehicles in Japan. About half of the foreign capital in the country was in joint concessions, particularly in the electrical goods and heavy engineering industries. There had been a big rise in Western companies' penetration after the First World War, and in Japan's borrowing from the West, particularly between 1924 (after the earthquake) and 1930. The latter year also saw the peak of foreign investment — ¥2,466 million. From this point the figure falls, as Japan tried to bring key sectors back under national control. In general, in spite of the depression and Inoue's gold standard blunder, Japan developed a strong external position during the 1930s. "In 1938 Japan's debt to the West was smaller than it had been in 1914; *per capita*, it was the lowest in the world next to China. With the exception of Turkey, Japan was the only important Asian country to reduce its indebtedness to the West between 1914 and 1938."[7] In the 1930s Japan was the only non-Western net creditor nation, though its attempts at setting up a yen bloc economy independent of the West were not a great success.

Moderate restrictions on foreign capital inside Japan were not particularly irritating to the Western powers. What did infuriate them was Japan's astounding export boom into hitherto reserved territories. The depression had something of the same medium-term advantageous effect as the First World War. Japan seized upon the breakdown *in the West* again. When Britain devalued the pound, Japan devalued the yen even more. The thirties saw Japan leaping forward from the advanced positions conquered during the World War, when it had consolidated its grip on Eastern markets. Now it expanded into the next ring of countries — India, the Dutch Indies and the British colonies in East Asia. While Britain's share of India's cotton cloth market fell from 97.1 per cent in 1913–14 to 47.3 per cent in 1935, Japan's share rose from 0.3 per cent (1913–14) to 50.9 per cent (1935) — taking over the entire British loss. Many of these countries retaliated with quotas and tariffs in the years 1933–34, whereupon Japan moved into Latin America. Exports to Central America increased from ¥3 million in 1931 to ¥41 million in 1936, and to South America from ¥10 million to ¥69 million in the same period. Britain's share of the South American cotton piece-goods market fell from 53.2 per cent in 1929 to 46.4 per cent in 1935, and Japan's rose from 4.5 per cent in 1929 to 38.6 per cent in 1935 (the share of Italy and the United States combined in the same period fell from 42.3 per cent to 15 per cent). The speed of the take-over terrified complacent Western bourgeoisies. For example, from virtually zero in 1931, Japan became the second largest exporter to Morocco by 1934, preceded only by France. The mere possibility of an alternative for the first time introduced a whole syndrome of previously ignored options for local traders in countries as diverse as Tanganyika and Palestine. Even where Japan did not take over a market, the high price of British exports often stimulated growth of local production, as in Egypt. Moreover, as a percentage of Japan's exports, semi-manufactures (including raw silk) fell from 51.8 per cent of the total in 1914 to 26.4 per cent in 1937; and between 1934 and 1936 the percentage of Japan's exports which went to free markets rose from 56 to 65 per cent.

This economic threat led Western business into startling revelations about factory conditions in Japan, particularly in Britain, which in 1929 had still been labouring under the hangover of the Anglo–Japanese Alliance. Books attacking working conditions in Japan began to appear. As well as the League of Nations, the International Labour Organisation (ILO) was mobilized in a particularly hypocritical campaign since Britain and France had expressly prevented ILO stipulations being applied to their sweat-shops in China when the organization was originally founded. What incensed the Western powers more than anything was Japan's refusal to kowtow to unilateral imperialist self-righteousness: Japanese delegates would turn up at international conferences and harangue the delegates with the history of the extermination of the American Indians or the development of the Lancashire textile industry, or contemporary colonialism in Hong Kong. It was Japan's insistence on denouncing *inequality among imperialists* which angered the West — not least because it was a line to which there was no ready answer. Ordinary imperialists were no problem; anti-imperialists could be written off as terrorists or demagogues; but a fellow imperialist who both refused to abide by the rules and in practice caused grave economic trouble was more than could be tolerated.

Finally, Japanese imperialism should be set in its comparative context. Japan greatly oppressed all the peoples it colonized, particularly the peoples of Korea and China. But Japanese colonialism was economically no worse than that of the Western powers. In 1940 Elizabeth Schumpeter wrote that "Japan has been more successful in increasing the purchasing power of these regions [Manchukuo and China] than all the outside powers there have ever been in China." Most of Japan's empire was acquired and held during wartime. But it is interesting that in areas where a peacetime comparison is possible, Japan emerges no worse than the white imperialists. Surveys indicate that in both early postwar south Korea and late-sixties Micronesia a majority of the inhabitants polled stated a preference for a return to Japanese rule over continued American occupation.

The existence of this empire naturally raises the questions: Who was in favour of expansion? Whom did it benefit? And what is the relationship between Japan's justifications for expansion and the general problem of economic development in a world dominated by imperialism?

The justifications advanced by Japan were multiple: the protection of interests acquired fighting Russia in 1904–5; the need to have access to raw materials which would otherwise be looted by Western capitalists; the need to protect investments (and later, citizens, in the well-known extension); access to markets, and their protection; the desire for a "Japanese sphere of influence," which was easy to argue since Japan's expansion, unlike that of the European and US imperialists, was limited to geographically adjacent areas; geo-political arguments, much used vis-à-vis the USSR., first over the invasion of Siberia, and later in Korea and China; general statements about the need to control Manchuria and Korea, sometimes combined with a plea that Japan was actually improving the territory; solidarity with the non-white peoples of Asia against the Caucasians; population pressure.

The population question merits a brief examination. In 1930 the population of Japan proper was 64,448,000 (71,253,000 by 1937). The density per square mile was 437 (468 in Great Britain, 670 in Belgium, 324 in Germany). Density in relation to arable land, however, was 2,774 per square mile (2,170 for Great Britain, 1,709 for Belgium, 806 for Germany.) The productive agricultural area of Japan proper was about the same as the area of West Virginia. Japan, therefore, was densely populated. Yet very few Japanese emigrated to the colonies or anywhere else. Whereas between 1910 and 1930 about 20 million Chinese moved into Manchuria, by 1929 there were only about 215,000 Japanese there — and 97 per cent of these lived in Kwantung, the Railway Zone and the Consular Jurisdiction areas: these were almost all administrative staff and suchlike, not settlers. In almost exactly the same period (up to 1928), more than four times as many Koreans had moved, usually as a result of either physical or financial force, into Manchuria. Similarly, after more than thirty years of colonization, there were only just over 200,000 Japanese in Taiwan (though this figure rose to some 300,000 by about 1940). The only other area where there was sizeable Japanese emigration was Brazil, which was not a colony: some 200,000 Japanese moved there between 1908 and 1940. Prior to the war, only a little over one million Japanese moved out of Japan to settle or reside abroad. Obviously, climate and housing as well as lack of adaptability, played their part. Migration to Hokkaido, Japan's Scotland rather than its golden West, was also very low. Japanese preferred to move to balmier climes like Hawaii; many would probably have chosen the United States if it had been possible. Taiwan was clearly more attractive than Manchuria.

The more general question of capitalist development in a world dominated by imperialism is more problematic. The experience of the last century indicates that there is no such thing as peaceful co-existence with imperialism. A non-socialist state has only a choice between attempting to combat other imperialist powers or forming an alliance with one or more of them (usually the most powerful). Japan was not the equal of the other powers in capital, and this plus Japan's relative lateness explains much of the recourse to military actions. There are no examples of non-socialist industrializing countries with Japan's lack of capital and lack of raw materials making their way in the modern world without using force overseas. Apart from capital, raw materials were Japan's biggest problem. After the Second World War, "pure" investment imperialism in other conservative countries became possible (e.g., Japanese investment in Australia, Kuwait, Alaska) — although this phase may itself now be drawing to a close. But before the war, Japan had good reason to think that major investment in Manchuria, Malaya, Indonesia and elsewhere could not be made and protected without some military presence. The type of imperialism Japan "required," investment imperialism, did not become "acceptable" until after the Pacific War.

What were Japan's requirements? Contrary to widespread opinion, Japan was broadly self-sufficient in food in the thirties — except for sugar which largely came from Taiwan. But Japan's farms were very dependent on fertilizers. In 1936 some 30 per cent of all commercial fertilizers were imported, about half from Manchuria. Japan had no phosphates at all. Other imported raw materials included bauxite, nickel and crude rubber (100 per cent for all three) and coal (10.8 per cent). A Brookings Institution report concluded that "Japan's military power is fundamentally dependent upon control of, or free access to, colonial and foreign sources of supply." In the imperialist jungle of the thirties, there was no such thing as "free access" without control. Japan's military force was, of course, less needed to cope with its imperialist rivals than to oppress the peoples of Asia.

From the Amur to Pearl Harbor

In the years 1937–39 Japan fought a series of brief but extremely costly encounters with the Soviet army. A large part of the Japanese army considered the Soviet Union to be its number one enemy, and Japanese encroachment and probing along the Soviet frontier from the Pacific to Mongolia, an independent socialist republic under Soviet "protection," had created the conditions for a serious clash. The first major outbreak of fighting came on the Amur River in 1937; the second at Changkufeng (Lake Khasan) in the summer of 1938; and the third, and largest, at Khalkhin Gol (Nomonhan) in 1939, where Japan suffered a major defeat of considerable strategic importance. The signing of the German–Soviet Pact brought the Nomonhan fighting to a halt.

Since Japan was informally allied with Germany, the German–Soviet Pact naturally inclined the Soviet Union to a similar arrangement with Tokyo. As the war progressed in Europe and Germany overran two of the key colonial powers with possessions in Southeast Asia, France and Holland, Japan shifted its attention more and more southwards. Germany's victories in Europe were followed shortly afterwards by the signing of a Triparite Pact between itself, Italy and Japan (September 27, 1940). In early 1941 Japan's Foreign Minister, Matsuoka Yōsuke, visited Berlin and, on his way back, Moscow, where he signed a non-aggression agreement with the Soviet government. This agreement, which infuriated the Germans, who were about to attack the U.S.S.R., was highly advantageous to both Moscow and Tokyo. The Japanese, although in alliance with Germany, scrupulously respected the non-aggression treaty with Moscow throughout the war, thus ensuring that the Soviet Union would not have to face a war on two fronts. The treaty was similarly advantageous for Tokyo, since it meant that it could concentrate on Southeast Asia without having to fight Russia at the same time.

The history of Japan's dealings with Russia, including the defeat at Nomonhan, are part of the background to Japan's entry into war with the West. In many ways, however, this was a prolongation of the war Japan was already fighting in China. In Japan the war is called "the fifteen years [i.e., 1931–45] war." And to a large extent Japan's attack on Southeast Asia and Pearl Harbor grew directly out of its activities in China.

The question of whether or not war (usually meaning war between Japan and the Western powers) could have been avoided is a highly vexed one, which is the subject of many extensive works. Schroeder, for example, argues that it could at least have been postponed. In an elegant excursus on American moralism, he stresses the extent to which U.S. policy was "designed to uphold principle and to punish the aggressor, but not to save the victim." The emphasis was on "meting out justice rather than doing good." America, he argues, went to war *over* China, but essentially to punish Japan. In a major piece of new research, Jonathan Marshall argues instead that "the United States and Japan fought over Southeast Asia, until then an 'obscure' corner of the world." Recent research and the loosening of wartime prejudice have led to renewed consideration of the operation of Japanese diplomacy and the extent to which Japan was prepared to compromise with the Western powers, and vice versa — against the peoples of Asia. The Brussels Conference of 1937 showed the Western powers profoundly divided on Far Eastern policy, as they continued to be throughout the Second World War. Britain, among, others, was anxious to appease Japan, and in September 1940 it agreed to close the Burma Road, the lifeline to the Kuomintang, at Japan's request. France agreed to let Japanese troops be stationed in Northern Indochina to complete the blockade the Nationalists.

Although most of Southeast Asia was in the hands of European powers, Japan's key negotiations were with the United States. This was not primarily because of America's colonial possession in Asia, the Philippines, but because of America's key role in Japan's trade, particularly in strategic raw materials. The United States began seriously to squeeze Japan in July 1940 when it introduced a licensing system for certain U.S. exports to that country. The two crucial items, crude oil and scrap iron, were added to the list after Japan occupied Northern Indochina in September 1940. A full embargo followed on July 26, 1941.

The American embargo, particularly on oil, severely limited Japan's ability to manoeuvre. Much of Japanese diplomacy prior to December 1941 was taken up with trying to secure supplies of oil: the long negotiations with the Dutch colonial regime in Batavia and Matsuoka's dealings with the Soviet Union whose oil, close to Japan's shores, was less vulnerable to attack during trans-shipment than that from the South Seas. Prior to Pearl Harbor, Japan had only about eighteen months' supply.

Without going into details of the negotiations between Tokyo and Washington, or into the wider political issues, it is well to remember that the clash between the West and Japan was the result not only of Japanese aggression against Asia, but also of the Western imperialists' refusal to accept Japan as an equal partner. In November 1941, when the talks with Washington were already well advanced, Japan proposed universal non-discrimination in commercial relations in the Pacific area, including China, if this principle were adopted throughout the world. To the United States (and presumably the other Western capitalist powers) this was "unthinkable." Japan was, on the whole, eager to reach a settlement and offered considerable concessions to this end. America could certainly have reached a temporary settlement within the framework of an imperialist carve-up which gave Japan slightly more than it had been granted at Washington in 1921–22. It was America which turned down the Japanese proposal for a summit meeting between Premier Konoe and Roosevelt in autumn 1941. And it was Secretary of State Cordell Hull's outright rejection of Japan's proposals of November 7, 1941 which brought negotiations to a halt.

It was Japan, of course, which attacked — not just at Pearl Harbor, but almost simultaneously throughout much of Southeast Asia. The skeleton of the Japanese plan was to incapacitate the American fleet long enough to enable Japan to take over Southeast Asia — the whole of which, with the exception of Thailand, whose regime was pro-Japanese, was a colonized area. All the colonial powers except the United States were either occupied by Japan's allies (Holland), or subordinated (Vichy

France), or direly threatened (Britain), or just plain inoffensive (Portugal). It is also important to remember that when the attack was launched on Pearl Harbor and Southeast Asia, most of the Japanese leaders, while hoping to achieve *some* gains from going to war, did not believe that they could defeat the United States. At the Liaison Conference on November 1, 1941, "the only thing the chiefs of staff of both branches, in spite of their strong stand, assured to the conferees was that Japan could keep on fighting favorably for two years, but the outlook after that was bleak."[8]

The question of Japanese "fascism"

Most Western writers on Japan accept the applicability of the term "fascist" to Japan for varying periods between some time in the later 1920s and 1945. The term is also used by Japanese Marxists.

The differences over dating immediately signal one obvious difficulty: if Japan had a fascist *regime*, what was its starting date? If Japan did not have a fascist regime, then what is the meaning of defining it as a fascist country? It is not enough to claim that there was a fascist *movement*. After all, there was a fascist movement in Britain in the 1930s, without Britain being a fascist country.

The term fascism raises some problems. Fascism as a political phenomenon is mainly associated with Europe, and particularly with Italy in the years 1922–1943/45 and Germany in 1933–45. It is a phenomenon which has not only political and ideological features, but also economic ones. While there is no universally accepted definition of fascism (one of the few terms used equally by Marxists and non-Marxists), it is generally agreed that the *minimum* characteristics involve the following: "the total, systematic suppression of every form of autonomous organization of the [working] masses", some form of mass petit bourgeois movement; rural discontent. While there is a wide measure of agreement over what constitutes fascist ideology, there is severe disagreement over two key questions: can fascism be produced by capitalism only at one stage of the latter's development? And can one talk of a fascist regime without either a recognizable fascist party or similar organization wielding state power?

As Togliatti and others warned during the fascist period in Europe, trying to over-generalize is pointless. If every form of reaction can be termed "fascism," the word loses its meaning. Fascism can be only a *specific* form of reaction. It seems an open question whether the most valuable approach is indeed to try to compare Japan with the European fascist states. While certain elements in Japan called themselves fascists and were purposefully imitating European fascism, and the Tokyo government was in *political* alliance with Berlin and Rome, posing the question "what was the nature of the Japanese regime?" exclusively in terms of "fascism" may be a Eurocentric approach which obscures the specific features of the Japanese regime.

Unlike the European fascist states, Japan had no successful coup d'état or putsch, such as the March on Rome in 1922 or Hitler's seizure of power in 1933. Equally, there was no violent or abrupt *end* to the wartime regime, which also raises questions about its nature. And there was no mass fascist party in Japan. Indeed, there was a degree of continuity in Japan, at least at the formal institutional level, which was quite unknown in Italy, Germany or Spain.

It is worth looking briefly at the arguments put forward by those who contend that Japan had a fascist state, and at the criteria adopted for this judgement. The only substantial Marxist work in English on Japanese fascism is the book by O. Tanin and E. Yohan, *Militarism and Fascism in Japan*, completed in early 1933. Tanin and Yohan follow the Kōza line and are cautious about applying the label "fascist" to the Japanese *regime*. Their book has an introduction by one of the Comintern's leading theoreticians, Karl Radek, specifically criticizing their theses from the standpoint of the Rōn faction, which coincided with the then official Comintern line. The difference between these two (the Tanin and Yohan text and the Radek introduction) illuminates some of the issues.

Tanin and Yohan ask if "the whole reactionary chauvinist movement" can be called "fascist" in the West European sense of the word and answer "no." First,

> West European fascism is primarily an instrument of finance capital, while the Japanese reactionary chauvinist movement, taken as a whole, is the instrument not only of finance capital but also of the Japanese monarchy which represents a *bloc* of two class forces: finance capital and semi-feudal landowners, and besides this possesses the logic of its own development, represented by the army and monarchist bureaucracy whose oppression has an independent significance. That is why at the center of the Japanese reactionary chauvinist movement we find principally the same people who head the system of Japanese military-feudal imperialism. Hence, the role of the army as the backbone of the reactionary chauvinist movement taken as a whole.

> The second distinguishing trait of the Japanese reactionary chauvinist movement, characteristic of the most important and so far the most influential wing of it, follows from this. It is the limited use of social demagogy by the reactionary chauvinist movement as a whole.

> . . . these peculiarities of the Japanese reactionary chauvinist movement as a whole, distinguishing it from West European fascism, are closely interwoven with the peculiarities of the social structure and the peculiar historical development of Japanese military-feudal imperialism.[9]

Radek takes issue with Tanin and Yohan on both points. On the first aspect, though, the difference is really about what stage Japanese capitalism has reached in its development. Discussing European fascism, Radek states that it "develops on the economic basis of the domination of monopoly capital, which . . . [inter alia] is feeling the approach of the social evolution." Radek asserts that fascism can exist only in a country which is dominated by finance capital. In a country not dominated by finance capital, reaction might share many features with fascism but would not be "homogeneous with fascism." Radek criticizes Tanin and Yohan on the grounds that they overrate the importance of the survivals of feudalism. Japan, he insists, is dominated by finance capital and has reached the stage of monopoly capital. As regards the economic base, therefore, Japan has reached the requisite stage to have a full, "classic" fascist regime. He does not say when the regime first qualified as fascist.

This disagreement among Marxists involves not the question "how reactionary was the Japanese regime?" but "had Japan reached the stage of development where the form of reaction could be qualified as fascist?" Radek says yes. Tanin and Yohan give a qualified no.

Another disagreement concerns not so much the nature of the state apparatus as such, but rather the relationship between the regime and the petit bourgeois masses. Tanin and Yohan go at great length into the many organizations which fall into what they call the "reactionary chauvinist movement." These they divide into two streams: the reactionary organizations of the privileged classes and reactionary organizations among the intermediate social strata. The latter stream is much closer to Western European fascism in its ideology but, though useful for the ruling group, it is also very doubtful that it will obtain power. Tanin and Yohan conclude that although there are a lot of fascist or quasi-fascist organizations in Japan, one cannot (1932–33) talk of a fascist party in the same way as in Germany or Italy.

Radek retorts that an actual fascist party is not a prerequisite. "The point is not whether the Japanese fascists have millions of adherents, united into special fascist organizations of a general patriotic nature, created by the bureaucrats and militarists. The decisive question is whether those people who control these mass organizations, although officially non-fascist, serve fascism or not, and what kind of ideas they propound in these organizations." The Japanese regime, he claims, *is* like those in Germany and Italy, in its "search for a bulwark among the broad petty bourgeois masses."

Radek asserts that there are no "primary" differences between European fascism and what he calls Japanese fascism, only "secondary" differences: first and most important, the role of the army as "organizer and leader of the fascist movement"; second, the role of landlords in organizing Japanese fascism in the spirit of the legends of the Middle Ages.

While Radek states that he is interested in both *"the resemblance and differences between Japanese and European fascism,"* the eminent Japanese political scientist, Maruyama Masao, on the other hand, has acknowledged that he is more interested in seeking out the differences between the Japanese and European experiences. Others have suggested that, while it is fair enough to attempt a comparison, an *exclusive* comparison with the West may be misleading. Japan might fruitfully be compared also with some contemporary Third World countries, and its political leadership to a *collective* form of modern nationalist movements.

Yet if Japan became a fascist country, then it must be possible to locate the transition, if not to one exact day, week or month, at least to some definable period. But this turns out to be very difficult. Where could the transition be located? Several liberal observers stress that "party cabinets" came to an end with the assassination of Premier Inukai in 1932. But these "party cabinets" can not be considered the *determinant* of a putative "democracy" as opposed to "fascism." Barrington Moore, seeking to locate the beginning of a "fascist" regime, acknowledges that these assassinations only "inaugurated a period of semi-military dictatorship rather than of outright fascism." Nor can one go by elections. In his discussion of periodization, Moore appears to adopt the 1932 election in Germany as a criterion for dating what he calls "a . . . distinction between a democratic and a totalitarian phase." But in Japan the 1936 election appears to have been relatively free, and even in the 1942 election opponents of the regime were elected (something impossible at that stage in Italy or Germany). It cannot, therefore, be said that there was a change in the political *system*. Paradoxically, proof of this lies not only in the absence of change on the way into the alleged "fascist" period, but also in the absence of change in the structures of the state in 1945.

In spite of what Radek and others have claimed, the Japanese state was a very different state from those in Germany and Italy. Both the monarchy and the military clearly played completely different roles. The survival of the monarchy as a locus of *real* power is part and parcel of the lack of change needed in the regime as a whole. The system has been described as "imperial absolutism," a reference not to the specific acts of the individual emperor, but to the place of the imperial institution in the structure of the state. The position of the imperial institution had important effects both on the forms of political organization selected by the ruling group, and on the absence of any figure comparable to Hitler or Mussolini.

Bourgeois democracy in Japan was much weaker than in either Germany or Italy, and the left-wing movement was not comparable either. The ruling group in Japan found it fairly easy to consolidate round the throne, and it did not need to develop a mass movement to achieve its ends. Indeed, consolidation round the throne was, in a way, the *opposite* of any form of political expression. The Imperial Rule Assistance Association, formally organized in October 1940 after all the political parties in the Diet had been dissolved, was the culmination of a process — the elimination of contesting organizations disturbing the nation's "harmony" — not an instrument of real mass mobilization.

In addition, the system of imperial absolutism led to definite limitations on those who were fascists. So powerful were both the ideology of the Emperor-system and the state structure that Japanese fascists could attack only the opposition. Otherwise they might "endanger" the Emperor himself. As was clearly shown in February 1936, the Emperor was literally unassailable. Thus, changes could only be brought about *through* the system, and the key problematic area is really the extent to which those with fascist ideas and objectives actually managed to get them implemented through the existing state personnel and machinery.

To decide this involves an evaluation of the role of the military, especially the army. The army certainly was more important politically in Japan than in Germany, Italy or even Spain, but it is by no means clear that it was qualitatively more important than it had been in the 1920s or even in the Meiji period. The army was important in Japanese expansionism in the 1930s and 1940s, but it had been important in moves overseas earlier. And, although expansion overseas was a central feature of the regime in the years 1931–42, expansionism and colonialism are not defining features of fascism. There can be non-expansionist fascism and non-fascist expansionism. What the military did was not simply to play a leading role in overseas expansion, but, while increasingly forming an alliance with the bureaucracy, simultaneously to nudge the

273

regime farther towards the right through the actions of its fascist individuals and groups. In addition, the military played an important role in ideology and "culture". The military were an "elite", fostering an ideology of "heroism." Together with that of Emperor-worship (or state-worship), this ideology helped create the conditions where a mass movement was neither needed nor wanted. In recent years there has been a major reassessment of the role of the Japanese military in the 1930s, and much emphasis has been placed on the fact that the military did not "succeed" in seizing power. This is technically correct. But there was also an element of "success through failure." The violence of the years 1931–36 was disorganized and did not represent the mainstream of the army, as Crowley stresses. On the other hand, there was extensive "seepage,", not only of ideas, but also of personnel. The "wild" elements in the army *did* influence policy enormously, even if not in immediately visible ways.

The main proponent of the thesis that there was a specific Japanese fascism radically different from European fascism is Maruyama Masao. Maruyama, while accepting the applicability of the term "fascism," also tends to stress the "uniqueness" of the Japanese case, and lays considerable emphasis on the aspects of "drift", particularly in foreign policy. Yet this somewhat neglects the remarkably direct and linear progression of Japanese foreign policy. Unlike in Germany and Italy, this can not easily be attributed to one man, but this does not mean it was not the result of identifiable class forces. Maruyama tends to base his acceptance of the term "fascism" on similarities in ideology between Japan and Europe, while playing down the dissimilarities of social and political structures.

In "The Ideology and Dynamics of Japanese Fascism" Maruyama singles out three specific features of the fascist movement in Japan: its family–system tendency; agrarianism; and the ideal of the emancipation of the peoples of Asia from European colonialism. The first is a permanent characteristic of Japanese society as a whole — it differentiates Japan as a whole from Europe; the last also marks off much of the Japanese political spectrum from comparable sectors in Europe though it hardly defines Japan in the 1930s as "fascist". The second feature, agrarianism, is more complex. Its potent ideological force is vividly shown by Tōjō's "anxious and pitiful" answer to a question from a Dietman in 1943, who had asked: "Are not the villages of Imperial Japan being endangered by the absorption of their labour power in the armament industries?" Tōjō answered:

> This is a point that truly worries me. On the one hand, I want at all costs
> to maintain the population of the villages at forty per cent of the total
> population. I believe that the foundation of Japan lies in giving
> importance to agriculture. On the other hand, it is undeniable that
> industry is being expanded, chiefly because of the war. It is extremely hard
> to reconcile these two factors. However difficult it may be, I am
> determined to maintain the population of the villages at forty per cent.
> But production must be increased. A harmony must be created by degrees
> between the two requirements. But, in creating this harmony, care must
> be taken to avoid making havoc of the Japanese family system. I must
> confess that things are not proceeding at present in an ideal manner. In
> the need for a rapid expansion of production large factories have been set

up in various places; their workers have to be hired from among farmers ... Although things are not proceeding ideally, I still believe that a method can and will be found to establish a proper harmony in the Japanese manner.[10]

Yet while Tōjō's remarks indicate that agrarianism as an ideological element had great potency, in practice "the agrarian current of traditionalist patriotism, expressed in such movements as *Nōhon-shugi*, was mainly a town and landlord affair, directed *against* peasant interests and aiming to keep the peasant frugal and contented — in a word in his place." Agrarianism was never powerful enough materially to alter the chosen orientation of business either at home or abroad. As far as can be seen it only marginally influenced the process of accumulation and investment. As for imperialism overseas, although the movement animated by Ishihara Kanji for agrarian colonies in Manchuria was active by the mid-twenties, the contours of Japan's imperialism were fundamentally unaffected by agrarianism as an ideology. On the contrary, the regime was swift to excise any threat from those who seemed to want to put a really radical right-wing programme through. Kita Ikki, the most famous exponent of aggressive expansion in Asia and a degree of internal "renovation" was executed, along with his main aide, Nishida Zei, on apparently trumped-up charges after the February 26th [1936] Incident. At home big business dominated policy.

The trouble with the term "fascism" is that it forces any examination of Japan into a Eurocentric category. It is virtually impossible to examine the phenomenon without constructing such an examination in terms of comparisons with Germany, Italy and Spain. Moreover, most of the criteria used to categorize Japan as fascist in, say, 1940 or thereabouts do not define specifically new phenomena within Japan. Maruyama is right to assert that the regime under Tōjō in 1942 was not qualitatively different from that under Inukai in 1932. This is why Japan could move *out* of "fascism" in 1945 as easily as it was able to move into it. Moore is correct to stress the unbroken dominance of big business, with agrarianism functioning at a purely ideological level; "big business needed fascism, patriotism, Emperor worship, and the military." Tanin and Yohan are correct to talk of imperial absolutism. If these factors are kept in mind, the others fall into place: the absence of a mass party, the role of the military, the continued importance of the Emperor, the absence of a Führer or Duce.

Did the Pacific War itself have some effect? Japan was a violent and aggressive country in Asia well before Pearl Harbor (1941) or the Mukden Incident (1931). The oppression of the working classes and political repression against proletarian militancy had been highly developed at least since the turn of the century. If Japan was "fascist" in 1941, it perhaps should be called "fascist" in 1915. There was a definite stepping up of the campaign to smash all autonomous organizations of the working class in the later 1930s, but this was not on the scale of the actions in Germany or Italy.

Although I would reject the term "fascist" for the regime, it is true that there was a fascist *movement* in Japan from the 1920s to 1945 in the sense that fascist *forces* were at work, and were effective, even if their relationship to state power did not take the same form as in Germany and Italy.

Notes

1. Saitō Takasi, "Japan's Foreign Policy in the International Environment of the Nineteen-Twenties," p. 695.

2. Crowley, "A New Deal for Japan and Asia," p. 240.

3. Iriye, *After Imperalism*, p. 207.

4. Jansen, "From Hatoyama to Hatoyama," p. 77; cf. Peter Duus, *Party Rivalry and Political Change in Taishō Japan* (Cambridge, Mass, Harvard University Press, 1968), pp. 199ff.

5. Crowley, *Japan's Quest*, p. 180. "The Saitō cabinet, in effect, marked the appearance of a new form of political oligarchy in which the authority and influence of the political parties, the Emperior's advisers, and the premier would be appreciably altered — in some instances, almost eradicated" (ibid, pp. 179-80). Saitō Makoto, a former governor-general of Korea, was premier from May 1932 until July 1934.

   While Crowley is correct to emphasize decentralization, it is hard to agree that the *pattern* of policy-making *determined* foreign policy, as he claims. Rather, the military and other right-wing elements exploited the existing "pluralism" of the system: see section below on "facism" and Tetsuo Furuya, "Naissance et dévelopment du fascisme japonais," *RHDGM*, No, 86, 22e année (April 1972), pp. 1-16. Also, the fact that the policies of the far right were *confused* and that those with fascist objectives did not succeed in imposing a unified political leadership does not mean that they were not *consistently* oppressive both at home and abroad.

6. Crowley, *Japan's Quest*, p. 269; after the February 26 [1936] Incident Aizawa was brought before a new court-martial and sentenced to death (Crowley, p. 274).

7. Woodruff, *Impact of Western Man*, p. 131.

8. Hosoya, "Japan's decision for War in 1941," p. 46; Hosoya is good on the psychological factors behind Japan's decision to attack.

9. Tanin and Yohan, *Militarism and Fascism in Japan*, pp. 266-67 (the title of the book indicates the authors' doubts).

10. Quoted in Maruyama, *Thought and Behaviour in Modern Japanese Politics*, p. 47.

16. Theory and Psychology of Ultra-Nationalism

Masao Maruyama

Translated by Ivan Morris

I

What was the main ideological factor that kept the Japanese people in slavery for so long and that finally drove them to embark on a war against the rest of the world? Writers in the West have vaguely described it as 'ultra-nationalism' or 'extreme nationalism'; but until now no one has examined what it really is.

Scholars have been mainly concerned with the social and economic background of ultra-nationalism. Neither in Japan nor in the West have they attempted any fundamental analysis of its intellectual structure or of its psychological basis. There are two reasons for this: in the first place, the problem is too simple; secondly it is too complex.

It is too simple because ultra-nationalism in Japan has no solid conceptual structure. Lacking such a structure it emerges instead in the form of shrill slogans, such as 'The Eight Corners of the World under One Roof' and 'Spreading the Emperor's Mission to Every Corner of the Earth'; for this reason scholars have tended to regard it as unworthy of serious examination.

Here we find a striking contrast to the situation in Nazi Germany, which, for all its emotionalism and illogicality, did in fact possess an orthodox, systematic *Weltanschauung* expressed in books like *Mein Kampf* and *The Myth of the Twentieth Century*. Yet the absence from Japanese ultra-nationalism of this sort of authoritative basis does not mean that is was weak as an ideology. Far from it: ultra-nationalism succeeded in spreading a many-layered, though invisible, net over the Japanese people, and even today they have not really freed themselves from its hold.

It is not merely the external system of coercion that determined the low level of political consciousness we find today in Japan. Rather, the key factor is the all-pervasive psychological coercion, which has forced the behaviour of our people into a particular channel. Since this has never had any clear theoretical form or any single intellectual pedigree, it is very hard to grasp in its entirety. We must therefore avoid dismissing slogans like 'the Eight Corners of the Earth under One Roof' as so much empty demagogy. These slogans are frequently manifestations of an underlying force; and in order to understand the true nature of ultra-nationalism we must grope through such manifestations to discover the common underlying logic.

This is certainly not a matter of exhuming our country's painful past out of some masochistic whim. As Ferdinand Lasalle puts it, 'The opening of a new era finds itself

Reprinted from *THOUGHT AND BEHAVIOUR IN MODERN JAPANESE POLITICS* by Masao Maruyama and edited by Ivan Morris (1963), pp. 1-24. Reproduced by permission of Oxford University Press.

in the acquisition of the consciousness of what has been the reality of existence.' This task may well be an essential condition for any true national reform. Indeed may we not say that a revolution is worthy of its name only if it involves an inner or spiritual revolution?

The following essay, then, is not a systematic explanation of ultra-nationalism, but rather a fragmentary attempt to indicate the *locus* and scope of the problem.

II

The first point is to determine why nationalism in our country evokes such epithets as 'ultra' and 'extreme'. The fact that modern States are known as 'nation-states' suggests that nationalism is no fortuitous aspect of these countries but rather their fundamental attribute. How then are we to differentiate between this type of nationalism, which is more or less common to all modern States, and the 'ultra' form of nationalism?

The distinction that may first come to mind is the presence of expansionist, militarist tendencies. The trouble is that during the period when nation-states first came into being *all* the countries that were under absolutist régimes blatantly carried out wars of external aggression; in other words a tendency to military expansion was an inherent impulse in nationalism long before the so-called age of imperialism in the nineteenth century.

It is quite true that in Japan nationalism was guided by this impulse to a stronger degree and that it manifested it in a clearer way than in other countries. But this is not merely a matter of quantity. Quite apart from any difference in degree, there is a qualitative difference in the inner motive power that spurred Japan to expansion abroad and to oppression at home; and it is only owing to this qualitative difference that Japanese nationalism acquired its 'ultra' aspect.

A comparison with European nationalism will lead us to the crux of the matter. As Carl Schmidt has pointed out, an outstanding characteristic of the modern European State lies in its being *ein neutraler Staat*. That is to say, the State adopts a *neutral* position on internal values, such as the problem of what truth and justice are; it leaves the choice and judgement of all values of this sort to special social groups (for instance, to the Church) or to the conscience of the individual. The real basis of national sovereignty is a purely 'formal' legal structure, divorced from all questions of internal value.

This resulted from the particular way in which the modern State developed out of the post-Reformation wars of religion that dragged on through the sixteenth and seventeenth centuries. The interminable struggle, which revolved about matters of faith and theology, eventually had two converse effects. On the one hand, it obliged the religious sects to give up the idea that they could realize their principles on the political plane. On the other, it confronted the absolute sovereigns of the time with a severe challenge. Until then the monarchs of Europe had brandished the slogan of the Divine Right of Kings, thus providing their own internal justification for ruling. Confronted now with severe opposition, they were obliged to find a new basis for their rule, namely, in the *external* function of preserving public order.

Thus a compromise was effected between the rulers and the ruled — a compromise based on distinguishing between form and content, between external matters and internal matters, between the public and the private domains. Questions of thought, belief, and morality were deemed to be private matters and, as such, were guaranteed their subjective, 'internal' quality; meanwhile, state power was steadily absorbed into an 'external' legal system, which was of a technical nature.

In post-Restoration Japan, however, when the country was being rebuilt as a modern State, there was never any effort to recognize these technical and neutral aspects of national sovereignty. In consequence Japanese nationalism strove consistently to base its control on internal values rather than on authority deriving from external laws.

Foreign visitors to Japan during the first half of the nineteenth century almost invariable noted that the country was under the dual rule of the Mikado (Tennō), who was the spiritual sovereign, and the Tycoon (Shōgun), who held actual political power. After the Restoration, unity was achieved by removing all authority from the latter, and from other representatives of feudal control, and by concentrating it in the person of the former. In this process, which is variously described as the 'unification of administration and laws' and the 'unification of the sources of dispensation and deprivation', prestige and power were brought together in the institution of the Emperor. And in Japan there was no ecclesiastical force to assert the supremacy of any 'internal' world over this new combined, unitary power.

It is true that in due course a vigorous movement arose to assert people's rights. Its advocates were soon engaged in a bitter struggle with the authorities, who in their resistance to the new theories tried to 'instil fear into the hearts of the people, brandishing the prestige of the armed forces in one hand and that of the police in the other, thus cowing the populace with power from above'.

Yet the struggle for people's rights was not concerned primarily with the right of ultimate judgement on such *internal* values as truth and morality. All that mattered to the fighters for popular rights was 'to secure the power of the Sovereign and to define the limits of the people's rights'. How frivolously they regarded the question of internalizing morality (a prerequisite of any true modernization) is suggested by the passage in which the leader of the Liberal Party, Kōno Hironaka, discusses the motives of his own intellectual revolution. The liberalism of John Stuart Mill was the decisive influence; yet he describes the process as follows:

> I was riding on horseback when I first read this work ['On Liberty']. In a flash my entire way of thinking was revolutionized. Until then I had been under the influence of the Chinese Confucianists and of the Japanese classical scholars, and I had even been inclined to advocate an 'expel the barbarian' policy. Now all these earlier thoughts of mine, *excepting those concerned with loyalty and filial piety*, were smashed to smithereens. At the same moment I knew that it was human freedom and human rights that I must henceforth cherish above all else.[1]

What really strikes one in reading this description is how glibly an outstanding Japanese liberal could, from the very outset of his deliberations, 'except' the concepts of loyalty and filial piety — concepts that must be squarely faced before any progress can possibly be made along the road to securing the internal freedom of the individual. Kōno does not show the slightest awareness that the retention of this traditional morality might pose a problem for liberalism.

The 'people's rights' approach, represented by early liberals of this kind, was from the beginning connected with theories about 'national rights'; and it was inevitable that it should in due course be submerged by them. Thus in the struggle for liberalism the question of the individual's conscience never became a significant factor in defining his freedom. Whereas in the West national power after the Reformation was based on formal, external sovereignty, the Japanese State never came to the point of drawing a distinction between the external and internal spheres and of recognizing that its authority was valid only for the former. In this respect it is noteworthy that the Imperial Rescript on Education should have been proclaimed just before the summoning of the First Imperial Diet. This was an open declaration of the fact that the Japanese State, being a moral entity, monopolized the right to determine values.

It is hardly surprising that the clash between Christianity and the policy of national education, which was so important in intellectual circles during the early part of the Meiji Period, should have taken the form of a heated controversy about this Imperial Rescript. Significantly it was at about this period that the word *étatisme* came into frequent use. The controversy was submerged in the wave of nationalist excitement that spread through the country at the time of the Sino–Japanese and Russo–Japanese wars. Yet the underlying problem was certainly not resolved; only the reluctance of the pro-Christian groups to avoid any open confrontation made it appear as though the issue of free conscience versus the total authority of the State had actually been settled.

Accordingly, until the day in 1946 when the divinity of the Emperor was formally denied in an Imperial Rescript, there was in principle no basis in Japan for freedom of belief. Since the nation includes in its 'national polity'[2] all the internal values of truth, morality, and beauty, neither scholarship nor art could exist apart from these national values. They were, in fact, totally dependent on them. The dependence, moreover, was less external than internal; for the slogans 'art for the nation' and 'scholarship for the nation' were not simply demands that art and scholarship be of practical value to the country. The essential point was that the final decision about the content of Japanese art, scholarship, and so forth, in other words, the definition of what was actually for the good of the country, was handed down by officials whose duty it was to give loyal service 'to His Majesty the Emperor and the Imperial Government'.

A natural consequence of this failure to draw any clear line of demarcation between the public and the private domains was the great extension in Japan of the scope of the law. 'Those things', writes Hegel, 'that are free in an interior sense and that exist within the individual subject must not enter into the purview of the law.' It was precisely the sanctity of such an interior, subjective sphere that the Japanese law failed to recognize. On the contrary, inasmuch as the law of the land in Japan arose from the 'national polity', which was an absolute value, it based its validity on inner or contentual, rather than on external or formal, norms and was thus free to operate in all those interior realms from which law in the West had been excluded.

Since the *formal* quality of the national order was not recognized in Japan, it was impossible by the very nature of things for any purely personal realm to exist apart from this order. In our country personal affairs could never be accepted *qua* personal affairs. The author of *The Way of the Subject* writes as follows on this point:

> What we normally refer to as 'private life' is, in the final analysis, the way of the subject. As such, it has a public significance, in that each so-called private action is carried out by the subject as part of his humble efforts to assist the Throne ... Thus we must never forget that even in our personal lives we are joined to the Emperor and must be moved by the desire to serve our country.

The ideology reflected in this passage did not emerge in Japan as part of the totalitarian vogue of the 1930s, but was from the outset immanent in the national structure. Private affairs accordingly always involved something shady and were regarded as akin, or even equivalent, to evil. This applied particularly to profit-making and to love.

Since the personal, internal quality of private affairs could never be openly recognized, people tried in one way or another to imbue these affairs with some national significance and thus to dispel the aura of shadiness. In Sōseki's *Since Then*, Daisuke and his sister-in-law have the following conversation:

> 'And what on earth did [Father] find to scold you about today ?'
>
> 'That's hardly the point. He always finds something. What really did surprise me was to hear that Father has been serving the nation. He told me that from the age of eighteen until today he has, gone on serving the country to the best of his ability.'
>
> 'I suppose that's why he's made such a success.'
>
> 'Yes, if one can make as much money as Father has by serving the nation, I wouldn't mind serving it myself.'

Now this father of Daisuke, whom the author presents with such trenchant irony, can be regarded as the typical Japanese capitalist. He represents 'The Road to Success and Prosperity', and it was precisely when the success motive joined forces with nationalism that modern Japan was able to embark on its 'rush towards progress'. Yet at the same time it was this very combination that led to Japan's decay. For the logic according to which 'private affairs' cannot be morally justified within themselves, but must always be identified with national affairs, has a converse implication: private interests endlessly infiltrate into national concerns.

III

In Japan, then, we are faced with a situation in which national sovereignty involves both spiritual authority and political power. The standard according to which the nation's actions are judged as right or wrong lies within itself (that is, in the 'national polity'), and what the nation does, whether within its own borders or beyond them, is not subject to any moral code that supersedes the nation.

This formulation will immediately bring to mind the Hobbesian type of absolutism. But there is a clear difference. The authority to which Hobbes refers when he writes: 'It is not the truth that makes laws, but authority' is a purely pragmatic decision and does not connote any value that can be regarded as normative. In his *Leviathan* there are no such things as right and wrong, good and bad, until they are enacted by a decision of the sovereign. 'The sovereign himself creates the norm; he does not bring into force a system of truth and justice that has already existed. What makes the laws valid in the Hobbesian State is exclusively the *formal* fact that they derive from the orders of the sovereign; and this stress on formal validity, far from involving any fusion of form and content (such as we find in Japanese thinking on the subject), leads to the modern theory of legal positivism. Even in Frederick the Great's Prussia, in which legitimacy (*Legitimität*) ultimately resolved itself into legality (*Legalität*), we can recognize a direct line of descent from the Hobbesian type of absolutism.

Japanese nationalism, on the other hand, was never prepared to accept a merely formal basis of validity. The reason that the actions of the nation cannot be judged by any moral standard that supersedes the nation is not that the Emperor creates norms from scratch (like the sovereign in Hobbes's *Leviathan*) but that absolute values are embodied in the person of the Emperor himself, who is regarded as 'the eternal culmination of the True, the Good, and the Beautiful throughout all ages and in all places'.[3]

According to this point of view, virtue arises only when this 'eternal culmination', which is in fact the essence of the 'national polity', starts to spread out in waves from its central entity, the Emperor, to the rest of the world. In the patriotic slogan, 'spreading the just cause throughout the world', the just cause (that is, virtue) is not regarded as something that could exist before the Japanese nation acted, nor is it something that developed afterwards. The just cause and national conduct invariably *coexist*. In order to spread the just cause it is necessary to act; conversely, when the nation acts, it is *ipso facto* in the just cause.

Thus it is characteristic of nationalist logic in Japan that the down-to-earth precept, 'It's always best to be on the winning side', should be subtly blended with the ideology, 'The righteous cause triumphs'. The Empire of Japan came to be regarded *per se* as 'the culmination of the True, the Good, and the Beautiful', and was by its very nature unable to do wrong; accordingly the most atrocious behaviour, the most treacherous acts, could all be condoned.

This point of view about the automatic righteousness of the nation's conduct can also be explained by the interfusion of ethics and power that occurred in Japan. National sovereignty was the ultimate source of both ethics and power, and constituted their intrinsic unity; this being the situation, Japanese morality never underwent the process of interiorization that we have seen in the case of the West, and accordingly it always had the impulse to transform itself into power. Morality is not summoned up from the depths of the individual; on the contrary, it has its roots outside the individual and does not hesitate to assert itself in the form of energetic outward movement. The 'total mobilization of the people's spirit' during the war was a typical manifestation of Japanese morality emerging as outward action.

Owing to this exteriorization of morality in Japan, the 'national polity' could never be discussed without immediately being brought to the level of a political conflict and involving the participants in a political clash. We can see this in the conflict, which has already been cited, of Christianity versus the Imperial Rescript on Education; essentially the same thing happened in the 'Shinto as a primitive religion' case, in the repercussions to Ozaki Yukio's speech about a Japanese republic, and in the Minobe case arising from his 'organ theory' of the Emperor. In all these instances the nationalist moralists carried out their attacks in the name of 'clarifying the national polity', a phrase that, far from implying any self-criticism or need to explain one's position, usually signified a method of putting pressure on one's political enemies.

This identification of morality with power meant that pure inner morality (as opposed to the external type) was always regarded as 'impotent' and therefore worthless. To be impotent meant not to have the physical strength to move other people — a type of strength, of course, that neither ethics nor ideals ever claim to possess.

We find a tendency, then, to estimate morality, not by the value of its content, but in terms of its power, that is, according to whether or not it had a power background. In the last analysis this was because the real *locus* of Japanese morality was not in the conscience of the individual but in the affairs of the nation.

This is most clearly revealed in Japan's relations with other countries. The following passage is significant:

> Our country's determination and military strength made [the principal Allied powers] unable to impose any sanctions whatsoever. When Japan seceded, the true nature of the League [of Nations] was revealed to the world. In autumn of the same year Germany followed our example and seceded, and later Italy took advantage of the Abyssinian question to announce its secession also, so that the League became nothing but an empty name. Thus since the autumn of 1931 our country made great strides in the vanguard of the forces struggling for world renovation.[4]

Two things set the tone of this passage: unconcealed scorn for the fact that the League was powerless to impose sanctions, and implicit admiration for Italy's dexterity in taking advantage of an opportunity. Neither the 'true nature' of the League nor the behaviour of Fascist Italy was judged according to any intrinsic set of values; the only criteria were real (that is, material) power and tactical skill. Here we see another aspect of the outlook of the Mombu Shō officials, those high priests of Japanese 'education'.

Now, at the same time that morality was being transformed into power, power was continuously being counteracted by moral considerations. Japanese politicians have never yet given vent to any open declarations of Machiavellism, nor have they ever (like some of their Western counterparts) boasted about resolutely trampling on *petit-bourgeois* morality. Inasmuch as political power in Japan based itself on ultimate

283

moral entities, the Japanese have never been able to recognize the 'satanic' aspect of politics for what it is.

Here we find a sharp difference between the Eastern and Western attitudes. The German people, as Thomas Mann has pointed out, have a latent sense that politics is essentially an immoral and brutal thing; but it is impossible for the Japanese to recognize this with any real conviction. Accordingly two types of politician are rarely to be found in our country: the genuinely idealistic politician who remains steadfastly faithful to truth and justice, and the Cesare Borgia type of politician who is prepared fearlessly to trample underfoot all accepted standards of morality. In Japan we find neither the humble, inwardlooking approach nor the naked lust for power. Everything is noisy, yet at the same time it is all most scrupulous. It is precisely in this sense that Tōjō Hideki can be regarded as representative of the Japanese politician.

This phenomenon, which we may term the diminutiveness of power or 'power dwarfing', does not apply to political power alone, but characterizes every type of control that operates with the State as its background. The ill-treatment of Allied prisoners during the Second World War provides a good example. (Later I shall discuss the atrocities committed in battle as involving a slightly different problem.) When one reads the reports about the beating and other ill-treatment meted out to the P.O.W.s, one is struck by the way in which almost all the Japanese defendants emphasized that they had worked to improve conditions in the camps. Of course these men were on trial and wanted to save their own skins. But I do not believe that is the whole story. Many of them were sincerely convinced that they were doing their best to improve the treatment of the prisoners. Yet at the very same time they were beating and kicking them. Acts of benevolence could coexist with atrocities, and the perpetrators were not aware of any contradiction. Here is revealed the phenomenon in which morality is subtly blended with power.

Those who have experienced life in a Japanese barracks should have no difficulty in understanding such a state of affairs. The people who exercised power in military establishments found the psychological basis of their control not in any secure self-confidence, but rather in an identification with the power of the nation. When later they were turned adrift and reverted to being lone individuals, no longer able to depend on superior authority, how weak and pitiful they showed themselves to be! At the war crimes trials Tsuchiya turned pale and Furushima wept;[5] but Göring roared with laughter. Among the famous war crimes suspects in Sugamo Prison how many are likely to display the arrogant impudence of a Hermann Göring?

The ill-treatment of prisoners was commonplace in both Germany and Japan. Yet the Japanese type of ill-treatment belongs to an entirely different pattern from the cold-blooded, 'objective' ill-treatment practised by the Germans when, for example, they sacrificed the lives of thousands of prisoners for the sake of medical experiments. In Germany, as in Japan, the State was of course the background against which the atrocities were perpetrated. Yet the attitude towards the victims was different. In Germany the relationship between the perpetrator and his victim was like that between a 'free' subject and a thing (*Sache*). In the case of Japan, on the contrary, the problem of relative position was always involved: in fine, the perpetrator was conscious of the comparative proximity of himself and of his victim to the ultimate value, that is, to the Emperor.

Now this sense of *degree of proximity* to the ultimate value or entity was immensely important in Japan: in fact it was the spiritual motive force that drove, not only the various individual power complexes (the military, the *zaibatsu*, etc.), but the entire national structure. What determined the behaviour of the bureaucrats and of the military was not primarily a sense of legality, but the consciousness of some force that was higher than they were, in other words, that was nearer the ultimate entity. Inasmuch as the formal quality of the national order was not recognized in Japan, it was inevitable that the concept of legality should be poorly developed. The law was not regarded as some general body of regulations that collectively circumscribed the ruler and the ruled, but simply as a concrete weapon of control operating in the hierarchy of authority of which the Emperor was the head.

Accordingly respect for the law mainly took the form of demands directed to those who were below, that is, who were further away from the head of the hierarchy. The application of the complex rules in the Military Service Regulations became increasingly lax as one went up in the hierarchy and increasingly severe as one went down. It is a well-known fact that the people who most brazenly flouted the provisions in the Code of Criminal Procedure regarding arrest, detention, preliminary hearings, and so forth were the Imperial officials themselves. Since the main objective was to preserve and strengthen concrete networks of control, the officials concerned with respect for the law were repeatedly told not to let themselves be hemmed in by 'minor details' in the laws and regulations.

The standard of values, then, that determined a person's position in society and in the nation was based less on social function than on relative distance from the Emperor. Nietzsche characterizes the aristocratic morality as 'the pathos of distance' (*Pathos der Distanz*); for the ruling class of Japan the consciousness of being separated from the 'humble' people increased in proportion with the sense of being near the ultimate value, that is, the Emperor.

Thus the pride of the nobility lay in being 'the bulwark of the Imperial House'; and the very lifeline of the Army and Navy was the independence of the prerogative of supreme command, 'based on the fact that the armed forces are under the personal leadership of His Majesty the Emperor'. What determined the everyday morality of Japan's rulers was neither an abstract consciousness of legality nor an internal sense of right and wrong, nor again any concept of serving the public; it was a feeling of being close to the concrete entity known as the Emperor, an entity that could be directly perceived by the senses. It was therefore only natural that these people should come to identify their own interests with those of the Emperor, and that they should automatically regard their enemies as violators of the Emperor's powers. This type of thinking certainly lay behind the hatred and fear that the leaders of the clan clique[6] felt for the Popular Rights Movement. And it continues to operate even today among the ruling class of Japan.

IV

The identification of morality with power and the constant stress on proximity to the Emperor have an important effect on people's attitudes to their duties. Pride in carrying out one's duties was based not so much on any sense of horizontal specialization (that is, division of labour) as on a consciousness of vertical dependence on the ultimate value. The various pathological phenomena that arose from this state of affairs are perfectly exemplified by the Japanese armed forces. The entire educational apparatus of the military establishment was directed towards cultivating this sort of 'vertical' pride. The primary policy was to identify the armed forces as being the mainstay of the nation, in that 'the military are the essence of the nation and occupy the principal position therein'. The sense of superiority that the military felt towards the 'provincials' (as they so pointedly described civilians) was unmistakably based on the concept of being an *Imperial* force.

Moreover the consciousness of being under the direct control of the Emperor led them to conclude that they were superior to other members of the community, not only in their position within the hierarchy, but in all values. According to General Araki, for example, men from the armed forces often acquire the reputation of being too honest, 'but such criticism in fact reveals the great discrepancy between the level of morality in the forces and that in society as a whole, which makes it difficult for military men to adjust themselves to society as it is now constituted'. Accordingly the military are required to 'purify the spirit of society at large and to strive for its amalgamation with the military spirit'. In the last war it was amply brought home to the Japanese people that there was a 'great discrepancy' between military and general morality — but in the very opposite sense from that intended by General Araki.

The armed forces were thoroughly imbued with this notion of superiority. According to a friend of mine, a pathologist, who was conscripted during the last war and who served for many years as a captain in the Medical Corps, professional medical men in the forces were almost all convinced that the level of medical science was far higher in the military establishment than anywhere in the 'provinces', including university medical centres. In fact the situation was exactly the reverse.

This self-centred pride of the military not only determined their attitude towards the 'provincials' but operated between the various branches of the forces themselves. In *Principal Rules of Strategy*, for example, we find the statement, 'Among the various branches of the armed forces the infantry is the main component and constitutes the nucleus of their association.' When I was mobilized to be drafted as a private in Korea, we had to recite this formula daily, and I can still hear the voice of a certain private when he shouted, 'D'you see? The infantry is the main component of the forces — right at the top! It says "main component of the forces", doesn't it? "Forces" doesn't mean just the Army. It includes the Navy too.' I am not suggesting that even this man actually believed the slogan; but a remark of this kind, however exaggerated, certainly reveals a psychological tendency that pervaded military education.

Thus the individual unit was inspired with a sense of superiority towards other units, the company towards other companies, the administrative squad towards other similar squads; at the same time the N.C.O.s insisted on the gulf that separated them from the 'soldier's nature', and the officers emphasized their superiority to the 'character of the N.C.O.'. Such an approach was the basis of the appalling reputation for self-righteousness and sectionalism that the armed forces acquired during the war.

This sectionalism was rampant not only in the Army and Navy but throughout the entire structure of the Japanese government. It has often been described as 'feudalistic', but that is an oversimplification. The feudalistic impulse to defend one's own particular sphere of interests had its origins in the efforts of each unit to entrench itself in a closed, self-sufficient world. Japanese sectionalism, however, derived from a system according to which every element in society was judged according to its respective connexion, in a direct vertical line, with the ultimate entity. This involved a constant impulse to unite oneself with that entity, and the resultant sectionalism was of a far more active and 'aggressive' type than that associated with feudalism. Here again the military provide a perfect example: while they relied at each point on the fortress provided by their prerogative of supreme command, they tried (in the name of total warfare) to interfere in every single aspect of national life.

We are faced, then, with a situation that might be described as the rarefaction of value. The entire national order is constructed like a chain, with the Emperor as the absolute value entity; and at each link in the chain the intensity of vertical political control varies in proportion to the distance from the Emperor. One might expect this to be ideal soil for the concept of dictatorship, but in fact it was hard for this concept to take root in Japan. For the essential premise of a dictatorship is the existence of a free, decision-making agent, and this is precisely what was lacking in our country: from the apex of the hierarchy to the very bottom it was virtually impossible for a truly free, unregulated individual to exist. Society was so organized that each component group was constantly being regulated by a superior authority, while it was imposing its own authority on a group below.

Much has been made of the dictatorial or despotic measures exercised by the Japanese military during the war; but we must avoid confusing despotism as a fact or a social result with despotism as a concept. The latter is invariably related to a sense of responsibility, and neither the military nor the civilian officials in Japan possessed any such sense.

This emerges in the question of responsibility for starting the war. Whatever may have been the causes for the outbreak of war in 1939, the leaders of Nazi Germany were certainly conscious of a *decision* to embark on hostilities. In Japan, however, the situation was quite different: though it was our country that plunged the world into the terrible conflagration in the Pacific, it has been impossible to find any individuals or groups that are conscious of having started the war. What is the meaning of the remarkable state of affairs in which a country slithered into war, pushed into the vortex by men who were themselves driven by some force that they did not really understand?

The answer lies in the nature of the Japanese oligarchy. It was unfortunate enough for the country to be under oligarchic rule; the misfortune was aggravated by the fact that the rulers were unconscious of actually being oligarchs or despots. The individuals who composed the various branches of the oligarchy did not regard themselves as active regulators but as men who were, on the contrary, being regulated by rules created elsewhere. None of the oligarchic forces in the country could ever become absolute; instead they all coexisted — all of them equally dependent on the ultimate entity and all of them stressing their comparative proximity to that entity. This state of affairs led one German observer to describe Japan as *Das Land der Nebeneinander* ('the land of coexistence'), and there is no doubt that it impeded the development of a sense of subjective responsibility.

During the Eighty-First Diet session,[7] when the extension of the Prime Minister's power was being considered by the Committee on Special Wartime Administrative Legislation, the Prime Minister, General Tōjō, was asked by Mr. Kita Sōichirō whether such power should be regarded as a dictatorship. He replied as follows:

> People often refer to this as a dictatorial government, but I should like to make the matter clear ... The man called Tōjō is no more than a single humble subject. I am just the same as you. The only difference is that I have been given the responsibility of being Prime Minister. To this extent I am different. It is only when I am exposed to the light of His Majesty that I shine. Were it not for this light, I should be no better than a pebble by the roadside. It is because I enjoy the confidence of His Majesty and occupy my present position that I shine. This puts me in a completely different category from those European rulers who are known as dictators.[8]

It is highly suggestive that the Prime Minister who spoke these words should have held greater power than any of his predecessors. For Tōjō's statement provides a candid revelation of the psychology of a timidly faithful Japanese subject: what instantly came to his mind was a proud feeling of superiority, based on the knowledge of being close to the ultimate authority, and a keen sense of being burdened by the spiritual weight of this authority.

In the absence of any free, subjective awareness the individual's actions are not circumscribed by the dictates of conscience; instead he is regulated by the existence of people in a higher class — of people, that is, who are closer to the ultimate value. What takes the place of despotism in such a situation is a phenomenon that may be described as the maintenance of equilibrium by the transfer of oppression. By exercising arbitrary power on those who are below, people manage to transfer in a downward direction the sense of oppression that comes from above, thus preserving the balance of the whole.

This phenomenon is one of the most important heritages that modern Japan received from feudal society. It has been aptly interpreted by Fukuzawa Yukichi as the result of 'attaching too great importance to power', which, as he says, 'has been the rule in human intercourse in Japan ever since the beginning'. Fukuzawa continues as follows:

> [The Japanese] make a clear distinction between the moral codes that apply to people above and to people below, and an equally clear distinction in the field of rights and duties. As a result every individual is in one capacity the victim of coercion, while in another capacity he metes out

coercion to his fellow-men. He both suffers and perpetrates oppression; in one direction he yields, in another he boasts ... Today's joy compensates for yesterday's shame, and thus dissatisfaction is evened out ... Peter is robbed to pay Paul.[9]

This too is reminiscent of military life. But, though the psychology described by Fukuzawa was most intensively expressed in the Army and Navy, it was not limited to these quarters; it was, in fact, embedded in every nook and cranny of the Japanese national order. For what happened in the Meiji Restoration was that by the union of authority with power the preponderant role of force in feudal society was systematically incorporated into the structure of modern Japan.

With the emergence of our country on the world stage the principle of 'transfer of oppression' was extended to the international plane. This can be seen in the campaign in favour of invading Korea, which flared up directly after the Restoration,[10] and in the subsequent dispatch of troops to Formosa. Since the latter part of the Tokugawa Period Japan had never ceased to be conscious of the close and heavy pressure of the Great Powers, and as soon as the country was unified it used its new strength to stage a small-scale imitation of Western imperialism. Just as Japan was subject to pressure from the Great Powers, so she would apply pressure to still weaker countries — a clear case of the transfer psychology.

In this regard it is significant that ever since the Meiji Period demands for a tough foreign policy have come from the common people, that is, from those who are at the receiving end of oppression at home. Again, when we examine the atrocities committed by Japanese forces in China and the Philippines, we are confronted with the unhappy fact that, whoever may have been ultimately responsible, the direct perpetrators were the rank-and-file soldiers. Men who at home were 'mere subjects' and who in the barracks were second-rank privates found themselves in a new role when they arrived overseas: as members of the Emperor's forces they were linked to the ultimate value and accordingly enjoyed a position of infinite superiority. Given the nature of Japanese society, it is no wonder that the masses, who in ordinary civilian or military life have no object to which they can transfer oppression, should, when they find themselves in this position, be driven by an explosive impulse to free themselves at a stroke from the pressure that has been hanging over them. Their acts of brutality are a sad testimony to the Japanese system of psychological compensation.

V

In the psychology of ultra-nationalism what, then, is the real status of the Emperor? Inasmuch as he is the centre of all authority and the fountainhead of all virtue, occupying the apical position in a hierarchy where each element from bottom to top relies progressively on the values belonging to a superior rung, would we be correct in concluding that he alone enjoyed subjective freedom? A comparison with absolute monarchs in the West will provide our answer.

In the early stages of modern European history the absolute monarch was freed from the limitations based on medieval natural law. No longer subject to the control of any contract, he was able to raise himself from being a mere protector of order (*Defensor*

289

Pacis) to being its creator (*Creator Pacis*), and thereby he emerged as the first 'free' individual in the modern period.

What happened at the beginning of modern Japanese history (that is, in the Meiji Restoration) was very different indeed. The amalgamation of spiritual authority with political power was regarded not as any new departure in the concept of sovereignty, but simply as a return to 'the ancient days of the Jimmu Foundation'. Though the Emperor was regarded as the embodiment of ultimate value, he was infinitely removed from the possibility of creating values out of nothing. His Majesty was heir to the Imperial line unbroken for ages eternal and he ruled by virtue of the final injunctions of his ancestors. The Imperial Constitution, granted to the people in 1889, was not regarded as having been created by the Emperor himself; rather it was a document that 'transmitted the immutable law according to which the land has been governed'.

Thus the Emperor too was saddled with a burden — in his case a tradition that derived from the infinitely remote past. It was only because his existence was inextricably involved with the ancestral tradition, in such a way that he and his Imperial Ancestors formed a single unit, that he was regarded as being the ultimate embodiment of internal values. The situation can be represented by a circle in which the Emperor is the centre and in which all the people, whose function it is to 'assist' the Emperor, are situated at their respective distances from the centre; now in this diagram the centre is not a single point but an axis of ordinates (the time dimension) running perpendicular to the plane of the circle. The endless flow of value from the centre towards the circumference is assured by the fact that the axis is infinite, as expressed in the familiar phrase, 'the prosperity of the Imperial Throne coeval with heaven and earth'.[11]

We are now in a position to have a clearer and fuller picture of the world from the standpoint of Japanese ultra-nationalism. Within Japan the standard of values is relative proximity to the central entity; by extending this logic to cover the entire world, the ultra-nationalists engendered a policy of 'causing all the nations to occupy their respective positions [*vis-à-vis* Japan]'. Japan, 'the suzerain country', placed each other country in an order that was based on social status. Once this order was secured there would be peace throughout the world. As one ultra-nationalist writer expressed it, 'The meaning of world history is that the august virtue of His Majesty should shine on all the nations of the world. This will indubitably be accomplished as a manifestation of the martial virtues of the Empire'.[12]

In such a scheme, where everything is based on the idea of an absolute central entity, there is no room for a concept like international law, which is equally binding on all nations. 'When the light of His Majesty's august virtue comes to illuminate the entire world in accordance with the ways of the Divine Land, there can be no such thing as international law.'[13]

The contemporaneousness of the myth of the national foundation has been expounded by Professor Yamada Takao: 'If we cut across the time axis, the events that occurred 2,600 years ago constitute the central layer . . . The happenings in Emperor Jimmu's reign are therefore no ancient tales but facts that exist at this very moment.'[14]

Here we find a truly skilful expression of ultra-nationalist logic according to which the extension of the axis of ordinates (time factor) represents at the same time an enlargement of the circle itself (space factor).

The fact of being 'coeval with heaven and earth' guaranteed the indefinite expansion of the range in which the ultimate value was valid, and conversely the expansion of the 'martial virtues of the Empire' reinforced the absolute nature of the central value. This process spiralled upwards from the time of the Sino–Japanese and Russo–Japanese Wars, through the China Incident and until the Pacific War. August 15 1945, the day that put a period to Japanese imperialism, was also the day when the 'national polity', which had been the foundation of the entire ultra-nationalist structure, lost its absolute quality. Now for the first time the Japanese people, who until then had been mere objects, became free subjects and the destiny of this 'national polity' was committed to their own hands.

Postscript

In this essay I concentrated on the configuration of Japanese nationalism during the Pacific War when it reached its most extreme form; and I tried, in as unified and consistent a way as possible, to identify within the post-Restoration structure of our country the various forces that governed the development of this nationalism. The result is an abstraction derived from historical facts. Accordingly I have deliberately avoided discussing the various stages in the development of the Emperor ideology and the relationship between constitutional and absolutist elements.

I leave it to the reader to decide whether or not the *schema* is arbitrary; but I have little doubt that an abstraction of this sort can be useful in measuring the degree to which the Emperor ideology was 'atomized' after the war.

*   *   *

In 1933 the *Mainichi* newspaper, in co-operation with the War Ministry, produced a film called *Japan in Emergency*. The film included a speech by General Araki, the War Minister; and a chart outlining the structure of the Imperial Way was shown by way of illustration. Since I later discovered that this chart agreed entirely with the theory suggested at the end of my present essay, I append it here.

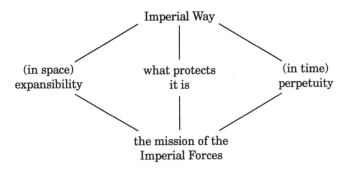

Some readers may conclude from reading this essay on its own that I have overlooked all the progressive momentum and universality in the development of Japan since the

Meiji Period and in nationalist thought as an ideology. I would certainly not wish to give the impression that I have discounted these aspects or that I have dismissed them as being 'pre-modern' or 'special' cases. In my lecture entitled 'Japanese Thought in the Meiji Period' and in *Kuga Katsunan: The Man and His Thought* I made an effort, albeit quite inadequate, to discuss these forward-looking and positive elements in Japanese society and thought.

Notes

1. Biography of Kōnō Hironaka (Baishū), Vol. I.

2. National Polity or *Kokutai*.

3. Araki Sadao, *The Spirit of Soldiers in the Emperor's Land.*

4. *The Way of the Spirit.*

5. Tsuchiya and Furushima were Class C War Criminals charged with atrocities against Allied prisoners of war.

6. The Meiji Oligarchs.

7. This session lasted from December 1942 to March 1943. The façade of constitutionalism was maintained throughout the militarist period.

8. *Ashahi Shimbun*, 6 February 1943.

9. Fukuzawa, *Outline Theory of Civilization,* Vol V.

10. Only four years after the Restoration there was a split in the government relations with Korea. One important group, led by Saigō Takamori, was in favour of sending a punitive expedition to the peninsula on the pretext that Korea had refused Japan's offer to establish relations. After a fierce controversy the 'peace' party won and Saigō and some of his supporters resigned from the government. However, two years later (in 1874) the government sent a small force to Formosa to deal with the aborigines who, it was alleged, had ill-treated Japanese sailors. The mission was successful.

11. Imperial Rescript on Education.

12. Satō Tsūji, *The Philosophy of the Imperial Way.*

13. *Chūō Kōron*. Dec. 1943, symposium, 'How We Must Face Our Country's Danger.'

14. *Ibid.*, Sept. 1943, 'The Mission of Divine Japan and the Resolve of Her People.'

17. Japanese and International Fascism
Karl Radek

The ominous rise of militarism in Japan and the slide of Japanese society into an increasingly authoritarian and nationalistic condition during the early 1930s was seen by two contemporary Soviet scholars, Tanin and Yohan, as reactionary chauvinism rather than fascism. In the introduction to their book, Militarism and Fascism in Japan, *a Marxist writer, Karl Radek, provided both a sustained attack on this view and a reassertion of the contemporary Soviet position which envisaged Japan as a growing fascist menace in the Far East. [Editor].*

. . . The military–fascist movement of Japan is one of those mechanisms which are to bring about the transition of Japan from a state of camouflaged war to one of open imperialist world war. It is necessary to uncover the fuse which leads to the explosives in the Far East hidden in the cause of peace . . .

I shall confine myself to one question put by the authors in the last chapter of their work, the question *of the resemblance and differences between Japanese and European fascism*, a question of great import for the appraisal of the perspectives of development in the Far East. Such comparison would not only permit us to draw attention to . . . the perspectives of the military–fascist movement in Japan, but would also give us the opportunity to emphasize more strongly the tremendous importance of those forces which, at present, rock imperialist Japan.

The authors ask: "Can this whole reactionary chauvinist movement be called 'fascist' in the West European sense of the word?" They answer this question in the negative, and they advance the following reason for their negative answer: ". . . if we investigate it [this movement] as a whole we find that it is characterized by two distinct traits in which it differs from, say, Italian or German fascism."

What are those distinct features?

The first difference amounts to this — that West European fascism is primarily an instrument of finance capital, while the Japanese reactionary chauvinist movement, taken as a whole, is the instrument not only of finance capital but also of the Japanese monarchy which represents a bloc of two class forces: finance capital and semi-feudal landowners, and besides this possesses the logic of its own development, represented by the army and monarchist bureaucracy whose oppression has an independent significance. That is why at the center of the Japanese reactionary chauvinist movement we find principally the same people who head the system of Japanese military–feudal imperialism. Hence, the role of the army as the backbone of the reactionary chauvinist movement taken as a whole.

Karl Radek: 'Can the Reactionary–Chauvinist Movement in Japan be called Fascist?' Extracts from the Introduction to *MILITARISM AND FASCISM IN JAPAN*, by O. Tanin and E. Yohan (Martin Lawrence, 1934; International Publishers, 1934), pp. 6–22. Reprinted by permission of Lawrence & Wishart and International Publishers Co.

The second distinguishing trait of the Japanese reactionary chauvinist movement, characteristic of the most important and so far the most influential wing of it, follows from this. It is the limited use of social demagogy by the reactionary chauvinist movement as a whole.

Before we put this motivation to an analysis, it is necessary to point out that only such phenomena may be compared with each other which have resemblance as well as points of difference. Phenomena having no resemblance cannot be compared at all. It is therefore methodologically wrong when the authors speak only of the distinctions between the military–fascist movement in Japan and European fascism, and say nothing about their resemblance, although the very term "military–fascist movement" indicates that they do see this resemblance. The failure to analyze the features of resemblance inevitably leads to one-sidedness which Lenin often called an "exaggeration of the truth."

Fascism is a phase in the development of monopoly capitalism at a certain stage in its decay, disintegration, crisis. Wherever monopoly capitalism was victorious it created a tendency to replace democracy, the hidden form of the dictatorship of big capital, by its more or less open forms. From the very moment of the rise of modern imperialism there were tendencies indicated in its policy which, as long ago as the end of the nineteenth and the beginning of the twentieth century, made it possible to talk about the crisis of democracy. Not only the representatives of the revolutionary proletariat, not only the representatives of petty-bourgeois opposition and rebellious currents — anarchists and syndicalists — spoke of this crisis, it was noted also by the representatives of feudal and semi-feudal reaction (*cf.* the literature of French royalists, of the German reactionary groups as, for instance, Delbruck), it was noticed by business men, who described the growing power of the finance oligarchy. The literature dealing with American internal politics at the end of the nineteenth and the beginning of the twentieth century abounds in works revealing the decay of bourgeois democracy.

The concentration of power in the hands of capitalist monopolies, trusts and cartels had led even before the war to a state where the decision on all basic questions of policy passed over from the government to uncontrolled, closed capitalist cliques, which influenced the government not through parliamentary channels, but by direct corruption, by the power within the bourgeois parties being transferred to small groups financing these parties and dictating their will to them. All these processes led not only to the weakening of parliamentary democracy, but to the actual curtailing of all so-called rights and liberties, without which bourgeois democracy would be unthinkable. Constant attacks upon the freedom of workers' organizations, upon the right of assembly, freedom of speech, etc., had taken place in the pre-war years in a number of capitalist countries, turning bourgeois democracy more and more into an empty shell, its contents removed.

This process continued at an accelerated tempo during the war, because the war had accentuated the class conflicts to such an extent that the bourgeoisie doubted whether it would be able to realize its aims by way of democracy at all. The military régime did not remove parliamentarism in the leading capitalist countries. Even in the most democratic countries, as, for instance, France, democracy became a means by which the most energetic imperialist cliques came to power (Clemenceau in France), but the "lower" base of bourgeois democracy was disappearing to a considerable extent. Democratic liberties were taken away immediately from proletarian groups *protesting against the imperialist war*. Even petty-bourgeois groups and Social-Democracy, which sided with imperialism, did not escape the same lot. The military cliques, realizing that large masses of the people are still behind the parties of the Second International, feared that the usual democratic liberties even when granted to Social-Democracy, which was supporting the war, would give vent to the discontent of the working masses through the Social-Democratic organizations. The Second International represented the situation as a matter of only a temporary sacrifice, a temporary surrender of democratic liberties, dictated by higher considerations — "Defense of the Fatherland." They asserted that after the war, the proletariat, as a reward for saving the fatherland, would be given an abundance of rights. They were even convinced that, together with this expected abundance of rights, a new era of social reforms would set in.

The years immediately following the world imperialist war, confirmed, as it seemed, these assumptions. They led to the expansion of women's suffrage in England, to the downfall of the empires of the Hohenzollerns and the Hapsburgs, to the creation of republics in the whole of central Europe and in a considerable part of eastern Europe, to the introduction of the eight-hour day and social insurance on a scale unknown before. In a number of countries, including even England, the parties of the Second International came to power. But even at that time this apparent growth of democracy in the countries where capitalism, fearing the proletarian revolution, was putting on democratic airs, was accompanied by violent suppression of the revolutionary movement and of the class organizations of the proletariat. If, in the pre-war period, monopoly capitalism, while emptying the shell of parliamentarism of its contents, outwardly left all the democratic rights of the workers intact (only curtailing them), the bourgeoisie now, with the power of monopoly capitalism constantly increasing behind the scenes, recognized the democratic rights only for those sections of the people which followed the parties supporting its rule. Bourgeois democracy became a democracy for slave-owners and for obedient slaves.

The rise to power of Italian fascism in 1922 marks a certain boundary line in the history of the decay of bourgeois democracy. Italian fascism outlawed not only the revolutionary, but also the reformist sections of the working class, and later even liquidated *Populare*, the reactionary petty-bourgeois party. It has openly abolished all the institutions of bourgeois democracy: parliament, the legal existence of bourgeois political parties, and all the principal democratic rights. Hurriedly waving aside and casting off all vestiges of syndicalist and socialist phrases, Italian fascism, using socialist criticism of liberalism, free competition and capitalist monopoly, has created the theory of the corporate state which, in practice, only covers up the rule of private capitalist organizations, slightly disguised as organs of state capitalist control. The victory of Italian fascism signified that the ruling sections of the bourgeoisie — from the landlords to the big bankers — no longer found it possible to retain power with bourgeois democracy in existence. The right to agitate and organize, which bourgeois democracy had formerly granted to the masses of the people, began to threaten the very existence of monopoly capitalism in those countries where conditions for the development of capitalism were most unstable. The seizure of factories by Italian workers in 1920 had been correctly interpreted by the Italian bourgeoisie as the approach of the proletarian revolution. It found itself helpless in the face of this movement. Giolitti, one of the cleverest statesmen of the Italian bourgeoisie, refused to use armed force against the workers in the occupied factories for two reasons: first, he knew that the army and police forces would not suffice, and, secondly, he realized that bringing troops into those factories might accelerate the approach of the revolution. The bourgeoisie was saved then by the reformist centrist leadership of the Italian Socialist Party, which had disorganized the entire movement. But the bourgeoisie understood too well that the consequence of the betrayal of the working class by the centrists and reformists would be the shifting of the working masses towards communism, the crystallization of a true revolutionary leadership which would secure victory during the next offensive of the working class. Therefore, the bourgeoisie decided to remove this danger once and for all by abolishing the entire democratic system, setting up an organization strong enough to safeguard capitalism from new dangers. This could not be the narrow organization of the conservative groups, as this organization would have met vehement resistance on the part of the workers and peasants, and could not have obtained any other support except that of the army and the police. The new counter-revolutionary organization had to be a mass organization, as its task was to fight the mass revolutionary movement. In order to become a mass organization, it had to make its appearance under a pseudo-revolutionary banner, use the slogans of social demagogy, and thus divert the social discontent of the backward vacillating masses away from monopoly capitalism.

The victory of Italian fascism accelerated the ripening of fascist ideas in almost all the capitalist countries. But only the gravest economic crisis, which broke out on the background of the general post-war crisis of capitalism, brought about the victory of the second mass fascist organization set up in a highly developed capitalist country, namely, in Germany. I shall not dwell here on the differences between German and Italian fascism, or on the distinctions of their development. My aim here is to stress their similarities. German capitalism is more highly developed than Italian. But, defeated in the World War, deprived of its big army, navy, naval bases and colonies, German capitalism proved unable to compete with the great imperialist powers — just as Italian imperialism, too, despite its pretensions, was unable to compete because of the insufficiency of its raw material base, its inadequate capitalist accumulations and the lack of rich colonies. This inability to compete with England, the United States and France put German post-war monopoly capitalism in a worse position in the struggle against the growing danger of a proletarian revolution, which in 1918–1923 had been disrupted by German Social-Democracy. In the period of the temporary stabilization of capitalism, during which German capitalism regained a considerable part of its old positions on the world market, the German bourgeoisie was still able to retain its power, thanks to the assistance of Social-Democracy and to the fact that any attempt at revolutionary action on the part of the working class was suppressed. While making use of Social-Democracy as its main bulwark, the German bourgeoisie supported the fascist movement, partly as a means of bringing pressure to bear on Social-Democracy and of forcing it to decrease its demands, partly as a substitute for Social Democracy in the future. The world economic crisis, which dealt the severest blows at Germany, confronted the German bourgeoisie with the problem of the imminent danger of a new revolution. No one could tell how long this crisis would continue. Its continuation carried with it the menace that the influence of German communism might grow to such an extent that the question of its winning over the majority of the working class — this main prerequisite of the struggle for the seizure of power — might become a question of the immediate future. Besides this, the crisis has let loose in all capitalist countries all centrifugal forces, tendencies to autarchy, i.e., to carve out from the capitalist world the largest possible slice of territory as a closed field of exploitation for the monopolist bourgeoisie of the given nation. The German bourgeoisie had to take care to remove the danger of a proletarian revolution and, simultaneously, to create conditions for the utilization of the growing imperialist contradictions in order to create its own autarchic economic organism, i.e., to conquer new colonies. These two problems could only be solved by destroying the remains of bourgeois democracy; without this, it was impossible either to defer or postpone the danger of a revolution, or to create the most favorable conditions for a new imperialist war.

The crisis, arousing a growing discontent among the broad petty-bourgeois masses, has created the necessary conditions for the victory of fascism as a mass organization and has, at the same time, made it impossible to struggle against the danger of revolution by any other means than fascist dictatorship. Hard hit by the crisis, the petty-bourgeois masses in town and countryside began to leave the ranks of the old bourgeois parties and fell under the influence of the Nationalist Party, which promised to save them from ruin while safeguarding private property. The disappearance of the old bourgeois parties was drawing nearer every day and made it impossible for them to continue their rule, even with the support of Social-Democracy; which gave up one democratic liberty after another in the name of the policy of the "lesser evil" — that is, in order to avoid a complete victory of fascism. This policy, on the contrary, has only weakened Social-Democracy as a bulwark of the bourgeoisie, because it has driven one section of the Social-Democratic workers after another into the camp of communism, thus increasing the danger of a proletarian revolution. The idea of the rule of a military–bureaucratic clique, which found its expression in the government of Von Papen and Schleicher proved an idle fancy, since it was impossible to rule by purely bureaucratic methods, relying only on the police and army, opposed by the revolutionary workers and by millions of the petty-bourgeois masses who had been drawn into the National-Socialist movement. In view of the spirit among the working masses, caused by Social-Democracy and not surmounted by the Communist Party, in view of the fact that the crisis had for the time being impelled considerable masses of the petty-bourgeoisie to go to the Right, into the ranks of fascism, the proletarian vanguard could not set itself the task of an immediate struggle for the seizure of power. This was how the victory of fascism became possible. The dictatorship of fascism is the dictatorship of monopoly capitalism and the task it sets itself is to seek a way out of the crisis, to escape revolution through an imperialist war and, as a result of this, to create a new German imperialist power, able to compete with other imperialist powers and to fight the revolutionary proletariat.

Summing up the phases of development of fascism in western Europe, it must be noted that its basic features are as follows: In the first place, fascism develops on the economic basis of the domination of monopoly capitalism, which is no longer able to solve the main economic problems facing society, which is feeling the approach of the social revolution and which is experiencing an ever-deepening crisis. That means that reaction in countries of undeveloped capitalism, which have not yet reached the stage of monopoly capitalism, is not homogeneous with fascism, although it possesses many features in common with fascism (combination of savage terrorism with social demagogy). The absence of the domination of finance capital as an economic basis of fascism prevents those reactionary régimes from being the last phase of development on the way to socialism. They can still be swept away by bourgeois-democratic revolutions of a sufficiently prolonged character or even by some hybrid democratic régime, which may appear as the heir to a bankrupt reactionary régime, even without a revolution.

The second feature of fascism consists in the fact that it is not merely the bureaucratic rule of reactionary cliques, but a dictatorship resting upon mass organizations, mostly petty-bourgeois; that it combines the greatest terrorism against workers and revolutionary peasants with an unbridled social demagogy, which tries to cause disintegration among the working class, to draw over the most backward *lumpen*-proletarian sections of the working class into the camp of fascism. Fascism is not a mere restoration of bourgeois power. Such a restoration is an idle fancy, because in all countries of developed capitalism the old bourgeois power rested upon the support of the broad masses of the petty-bourgeoisie and even of the backward workers, who supported all bourgeois and "Socialist" parties whose platform was the reform of capitalism. These masses were subordinated to the bourgeoisie through the medium of bourgeois democracy. Wherever bourgeois democracy has been done away with, it occurred precisely because the masses of the petty-bourgeoisie and of the proletariat have lost their faith in the stability of the capitalist system and have been leaving the ranks of the bourgeois parties in greater numbers every day.

Fascist dictatorship is not simply a reactionary dictatorship, like the régime of Horthy or Tsankov.* It is a dictatorship of finance capital, which has been able, by employing a number of new methods, to secure for itself the support of the petty bourgeoisie by means of a demagogic policy and mass organizations.

Do these two features of fascism — (1) the domination of a monopoly capitalism, which has already been shaken, which fears a proletarian revolution, which is seeking an escape from it by way of a fascist state organization within the country, and a new war with the object of a redivision of the world, and (2) a striving to create, as a bulwark for capitalism, a mass petty-bourgeois movement, hoodwinked by Social-Democratic slogans — exist in Japan? Undoubtedly these two features do exist. Finance capital rules in Japan. Students who stress the peculiar traits of the rule of finance capital in Japan — the fact that it still rules to a large extent through the monopoly of banks, through the exploitation of the small and middle *entrepreneurs* and the scattered small farmers by the banks, the fact that it has merged to a great extent with the survivals

* Reactionary dictatorships in Hungary and Bulgaria.—Ed.

of feudalism — such students are absolutely right. For instance, the book by J. Orchard [*Japan's Economic Position.* — Ed.], pointing out this peculiarity in the rule of monopoly capitalism in Japanese industry, as well as G. Safarov's foreword to this book, giving as it does a concrete description of the survivals of feudalism on the Japanese countryside and their intertwining with the rule of monopoly capitalism, correctly indicate, despite some exaggerations, those peculiarities which will acquire great significance in the further development of the Japanese crisis. The importance of these factors lies, first, in the fact that insufficient concentration and inadequate technical modernization of Japanese industry do not allow Japanese finance capital to develop that strength without which Japanese imperialism, to employ the correct expression of one of our students of Japanese affairs, may prove a "powerful fist upon very feeble muscles." The Japanese militarists are well aware of this weakness and during the last two years they have done all in their power to concentrate industry and equip it with modern technique. Nevertheless, despite the large sums invested in industry during the last two years by the Japanese government and Japanese financial trusts, they have not succeeded in removing this backwardness to any considerable extent. The exceptional parasitism of the Japanese landlord, who squeezes out of the countryside 50 per cent of its annual income, and the presence of survivals of feudalism in all spheres of rural life, are a pledge that the future will bring with it a broad upswing of the democratic revolutionary movement among the peasantry. However, important as these peculiarities are, we cannot evade that question which is indeed the crux of all questions. And in considering Japanese imperialism and Japanese fascism, the question is: Who is economic master in Japan — monopoly capitalism or the survivals of feudalism? To this question there can be only one answer.

The development of Japan since 1868 denotes the rise and triumph of industrial capitalism, its transition to monopoly capitalism. The landowner class of Japan — a survival of the feudal class which was not swept away in 1868 — has managed to retain, though in a modified form, its right to collect tribute from the peasantry. To this end they have used the state power, which they have retained to a considerable extent in their own hands. But this power has at the same time served as a means of strengthening finance capital, has served to assist its victory over all other classes in Japan, has served as a weapon in its struggle for the world market and for winning positions on the Asiatic continent. The landowner class, which invests in industry and banks the capital which it squeezes out of the peasantry, is itself a part of the monopolist bourgeoisie. Inasmuch as its interests as a rent collector have conflicted with its interests as a profit owner, it could get its own specific interests served at the expense of the general development of the economic forces of the country. But the landowner class of Japan, thus strengthening the role of monopoly capital as a brake on the development of the productive forces, could not rule in contradiction to the basic interests of monopoly capitalism. From the capitalist development of Japan the landowner tried to snatch for himself as much as possible, but he could not pursue a policy which did not conform to the basic interests of monopoly capitalism.

The entire economic and political crisis of Japan is unfolding against a background formed by the crisis of monopoly capitalism, although this crisis is deepened and complicated by the presence of survivals of feudalism. The social and political crisis of

Japan has the same causes as the crisis of the entire capitalist system. Monopoly capitalism has lost the ability to secure the development of the productive forces. Every one of its attempts to do this by way of improved technique or rationalization leads to a tremendous intensification of the distress and unemployment of the masses, enhances the social crisis. The attempt of Japanese monopoly capitalism to conquer new markets for the sale of its products leads to the tremendous sharpening of international imperialist antagonisms, compels it to arm at frantic speed. These armaments, undermining as they do the economic forces of the countryside, impose an unheard-of burden on the masses of the working class and of the urban and petty bourgeoisie, and, in their turn, weaken the productive forces of the country. The attempt to conquer parts of China, in order to create an autarchic Japanese colonial empire on the continent, having its own iron and coal and forming a market closed to other imperialist powers, leads to increasing conflict with the masses, who do not want to become the colonial slaves of Japan, and to a conflict with other imperialist powers, above all with the United States.

Such are the bases of the crisis which Japan is experiencing. It is only a modification of the general crisis which is being experienced by monopoly capitalism. Under the circumstances, the danger of a proletarian revolution in Japan is beyond doubt and arises from fundamentally the same sources as in other countries — from the domination of monopoly capitalism. Survivals of feudalism in Japan, sharpening as they do the antagonisms of interests between the peasantry and the landlord class, create the danger of revolutionary peasant movements and thus create conditions for the support of a proletarian revolution by a peasant war. No matter whether the outcome of the political crisis in Japan begins with a peasant war or with proletarian revolutionary movement, the existence of survivals of feudalism makes the solution of the problems of the democratic revolution in Japan indispensable and inevitable. The development of a proletarian revolution in Japan will be the consequence of the democratic revolution growing over into a socialist revolution. The fundamental significance of the idea of this process of growing over is that it should teach the proletariat not to skip over the tasks of the democratic revolution, not to forget for a moment that the peasantry is one of the motive forces of the Japanese revolution, that an alliance with the peasantry is the condition for the coming victory of the proletariat.

However, the fact that survivals of feudalism exist in Japan, and that consequently there is a prospect of a proletarian revolution in Japan growing out of the bourgeois-democratic revolution, does not do away with the fact that the degree of development reached by Japanese capitalism is one of monopoly capitalism. The outcome of the crisis of monopoly capitalism can only be a social revolution, no matter through how many stages it will have to pass. The crisis in Japan is developing on the basis of monopoly capitalism, and the Japanese bourgeoisie, seeking a way out of the crisis by way of imperialist aggression and fascism, is seeking salvation from a proletarian revolution and is struggling for such terms of competition with other imperialist powers as may enable her to avoid a proletarian revolution in the future as well. There is, therefore, not the slightest doubt that Japanese fascism is in the main trying to solve those very problems which German and Italian fascism are also trying to solve. When the authors of this book write that:

> West European fascism is in the main a tool of finance capital, while the
> Japanese reactionary chauvinist movement, taken as a whole, is a tool not
> of finance capital alone, but also of Japanese monarchy, which represents
> a *bloc* of two class forces — finance capital and semifeudal landlords,

they are mistaken both with regard to western European and with regard to Japanese fascism in that they contrast the landlords to finance capitalism.

The Italian landowners, trying to escape the onslaught of the farm laborers and small tenants, played a great role in the victory of Italian fascism. The role of the German *Junkers* in the victory of German fascism is known to the whole world. Detachments of fascist murderers were reared on the Mecklenburg, Pomeranian and East-Elbian estates, long before gold from the iron safes of captains of industry began to pour into the pockets of fascism. A good many of the leaders of German fascism are sons of landowners. German fascism came to power easily thanks to the support given it by the Prussian *Junker*, Field-Marshal Hindenburg, and the officers of the *Reichswehr*, who consisted of Prussian *Junkers*. That is why German fascism does not dare to infringe upon the interests of the East-Elbian landowners, notwithstanding the fact that it has to play the role of a party whose alleged aim is to save the peasantry. Owing to the fact that the survivals of feudalism in Japan are stronger than in Italy and even in Germany, the role of the landlords in the military–fascist movement of Japan is surely more powerful. But, in the main, it cannot differ from the role of the landowners in the European fascist movement, because fascism in Japan, by its armaments policy, is above all filling the pockets of finance capital. Having seized power completely, the policy which it pursued in the economic sphere could only be one which in the main suited the interests of monopoly capital. By their participation in the fascist movement, the landowners have secured for themselves a special portion of the general imperialist loot, just as the German and Italian landowners did. It is possible that their share in the partition of the temporary plunder will be even larger. But that does not mean that any of the bases of Japanese fascism are fundamentally different from the fascism of western Europe.

The second feature of the fascist movement, namely the search for a bulwark among the broad petty-bourgeois masses, who are attracted by a broad demagogic social program, is to be observed in Japan no less than in Europe.

This very book offers thousands of proofs that there is not one social idea, promulgated for demagogic purposes by European fascism, which is not to be found in the arsenal of the fascist movement in Japan. Could there be a better example of social demagogy than when Japanese noblemen spoke at the trial of Inukai's murderers as defenders of workers and peasants? It is precisely thanks to this social demagogy, that Japanese military–fascist organizations have succeeded in mobilizing huge masses of the petty bourgeoisie who have been set in motion by the social and political crisis in Japan. The authors of this book are right when they prove that the figures produced by Japanese fascists to show the strength of their organization are greatly exaggerated. But it would also be a mistake to underrate these forces. The point is not whether the Japanese fascists have millions of adherents, united into special fascist party organizations, or whether these millions are in mass organizations of a general patriotic nature, created by the bureaucrats and militarists. The decisive question is whether those people who control these mass organizations, although officially non-fascist, serve fascism or not, and what kind of ideas they propound in these organizations. The German Steel Helmet organization was not a fascist party organization; it was an organization which a part of the German landowners and a part of German industry tried to oppose to the fascist organization. The Steel Helmets were at one time more numerous than Hitler's storm troops. But as the Steel Helmets, with the party of the German Nationalists behind it, did not have any ideas which distinguished them from the Hitlerites or which they might have opposed to the Hitlerites, they finally became subordinate to Hitler and, from an organization competing with him, turned into an additional reservoir for the forces of German fascism. The distrust felt by the bureaucratic military leaders of Japan for an organization of the petty-bourgeois masses, their fear of this organization, is driving the military clique towards an attempt to seize power without any organization of a fascist mass party, just as in Germany this same fear of the petty-bourgeois masses led to the formation of the government of von Papen and Schleicher, who tried to retain power without Hitler, and, to some extent, against him. But that government was no more than an episode, for, without the support of mass fascist organizations, it was left hanging in the air. The course of development in Japan is difficult to foretell, but if the Araki group seizes complete power by way of backstairs machinations, backed by the pressure of the upper strata of the officers, then this group will have to look for support to the fascist organizations. Whether it is a government basing itself on fascist organizations, or whether it develops into a government of the fascist organizations — its social composition will be the same: it will be a dictatorship of monopoly capitalism, forced to give great consideration to the interest of the landowners; and in either case the petty bourgeoisie will not govern, but serve only as a mass bulwark for the domination of monopoly capitalism.

The peculiarities of Japanese fascism consist to a certain extent in the more considerable part played by the landlords in the organization of Japanese fascism in the spirit of the Middle Ages, or, to speak more exactly, of those legends about the Middle Ages with which the leaders of Japanese fascism are trying to imbue the masses of the people. Here, however, we are dealing with secondary, not with primary differences. The most important, though still not the main, difference is the role of the Japanese army as organizer and leader of the fascist movement. In Italy the army officers did not play this role, although a number of the higher commanders sided with fascism. The Italian army did not come out of the World War crowned with glory, while the masses of the Italian people were utterly war-weary. It was therefore only after its victory that Italian fascism got the army under its control. In Germany it was only the younger generation of the former imperial army — those who had not entered the *Reichswehr* — who played a leading role in the fascist movement. The *Reichswehr* secretly rendered aid to the fascist organizations, supplying them with arms and instructors. However, from military–political considerations and partly owing to its connection with the old bourgeois parties and their regime, it was unable to play a leading role in the rise and victory of German fascism. In Japan, however, we see the higher officers playing this leading role in the organization of fascist forces. This is going so far that even the split in the ranks of Japanese Social-Democracy and the formation of an open fascist "socialist" party are effected with the direct participation of extreme fascist elements from among the higher Japanese officers (the group of Colonel Hasimoto of the general staff). This role of the Japanese officers in the organization of fascism is to be explained, on the one hand, by the halo which surrounds them as the organizers of the victorious war against Russia in 1904–05, and on the other hand, by the fact that the ruin of a considerable part of the small and middle landowners, from whom the most of the officers are recruited, and the degradation of Japanese agriculture are creating social unrest among the officers, allying them with the discontented petty-bourgeoisie, from whom a part of the officers also comes. The role of the Japanese officers as leaders of the fascist movement has created among the higher circles of these officers, rallied around General Araki, the illusion that this group can seize power alone, without the participation of fascist petty-bourgeois organizations, which the Araki group does not try to unite apparently from fear of giving them too much importance. But this policy arouses discontent among a section of the junior officers, headed by the former military attaché to the U.S.S.R., Colonel Hasimoto, who declares that the officers are not able to rule Japan and that unless they create a mass fascist party as their bulwark, they will be routed by communism which is undoubtedly developing into a mass organized power. The purely fascist tendency represented by Hasimoto, which will increase in strength with the growth of the social crisis in Japan, shows that here too there are forces which (as far as the role of the army in the fascist movement is concerned) bring Japanese fascism close to the European type.

The mistakes committed by the authors of this work flow from two sources. One of these is that from a legitimate fear of underrating the importance of survivals of feudalism they have in their final formulations been guilty to a certain extent of going to the other extreme. The other is that the historical exposition of the development of the Japanese fascist movement leaves an excessively marked imprint on their theoretical deductions. The fascist movement in Japan has its roots in the bureaucratic–military organization of the Black Dragon, which in the past was the main secret organization of budding Japanese imperialism. But despite its landowner–bureaucratic composition this organization, serving as it did the aims of Japanese expansionism, was in the last analysis a tool of monopoly capitalism. Here we may observe a strong analogy with the development of the Pan-German League, which played such a tremendous part in the history of German imperialism. The Pan-German League was formed by bureaucratic and military circles; the part played in it by the nobility was a very significant one, but it served as a pioneer of German imperialism, which was the result of the development of German monopoly capitalism. Marxist analysis cannot of course disregard the social composition of any political organization, but it does admit that this social composition is the decisive factor in determining the social character of a given movement; it asks what class interests in the last analysis are directing this movement. The parties of the Second International in all capitalist countries are in the majority of cases still workers' parties in their composition, but they are bourgeois parties in the character of their policy, because, renouncing the revolutionary struggle, they cannot pursue any other policy than that dictated by the interests of the bourgeoisie. The fascist parties in western Europe are, in their composition, petty-bourgeois parties. Their leading strata in them are to a large extent landowners, but they pursue a policy of defending the interests of finance capital, which represents the leading force of a capitalist society which has reached the stage of monopoly capitalism. And the same holds true of Japan, although the leading role in the fascist movement of that country is played by the landowners and the higher bureaucracy.

18. Plan for the Reorganization of Japan
Kita Ikki

An Outline Plan for the Reorganization of Japan (Nihon Kaizō hōan taikō) *contained Kita's suggestions for changes necessary in Japanese society. Written in 1919 while Kita was still in Shanghai, the book was printed secretly and passed from hand to hand by Kita's associates. In 1920 its distribution was forbidden by the police. In 1923, after major excisions, the book was published, only to be banned again shortly afterward. A third edition came in 1926, but it too was later banned.*

The Outline Plan, *of which the opening section is given below, consists of cryptic announcements of steps to be taken followed by notes which justify the steps and anticipate probable objections.*

[From *Nihon Kaizō hōan,* pp. 6–14]

Kita Ikki (1884–1937) was a major ideological influence on the Imperial Way faction within the armed forces and he is often taken to be the founder of Japanese fascism. Kita's radical right-wing ideas comprised both a hatred of the big capitalist zaibatsu *and a desire for greater economic equality along with supreme reverence for the Emperor and a belief in Japan's mission in Asia. These ideas had inspired army officers to instigate a number of attempted coup d'états in the 1930s but Kita's involvement in the insurrection and assassinations that occurred during one such incident in Central Tokyo in February 1936 led to his trial and execution. [Editor]*

At present the Japanese empire is faced with a national crisis unparalleled in its history; it faces dilemmas at home and abroad. The vast majority of the people feel insecure in their livelihood and they are on the point of taking a lesson from the collapse of European societies, while those who monopolize political, military, and economic power simply hide themselves and, quaking with fear, try to maintain their unjust position. Abroad, neither England, America, Germany, nor Russia has kept its word, and even our neighbor China, which long benefited from the protection we provided through the Russo–Japanese War, not only has failed to repay us but instead despises us. Truly we are a small island, completely isolated in the Eastern Sea. One false step and our nation will again fall into the desperate state of crisis — dilemmas at home and abroad — that marked the period before and after the Meiji Restoration.

The only thing that brightens the picture is the sixty million fellow countrymen with whom we are blessed. The Japanese people must develop a profound awareness of the great cause of national existence and of the people's equal rights, and they need an unerring, discriminating grasp of the complexities of domestic and foreign thought. The Great War in Europe was, like Noah's flood, Heaven's punishment on them for arrogant and rebellious ways. It is of course natural that we cannot look to the Europeans, who are out of their minds because of the great destruction, for a completely detailed set of plans. But in contrast Japan, during those five years of

Kita Ikki: 'Plan for the Reorganization of Japan' from *SOURCES OF JAPANESE TRADITION*, edited by William Theodore DeBary (Columbia University Press, 1958), pp. 6–14.

destruction, was blessed with five years of fulfilment. Europe needs to talk about reconstruction, while Japan must move on to reorganization. The entire Japanese people, thinking calmly from this perspective which is the result of Heaven's rewards and punishments, should, in planning how the great Japanese empire should be reorganized, petition for a manifestation of the imperial prerogative establishing "a natural opinion in which no dissenting voice is heard, by the organization of a great union of the Japanese people." Thus, by homage to the emperor, a basis for national reorganization can be set up.

Truly, our seven hundred million brothers in China and India have no path to independence other than that offered by our guidance and protection. And for our Japan, whose population has doubled within the past fifty years, great areas adequate to support a population of at least two hundred and forty or fifty millions will be absolutely necessary a hundred years from now. For a nation, one hundred years are like a hundred days for an individual. How can those who are anxious about these inevitable developments, or who grieve over the desperate conditions of neighboring countries, find their solace in the effeminate pacifism of doctrinaire socialism? I do not necessarily rule out social progress by means of the class struggle. But still, just what kind of so-called science is it that can close its eyes to the competition between people and nations which has taken place throughout the entire history of mankind? At a time when the authorities in the European and American revolutionary creeds have found it completely impossible to arrive at an understanding of the "gospel of the sword" because of their superficial philosophy, the noble Greece of Asian culture must complete her national reorganization on the basis of her own national polity. At the same time, let her lift the virtuous banner of an Asian league and take the leadership in a world federation which must come. In so doing let her proclaim to the world the Way of Heaven in which all are children of Buddha, and let her set the example which the world must follow. So the ideas of people like those who oppose arming the nation are after all simply childish.

Section One: The People's Emperor

Suspension of the Constitution. In order for the emperor and the entire Japanese people to establish a secure base for the national reorganization, the emperor will, by a show of his imperial prerogative, suspend the Constitution for a period of three years, dissolve both houses of the Diet, and place the entire nation under martial law.

(Note 1: In extraordinary times the authorities should of course ignore harmful opinions and votes. To regard any sort of constitution or parliament as an absolute authority is to act in direct imitation of the English and American semisacred "democracy." Those who do so are the obstinate conservatives who hide the real meaning of "democracy"; they are as ridiculous as those who try to argue national polity on the basis of the [Shintō mythological] High Plain of Heaven. It cannot be held that in the discussion of plans for naval expansion Admiral Tōgō's vote was not worth more than the three cast by miserable members of the Diet. The effect of government by votes which has prevailed hitherto is really nothing more than a maintenance of the traditional order; it puts absolute emphasis on numbers and ignores those who would put a premium on quality.)

(Note 2: Those who look upon a *coup d'état* as an abuse of power on behalf of a conservative autocracy ignore history. Napoleon's *coup d'état* in refusing to cooperate with reactionary elements offered the only out for the Revolution at a time when the parliament and the press were alive with royalist elements. And even though one sees in the Russian Revolution an incident in which Lenin dissolved with machine guns a parliament filled with obstructionists, the popular view is still that a *coup d'état* is a reactionary act.)

(Note 3: A *coup d'état* should be looked upon as a direct manifestation of the authority of the nation; that is, of the will of society. The progressive leaders have all arisen from popular groups. They arise because of political leaders like Napoleon and Lenin. In the reorganization of Japan there must be a manifestation of the power inherent in a coalition of the people and sovereign.)

(Note 4: The reason why the Diet must be dissolved is that the nobility and the wealthy upon whom it depends are incapable of standing with the emperor and the people in the cause of reorganization. The necessity for suspension of the constitution is that these people seek protection in the law codes enacted under it. The reason martial law must be proclaimed is that it is essential for the freedom of the nation that there be no restraint in suppressing the opposition which will come from the above groups.

However, it will also be necessary to suppress those who propagate a senseless and half-understood translation of outside revolutionary creeds as the agents of reorganization.)

The True Significance of the Emperor. The fundamental doctrine of the emperor as representative of the people and as pillar of the nation must be made clear.

In order to clarify this a sweeping reform of the imperial court in the spirit the Emperor Jimmu in founding the state and in the spirit of the great Meiji emperor will be carried out. The present Privy Councillors and other officials will be dismissed from their posts, and in their place will come talent, sought throughout the realm, capable of assisting the emperor.

A Consultative Council (*Kōmonin*)will be established to assist the emperor. Its members, fifty in number, will be appointed by the emperor.

A member of the Consultative Council must tender his resignation to the emperor whenever the cabinet takes action against him or whenever the Diet passes a vote of nonconfidence against him. However, the council members are by no means responsible to either the cabinet or to the Diet.

(Note 1: Japan's national polity has evolved through three stages, and the meaning of "emperor" has also evolved through three stages. The first stage, from the Fujiwara to the Taira, was one of absolute monarchy. During this stage the emperor possessed all land and people as his private property in theory, and he had the power of life and death over the people. The second stage, from the Minamoto to the Tokugawa, was one of aristocracy. During this period military leaders and nobility in each area brought land and people of their locality under their personal control; they fought wars and made alliances among themselves as rulers of small nations. Consequently the emperor's significance was different from what it had been. He now, like the Roman pope, conferred honor upon the *Bakufu*, the leader of the petty princes, and showed himself the traditional centre of the national faith. Such a development can be compared with the role of the Roman pope in crowning the Holy Roman Emperor, leader of the various lords in the Middle Ages in Europe. The third stage, one of a democratic state, began with the Meiji Revolution, which emancipated the samurai and commoners, newly awakened, from their status as private property of their shōgun and feudal lords. Since then the emperor has a new significance as the true center of government and politics. Ever since, as the commanding figure in the national movement and as complete representative of the modern democratic country, he has become representative of the nation. In other words, since the Meiji Revolution Japan has become a modern democratic state with the emperor as political nucleus. Is there any need whatever for us to import a direct translation of the "democracy" of others as though we lacked something? The struggle between those who stubbornly talk about national polity and those who are infatuated with Europe and America, both without a grasp of the background of the present, is a very ominous portent which may cause an explosion between the emperor and the people. Both sides must be warned of their folly.)

(Note 2: There is no scientific basis whatever for the belief of the democracies that a state which is governed by representatives voted in by the electorate is superior to a state which has a system of government by a particular person. Every nation has its own national spirit and history. It cannot be maintained, as advocates of this theory would have it, that China during the first eight years of the republic was more rational than Belgium, which retained rule by a single person. The "democracy" of the Americans derives from the very unsophisticated theory of the time which held that society came into being through a voluntary contract based upon the free will of individuals; these people, emigrating from each European country as individuals, established communities and built a country. But their theory of the divine right of voters is a half-witted philosophy which arose in opposition to the theory of the divine rights of kings at that time. Now Japan certainly was not founded in this way, and there has never been a period in which Japan was dominated by a half-witted philosophy. Suffice it to say that the system whereby the head of state has to struggle for election by a long-winded self-advertisement and by exposing himself to ridicule like a low-class actor seems a very strange custom to the Japanese people, who have been brought up in the belief that silence is golden and that modesty is a virtue.)

(Note 3: The imperial court today has restored corrupt customs of the Middle Ages and has moreover added others which survived in European courts; truly it has drifted far from the spirit of the founder of the nation — a supreme commander above an equal people. The revolution under the great Meiji emperor restored and modernized this spirit. Accordingly at that time a purification of the imperial court was carried out. The necessity for doing this a second time is that when the whole national structure is being reorganized fundamentally we cannot simply leave the structure of the Court in its present state of disrepair.)

(Note 4: The provision for censure of members of the Consultative Council by cabinet and Diet is required in view of the present situation in which many men do as they wish on the excuse that they are duty-bound to help the Emperor. The obstinacy and arrogance of the members of the Privy Council is not very different from that of the court officials in Russia before the revolution. The men who cause trouble for the emperor are men of this kind.)

The Abolition of the Peerage System. The peerage system will be abolished, and the spirit of the Meiji Restoration will be clarified by removal of this barrier which has come between the emperor and the people.

The House of Peers will be abolished and replaced by a Council of Deliberation (*Shingiin*), which shall consider action taken by the House of Representatives.

The Council of Deliberation will be empowered to reject decisions taken by the House of Representatives a single time. The members of the Council of Deliberation will consist of distinguished men in many fields of activity, elected by each other and appointed by the emperor.

(Note 1: The Restoration Revolution, which destroyed government by the aristocracy, was carried out determinedly, for it also confiscated the estates of the aristocracy. It went much farther than did European countries, for with the single exception of France they were unable to dispose of the medieval estates of earlier days. But with the death of men like the great Saigō, who embodied the revolutionary spirit, men like Itō Hirobumi, with no understanding of our advancement, and men who simply acted as attendants in the Revolution, imitated and transplanted backward aristocratic and medieval privileges which had survived in Western countries. To abolish the peerage system is to abandon a system translated directly from Europe and to return to the earlier Meiji Revolution. Do not jump to the conclusion that this is a shortcoming we are seeking to correct. We have already advanced farther than some other countries as a democratic country.)

(Note 2: The reason a bicameral system is subject to fewer errors than a unicameral system is that in very many cases public opinion is emotional, uncritical and changeable. For this reason the upper house will be made up of distinguished persons in many fields of activity instead of medieval relics.)

Universal Suffrage. All men twenty-five years of age, by their rights as people of Great Japan, will have the right, freely and equally, to stand for election to and to vote for the House of Representatives. The same will hold for local self-government assemblies.

Women will not have the right to participate in politics.

(Note 1: Although a tax qualification has determined suffrage in other countries and this system was first initiated in England, where the Parliament was originally set up to supervise the use of tax money collected by the Crown, in Japan we must establish it as a fundamental principle that suffrage is the innate right of the people. This universal suffrage must not be interpreted as a lowering of the tax qualification on grounds that all men pay at least indirect taxes. Rather, suffrage is a "duty of the people" in the same sense that military service is a "duty of the people.")

(Note 2: The duty of the people to defend their country cannot be separated from their duty to participate in its government. As this is a fundamental human right of the Japanese people, there is no reason why the Japanese should be like the slaves in the

Roman Empire or like the menials driven from the imperial gates during the monarchical age — simply ruled, having to live and die under orders from a ruling class. Nothing can infringe upon the right and duty of suffrage under any circumstances. Therefore officers and soldiers on active service, even if they are overseas, should elect and be elected without any restrictions.)

(Note 3: The reason for the clear statement that "Women will not have the right to participate in politics" is not that Japanese women today have not yet awakened. Whereas the code of chivalry for knights in medieval Europe called for honoring women and gaining their favor, in medieval Japan the samurai esteemed and valued the person of woman on approximately the same level as they did themselves, while it became the accepted code for women to honor the men and gain their favor. This complete contrast in developments has penetrated into all society and livelihood, and continues into modern history — there has been agitation by women for suffrage abroad while here women have continued devoted to the task of being good wives and wise mothers. Politics is a small part of human activity. The question of the place of women in Japan will be satisfactorily solved if we make an institutional reorganization which will guarantee the protection of woman's right to be "mother of the nation and wife of the nation." To make women accustomed to verbal warfare is to do violence to their natural aptitude; it is more terrible than using them in the line of battle. Anyone who has observed the stupid talkativeness of Western women or the piercing quarrels among Chinese women will be thankful that Japanese women have continued on the right path. Those who have developed good trends should let others who have developed bad trends learn from them. For this reason, one speaks today of a time of fusion of Eastern and Western civilization. But the ugliness of direct and uncritical borrowing can be seen very well in the matter of woman suffrage.)

The Restoration of the People's Freedom. The various laws which have restricted the freedom of the people and impaired the spirit of the constitution in the past — the Civil Service Appointment Ordinance, the Peace Preservation police law, the Press Act, the Publication Law, and similar measures — will be abolished.

(Note: This is obviously right. These laws work only to maintain all sorts of cliques.)

The National Reorganization Cabinet. A Reorganization Cabinet will be organized while martial law is in effect; in addition to the present ministries, it will have ministries for industries and several Ministers of State without Portfolio. Members of the Reorganization Cabinet will not be chosen from the present military, bureaucratic, financial, and party cliques, but this task will be given to outstanding individuals selected throughout the whole country.

All the present prefectural governors will be dismissed from their offices, and National Reorganization Governors will be appointed by the same method of selection as above.

(Note: This is necessary for the same reasons that the Meiji Revolution could not have been carried out by the Tokugawa shogun and his vassals. But a revolution cannot necessarily be evaluated according to the amount of bloodshed. It is just as impossible to say of a surgical operation that it was not thorough because of the small amount of blood that was lost. It all depends on the skill of the surgeon and the constitution of the patient undergoing the operation. Japan today is like a man in his prime and in good health. Countries like Russia and China are like old patients whose bodies are in total decay. Therefore, if there is a technician who takes a farsighted view of the past and present, and who draws judiciously on East and West, the reorganization of Japan can be accomplished during a pleasant talk.)

The National Reorganization Diet. The National Reorganization Diet, elected in a general election and convened during the period of martial law, will deliberate on measures for reorganization.

The National Reorganization Diet will not have the right to deliberate on the basic policy of national reorganization proclaimed by the emperor.

(Note 1: Since in this way the people will become the main force and the emperor the commander, this *coup d'état* will not be an abuse of power but the expression of the national determination by the emperor and the people.)

(Note 2: This is not a problem of legal philosophy but a question of realism; it is not an academic argument as to whether or not the emperors of Russia and Germany were also empowered with such authority, but it is a divine confidence which the people place only in the Emperor of Japan.)

(Note 3: If a general election were to be held in our present society of omnipotent capital and absolutist bureaucracy the majority of the men elected to the Diet would either be opposed to the reorganization or would receive their election expenses from men opposed to the reorganization. But, since the general election will be held and the Diet convened under martial law, it will of course be possible to curb the rights of harmful candidates and representatives.)

(Note 4: It is only because there was such a divine emperor that, despite the fact that the Restoration Revolution was carried out with greater thoroughness than the French Revolution, there was no misery and disorder. And thanks to the existence of such a godlike emperor, Japan's national reorganization will be accomplished a second time in an orderly manner, avoiding both the massacres and violence of the Russian Revolution and the snail's pace of the German revolution.)

The Renunciation of the Imperial Estate[1]. The emperor will personally show the way by granting lands, forests, shares, and similar property owned by the Imperial House to the nation.

The expenses of the Imperial Household will be limited to approximately thirty million yen per year, to be supplied by the national treasury.

However, this amount can be increased with consent of the Diet if the situation warrants such action.

(Note: The present imperial estate began with holdings taken over from the Tokugawa family, and however the true meaning of the emperor might shine forth, it is inconsistent to operate such medieval finances. It is self-evident that every expense of the people's emperor should be borne by the nation.)

Note

1.   This entire section was censored in pre-war editions.

19. Tenancy and Aggression

Ronald Dore

In the Tokyo War Crimes Trials individual politicians and generals were placed in the dock and accused of plotting crimes against humanity. It is, perhaps, easier and more emotionally satisfying to contemplate evil incarnate in individual men than in some amorphous thing called historical inevitability, and in any case systems cannot be put on trial. Nevertheless, in the background to the reforms which the Occupation Army carried out in order to 'prevent Japan from ever again becoming a menace to the peace of the world', there is traceable a widespread belief that the social and economic condition of the Japanese countryside was a powerful causal factor in bringing about Japan's aggressive policies in Asia. The foregoing summary of events in the 1920's and 1930's has perhaps provided some of the material necessary for a discussion of some of the causal connexions which often are, explicitly or implicitly, inferred.

The first question to be disposed of is: how far was the system of land tenure responsible for economic distress in rural areas? The answer must be: to a large extent, but not entirely. In the first place, the landlord system, with the high rent levels which it involved, drained off a certain proportion of the income derived from agriculture to the absentee landlords in the towns. Secondly, the income which reached the villages was very unequally distributed as between landlords and tenants. Had the distribution been more equal, the distress of the tenants would not have been so severe. (On the other hand the rate of capital accumulation, in which the landlords played a leading role in the Meiji period, would have been slower, and hence also the rate of industrial development with, consequently, a greater pressure of population on the land.) Thirdly, there is the probability that had the peasants all been owner-farmers their incentives and their economic ability to carry out agricultural improvements would have been greater — and consequently their productive capacity and their income as well. Fourthly, there is the possibility that, had the village population been more homogeneous from the point of view of economic level and economic interest, farmers would have developed stronger political representation and stronger economic organizations on the lines of the Agricultural Co-operatives and so, by improving their position in the market, have increased the income derived from a given volume of agricultural production.

On the other hand the basic ratio of agricultural population to land resources would have been no different. The average size of holding would still have been only slightly more than 1 chō[1]. Cultivation was already intensive and however much higher the level of agricultural investment, however much improved the agricultural techniques, there was a limit to the possibilities of an increase in the amount of agricultural production per worker. And, given the pressure of foreign competition for a wide range of agricultural products, the exchange value of the farmer's marketable surplus could

Ronald Dore: 'Tenancy and Aggression' from LAND REFORM IN JAPAN (Oxford University Press, 1959), pp. 115–125. Published by Oxford University Press for the Royal Institute of International Affairs, London. Copyright © Royal Institute of International Affairs 1959.

only have been improved by strong protective measures which would have borne heavily on the working classes of the towns.

To sum up, then, the landlord system was responsible for the extremes of poverty among the tenants. Its reform would not, however, by itself have brought prosperity to the countryside.

What then of the possible links between agrarian distress — including tenancy as one component element — and the rise of totalitarianism at home accompanied by expansion abroad? A few hypotheses will be enumerated and discussed in turn.

1. *That a powerful motive for expansion was to secure opportunities for emigration in order to relieve the pressure of population at home. Whereas by suitably adjusting the system of land tenure the worst distresses of the tenants could have been relieved, exclusive emphasis on the shortage of land as the cause of rural poverty by those who were unwilling to touch the vested interests of the landlords made emigration seem the only solution. As a report issued by the Natural Resources Section of the Occupation Army states, 'Repulsed in their demands for remedial legislation, farmers, during the decade preceding World War II, consciously and unconsciously gave strong support to the military group which held out the promise of new lands and prosperity to be won through aggressive war.'[2]*

There may well be something in this. The possibility of continental emigration as a solution to the land problem was already being discussed before the First World War and by the late 1930's the importance of Manchuria as an outlet for Japan's surplus rural population was accepted as axiomatic. Count Arima, for instance, speaking as Minister of Agriculture in the Diet in 1937 on the prospects for the Owner-Farmer Establishment Scheme he was introducing, mentioned the current plan to transfer a million families to Manchuria in the next twenty years as providing a possible means of 'getting round' the problem of establishing owner-farmers. But this is not to say that this was a powerful motive among those who engineered the Manchurian Incident or those who condoned and supported their action at home. It was only in the late 1930's that such plans came to be widely talked of, and that it was hardly uppermost in men's minds at the beginning of the decade seems a fair inference from the lengthy interview, considered to be of somewhat sensational frankness, given by Mori Kaku, one of the most powerful politician supporters of the Army's expansionist policies, some months after the Manchurian Incident. He mentioned, in the course of this interview, the possibilities of solving Japan's population problems by expansion in Asia. But he saw the means of solution as lying in the development of Japanese industry which would be assured if Japan were able to 'act freely' in Asia. He made no mention of emigration except to say that such a development of industry would be a better solution of the population problem than emigration to the Americas. Though not necessarily relevant to the question of how far the need for emigration provided a motive for expansion, it is worth remarking that the opportunity offered by Manchuria was never fully utilized.

2. *That the maldistribution of income kept at a low level the purchasing power of the mass of the peasants. Rural poverty, at the same time, implied an extremely low 'floor' for industrial wages, the merest pittance being enough to recruit labour from depressed peasant families. Hence, the home market for consumption goods was*

314

extremely constricted, while at the same time the high profits of the landlords helped to swell the flow of savings available for industrial investment. Hence an expanding Japanese industry was obliged to look for external markets and, where they could only be effectively secured by force, force was used.

This argument makes sense. It is elaborated by such pre-war writers as Freda Utley[3], and it was reiterated by a Socialist Member during the Diet discussions of the Land Reform Bill as a horrible warning for the future. And there is evidence — in, for instance, speeches such as that of Mori Kaku quoted above — that this was a conscious preoccupation of those who planned and aided the expansionist policies. It needs to be modified, however, by the reminder that although there were some industrialists whose fortunes were from the very first linked with the Army — the so-called New *Zaibatsu* men typified by Kuhara Fusanosuke — the big industrial concerns like Mitsui and Mitsubishi were lukewarm towards the Manchurian adventure and supported Shidehara's 'peaceful diplomacy'. For them at that time the prospects of advantage to be derived from monopolizing and developing the Manchurian market were outweighed by the prospect of reprisals from Britain and America against Japanese trade in other areas. They jumped on the bandwaggon later on, but still probably the most important connexion between industrialists and the Army's expansion policies was the usual one — that development of the armament industries offered them, directly and indirectly, higher profits.

3. *That the ruling groups — of army leaders, elder statesmen, politicians, industrialists, and bureaucrats in a position to influence policy — though at loggerheads in many respects, were at one in being alarmed at the growing signs of disaffection evident in the tenancy disputes and industrial disputes of the 1920's. As a means of countering the threat to their own power they deliberately adopted a policy of overseas expansion hoping thereby to (a) divert attention from distress at home, and (b) heal rifts in the social structure by fostering a sense of national unity in the face of a common danger.*

Such runs the contention of a number of left-wing historians such as Andrew Roth[4] and the recent Japanese authors of a popular modern history,[5] and there is a good deal of indirect evidence for it. The need for national unity is certainly a common theme in the speeches of those concerned with the furthering of expansion policies. There are, too, good precedents in recent Japanese history which must have occurred to Japanese statesmen. The opportunity which the Sino–Japanese War offered of quelling a recalcitrant Diet is generally thought to have been one of the war's major attractions in the eyes of the oligarchy at the time. But, perhaps in the nature of the case, it is difficult to find any direct evidence that the sort of calculation outlined above went on in the mind of anyone in control of policy. In any case it is hardly likely to have been more than a subsidiary contributing motive on the part of the Army leaders and right-wing nationalists who provided the main driving force for expansion. Their chauvinism has a much too genuinely ideological ring to be merely expediential and their heart-felt disapproval of social disunity is as likely to have been a consequence of their concern for national military strength and of their military ambitions as vice versa.

It may well be, however, that considerations such as these made those who were temperamentally moderates in foreign policy matters but concerned at threats to their interests at home less anxious to restrain the hot-heads, and that in order to suppress possible threats to their interests, they committed themselves to propaganda slogans and to factions which were bent on foreign expansion. It is no accident, for instance, that Hiranuma's Kokuhonsha — the right-wing group formed in the early 1920's — contained prominent industrialists as well as generals and admirals among its leaders, was specifically a counter-movement against the growth of left-wing movements at the time, and proclaimed as its objective the harmonization of the interests of capital and labour, as well as 'nourishing and developing the national spirit'.[6]

Post hoc does not argue *propter hoc*, but, at any rate, if overseas expansion was adopted as a cure for internal conflicts the remedy may be said to have worked. Class tensions in the villages did decrease with the growing emergency, as the decline in the number of tenancy disputes after 1935 shows.

4. *That the right-wing nationalists and the Army — in particular the Young Officers — succeeded, by their advocacy of internal reform, in tapping the latent demand for a reform of the land-tenure system on the part of the distressed tenants and so both prevented the development of a genuine reform movement and won the support of the peasants which carried over to support for their external policies as well.*

This argument, or something like it, is used by L. I. Hewes in his work on the Japanese land reform,[7] but it cannot be accepted without modification.

In the first place, neither the Young Officers nor the Army leaders placed much emphasis on creating a mass movement or seeking the support of the peasants as a means of gaining power. It is true that in the abortive October rising of 1931 Okawa Shumei was to provide a mass demonstration of rightist trade unionists, and that some branches of the radical right-wing movement sought to create mass organizations in such bodies as the Japanese National-Socialist Party, the Great Japan Production Party, and in the federated organization of the Patriotic United Action Association of 1930. But these never formed the main stream of the right-wing revolutionary movement which was throughout directed by small groups of scheming revolutionaries who saw themselves as an *élite* destined to seize power by a top-level coup and having no need of mass followers. After the February 1936 incident one of the Young Officers writes in his diary that this neglect to tap the revolutionary energies of the masses was one of the causes of their failure.

Secondly, what mass support was organized for these ultranationalist parties by such organizations as the National Socialist Party was mostly urban.

Thirdly, such promises of internal reform as these movements held out were extremely vague. Their appeal to the masses (in so far as they did appeal, at the time, for instance, of the trials of the May 1932 revolutionaries) lay in their formulation of a general resentment against the capitalists and the political parties. ('Fierce Attack on Decadence of the Ruling Class' said the headlines of a national newspaper at the time.) They did not specifically advocate a reform of the land system to benefit the tenants.

That, nevertheless, the depression and the events of the 1930's did help to make the peasants as a whole — as distinct from just the tenants — favourably disposed towards the Army and by extension to the ideals and policies it stood for, was argued in the last chapter. It is also clear that the Army was at pains to cultivate mass support by its championship of relief measures and its direct publication of propaganda pamphlets in large editions. It is doubtful, however, how far such support was *necessary* to the Army in seizing control of the State. Organized opposition might have made its task more difficult, but, given the authoritarian structure of Japanese society, it was enough to gain control at the centre: the rest followed.

These arguments are, however, intended only to qualify the assertion of a direct causal connexion between the Army's rise to power and the desire for reform on the part of the *mass* of the peasants. There are, at the same time, good reasons for thinking that the land problem and agrarian distress, and the fact that the Army and the right-wing radical movements associated with it seemed to offer the best hopes of reform, did help to gain the latter sympathy among some elements of what might be called the informed public opinion of the time — among, that is to say, the sort of people in universities and newspaper offices and government departments whose temperament and outlook were such that had they been Americans they would have been supporters of the New Deal and had they been British they would have been counted among the middle-class intellectuals in the ranks of the Labour Party.

At the very least the existence of these agrarian problems and the unwillingness of successive Governments to tackle them served to alienate these bodies of opinion from the political parties — the only potential focus of effective opposition to the military power. The sense of disillusionment with the fruits of 'party government' is well expressed in a book published in 1931 entitled *How to Save the Villages*. The author, who makes sweeping proposals for a land reform, devotes a good deal of space to attacks on the ruling politicians whose factional squabbles and corrupt favouritism of their capitalist friends prevented any action to save the countryside. He speaks with nostalgia of the days of Meiji absolutism when the ruling oligarchy did, at least, have the interests of the nation at heart. It was attitudes such as these which created a favourable climate for the Army to make its bid for power, for it too attacked the political parties and claimed to speak, like the Meiji oligarchs, not for sectional interests, but for the nation. It was no accident that some of the active intellectual left-wingers of the 1920's should have swung round to whole-hearted support of the military radicals in the 1930's. (Akamatsu Katsumaro, for instance, who started as a Marxist and ended as the leader of the National-Socialist Party.) The hundred-and-eighty-degree implications of the terms 'a switch from the "left" to the "right"' certainly exaggerate the nature of this conversion. Hostility towards the political parties and the capitalists remained a consistent theme throughout the intellectual history of these men.

5. *That it was concern for the distress of the peasants which inspired the Young Officers in their revolts which paved the way for the Army to gain power.*

Some of the evidence for this was presented in the last chapter. It might, however, be misleading to carry this argument to the extent of suggesting that had the peasants been well-fed and contented there would have been no Young Officer revolts. Men with the backgrounds and ideas of Kita Ikki and Okawa Shūmei could hardly have lived without revolutionary intrigue, distressed peasants or no distressed peasants, and given the nature of Army education it would have been odd if there had not been some young officers ready to be influenced by them. And in the early incidents of 1931 which set the pattern for the later bigger ones resentment against disarmament and pay-cuts seems to have provided an important motive. Nevertheless, there is plenty of evidence of the stimulus provided by rural poverty.

6. *That the structure of social relations in the villages which the landlord system preserved provided a natural base for totalitarianism.*

This argument can take a number of forms all of which have considerable plausibility. First, the paternalistic authoritarianism of the relations between landlord and tenant and the strict observance of status distinctions which they involved formed the dominant element in the whole social structure of villages where landlordism was common. People born into, and trained to survive in, such an atmosphere inevitably had an inbred susceptibility to authoritarian leadership of any sort, whether it came from their immediate master, the landlord, or from their remoter masters, 'the authorities' and the Emperor. It simply did not pertain to the tenant's situation in life to consider the actions of his superiors in a critical spirit. According to this argument the actual direction in which the ruling class led the nation was irrelevant. It was enough that the disposition to be led was there.

Secondly, it might be argued that the system of values which was supported by the landlord class — most articulately by the landlord paternalistic-didactic of Chapter II — were, with their simple emphasis on hard work and the loyal performance of duty without selfish regard for personal profit, an eminently suitable base for the kind of ideology with which the authorities attempted to bring the peasants into the 'spiritual mobilization' campaign of the 1930's. The connexions between the landlord ideology, the ideals of *Nōhon-shugi*, and the Rehabilitation Movement were discussed in the last chapter.

Thirdly, the all-inclusive and self-contained nature of the geographically concentrated hamlet community, together with the traditional emphasis on a complete harmony of neighbour relations, produced strong pressures for social conformity. This made it difficult for clashes of economic interest to be brought into the open, or for interest groups formalizing conflict to be created. At the same time any deviant individuals who did not have the psychological 'disposition to be led' and showed tendencies to react against authority were easily made to toe the line. It was always much more difficult to harbour slightly dangerous thoughts in the villages than in the towns.

Some empirical confirmation of these arguments may be found in the results of the questionnaire survey conducted in 1956 and described in [Chapter XVI and Appendix II]. There was a high correlation between what are there called 'submissive', 'holistic', and 'nationalistic' attitudes. That is to say, those whose replies showed them to be most unquestioningly susceptible to authoritarian leadership in the context of the village tended also to express the most nationalistic sentiments and to agree with statements suggesting that the proper duty of the citizen lies in suppressing individual interests for the sake of the State. One might also expect to find regional differences in this respect, with the more landlord-dominated villages of the north-east showing more obedient co-operation with the authorities than villages with a more egalitarian structure such as predominated in the south and west. (It was, for instance, generally held that the farmers from the north-east made the best soldiers.) In so far as the questionnaire answers are concerned, however, there is no apparent correlation, among the six villages studied, between the presence or absence of paternalistic landlords in 1945 and the predominance of 'nationalistic' or 'holistic' attitudes in 1956. Perhaps too much water had flowed under the bridges in these eleven years for clear relations still to be apparent, and the number of villages was in any case too small for conclusive results to be obtained. As far as individuals are concerned, then, the relationship between these clusters of attitudes is clear, but as far as the relation between all these attitudes and the social structure of the village is concerned the verdict must be 'not proven'.

7. *Finally, there are the usual psychological arguments relating the frustrations of poverty with aggressiveness.*

The argument would run thus: in the state of economic hardship in which the peasants found themselves, war and overseas expansion, and the sense that they were members of a nation which was achieving glory in which they themselves shared, provided a sort of psychological compensation for which, had they been better off, they would have had less need. Again, however, even if the psychological assumptions of this argument are correct, it still remains a question how far the wishes or the psychological needs of the mass of the people had a direct bearing on the course of events.

Speculation concerning the 'causes' of historical events is fraught with many pitfalls and must in the nature of the case, the experimental reproduction of situations being impossible, remain mere speculation. The 'ifs' will always remain to tantalize. Supposing the Governments of the early 1920's had carried out a radical adjustment of the distribution of landownership, would the subsequent history of Japan have been entirely different? It is impossible to say more than that there are some fairly plausible reasons for thinking that it might have been.

Notes:

1. 1 chō = about 2.5 acres or about 1 hectare [editor]

2. SCAP, Natural Resources Section, *The Japanese Village in Transition*, by A.F. Raper and others (Tokyo, 1950), p. 259.

3. *Japan's Feet of Clay* (London, 1936), p. 97.

4. A. Roth, *Dilemma in Japan* (Boston, 1945), pp. 162, 177–85.

5. Tōyama Shigeki and other, *Shōwa shi* (1955), pp. 21, 54, 61. ff.

6. Scalapino, *Democracy and the Party Movement in Pre-War Japan*, p. 360.

7. L.I. Hewes, Jr.: *Japan: Land and Men* (Iowa, 1955), pp. 36–37

20. Agriculture and the Villages before World War II

Tadashi Fukutake

Translated by Ronald Dore

Agriculture and the development of capitalism

The modern history of Japan begins less than one hundred years ago. It was in 1868, with the Meiji Restoration, that she set out on the road of development which was to make her a modern capitalist state.

For the preceding two and a half centuries Japan had been a feudal society, a society whose pattern had been evolved by the Tokugawa Shogunate, the government of the ruling family which seized control of the country at the beginning of the seventeenth century. The farmers had been peasants subject to the restrictions of a rigid system of social barriers between 'estates' — between the 'four orders' of society defined, in order of social honour, as: the samurai, the peasants, the artisans and the merchants. They were forbidden to sell their land; their right to sub-divide it was limited; they had no freedom to change their place of residence, and even the crops they could grow were restricted in order that they should be able to pay their taxes in rice. Practically forced into a self-sufficient subsistence economy in small villages, and bearing collective responsibility for the annual payment of their rice taxes, the individual was submerged in an isolated and exclusive community.

There was, however, in the latter half of the period, though only in certain districts, an increasing production of cash crops and an increasing penetration of the monetary economy into the villages. There were some new developments in agricultural implements, and fish manure came to be used as fertilizer. With this penetration of the commercial economy, some farmers expanded their production or entered trading activities themselves, thereby accumulating wealth, while others, on the other hand, declined into poverty, mortgaged their land, and eventually lost it to the landlords whose tenants they became. With this process of class division among the peasants the stability of feudal society came to be threatened.

However, it would be wrong to say that in the century before the Meiji Restoration conditions had matured for the spontaneous dissolution of feudalism and for the internal development of a capitalist economy. There were, indeed, by the end of the Tokugawa period, what can properly be described as manufacturing establishments, but these were by no means common. As far as internal factors are concerned, Japanese feudalism, while losing its stability, was still capable of survival. The fact that feudalism was brought to an end nevertheless with the Meiji Restoration must be attributed to the stimulus of foreign powers. England, the pioneer capitalist country, had already begun her industrial revolution a century before, and the shock waves of

Tadashi Fukutake: 'Agriculture and the Villages before World War II' from *JAPANESE RURAL SOCIETY* (Oxford University Press, 1967), pp. 3–15, translated by R.P. Dore. Reprinted with permission.

expanding capitalism spread from England and the other European powers to Japan's Pacific islands, threatening the security of her two centuries of dreamy seclusion as demands became more insistent that she should open her doors for trade. As Japanese history and world history came together, the disparities in their stages of development became obvious, and it was equally obvious that unless this gap were bridged Japan was in danger of becoming a colony of the advanced capitalist powers.

Thus it was that, after the Restoration, as well as re-ordering her political structure on modern lines, Japan pursued the policy of — to quote the contemporary slogan — 'enriching the country and strengthening the army', and set about the process of forced-draft capital accumulation. As a result Japanese capitalism developed at great speed, and she achieved a rate of economic development which has attracted world-wide attention. By the 1890's, capitalism was firmly established and from then until the development of monopoly capital in the second decade of this century she showed an astonishing rate of growth. At the same time, along with this economic development, went development as a military power. By the First World War, Japan had become one of the world's five Great Powers, and soon, in their vainer moments, the Japanese counted their country along with America and England as one of the Big Three.

Such rapid development necessarily created great strains and distortions and on no section of the economy did they press more heavily than on agriculture. It would be no exaggeration to say that the Japanese economy developed at the expense of agriculture.

To start with, in the period immediately after the Meiji Restoration the peasants, who made up 80 per cent of the population, paid in land taxes some 80 per cent of the total revenue of the Meiji government, and it was this which provided the basis for the construction of a capitalist state. At a time when Japan had little industry to speak of, it was only by converting the feudal revenues (formerly paid in kind to local lords) into land taxes paid in cash to the central government, without any reduction in the level of taxation, that it was possible for the state to pursue its policies of protecting and developing the mining and manufacturing industries.

Secondly, because — as is generally the case in late-developing capitalist countries — Japanese industry was from the very beginning of a relatively modern and highly capitalized kind, it was unable to absorb a great deal of labour from agriculture. Since Japan did not pass through the period of simple manufactures but began industrial production with the import of advanced machines from abroad, labour requirements were not especially heavy. In the light industries, in particular, young female labour was adequate to satisfy all requirements. Hence, although industry developed it did not exert a sufficient pull to reduce the agricultural population. Agriculture always held a reservoir of surplus population and it was this which made possible the low wage rates of world-wide fame and which gave Japan the strength to compete with the advanced capitalist powers.

Moreover agriculture, as well as aiding the development of industry by supplying labour, also bore the social policy costs for mining and manufacturing. It is often said that Japanese workers were migrant workers. The patriarchal family system of the peasant family preserved social bonds which in some sense linked these industrial workers to their native families. The fact that in times of depression unemployment could be absorbed without too much disorganization was largely due to these familial ties; workers could return to their native village or at least call on their families for assistance.

In these circumstances there was no remedy for the great defect of Japanese agriculture — the small size of holdings. Despite the rapid development of a capitalist economy, the number of farm families in Japan remained throughout at around the 5½ million mark. And in a country which had for so long been under cultivation there was very little possibility of expanding the total cultivated area. Consequently the average size of a holding was never much greater than 1 hectare and Japanese agriculture continued to be characterized by the minute size of family holdings. As we shall see, in the economic disruptions of the early Meiji period a good deal of land passed into the hands of landlords, but as long as there was an abundance of farm families unable to move out of agriculture it was always more profitable for the landlord to lease his land to tenants than to cultivate it himself on an extensive scale. Thus it was that capitalist agriculture never became of any importance in Japan.

Table 1   Farm households by size of operated holding (percentages): 1908–40

	Size of holding (has.)*					
Year	— 0.5	— 1.0	— 2.0	— 3.0	— 5.0	5.0+
1908	37.3	32.6	19.5	6.4	3.0	1.2
1910	37.6	33.0	19.3	5.9	2.9	1.3
1920	35.3	33.3	20.7	6.1	2.8	1.6
1930	34.3	34.3	22.1	5.7	2.3	1.3
1940	33.4	32.8	24.5	5.7	2.2	1.4

It will be seen from Table 1 just how few big holdings there were—never as many as 2 per cent containing 5 hectares and with nearly 70 per cent of farmers cultivating less than a single hectare. There was a slight increase in the proportion cultivating between 1 and 2 hectares and some decrease in the proportion with less than half and more than 2 hectares, so that one can speak of a tendency towards concentration in the medium size class, but these trends are slight ones and broadly speaking the picture is one of stability.

Inevitably such small holdings meant poverty. It was impossible to make a living from less than half a hectare, and in consequence, these farmers were forced to supplement their income by additional work outside agriculture. Even the inadequate agricultural statistics which are available show the proportion of part-time farmers as never less than 30 per cent. According to a farm household survey in 1938, 24 per cent of farm households relied less on agriculture than on other occupations and another 31 per cent received some income from non-agricultural work. Thus less than half of Japanese farm households could be called full-time farmers.

* ha. or hectare is equal to 10,000 m² or 2.47 acres. [Editor]

Certainly it is possible for the farmers' level of living to rise even without an expansion in the size of holdings if there is an increase in agricultural productivity. And it is true, if we take for instance rice, the main staple of Japanese agriculture, that in the second decade of the century production per acre was already 50 per cent higher than in the early years of the Meiji period and by about 1930 some 70 per cent higher. However, these increases in yield were all but cancelled out by the relative fall in agricultural prices and by the rise in the general standard of living. Clinging desperately to their land for lack of any opportunity to find a job in industry, the farmers continued to produce as long as there was any possibility of scraping a bare living out of agriculture. Consequently it was easy to keep agricultural prices at a low level. With the self-sufficiency of their economy destroyed, now fully involved in the commercial economy, they were unable, even though they achieved some increase in income, to catch up with the increase in living levels in Japanese society as a whole.

Since they had no capital with which to buy machines and so raise the productivity of their labour, farmers' attempts to raise their level of living were directed towards increasing the productivity of their land. The increase in agricultural production was achieved chiefly by the use of improved crop strains and by increased fertilization. By the third decade of this century, admittedly, there was already a certain amount of mechanical power in use, but there was still no machine tillage, and agriculture was still predominantly at the stage of reliance on the labour of bare human hands.

Thus developed the image of Japanese farmers as doomed to perpetual poverty however hard they might work. There was, of course, in the slums of the cities a stratum of population even poorer than the farmers and the income of a farmer of middling to upper status made him by no means poor in the context of the general Japanese situation. However, that income was achieved only by using the total labour of the whole family, and the level of income per worker was still extremely low. Japanese agriculture was left behind in the development of the Japanese economy and seemed unable to escape from its depressed position.

Being unable to escape from this poverty, and practising an agriculture which was still essentially no different from that of the feudal period, it is hardly surprising that the farmers who made agriculture their livelihood, and the rural society which those farmers created, should have been of an old-fashioned character. The astonishing development of Japanese capitalism was supported by the mechanism of cheap rice and cheap wages but it did not confer any fringe benefits on the villages. Rather, its development depended on keeping Japanese agriculture and Japanese villages firmly entrenched in their old-fashioned mould. It was as if Japan could not afford the time or the energy to think of modernizing her villages.

Landlords and village society

Approximately two-thirds of Japanese farmers before the war were tenants. Hence, not only were they never liberated from the poverty caused by lack of sufficient land; they were also tormented by the burden of rents. The relation between landlord and tenant was the most important single social relationship in the pre-war Japanese village, and no account of Japanese village society can ignore the landlord system.

In the Tokugawa period the majority of the peasants were *honbyakushō*, that is, peasants who had registered cultivating rights to certain pieces of land and the duty of paying feudal dues for that land to the lord of their fief. In very general terms what happened in the transition to the Tokugawa form of feudalism was that, by the separation of the farmers from the warrior class, the former landed squire became a samurai living in the castle town, while the actual cultivators, who had until then rendered him serf-like labour dues, became the *honbyakushō*. However, in the more remote districts of Japan and particularly in mountainous areas, some of these landed knights did not become samurai but instead became themselves *honbyakushō*, their serfs remaining serfs. Later in the period this system changed and the serfs, instead of cultivating their master's land under his direction, became independent tenants. Here was one of the origins of the landlord system. However, there were other routes to landlordism too. As the monetary economy began to penetrate the villages in the latter half of the Tokugawa period some merchants and moneylenders managed to acquire fairly considerable holdings of land. In some districts such merchants acquired land through the financing of land reclamation operations. And generally throughout the country it happened that some among the small farmers subject to the harsh exactions of their feudal lords and to the vagaries of uncertain harvests, mortgaged and sold their independent cultivating rights as *honbyakushō*. They became what were known as 'water-drinking farmers' (*mizunomi-byakushō*), while others more fortunate than they acquired their land and became their landlords. In these various ways one can consider the landlord system to have been already fairly well established by the end of the Tokugawa period.

By the beginning of the Meiji period already more than a quarter of the arable area was tenanted land. And this proportion rapidly increased after the Meiji Restoration. The reasons lay in the reform of the land tax system which began in 1873 and in the economic fluctuations which followed it. As a result of the new tax system farmers who until then had paid their feudal dues in rice were now required to pay, in cash, a fixed annual tax calculated on the basis of the value of their land. Since they now had to sell their crops in order to acquire the money to pay their taxes, they were to that extent drawn more closely into the monetary economy. Too many farmers found themselves unable to adjust to the successive waves of inflation and deflation which followed. As the price of rice became inflated while their taxes remained fixed their standards of living rose, but when the reverse process set in, in the 1880's, their income fell rapidly. A large number of farmers lost their land in the process. The area under tenancy, estimated to be about 29 per cent in 1872 before the new land tax was instituted, approached 40 per cent only fifteen years later. This percentage continued to increase gradually, and at its peak in 1930 reached 46.7 per cent — nearly half of the total area.

This tenanted land was shared between about 70 per cent of the total number of farmers, 30 per cent of them classified in the official figures shown in Table 2 as 'tenants' (i.e., those who owned less than one-tenth of the land they cultivated) and some 40 per cent as 'part-tenants' (those who owned less than 90 per cent but more than 10 per cent of the land they cultivated). In detail the figures show that during the Meiji period there was an increase in the number of tenants, while after about 1920 a bigger increase came in part-tenants, but it remains true for the whole period since the late nineteenth century that owner-farmers made up less than a third of the total. The landlord-tenant relationship was a crucial one for village society, not simply because of the high proportion of tenanted land, but because of the very high proportion of farm households which were involved.

Table 2   Farm households by ownership status (percentages): 1888–1940

Year	Owner-farmers	Part-owners, part-tenants	Tenants
1888	33.4	46.0	20.6
1910	32.8	39.5	27.8
1920	30.7	40.9	28.4
1930	30.6	42.6	26.8
1940	30.5	42.4	27.1

There were, however, among the landlords thus involved with such a large proportion of the farmers, a variety of types. There were the local magnates of long standing, descended from the medieval squires mentioned above. There were the merchant–moneylender landlords. And then there were the peasant landlords, the owner–farmers who by their own efforts had managed to secure extra land which they leased to tenants. Some among them, particularly the merchant–moneylender type, owned very large estates (by Japanese standards), but for the most part landlords of whatever type held modest holdings. There were no more than about 3,000 in the whole of Japan who owned more than fifty hectares of land, and about 50,000 with more than ten. Even the number holding five or more hectares of leased-out land was only about 100,000; which means, if we assume a total number of about 150,000 hamlet settlements, that there was less than one per hamlet. However, if we include the small landlords owning between one and five hectares of tenanted land, the total number of landlords becomes 380,000 of whom more than 160,000 were themselves cultivating farmers. If one takes into account the fact that the owners of very large tracts of territory appointed managers of their land in hamlets in which they did not themselves live — the manager in this case performing much the same kind of social role as the landlord — it is a fairly safe assertion that there was hardly a single hamlet in Japan from which landlord domination was absent.

The concrete nature of this landlord dominance varied, of course, according to the type of landlord, but certain common characteristics were shared in all cases and may be considered typical of Japanese landlord–tenant relations. They are as follows.

In the first place, rents for rice land were usually fixed in kind at so much per unit area and they were fixed at the same high level as the feudal dues of the Tokugawa period. From around 1930 rent rates began to show a slight decline, and since yields were improving there was an additional slight decline in the proportion of the crop paid in rent, but even so it would be no exaggeration to say that rents generally amounted to as much as half the crop.

Secondly, tenancy contracts were for the most part verbal, and written contracts were rare except in the case of very large landlords and in districts where there had been tenancy disputes. Moreover, except for a small number of cases where rights of permanent occupancy were recognized by custom, the term of the contract was rarely specified. This did not mean that the tenant was able to stay indefinitely on the land; it meant rather that his cultivating rights were insecure since the landlord could always evict him at his own convenience. For a tenant family the prospect of being forced off its land meant immediate privation, and in a situation of surplus population with consequent keen competition for tenancy rights, this further strengthened the position of the landlord.

Then, thirdly, the agreed rent rate though expressed in terms of a fixed amount of rice, was by general custom open to reduction in years of bad harvest. The usual procedure was for the tenant to ask the landlord for a reduction, and for the latter then to inspect the crop and grant relief according to the degree to which it fell below the normal yield. But whether such a reduction was granted or not, and if so by how much, was entirely left to the discretionary benevolence of the landlord.

For these various reasons, the tenant–farmer was in a weak position *vis-à-vis* the landlord. If he offended his landlord he might be evicted from his land; at the very least it would become difficult for him to ask for a rent reduction if his crop failed. Except for tenants of the local magnates of feudal origin, or of other large landlords who held something like monopoly rights over land in certain districts, it was usual for tenant–farmers to rent parcels of land not from a single landlord but from several. In other words, tenants who depended on a single landlord were in a minority. But despite this diffusion of dependency the tenant was still unable to treat on equal terms with his landlords because of those characteristics of the landlord–tenant relationship outlined above. The patron–client relationships typically found in districts where there were old-style local magnates with tenants who had only in recent centuries evolved from a more direct form of serfdom, represent only a more exaggerated form of the landlord–tenant relationships typical of the whole of Japan.

However, the pattern of landlord control in the villages changed slowly. The big and medium landlords who accumulated land after the Meiji Restoration gradually, around the turn of the century when the foundations of Japanese capitalism were established, reduced the size of their own cultivated holdings or gave up agriculture altogether, thus becoming purely parasitical landlords. Even among those with smaller holdings there were a number whose children were sent away to receive higher education, often coming back to become school teachers or village officials and give up farming. These tendencies weakened the authority of the landlords in the villages. As a consequence — and as a result, too, of changing attitudes on the part of tenants caused by the spread of literacy, their military experience as conscripts, and the proselytizing activities of leftwing intellectuals — from around 1920 there were frequent outbreaks of tenancy disputes. There developed an organized tenants' movement which gradually gathered strength as the tenants' demands increased — from rent reductions for a particular bad harvest to permanent reductions in rental rates and the guarantee of secure tenure.

This tenants' movement, however, never succeeded in destroying the landlord system. Even at the peak of its activity it did not extend over the whole country. Even if the larger and medium landlords did come to play a purely parasitical role, and even if a number of the smaller landlords did move out of farming, the majority still continued to be peasant landlords cultivating a holding of their own. They continued to function as the ruling stratum of the village.

Thus, despite changes in the landlord system *pari passu* with the social and economic development of Japanese society after the Meiji Restoration, the landlord remained the dominant element in rural society. One should, however, distinguish between those who were responsible for progress in agricultural technology and for the creation of Agricultural Associations in the Meiji period or who played a major role in developing local self-government after the system was founded in 1888, and on the other hand, those who, in the 1930's, carried through the remoulding and strengthening of the traditional village social order and so prepared a firm basis for putting the country on a war footing—the landlords, that is, who were active in the producers' co-operatives and organized the new Farmers' Associations. Though both types bear the name landlords, their character was different. As the former ceased to farm and gradually lost their control of the villages, the latter, as farming landlords, came to play the major role in dominating them. These changes over time in the ruling stratum necessarily brought, of course, simultaneous changes among the tenants and part-tenants — the stratum of the ruled. But for these changes to take any conclusive form it was not enough simply for the landlord system to change; it had to be entirely destroyed. This was postponed until after the war. The landlord system, though changing in character, continued until the defeat in World War II to be the main determinant of the structure of Japanese village society.

21.   "If Only We Might Fall . . ."
Ivan Morris

If only we might fall
Like cherry blossom in the Spring —
So pure and radiant!

*Haiku by a kamikaze pilot of the Seven
Lives Unit, who died in combat in February
1945 at the age of twenty-two*

. . . The aircraft was of simple design and construction without
refinements and appropriate for its use. Three solid-fuel rocket motors
were installed in the rear fuselage and operated for the final phase of the
flight. The [aircraft] was usually carried by a twin-engined Mitsubishi
bomber and released at high altitude some distance from the target. When
within striking distance the rocket motors were ignited for the final
high-speed dive through the defensive screen of the target.

Description: Single seat, mid-wing monoplane. Wood and mild steel
construction. Span 16'5"; length 19'18½"; weight empty 970 lbs, loaded
4,700 lbs; weight of high explosive in nose 2,600 lbs.

Performance: The aircraft could glide 50 miles at 230 m.p.h. after release
from mother aircraft at 27,000'. With motors operating the aircraft dived
at 570 m.p.h.

Power plant: 3 solid-fuel rocket motors giving a total thrust of 1,764 lbs.
for 9 seconds.

Thus the visitor to the Science Museum in London is introduced to one of the strangest
and most poignant weapons in the history of warfare. Suspended by three slender
cables, it hovers inconspicuously in the back of the third floor, where it is over
shadowed by sturdy-looking Hawker Hurricanes, Supermarine Spitfires, and Gloster
Turbojets — a delicate green cocoon, smaller and frailer and simpler than the nearby
V-1 flying bomb, yet, unlike its German counterpart, equipped to carry a human
warrior to his fiery destination.

"Ōka" it was named by the Japanese — "cherry blossom," the ancient symbol of purity
and evanescence. The Americans, against whom this diminutive craft was designed,
dubbed it the "*baka* [idiot] bomb," as if by denigrating this eerie weapon they might
neutralize the unease it instinctively evoked.

From *THE NOBILITY OF FAILURE* by Ivan Morris. Copyright © 1975 by Ivan Morris. Reprinted by
permission of Georges Borchardt, Inc. for the Estate of Ivan Morris.

From any common-sense viewpoint it was indeed something of an absurdity. That hundreds of young pilots should have clambered into these contraptions — mere wooden torpedoes with toy-like fuselage and stubby wings — to pit themselves against the leviathan carriers and battleships of the American navy would truly appear idiotic, even incredible, to those unfamiliar with Japan's ancient heroic tradition and the nobility that tradition attributed to forlorn ventures inspired by sincerity.

The principle was simple enough: as conventional methods of aerial warfare were rapidly becoming ineffective, Japan would have recourse to a one-way glider which would be transported at high altitude close to the target and would then dive down at enormous speed to detonate its warhead onto the enemy ship. The use of such dirigible manned bombs would thus allow the transporting aircraft, the mother plane, to return safely to base and be available for future missions. The suicide craft itself with its ton of tri-nitro-anisol would sink, or at least incapacitate, the ships of the enemy navy, which were now slowly strangling the home islands; in addition, the use of this new secret weapon would overawe and demoralize the foreigners, who were psychologically unprepared for such methods.

The Ōka was designed so that it could be tucked snugly under the fuselage of the mother plane, usually a converted Mitsubishi G4 M.2e bomber or, in the homely nomenclature of the enemy, a "Betty." During the main part of the flight towards the target, the kamikaze fighter would sit with the pilot of the carrying plane. As they neared the area where American ships had been sighted, he would briskly make his last farewell, exchange salutes, then climb through the bomb bay of the mother plane into the cramped cockpit of the flying coffin where he would spend the remaining minutes of his life. His equipment, limited, to bare essentials, included a steering device and a voice tube that allowed him to communicate with the bomber pilot until the moment of separation. When the target was verified, usually at a distance of some twenty-five miles, the kamikaze fighter would pull the release handle. His craft would then drop from the belly of the mother plane and glide downwards at a gradual angle gaining a speed of about two hundred and thirty miles an hour. Approaching the enemy ship, a rapidly growing dot in the ocean, he would activate the booster rockets, which were installed directly behind his seat without any protection. They instantly increased his velocity, which soon approached six hundred miles an hour (a fantastic speed for the time) and helped protect his precious cargo from enemy fighters and anti-aircraft fire. Preparing for his suicide dive, the pilot would increase his downward angle to about fifty degrees; and, as he plummeted towards his prey, he was supposed to keep his eyes wide open until the last second, for a final adjustment in course could determine the outcome of his sacrifice.

The first Oka attacks were launched towards the end of March 1945 as the American navy prepared to invade Japan's last line of defence, the island stronghold of Okinawa. At dawn on the 21st a mighty force of enemy ships, including seven aircraft carriers (the prime kamikaze target), had been sighted three hundred miles southeast of Kyushu. Vice Admiral Ugaki, the zealous commander of the Fifth Naval Air Fleet, who had been involved with kamikaze tactics since their inception, decided that the time had come to use the new weapon and to launch the Divine Thunder Unit on its first operation. Almost immediately there was a dispute, of a type common in the annals of samurai warfare, to decide who should lead the attack. After some heated wrangling the honour was awarded to Lieutenant Commander Nonaka, an expert on torpedo bombing. The force consisted of eighteen twin-engine Mitsubishi bombers, of which all but two had Ōka dirigible bombs attached to their bellies, escorted by fifty-five Zero fighters (an absurdly inadequate defence for such a momentous mission). Soon the roll of drums, the sound that traditionally precedes the hero's departure for battle, announced that the planes were ready to take off. The bomber crews hurried onto the field, and the sixteen Ōka pilots ran towards the mother planes that were to transport their little craft. Under the standard flight uniforms all wore white scarves, and in conformity with samurai custom each man, as he prepared for his last sortie, tightened around his helmet a white *hachimaki* cloth — the antique symbol of determination and derring-do. Above them fluttered the unit's pennant, a white banner emblazoned with the slogan HI RI HŌ KEN TEN. These characters referred to a favourite saying by Kusunoki Masashige:

> Wrong [*Hi*] cannot prevail over Truth [*Ri*];
> Nor Truth conquer the Law [*Hō*];
> The Law cannot prevail over Power [*Ken*];
> Nor Power conquer Heaven [*Ten*].

Masashige's disastrous last battle, in which the Emperor's forces were routed by the enemy, was clearly in Nonaka's mind as he prepared to board his lead plane: "This," he said with a smile, "is my Minatogawa." While Admiral Ugaki watched from his command post, the young Ōka pilots climbed into the cockpits of the mother crafts, shouting their farewells and their thanks for being included in the momentous mission. Led by Nonaka's plane, the bombers started taking off at half past eleven. As the last craft left the ground, the beat of drums ceased abruptly.

Almost at once it became clear that this might indeed be a Battle of Minato River. So defective was the equipment at this stage of the war that only about half of the escorting planes were able to accompany the mission. Many of them could not take off at all, while others had to turn back owing to engine trouble. Next it was learnt from reconnaissance reports that the enemy force was a great deal more powerful than originally believed, and thus it would be harder than ever to break through their defence screen. Vice Admiral Ugaki could still have called back his planes but he evidently decided that after so many months of feverishly preparing this first Ōka venture, such a move could have a devastating effect on morale.

The fatal hour came at two o'clock in the afternoon, when the mother planes, now some fifty miles from target, were suddenly intercepted by fifty Grumman fighters. In an attempt to gain speed the pilots jettisoned their Ōka craft; but they were still not sufficiently manoeuverable, and there were far too few fighters to provide adequate protection. The Americans furiously assaulted one bomber after another. As each of the huge planes caught fire and broke formation, the pilot would wave a final salute to his leader, Lieutenant Commander Nonaka, before spiralling down to the ocean. Soon every single bomber had been destroyed, and only a few Zero fighters remained to return to base with details of the disaster. Nonaka's bomber had disappeared behind a cloud bank, but one of the fighters reported that he later saw it burst into flames and plunge into the water like a meteor. The attack of 21st March was a gloomy augur for the final weapon that was to save Japan: not a single Ōka craft had even approached its target, let alone caused any damage. When Ugaki, the commanding admiral, heard the news, he is said to have wept openly.

After American forces started their invasion of Okinawa, further Ōka attacks were launched from the same airfield in the desperate hope that this time the new tactic might justify all the effort it had entailed. A major operation of 12th April included 333 aircraft and was designated as "Kikusui Number 2" in typical reference to the chrysanthemum emblem used by Masashige. With its eight Ōka-carrying bombers the force headed south towards Okinawa, the planes choosing different courses in order to approach their targets from various directions and confuse the enemy. In the base headquarters the senior officers listened anxiously to radio messages from the mother planes. Commander Nakajima, an expert on kamikaze operations, was particularly interested in the fate of a certain Lieutenant Doi, an Ōka pilot who had recently graduated from normal school in Osaka. Doi had distinguished himself at the base by organizing an energetic house-clearing operation to improve the sordid conditions in the barracks, and his immediate reaction on being informed that he had been chosen for the next day's mission was to tell Commander Nakajima, "I have ordered six beds and fifteen straw mats. They are supposed to arrive today. May I ask that you watch for them and make sure they go to the billet?"

Messages came in rapid succession from the mother plane that was now carrying Doi and his green flying bomb to their target: "Enemy fighters sighted" was the first report, shortly followed by the encouraging news, "We have bypassed enemy fighters"; next came the messages, "Standing by to release Ōka . . . Targets are battleships," and, a few seconds later, "Released!" "I visualised the scene," writes Commander Nakajima "as Doi plummeted toward a great battleship, his speed boosted by rocket thrusts, and the final successful direct hit." The reality was somewhat different. Only one of the eight mother planes succeeded in returning to base. As it happened, this was the bomber that had transported Lieutenant Doi, and the crew was able to provide detailed news of his last hours. Shortly after take-off the young man announced that he wanted to take a nap and asked to be called half an hour before reaching the target area. He stretched out on a makeshift canvas cot and despite the noise and the rather tense nature of the situation, promptly fell asleep. On being awakened, he remarked with a smile, "Time passes quickly, doesn't it?" Lieutenant Doi then shook hands with the commander of the mother plane and climbed through the bomb bay into his Ōka craft. Approaching the battleship that had been selected as his target, he waited for the optimum position (altitude twenty-thousand feet, distance fifty thousand feet), then he pulled the release handle. In accordance with Ōka tactics the mother plane was obliged to withdraw rapidly from the scene of action, but the crew reported that they had seen Doi's bomb hurtling down towards its target and afterwards a pillar of heavy smoke had risen some fifteen hundred feet from the general position of the battleship. It was not a signal of success: from official United States Navy reports we know that Lieutenant Doi missed his target, for not a single capital ship was hit by a piloted bomb on that day. The sortie did, however, provide at least an intimation of hope since one American destroyer was damaged. Destroyers were certainly not the most worthy targets for suicide bombs, but without this scintilla of encouragement the Imperial High Command might well have abandoned the entire Ōka venture.

Ōka bombs, though the most dramatic manifestation of Japan's suicide tactics in The Pacific war, by no means dominated the kamikaze epic. The history of organizing suicide units as a major part of military strategy had started about half a year before Ōka bombs were first used. On 17th October 1944, as Japanese forces in the Philippines prepared to meet an all-out American attack, a new commander, Vice Admiral Ōnishi, arrived from Tokyo to take over the First Naval Air Fleet in Manila. Two days later he visited Mabalacat, a little town some fifty miles northwest of the capital, and the headquarters of the 201st Air Group. The base at Mabalacat now became the scene of one of the most fateful conferences in the Pacific war.

The central figure, Ōnishi Takijirō, had made a name for himself from the outset of hostilities when he had cooperated with the eminent Admiral Yamamoto in planning the attack on Pearl Harbor. In the Imperial Navy he and Yamamoto were the two most fervent exponents of aviation as the key to Japan's strategy in the Pacific, and they had worked in close partnership until Yamamoto's sudden death in 1943. Ōnishi himself flew every type of aircraft, and during the early, successful part of the war he exercised personal command as Chief of Staff for land-based air operations in action over the Philippines and in the sea battle off Malaya. When Japan's situation became critical in 1944, he was appointed to a key position in the aviation department of the Munitions Ministry and soon came to realize his country's hopeless inferiority in the production of aircraft compared with the enemy's boundless capacity. Like Yamamoto he had a resourceful and imaginative mind, and it was no doubt during this time that he began to seek some new form of aviation strategy that might help offset the absurd material discrepancy between Japan and America.

Considering his key role in the latter part of the war, remarkably little is known about Vice Admiral Ōnishi. The few published pictures show a large, kindly-looking man with round, somewhat puffy features. He certainly does not resemble the impassive, grim-looking Japanese officers who glare at us from most photographs of the time. In the Imperial Navy he was a controversial figure with a "maverick" reputation much like Admiral Yamamoto's. A poor politician, blunt, straightforward, uncompromising, he was endowed with the type of simple-hearted sincerity so often encountered among heroic nonconformists in Japanese history. Like Saigō Takamori and earlier representatives of the tradition, he stressed the importance of resolute action as opposed to talk, and of spirit over "systems." Again like Saigō, he became known as a masterful calligrapher; he was also a keen (though not especially talented) composer of haiku.

Ōnishi's soft appearance belied the toughness of a man who demanded much from others and still more from himself. He was noted for his dynamic energy and for a courage that bordered on foolhardiness: Vice Admiral Ōnishi was the first military man in Japan to practise parachuting and often during the war he seemed to court physical danger. In almost every respect he was the ideal leader for organized kamikaze strategy.

333

Though recognized as Japan's foremost officer in naval aviation, Ōnishi was not altogether popular in the corridors of power. Owing to his outspoken, somewhat tactless nature, many regarded him as aggressive, arrogant, even dangerous — the typical "nail that sticks out" and needs a sharp knock on the head.

Among his own men, however, especially the young pilots, he appears to have been loved, and he reciprocated their admiration by extolling them as "the treasure of the nation" and declaring, in his powerful calligraphy, that "The purity of youth will usher in the Divine Wind."

These were the young men whose deliberate and systematic sacrifice he was to propose at the meeting on 19th October. The Admiral was tired and in poor health when he reached the headquarters at Mabalacat, and the extraordinary nature of the conference must have added to the strain. Facing the assembled officers, he started by rehearsing the all too familiar facts about Japan's material shortages. Having presented a seemingly insoluble problem, he offered the idea that had been forming in his mind during the past months: "In my opinion, there is only one way of assuring that our meagre strength will be effective to a maximum degree. That is to organize attack units composed of Zero fighters armed with two-hundred-fifty-kilogram bombs, with each plane to crash-dive into an enemy carrier . . . What do you think?"

Captain Inoguchi, a senior staff officer who was present at the conference, has described the moment: "The Admiral's eyes bored into us as he looked around the table. No one spoke for a while, but Admiral Ōnishi's words struck a spark in each of us." The decision had to be made at once, for time was rapidly running out. Responsibility devolved upon Commander Tamai, the executive officer of the 201st Air Group, who now excused himself and left the room with an aide in order to assess the probable reactions of the pilots themselves. Tamai returned shortly and said, "Entrusted by our commander with full responsibility, I share completely the opinions expressed by the Admiral. The 201st Air Group will carry out his proposal. May I ask that you leave to us the organization of our crash-dive unit?" Not a single officer at the meeting demurred.

The decision to adopt organized suicide tactics had been made in a matter of minutes, though the psychological groundwork had been laid during many centuries. In less than a week the first kamikaze planes took off from Mabalacat to attack the American navy. Captain Inoguchi ends his description of the meeting as follows: "I well remember Admiral Ōnishi's expression as he nodded acquiescence. His face bore a look of relief coupled with a shadow of sorrow." Ōnishi was indeed the father of the kamikaze units, but he had mixed feelings about his progeny. He knew, of course, that with ordinary tactics there was no longer the slightest chance of stopping the enemy. In addition he attached great importance to the "spiritual" aspect of the operations, quite apart from any practical effect they might have. In a speech delivered a few months later to members of the first kamikaze unit in Taiwan he declared, "Even if we are defeated, the noble spirit of the kamikaze attack corps will keep our homeland from ruin. Without this spirit, ruin would certainly follow defeat."

These might appear surprising sentiments for a commanding officer at a period when "defeatism" was officially considered the most heinous of crimes; yet clearly they belong to the Japanese heroic tradition that places sincerity of purpose above practical efficacy. At the same time we know that Ōnishi regarded the kamikaze operations as a tragic necessity rather than a source of satisfaction. One morning shortly after the formation of the first units, when he was crouching in an air-raid shelter with Captain Inoguchi, he recalled that similar tactics had been mooted earlier in the war but that he had then refused to countenance them. "He stared fixedly at the wall during the burst of machine-gun fire and continued, 'The fact that we [now] have to resort to [such a method] shows how poor our strategy has been since the beginning." Ōnishi paused for a moment, then suddenly let drop the remark, "You know, this really is a violation of [proper] command."

If Ōnishi, the single man in Japan most responsible for initiating the suicide strategy, could harbour such hesitations, it is hardly surprising that more conventional military leaders should have had their doubts. Imperial Headquarters in Tokyo, though giving official approval to the organization of kamikaze units, tended at first to view the plan with misgivings. This was not, of course, due to any humanitarian scruples, but because they were frankly sceptical about Ōnishi and the feasibility of his new tactics and, perhaps more important, because these tactics represented a disturbing departure from orthodox principles and procedures, which were still based on the principle of "great warships and big guns" (*taikan-kyohō-shugi*).

As the months passed and kamikaze attacks became an established way of warfare, Japan's leaders increasingly accepted their necessity. The practical advantages were obvious. Now that the Imperial Navy was crippled and the air force rapidly dwindling, here was a method that allowed pilots with minimal experience, flying almost any kind of craft, to damage, perhaps even sink, the seemingly impregnable carriers, the core of the American threat. The young men in their disposable planes merely had to take off on their one-way missions, follow their flight leader, and steer their lethal cargo straight onto the target. Youth, speedy reactions, and, above all, zeal were the prime requirements, and there was no need for special skills or elaborate training. The Americans, being unprepared for such unconventional methods, had not yet invented anti-aircraft batteries capable of destroying a plane as it hurtled down in a full-throttled dive, and they therefore had to improvise zig-zagging manoeuvres and other evasive tactics which were far from foolproof. There was also a psychological element. Japan's military leaders managed to convince themselves that their enemy would be daunted by the spiritual strength of the kamikaze. As it turned out, they grossly misjudged American reactions and overestimated the demoralizing effect of Ōka and other suicide weapons. But in the last desperate phase of the war the idea that the Japanese spirit (*Yamato-damashii*) was the trump card that could counter the enemy's material force had become an article of faith. Thus when General Ushijima addressed his troops in Okinawa he insisted that their ultimate strength lay in moral superiority. And the eagerness of young kamikaze volunteers to make an oblation of their lives served as dramatic evidence of this supposed advantage.

The initial doubts of the men in high places were certainly not shared by the pilots in the Philippines, who appear to have responded to Ōnishi's challenge with spontaneous enthusiasm. We are told that every single member of the 201st Air Group volunteered for the new kamikaze units in a frenzy of elation; and, while the outsider may be permitted to wonder what would have happened to the rare dissenting pilot who preferred to continue orthodox operations, there can be no doubt about the general reaction. Once it was clear that the candidates for self-sacrifice were available, a leader had to be chosen for the historic first mission. Captain Inoguchi and the Executive Officer of the 201st Air decided on a fervent young lieutenant called Seki, who had frequently volunteered for dangerous missions, and the young man was promptly summoned. Inoguchi's description evokes the highly charged atmosphere of the time:

> The Philippine night was dark and quiet. We sat silently in the officers' lounge as the sound of the orderly's footsteps faded upstairs. I thought of Seki, deep in slumber, and wondered what his dreams might be. Quick steps soon descended the stairs and the tall figure of the lieutenant appeared in the doorway. It was evident that he had hurried, for his jacket was still not completely buttoned. He addressed Commander Tamai: "Did you call me, sir?"

> Beckoned to a chair, the young man sat down facing us. Tamai patted him on the shoulder and said "Seki, Admiral Ōnishi himself has visited the 201st Air Group to present a plan of greatest importance to Japan. The plan is to crash-dive our Zero fighters, loaded with 250-kilogram bombs into the decks of enemy carriers . . . You are being considered to lead such an attack unit. How do you feel about it?"

> There were tears in Commander Tamai's eyes as he ended.

> For a moment there was no answer. With his elbows on the table, hands to his head, jaws tight shut and his eyes closed, Seki sat motionless, in deep thought. One second, two seconds, three, four, five . . . Finally he moved, slowly running his fingers through his long hair. Then, calmly raising his head, he spoke, "You absolutely must let me do it." There was not the slightest falter in his voice.

> "Thank you," said Tamai.

During the following hectic week four kamikaze units were formed in Mabalacat, and detailed arrangements made for their maiden sortie on 25th October. As the news spread among other pilots in the area, further units were rapidly created, notably by members of the Second Air Fleet, who in less than a week managed to organize several Special Attack units of their own. In these early days most of the initiative and detailed planning came from pilots themselves, the principal role of the superior officers being to coordinate and supervise the new tactics. Early on the morning of the 25th the two dozen men chosen to take part in the first attack from Mabalacat ate a quick breakfast and lined up on the airfield, with Lieutenant Seki a step ahead of the others, to hear their first and final instructions from Vice Admiral Ōnishi. According to Inoguchi's description, the Admiral looked pale and, as he started to speak, his words were slow and troubled:

> "Japan is in grave danger. The salvation of our country is now beyond the powers of the ministers of state, the General Staff, and lowly commanders like myself. It can come only from spirited young men such as you. Thus,

on behalf of your hundred million countrymen, I ask of you this sacrifice, and pray for your success." He paused for a while and tried to regain his composure, then continued, "You are already gods, without earthly desires . . . I shall watch your efforts to the end and report your deeds to the Throne. You may all rest assured on this point." His eyes were filled with tears as he concluded with the words, "I ask you all to do your best."

Just before take-off, Lieutenant Seki pulled out a handful of crumpled bank-notes from his pocket and handed them to an officer who was staying behind, asking that they be sent to Japan and used to build new planes. A few minutes later the twenty-four pilots started on their one-way journeys. Seki's plane was in the lead, and his was the first to crash into its target. The unlucky victim was the American escort carrier *St. Lo*, which, after being hit in the flight deck by another suicide plane, sank following a fierce succession of internal explosions. On this opening day, altogether the most encouraging in the entire history of kamikaze operations, half a dozen other American escort carriers were struck by suicide planes and damaged. The sensational news of the attack — the one favourable development for Japan at a time of almost unrelieved setbacks — was instantly signalled to Tokyo and conveyed to the Emperor. His reaction, as reported to Ōnishi and members of the kamikaze units, was typically ambiguous. Captain Nakajima describes the scene at Mabalacat when he ordered all his men to assemble at the command post:

As they gathered I could see that their spirit and morale were high, despite the intense day-and-night effort demanded of them. Holding [Vice Admiral Ōnishi's cablegramme] in my hand I addressed them: "I relay to you His Majesty's words upon hearing the results achieved by the Kamikaze Special Attack corps." Everyone snapped to attention, and I read the message from Admiral Ōnishi: "When told of the special attack, His Majesty said 'WAS IT NECESSARY TO GO TO THIS EXTREME? BUT THEY HAVE CERTAINLY DONE A GOOD JOB.' His Majesty's words suggest that His Majesty is greatly concerned . . . We must redouble our efforts to relieve His Majesty of this concern. I have pledged our every effort toward that end."

22.   An Empire Won and Lost, 1939–1945
W.G. Beasley

Once Japanese strategists were convinced that the United States would not stand idly by while the countries of South East Asia were invaded, it became axiomatic that the American Pacific fleet, the only force capable of threatening Japan's communications with the south, must become the first object of attack. Accordingly, a major air strike was directed at its Hawaiian base, Pearl Harbour, on the morning of Sunday, December 7, 1941, by planes from a naval squadron which had left the Kuriles ten days earlier. Surprise was complete and success phenomenal. Eight battleships were sunk or damaged, as were seven other vessels. Ninety per cent of America's air and surface strength in the area was immobilized or destroyed. Simultaneously, attacks were launched against targets in Wake, Guam, Midway, the Philippines and Hong Kong, all of them successful, while soon after a British battleship and battle cruiser from Singapore were attacked and sunk at sea.

These operations, carefully planned and brilliantly executed, opened the way for a series of rapid campaigns in South East Asia. Hong Kong was forced to surrender on Christmas Day. Landings on Luzon brought the capture of Manila on January 2, 1942, followed quickly by the occupation of the whole of the Philippines, though an American force in Bataan held out until the beginning of May. Other Japanese troops landed on the east coast of Malaya, crossed the Kra isthmus, and advanced down both sides of the peninsula, taking Kuala Lumpur on January 11 and Singapore — supposedly impregnable — on February 15. This freed men for an assault on the Netherlands Indies, where Dutch troops capitulated on March 9, and on Burma, which was largely overrun by the end of April. At this point, therefore, Japan controlled everything from Rangoon to the mid-Pacific, from Timor to the Mongolian steppe.

Her war plans, drawn up in November 1941, had envisaged turning the whole of this area into a Greater East Asia Co-prosperity Sphere, with Japan, north China and Manchukuo as its industrial base. The other countries were to provide raw materials and form part of a vast consumer market, building a degree of economic strength that would enable Japan, first, to meet and contain any counter-attack from outside, then, if all went well, to incorporate India, Australia and Russia's Siberian provinces by further wars at a later date.

To achieve these ends it was necessary that Japanese domination be substituted for domination by the West, at least initially, a decision that led to a cultural crusade — widespread teaching of the Japanese language, reforms of education to eliminate 'undesirable' influences, the organization of literary and scientific conferences, even attempts to abolish the siesta and jazz — as well as the creation of a network of new political alignments. Some countries were from the beginning left a large measure of independence. Indo-China, for example, was left in the hands of the French, and Siam

W.G. Beasley: Extract from 'An Empire Won and Lost, 1939–1945' from *THE MODERN HISTORY OF JAPAN* (Weidenfeld & Nicolson, 1973), pp. 271–278.

(Thailand), after signing a treaty of alliance, retained its own monarchy and administration, though both had to grant a number of special favours to Japan. Occupied China, as represented by Wang Ching-wei's regime, had already signed a peace agreement in November 1940 and was eventually persuaded to declare war on America and Britain in January 1943. This heralded an era of greater formal equality with Japan, marked by the abolition of Japanese concessions in the old treaty ports later in the year. Manchukuo, of course, had always been nominally an independent state, despite the authority of the Kwantung Army there. This situation, like the colonial status of Korea, remained unchanged.

Of the territories that had been newly conquered, Burma produced a puppet leader, Ba Maw, who was made head of a Japanese-sponsored administration on August 1, 1942. However, real power was in the hands of his military advisers and they retained it after the country was given independence in the following year, when it declared war and concluded an alliance in its turn. The Philippines, with the help of pro-Japanese collaborators, achieved independence on October 14, 1943, though its government was able to avoid declaring war on the allies until September 1944. In Malaya and the Netherlands Indies, on the other hand, because they were economically vital, Japan was more reluctant to relinquish direct control. Each was put under military administration, centralized and bureaucratic in its methods, which replaced the officialdom of the former colonial powers. Nor were freedom movements of any kind encouraged in the first two years. Even thereafter no very extensive promises were made, though regional councils were established and local residents were allowed to play some part in government. In Malaya, in fact, this was as much as was done for the rest of the war, though in the Indies a nationalist movement developed and was at last recognized by the Japanese when their defeat was obvious in 1945, a fact that enabled its leader, Dr Soekarno, to declare Indonesian independence immediately after Japan's surrender in August of that year.

Apart from the long-term problem of maintaining these states as dependencies, Japan's colonial policy was also directed to the task of exploiting their anti-Western sentiments and economic resources in support of her own defence. In this she was a great deal less successful. For one thing, the harshness of her rule tended to alienate the very people whose sympathy she was trying to win. All too often executions and torture produced, not co-operation, but hatred and resistance, which her enemies found it easy to put to use. There was a good deal of inefficiency, too, since the Greater East Asia Ministry, established in November 1942, recruited most of its staff from the diplomats and commercial representatives whom the war had brought back from Europe and elsewhere, or from journalists and traders whose jobs had given them a nodding acquaintance with the areas to be governed. The former lacked local knowledge, the latter administrative experience and expertise, while both found it impossible to pursue any policy which conflicted with the views of army commanders. To this handicap was added a lack of trained technicians capable of restoring the trade and industry of South East Asia, especially the production of oil, to their former efficiency, so that the plan for creating a powerful and self-sufficient economic bloc experienced difficulties from the very start.

They were increased by the consequences of military failure. Allied submarine attacks interfered seriously with sea communications among the islands as early as 1942. When they were supplemented by an air offensive later in the war, Japan found herself almost completely cut off from her more distant — and more valuable — possessions. Three-quarters of her merchant marine had been lost by the summer of 1945 in an attempt to keep the sea lanes open. One result was to handicap industrial production at home, so that the traditional rivalry between army and navy was accentuated by disputes over the allocation of equipment, to a point at which even the co-ordination of their respective operations was affected. Their quarrels did much to render useless the fanatical courage with which Japanese units fought.

Indeed, it was soon apparent that it was not going to be easy for the services to fulfil the role which had been assigned them, namely, of holding an extended perimeter while Japan replenished her reserves, so that America could be persuaded to accept a compromise peace. Not only was the economic development of the Co-prosperity Sphere much slower, but the American counter-offensive was much faster than had been expected. The naval battles of the Coral Sea at the beginning of May 1942 and of Midway a month later foiled Japanese thrusts towards Australia and Hawaii respectively, the former being confirmed by the successful Australian defence of southern New Guinea in the rest of the year. Then, as Japan's first major repulse on land, came the American recapture of Guadalcanal in the Solomon islands, ending after six months' bitter fighting in February 1943. These operations, it later appeared, marked a strategic turning-point.

During them, moreover, a new pattern of warfare was evolving: in naval engagements, action at long range, using aircraft from carriers as the main offensive weapons — a development which largely offset Japan's initial advantage in capital ships — and in island campaigns, close co-operation between land, sea and air forces, preferably under unified command. These became the main ingredients in an American 'island-hopping' technique designed, not to regain territory in any general sense, but to win bases from which ships and aircraft could dominate wide areas of the west Pacific.

In January 1943 allied leaders met at Casablanca and agreed to divert more resources to the war against Japan. In August they followed this up at Quebec by naming their commanders and outlining the strategy to be used. Within a few months forces under Admiral Chester Nimitz, acting in accordance with these decisions, had attacked the Marshall islands in the central Pacific, demonstrating for the first of many times the overwhelming weight of metal that could be brought against an island target and the speed with which it could be reduced if enemy reinforcement were made impossible. The key base of Kwajalein was captured in ten days' fighting in February 1944. Saipan in the Marianas took a little longer (mid-June to early July 1944) and involved a full fleet action, the battle of the Philippine Sea, to cover the landings. This broke the back of Japanese naval resistance, however, and made even more rapid progress possible elsewhere. Guam fell in August, the Palau group in September, completing an 'advance' of over two thousand miles in less than a year.

The emphasis now swung to the South West Pacific, where General Douglas MacArthur was in command. In September 1944, simultaneously with the attack on

Palau, his forces landed on Morotai off the northern coast of New Guinea. A month later they reached the Philippines, completing the occupation of Leyte by the end of December and invading Luzon in January 1945. Manila was captured on February 5. From this point the two commands were able to act together, their first target being Okinawa in the Ryukyu islands, which was secured by late June, their next an invasion of Japan itself. The Japanese fleet was no longer a serious threat, having been virtually destroyed in a further naval battle in the Leyte Gulf in October 1944. This left the offshore defence of the homeland to the suicide tactics of planes and midget submarines, a kind of fighting which experience at Okinawa had shown to be terrifying, but not fully effective. Since a land campaign had also begun in Burma, which, together with the guerilla activities of Chinese communists and nationalists, was engaging the attention of a substantial proportion of Japan's available troops, success for an invasion seemed highly probable, the more so as Germany's surrender in May 1945 enabled the allies to devote all their efforts to it.

The first stage of preparation was the bombing of Japanese industries and cities. The use of land-based aircraft for this purpose had begun from Saipan the previous autumn and was made easier by the capture of Iwojima in March 1945. Then operations began from Okinawa, growing rapidly in frequency and extending to the whole of Japan, so that by the summer the country was in a state of siege. Shipping to and from the mainland almost ceased. Most industrial centres, despite attempts at dispersal, suffered heavy damage, while incendiary raids on urban areas, made as an attack on Japanese morale, brought casualties which included over 200,000 killed. Rail transport, suffering not only from bombing but from lack of maintenance, began to deteriorate rapidly, contributing to a situation in which production, even of munitions, dropped sharply from its wartime peaks. Consumer goods became wellnigh unobtainable. Food was scarce, prices rising, black markets everywhere. Nor was there much that was encouraging in the visual scene. People in the streets were drab, the men in a kind of khaki suiting that was virtually a civilian uniform, the women in dark working-trousers or the dullest of kimono. Vehicles were ramshackle, buses having been converted to charcoal-burning to save fuel and their windows, like those of trains and trams, boarded up to save replacing glass. With it all, the population was required to work harder, and for less reward, than ever before. Education had been curtailed to get more students into the army and the factories. Restrictions on child and female labour had been abolished. Even the regulations which limited working hours, mild though they were, had been swept away.

Despite the evidence around them, press and radio constantly assured the Japanese that they could win the war, if only they would make a supreme effort — sometimes it was called a supreme sacrifice — in their own defence. The enemy had over-extended his communications; he had underestimated Japanese strength; he would never accept the casualties which a determined people could make him suffer. All these arguments and many more were used to justify — and make possible — a last-ditch stand.

Nevertheless, most of Japan's leaders had by this time few illusions about the fact of military defeat. Some of them, like Yoshida Shigeru, Shigemitsu Mamoru and others with a diplomatic background, had begun to think of a compromise peace as early as 1943; and their influence, together with a secret war study prepared by a member of the Naval General Staff, which clearly indicated that victory was unattainable, won over men close to the emperor, including the former Prime Minister, Konoe Fumimaro. When Saipan was captured in 1944 they moved to bring about Tojo's fall, helping to force the resignation of his cabinet on July 18. His successor, General Koiso Kuniaki, another member of the Kwantung Army group, proved no more amenable, but he, too, could not survive for long in the face of a deteriorating military situation. Air raids on Tokyo and news of the landings on Okinawa brought his resignation on April 5 1945. This made way for an aged and much respected admiral, Suzuki Kantaro, who was known privately to favour ending the war, if it could be done with honour.

The War Minister, Anami Korechika, backed by Tojo and the high command, was still resolutely opposed to any peace moves. Accordingly, the talks now undertaken with the Russian ambassador in Japan, which superseded earlier approaches made in Konoe's name to the Swedish minister, were officially to seek a basis for improving Russo–Japanese relations, though many senior statesmen were clearly hoping to get Russian mediation in the Pacific war. Towards the end of June they succeeded, albeit with difficulty, in getting this second purpose formally avowed, only to find Russia unresponsive. Despite a proposal that Konoe should go to Moscow as an imperial envoy to negotiate a peace, no progress had been made in the discussions when the allied powers, with Russia's concurrence, issued the Potsdam Declaration on July 26.

The declaration, made in the names of Britain, America and China, called for the unconditional surrender of Japan, to be followed by military occupation, demilitarization and loss of territory. This left little prospect of the kind of settlement which the uncommitted in Japan, especially in the services, might have been persuaded to accept. Indeed, it brought a temporary closing of the ranks behind those who were willing to go down fighting. This, however, lasted only for about a week. On August 6, 1945, the first atom bomb was dropped on Hiroshima and three days later another destroyed most of Nagasaki, the second coming less than twenty-four hours after a Russian declaration of war upon Japan. To the great majority, these events made surrender imperative — and at once.

Even so, the War Minister and the two Chiefs of Staff refused to give way, arguing throughout meetings of the Supreme War Council and the cabinet on August 9 that conditions must be attached to any acceptance of the allied ultimatum. The result was deadlock, broken at last by the emperor at an imperial conference after midnight, when he gave a ruling in favour of those who urged that surrender be subject only to a reservation of his own prerogatives as sovereign ruler. In this form the message was handed to Swiss representatives on August 10 for transmission to the allies. The latter's reply, making no mention of the imperial prerogative, precipitated another series of disputes in the next few days, which were resolved, like the previous ones, by the emperor's intervention. The decision to surrender on the allies' terms was therefore made public on August 15, 1945.

This was not quite the end of the story, for Japan's career of conquest was to end, as it had begun, with attempted mutiny and disorder. Officers of the War Ministry and General Staff, determined to prevent the emperor from broadcasting the announcement of defeat, broke into the palace on the night of August 14 to search for the recording of his speech, though they did not find it. Others set fire to the homes of the Prime Minister and President of the Privy Council. When all this failed to reverse the decision, many, including War Minister Anami himself, committed suicide, several doing so on the plaza opposite the palace gates. It was in this turbulent atmosphere that orders were given for a ceasefire on August 16 and a new government, headed by an imperial prince to give it greater prestige, formed the following day to see that they were carried out. By September 2, when members of it signed the instrument of surrender aboard the American flagship in Tokyo Bay, American troops had already begun to arrive for the occupation of Japan.

Post-war Reconstruction and the Economic Miracle

The principal question posed at the beginning of this volume — why has Japan succeeded? — is the problem which must be returned to now. But it is only by approaching this issue within its full context, which involves scrutiny of both geo-political and domestic factors, that a comprehensive understanding can be gained. Japan's rapid, phoenix-like recovery in the aftermath of the Pacific War, and the subsequent economic miracle of the 1960s, were products of the complex interaction of international relations and internal causes.

In defeat Japan was occupied by the Supreme Command Allied Powers (SCAP), which in theory represented the consortium of Western allies opposed to the Axis countries but in practice was synonymous with America alone. In all its history Japan had never been invaded and the trauma of such an impending catastrophe was envisaged by emperor Hirohito as 'enduring the unendurable and suffering what is insufferable'. But despite Japanese expectations the American occupation from 1945 to 1952 proved to be benign and dynamic in terms of the reform and social change it initiated. For America, though, these policies were driven as much by fears of contemporary developments on the Asian mainland as by desires to preserve peace. The victory of the Chinese revolution in 1949 was sudden and unexpected and in these early phases of the Cold War the spread of communism to China, and then conceivably to Korea, produced the greatest alarm among American policy-makers.

Economic recovery in Japan was to be heavily influenced by America's post-war preoccupation with stemming the tide of communism. Japan was to enter into a special relationship with America as a subordinate partner in East Asia. Resurgent industry was to be given large and lucrative orders for armament production for American forces to use in the Korean War from 1950 to 1953 and then in the Vietnam War in the 1960s and 1970s. As junior partner in an alliance with America, Japan's economy was to benefit on all fronts, but the constraints which this was to place on social development produced a high tide of political opposition and lingering resentment that resonates within popular consciousness to this day.

In no sense, however, does this special relationship fully explain Japanese economic recovery. It is true that the $2 billion of American aid, provided from 1946 to 1951 for use in pump-priming Japan's economy, was of inestimable value to a war shattered industry and infrastructure. But the fact that Japan paid America $4 billion in the same period as costs of the SCAP occupation, shows that the rapid growth of the economy cannot be attributed to injections of foreign capital alone and further enquiry is required. Apart from the level of GDP, Japan in the 1940s was not like a Third World country struggling to emerge from a state of underdevelopment. Japan had a well established urban-industrial tradition: the workforce was highly skilled, literate and disciplined and there were no barriers to economic development posed by religious, ethnic or cultural divisions. Population growth declined rapidly after the war as a result of government policy, which eased the need for capital accumulation for social

345

investment. A long tradition of poor social service provision has always meant that Japan has had a high personal savings to income ratio, which provided an additional source of available capital for reinvestment. But these positive factors were also present in a variety of other post-war economies and while they are necessary aspects of growth they do not in themsleves constitute sufficient cause of growth.

SCAP ended several decades of dictatorship causing a surge of popular political expression. Trade union membership rose from near zero to six million in less than the first two years of the occupation. Both socialists and communists, who had faced banning and exile until 1945, became free to organise their political parties, which grew rapidly in size and influence. Working-class militancy also grew in conditions of rampant inflation and high unemployment, aggravated by the final return of Japanese migrants and military personnel from Asia. The new-found power of Japan's masses expressed a range of social grievances — that had remained suppressed for several generations — in a wave of strikes, factory occupations and demonstrations. Growth of left-wing political power led to mounting fear among the forces of the largely unpurged establishment right that Japan would join the socialist bloc on a wave of popular support.

Having unwittingly unleashed this militancy, SCAP's main objective in the early 1950s was to rein it in by the reconstitution and reform of the conservative political and business élites. Above all SCAP intended to 'make Japan safe from communism', and this was to be achieved through a mixture of liberal capitalist reforms and the refurbishment and reinstatement of the state apparatus in a modified form. Halliday presents an overview and analysis of this critical period of social development and in particular he provides convincing reasons that explain why Japan's weakened industrial working class came to lack mass militancy after the 1960s. His examination also leads us to the fact that in Japan the lack of any effective political opposition to a parliamentary élite, which has retained its power base for over forty years, has allowed government policies for economic growth to dominate all other considerations. A government able to do almost whatever it likes has a much greater chance of single-mindedly promoting successful economic policies than one impeded by countervailing pressures within a truly democratic system.

There are, however, other equally significant factors which explain Japan's economic ascent. The first of these is the structure and organisation of Japanese industry and the second concerns the relationship between the state and the large business corporations.

Japan's pre-war industrial structure had been dominated by the *zaibatsu* or 'financial cliques', vast, monopolistic industrial giants that controlled whole sectors of the economy, such as metals or chemicals, through a labyrinth of subsidiary companies. Zaibatsu operations often comprised an integrated set of production functions which included the original extraction of raw material, its transportation, refinement, eventual manufacture and even its final marketing. Even the finance of a zaibatsu was part of the integrated conglomeration since this was based upon a bank that was both owned by and dedicated to the group alone. Zaibatsu ownership was normally in the hands of a single holding company that was itself frequently owned by a single family. The lack of any intervening stock-holding class that might have ameliorated zaibatsu policies, and in particular prevented its close association with Japan's military élite and their imperialistic aggression, was seen by SCAP as a reason for reforming these monopolies.

In doing so SCAP ushered in a new breed of industrial giant, the *keiretsu* or 'enterprise group', a form of corporate organisation which has been largely responsible for producing the economic miracle. The zaibatsu had been conceived soon after the founding of modern Japanese industry and in these early times provided a valuable concentration of scarce capital and skill, but by 1945 they had become industrial dinosaurs. The American reforms had the effect of ending the gross inefficiencies of the zaibatsu by substituting a new system of industrial organisation in which autonomous and competing companies combined for mutual advantage. Under the keiretsu system groups of independent companies effectively pool their resources by providing each other with goods and services at preferential rates to those offered by companies belonging to other groups. All aspects of production including marketing, distribution, exporting, design, storage and transport are performed by the keiretsu's co-operating companies. Financial services for research and development as well as specific projects and the investment of enterprise capital is generated by banks within each keiretsu. These competing oligopolies, exemplified by rival groups in a range of industries, have been the efficient means by which the economic miracle has been achieved.

Japan's long tradition of co-operation between government and industry must also be seen in this context. Since the 1950s the keiretsu and smaller associated companies have operated within a close state-industry relationship. To a large extent the Japanese state planned and managed the dramatic period of economic growth of the 1960s and 1970s and continues to be closely involved with the activities of the large corporations. But the state-industry relationship in Japan goes further than involvement and co-ordination, which are frequent aspects of modern industrial policy, because to a large extent the state directs the economy. Special units within the civil service provide targeted sectors of industry with guidance and nurture. A company that is adopted for official direction may be given help and protection in the form of low interest finance, subsidies, special tariff rates on its imports of critical equipment, lower taxes and a host of specialist services including finance and export intelligence. The implementation of this economic strategy is the theme followed in the extracts taken from the works of Johnson and Eccleston.

This is the form of economic organisation which has produced long-term sustained growth, however, the *social effects* of the strategy adopted by the Japanese government have not been entirely beneficial to the country as a whole. The slogan *fukoku hinmin* — enrich the country: impoverish the people — is cynically used to describe modern Japan. Fukutake provides an outline of the social and environmental costs of Japan's rapid economic ascent.

Historians of the future will be obliged to explain Japan's economic miracle in terms of at least some of the factors that have been discussed here. But they are also likely to be struck by the irony that it was the Japanese state which successfully planned its capitalist economy, and that this was done with a thoroughness and efficiency which put socialist planning systems in the former Eastern bloc to shame.

23. The Destruction of the Sanbetsu Kaigi and the Formation of Sōhyō

Jon Halliday

With the collapse of the Ashida cabinet, a caretaker government was formed under Yoshida, who quickly called a new general election to capitalize on the Socialists' disarray. The election on January 24, 1949, shattered the Socialist Party, whose seats fell from 143 to 48 in the Lower House, while the Communist Party was enormously strengthened, winning 35 seats and nearly 10 per cent of the vote. The overall result, however, was a swing to the right and Yoshida became premier of the new post-election government, a post he was to hold for nearly six years. Yoshida, with SCAP backing, now moved the anti-union struggle into higher gear. This took the form of a linked attack on two fronts: extensive subversion of left-wing unions from within, via so-called "democratization leagues" or *mindō* and an "anti-inflationary" policy, one of whose chief features was retrenchment and wholesale dismissals of militant workers.

As early as the end of 1946, a concerted effort began to weaken the Sanbetsu and the left-wing unions by forming right-wing cells within them. The main element in this tactic was an appeal to anti-communism, a slogan which had several components: on the one hand, it was alleged that the Communist Party was somehow manipulating the unions, turning their struggle into a "political" one; further, the JCP was alleged to be subservient to Moscow. SCAP's Labor Section took an active role in promoting the *mindō*, part of a global struggle to split the world union movement which had recently united under left-wing leadership in the World Federation of Trade Unions. SCAP was aided by Japanese police intimidation and open intervention on the shop floor, as well as by management and government pressures of dismissal, pay and promotion. Special efforts were made to split the National Railway Workers' Union, one of the key militant organizations, in which over 100,000 workers were later fired, and in the All Communications Employees' Union. Estimates vary of the number of workers who joined *mindō*, but there is no doubt that the leagues, in conjunction with deflation, mass layoffs and repression, were an important instrument in weakening the left. Sōhyō, the biggest union federation in Japan for more than the past twenty years, was originally founded as part of the anti-communist drive which began with the *mindō*.

Even before the Dodge Plan, Ashida had carried out a major round of dismissals after the events in July 1948. But it was the implementation of the Dodge proposals which led to firings and layoffs on a really large scale. This retrenchment programme, again, is often presented under the technical guise of a "deflationary" policy. But it was much more than this, for it was specifically designed to eliminate a large sector of the militant left, and to reorganize and strengthen oligopoly capital. In 1949 alone, 435,465 workers were dismissed from their jobs, and the figure for the whole 1949–50

Jon Halliday: 'The Destruction of the Sanbetsu Kaigi and the Formation of Sōhyō' from *A POLITICAL HISTORY OF JAPANESE CAPITALISM* (Monthly Review Press, 1975), pp. 217–234. Copyright © 1975 by Jon Halliday. Reprinted by permission of Monthly Review Federation.

retrenchment was about 700,000. Although, on the whole, the Dodge programme involved expanding big industry and therefore employment in big industry, the reorganization was used carefully to weed out militant workers in these expanding sectors, and to weaken the union movement overall by cutting total employment. In roughly the same period as 700,000 workers lost their jobs, the number of unions fell by more than 5,500 and union membership by 880,000. The government purges were accompanied by direct promotion of the anti-communist *mindō*, which were thus enabled to take over the union leadership through this double-barrelled operation.

This retrenchment was extremely important in assisting management to consolidate its dominant position over the working class. The many dismissals naturally made employees more desperate to hold on to their jobs. The figures on the disappearance of unions and the precipitous fall in union membership cover a multiplicity of personal tragedies among the proletariat. As jobs became more and more scarce, and unions which would back the workers' interests weaker and weaker, the pressures to compromise with management by acceding to the latter's version of the enterprise union became stronger and stronger. Whereas in the early postwar period an enterprise union had usually contained all the employees in a plant, management now seized the initiative and demanded that the union grant membership only to a limited number of the enterprise's employees viz., usually the *minimum* work force which the company would want to employ at the period of maximum retrenchment. Workers, desperate to keep their jobs, were obliged to go along with this definition of the union, which thus became limited to so-called "permanent" workers. Correspondingly, there was now a re-expansion of the number of "temporary" workers, as there had been in the 1930s, on similarly disadvantageous conditions.

As Taira has shown, the inordinately large wage differentials between big and smaller industry which have been specific to Japan developed very quickly in the years 1945–51, in spite of high inflation during most of the period. He ascribes this to the strength of the enterprise unions in the early period. What is surprising is that the tendency accelerated during the period of deflation. The upshot of the growth in wage differentials, however, was a counter-offensive by management, paradoxically. By restricting membership of the enterprise unions during the Dodge Line period, business both cut down the number of employees who had a (relatively) high guaranteed wage, and correspondingly increased its own chances of exploiting "temporary" and other non-"permanent" labour, and of devolving work to subcontracting firms, where unions were much weaker, or non-existent, and wages far lower. This constellation of factors had very important effects on the structure of postwar Japanese industrialization, since labour costs, unionization and company size all formed a nexus determining the structure of investments and work allocations. In brief, in return for guaranteeing a relatively high wage to a limited number of workers, protected by a union and a negotiated agreement, business ensured itself a much larger pool of labour ("temporary," casual, subcontracted, etc.) which was almost wholly un-unionized, employed in small and medium enterprises, and heavily discriminated against. Business's main goals included not simply cheap labour, but also *weak* labour. The discriminatory wage *and union* system, which was largely the work of management, ensured both these, but also involved business in the apparently curious

350

situation of securing its own expansion by maintaining an archaic industrial structure, with a relatively small number of large enterprises, with high unionization and high wages, while the large majority of workers continued to be employed in very small factories, almost wholly un-unionized, and with much lower wage levels. The success of business's low-wage, anti-union policy has been a major element in Japan's postwar expansion, and in the right's retention of political power at the centre.

The assault on the militant working class on the shop floor was accompanied by action at other levels: in education, where a major purge had been launched by SCAP and the Yoshida regime from the beginning of 1949, in the media, and at the party political level. In May–June 1950, before the outbreak of the Korean War, MacArthur launched a direct attack on the leadership of the Communist Party and on its newspaper, *Akahata (Red Flag)*. This purge of political leaders on the left started well before the outbreak of the Korean War, and it was a direct continuation of the dismissals of militant workers which had marked the overall drive to cripple the left.

MacArthur's announcement on May 3, 1950 of a stepped-up drive to root out "destructive communist elements," often referred to as the "Red Purge," took on the proportions of a nationwide witchhunt. Though this phase of the operation tends to be better known than others because it hit prominent political and media figures, the really crucial part of crippling the left was the destruction of Sanbetsu and Zenrōren, the wholesale wrecking of the militant unions and the dismissal of hundreds of thousands of workers who were the backbone of the struggle. As the Sanbetsu and the left were being gravely weakened, the Yoshida government, the Employers' Federation (Nikkeiren) and SCAP worked towards a new union coalition based largely on the *mindō*. The new federation, Sōhyō, was founded in July 1950, immediately after the purge of the JCP and the start of the Korean War. As the head of Sōhyō wrote to George Meany in 1965: "the history of the foundation of Sōhyō is closely connected with the fight against the domination of the Japanese trade unions by the Communist Party." Just after the formation of Sōhyō, Sanbetsu membership dropped to 47,000, and in 1953 it went down to 13,000. The Federation was dissolved on February 15, 1958.

Although Sōhyō moved to the left on a number of issues connected with foreign policy and U.S. imperialism shortly after it was founded, it retained a cautious position on domestic matters related to industrial relations. Sōhyō's domestic platform and the wrecking of the Sanbetsu were a big victory for business in imposing the seniority-wage system and intra-enterprise unions, which Sōhyō began to challenge only in the mid-fifties. However, on other questions Sōhyō took up a fairly militant stance. It opposed the terms of the San Francisco Treaty and the Security Treaty. It also opposed attempts to force it into the anti-communist International Confederation of Free Trade Unions, which had recently seceded from the World Federation of Trade Unions. Sōhyō lined up with the JCP and the left of the JSP in opposing the terms under which the United States conceded formal independence, and this experience determined the outlook of the federation in the years ahead. Sōhyō, for example, took a leading part in the 1959–60 struggles against revision of the Security Treaty with the United States.

The union movement since formal Independence (1952)

Although business succeeded in re-establishing its dominant position after the immediate post-surrender period, this dominance has not gone unchallenged, and important changes have taken place both in the methods of struggle and in the balance of power between labour and capital since that early period. The Korean War brought about a large upsurge in employment and in output. In many cases this involved reactivating old equipment in conditions where employers felt unsure of the future. Business insisted that many of the workers taken on be employed on a "temporary" basis, since, it claimed, it could not guarantee the regular employment which the unions were demanding. Business continued to use much the same arguments against the unions in the years after 1955 when a new wave of "temporary" employees was hired in the wake of technological innovations. At this stage the unions were too conservative, and too much on the defensive, to react.

Taira, following Magota, periodizes the history of the Japanese unions so that the postwar enterprise unionism forms a unit with the wartime Sampō; and this stage interpenetrates from the mid-1950s with a new stage — that of the "spring offensive" or Shuntō, which is now the main feature of Japanese union activity. Shuntō is a peculiarly Japanese phenomenon. It can be explained as a means to counter the weakness of the enterprise system. Since individual enterprise unions had such difficulty organizing across enterprise lines, a group of Sōhyō leaders took the initiative, in 1955, of trying to organize a joint offensive rather than a lasting federation. This offensive has been repeated every spring and began to show results about 1960. Each year the Shuntō organizers, Sōhyō and the Chūritsurōren, choose a lead-off union, one which is in a particularly strong bargaining position either because of its internal strength or because of its crucial place in the economy. The Private Railway Workers' Union and the Iron and Steel Workers' Union have most often been chosen to "go first." The settlement achieved by this union, which is backed up by other unions, tends to set the standard for agreements between management and the other unions involved in the Shuntō: average wage increases achieved in this way rose steadily from 1965 to hit 17 per cent in 1970, falling to around 15 per cent in 1971 and 1972, but going back up to almost 20 per cent in 1973. Clearly the acute labour shortage from the late 1960s was an important factor in increasing wages. But there are a number of other factors specific to Japan which explain the Shuntō's success.

Because of the high ratio of credit financing on which Japanese companies tend to operate, plus the crucial importance of maintaining a given market share, Japanese firms are very badly placed to survive a long strike. This strengthens the position of the unions who, through the "spring offensive," have been able not just to win an increase for one union, but by the mechanism of trans-enterprise solidarity, persuade other firms to make quick settlements along the lines achieved by the lead union. In fact, the average length of strikes in the Shunto has been only between 2.0 and 3.3 days. In theory, of course, any individual union could win a big wage increase by striking against a firm which could not afford a long strike, but it has been precisely the element of solidarity which has given the Shuntō its strength.

To a Western observer, the curious factor is probably why the unions strike *before* negotiations, or at any rate before a stalemate has been reached. There may be an element of ceremony here, but there is also an important economic–cultural factor at work. Fundamentally, Japanese business has still not accepted a union's right to speak for its members. In innumerable ways a union is still treated as a body which is sabotaging the enterprise's harmony and the "beautiful" relations between exploiters and exploited. Because of the broad gamut of discriminations against unions, they more or less have to prove each year that they do represent the workers they claim to represent, and that these workers are united behind a given goal. Through the Shuntō the unions try to tell management that they do represent the workers; management then has only a short time, usually, to come to a settlement.

Japanese unionism is in a transitional stage. Enterprise unions still are the dominant form of union; but at the same time the Shuntō provides a solid form of multi-union coalition which can be mobilized annually, even if it is not an all-year institution like a union confederation in the Western countries. In some ways, the Shuntō is clearly stronger than most Western confederations .

But the relative success of the Shuntō needs to be set in perspective. First, labour's share of gross value added. Over the entire period of the postwar boom as a whole, wages have risen considerably more slowly than productivity; moreover, wages have moved across a much narrower band than productivity. The crucial fact is that labour's share of gross value added has been falling constantly whereas it has risen in all the other major capitalist countries. Labour's share in Japan fell from 39.6 per cent in 1953 to 33.8 per cent in 1966, and an estimated 33.7 in 1970. This compares with figures of over 50 per cent for Canada, Sweden, Holland and the United Kingdom. Thus, not only is labour's share of gross value added much lower than in comparable capitalist countries, but this share is falling constantly. The gap between the rich and the poor, in spite of government rhetoric, is constantly growing.

In addition, Japanese workers as of 1970 had, on average, the longest working week of any of the advanced capitalist countries: 43.1 hours (45.0 in an ordinary week), compared with 39.1 hours in West Germany, and 37.5 in the United States. For this they were paid less, absolutely, than workers in these other countries.

As of 1970, only about 35 per cent of all industrial workers were unionized (the U.K. figure is about 40 per cent). Of unionized workers, some one-third did not then belong to any of the four main federations. Unionization still depends very much on the size of the plant: 63 per cent of companies employing more than 500 people had unions; one-third of those employing 100–500 had unions; but less than 10 per cent of those employing 30–100 workers had a union, and for smaller companies the figure was 4 per cent. In the same year (1970), 58,000 unions were organized on an enterprise basis, though the number of unions combining blue- and white-collar workers had fallen considerably, to below half.

There is, therefore, a direct correlation between company size, degree of unionization, wage levels and employment systems. In fact, in the context of the government's overall economic policy, and business's decisions about investment, it is clear that unionization is only a partial index of the strength of the working class. Indeed, it is fair to say that formal unionization does not represent the fully autonomous aspirations of the working class, but rather the common ground between labour and capital, and that within the total context of Japanese industrialization the unions represent instruments of conciliation, in the last instance, between the two sides.

The weakness of Sōhyō

Although Sōhyō has moved quite a long way from its starting point in 1950, it has never fully escaped from the limitations which marked its inception or formed a really cohesive central organization. Thus in the 1960s when big business launched a major subversive drive against it, business was able to undermine the federation by setting up new "democratization leagues," which soon combined to form a new, more right-wing federation, the Dōmei-kaigi (reorganized in November 1964 as Dōmei), which soon became the second biggest in the country. By mid-1971 Dōmei had well over two million members and, what is more important, overtook Sōhyō in private industry in 1967. In 1970 Sōhyō had only 39 per cent of its members in private industry, while Dōmei had no less than 93 per cent, being especially strong in the electronic, automobile and textile industries. Thus, although Sōhyō has been responsible for a very high proportion of the registered strikes and other industrial disputes, it has not mounted any major challenge to capital.

On the contrary, Sōhyō has pursued a centrist and essentially collaborationist policy on the shop floor. It has refused, or been unable, to make the leap across such capitalist-imposed barriers as those dividing "permanent" from "temporary" and other workers. Sōhyō-affiliated unions have supinely accepted management directives to exclude "temporary" workers from membership, even in the stage of high growth, and consequent labour shortage. Sōhyō's role in the key sector of steel is exemplary. The Yawata–Fuji (re-)merger produced the biggest steel firm in the world, Nippon Steel. The local union at Yawata, affiliated to the Federation of Steel Workers' Union (which is in Sōhyō), was completely debilitated from within by the company, which systematically isolated the militant members. At the time of the re-merger, the union was entirely in the hands of the company's representatives, and yet was still accepted by Sōhyō.

Sōhyō went along with the JSP and the JCP in excluding members of the militant workers' group, the Hansen Seinen Iinkai, from its ranks. It also cut its ties with Beheiren, the loose-knit, but dynamic and influential anti-imperialist movement that grew up at the time of the Vietnam War. As one observer recently stated, Sōhyō has aided the integration of the working class into capitalism: "real disruption would be more likely without this organization."

THE MECHANISMS OF CAPITALIST CONTROL

The exploitation of women

The exploitation of women has been absolutely central to the whole development of Japanese capitalism: low-wage female labour has been a key factor in the accumulation of capital since the beginning of industry in Japan. Moreover, discrimination against women in wages, terms of employment and pensions is still qualitatively more severe in Japan than in the other advanced capitalist societies.

First, there is the whole area of housework and other completely unpaid labour. In the late 1960s only 63 per cent of the employed labour force were actually classed as employees at all, and about 17 per cent of the employed were unpaid family workers (including some 8 per cent of those employed outside agriculture and forestry). A high proportion of these can reasonably be assumed to be women. Moreover, it is impossible even to know how many women are *unemployed*, since government statistics describe most people who are not working as "without occupation" rather than "unemployed." A 1969 survey found that nearly one-quarter of those women classified as "without occupation" wanted "employment."

But it is in factory work that women play the biggest role. In 1972 women accounted for 32.4 per cent of all employed workers in the economy as a whole (11.2 million out of 34.52 million), but they accounted for no less than 57.5 per cent of all factory workers — and 46.8 per cent of all office workers, the next biggest area. The importance of the exploitation of women can be seen from the fact that, while they provide well over half the factory workers in Japan, the average woman's wage is only 48.2 per cent of the average man's wage. Moreover, women are excluded from the *nenkō* system and are forced into *formal* retirement much earlier than men — often being statutorily dismissed at the age of thirty, or at marriage. By firing women so early, and by excluding them from any system of guaranteed wage increases, business can then re-hire them cheaply after marriage or in old age at particularly low rates, a practice which became increasingly common as the labour shortage became more acute. This barrage of discriminatory measures against women not only helps management keep their wages down, but also has aided management in preserving sexist exclusionism in the unions, which have been appallingly passive on this issue. Organized action against this system is now beginning, with attention focused on the early obligatory "retirement," but this action is largely taking place outside the established union framework. Further, as Kaji Etsuko trenchantly notes, both sexist ideology and the whole "division of labour" between the state and private industry stand in the way of any major improvement in women's lot: "in Japan, the strength of the sexist ideology is reflected in an appalling lack of social services for children to make women *prefer* grossly underpaid jobs as temporary workers, because this is the only way they can combine work with childcare" – which the ideology promotes as their main function.

General mechanisms for weakening the proletariat: the organization of the work force

One of the most striking features of the Japanese economy is that although in terms of GNP it is the third largest in the world, as of the late 1960s two-thirds of all employees in manufacturing were still employed in small and medium enterprises. This is partly the result of the historical formation of Japanese industry, with many plants sited in rural areas, with only limited labour and raw materials available, very bad transportation, and, until recently, very few people in urban areas. But it also represents a deliberate option by capitalism, since the smaller the enterprise the lower the wages which employers have had to pay (although productivity has also been lower). Smaller enterprises, being proportionately less unionized, have also allowed management greater freedom of action in reducing wages and firing workers, as well as sources for cheap labour which can be used in subcontracting outside *and inside* bigger plants. There are also other economic factors connected to credit and cash-flow which have made it advantageous for big business to maintain smaller, subordinate companies.

Even with this advantageous big/small industry division, business has worked to maintain the key elements in its wage and employment system: the special discrimination against women, the division of workers into "permanent" and others, and the division of pay into "basic" and other. In this way, *pace* Abegglen, both labour force and wages have been kept variable, at management's wishes, providing a *double* cushion.

Outside the core of "permanent" employees, business has developed a flexible band of non-"permanent" workers. These are: "temporary" workers, some of whom are *permanent* temporary workers; day-labourers and casual workers; *shagaikō* (extra workers); and subcontractors. There is not universal agreement on how many people are covered by the guaranteed employment system. According to one source, in the early 1960s it covered only one-fifth of all wage-earners in manufacturing. Another source, referring to the late 1960s, states that it covers "perhaps not even a majority" of Japanese workers. Those who are covered by it include most regular workers in large corporations, governmental employees, including those in governmental corporations, and university employees. Those excluded are all temporary employees of large corporations, day-labourers, and most employees of medium and small industry. Probably nearly all the long-term employees in big private industry are covered by some kind of guarantee system. But conditions vary enormously in small and medium plants, where it would seem that firms subcontracting to bigger enterprises, or otherwise closely subordinate to them, tend not to have a *nenkō*-type system, whereas independent smaller industries do.

This cushioning system is almost invulnerable. The stipulation that unions may usually only enroll permanent workers in effect enlists the unions' aid in perpetuating the discriminations, and in fragmenting the working class.

The use of "temporary," subcontracted and other types of labour at much lower wages varies greatly between different sectors of industry, and, by size of enterprise. The highest number of temporary workers is employed in *big* industry, where the "saving" tends to be highest. The car industry has had a particularly high proportion of "temporary" workers, an average of 19 per cent for the whole sector in 1957, with Toyota showing the staggering figure of 52 per cent of all employees being "temporary" in 1961. Business also invented the category of "permanent temporary" workers, who were just kept on low pay in spite of being employed for very long periods by one enterprise. The number of "temporary" and day workers reportedly dropped towards the mid-1960s, amounting to 5 per cent of all employees in private establishments as of mid-1966.

Probably more important than the "temporary" worker ploy is the extensive use of subcontracting. This involves not only putting work out to smaller enterprises which pay lower wages, but also using workers from these smaller plants *in* the "parent" plant, where they are paid less than the big enterprise's permanent workers for exactly the same job. This practice appears to be particularly prevalent in the shipbuilding and construction industries, although it is impossible to get precise figures on "internal subcontracting." By paying all these non- "permanent" workers considerably less, and by keeping them in a situation where there is no job guarantee, business protects itself against recessions, as well as against other troubles such as strikes, allowing it to "adjust" at its discretion.

The other key element in this is the structure of wages. For male permanent workers, management makes a calculation which in essence boils down to this: we will pay you x amount of money for the "lifetime" you spend with us (i.e., from hiring date to compulsory retirement date), but we will pay it out to you at our own rate, which *starts* very low, but will rise fairly steadily to about age 40–44 and then fall again gradually until retirement in the mid- to late 50s (and very steeply after that). In this way, business, holding out the carrot of "fair" wages only in return for a long-term commitment by a worker, secures a cheap labour force. Moreover, as well as usually being the most productive, younger workers are often the most militant, and the seniority-wage system, on the whole, strengthens the position of older employees. The Shuntō and other actions seem in the context of a growing labour shortage to have had a good deal of effect on the gap in *starting* wages between big and small industry, but not on the *internal* pay differentiations in either big or small enterprises, which have stayed very much the same. Starting wages for all sizes of enterprises are now much closer to each other, but wages in big industries rise much more steeply.

But the pay system is not simply an automatic one. It is important not to overemphasize either age, or even years of service, as the criteria either for wage increases or for promotion. Recently, non-*nenkō* factors have been becoming more and more important in wage assessments. This has not necessarily weakened management's power, since a system of wage fragmentation has been devised to maximize control. In one of the factories that Robert Cole studied, wages in the late 1960s were made up of fourteen different components: six of the standard wage, and eight of the supplementary wage. This fragmentation of pay makes it very much more difficult for any workers, whether unionized or not, to bargain effectively over wages, since management has so many categories with which to juggle. In addition, the supplementary wage sector can be manipulated either to repress a combative work force or to increase capital accumulation through lower wages.

A word should be said about management's ability to "adjust," particularly as this is a subject which has been rather obfuscated in many Western sources. There is no evidence that Japanese business has had difficulty dealing with recessions or other questions (such as accelerating capital accumulation) through manipulating the labour force. In the 1962 slump employers used a whole gamut of measures ranging from shortening working hours, via curtailment of external employment and reallocation of ordinary employees, to straight dismissals. The restricted dimensions of the *nenkō* and "life employment" (*shūshin koyō*) systems give an indication of the extent of the protective cushioning which business has established. Of course, there are compromises in the set-up. In some cases, for example, an employer will keep *some* employees on something around 60–70 per cent of *basic* pay over a relatively long layoff

357

(say, six months); but there is no reason to think this may not be a self-protective measure against the next wave of the boom.

The idea, too, that there is no mobility of labour in Japan is a myth. The seniority-wage system and other devices have definitely served to restrict labour mobility by Western standards. But there is fairly high mobility among young workers, both male and female, with low mobility among experienced workers. Roughly half the labour force changes jobs at least once in a decade, with about half these moves involving inter-industry mobility. Thus, in Evans's words, "it would appear that the elasticity of labour supply has been quite extensive. Mobility has been growing very fast in the last decade or so, particularly among blue-collar workers. Government policy, aimed at countering the effects of the labour shortage, has been designed to promote mobility among certain categories of workers in the interests of big business. Since the various guarantee systems cover at most half the labour force, and probably much less, these requirements are by no means in conflict with each other.

To sum up: as Kaji so correctly emphasizes in her discussion of the capitalist exploitation of women, the wage and employment systems are integrally tied to ruling class ideology and to the Japanese social system itself. Unless these are changed, although there will probably be a gradual trend towards less inequality, an increase in job-related factors in assessing pay, and more mobility, the system is likely to remain an adjusted mix of *nenkō*, personal and job factors.

The context of opposition: the division of repression between government and business

The system of capitalist rule does not, of course, depend only on these relatively "technical" mechanisms. It rests on class struggle — class struggle in which the ruling class wages an unrelenting battle against the working masses at every level, with ideology, law, physical repression and straight exploitation. The legal system has failed to support the idea of a contract; and official ideology fosters the ideal that employers have rights over their employees, but not vice versa, and that these rights are open-ended, while employees have only duties towards their employers.

It is in this context that one should consider the high degree of repression and exploitation in Japanese industry. Japanese factories have an extremely high number of supervisory staff. Repression inside the plant is sustained through constant espionage on militant workers and the sabotage of contesting workers' organizations — such as splitting a combative union or forming a subsidized "second" union to bribe or terrorize away wavering workers from the militant line — and also through the constant "family-like" interference in workers' everyday lives. In many cases companies hire gangsters and goon squads, which operate off the shop floor as well as on it. Terror in and around the plant by private companies is complemented by massive police repression against militants in society in general.

The working conditions of the most exploited workers in postwar Japan are rarely reported in detail in the West. An account of the life of coalminers in Kyushu in the late 1950s describes how the most dangerous work in the mines was done by "temporary" workers employed by a gang-boss hired by the company. These workers were paid at most half the regular wage, sometimes getting only a small bag of rice for an entire month's work; when factory inspectors visited the mine, these workers were sealed into remote areas of the pits for the duration of the visit. They were housed in hovels patrolled by armed guards, and visitors were rigidly excluded. The union refused to intervene.

Again, much has been written in the West about air and sea pollution in Japan, but little about "pollution" and danger *inside* the factories and mines where most workers spend half of their waking life. A 1968 government survey (which may understate the case) showed nervous fatigue in 80–96 per cent of all workers; "great fatigue" after each day's work in some 80 per cent; fatigue frequently lasting over till the next day in well over half. Over 6,000 people were killed in industrial accidents in 1968, and 6,200 in 1969. Compensation for death at a big company like Nissan at the time could be a mere ¥50,000 (£50 at that date).

As the study of the Hitachi mine cited above showed, old workers and members of the families of workers injured frequently have to take up badly paid work to make ends meet. But the statistics on fatigue indicate that nervous troubles extend right through the work force. Japanese capitalism is well aware of this, as is shown by the case of Matsushita Kōnosuke and the "self-control room" he has set up in one of his factories. This room, the approach to which is lined with distorting mirrors "to help workers relax and perhaps even laugh at themselves" (in the words of *Time*), contains a stuffed dummy of Matsushita himself on which workers can unleash aggression with bamboo staves provided by the company. At another level, such institutions as the obligatory singing of the company song and physical exercise, far from being the expression of "harmony," are management-imposed devices to facilitate exploitation by creating a climate of bogus enterprise solidarity where dissidence and revolt are made difficult.

As in the Meiji era, business continues to talk about "serving the nation," claims to eschew profit (and the profit motive), and veils exploitation in a vocabulary of "harmony" and "love." Yet the facts tell a different story. The labour share is the lowest in any of the advanced capitalist countries, the rate of capital accumulation is the highest and, contrary to widely accepted belief, the real rate of after-tax profits is about the same as in the other major capitalist economies.

An important element in the preservation of this situation has been the ruling class's success in establishing the ideology of Japan as a "classless" society. It must be emphasized that this denial of class is in a qualitatively different league from the efforts in the same direction undertaken by the Western bourgeoisies and their ideologists.

An exceptionally sophisticated expression of this ideology has been provided by the sociologist Nakane in *Japanese Society*:

> The overall picture of society . . . is not that of horizontal stratification by class or caste but of vertical stratification by institution or group of institutions . . . Even if social classes like those in Europe can be detected in Japan, and even if something vaguely resembling those classes that are illustrated in the textbooks of western sociology can also be found in

Japan, the point is that in actual society this stratification is unlikely to function and that it does not really reflect the social structure. In Japanese society it is really not a matter of workers struggling against capitalists or managers but of Company A ranged against Company B. The protagonists do not stand in vertical relationship to each other but instead rub elbows from parallel positions . . . The antagonism and wrangling between management and labour in Japan is unquestionably a "household" problem, and though their basic divergence is the same as it is the world over, the reason it cannot develop in Japan into a problem intimately and powerfully affecting society as a whole is to be found in the group structure and the nature of total Japanese society.[1]

The plain fact is that while the workers in a factory are *subjected* to this ideology, management shows no "enterprise solidarity." The simplest evidence of this is the superb trans-enterprise organization of Japanese big business, which has the most powerful federations in the capitalist world. Group solidarity is an ideological weapon, where the capitalist class operates class solidarity within itself and fragmentation among the working class. Nakane shows that this condition is brought about and maintained by violence: "each member [of a group] is shaped to more or less the same mould, and forced to undergo the kneading effects of group interaction whether he likes it or not. The individual Japanese has little opportunity to learn sociability. Whatever security he feels is derived from aligning and matching himself with group purpose and plan. As Nakane notes later, "there is a cruelly heavy handicap against the powerless and the socially inferior."

The government fosters the preservation of these conditions not only by promoting such ideology in schools, but by directly and indirectly creating the conditions where business can continue to exploit the working masses. Here government action and inaction over the labour laws have both been extremely important.

Under the Occupation, the Japanese regime was able both to enact anti-working class legislation and to refuse to apply SCAP laws of which it disapproved. The Labour Standards Law of 1947, for example, which included equal pay for equal work, was almost completely ignored. In 1949 alone, according to Premier Yoshida, there were 1,200,000 violations of the law brought before the authorities, of which only a derisory number were actually proceeded upon. After independence the government revised the labour laws in an anti-working class direction and made particularly extensive use of MacArthur's measures depriving public employees of the right to strike. Until 1965 the government refused to ratify ILO Convention 87, which calls for unrestricted rights for all workers to organize and bargain, including the designation of bargaining representatives. The government finally ratified the Convention and then simply refused to apply it. The Ministry of Labour has played the lead, along with the Ministry of International Trade and Industry, in these machinations, which have been accompanied by much rhetoric about aiding labour and management to meet on an equal basis to solve labour problems.

On a wider scale, too, the state, by keeping down spending on social services, has actively fostered the conditions under which business has been able to seize and hold labour; protecting insecurity outside the enterprise, it enhanced the appeal of such company services as housing. In more complex ways, too, the state has played an active role, particularly over pensions. By refusing to provide care for the aged, the state has not simply strengthened the appeal of private companies' pension schemes, but also worked to force more older people back into jobs after the statutory retirement age (and therefore on much lower pay). Further, by keeping the prospect of a poverty-stricken old age ever-present, the regime stimulated the highest savings rates in the world, double those (proportionate to earnings) in any other advanced capitalist country, among all income groups. The vast majority of these savings have gone not into assets, but straight to the banks whence they have been redirected largely to favoured private industry rather than towards public services. In 1964, for example, government outlay on social services per capita was about the same as in Tunisia or Sri Lanka.

It is important to realize that this situation represents a consistent long-term policy for a specific form of high capital accumulation based on low wages and a rigidly controlled work force. But, though control of the work force has been largely achieved, the economic options of the ruling class and the state have themselves created acute new contradictions, particularly at the social level, which have given political struggle in Japan its unique configuration.

The neglect of social services and assistance has had striking effects in Japan. The refusal to allocate money for such things as sewers and urban improvements has made many working class areas in the cities into slums or quasi-slums. A 1969 survey showed that only 9.2 per cent of Japanese houses had flush toilets (98.2 per cent in the United Kingdom); the sewer service saturation rate was only 17 per cent (90 per cent in the United Kingdom); the percentage of roads paved was a mere 10.8 per cent. There were only 0.9 square meters of park per urban citizen (compared with 19 in the United States). Swift economic "growth" partly masked this situation and the dire poverty in which many Japanese have been living during the so-called miracle. A 1963 Ministry of Welfare publication showed that 20 per cent of all households were living below the officially-defined poverty line (defined as an income of about the then equivalent of 45 U.S. cents per person per day). In one *burakumin* village studied, not only was the population density ten times that of its non-*burakumin* neighbouring village, but the average income of the *burakumin* village was one-twentieth that in the village next door. Moreover, in the early 1960s about 60 per cent of all the fully unemployed persons in Japan were *burakumin*.

Alongside this failure to reallocate the fruits of economic growth, the government has assisted capital accumulation by allowing industry to use maximally untrammeled methods in its operations. It is important to stress that a very large part of Japan's overall "pollution" problems are the direct result of a chosen policy for capital accumulation and not the unavoidable "by-products" of development, as they are frequently presented. This contradiction has now reached acute political proportions, with pollution in Japan now worse than anywhere else in the world except the Seoul area of south Korea. The crucial political factor is that the noxious effects of big business's "high growth" policies have spilled over from the shop floor and the mines into society as a whole, and this has had important effects on the class struggle.

Government attempts to defuse mass opposition to its economic policies by spreading pollution under the guise of decentralization have been dismal failures.

The ruling class's economic policies have increasingly blighted much of Japan and increasingly *destroyed* the livelihood of many Japanese — for example, those who lived off fishing. Several of the biggest struggles of recent years have been against "development" plans which threatened to wreck local communities. The most famous was the struggle against the new Tokyo airport at Narita, which lasted several years. This struggle is particularly important both because of the high level of combativity and because it fused the domestic fight against Japanese capitalism with the fight against U.S. imperialism.

With the escalation of U.S. aggression against the peoples of Indochina, Tokyo's main airport, Haneda, became overloaded. This was because between one-third and half of the traffic there was made up of U.S. military charter and other related flights tied to the war against Indochina. The "need" for a new airport was thus a direct result of U.S. imperialism's activities and the Tokyo government's relationship to the United States.

In July 1966 the Satō government, without consulting the local inhabitants, decided to put a new airport at Sanrizuka, a small village about forty miles north of Tokyo. One reason Sanrizuka was chosen was that the Emperor owned 500 hectares there and the authorities would have the Emperor's land as a secure base from which to start. The fight against the construction of the new airport was waged for over five years on the interconnected issues of the farmers' determination not to be evicted from their rich farmland and the popular rejection of a new airport designed largely to assist U.S. aggression.

After a first attempt to seize the land, in which the police terrorized the local population and beat up the farmers' elderly leader, Tomura Issaku, the farmers organized local defences and publicized their struggle, which became a national issue. Support flooded in from thousands of workers and students from all over the country, and a solid farmer–worker–student alliance was formed. The defenders built an extensive system of trenches and interconnecting tunnels, guarded by watch-towers, palisades and block-houses, protected by cadres armed with grenades and staves. A survey team which tried to penetrate the area on February 19, 1970 had to be accompanied by three thousand armed riot police (Kidōtai) and plainclothesmen, yet was still held off by the farmers and their supporters. In February 1971 the government decided to launch a full-scale attack to carry out further expropriations: four thousand Kidōtai assaulted the farmers with watercannon, bulldozers and baton-charges. Fourteen hundred people were injured, at least two hundred seriously. Goon squads employed by the construction companies also went on the rampage at the same time, unwisely beating up two JSP Dietmen. In September 1971, after a further police attack on the area, three policemen were killed. More than one year after that, several years behind schedule, the last farmers were finally evicted.

The portrayal of events at Sanrizuka as a rearguard fight by backward peasants against innocent progress is a classic travesty of the struggle, which was a vanguard struggle on a highly political issue. The struggle aroused an unprecedented wave of mass support throughout the country: it showed that the regime's alliance with U.S. imperialism meant literally the destruction of people's livelihood and of the Japanese countryside. Particularly terrifying to the regime was the fact that the high level of militancy shown by the defenders at Sanrizuka found such a widespread echo in the society at large.

Another big struggle surged up over plans to build a new industrial area at Rokkasho in the far north of Honshu Island. Again issues of "pollution" enter into the struggle, but it is basically one by the local inhabitants against exploitation of their land, their labour and their lives. Many of the big struggles against the U.S. presence in Japan and on Okinawa have been against both the U.S. exploitation of Japan for its imperialist activities and the appalling effects of the U.S. bases and personnel on life in Japan itself.

The Japanese left has consistently been able to mount extensive demonstrations and active interventions against U.S. and Japanese imperialism: strikes among the base workers on Okinawa and at the big U.S. bases in Japan proper; actions by railway workers to block the transportation of U.S. military equipment, including petrol and armaments for use in Indochina; actions by local government authorities to prevent the transit of tanks for the Saigon regime in 1972; attacks on U.S. bases, including the destruction of American military equipment in the bases and of U.S. property outside, as well as attacks on U.S. military personnel. On the occasion of Premier Satō's departure for a trip to the United States, the government had to mobilize 75,000 armed police to ensure his passage to Tokyo airport — five times the total number of British troops in Northern Ireland.

Yet this strength on issues of imperialism goes together with considerable isolation. Some of this isolation is due to problems of distance and language. But more important, and little appreciated outside Japan, are the systematic government efforts to isolate the Japanese left from contact with progressive forces in the rest of the world, particularly in East Asia, and to prevent militants from other countries getting into Japan. The new Immigration (Control) Bill, which the LDP government has in draft form, is designed to make it very hard for anyone the Japanese government does not like to enter Japan. It lays down extremely strict conditions for being in Japan, combined with a degree of vagueness so that almost anyone can be deported. The Japanese police have been particularly diligent in rounding up critics from south Vietnam, south Korea and Taiwan. There is no recognized legal redress against being held in one of the two detention centres (Omura in Nagasaki, and Yokohama), or against deportation.

Notes

1. Nakane, *Japanese Society*, p. 87; the same sort of attempts to conjure away the class struggle are to be found in Kahn, Brzezinski, et al.; the most repugnant elucubrations on the subject are those by Brian Beedham, the foreign editor of the *Economist* (see Beedham, "A Special Strength: A Survey of Japan," *Economist*, March 31, 1973, Survey, pp. 8-11).

24.   The Japanese "Miracle"
[from Chapter 1 — MITI and the Japanese "Miracle"]
Chalmers Johnson

By common agreement among the Japanese, the "miracle" first appeared to them during 1962. In its issues of September 1 and 8, 1962, the *Economist* of London published a long two-part essay entitled "Consider Japan," which it later brought out as a book that was promptly translated and published in Tokyo as *Odorokubeki Nihon* (Amazing Japan). Up to this time most Japanese simply did not believe the rate of economic growth they were achieving — a rate unprecedented in Japanese history — and their pundits and economists were writing cautionary articles about how this boom would fail, about the crises to come, and about the irrationality of government policy. Yet where the Japanese had been seeing irresponsible budgets, "overloans," and tremendous domestic needs, the *Economist* saw expansion of demand, high productivity, comparatively serene labor relations, and a very high rate of savings. Thus began the praise, domestic and foreign, of the postwar Japanese economy — and the search for the cause of the "miracle."

First, some details on the miracle itself. Table 1 presents indices of industrial production for the entire period of this study, 1925 to 1975, with 1975 as 100. It reveals several interesting things. The miracle was actually only beginning in 1962, when production was just a third of what it would be by 1975. Fully half of Japan's amazing economic strength was to be manifested after 1966. The table also shows clearly the "recessions" of 1954, 1965, and 1974 that spurred the government to new and even more creative economic initiatives; and it demonstrates the ability of the Japanese economy to come back even more strongly from these periods of adversity. Intersectoral shifts are also recorded: the decline of mining as coal gave way to oil and the movement from textiles to machinery and finished metal products, a movement the Japanese call heavy and chemical industrialization (*jūkagaku kōgyōka*).

If we use a slightly different base line — for example, if we take 1951–53 to be 100 — then the index of gross national product for 1934–36 is 90; for 1961–63, 248; and for 1971–73, 664; and the index of manufacturing production for 1934–36 is 87; for 1961–63, 400; and for 1971–73, 1,350. Over the whole postwar era, 1946 to 1976, the Japanese economy increased 55-fold. By the end of our period Japan accounted for about 10 percent of the world's economic activity though occupying only 0.3 percent of the world's surface and supporting about 3 percent of the world's population. Regardless of whether or not one wants to call this achievement a "miracle," it is certainly a development worth exploring.

Reprinted from *MITI AND THE JAPANESE MIRACLE* by Chalmers Johnson with the permission of the publishers, Stanford University Press. © 1982 by the Board of Trustees of the Leland Stanford Junior University.

Table 1
Indices of Japanese Mining and Manufacturing Production, 1926–1978
(1975 = 100)

Manufacturing Industries

Year	All industry	Public utilities	Mining and manufacturing	Mining	All manufacturing	Iron and steel	Non-ferrous metals	Metal finished goods	Machinery	Ceramics and cement	Chemicals	Petroleum and coal products	Pulp and paper	Textiles	Wood and wood products	Food
1926		2.5		54.5		1.5	4.0				1.5	0.7	4.9	17.4		
1927		2.8		59.7		1.7	4.1				1.7	0.8	5.3	18.8		
1928		3.3		62.0		2.0	4.6				1.8	1.0	5.8	18.1		
1929		3.6		63.2		2.2	4.6				2.2	1.0	6.4	18.9		
1930	5.5	3.9	5.8	62.0	5.3	2.1	4.8		1.4	8.4	2.5	1.0	5.5	21.8	15.8	21.0
1931	5.0	4.0	5.2	58.8	4.7	1.8	4.4		1.1	8.5	2.6	1.1	5.3	23.0	15.2	19.0
1932	5.3	4.3	5.5	60.0	5.0	2.3	4.9		1.0	9.2	3.2	1.2	5.3	24.9	16.0	20.8
1933	6.4	4.9	6.7	68.6	6.1	3.1	5.7		1.4	10.3	3.7	1.4	5.8	28.6	18.8	22.3
1934	6.9	5.3	7.2	75.1	6.5	3.7	5.6		1.4	10.0	4.3	1.7	5.4	31.5	24.0	22.5
1935	7.3	6.0	7.6	81.0	6.9	4.4	6.7		1.4	11.6	5.2	1.8	5.9	33.4	26.4	22.5
1936	8.2	6.5	8.6	89.6	7.8	4.9	7.4		1.7	12.0	6.2	2.1	7.0	35.8	27.6	23.0
1937	9.6	7.1	10.0	97.5	9.2	5.7	8.7		2.3	12.7	7.1	2.5	8.0	40.8	27.9	25.2
1938	9.9	7.7	10.3	103.8	9.4	6.5	9.1		2.5	13.5	8.1	2.7	7.2	33.6	27.5	25.5
1939	10.9	8.1	11.4	108.8	10.5	7.2	10.3		3.1	14.2	8.6	3.2	8.3	33.6	32.2	26.1
1940	11.4	8.3	12.0	116.7	11.0	7.3	10.1		3.8	14.7	8.5	3.4	8.3	30.4	26.8	22.7
1941	11.8	9.1	12.4	117.1	11.3	7.5	9.6		4.4	13.1	8.5	4.0	8.5	24.6	33.5	19.7
1942	11.5	9.1	12.0	114.4	11.0	7.9	10.9		4.5	10.8	7.1	4.0	6.7	19.5	31.7	17.5
1943	11.7	9.2	12.1	115.5	11.1	8.9	13.3		5.0	9.6	6.1	4.0	5.7	12.7	28.0	14.5
1944	11.9	9.0	12.4	105.1	11.4	8.3	14.7		5.8	7.5	5.7	3.2	3.3	6.8	24.8	11.9
1945	5.2	5.4	5.3	55.5	4.8	2.9	5.5		2.5	2.9	2.3	0.9	1.6	2.6	14.8	7.9
1946	2.3	6.9	2.2	40.9	1.8	1.0	2.9		0.8	3.1	1.4	0.4	1.7	4.3	22.7	7.0
1947	2.9	7.8	2.7	54.0	2.3	1.3	4.0		0.9	3.8	1.9	0.5	2.4	5.8	29.9	6.3
1948	3.8	8.5	3.6	66.2	3.0	2.1	5.5		1.4	5.8	2.5	0.8	3.5	6.6	34.7	7.7
1949	4.8	9.6	4.6	75.7	4.0	3.7	6.3		1.7	7.6	3.5	0.9	4.9	8.9	34.8	11.7
1950	5.9	10.3	5.7	80.0	5.1	5.1	7.3		1.8	9.0	4.7	1.7	6.7	12.6	36.5	13.1
1951	8.0	11.0	7.8	91.4	7.1	6.9	8.8		2.9	12.5	6.3	2.8	9.1	17.9	54.7	16.8
1952	8.6	11.9	8.4	94.4	7.7	7.1	9.3		3.0	13.0	6.9	3.6	10.4	20.3	58.2	17.2
1953	10.4	12.7	10.2	101.2	9.5	8.4	9.9		3.8	15.4	8.6	4.6	13.3	24.4	55.7	26.3
1954	11.2	13.5	11.1	97.5	10.4	8.8	11.5		4.3	17.5	9.8	5.4	14.5	26.5	54.6	28.5
1955	12.1	14.5	11.9	98.0	11.3	9.8	12.2		4.3	17.7	11.3	6.2	16.6	29.6	54.4	30.3
1956	14.9	16.7	14.6	108.3	13.9	12.0	14.7		6.2	21.5	13.6	8.0	19.2	35.2	60.8	32.0
1957	17.3	18.6	17.3	119.3	16.5	13.6	16.4		8.7	25.3	16.0	9.6	21.7	38.9	64.1	30.7
1958	17.4	19.7	17.3	115.7	16.6	12.8	16.4	15.6	9.3	23.9	16.0	10.0	21.3	34.8	61.8	35.6
1959	20.9	22.6	20.8	114.6	20.1	17.0	21.0	19.2	12.0	28.3	18.5	12.4	27.9	40.6	65.9	37.7
1960	26.0	26.5	25.9	125.2	25.3	22.4	27.8	24.4	16.5	25.7	22.3	15.8	33.6	47.9	73.2	39.9
1961	31.0	30.8	31.0	134.0	30.4	28.3	33.3	28.8	21.4	41.5	25.5	19.0	40.5	51.7	77.5	43.1
1962	33.5	32.9	33.6	137.0	32.9	28.3	32.5	30.3	24.0	45.3	29.2	21.4	43.4	54.5	79.3	46.6
1963	37.3	36.0	37.4	135.9	36.7	31.9	37.2	34.0	26.5	48.1	32.2	25.6	48.0	58.6	83.8	57.8
1964	43.2	40.6	43.3	137.1	42.6	39.7	45.6	39.6	32.3	55.5	36.6	30.3	54.5	64.8	88.9	62.7
1965	44.9	43.3	44.9	135.2	44.3	40.8	45.3	40.5	32.8	57.1	40.1	34.8	55.7	69.4	90.0	66.7
1966	50.7	47.6	50.8	143.1	50.2	47.2	51.0	48.0	38.1	62.2	45.3	40.0	62.5	76.4	95.4	73.1
1967	60.5	54.0	60.7	141.0	60.2	61.1	61.6	58.6	49.6	72.8	53.0	48.1	69.6	83.3	102.5	76.8
1968	69.7	59.6	70.1	142.1	69.6	68.4	74.3	71.0	61.5	81.4	62.6	56.9	76.9	88.4	107.0	78.7
1969	80.7	67.0	81.3	142.9	80.9	82.6	86.6	84.0	74.8	90.3	73.7	67.9	86.6	97.0	113.9	83.6
1970	91.8	75.9	92.5	139.2	92.2	94.2	93.8	96.9	87.7	101.0	86.8	79.8	98.2	105.2	118.7	89.9
1971	94.3	80.6	94.9	131.6	94.6	91.2	95.7	100.1	89.8	102.6	91.6	87.4	100.6	109.4	117.1	92.6
1972	101.1	87.4	101.8	121.9	101.6	98.7	108.4	111.0	87.3	109.5	97.2	91.5	106.7	110.8	120.7	97.8
1973	116.2	97.4	117.0	112.8	117.0	118.8	128.6	133.4	117.4	126.5	110.2	106.6	113.3	118.5	122.1	98.6
1974	111.7	97.3	112.3	105.8	112.4	116.9	112.6	123.0	116.2	117.0	109.9	104.4	113.7	106.1	109.1	97.5
1975	100.0	100.0	100.0	100.0	100.0	100.0	100.0	100.0	100.0	100.0	100.0	100.0	100.0	100.0	100.0	100.0
1976	111.0	108.5	111.1	100.0	111.2	109.5	119.3	116.8	113.7	110.4	111.5	102.7	113.3	108.4	106.8	101.1
1977	115.6	113.7	115.7	103.1	115.7	108.1	125.0	124.9	121.3	115.2	117.2	104.7	115.3	106.7	104.4	104.6
1978	122.7	119.9	122.8	105.9	123.0	110.1	135.0	134.9	131.5	121.0	131.0	104.0	120.8	107.7	107.0	106.1

Source: Mainichi Shimbun Sha. ed. *Shōwa shi nten* (Dictionary of Shōwa History), Tokyo, 1980. p.457

Many voyagers have navigated these waters before me, and a survey of their soundings is a necessary introduction to this study and my particular point of view. The task of explaining Japanese economic growth — and its repeated renewals after one or another set of temporary advantages had been exhausted or removed — is not easy, as the frequent use of the term "miracle" suggests; and the term cannot be isolated and applied only to the high-speed growth that began in 1955. As early as 1937 a much younger Prof. Arisawa Hiromi (b. 1896), one of the people who must be included on any list of the two or three dozen leading formulators of postwar industrial policy, used the phrase "Japanese Miracle" to describe the increase of 81.5 percent in Japanese industrial output from 1931 to 1934. Today we know why that particular miracle occurred: it resulted from the reflationary deficit financing of Finance Minister Takahashi Korekiyo, who at 81 was assassinated by young military officers on the morning of February 26, 1936, for trying to apply the brakes to the process he had started.

This earlier miracle is nonetheless problematic for scholars because of what Charles Kindleberger refers to as "the riddle" of how Japan "produced Keynesian policies as early as 1932 without a Keynes." Some Japanese have not been overly exercised by this riddle; they have simply settled for calling Takahashi the "Keynes of Japan." As I hope to make clear in this book, this kind of sleight of hand will not do; there was more to state intervention in the thirties than Keynesianism, and Arisawa and his colleagues in the government learned lessons in the formative years that are quite different from those that make up what has come to be known in the West as mainstream governmental fiscal policy.

Kindleberger's "riddle" does serve to draw attention to the projectionists, one major category among modern explorers of the Japanese economic miracle. These are writers who project onto the Japanese case Western — chiefly Anglo–American — concepts, problems, and norms of economic behavior. Whatever the value of such studies for the countries in which they were written, they need not detain us long here. This type of work is not so much aimed at explaining the Japanese case (although it may abstract a few principles of Japanese political economy) as it is at revealing home-country failings in light of Japan's achievements, or at issuing warnings about the possible effects of Japan's growth on other parts of the world. Even the *Economist's* brilliant little tract of 1962 might better have been called *Consider Britain in the Light of What the Japanese are Doing*, which was in any case its true purpose. Successors to the *Economist* include Ralph Hewins, *The Japanese Miracle Men* (1967), P. B. Stone, *Japan Surges Ahead: The Story of an Economic Miracle* (1969), Robert Guillain, *The Japanese Challenge* (1970), Herman Kahn, *The Emerging Japanese Superstate* (1970), and Hakan Hedberg, *Japan's Revenge* (1972). Perhaps the most prominent work in this genre, because it is so clearly hortatory about what Americans might learn from Japan rather than analytical about what has caused the phenomenal Japanese growth, is Ezra Vogel's *Japan as Number One: Lessons for Americans* (1979). My study does not follow these earlier works in advocating the adoption of Japanese institutions outside of Japan. It does, however, try to lay out in their full complexity some of the main Japanese institutions in the economic field so that those who are interested in adopting them will have an idea of what they are buying in terms of the Japanese system's consequences – intended, unintended, and even unwanted.

A second and entirely different set of explanations of the Japanese miracle belongs to the socioeconomic school, or what I have sometimes called the "anything-but-politics" approach to "miracle" research. This broad school includes four major types of analysis that often overlap with each other but that are clearly isolable for purposes of identification, although they rarely appear in pure form. These are the "national character — basic values — consensus" analysis favored by humanists in general and the anthropologically oriented in particular; the "no-miracle-occurred" analysis, chiefly the work of economists; the "unique-structural-features" analysis promoted by students of labor relations, the savings ratio, corporate management, the banking system, the welfare system, general trading corporations, and other institutions of modern Japan; and the various forms of the "free-ride" analysis, that is, the approach that stresses Japan's real but transitory advantages in launching high-speed growth in the postwar world. Before proceeding to sketch the qualities of these types of analysis, let me say that to a certain extent I can agree with all of them. My interest is not in disputing the facts that they have revealed nor in questioning their relevance to the miracle However, I believe it can be shown that many of them should be reduced to more basic categories of analysis, particularly to the effects of state policy, and that they need to be weighed according to standards different from those used in the past, thereby giving greater weight to the state and its industrial policy.

The national-character explanation argues that the economic miracle occurred because the Japanese possess a unique, culturally derived capacity to cooperate with each other. This capacity to cooperate reveals itself in many ways — lower crime rates than in other, less homogeneous societies; subordination of the individual to the group; intense group loyalties and patriotism; and, last but not least, economic performance. The most important contribution of the culture to economic life is said to be Japan's famous "consensus," meaning virtual agreement among government, ruling political party, leaders of industry, and people on the primacy of collective objectives for the society as a whole — and on the means to obtain those objectives. Some of the terms invented to refer to this cultural capability of the Japanese are "rolling consensus," "private collectivism," "inbred collectivism," "spiderless cobweb," and "Japan, Inc".

My reservations about the value of this explanation are basically that it is overgeneralized and tends to cut off rather than advance serious research. Consensus and group solidarity have been important in Japan's economic growth, but they are less likely to derive from the basic values of the Japanese than from what Ruth Benedict once called Japan's "situational" motivations: late development, lack of resources, the need to trade, balance of payments constraints, and so forth. Positing some "special capacity to cooperate" as an irreducible Japanese cultural trait leads inquiry away from the question of *why* Japanese cooperate when they do (they did not cooperate during almost half of the period under study here), and away from the probability that this cooperation can be, and on occasion has been, quite deliberately engineered by the government and others. David Titus's research into the use of the Imperial institution in prewar Japan to "privatize" rather than to "socialize" societal conflict is one creative way to look at this problem of consensus.

Many instances to be discussed later in this study illustrate how the government has consciously induced cooperation among its clients with much better results than during the Pacific War, when it sought to control them. In the final analysis it is indeed probable that Japanese basic values are different from those of the Western world, but this needs to be studied, not posited; and explanations of social behavior in terms of basic values should be reserved for the final analysis, that is, for the residue of behavior that cannot be explained in other more economical ways. Actually, the explanation of the Japanese economic miracle in terms of culture was more prevalent a few years ago, when the miracle had occurred only in Japan. Now that it is being duplicated or matched in the Republic of Korea, Taiwan, Hong Kong, and Singapore — and perhaps even in some non-East Asian nations — the cultural explanation has lost much of its original interest.

Exemplars of the "no-miracle-occurred" school of analysis do not literally assert that nothing happened to Japan's economy, but they imply that what did happen was not miraculous but a normal outgrowth of market forces. They come from the realm of professional economic analyses of Japanese growth, and therefore in their own terms are generally impeccable, but they also regularly present extended conclusions that incorporate related matters that their authors have not studied but desperately want to exclude from their equations. Hugh Patrick argues, "I am of the school which interprets Japanese economic performance as due primarily to the actions and efforts of private individuals and enterprises responding to the opportunities provided in quite free markets for commodities and labor. While the government has been supportive and indeed has done much to create the environment for growth, its role has often been exaggerated." But there is a problem, he concedes. "It is disturbing that the macro explanations of Japanese postwar economic performance — in terms of increases in aggregate labor and capital inputs and in their more productive allocation — leave 40 percent plus of output growth and half of labor productivity growth unexplained." If it can be shown that the government's industrial policy made the difference in the rate of investment in certain economically strategic industries (for instance, in developing the production and successful marketing of petrochemicals or automobiles), then perhaps we may say that its role has not been exaggerated. I believe this can be demonstrated and I shall attempt to do so later in this study.

Many Japanese would certainly dispute Patrick's conclusion that the government provided nothing more than the environment for economic growth. Sahashi Shigeru, former vice-minister of MITI (the Ministry of International Trade and Industry), asserts that the government is responsible for the economy as a whole and concludes, "It is an utterly self-centered [businessman's] point of view to think that the government should be concerned with providing only a favorable environment for industries without telling them what to do." There have been occasions when industries or enterprises revolted against what the government told them to do — incidents that are among the most sensational in postwar politics — but they did not, and do not, happen often enough to be routine

Discussions of the Japanese economy in purely economic terms seem to founder on their assumptions rather than on their analyses. It is assumed, for example, that the Japanese developmental state is the same thing as the American regulatory state. Philip Treizise argues, "In essentials, Japanese politics do not differ from politics in other democracies." But one way they differ is in a budgetary process where appropriations *precede* authorizations and where, "with the single exception of 1972, when a combination of government mishandling and opposition unity led to small reductions in defense spending, the budget has not been amended in the Diet since 1955"; before that there was no pretense that the Diet did anything more than rubber-stamp the bureaucracy's budget.

369

Another difference between Japan and the United States is to be found in the banking system. Before the war the rate of owned capital of all corporations in Japan was around 66 percent — a rate comparable to the current U.S. rate of 52 percent — but as late as 1972 the Japanese rate of owned capital was around 16 percent, a pattern that has persisted throughout the postwar period. Large enterprises obtain their capital through loans from the city banks, which are in turn overloaned and therefore utterly dependent on the guarantees of the Bank of Japan, which is itself — after a fierce struggle in the 1950s that the bank lost — essentially an operating arm of the Ministry of Finance. The government therefore has a direct and intimate involvement in the fortunes of the "strategic industries" (the term is standard and widely used, but not in the military sense) that is much greater than a formal or legal comparison between the Japanese and other market systems would indicate. MITI was not just writing advertising copy for itself when in 1974 it publicly introduced the concept of a "plan-oriented market economy system," an attempt to name and analyze what it had been doing for the previous twenty years (the twenty years before that it had spent perfecting the system by trial and error). The plan-oriented market economy system most decidedly includes some differences from "politics in other democracies," one of them being the care and feeding of the economic miracle itself.

The "no-miracle-occurred" school of miracle researchers agrees that Japanese economic growth took place but insists that this was because of the availability of capital, labor, resources, and markets all interacting freely with each other and unconstrained in any meaningful ways. It rejects as contrary to economic logic, and therefore as spurious, all the concepts that the Japanese have invented and employed continuously in discussing and managing their economy — such concepts as "industrial structure," "excessive competition," "coordination of investment," and "public-private cooperation." Most seriously, from a historical point of view, this explanation short-circuits attempts to analyze what difference the government's intervention has actually made by declaring in advance and as a matter of principle that it made no difference. The result is, as John Roberts has put it, that Japan's "miraculous" emergence as a first-rate economic power in the 1960s has been described exhaustively by Japanese and foreign writers, and yet very little of the literature provides credible explanations of how it was done, or by whom. This study is an attempt to answer these questions.

The third prevalent type of analysis of the Japanese miracle — stressing the influence of unusual Japanese institutions — is by far the most important of the four I have isolated, and the one that has been most thoroughly discussed in Japan and abroad. In its simplest form it asserts that Japan obtained a special economic advantage because of what postwar Japanese employers habitually call their "three sacred treasures" — the "lifetime" employment system, the seniority (nenkō) wage system, and enterprise unionism. Amaya Naohiro of MITI, for example, cites these three institutions as the essence of what he terms Japan's uchiwa (all in the family) economic system; and in reporting to the Organization for Economic Cooperation and Development's Industry Committee during 1970, the former MITI vice-minister Ōjimi Yoshihisa referred to various "typically Japanese phenomena" that had helped Japan to obtain its high-speed growth — the phenomena again being the three sacred treasures. Because of these institutions, the argument goes, Japan obtains greater labor commitment, loses fewer days to strikes, can innovate more easily, has better quality control, and in general produces more of the right things sooner than its international competitors.

This argument is undoubtedly true, but it has never been clearly formulated and is, at best, simplistic. There are several points to be made. First, the three sacred treasures are not the only "special institutions," and they are certainly not the most sacred. Others include the personal savings system; the distribution system; the "descent from heaven" (*amakudari*) of retired bureaucrats from the ministries into senior management positions in private enterprises; the structure of industrial groupings (*keiretsu*, or the oligopolistic organization of each industry by conglomerates); the "dual economy" (what Clark usefully terms the system of "industrial gradation") together with the elaborate structure of subcontracting it generates; the tax system; the extremely low degree of influence exercised over companies by shareholders; the hundred-odd "public policy companies" (public corporations of several different forms); and, perhaps most important of all, the government-controlled financial institutions, particularly the Japan Development Bank and the "second," or investment, budget (the Fiscal Investment and Loan Plan).

It is unnecessary here to describe each of these institutions. Most of them are quite familiar even to novice Japan watchers, and others will be analyzed in detail later in this book since they constitute some of the primary tools of the government for influencing and guiding the economy. What needs to be stressed is that they constitute a system — one that no individual or agency ever planned and one that has developed over time as ad hoc responses to, or unintended consequences of, Japan's late development and the progrowth policies of the government. Taken together as a system, they constitute a formidable set of institutions for promoting economic growth (a "GNP machine," in Amaya's metaphor), but taken separately, as they most commonly are, they do not make much sense at all. And this is the primary reservation that one must make about the unique-institutions explanation: it never goes far enough and therefore fails as anything more than a partial explanation.

Let us take one example. As a result of the recognition of the Japanese miracle around the world, some American professors of business administration have begun to recommend to American entrepreneurs that they experiment with one or all of the three sacred treasures. Sometimes Japanese practices, suitably modified, travel well. However, an American businessman who really attempted to institute "lifetime" employment without the backing of the other institutions of the Japanese system would soon find himself bankrupt. Among other things, lifetime employment in Japan is not for life but until the middle or late fifties; and although wage raises are tied to seniority, job security is not: it is those with most seniority who are the first fired during business downturns because they are the most expensive. Lifetime employment also does not apply to the "temporaries," who may spend their entire working lives in that status, and temporaries constitute a much larger proportion of a firm's work force than any American Union would tolerate (42 percent of the Toyota Motor Company's work force during the 1960's, for example).

Even if these problems could be taken care of, the American employer still would not have below him the extensive enterprise sector of medium and smaller contractors that his Japanese counterpart can squeeze in difficult times. Tomioka calls the subcontractors the "shock absorbers" of the Japanese business cycle — the smaller firms on the receiving end when large firms find they can no longer carry the fixed costs of their labor force and must "shift the strain" (*shiwayose*). On the other hand, the American employee would not have Japan's extensive if redundant distribution system to fall back on in case he did get laid off. The distribution system in Japan serves as a vast sponge for the unemployed or underemployed when economic conditions require it. As testimony to the layers of middlemen in Japan, the volume of transactions among Japanese wholesalers in 1968 exceeded the total of retail sales by a ration of 4.8 to 1, whereas the United States figure was 1.3 to 1. It is not surprising that many knowledgeable Japanese do not want to change the distribution system, despite protests from foreign salesmen who have trouble breaking into it, because it performs other functions for the society than distribution, not the least of which is reducing the tax burden necessary to provide adequate unemployment insurance.

Lifetime employment, Japanese style, offers many advantages from the point of view of economic growth: it provides a strong incentive to the employer to operate at full or close to full capacity; it inhibits a horizontally structured trade union movement; and, in the words of Ohkawa and Rosovsky, it gives the Japanese entrepreneur "a labor force without incentives to oppose technological and organizational progress even of the labor-saving type." But it does not exist in isolation and would not work without the rest of the system of "unique institutions."

The second main point about these special institutions concerns the date of their origins and how they are maintained. It is here that this school of explanations of the miracle sometimes blends imperceptibly with the first school, which says that Japanese culture and the Japanese national character support the economy. Amaya, for example, traces the three sacred treasures to the traditional world of family (*ie*), village (*mura*), and province (*kuni*), which he believes have all been homogenized and reincarnated today within the industrial enterprise. It has to be stated that assertions of this type are a form of propaganda to defend these special institutions from hostile (often foreign) critics. Extensive research by scholars in Japan and abroad has demonstrated that virtually all of the so-called special institutions date from the twentieth century and usually from no earlier than the World War I era.

Lifetime employment, for example, has been traced to several influences, including the efforts during World War I to inhibit the growth of a left-wing social reform movement; the introduction of large numbers of Korean and Taiwanese laborers during the 1920's, which caused Japanese workers to seek job security at all costs; and the wartime munitions companies, which had to guarantee the jobs of their best employees in order to keep them. R. P. Dore, one of the leading authorities on Japanese industrialism, summarizes the state of research on this subject as follows:

> "Japan's employment system in 1900 was pretty much as market-oriented as Britain's. It was conscious institutional innovation which began to shape the Japanese system in the first two decades of this century,

perfected the system of enterprise familism (or what one might call corporate paternalism) in the 1930s, and revamped the system to accommodate the new strength of unions in the late 1940s to produce what is called [by Dore] the 'welfare corporatism' of today."

Nakamura Takafusa finds the roots of a whole range of important institutions in the wartime control era — including the bank-centered keiretsu (industrial groups based on the Designated Financial Organs System of the time) and the subcontracting system, which though it existed before the war was greatly strengthened by the forced mergers of medium and small enterprises with big machinery manufacturers (the so-called *kigyō seibi*, or "enterprise readjustment," movement).

There are several ways in which the government has influenced the structure of Japan's special institutions. Many of these institutions it created directly in the course of its "industrial rationalization" campaigns of the 1930's or in the prosecution of the Pacific War. When the government did not create them directly, it nonetheless recognized their usefulness for its own purposes and moved to reinforce them. The savings system is an example. It is possible, as many commentators have urged, that the savings of private Japanese households — the highest rate of savings as a share of GNP ever recorded by any market economy in peacetime — is due to the natural frugality of the Japanese. But there are some strong external pressures that encourage the Japanese to save: a comparatively poor social security system; a wage system that includes large lump-sum bonus payments twice a year; a retirement system that cuts a worker's income substantially before he reaches the age of 60; a shortage of new housing and housing land, as well as a premium on university education for one's children, both of which require large outlays; an underdeveloped consumer credit system; a government-run postal savings system with guaranteed competitive interest rates; the lack of a well-developed capital market or other alternatives to personal saving; and a substantial exemption from income taxes for interest earned on savings accounts. The government is quite aware of these incentives to save and of the fact that money placed in the postal savings system goes directly into Ministry of Finance accounts, where it can be reinvested in accordance with government plans. Innate frugality may indeed play a role in this system, but the government has worked hard at engineering that frugality.

The theory of the "free ride," our fourth category of explanations, argues that Japan is the beneficiary of its postwar alliance with the United States, and that this alliance accounts at least for the miraculous part of Japan's rapid economic growth, if not for all of it. There are three ways in which Japan is said to have enjoyed a free ride: a lack of defense expenditures, ready access to its major export market, and relatively cheap transfers of technology.

Although it is true that Japan has not had to devote much of its national income to armaments, this factor cannot have influenced its growth rate significantly. If Japan's overall rate of investment had been very low — as low, for example, as it was in China — then the demands of defense could have had a retarding effect. But in Japan, where capital formation exceeded 30 percent of GNP during high-speed growth, the effect of low defense expenditures was negligible. The cases of South Korea and Taiwan, which have been pursuing the high investment strategy of the Japanese with equal or even more spectacular results, illustrate this point: their very high defense expenditures have had little or no impact on their economic performance.

The case of exports is more important. Japan profited enormously from the open trading system that developed throughout the world after World War II, and Japanese government leaders have repeatedly acknowledged the favorable effects for them of such institutions as the General Agreement on Tariffs and Trade, the International Monetary Fund, and, until 1971, stable exchange rates — all institutions that they had no role in creating. In fact, in their more pessimistic moods MITI leaders have speculated on the historical observation that Japan's great economic achievements came in the relatively open periods of world commerce — from the Meiji Restoration to World War I and from 1945 to 1970 — and they have expressed concern that the post-1970's era could look like 1920–45 when seen in historical perspective.

Nonetheless, the important point for our discussion is that Japan's growth did not depend nearly so much on exports as it did on the development of the domestic market (a market half the size of the United States' in terms of population). Eleanor Hadley notes that although Japan's economy in the early sixties was roughly three times the size of the 1934–36 economy, exports as a proportion of GNP were only about two-thirds what they had been in the mid-1930's. By the late 1960's Japan's exports were only 9.6 percent of GNP, compared for example with Canada's 19.8 percent. From 1953 to 1972 Japan had a consistently lower dependency on exports and imports as a percentage of GNP at constant prices than France, Germany, Italy, Britain, or OECD Europe as a whole. Japan's exports ran at about 11.3 percent of GNP, and its imports at 10.2 percent, whereas the OECD European figures were 21.2 percent and 20.9 percent respectively. There is no question that Japan, as a heavily populated resource-deficient country, has to export in order to pay for its vital imports, but foreign sales were not the main factor driving its economic activity during high-speed growth.

Home demand led Japan's growth for the twenty years after 1955. The demand was there, of course, before 1955, but with the coming to power of the Ishibashi government in December 1956 and Ikeda Hayato's return to the post of minister of finance, Ishibashi and Ikeda launched the policy of "positive finance." Under the slogan "a hundred billion yen tax cut is a hundred billion yen of aid" as the basis for the fiscal 1957 budget, Ikeda opened up domestic demand as it had never been opened before. Balance of payments problems slowed positive finance during the "bottom-of-the-pot" recession (with its trough in June 1958), but the economy responded quickly to government discipline and rebounded in the Iwato Boom (July 1958–December 1961), during which Ikeda became prime minister and launched the Income-doubling Plan. The propelling force of the economy in this and later periods was private corporate investment nurtured by favorable expectations for the longer term that were created by the government; it was not export sales.

Technology transfers — the third alleged "free ride" — were not exactly free, but there can be no question that they were crucial to Japanese economic growth and that the prices paid were slight compared with what such technology would cost today, if it could be bought at any price. Japan imported virtually all of the technology for its basic and high-growth industries, and it imported the greater proportion of this technology from the United States. But it is trivial and misleading to refer to this movement of patent rights, technology, and know-how across the Pacific and from Europe as a "free ride." It was, in fact, the heart of the matter.

The importation of technology was one of the central components of postwar Japanese industrial policy, and to raise the subject is to turn the discussion to MITI and the Japanese government's role. Before the capital liberalization of the late 1960's and 1970's, no technology entered the country without MITI's approval; no joint venture was ever agreed to without MITI's scrutiny and frequent alteration of the terms; no patent rights were ever bought without MITI's pressuring the seller to lower the royalties or to make other changes advantageous to Japanese industry as a whole; and no program for the importation of foreign technology was ever approved until MITI and its various advisory committees had agreed that the time was right and that the industry involved was scheduled for "nurturing" (*ikusei*).

From the enactment of the Foreign Capital Law in 1950 (it remained on the books for the next thirty years), the government was in charge of technology transfers. What it did and how it did it was not a matter of a "free ride" but of an extremely complex process of public-private interaction that has come to be known as "industrial policy." MITI is the primary Japanese government agency charged with the formulation and execution of industrial policy.

Thus I come to the final school, in which I place myself, the school that stresses the role of the developmental state in the economic miracle. Although the rest of this book is devoted to this subject — and to some of the non-miracles produced by the developmental state in its quest for the miracle — several further points are needed by way of introduction. What do I mean by the developmental state? This is not really a hard question, but it always seems to raise difficulties in the Anglo–American countries, where the existence of the developmental state in any form other than the communist state has largely been forgotten or ignored as a result of the years of disputation with Marxist–Leninists. Japan's political economy can be located precisely in the line of descent from the German Historical School — sometimes labelled "economic nationalism," *Handelspolitik*, or neomercantilism; but this school is not exactly in the mainstream of economic thought in the English-speaking countries. Japan is therefore always being studied as a "variant" of something other than what it is, and so a necessary prelude to any discussion of the developmental state must be the clarification of what it is not.

The issue is not one of state intervention in the economy. All states intervene in their economies for various reasons, among which are protecting national security (the "military-industrial complex"), insuring industrial safety, providing consumer protection, aiding the weak, promoting fairness in market transactions, preventing monopolization and private control in free enterprise systems, securing the public's interest in natural monopolies, achieving economies of scale, preventing excessive competition, protecting and rearing industries, distributing vital resources, protecting the environment, guaranteeing employment, and so forth. The question is how the government intervenes and for what purposes. This is one of the critical issues in twentieth-century politics, and one that has become more acute as the century has progressed. As Louis Mulkern, an old hand in the Japanese banking world, has said, "I would suggest that there could be no more devastating weakness for any major nation in the 1980s than the inability to define the role of government in the economy." The particular Japanese definition of this role and the relationship between that role and the economic miracle are at once major components and primary causes of the resurgent interest in "political economy" in the late twentieth century.

Nowhere is the prevalent and peculiarly Western preference for binary modes of thought more apparent than in the field of political economy. In modern times Weber began the practice with his distinction between a "market economy" (*Verkehrwirtschaft*) and a "planned economy" (*Planwirtschaft*). Some recent analogues are Dahrendorf's distinction between "market rationality" and "plan rationality," Dore's distinction between "market-oriented systems" and "organization-oriented systems," and Kelly's distinction between a "rule-governed state" (*nomocratic*) and a "purpose-governed state" (*telocratic*). I shall make use of several of these distinctions later, but first I must stress that for purposes of the present discussion the right-hand component of these pairs is *not* the Soviet-type command economy. Economies of the Soviet type are not *plan rational* but *plan ideological*. In the Soviet Union and its dependencies and emulators, state ownership of the means of production, state planning, and bureaucratic goal-setting are not rational means to a developmental goal (even if they may once have been); they are fundamental values in themselves, not to be challenged by evidence of either inefficiency or ineffectiveness. In the sense I am using the term here, Japan is plan rational, and the command economies are not; in fact, the history of Japan since 1925 offers numerous illustrations of why the command economy is not plan rational, a lesson the Japanese learned well.

At the most basic level the distinction between market and plan refers to differing conceptions of the functions of the state in economic affairs. The state as an institution is as old as organized human society. Until approximately the nineteenth century, states everywhere performed more or less the same functions that make large-scale social organization possible but that individuals or families or villages cannot perform for themselves. These functions included defense, road building, water conservancy, the minting of coins, and the administration of justice. Following the industrial revolution, the state began to take on new functions. In those states that were the first to industrialize, the state itself had little to do with the new forms of economic activity but towards the end of the nineteenth century the state took on *regulatory* functions in the interest of maintaining competition, consumer protection, and so forth. As Henry Jacoby puts it, "Once capitalism transformed the traditional way of life, factors such as the effectiveness of competition, freedom of movement, and the absence of any system of social security compelled the state to assume responsibility for the protection and welfare of the individual. Because each man was responsible for himself, and because that individualism became a social principle, the state remained as almost the only regulatory authority."

In states that were late to industrialize, the state itself led the industrialization drive, that is, it took on *developmental* functions. These two differing orientations toward private economic activities, the regulatory orientation and the developmental orientation, produced two different kinds of government-business relationships. The

United States is a good example of a state in which the regulatory orientation predominates, whereas Japan is a good example of a state in which the developmental orientation predominates. A regulatory, or market-rational, state concerns itself with the forms and procedures — the rules, if you will — of economic competition, but it does not concern itself with substantive matters. For example, the United States government has many regulations concerning the antitrust implications of the size of firms, but it does not concern itself with what industries ought to exist and what industries are no longer needed. The developmental, or plan-rational, state, by contrast, has as its dominant feature precisely the setting of such substantive social and economic goals.

Another way to make this distinction is to consider a state's priorities in economic policy. In the plan-rational state, the government will give greatest precedence to industrial policy, that is, to a concern with the structure of domestic industry and with promoting the structure that enhances the nation's international competitiveness. The very existence of an industrial policy implies a strategic, or goal-oriented, approach to the economy. On the other hand, the market-rational state usually will not even have an industrial policy (or, at any rate, will not recognize it as such). Instead, both its domestic and foreign economic policy, including its trade policy, will stress rules and reciprocal concessions (although perhaps influenced by some goals that are not industrially specific, goals such as price stability or full employment). Its trade policy will normally be subordinate to general foreign policy, being used more often to cement political relationships than to obtain strictly economic advantages.

These various distinctions are useful because they draw our attention to Japan's emergence, following the Meiji Restoration of 1868, as a developmental, plan-rational state whose economic orientation was keyed to industrial policy. By contrast, the United States from about the same period took the regulatory, market-rational path keyed to foreign policy. In modern times Japan has always put emphasis on an overarching, nationally supported goal for its economy rather than on the particular procedures that are to govern economic activity. The Meiji-era goal was the famous *fukoku-kyōhei* (rich country, strong military) of the late nineteenth and early twentieth centuries. This was followed during the 1930's and 1940's by the goals of depression recovery, war preparation, war production, and postwar recovery. From about 1955, and explicitly since the Income-doubling Plan of 1960, the goal has been high-speed growth, sometimes expressed as "overtake Europe and America" (*Ōbei ni oikose*). Amaya lists the goals of the past century in detail: *shokusan kōgyō* (increase industrial production), *fukoku-kyōhei* (rich country, strong military), *seisanryoku kakujū* (expand productive capacity), *yushutsu shinkō* (promote exports), *kanzen koyō* (full employment), and *kōdo seicho* (high speed growth). Only during the 1970's did Japan begin to shift to a somewhat regulatory, foreign-policy orientation, just as America began to show early signs of a new developmental, industrial-policy orientation. But the Japanese system remains plan rational, and the American system is still basically market rational.

This can be seen most clearly by looking at the differences between the two systems in terms of economic and political decision-making. In Japan the developmental, strategic quality of economic policy is reflected within the government in the high position of the so-called economic bureaucrats, that is, the officials of the ministries of Finance,

377

International Trade and Industry, Agriculture and Forestry, Construction, and Transportation, plus the Economic Planning Agency. These official agencies attract the most talented graduates of the best universities in the country, and the positions of higher-level officials in these ministries have been and still are the most prestigious in the society. Although it is influenced by pressure groups and political claimants, the elite bureaucracy of Japan makes most major decisions, drafts virtually all legislation, controls the national budget, and is the source of all major policy innovations in the system. Equally important, upon their retirement, which is usually between the ages of 50 and 55 in Japan, these bureaucrats move from government to powerful positions in private enterprise, banking, the political world, and the numerous public corporations – a direction of elite mobility that is directly opposite to that which prevails in the United States. The existence of a powerful, talented, and prestige-laden economic bureaucracy is a natural corollary of plan rationality.

In market-rational systems such as the United States, public service does not normally attract the most capable talent, and national decision-making is dominated by elected members of the professional class, who are usually lawyers, rather than by the bureaucracy. The movement of elites is not from government to the private sector but vice versa, usually through political appointment, which is much more extensive than in Japan. The real equivalent of the Japanese Ministry of International Trade and Industry in the United States is not the Department of Commerce but the Department of Defense, which by its very nature and functions shares MITI's strategic, goal-oriented outlook. In fact, the pejorative connotations in the United States of terms such as "Japan, Inc." are similar to those surrounding the domestic expression "military-industrial complex" referring to a close working relationship between government and business to solve problems of national defense. (Not to be outdone, some Japanese have taken to calling the Japanese government-business relationship a "bureaucratic-industrial complex."). American economic decisions are made most often in Congress, which also controls the budget, and these decisions reflect the market-rational emphasis on procedures rather than outcomes. During the 1970's Americans began to experiment with industrial policy bureaucracies such as the Department of Energy, but they are still rather wary of such organizations, whose prestige remains low.

Another way to highlight the differences between plan rationality and market rationality is to look at some of the trade-offs involved in each approach. First, the most important evaluative standard in market rationality is "efficiency." But in plan rationality this takes lower precedence than "effectiveness." Both Americans and Japanese tend to get the meanings of efficiency and effectiveness mixed up. Americans often and understandably criticize their official bureaucracy for its inefficiency, failing to note that efficiency is not a good evaluative standard for bureaucracy. Effectiveness is the proper standard of evaluation of goal-oriented strategic activities. On the other hand, Japanese continue to tolerate their wildly inefficient and even inappropriate agricultural structure at least in part because it is mildly effective: it provides food that does not have to be imported.

Second, both types of systems are concerned with "externalities," or what Milton Friedman has called "neighborhood effects" — an example would be the unpriced social costs of production such as pollution. In this instance, however, the plan-irational system has much greater difficulty than the market-rational system in identifying and shifting its sights to respond to effects external to the national goal. The position of the plan-rational system is like that of a military organization: a general is judged by whether he wins or loses. It would be good if he would also employ an economy of violence (be efficient), but that is not as important as results. Accordingly, Japan persisted with high-speed industrial growth long after the evidence of very serious environmental damage had become common knowledge. On the other hand, when the plan-rational system finally shifts its goals to give priority to a problem such as industrial pollution, it will commonly be more effective than the market-rational system, as can be seen in the comparison between the Japanese and American handling of pollution in the 1970's.

Third, the plan-rational system depends upon the existence of a widely agreed upon set of overarching goals for the society, such as high-speed growth. When such a consensus exists, the plan-rational system will outperform the market-rational system on the same benchmark, such as growth of GNP, as long as growth of GNP is the goal of the plan-rational system. But when a consensus does not exist, when there is confusion or conflict over the overarching goal in a plan-rational economy, it will appear to be quite adrift, incapable of coming to grips with basic problems and unable to place responsibility for failures. Japan has experienced this kind of drift when unexpected developments suddenly upset its consensus, such as during the "Nixon shocks" of 1971, or after the oil shock of 1973. Generally speaking, the great strength of the plan-rational system lies in its effectiveness in dealing with routine problems, whereas the great strength of the market-rational system lies in its effectiveness in dealing with critical problems. In the latter case, the emphasis on rules, procedures, and executive responsibility helps to promote action when problems of an unfamiliar or unknown magnitude arise.

Fourth, since decision-making is centered in different bodies in the two systems — in an elite bureaucracy in one and in a parliamentary assembly in the other — the process of policy change will be manifested in quite different ways. In the plan-rational system, change will be marked by internal bureaucratic disputes, factional infighting, and conflict among ministries. In the market-rational system, change will be marked by strenuous parliamentary contests over new legislation and by election battles. For example, the shift in Japan during the late 1960's and throughout the 1970's from protectionism to liberalization was most clearly signaled by factional infighting within MITI between the "domestic faction" and the "international faction." The surest sign that the Japanese government was moving in a more open, free-trade direction was precisely the fact that the key ministry in this sector came to be dominated by internationalistic bureaucrats. Americans are sometimes confused by Japanese economic policy because they pay too much attention to what politicians say and because they do not know much about the bureaucracy, whereas Japanese have on occasion given too much weight to the statements of American bureaucrats and have not paid enough attention to Congressmen and their extensive staffs.

Looked at historically, modern Japan began in 1868 to be plan rational and developmental. After about a decade and a half of experimentation with direct state operation of economic enterprises, it discovered the most obvious pitfalls of plan rationality: corruption, bureaucratism, and ineffective monopolies. Japan was and remained plan rational, but it had no ideological commitment to state ownership of the economy. Its main criterion was the rational one of effectiveness in meeting the goals of development. Thus, Meiji Japan began to shift away from state entrepreneurship to collaboration with privately owned enterprises, favoring those enterprises that were capable of rapidly adopting new technologies and that were committed to the national goals of economic development and military strength. From this shift developed the collaborative relationship between the government and big business in Japan. In the prewar era this collaboration took the form of close governmental ties to the zaibatsu (privately owned industrial empires). The government induced the zaibatsu to go into areas where it felt development was needed. For their part the zaibatsu pioneered the commercialization of modern technologies in Japan, and they achieved economies of scale in manufacturing and banking that were on a par with those of the rest of the industrial world. There were many important results of this collaboration, including the development of a marked dualism between large advanced enterprises and small backward enterprises. But perhaps the most important result was the introduction of a needed measure of competition into the plan-rational system.

In the postwar world, the reforms of the occupation era helped modernize the zaibatsu enterprises, freeing them of their earlier family domination. The reforms also increased the number of enterprises, promoted the development of the labor movement, and rectified the grievances of the farmers under the old order, but the system remained plan rational: given the need for economic recovery from the war and independence from foreign aid, it could not very well have been otherwise. Most of the ideas for economic growth came from the bureaucracy, and the business community reacted with an attitude of what one scholar has called "responsive dependence." The government did not normally give direct orders to businesses, but those businesses that listened to the signals coming from the government and then responded were favored with easy access to capital, tax breaks, and approval of their plans to import foreign technology or establish joint ventures. But a firm did not have to respond to the government. The business literature of Japan is filled with descriptions of the very interesting cases of big firms that succeeded without strong governmental ties (for example, Sony and Honda), but there are not many to describe.

Observers coming from market-rational systems often misunderstand the plan-rational system because they fail to appreciate that it has a political and not an economic basis. During the 1960's, for example, when it became fashionable to call the Japanese "economic animals," the most knowledgeable foreign analysts avoided the term because, in Henderson's words, there was "no doubt that Japan's center of gravity is in the polity not the economy — a source of puzzlement for Japan's numerous economic determinists of various Marxist stripe in academia and opposition politics." One did not have to be an economic determinist or a Marxist to make this error; it was ubiquitous in English-language writing on Japan.

J. P. Nettl's comment on Marx is relevant to this point: "The notion that 'the modern state power is merely a committee which manages the common business of the bourgeoisie' is one of the historically least adequate generalizations that Marx ever made." It is not merely historically inadequate; it obscures the fact that in the developmental state economic interests are explicitly subordinated to political objectives. The very idea of the developmental state originated in the situational nationalism of the late industrializers, and the goals of the developmental state were invariably derived from comparisons with external reference economies. The political motives of the developmental state are highlighted by Daniel Bell's observation — based on Adam Smith — that there would be little stimulus to increase production above necessities or needs if people were ruled by economic motives alone. "The need for economic growth in a developing country has few if any economic springs. It arises from a desire to assume full human status by taking part in an industrial civilization, participation in which *alone* enables a nation or an individual to compel others to treat it as an equal. Inability to take part in it makes a nation militarily powerless against its neighbors, administratively unable to control its own citizens, and culturally incapable of speaking the international language."

All of these motives influenced Meiji Japan, and there were others that were peculiar to Japan. Among these was one deriving from the treaties Japan was forced to conclude after its first contacts with Western imperialism in the nineteenth century: Japan did not obtain tariff autonomy until 1911. This meant that Japan was not able to aid its developing industries by the protective duties and other practices recommended by the market-oriented theories of the time, and the Meiji government consequently concluded that it had to take a direct hand in economic development if Japan was ever to achieve economic independence.

A second special problem for Japan lasted until the late 1960's, when it temporarily disappeared only to return after the oil crisis of the 1970's; this was a shortage in its international balance of payments and the resultant need for the government to manage this most implacable of ceilings in a country with extremely few natural resources. As early as the 1880's, Tiedemann writes that in order to keep foreign payments in balance with customs receipts, "all agencies were required to prepare a foreign exchange budget as well as their normal yen budget." Such a foreign exchange budget came into being again in 1937 and lasted in one form or another until 1964, when trade liberalization was carried out. In the era of high-speed growth, control of the foreign exchange budget meant control of the entire economy. It was MITI that exercised this controlling power, and foreign currency allocations were to become its decisive tool for implementing industrial policy.

The political nature of plan rationality can be highlighted in still other ways. MITI may be an economic bureaucracy, but it is not a bureaucracy of economists. Until the 1970's there were only two Ph.D.'s in economics among the higher career officials of the ministry; the rest had undergraduate degrees in economics or, much more commonly, in public and administrative law. Not until Ueno Kōshichi became vice-minister in June 1957 was modern economic theory even introduced into the ministry's planning processes (Ueno studied economics during a long convalescence from tuberculosis before assuming the vice-ministership). Amaya Naohiro reflects this orientation of the ministry when he contrasts the views of the scholar and of the practitioner and notes that many things that are illogical to the theorist are vital to the practitioner — for instance, the reality of nationalism as an active element in economic affairs. Amaya calls for a "science of the Japanese economy," as distinct from "economics generally,"

381

and pleads that some things, perhaps not physics but certainly economics, have national grammars. One further difference between the market-rational state and the plan-rational state is thus that economists dominate economic policy-making in the former while nationalistic political officials dominate it in the latter.

Within the developmental state there is contention for power among many bureaucratic centers, including finance, economic planning, foreign affairs, and so forth. However, the center that exerts the greatest *positive* influence is the one that creates and executes industrial policy. MITI's dominance in this area has led one Japanese commentator to characterize it as the "pilot agency," and a journalist of the *Asahi* who has often been highly critical of MITI nonetheless concedes that MITI is "without doubt the greatest concentration of brain power in Japan." MITI's jurisdiction ranges from the control of bicycle racing to the setting of electric power rates, but its true defining power is its control of industrial policy (*sangyō seisaku*). Although the making and executing of industrial policy is what the developmental state does, industrial policy itself — what it is and how it is done — remains highly controversial.

Industrial policy, according to Robert Ozaki, "is an indigenous Japanese term not to be found in the lexicon of Western economic terminology. A reading through the literature suggests a definition, however: it refers to a complex of those policies concerning protection of domestic industries, development of strategic industries, and adjustment of the economic structure in response to or in anticipation of internal and external changes which are formulated and pursued by MITI in the cause of the national interest, as the term 'national interest' is understood by MITI officials." Although this definition is somewhat circular — industrial policy is what MITI says it is — Ozaki makes one important point clear: industrial policy is a reflection of economic nationalism, with nationalism understood to mean giving priority to the interests of one's own nation but not necessarily involving protectionism, trade controls, or economic warfare. Nationalism *may* mean those things, but it is equally possible that free trade will be in the national economic interest during particular periods, as was true of Japan during the 1970's. Industrial policy is, however, a recognition that the global economic system is *never* to be understood in terms of the free competitive model: labor never moves freely between countries, and technology is only slightly more free.

There are two basic components to industrial policy, corresponding to the micro and macro aspects of the economy: the first the Japanese call "industrial rationalization policy" (*sangyō gōrika seisaku*), and the second, "industrial structure policy" (*sangyō kōzō seisaku*). The first has a long history in Japan, starting from the late 1920's, when it was quite imperfectly understood, as we shall see later in this book. MITI's *Industrial Rationalization Whitepaper* (1957) says that industrial rationalization subsumes a theory of economic development in which Japan's "international backwardness" is recognized and in which "contradictions" in the areas of technology, facilities, management, industrial location, and industrial organization are confronted and resolved.

Concretely, according to the *Whitepaper*, industrial rationalization means: (1) the rationalization of enterprises, that is, the adoption of new techniques of production, investment in new equipment and facilities, quality control, cost reduction, adoption of new management techniques, and the perfection of managerial control; (2) the rationalization of the environment of enterprises, including land and water transportation and industrial location; (3) the rationalization of whole industries, meaning the creation of a framework for all enterprises in an industry in which each can compete fairly or in which they can cooperate in a cartellike arrangement of mutual assistance; and (4) the rationalization of the industrial structure itself in order to meet international competitive standards. (The last element of the definition was included before the concept of "industrial structure" had been invented by MITI. After about 1960 it was no longer included in the concept of industrial rationalization.)

The short definition is that industrial rationalization means state policy at the micro level, state intrusion into the detailed operations of individual enterprises with measures intended to improve those operations (or, on occasion, to abolish the enterprise). Nawa Tarō says that in its simplest terms industrial rationalization is the attempt by the state to discover what it is individual enterprises are already doing to produce the greatest benefits for the least cost, and then, in the interest of the nation as a whole, to cause all the enterprises of an industry to adopt these preferred procedures and techniques.

Industrial rationalization in one form or another is an old and familiar movement going back to Frederick W. Taylor's system of "scientific management" of the progressive era in the United States (1890–1920); it exists or has appeared in every industrialized country, although it probably lasted longer and was carried further in Japan than in any other country. Industrial structure policy, on the other hand, is more radical and more controversial. It concerns the proportions of agriculture, mining, manufacturing, and services in the nation's total production; and within manufacturing it concerns the percentages of light and heavy and of labor-intensive and knowledge-intensive industries. The application of the policy comes in the government's attempts to change these proportions in ways it deems advantageous to the nation. Industrial structure policy is based on such standards as income elasticity of demand, comparative costs of production, labor absorptive power, environmental concerns, investment effects on related industries, and export prospects. The heart of the policy is the selection of the strategic industries to be developed or converted to other lines of work.

Robert Gilpin offers a theoretical defense of industrial structure policy in terms of a posited common structural rigidity of the corporate form of organization:

> The propensity of corporations is to invest in particular industrial sectors or product lines even though these areas may be declining. That is to say, the sectors are declining as theaters of innovation; they are no longer the leading sectors of industrial society. In response to rising foreign competition and relative decline, the tendency of corporations is to seek protection of their home market or new markets abroad for old products. Behind this structural rigidity is the fact that for any firm, its experience,

existing real assets, and know-how dictate a relatively limited range of investment opportunities. Its instinctive reaction, therefore, is to protect what it has. As a result, there may be no powerful interests in the economy favoring a major shift of energy and resources into new industries and economic activities.

Whether this is true or not, MITI certainly thinks it is true and considers that one of its primary duties is precisely the creation of those powerful interests in the economy that favor shifts of energy and resources into new industries and economic activities. Like Gilpin, MITI is convinced that market forces alone will never produce the desired shifts, and despite its undoubted commitment in the postwar era to free enterprise, private ownership of property, and the market, it has never been reticent about saying so publicly (sometimes much too publicly for its own good).

Although some may question whether industrial policy should exist at all in an open capitalist system, the real controversy surrounding it concerns not whether it should exist but how it is applied. This book is in part devoted to studying the controversy over means that has gone on in Japan since industrial policy first appeared on the scene. The tools of implementation themselves are quite familiar. In Japan during high-speed growth they included, on the protective side, discriminatory tariffs, preferential commodity taxes on national products, import restrictions based on foreign currency allocations, and foreign currency controls. On the developmental (or what the Japanese call the "nurturing") side, they included the supply of low interest funds to targeted industries through governmental financial organs, subsidies, special amortization benefits, exclusion from import duties of designated critical equipment, licensing of imported foreign technology, providing industrial parks and transportation facilities for private businesses through public investments, and "administrative guidance" by MITI. These tools can be further categorized in terms of the types and forms of the government's authoritative intervention powers (its *kyoninkaken*, or licensing and approval authority) and in terms of its various indirect means of guidance — for example, its "coordination of plant and equipment investment" for each strategic industry, a critically important form of administrative guidance.

The particular mix of tools changes from one era to the next because of changes in what the economy needs and because of shifts in MITI's power position in the government. The truly controversial aspect of these mixes of tools — one that greatly influences their effectiveness — is the nature of the relationship between the government and the private sector. In one sense the history of MITI is the history of its search for (or of its being compelled to accept) what Assar Lindbeck has called "market-conforming methods of intervention." MITI's record of success in finding such methods — from the founding of the Ministry of Commerce and Industry (MCI) in 1925 to the mid 1970's — is distinctly checkered, and everyone in Japan even remotely connected with the economy knows about this and worries about MITI's going too far. MITI took a long time to find a government business relationship that both enabled the government to achieve genuine industrial policy and also preserved competition and private enterprise in the business world. However, from approximately 1935 to 1955 the hard hand of state control rested heavily on the

Japanese economy. The fact that MITI refers to this period as its "golden era" is understandable, if deeply imprudent.

Takashima Setsuo, writing as deputy director of MITI's Enterprises Bureau, the old control center of industrial policy, argues that there are three basic ways to implement industrial policy: bureaucratic control (*kanryō tōsei*), civilian self-coordination (*jishu chōsei*), and administration through inducement (*yūdō gyōsei*). Between 1925 and 1975 Japan tried all three, with spectacularly varied results. However, at no time did the Japanese cease arguing about which was preferable or about the proper mix of the three needed for particular national situations or particular industries. The history of this debate and its consequences for policy-making is the history of MITI, and tracing its course should give pause to those who think that Japanese industrial policy might be easily installed in a different society.

What difference does industrial policy make? This, too, is part of the controversy surrounding MITI. Ueno Hiroya acknowledges that it is very difficult to do cost-benefit analyses of the effects of industrial policy, not least because some of the unintended effects may include bureaucratic red tape, oligopoly, a politically dangerous blurring of what is public and what is private, and corruption. Professional quantitative economists seem to avoid the concept on grounds that they do not need it to explain economic events. For example, Ohkawa and Rosovsky cite as one of their "behavioral assumptions . . . based on standard economic theory and observed history . . . that the private investment decision is mainly determined by profit expectations, based among other things on the experience of the recent past as affected by the capital-output ratio and labor-cost conditions."

I cannot prove that a particular Japanese industry would not or could not have grown and developed at all without the government's industrial policy (although I can easily think of the likely candidates for this category). What I believe can be shown are the differences between the course of development of a particular industry without governmental policies (its imaginary or "policy-off" trajectory) and its course of development with the aid of governmental policies (its real or "policy-on" trajectory). It is possible to calculate quantitatively, if only retrospectively, how, for example, foreign currency quotas and controlled trade suppress potential domestic demand to the level of the supply capacity of an infant domestic industry; how high tariffs suppress the price competitiveness of a foreign industry to the level of a domestic industry; how low purchasing power of consumers is raised through targeted tax measures and consumer-credit schemes, thereby allowing them to buy the products of new industries; how an industry borrows capital in excess of its borrowing capacity from governmental and government-guaranteed banks in order to expand production and bring down unit costs; how efficiency is raised through the accelerated depreciation of specified new machinery investments; and how tax incentives for exports function to enlarge external markets at the point of domestic sales saturation. Kodama Fumio has calculated mathematically the gaps between the real trajectory and the policy-off trajectory of the Japanese automobile industry during its infant, growing, and stable phases (the data are of course not yet available for a future declining phase). His measures are also tools for analyzing the appropriateness and effectiveness of the various governmental policies for the automobile industry during these phases.

The controversy over industrial policy will not soon end, nor is it my intention to resolve it here. The important point is that virtually all Japanese analysts, including those deeply hostile to MITI, believe that the government was the inspiration and the cause of the movement to heavy and chemical industries that took place during the 1950's, regardless of how one measures the costs and benefits of this movement. A measurement of what MITI believes and others consider to be its main achievement is provided by Ohkawa and Rosovsky: "In the first half of the 1950s, approximately 30 percent of exports still consisted of fibres and textiles, and another 20 percent was classified as sundries. Only 14 percent was in the category of machinery. By the first half of the 1960s, after the great investment spurt, major changes in composition had taken place. Fibres and textiles were down to 8 percent and sundries to 14 percent, and machinery with 39 percent had assumed its position of leading component, followed by metals and metal products (26 percent)."

This shift of "industrial structure" was the operative mechanism of the economic miracle. Did the government in general, or MITI in particular, cause it to occur? Or, to put it more carefully, did they accelerate it and give it the direction it took? Perhaps the best answer currently available is Boltho's comparative appraisal:

> "Three of the countries with which Japan can most profitably be compared (France, Germany, and Italy) shared some or all of Japan's initial advantages — e.g., flexible labor supplies, a very favorable (in fact even more favorable) international environment, the possibility of rebuilding an industrial structure using the most advanced techniques. Yet other conditions were very dissimilar. The most crucial difference was perhaps in the field of economic policies. Japan's government exercised a much greater degree of both intervention and protection than did any of its Western European counterparts; and this brings Japan closer to the experience of another set of countries — the centrally planned economies."

If a prima facie case exists that MITI's role in the economic miracle was significant and is in need of detailed study, then the question still remains why this book adopts the particular time frame of 1925–75. Why look at the prewar and wartime eras when the miracle occurred only in postwar Japan? There are several reasons. First, although industrial policy and MITI's "national system" for administering it are the subjects of primary interest in this study, the leaders of MITI and other Japanese realized only very late in the game that what they were doing added up to an implicit theory of the developmental state. That is to say, MITI produced no theory or model of industrial policy until the 1960's at the earliest, and not until the creation of the Industrial Structure Council (Sangyō Kōzō Shingikai) in 1964 was analytical work on industrial policy begun on a sustained basis. All participants are agreed on this. Amaya quotes Hegel about the owl of Minerva spreading her wings at dusk. He also thinks that maybe it would have been just as well if the owl had never awakened at all, for he concludes with hindsight that the fatal flaw of MITI's prized but doomed Special

Measures Law for the Promotion of Designated Industries of 1962–63, was that it made explicit what had long been accepted as implicit in MITI's industrial policy.

As late as 1973 MITI was writing that Japan's industrial policy just grew, and that only during the 1970's did the government finally try to rationalize and systematize it. Therefore, an individual interested in the Japanese system has no set of theoretical works, no locus classicus such as Adam Smith or V. I. Lenin, with which to start. This lack of theorizing has meant that historical research is necessary in order to understand how MITI and industrial policy "just grew." Certain things about MITI are indisputable: no one ever planned the ministry's course from its creation as the Ministry of Commerce and Industry (MCI) in 1925, to its transformation into the Ministry of Munitions (MM) in 1943, to its reemergence as the MCI in 1945, down to its reorganization as MITI in 1949. Many of MITI's most vital powers, including their concentration in one ministry and the ministry's broad jurisdiction, are all unintended consequences of fierce intergovernmental bureaucratic struggles in which MITI sometimes "won" by losing. This history is well known to ministerial insiders — it constitutes part of their tradition and is a source of their high esprit de corps — but it is not well known to the Japanese public and is virtually unknown to foreigners.

Another reason for going back into history is that all the insiders cite the prewar and wartime eras as the time when they learned *how* industrial policy worked. As will become clear in subsequent chapters, there is direct continuity between prewar and postwar officials in this particular branch of the Japanese state bureaucracy; the postwar purge touched it hardly at all. The last vice-minister during the period of this study, Komatsu Yūgorō, who held the office from November 1974 to July 1976, entered the ministry in the class of 1944. All postwar vice-ministers previous to him came from earlier classes, going back to the first postwar vice-minister, Shiina Etsusaburō of the class of 1923. Wada Toshinobu, who became vice-minister in 1976, was the first without any experience of the Ministry of Munitions era.

Nakamura Takafusa locates the "roots" of both industrial policy and administrative guidance in the controlled economy of the 1930's, and he calls MITI the "reincarnation" of the wartime MCI and MM. Arisawa Hiromi says that the prosperity of the 1970's was a product of the "control era," and no less a figure than Shiina Etsusaburō, former vice-minister, twice MITI minister, and vice-president of the Liberal Democratic Party, credits the experiences of old trade-and-industry bureaucrats in Manchuria in the 1930's, his own and Kishi Nobusuke's included. Tanaka Shin'ichi — who was one of the leading officials of the Cabinet Planning Board (Kikaku-in) before it was merged with MCI to form the MM, and who became a postwar MITI official — argues that wartime planning was the basis for the work of the postwar Economic Stabilization Board (Keizai Antei Honbu) and MCI. And Maeda Yasuyuki, one of Japan's leading scholars of MITI, writes that "the heritage of the wartime economy is that it was the first attempt at heavy and chemical industrialization; more important, the war provided the 'how' for the 'what' in the sense of innumerable 'policy tools' and accumulated 'know-how.'"

Even more arresting than these comments from participants and analysts is the fact that the Japanese economy began to change in quite decisive ways around 1930. It is true that industrial policy in one form or another goes back to the Meiji era, but it is also true that after the turn of the century the government moved progressively away from its former policies of interference in the domestic economy (if not in those of the colonies or dependencies), and that for about thirty years an approximation of laissez faire was in vogue. Rodney Clark's observation is startling but true: "The organization of Japanese and Western industry was probably more similar in 1910 than in 1970."

MITI and modern Japanese industrial policy are genuine children of the Shōwa era (1926–), and the present study is for that reason virtually coterminous with the reign of Emperor Hirohito. To carry the story back any further is to lose focus on the postwar economic miracle, but to fail to incorporate the history of the prewar MCI is to ignore MITI's traditions and collective consciousness. MITI men learned their trade in MCI, MM, and the Economic Stabilization Board. These were once such fearsome agencies that it was said the mere mention of their names would stop a child from crying. Admirers of the Japanese miracle such as I have a duty to show how the disastrous national experiences of the 1940's gave birth to the achievements of the 1950's and 1960's.

25.   A Planned Market Economy
Bernard Eccleston

Eulogies for a liberal market economy

Over the past decade there has been a tendency among economists to minimize the role of the state in the contemporary Japanese economy. This trend seems to be closely connected to the general revival of support for the ideology of free market forces with its corollary of rolling back the growth of state interference. The Japanese example of limited state expenditure with consequentially lower tax burdens, has been linked in a causal fashion to its higher rates of economic growth in order to highlight 'this secret of strong growth for a shining future' (President Reagan addressing Japan's National Diet November 1983 — quoted in K. Sato 1985 p.105).[1] The publication of *Asia's New Giant* edited by two of the most distinguished US students of Japan most clearly confirmed the greater importance of market forces. 'The Japanese government has never taken the lead in directly encouraging the transfer of resources away from inefficient uses; rather this has occurred through the operations of the market place' (Patrick and Rosovsky 1976 p.46).[2]

In the spirit of other Western studies of Japan at this time, the contributors to the Patrick and Rosovsky volume devoted part of their energies to establishing the lessons that the West can learn from Japan. This theme of learning lessons developed into a popular pastime after Vogel portrayed Japan as the *Number One* society in which the state merely provides a supportive 'framework within which private business can prosper' (1979 p.67).[3] Following the lead given by both of these works, a great deal of recent analysis has sought to divert attention away from industrial policies which smooth the process of change in particular industries toward the impact of freer competition. Gone is the emphasis on growth-promoting trade controls and specially targeted sectors which have had little effect in comparison to the 'actions and efforts of private individuals and enterprises responding to the opportunities provided in quite free markets for commodities and labour' (Patrick 1977 p.239).[4] Instead much greater weight in explaining Japanese economic performance is given to aggressive business attitudes to the importance of high levels of investment and to very high rates of individual saving. In addition more cooperative labour-management relations are founded on an individual work ethic unaffected by the disincentives that are said to follow in the wake of an over-burdening welfare state. Japan's remarkable rates of economic growth are then to be explained not by overt state intervention but by 'the huge 30–35 per cent of GNP that Japan has invested in the past several decades' (Schultze 1983 p.17).[5]

Although the main thrust of the analysis which depicts Japan as the epitome of a liberal free market has come from the US, this interpretation is also popular among Japanese commentators. If there is any difference of emphasis on the role of market

Bernard Eccleston: 'A Planned Market Economy' from *STATE AND SOCIETY IN POST-WAR JAPAN* (Polity Press, 1989), pp. 88–104. Reprinted by permission of Basil Blackwell Publishers.

forces, it is based not on the current scene, but on the part the state played in the economic recovery of the 1950s. Liberalization starting in the 1960s and continuing at an accelerating rate in the 1970s, thereafter reduced the extent of state licensing controls over imports, foreign exchange, investment programmes and the use of foreign technology. Until the current era of unbridled international economic relations, the state undertook developmental functions to foster speedy recovery, but these functions have since been passed to the free market. In contemporary Japan 'most of the country's industrial activity is developing without the hand of government in a competitive economy . . . under the harsher more entrepreneurial conditions of the market' (Tsuruta 1983 p.48).[6] Thus both in the West and in Japan analysis of the contemporary economy stresses the workings of unfettered free private enterprise.

Acceptable quantitative indicators of the size let alone the extent of state influence over the private markets in capitalist economies are, as we shall see, fraught with difficulty. Ultimately therefore any evaluation of the relative importance of private market forces against public intervention depends as much on normative values as it does on positive measurements. It is clear for instance that the shift in intellectual opinion on the need to diminish the role of the state has gathered support from the economic achievements of East Asian countries like Hong Kong, Japan, Singapore, South Korea and Taiwan where the 'invisible hand' of the market is said to reign supreme. The economic performance of these countries has received 'much admiration and many eulogies' (Sen 1983 p.12)[7] which has then led to suggestions that their market-based systems should provide the guiding path for the West. In particular monetarist and supply-side economists have stressed the way a small state requires small contributions in the form of taxes which places less constraints on individual incentives. This also leaves capital markets free to supply funds for private investment rather than purchasing vast quantities of state bonds.

Equally important in the US context has been the desire to use the Japanese example to challenge the assumptions of those in Congress and the labour unions who see stringent trade controls and a forceful industrial policy as the way to revitalize manufacturing industry. If it can be shown that Japan's vastly superior exports record is the result not of more state intervention but less, then it is argued that current US problems can only be corrected by restoring the supremacy of the market and reducing the distorting effect of Federal budget deficits. Therefore interpreting Japan as *the* model of successful market capitalism allows the judgement that interventionist policies are unnecessary. At the same time if Japanese experience goes to show what can be achieved with limited state involvement, this justifies the need to cut back interference by public agencies. If Japan could become so efficient without an overburdening state carefully planning industrial change, why should its competitors not do the same?

Within Japan there is, [as we saw in Chapter 1], a good deal of self-satisfaction about Western adulation of its society as the model of vigour and private initiative. Particular pleasure is taken from Japanese immunity from the Western disease of a diminishing work ethic and low productivity caused, so it is said, by excessive taxation and an over-protective welfare state. This view has been especially vibrant among business leaders who have been at the centre of LDP policies to reduce even further the number of public employees in a programme of privatizing state enterprises in telecommunications and on Japan National Railways.

State officials have had a particular interest in derogating the extent of their own influence over economic affairs. In the recurrent bouts of Western complaints about the scale of Japanese trade surpluses, LDP ministers insist that the imbalance in trade is essentially due to the inefficiency of Western products and lack of marketing effort by overseas exporters rather than import restrictions. It is of course enormously helpful for the Japanese then to be able to support their case by referring to the analysis of Western commentators who confirm that 'the average level of tariff was lower in Japan than in the US and all members of the EEC' (OECD 1985 p.40).[8] In the absence of tariffs, Japanese trade surpluses are portrayed as the outcome of rational domestic preferences for superior home-produced goods in a competitive market. Equally, those Western writers who have focused on the economic advantages of Japan's small state have provided invaluable evidence to support the case for cutting public expenditure to maintain the vigour of the private sector.

The association of Japan's economic performance with unfettered private enterprise has then provided justification for normative comments on the future role of the state both inside Japan and in the West. What has given these comments added credence has been the intellectual shift in favour of greater market incentives and the debate about how Japan managed to recover more quickly from the 1974 oil crisis. As many in the West have blamed their sluggish recovery on the distorting effects of increased public expenditure, the example of successful market-dominated economies like Japan holds a crucial position in the general debate on the appropriate balance between state intervention and free markets. In the rest of this chapter I will attempt to explore in more detail some of the assumptions and implications that follow from the current emphasis on a more limited economic role for the Japanese state.

In particular we need to ask in what sense is the Japanese state less interventionist than in other Western economies? Quantitative measures provide ambiguous evidence because although the Japanese state does indeed *consume* a smaller proportion of GNP in spending on public administration, defence, healthcare or housing, public *investment* is actually higher than other OECD countries. Placing more emphasis on Japan's peculiarly high rates of saving and investment also begs questions about how these high levels are maintained. To what extent are high levels of household savings themselves the result of state policies and how important have public financial institutions been in transferring savings to companies who need to borrow to finance their high investment levels?

Recent attempts to show that Japanese experience illustrates why interventionist policies are not necessary for rapid economic growth has tended to focus the debate fairly narrowly on industrial policy. Nurturing the expansion of new sectors and smoothing the decline of others is only one element of economic policy and the whole array of state management activities ought to be considered. For example one crucial reason why labour costs have been tied more closely to productivity levels in Japan has been the operation of an informal incomes policy where the state coordinates national norms for the annual spring wage offensive — *shunto*. In some ways this informal

391

process has been more influential because it has not been tied to specific public agencies; instead it builds in the expectation that the national interest requires a coordinated approach to wage increases. What matters is the effect this process has had on relative labour costs. Whether the desired result is achieved by informal or indirect state coordination as opposed to formal or direct policy is in the end less significant.

The distinction between formal power and informal influence is crucial, though, to the argument that trade liberalization has eroded the ability of the Japanese state to intervene in the economy. While it is true that important controls have to a large extent been loosened and investment authorization schemes dismantled, this need not imply any lessening of state involvement. Formal power to intervene may have been eroded but informal cooperation and consultation remains pervasive. From a Western perspective the strength of the ideology of liberalism encourages antagonistic reactions from private firms who resent state interference with the rights of free enterprise. Hence more attention tends to be focused on formal powers needed to overcome such resentment. Such an adversarial framework may well be related to the way many Western states are said to have encroached on the rights of free enterprise after the unhindered market system provided the basis for industrialization in the last century. But Japan never experienced a *laissez-faire* stage of economic development and its history since the 1860s has been marked by more cooperative relations between the state and private business. This heritage, supported by specific institutions, has built up different attitudes to the legitimacy of state involvement. Therefore the erosion of formal state powers over Japanese industry since the 1960s has to be balanced by an examination of institutions which maintain the higher degree of collaboration between state officials and business representatives.

First, though, we should look at the sort of supportive environment the Japanese state has maintained to assist economic growth and how it merely 'accelerated trends already put into motion by the private market' (Patrick and Rosovsky 1976 p.47).

The state as investor rather than consumer

A generally accepted measure for the size of the public sector is difficult to find not least because of differences in the way aggregate economic data is presented. However the OECD has attempted to standardize the national accounts of its 24 members who are the leading capitalist economies. Table 1 presents data on the equivalent shares in each country's GDP for the main categories of government expenditure in the 25 years from 1960–86. Column 1 covers current spending on goods and services and the contrast over the whole period between Japan and the average for the other six largest OECD countries is illustrated in Figure 1. The gap on current spending has remained fairly stable such that the Japanese state has rarely consumed resources at more than half the level of the other major economies. In complete contrast Figure 2 shows that as a proportion of gross domestic product government investment in Japan has consistently exceeded the average of the other six by an equally wide margin. There are some problems with the US data because part of their public investment is included under public consumption. Nevertheless Japan's larger share of state expenditure devoted to public investment rather than consumption seems to be quite different than the general OECD pattern.

Table 1   **Government expenditure as a percentage of GDP in the big seven OECD economies, annual average, 1960–86.**

	Consumption +	Investment +	Transfers =	Total outlay
United States	18.2	1.9	12.3	32.4
Japan	8.8	7.3	10.3	26.4
West Germany	17.3	3.9	19.2	40.4
France	14.3	3.9	24.4	42.6
United Kingdom	19.2	4.2	18.0	41.4
Italy	16.3	4.2	20.3	40 8
Canada	18.3	3.7	15.3	37.3
Smaller OECD av.	15.2	3.8	18.0	37.0

Source: OECD *Economic Outlook*, December 1982 and 1987

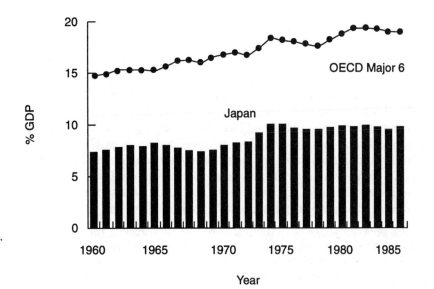

Figure 1   **Government consumption expenditure as a percentage of GDP in the Big Seven OECD economies, 1960–86.**

Source: *Economic Outlook*, OECD, December 1982 and 1987.

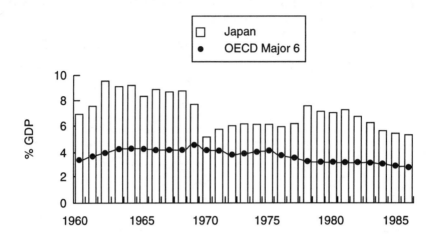

Figure 2   Public investment as a percentage of GDP in the Big Seven OECD economies, 1960–86.

Source: *Economic Outlook*, December 1982 and 1987.

When considering the lower levels of government consumption in Japan many economists choose to exclude defence spending because of the unusual constitutional limitations bequeathed by the US occupation. Until recently Japanese defence expenditure has been restricted to 1 per cent of GDP in contrast to about 5 per cent in the US and about 3 per cent in Europe. Therefore allowing for defence does close the gap in government consumption, but if we assume that some public investment goes on defence this should in theory widen the gulf between Japan and others who have no formal limit on defence spending. However we juggle the data, we are still left with Japan's noticeable 'enthusiasm for investing in the public sector' (Simon 1986 p.9)[9] in contrast to more limited current purchases of goods and services.

Throughout the past 25 years then Japanese public investment has been about twice the level of other Western economies and despite the cuts imposed on public spending in Japan during the mid-1980s the differential remains significant. A large proportion of this investment has been devoted to improving the infrastructure, especially in transport. Construction of roads, railways and new port facilities have been a priority in order to sustain the expansion of industry. Equally important has been public investment in the preparation of sites for private companies who are then able to re-locate their plant into integrated industrial complexes. Even in the service sector public investment has been important in developing real estate utilities around new railway stations to house department stores, hotels and offices.

One feature of rapid industrial expansion in Japan has been the ability of companies to lower average costs and increase productivity by operating within integrated units which house their own production facilities and that of subcontractors. Public investment in necessary utilities such as drainage and roads has sustained this process of integration by providing private companies with the opportunity to earn external economies of scale that follow from concentrating related firms within close spatial proximity. It is difficult to separate industrial from other beneficiaries of infrastructure investment, but the priorities appear to have been weighted towards activities that sustain increases in the private capital stock rather than social overhead investment. One could no doubt argue that individual citizens benefit from better transport facilities, but in general the comfort of passengers has had a lower priority than the needs of industrial users. It is not possible to cram more steel into a given piece of rolling stock but 'it is possible to crowd in three times the passenger capacity into an electric train'! (Economic Survey of Japan, *EPA* 1963 p.35). Media coverage of rush-hour trains in urban Japan show that this overcrowding is not a thing of the past.

Despite the abrupt shift of concern about environmental pollution in Japan during the 1970s, public spending to correct negative externalities (such as congestion) or to provide more public goods with positive externalities, remains less significant. The lower levels of current spending by the state and the smaller share of public investment in social capital reflect this trend and provision for education, housing and healthcare are left more to the private market than in many Western countries. The public share of fixed investment in housing as a proportion of Japan's GNP has since the 1960s been about one-fifteenth of the total. State spending on education is approximately two-thirds of total spending compared to 90 per cent in the main OECD countries; public outlays on health and social security are but 60 per cent of outlays in the leading Western nations.

The Japanese state still maintains a preference for holding back as far as possible its own current spending and being relieved of the burden of higher defence spending enables the Government's current account to be kept in surplus. Because rising state revenues from taxation have kept pace with the limited expansion in current spending the current account surplus is one source of funds for public investment. Although rates of direct taxation are lower in Japan they are steeply progressive which makes tax liability very sensitive to increases in income. So for example when incomes were rising very quickly up to 1973, so also did state revenues from taxation. Indirect tax revenues are also sensitive to changes in income because they are dependent on sales of more expensive goods. State revenues grew so quickly before the first oil crisis that frequent cuts were made in taxation rates, although tax bands or thresholds were adjusted less frequently meaning that the overall revenue yield continued to grow. The net results of expenditure limitation with rising revenues meant that the state for many years was a contributor to aggregate savings. Part of the background to a cautious fiscal policy can be explained by the legal requirement to balance budgets which was inherited from the US Occupation's anti-inflation programme. In fact cautious spending and healthy revenues meant that the current budget rarely balanced but was in surplus for almost every one of the past 30 years.

The excess of revenue over current spending or consumption provided one source of resources for public investment. But the biggest source has been the accumulated saving of households which since 1975 has been supplemented by substantial issues of government bonds. Household savings in Japan have been approximately 75 per cent higher than in the West over the past 25 years, and the state has occupied a pivotal position in transferring these savings into investment by the public and private sectors. The central mechanisms for this transfer is the Fiscal Investment and Loan

Programme (FILP) which lends at lower than market interest rates to a variety of public agencies. These include local governments, public enterprises in transport and communications and public finance institutions who in turn lend funds to private companies. So all Japanese companies have direct or indirect access to FILP from public corporations, to those with mixed public and private ownership to those wholly owned by the private sector.

The size of FILP at 40–50 per cent of the State's current account budget is very significant as may be expected given the resources available from very high household savings. Indeed Eiichi has argued that 'FILP is the key to the economic growth of our country' (quoted in Johnson 1978 p.81).[10] As a programme which is administered separately from the 'official' budget, FILP allocations tend to be freer from the major political wrangles that surround budget decisions. In fact until 1973 FILP accounts were not subject to Diet consent. We will see later how FILP acts as a vital intermediary in the supply of investment funds to private companies, but at this stage we need to recognize the way FILP uses savings to finance the investment activities of a variety of public agencies.

Until 1975 FILP funds and the current budget surplus were sufficient to cover the finance needed for public investment. Since then lower growth rates, smaller increases in incomes have meant a less rapid growth of revenue from taxation which, in the absence of any marked fall in public investment, required high levels of state borrowing. Although the issue of state bonds increased massively even this level of borrowing was more than matched by the continued flow of household savings. In fact with a slower increase in private investment only heavy state borrowing prevented the emergence of excess saving which would have plunged Japan into a serious recession (Y. Sato 1984 p.128).[11]

Reluctant state intervention on transfer payments

For most of the post-war period high levels of public investment were possible because of cautious attitudes to current state spending especially on the provision of public goods, because taxation revenues rose quickly and because the state had access to household savings. In managing the national accounts the Japanese state in contrast to other leading OECD members chose to minimize its own consumption and give a lower priority to transfer payments. There was a change to the pattern of state finances during the mid-1970s which is frequently associated with the massive increase in public borrowing. As Figure 3 illustrates, transfer payments began to increase markedly as a proportion of GDP after 1974.

This increase reflected greater state involvement in reshuffling purchasing power from one group of citizens to another — most commonly associated with transfers from the employed to the unemployed, the sick or the aged. Despite the fanfares which Japanese politicians sounded on the arrival of a superior welfare system, there is little doubt that improved public welfare provision was introduced with reluctance. Business leaders and state officials forecast grave consequences for individual initiative, the work ethic and savings levels once 'the warmth of the Japanese family [was replaced] by the cold and impersonal bureaucratic welfare state' (Campbell 1984 p.57).[12] Warnings were issued that better public welfare would mean bigger public expenditure which would inevitably mean higher taxes and consequently a lower rate of economic growth.

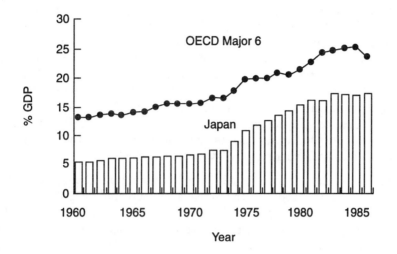

Figure 3   Government transfers as a percentage of GDP in the Big Seven OECD economies, 1960–86

Source: Economic Outlook, December 1982 and 1987.

It is evident that from the later 1960s as rapidly rising incomes went some way towards satisfying the demand for private consumer goods, the demand for goods and services of a social or public nature became much more active. In part this reflected general dissatisfaction with the external costs of rapid industrial growth seen especially in environmental pollution. But there was also disenchantment with the under provision of public services which were seen to have been sacrificed in the cause of promoting high rates of industrial investment. A sharp decline in support for the LDP was a catalyst in securing 'improvements in social security provision that led to a large increase in real transfers (OECD 1985 p.91). This judgement about transfers and an improved social security system does though need to be qualified by noting that increases in welfare spending were accommodated by increases in individual contributions and that social security outlays are only one element in total transfer payments.

Social security outlays did rise fivefold between 1974 and 1984 but their share of total transfers actually fell from 75 to 64 per cent and the share of subsidies to local government and public enterprises also fell. The most significant increase came in interest payments to holders of public debt which grew twice as fast as the social security component. Thus an important element of the overall increase in transfer payments went not to households who own a tiny amount of public debt, but to financial institutions and corporate enterprises.

Alongside larger social security disbursements has gone an equivalent growth in contributions which increased by nearly 40 per cent between 1980 and 1985. The objective is to minimize the extent to which public subsidies are needed and thereby make the social security accounts balance. In practice the accounts have regularly shown a huge annual surplus equivalent to 3 per cent of GNP as the accumulated pension surpluses from earlier years are invested to produce substantial interest earnings. The excess of income over expenditure is transferred to FILP for loans to public institutions and thence to the private sector. In the process of managing these welfare funds the state is making crucial decisions on behalf of civil society about contribution and payment rates and on the allocation of surplus funds. The priorities expressed in these decisions have stressed individual responsibility for adequate welfare cover, rather than providing resources from the public purse, i.e. from general tax revenues. To reduce still further the chance that social security spending in the future will exceed contributions, changes have been made which not only increase contributions but will limit spending by lowering standards.

An improved state pension scheme in 1973 set the retirement benefit level at 50 per cent of average earnings — although the average pension paid in 1983 was only 40 per cent because the scheme was fairly new and contributions were incomplete. Changes introduced in the early 1980s reduced the retirement pension norm by one-sixth, lengthened the required period of contributions from 32 to 40 years and raised the pensionable age from 60 to 65. As we have seen [in Chapter 3] most people 'retire' well before 65 and so the pressure to find other paid work until they reach pensionable age is maintained. Indexation of pensions was a vital part of the 1973 scheme but now this is to be initiated *only* if consumer prices rise by more than 5 per cent *per annum*. Inflation at this level has been rare in recent years, but even price increases of 2 or 3 per cent when accumulated over a number of years significantly erode the real value of payments made.

The other main element in social security is healthcare where again the main objective is to make expenditure and revenue balance. So to match increases in healthcare spending patients have had since 1984 to pay the first 10 per cent of their medical expenses. Not surprisingly spending dropped, especially among the elderly who had previously been accused of 'over-using medical services because they were free' (Campbell 1984 p.57).

As a managing trustee for the social security schemes, the state has established ground rules which will ensure that public welfare is largely self-financing. Prudence dictates that individual responsibility should be the basis of a welfare system that offers what Vogel called 'security without entitlement' (1979 Chapter 9). This system reflects the view that entitlement produces over-reliance on the state which undermines initiative and the propensity of individuals to save. Transferring income from employees to the sick or elderly means moving purchasing power to groups with lower saving propensities thus raising fears that aggregates will fall. Equally the saving habits of employees may be changed as the 'guarantee of a state pension is likely to reduce one important motive for household saving' (OECD 1985 p.48).

Concern about the level of personal savings has been heightened because household tax burdens have risen. Although compulsory social security contributions are now bigger than direct tax payments both have risen sharply in the 1980s. Rates of taxation have been reduced on several occasions recently but tax thresholds have not and the minimum taxable income has been frozen since 1977, when to keep pace with inflation it should have fallen by a third. For employees extra tax and social security payments meant a slower growth of disposable incomes between 1980 and 1985 thus the spectre of falling savings levels loomed large. In this scenario the state has sought to confirm the Japanese tradition of self-help as opposed to public entitlement to maintain personal savings and prevent any erosion of FILP reources.

The Japanese savings rate

At first sight fears that better public welfare provision would depress saving seem to be confirmed as the proportion of disposable income saved by Japanese households fell from 24 per cent in 1974 to 17 per cent in 1984. However it should be noted that the 1974 figure was a record and came in the wake of a record increase in money incomes around that time. It is significant that although the aggregate savings ratio fell markedly in the decade after 1974 the ratio for employee households fell only marginally from 25 to 23 per cent (OECD 1986 p. 13). Thus for that half of Japanese households who depend on wage earning rather than income from property and/or who are retired, saving ratios declined only slightly despite a slower growth in gross incomes and despite increased tax and social security contributions.

Even with some decline in the propensity to save, the Japanese still manage to save at levels some 50–40 per cent higher than the OECD average. The debate over why the Japanese apparently prefer to save rather than consume has thrown up numerous explanations which usually highlight unique cultural frugality or peculiar social practices. For example paying a proportion of wages in bi-annual lump-sum bonuses and an underdeveloped consumer credit system are said to encourage saving. It is difficult to see though why lump-sum bonuses, which make an ideal source for purchasing consumer durables, are not used as an alternative to the inadequate consumer credit facilities. Neither is it obvious why the higher paid who receive bigger lump-sum bonuses tend to have a lower marginal propensity to save.

A favoured explanation among monetarist or supply-side economists suggests that the lower direct tax levels in Japan are crucial in generating higher personal savings. But there are several problems with this not least how to account for the relative stability of employee saving ratios despite the increasing direct tax burden in the first half of the 1980s. Over the longer term we also need to explain why those earning higher incomes, whose marginal rate of tax is lower than in the West, actually save a small proportion of their disposable income. At the other end of the scale we find that low income families who have not reached the minimum tax threshold and so are not affected by lower direct tax rates, also save large amounts. Therefore saving ratios may actually 'be insensitive to the tax burden' (K. Sato 1985 p. 120).

Some have argued that higher personal saving in Japan is really an exaggerated phenomenon because the personal sector includes larger numbers of the self-employed whose saving should really be counted in the corporate sector. As access to external finance for small firms is limited, the self-employed are forced to save more to support their businesses. The self-employed do save at higher rates and there are more self-employed workers in Japan, although the number has fallen in recent years and one would expect this to have a diminishing effect on aggregate saving. Even conceding the role of the self-employed still leaves us to explain why households which depend on outside paid employment save at higher rates.

Socio-cultural theories about unique Japanese practices are common to a whole host of issues, and a traditional preference for frugality has been used to highlight the continuity in saving habits since the pre-war era. These theories are more difficult to confront because they tend to be so general and at first sight so appealing. For instance the incidence of typhoons and earthquakes may be common enough to encourage the Japanese to place more emphasis on precautionary motives for saving. But such long-standing habits surely need other supporting processes to maintain cautious attitudes to spending as opposed to saving. Inducements to save whether through tax exemptions, compulsory social security contributions or through the extensive network of state post offices, have to be considered along with apparently long-standing traditional preferences. One can only speculate whether the traditions could have survived without a supportive institutional environment to maintain cautious attitudes to consumption.

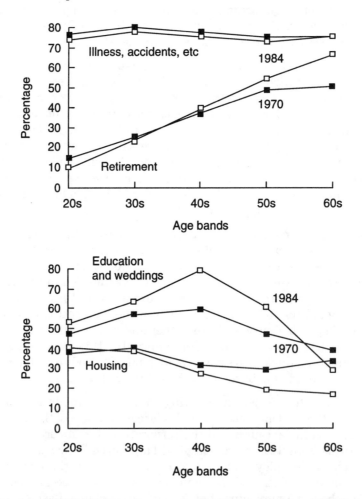

Figure 4   (a) and (b) Motives for personal savings in Japan, 1970 and 1984.

Source: OECD 1985.

The motives of Japanese savers are surveyed regularly and Figure 4 compares the main reasons given in 1970 and 1984 according to age group. These particular years may have been untypical but the general features have been confirmed in other surveys using alternative sources. For example the high ranking of precautionary motives to provide for illness or accidents which incur medical costs at the same time as earnings fall through temporary absence from employment. This category is the one which 'registers the highest rate of response (60–80 per cent) in all age groups' (1985 Survey on Savings *FPC* p.3).[13]

A noticeable change in saving for retirement is the increase in its ranking for those over 50 which to a large extent reflects the lengthening gap between the earlier age at which many workers leave their tenured jobs and the age when state pensions begin. Older workers may not have sufficient years of contributions to the scheme and so receive a smaller pension; this explains why more elderly people continue to rely on employment than in the West. Growing awareness of the inadequacy of state benefits seems to be reflected in the continuing importance of saving for retirement throughout the age range.

Perhaps the most significant change in responses between 1974 and 1984 concerns the need to provide for children's education and weddings especially for those in the 45–55 age group. Weddings in 1983 according to one survey cost on average a staggering 7 million yen which was equivalent to one and a half times the average wage (*JTW* 4/8/84).[14] This is clearly one place where cultural traditions do play a part in sustaining savings.

In a similar way it could be argued that Japan's meritocratic ideology sustains traditional motives to save for education. Education expenses depend very much on the mix of public and private facilities chosen by parents; one bank survey for 1984 estimates the cost of a mainly state route at 17.5 million yen and a more private one at 25.3 million (*JTW* 6/4/85). Ministry of Labour statistics show that at their peak educational expenses take up 20 per cent of average income in the age range 47–53, and the rising trend in education expense accounts for the increasing importance of this category of savings motives. As we saw in the discussion of labour markets access to tenured employment in larger companies who pay more and offer better welfare benefits, depends on performance in and attendance at prestigious universities. Entrance to such institutions requires parental planning to set their children on the appropriate route from kindergarten onwards to be able to pass the entrance examinations to selected schools. With so much at stake in these examinations, parents pay for additional tuition at weekends, in the evenings and in vacations at private crammer schools known as *juku*.

Individual opportunities in Japan are very much a matter of competition for places at selected schools which have established a good track record of examination passes. Given the importance of educational credentials in the life chances of their children, even younger parents save to be able to meet 20 years of education expenses. These expenses are increased by the relative under provision of places in state establishments at the extreme ends of the child's educational career: before the age of compulsory schooling at six and in higher education. In both of these sectors the state provides only

401

one-quarter of places yet in both Japan has one of the highest enrolment rates. For example one-third of three-year-olds, 80 per cent of four-year-olds and 95 per cent of five-year-olds attend kindergarten and 36 per cent of the relevant age group go on to higher education. If we add the costs of attendance at *juku* the average parent faces escalating educational costs rising from 6 per cent of disposable income for children under six to 30 per cent for children attending private universities.

A pronounced demand for educational credentials extends across all income brackets and arguably creates more pressure on poorer families because education is seen to be the key to upward mobility. The Japanese state has actively participated in maintaining the ideology of a meritocracy without, as we shall see, paying as much attention to equality of opportunity in the sense of subsidies to low income households. By failing to provide an adequate supply of places in its own institutions especially in the early and later stages of educational careers, the state forces people into the private market. Equally by holding down public spending, parents have to pay higher costs even in state schools. Both tendencies reinforce the need to save to meet expenses which are known to last throughout the educational career of their children.

Saving to buy land or housing has a lower response rate and one which 'has declined sharply in recent years' (1985 Survey on Savings, *FPC* p.2). Two of the main factors causing this decline have been firstly the increased availability of housing loans and secondly the emergence in the 1980s of a switch to rented housing. The state's role in the housing market has been less concerned with the supply of housing itself than with satisfying part of the demand for finance where FILP funds are used through the Housing Loan Corporation (HLC). Apart from a meagre level of tax deductibility for housing loans, the HLC provides finance at a subsidized rate of interest; funds are obtained from FILP at 7.5 per cent and HLC then lends at 5.5 per cent for up to a half of the cost of house purchase. Of the remainder about 20 per cent comes from bank loans and 30 per cent from purchasers deposits. Up to the early 1980s, then, relatively better access to housing loans eased the pressure on individuals to save for house purchase.

Since then there has been a noticeable slackening in the demand for loans to purchase houses. The HLC interest rate subsidy has been cut and as house prices have risen much more quickly than incomes, the maximum proportion borrowable from public or private institutions has fallen. Hence bigger down payments by purchasers are needed. This trend has not increased personal saving for house purchase, rather it has reduced the demand for loans and caused a rise in the demand for and supply of rented housing. This switch reflects other pressures on disposable incomes and the massive increase in house prices. Relative to construction, the cost of land makes up two-thirds of the total price compared to one-quarter elsewhere in the OECD. Given a scarce supply of land available for housing the average price of a house in urban Japan is equivalent to eight years average income or twice the ratio in Europe or the US.

Ostensibly the state has lubricated the housing market mechanism, but it has concentrated more on the demand side. Where action has been more limited is in public construction but particularly in doing little to improve the availability of land. An over-protected agricultural sector not only results in higher food prices for consumers but inhibits the release of poorer quality land for housing. Lubricating just one side of the market has then produced a move towards renting accommodation in order to preserve savings for ill-health, retirement and education.

Higher personal savings may indeed be a matter of Japanese cultural proclivities but we need to consider how such traditions are maintained. Choosing to save appears to be a matter of personal decisions to sacrifice present consumption to pay for future spending whether this is predictable, for expected education expenses, or unpredictable for sickness. However what the state does or does not provide in these areas has crucial implications for individuals. Even with a limited amount of public enterprise employment, the Japanese state has guided individual decisions by moulding the social environment within which these decisions are made. The end result of this guidance has been the accumulation of huge savings over which the state acts the part of managing trustee. In an aggregate sense the personal sector is the major source of savings which have gone to finance the enormous borrowing requirements of private industry. A smooth flow of funds from savers to borrowers could not have been made as effectively without state management because 'there was no market mechanisms to automatically channel private saving into growth-promoting investment' (K. Sato 1985, p.128). Supporting a smooth transfer from net lenders to net borrowers has been the main responsibility of the FILP.

Notes

1. Sato, K. (1985) 'Supply-Side Economics'. *J. of Japanese Studies*. Vol. II, No. 1.

2. Patrick, H.T. & Rosovsky, H. (1976) *Asia's New Giant*. Washington D.C., Brookings Institution.

3. Vogel, E.F. (1979) *Japan as Number One*. Cambridge, Mass., Harvard University Press.

4. Patrick, H.T. (1977) 'The Future of the Japanese Economy'. *J. of Japanese Studies*. Vol. III, No. 2.

5. Schultze, C.L. (1983) 'Industrial Policy: A Dissent'. *The Brookings Review*. No. 2. Fall.

6. Tsuruta, T. (1983) 'The Myth of Japan Inc.', *Technology Review*. Vol. 86, No. 7.

7. Sen, A. (1983) 'The Profit Motive'. *Lloyds Bank Review*, 147

8. OECD (1985) *Economic Survey: Japan*, Paris, OECD.

9. Simon, O. (1986) 'Investing in Infrastructure'. *National Westminster Bank Quarterly Review*, May.

10. Johnson, C. (1978) *Japan's Public Policy Companies*. Washington D.C., American Enterprise Institute.

11. Sato, Y. (1984) 'The Subcontracting Production System in Japan'. *Keio Business Review*. No. 21.

12. Campbell, J.C. (1984) 'Problems, Solutions, Non-solutions and Free Medical Care for the Elderly in Japan'. *Pacific Affairs*, Vol. 57, No. 1.

13. *Foreign Press Centre (FPC)* (1985) *Survey on Savings*.

14. *Japan Times Weekly (JTW)* Overseas Edition, Tokyo.

26.   Social Ills and Destruction of the Environment

Tadashi Fukutake

Old and new poverty

Although Japan was once very poor, its agricultural productivity has always been high compared with other Asian countries. For this reason it is the single Asian nation that has been able to achieve industrial development and growth of a capitalist economy with no outside assistance.

A policy aimed at increasing national wealth and military strength was the motivating force behind this development. Special favors and encouragements were given to industry, and higher productivity and large sums of money were invested in building a modern military force. The poverty that was left in the wake of Japan's spectacular national economic development was given scant attention, however. To most it was inevitable and therefore seemed hopeless — a necessary by-product of industrialization. The poverty of the urban lower classes was no less abject than the destitution of tenant farmers in the villages, nevertheless with the exception of the rice riots following World War I, conditions of the poor in Japan never erupted in social outbreaks violent enough to force recognition of a basic social problem.

Measures for alleviating what had become an urgent problem were not taken. Within the very framework of Japanese society there existed devices for absorbing or ignoring poverty; there was a strong tendency, for instance, to regard poverty as a misfortune that one must simply become resigned to, and there was a lack of awareness of the social causes of poverty. The idea that society itself should be responsible for relieving that which it had caused never occurred to most. The Meiji government made a beginning in helping the poor with the establishment of the Relief Regulations in 1874; and in 1929 a national aid system, the Relief and Assistance Law, was adopted. But these measures fell far short of providing real relief. Also, the people had a deeply-rooted tendency to regard relief as shameful; poverty was something for the family and relatives to take care of themselves. Poverty which could not be handled in this way was considered a problem of unfortunates to be taken care of by charitable activities. Those who lacked even relatives to help them were simply pitied as the lowest of the unfortunate. The attitude that people had a right to assistance from society through a national welfare system simply did not exist.

After the war these attitudes underwent great change. At the end of 1945, when poverty was rampant, the general outlines of emergency relief for the needy were set up in a Cabinet meeting and the Daily Life Security Law went into effect. This law provided for national aid to the poor and needy on an equal basis without discrimination. The idea that it was a disgrace to become a "card-carrier," one who was

Tadashi Fukutake: 'Social Ills and Destruction of the Environment' from *JAPANESE SOCIETY TODAY* (University of Tokyo Press, 1974), pp. 106–119. Reprinted by permission of University of Tokyo Press.

entitled to government assistance, began to fade, and most began to take it for granted that those in need should receive help from government welfare policies. Relief from relatives, who now had no legal or even social obligation to help their cousins and nephews decreased. Whereas before the war they would have been ashamed not to help, it was not long before they refused to help at all. Just after the war, nearly three million persons were receiving government assistance, 27 out of every 1,000. When Japan's economy entered its period of growth in 1955, these figures dropped to 1.7 or 1.8 million, or 20 out of every 1,000 and more recently, to 1.4 million, or 13 out of every 1,000. The increasing employment opportunities and rising wages that accompanied rapid economic growth have meant that many people have gone off relief. As a result, most families who now receive assistance are old people, mothers and children with no father, the mentally or physically handicapped or the disabled. Such people make up almost 80 percent of the families on relief. In nearly 70 percent of those households no member is capable of working. It is especially noteworthy that while ten years ago the head of the household was working in 40 percent of families receiving relief, this ratio has now dropped to a little over 20 percent.

These statistics indicate that while poverty as such is decreasing, it is becoming more and more necessary for the aged, the mentally or physically handicapped and the disabled to be given long-term assistance. Assistance has increased steadily year after year, but the richer society as a whole becomes, the more keenly people feel their own poverty. This applies not only to those receiving public assistance but also to those whose economic level brings them down to the so-called borderline stratum. As part of a society that is growing increasingly more affluent, these people are painfully aware of their poverty. In this country which has risen to thirteenth in the world in per capita income, the low-income strata that embrace these groups come to over one-tenth of the population.*

Thus, modern Japanese society has not eliminated 'its old poverty; indeed, its huge economic growth is responsible for having created a new kind of poverty. Mixed in with the "old poor" — those on relief and others only a shade better off — are the "new poor," for whom their condition is all the more painful in an age of affluence and high mass consumption. New burdens on those left out of Japan's prosperity have been added to the old — psychological burdens. The prewar attitude of resignation to one's lot and of an unconcern for human rights is no longer possible, so, though the poor remain poor, it is more difficult for them to accept their lot.

In addition to poverty in the conventional sense of the word, Japanese society is becoming increasingly poor in a spiritual sense; although materially rich, something is lacking in the quality of life. Commercialized mass culture, hedonistic in its pursuit of

---

* Today Japan has the highest GDP per capita of all industrial economies with large populations. However, while the absolute poverty of the early post-war period has been largely alleviated, marked differences in life chances persist as considerable income inequalities remain. Income differentials between the lowest twenty percent and the top twenty percent of households has remained constant throughout the era of rapid economic growth. More than sixty per cent of all Japanese households have consistently received less than the average national income and twenty per cent have less than half the average income. [Editor]

pleasure, demonstrates a kind of cultural Gresham's law. Compared with "high-quality culture" there is no denying the energy of Japan's masses is not developing to the fullest but is being degraded for commercial ends. Mass amusements, which provide an outlet for sexual desire, and gambling, which becomes an escape from reality, only increase spiritual poverty, or even in cases of the materially affluent, crime and delinquency start to increase.

In addition, extraordinarily rapid economic growth is destroying the natural environment itself. What was once a rich, verdant nature is becoming an impoverished nature. This is causing a deterioration of the essential quality of human life. In the face of such jeopardy to the natural environment, we are beginning to realize that human life should be valued above all else. How long will it take for the idea of the ultimate worth of man to become embodied in social policy.

Those left behind

Before the war the physically or mentally handicapped, orphans and solitary old people without relatives managed to sustain themselves either through the help of relatives or by receiving charity from their localities. The few who had no relatives and could not support themselves by any means received aid from private social work. Public aid facilities were scanty, and most such social work as the charitable undertakings of religious organizations or of philanthropists could just barely struggle along.

This situation improved considerably after the war, and at present social welfare work is based on the Five Social Welfare Laws. This is the general name for individual welfare laws enacted for children, the aged, the physically handicapped, the mentally retarded, and mothers with children who are without the support of a father, respectively. The fact that relief and aid are now provided by law is a great change from the prewar situation, even though welfare facilities and personnel remain inadequate. Of the five laws, those for child welfare and for the physically handicapped were enacted soon after the war, in 1947 and 1949, respectively. Legislation for the mentally retarded, the aged and for fatherless families were effected fairly recently, in 1960, 1963 and 1964, respectively.

The unfortunate people for whom these laws are designed are apt to be left behind in the surge of economic growth. Their voice in society is weak, legal measures to provide for them have lagged, and public welfare expenditures have not been given enough weight in the national budget. The first order of business in the government is growth in the economy. Social welfare work has, nontheless, made great strides since the end of the war. The establishment of welfare offices in prefectures and cities had become obligatory, and about a thousand or more are now in operation. They are short of personnel, however; their activities are directed mainly toward assuring subsistence for the poor, and they do not get around to many other aspects of social welfare work. Although the number of caseworkers has recently gone up they are still too few. In the present situation subsidies for personnel expenditures are so small that agencies depend on the cooperation of social welfare councils. These are established on three levels: national; prefectural; and city, ward, town and village. Broadly classified, social welfare facilities may be divided into those for the care of the needy, welfare for the aged, rehabilitation of and assistance to the physically handicapped, protection of women, children's welfare, aid to the mentally retarded, mothers' welfare, etc. A more detailed classification would include fifty different kinds of facilities. The total number of such facilities at present is about 24,000, but 14,000 of them are day nurseries. Since two-thirds of the total number are public facilities and one-third private, in general the proportion of private social work is the reverse of what it was before the war.

The organization of social work is expanding, and the number of facilities is gradually increasing year by year, but the work as a whole is still far from adequate. Compared with the striking rise in the standard of living of the population as a whole, the misery of uncared-for physically or mentally handicapped children and fatherless families has worsened. The increase in the proportion of the aged in the total population and the trend toward nuclear families have resulted in more and more elderly people who require social welfare. Physically and mentally these people are being excluded from the modern, economic society. Changes in methods of production and new applications of technology have the effect of depressing still further the lives of the handicapped and retarded.

There are not enough facilities to accommodate those who need institutional care. Even if they were admitted to an institution it is likely to be short of personnel so that they would not get the kind of attention they need. For example, nursing homes for the aged can accommodate less than 30 percent of those who need such care. The same proportion applies to institutions for children who are seriously handicapped mentally or physically, and the number of institutions for severely mentally retarded and physically handicapped people comes nowhere near meeting the need, for they can accommodate only about 15 percent of those who should be admitted.

These institutions should be always staffed with trained, competent personnel, but the present labor shortage makes it possible for people to select jobs that have better remuneration and working conditions. Japan is backward both in establishing institutes for specialist technical training and also in providing salary scales appropriate to these specialities. The pay, working conditions, and benefits in private institutions are well below the level in public ones. Strenuous efforts are urgently needed to raise salaries according to the work performed. If the people who take care of the needy are themselves left behind in the upward surge of the economy, there is a dark future awaiting social welfare work in Japan.

It is not only the elderly, the orphaned and the handicapped who have been left behind. Day laborers with irregular employment have been part of Japanese society since the beginning of industrial society. Although their numbers have decreased with the development of industry, many are still without the security of daily jobs, many cannot marry and support a family, and many have failed completely in trying to establish themselves in a job. The rapid growth of the economy has greatly expanded opportunities for employment, but it is difficult for the old or middle-aged man to change his occupation. Some were unable to shift from farming or coal mining, and in the course of long periods of working at jobs away from home they turned to casual labor. Many such people settle in the slums of the large cities; Tokyo's Sanya district and Osaka's Kamagasaki district are examples of such settlements. The very fact that these cheap lodging-house districts still exist illustrates one serious imbalance in Japanese society.

This group has been alienated, and rebellion against alienation sometimes leads to unhealthy mob riots. Outbursts at bicycle races (even though the fans are not necessarily slum-dwellers) are also rebellions against alienation by people who feel constantly frustrated. Such pathological social phenomena may occur at other places as well. Latent hostility has built up in those left behind by the economy; these people are on the lowest rung of a society which appears wealthy. The more wealthy the society, the more explosive this group is likely to become.

Crime and delinquency

Crime and delinquency are the clearest manifestations of a socially pathological condition. Throughout the advanced world, these symptoms increase as income level rises. Crimes and misdemeanors can only be counted if they are first detected and prosecuted. Crimes that are never detected cannot become part of general statistics. In order to look at the trends and transitions in this area we need at least police statistics. According to these statistics, the total number of crimes by adults reached a peak in 1950, decreased thereafter, and have recently been on the rise again. Juvenile crimes followed the same pattern. In adult crime there has been an abrupt increase in cases of involuntary homicide and personal injury due to automobile accidents; the improvement in social and economic conditions has, on the other hand, been accompanied by only a slight decrease, or no change at all, in the amount of ordinary crime. The incidence of juvenile crime is rising rapidly. Exclusive of involuntary homicide and injury, there have been over 40 juvenile crimes to every 100 committed by adults. Taking into account the proportion of youths in the population, juvenile crime occurs three times more often than that of adults. This increase is striking, considering that slightly over ten years ago it was about the same as that of adults.

Crimes against property, mainly theft, make up half of the total, while violent crimes such as assault, personal injury, intimidation and extortion account for one-fourth. As a general trend, crimes against property and crimes of brutality are decreasing, while crimes of negligence (chiefly from automobile accidents) and sex offenses are increasing. There is a great deal of variation between cities and rural areas in the incidence of crime, but urban crime tends to be similar regardless of size of city. In general, urbanization is causing a diffusion of crime throughout the nation. The ratio of crimes committed by people with steady jobs and no previous criminal records is increasing, and crimes connected with traffic accidents have soared with greater motorization. Use of automobiles as an instrument of crime, has become more widespread.

These trends may be a reflection of changes and growth in the economy but the pattern here of an overall falling crime rate stands in contrast to foreign countries during the 1960s, where there was a direct correlation between the rise in incomes and the crime rate. Perhaps Japan is experiencing the peaceful conditions of a modern "Genroku," supported by the growth of the economy. (Genroku, 1688–1704, was a period of peace and prosperity that gave rise to the merchant class.) Practically, however, Japan differs from other countries only in that it has reached the stage where income levels are high enough to allow people to dissipate their day-to-day frustrations in recreation and pleasure. If in the future rising demand cannot be adequately fulfilled, it is possible that Japan will duplicate the pattern that has occurred in other countries.

A sensitive indicator of this trend is the increase in and changing nature of juvenile crime. In the past the main causes of juvenile crime were family poverty, some deficiency in the family (such as only one parent), or a negative environment within or outside the family. But today families with both parents at home and incomes well above the poverty level are producing juvenile criminals. About ten years ago 50 percent or less of the juveniles who came under the general guardianship of the courts were from families with both parents; recently this proportion has surpassed 70 percent, while the proportion of juvenile wards from broken families dropped from 35 to 15 percent. The proportion of juvenile delinquents from families who are poor or needy is decreasing. Recently the proportion of juvenile criminals from "ordinary" families rose to 80 percent.

These trends in juvenile crime cannot be divorced from the many changes in family life that have occurred since the war, in addition to the permissiveness, overprotection and pampering of children that have accompanied rising income and consumption, and the spread of small families. Another factor is that, as material life becomes more abundant, young people's wants and expectations also rise, and when their purchasing power cannot satisfy their demands, they are likely to feel thwarted. As a general rule the young are most vulnerable to social imbalances. Their very sensitivity makes them particularly susceptible to the distortions of mass culture. The crime rate among working juveniles, compared with students, for example, has been increasing. The rising rate of crimes of brutality among employed juveniles is particularly marked among those who shift from one job to another, a phenomenon often seen in high-growth periods.

Juvenile delinquency, or destructive, harmful acts which do not amount to crime, is also spreading. Delinquency is a general term applied to problematic conduct and anti-social acts of juveniles. In this limited meaning it applies to crimes committed by youths between 14 and 19, lawbreaking behavior of persons under the age of 14, and juveniles with criminal tendencies who are considered potentially capable of criminal acts in the future. All these are lumped together in the term "delinquents." Very often these juveniles have associated with other problem children or groups of delinquents. This trend is evidenced by the fact that, of all the criminal offenses investigated in 1970, 15 percent of those by adults were committed by two or more persons, while one-third of those by juveniles involved two or more. Among them were cases involving gangs of young hoodlums, many of them linked with established gangster groups.

The connection of these gangster groups with crime is an important factor in many aspects of social life. When police control becomes strong, the groups go underground or disperse; when such control is relaxed, they come out into the open again. It is difficult to say whether statistics show the real situation, but if police surveys can be relied on, the number of gangs has decreased since 1960, although the number of gang members has increased. It is impossible to predict whether the slight decrease in the number of groups will continue. The crimes of these gangs mainly involve personal injury, intimidation, assault and gambling. Of the total number of crimes of personal injury and intimidation, 30 percent are allegedly gangster crimes. Even more indicative of an ailing society is the growing incidence of blackmail and extortion, whereby a company or organization suffers at the hands of gangsters. Only a few of these cases ever reach the courts. Strong-arm men hired to intimidate stockholders or company representatives are, in this area, only slightly different from gangsters. They are hired to attend general stockholders meetings disguised as stockholders, to 'preserve order" and to "assure" that the meeting proceeds as planned by the directors, with no embarrassing questions or rebellion by the legitimate stockholders.

Drugs and prostitution are a common source of funds for gangs. It was only after the war that drugs became a significant social problem. Drug sales are very strictly controlled and for that reason alone their price is high. The gangs make their way into illicit sales organizations and use this traffic as a source of funds. Gangs formerly were closely connected with prostitution, but since the antiprostitution law went into effect this source of funds has decreased. Prostitution is still difficult to eradicate, and the more strictly it is prohibited, the greater are the potential profits to be gained by clever evasion of the law. Gangs are still involved in such activities.

These darker aspects of society exist in every era; a society without crime or delinquency can hardly be hoped for, but a sound and healthy society can keep them to a minimum. An increasing crime rate is a sign that social development is not keeping pace with economic growth. Although the dark clouds which hang over our society have covered the world since World War II, and even though the situation in Japan is not uniquely bad, our society still has room for improvement.

Destruction of the natural environment

Japan's economic development has not only aggravated unhealthy social conditions; it has also been destroying the natural environment. This newly dubbed "polluted archipelago" now leads the world in the rate of pollution.

The Japanese word most often used for pollution (kōgai) is similar to the English term "public nuisance." Though literally kōgai is a calamity inflicted on society as a whole by an unspecified large number of individuals or enterprises, it has come to connote the pollution resulting from the discharge of smoke and water from specified industries. But what is this thing we call kōgai?

Pollution long antedates World War II. Exhaust from factories rained soot upon every neighborhood, and smoke from mines stripped the mountains of their verdure. Polluted water contaminated the soil and damaged agricultural products. The soot and smoke of industrial cities were, nonetheless, accepted as symbols of industrial progress and those who suffered damage had to be content with trifling amounts paid in compensation. From the Meiji period on, the government maintained a policy of increasing production and encouraging industry. The development of mining and manufacturing was considered necessary for the development of Japan, and whatever damage was caused had to be endured. Local governments regarded such damage as a necessary evil to be tolerated for the sake of regional prosperity. The political and social climate allowed industrial enterprises to feel no distress over the pollution they

411

were spreading. The same attitudes continued after the war. Heavy and chemical industrial growth and the shift from coal to oil as a source of power increased pollution until discharges from the factories began to destroy the cycle of nature itself.

Sulfuric acid gas has replaced smoke and dust as the main contaminants in polluted air. Industrialized urban areas are so polluted now that, with added exhaust from heating installations and automobile gases, city people are coughing and gasping for breath and complaining of smarting eyes from photochemical smog.

Water pollution has also become an urgent problem. Since before the war the lack of adequate sewage systems has contributed to the contamination of water by household waste. Failure to plan facilities for disposal of industrial waste, moreover, has turned rivers into sewers and "killed" large areas of our coastal seas. Pollution of rivers is reaching a level where they can no longer purify themselves naturally. Using rivers as sources of water supply has required great sums of money for water purification systems, and in some cases contamination has exceeded the limits beyond which water cannot be used at all. The waste waters from industrial plants have passed the stage where they merely damage farm crops or curtail fishing; they are now eating away at the bodies of human beings themselves. Such maladies as the Minamata disease and *itai-itaibyō* (the "ouch-ouch disease," a bone disease caused by cadmium poisoning) are making polluted Japan infamous throughout the world. Extraction of water for industrial use, moreover, has caused areas of land to sink in some places. The most notable cases are to be found in Tokyo and Osaka. Noise and vibration produced by factories, trains, highway transport and other sources comprise another area of disturbance that is not only destroying the natural environment but normal human life as well.

Even farm villages, which, if anything, were once the victims of pollution, have now become the source of pollution. The postwar emphasis on increased production encouraged wide use of agricultural chemicals and insecticides, and the accumulative effects has made chemical pollution a serious problem. In addition, the development of recreational areas to attract vast numbers of tourists is further promoting the destruction of the environment, as mountains are cleared for roads and land cut up for cheap recreational facilities. If this rate of destruction continues unabated, the natural environment cannot be preserved, and man's very existence on the soil of Japan may be endangered.

Postwar Japanese governments have been tolerant of environmental destruction, making development of industry their first priority. At a time when rapid increase in production was also causing a rapid increase in pollution, the Ministry of Health and Welfare prepared a bill to prohibit contamination and destruction of the environment. It was pigeonholed as premature. The Water Quality Preservation Law and the Industrial Plant Waste Water Regulations Law came out in 1958; the Soot and Smoke Regulations Law belatedly went into effect in 1962. In 1964 a Pollution Section was established in the Ministry of Health and Welfare. In 1965, when pollution could no longer be ignored, the Pollution Prevention Corporation was formed. Finally, in 1967, the Basic Law on Pollution was drawn up. The Basic Law stressed the need for development of the economy in harmony with nature and set up standards with regard to air, water, and noise levels, but it was not grounded in a basic concern for the people or the country as a whole. Instead, there were noticeable compromises with the existing situation. After a period of extreme pollution, in 1970 the pressure of public opinion succeeded in eliminating those articles in the law which made concessions to economic development. The argument still persists, nonetheless, that preservation of the environment must be reconciled with sound development of industry — even today the latter tends to be given precedence.

The people of the nation and the residents of polluted areas who have allowed environmental destruction to run its course must bear some of the responsibility for it. The attitude which equates industrial and social development still persists, and popular acquiescence to the destruction of the environment for the sake of the region as a whole has made Japan the most polluted of countries. Both national and local governments tend to look at the problem from the point of view of the polluting enterprises rather than from that of the citizen. At the present time, concern over pollution has increased; citizens' opposition to the location of polluting industries in their areas has increased considerably, but movements to prevent pollution by established enterprises and demand compensation for damage already caused are very difficult for local residents to promote. Workers in the polluting enterprises hesitate to cooperate with popular movements, knowing that they will be working against their own companies and their own interests. Old established local organizations such as the neighborhood associations are reluctant to join for fear that they will be used for partisan purposes. The soil of Japan, where old social cohesiveness has broken down and where solidarity of regions as democratic communities is a thing of the future, is not fertile ground for citizens' movements. When a proposal is made to strip natural greenery for a new tourist site, most join the destroyers, hoping to share in the profits from the tourist industry, even in the face of conservation-minded opposition.

To preserve the natural environment of Japan and maintain the health of its people, environmental destruction must be stopped and nature must be restored. This will not be easy. Yet despite the predisposition to give priority to the economy, since the 1970 anti-pollution campaign a change is taking place in the attitude of the Japanese people toward pollution. Recent court decisions against pollution-causing industries have given impetus to this change. The number of people who now stress the importance of preserving the environment is rapidly growing. The will to preserve the natural environment must take priority and serve to reinforce efforts to provide a complete and enriching life environment. While people have become more aware of the need for the former, there are still very few in our country who can see the connection between the poor efforts being made by politicians, and their lack of desire even to do so, and the provisions such a life environment. It may be a question of political education. Today there are not too many people who have the intention of reforming the socio-political structure of the country; we must encourage many more to realize how our political and economic systems can be used toward a better natural and social environment.

Society and Economy in Japan Today

With economic growth roaring ahead at an unprecedented rate of 13 per cent each year between 1965 and 1970 following the implementation of the Income Doubling Plan, Japan seemed to have gained on all fronts. Economic recovery was complete; new products made by revolutionary industrial methods were developed for growing world markets. The technology gap between Japan and the Western industrialised countries was closed decisively with Japanese leadership apparent in some branches of science. Export performance — which like production had been officially planned — was encouraging and indicated that Japanese goods and their methods of manufacture and sale were well suited for international trade. Inflation, gross poverty and destitution had been ended, labour relations were calm and reassimilation within the international community was fully achieved after the Tokyo Olympiad in 1964.

Social conditions, especially diet, health and housing were steadily improving. The population had become taller and heavier, and by the 1980s Japan was to have the longest life expectancy of any country in the world. With full employment, rising productivity, low labour turnover and less time lost due to industrial disputes than in competitor nations there appeared to be every indication of a committed workforce that was dedicated to both company and product.

In present day Japan authority figures and established institutions seem to have retained their respect. Crime rates remain low and the wave of counter-culture which swept in from the West has been absorbed without arousing widespread contempt and cynicism among the young. Even the Japanese chapters of the Hell's Angels cult are rigorous about their personal hygiene: they bow politely to policemen and drive in an organised convoy. Since the 1970s the clear signs of economic success and the lack of any serious political opposition to the seemingly endless conservative rule of successive Liberal Democratic governments have been taken as confirmation that Japan is a consensus society.

Ideas of contemporary Japan as conflict free, and of a society that has been calmed after its industrial transformation by renewed contact with its unique historical roots and by the resurgence of tradition, have been effectively disseminated by the ruling élite and given support by official data. In 1993 a social survey by the office of the Prime Minister found that the self-perceptions of social class held by Japanese households indicated that 89 per cent of the population saw themselves as middle or upper class, and that less than 6 per cent admitted belonging to the working class. The low incidence of industrial conflict in many Japanese firms, together with a system which apparently guarantees life-time employment and the absence of many of the culturally maintained boundaries between management and workers which are prevalent in the West, tends to reinforce the view of a placid and acquiescent work-force who fully identify with corporate aims. After all Japanese workers and their bosses do dress alike, share facilities and regularly participate in shop-floor discussions on working practices and productivity. In the case of office workers, they all occupy the same room and even work at the same long desk. Wage differentials within large companies tend to be less severe than in the West. Top executives earn far less than their Western counterparts, and the example of the American director of Sony USA earning more than the Japanese president of the Sony Corporation itself has been taken to indicate a trend toward social equality. Many of the keiretsu and other large corporations provide a range of social services that go with the job. Health care and housing, holidays, and even marriage-broking services and a place in the company's cemetery are frequently available for employees leaving an impression of corporate benevolence and worker fidelity which has been widely projected abroad.

However, this image of Japan as a consensus society with a workforce whose compliance is a product of its commitment to collective social values is not one which survives careful scrutiny. As both Kamata and Eccleston show, the Japanese élite has consistently refused to extend its power and prosperity to larger sections of society. Greater participation in the political process at a variety of levels, including shop-floor organisation and pressure groups, has been consistently opposed, and despite the fabulous wealth amassed in the last few decades society has remained poor with living conditions and social provision well below that which the economy might easily support. Food prices remain exceptionally high, partly because of the unreformed nature of Japanese agriculture, as Bernier explains, and partly because of the unofficial alliance between the Liberal Democratic Party and the peasantry who continually re-elect conservative governments. Visitors to Japan often comment on pollution and the tacky urban structure. An acute lack of social and cultural infrastructural investment is immediately evident in the absence of parks and social spaces, and in the Lilliputian homes of most Japanese. After more than a century of development the real benefits of industrialisation have yet to be fully realised in Japanese society as a whole. The lion's share of post-war economic growth has gone to the state and large businesses, whose goals are biased toward yet further economic expansion and world market dominance rather than human investment.

As a result, social divisions are marked and inequalities remain pronounced. Women, who make up over a third of all salaried workers and more than half the casual labour force, have for decades received little more than half the male wage despite legislation for equality. Hunter examines the historical and cultural background of sexual inequality in Japan, together with the changing domestic roles embraced by women. Working hours in industry as a whole are longer than in other industrial societies — a six day working week is common for many workers — and far less holidays are taken than in Europe or America. McCormack explores some of the social effects of this meagre leisure. Steven shows that the Japanese working class is riven with social divisions that have been created by the economic system itself and is politically weak as a result. Within a company the position of individual workers is made insecure by a complex pay structure which does not recognise the basic principle of equal pay for equal work. The absence of this fundamental axiom of collective bargaining makes effective negotiations over pay and conditions difficult. But this problem is compounded by the fact that in Japan it is usually only the enterprise-based employees associations, rather than national unions based on specific trades and industries, that are recognised for negotiations. The comparison between Western and Japanese industrial cultures is taken further in the extract by Clark.

Other forms of social division, which are far less apparent to the outside observer, are highlighted by Herzog who shows that Japan's image of social homogeneity is false. Japan has a long-standing Korean minority who are still the objects of systematic discrimination after several generations of residence. Like all advanced industrial societies Japan has attracted migrant labour and, in the past twenty years, worker communities from the Indian sub-continent and South East Asia have arisen with the increasing ability of the home work-force to move toward the more prestigious and higher paid work. However, the persistence of an indigenous outcast group, the *burakumin*, who are regarded as heavily polluted and ritually unclean by virtue of their origins alone — which are pure Japanese — comes as a surprise to many Westerners.

Japanese workers face heavy demands for moral compliance from their employers. Heart and soul dedication to the aims and products of a corporation, or at least a semblance of this, is as much a prerequisite for continued employment or advancement as the work itself. Management techniques place great emphasis on the instillation of traditional Confucian virtues in the industrial context. Social harmony, loyalty to the company and subordination to hierarchical authority are combined with uniquely Japanese practices which bind workers and management together in patron-protege ties — the *oyabun-kobun* relationship — that are sometimes expressed in kinship terms. Work group members are encouraged to adopt familial-like relationships reminiscent of a feudal clan and identify each other and their supervisor as relatives. Such 'beautiful customs', as they are perceived in managerial ideology, clearly serve as a means of inculcating values which directly serve the interests of the state and business élites. An outward appearance of social tranquillity in the working environment is paramount for Japanese management and no form of conflict or any democratic means of resolving it is accepted as legitimate. Genuine grievances, including the underlying divergence of real interest between workers and their employer, are obscured in this manner and managerial authority and its considerable oppression remains wrapped in apparent benevolence.

Beautiful customs, which also include the life-time employment system, have been taken by some industrial sociologists in the West to be no more than the result of surviving feudal customs. But persistence, like change, requires explanation and what appears as the simple continuation of traditional social customs in the modern work place should be treated with caution. Since the normal processes of social decay which accompany industrialisation have eliminated the majority of archaic feudal practices, it seems ironic that those which serve the ends of management have endured intact. In fact such work practices are not the simple remnants of the feudal era. These ostensible hangovers from the age of the shoguns represent in actuality the conscious attempts of the Japanese industrial élite to modify, preserve and even invent traditions and customs as a means of securing their own political interests.

This is nowhere more evident than in the custom of the life-time employment system which is often presented as a treasured aspect of Japan's cultural inheritance and is analogous with the unswerving loyalty of the samurai to his lord. Life-time employment is, in fact, a restricted privilege that is enjoyed by only a minority of male workers employed in large corporations. These firms do provide long-term employment

417

for workers from the point of leaving education until their retirement at about fifty-five. But such workers should be seen as a labour aristocracy since they work alongside other workers employed on short-term contracts who have none of their security, pay or privileges, such as pensions or graduated salary scales. In the backward sector of the economy, which employs the majority of the work-force and pays lower wages, there is no such confidence in continuous employment. Large companies sub-contract work to small businesses in the backward sector and take on or dismiss extra labour when demand for their products varies. This form of flexible labour market allows large firms to retain a core of life-time employees, even during a downturn in the business cycle. Finally, it is important to realise that the life-time employment system does not derive from feudal custom: it is in fact an artifact of early twentieth century industrial organisation which arose with the need to retain skilled labour in key sectors of the economy.

Japanese workers have only a restricted mobility for their labour. Job changing remains difficult and is usually equated with personal instability or disloyalty. A Japanese employer's authority extends far beyond that found in the West, and control over both work and leisure time is an accepted part of the industrial social contract. The source of many of the things which sustain everyday life — housing, health, and at times even education — lies with employers and a worker will find that any reluctance to conform to company values and work norms may jeopardise these vital social services for both self and family. Occupational pensions are meagre and even though the Japanese are assiduous savers retiring workers are usually forced to take a new job at lower pay in their mid-fifties when corporations shed labour. An employee in Japan is tied by a series of tight economic and ideological ropes that act to stifle independent thought and action. Social conformity is much more the result of these political and economic factors than imaginary constraints imposed by a unique cultural tradition. The absence of effective opposition to conservative élite values is therefore not an indication of a consensus society: conformity here is more a product of coercion than conviction.

Yet there are strong signs that Japan also contains a growing number of independent minds and creative forces which wish to break free from this constricting social mould and reconstruct society on a new basis. Japan has a rich and varied historical tradition and, as we have seen in the course of this book, the ingenious adaptiveness of the Japanese people has already been capable of making at least two profound social transformations within a century. Another such transformation of Japan is both inevitable and overdue. And these surely are the leading reasons why the study of this dynamic and resourceful country has always been so exciting.

27.   Japan in the Passing Lane
Satoshi Kamata

Toyota Hall stands near the Toyota Motor Company's Head Office Building in an area where the hills were once covered with red pines. Now everything is different. Even the place names have been changed to honor the Toyota family, and it has become the keep of their "castle town." The two-story hall itself was built in November 1977 to commemorate the company's fortieth anniversary. It's an enormous Toyota show-case.

I arrived yesterday, January 7, 1980, the first working day of Toyota's new year. Today, however, since I don't have any appointments with workers or any other plans, I decided to pay my first visit to this showy hall — not so very different from a penny arcade. A big sign in the hall showing "The Number of Toyotas Produced up to the Present" lights up quite impressively. Its electronic panel displays a long row of figures: 29,894,140. Twenty-nine million eight hundred ninety-four thousand one hundred and forty Toyotas! This is the total number of vehicles produced since Toyota shipped out its first trial automobile in May 1935. Of course, this figure is only as of 11:15 A.M. As I watch, the last digit continually increases. Timing it, I realize that the number is changing every six seconds. Two weeks from now, the 30 millionth car will be recorded. The 20 millionth came in July 1976. According to the guide, this figure includes all the cars and trucks finished at the five Toyota plants as well as Toyota Chassis, Arakawa Chassis, Hino, and Daihatsu–Toyota-affiliated firms. One new vehicle every six seconds!

The computer in the control room, which occupies one corner of the Head Office Building, assesses the rate of production through circuits linking the various plants, and quickly computes the number on the panel. It is the perfect symbol of mass production. Standing in front of it, an executive would probably nod in satisfaction — or would he feel impatient seeing that the six seconds have not yet been reduced to five?

Watching the figure increase with each passing second, I feel all choked up. I can see it: the conveyor belts moving along mercilessly; the workers moving frantically as they try to keep up. I can hear their sighs. One vehicle every six seconds. The conveyor belts never stop. Workers are already dead tired. Figures racking up on the panel without a break. For a few moments, I just stand there stunned.

The wind carries shouts from the adjacent athletic field. Preparations are under way for the New Year's Parade of Security Division Fire Brigades, which is scheduled for the afternoon. In the empty Exhibition Hall (where the first visitors of the year have not yet appeared), part-time women workers are polishing cars. The 1980 auto-production competition is just about to start.

From *JAPAN IN THE PASSING LANE* by Satoshi Kamata. Translation copyright © 1982 by Tatsuru Akimoto. Reprinted by permission of Pantheon Books, a division of Random House, Inc.

Yesterday, the president's annual New Year's address was delivered in this hall's big auditorium. Eiji Toyota spoke to his seven hundred middle- and top-management employees: "We already depend on overseas markets for about one-half of our products. Overseas markets are extremely important. I ask you to see things from a broad international point of view, and I also want you to carry out your daily work always keeping in mind the overseas situation."

Last year's sales of Japanese automobiles (Toyotas, Datsuns, and others) in the United States reached 1,710,000, a 30.5 percent increase over the previous year. Both General Motors and Ford have been preparing full-scale production of compact and sub-compact cars since the autumn, in an effort to compete with Japanese manufacturers. To protect the American automobile industry, Douglas Fraser, head of the United Automobile Workers, is both pressing the United States government to pass legislation requiring Japanese automakers to build automobile plants within the United States and strongly insisting on Japan's self-restriction of exports. Honda has decided to launch production of cars in the United States, and Datsun will follow with the production of small-sized trucks. Toyota has also been forced to decide to begin manufacturing in the United States in order to avoid being criticized for flooding the market in the United States and Europe. In his New Year's address to his managers, President Toyota called for the "establishment of an epoch-making management system" and the "lowering of costs from the ground up." Rationalization will certainly become more severe.

A certain foreman is said to have grumbled, on his way to the auditorium, "Last year we were pushed to wring water out of a dry towel. What will they tell us to do this year?" The punch line in the address that day was "If there is a steep mountain ahead of us, let us call the mountain to us, level it, and endure difficulties." It seems that Toyota-style rationalization is going to become even more high-handed.

Toyota's production in 1979 reached 2,996,000 units, a 4.9 percent increase over the preceding year. With knockdown* sets included, the number reached 3,070,000 — a new record. The ordinary profit for the first half of this year is forecast at $1.1 billion, or an increase of 26 percent over the same period of last year. This, too, is the highest in the company's history. As a result, profit, after taxes, will amount to $590 million. This means that a day's operation will bring to Toyota more than $1.8 million profit.

As of June 1979, the Toyota Motor Company employed 45,233 workers. The increase is only 30 people over the same month last year. On the other hand, the increase in production is marked, an increase of 140,000 vehicles, from 2,930,000 to 3,070,000. Calculated in terms of finished vehicles, this means each worker produces 66 vehicles a year. Ten years ago, the equivalent figure was 49. Even by simple calculation (and taking into account some automation at work), it's clear that labor has been intensified enormously. Furthermore, in those few years Toyota hired few seasonal workers.

It was only twelve years ago that red-and-white sweet rice jelly was handed out to all employees to commemorate the achievement of the production level of 100,000 vehicles

* Knockdown sets are the vehicles that are sold and exported disassembled to be assembled in another country.

per month. Clearly, these recent records have been achieved at the expense of the exhaustion of the regular workers. This year the production goal is 3,220,000. The electric lights on the panel will flash on and off still more rapidly.

The keynote of Toyota rationalization is the elimination of all waste:
1. Waste from overproduction
2. Waste in waiting
3. Waste in the shipping process
4. Waste in processing
5. Waste in inventories
6. Waste in motions
7. Waste from producing defective products*

The rationalization here is not so much to eliminate work as, more directly, to eliminate workers. For example, if 33 percent of "wasted motion" is eliminated from three workers, one worker becomes unnecessary. The history of Toyota rationalization is a history of the reduction of workers, and that's the secret of how Toyota shows no increase in employees while achieving its startling increases in production. All free time during working hours has been taken away from assembly-line workers as wasteful. All their time, to the last second, is devoted to production. Subcontractors deliver parts directly to the conveyor belts. Assembly conveyors in each plant are subordinate to the main conveyors that ship out finished cars, and the conveyor belts in subcontracting firms are "synchronized" to the conveyor belts in each Toyota plant. This "kanban method," which has been widely heralded in the mass media, is meant to compel subcontractors to deliver parts exactly on time, which is just another sign of the increasing "synchronization" in the industry. Even the streets between the subcontractors and Toyota's plants are regarded as conveyor belts connecting the actual conveyor belts within the plants. The Toyota method of production appears to the outside world as the systematization of "the relationship of a community bound together by a common fate" (Ohno, *Toyota Method of Production*). But truthfully, it's nothing more than the absolute determination to make all movement of goods and people in and out of these plants subordinate to Toyota's will.

It was the silent coercion of the conveyor belt that I felt most strongly while I was working at Toyota. More precisely, it was the merciless directions from the control room at the Head Office. The number and type of vehicles to be produced are probably allocated to each shop through consultation between Toyota and the Toyota Motor Sales Company Ltd. In the transmission assembly shop where I worked, iron flags (a variety of kanban) came down the conveyor belts to designate the type of cars to be produced. These were sent in accordance with the instruction printed out on tapes by the control room. Seeing the color and shape of the flags, workers chose appropriate parts from those on hand. If production was lower because of some minor malfunction of machines, the conveyor speed was increased to make up the delay. If production was delayed owing to a fellow worker's absence, overtime became necessary. Even without

* Taiichi Ohno, *The Toyota Method of Production*.

such incidents, production goals were always just beyond what seemed like the human capacity to produce, and no worker knew what time he might go home once he was in the shop. The workers were bound to the conveyors until they stopped, and the conveyors never stopped until the production goal for the day was achieved.

Books praise the "kanban method" to the skies, but the real things that make Toyota run haven't changed since I was there in 1973. Basically, Toyota's great leaps in production are achieved through production allowances and a work-quota system. At Toyota, an employee's total monthly wage includes a relatively low basic wage, overtime pay, a production allowance, and various other allowances. The production allowance is that part of an employee's monthly pay which is calculated against the number of work units (that is, the number of workers multiplied by the number of working hours) it takes a team to reach a certain production goal. Basically, wages for the month will increase if the team exceeds the production goal in fewer hours and with less manpower. One worker's monthly wage could fluctuate from month to month by as much as $45, even with the same number of working days and the same amount of overtime. Nobody except the Personnel Department really knows how the wages are computed. In some plants, announcements like the following are made during working hours:

TODAY'S PRODUCTION GOAL IS 565 VEHICLES.
THE LINE HAS STOPPED SIXTY MINUTES.
WORKER TROUBLE RESPONSIBILITY THIRTY MINUTES.

With more hours of "trouble responsibility," the month's wages would naturally decrease. Should someone in the team make a mistake, the wage would decrease correspondingly. Tied to the conveyor belts, everyone works desperately, hoping that he is not a burden to others. This is the "relationship of a community bound together by a common fate."

A worker says: "I worked four or five hours of overtime last month. This month I worked twelve hours. But the total earnings differ only by $4.50." This is not a rare case at all. The basic wage for a worker who is a high school graduate with eleven years of service is $285 a month. However, the "basic wage-production allowance" as printed on the pay slips fluctuates as follows:

July 1979:	$652
October 1979:	$647
December 1979:	$650

These figures are for a worker off the assembly line, and therefore his productivity can't be measured in the manner outlined above. Nevertheless, his wage fluctuates as shown above.

The pay slips of workers at the conveyor lines — where work quotas are assigned — are not available. But I have heard that their basic pay, including production allowance, would be about twice the basic wage, and that the production allowance would go up and down by a margin of 40 percent. In other words, if a worker's basic wage is $318, his pay will fluctuate between $636 and $763. The quota and production allowance constantly spur workers to increase their output. If the teams put in too much overtime, the production allowance is reduced "because they are inefficient." If the teams should have a successive three-month increase in the production allowance, the number of workers is reduced "because they have too many workers." This is the essence of the Toyota method of production. Introduced around 1960, this is functionally a piecework payment system.

Workers are urged on to production, day and night. So tightly are their lives bound to the conveyor belts in the plants that they cannot even take days off when they want to. The thoroughgoing enforcement of rationalization has eliminated all relief workers. Not only team leaders, the lowest management people, but also unit leaders have been required to work on conveyor lines. Even foremen, normally part of higher management, may sometimes put on working gloves and lend a hand. Then these men have to take home their paperwork such as the writing of daily reports and the calculation of day-by-day work units. Through it all the conveyor belts are kept running, with the absolute minimum number of men necessary.

I can remember times when I was absent from work and someone from the Personnel Department came to the dormitory to get me. One worker, who had to attend to an urgent matter, took a day off only after going to the shop to confirm that all the other workers had arrived. Another worker, who was absent because of illness, was called out to work only to collapse on the line. You could easily find many similar absurd but true stories. The other side of rationalization is compulsory labor.

Workers in Japan are guaranteed annual paid personal holidays (APPH) by the Labor Standards Act. However, 30 percent of Toyota workers were not able to take even a day off in three months. Taking one month, September 1979, as an example, the no-leave rate reached 49 percent for the entire company. The rate was highest at the plants producing the most popular models. Management and union both have encouraged workers to submit requests for leaves once every three months. In other words, by making workers apply for leaves three months in advance, the corporation controls holiday as well as work time. The union's goal is "to make sure that everyone can take planned APPHs once in three months." The company's idea on APPHs, transmitted to workers at before-work meetings, is "APPHs are not a right but a favor given by the company." "Vacation without causing a burden for others" is the slogan repeatedly stressed at Toyota. The number of holidays taken is an important factor in performance appraisals. A sudden absence is called an "unexpected annual leave," and is not only harmful to the worker's future career but may also result in a car from the plant coming to get him within minutes.

In 1979, an issue of the *Toyota Weekly* carried the following part of a question-and-answer article.

Q: It is difficult to take days off since the boss looks displeased and absences will influence my record, won't they?

A: If there are many "unexpected leaves" or if specific people take too many days off, this will mean trouble for your fellow workers, and your boss will indeed be displeased. The mood that you complain of would be dispelled if everyone took leaves in a planned and impartial way. As long as this happens, the management will prove understanding and co-operative.

The root of the workers' difficulty in taking annual paid personal holidays is the extreme reduction of manpower. However, the union's policy is not to demand abolishment of the reward system or the production allowance, which together form the piecework wage system supporting Toyota's incredible increase in productivity. Nor does the union demand more workers. Rather the policy is always "to have talks to promote understanding and cooperation." In 1962 Toyota management and labor issued a "Management–Union Declaration," in which they called for the reduction of costs and the establishment of a mass-production system "in order to overcome this difficult situation with determination." Since then, the labor union has been "resolutely" complying with rationalization. Big headlines — "New Record in Production" — can be found in almost every issue of the *Toyota*, which calls on workers to "challenge the highest peaks with our all-out efforts" (January 1, 1980). For more than ten years management has been spurring workers on at meetings: Don't be caught up by Datsun. Don't drop the market share. Don't be defeated in the small-car war. Don't be a second Chrysler.

In a speech at a management–union convention in early November 1979, President Toyota stressed that "we cannot afford to lose in the competition of the 1980s," and concluded: "The competitors closely following us will make inroads if we lose the spirit of challenge."

The rationalization policy proposed on that day was to make bold and resolute decisions on "strategic investments," such as new plant construction, but to refrain from "investments for the increase of production capacity." This is no more than a fancy way to repeat the Toyota ideology: "With ingenuity and good ideas, we can find a solution to increased orders even beyond our present full capacity, though we know how hard it is." In other words, Toyota will expand its assembly-line facilities, but any increase in production should be managed through the intensification of labor. Speeding up the conveyor belts does not cost money.

When I left Toyota in February 1973, assembly time at the Main Plant for transmissions was one minute and fourteen seconds. This had been shortened by six seconds in the six months since I had begun, while production had been increased by 100 to 415 units. Now, seven years later, the assembly time is forty-five seconds and the production is 690 units. This increase was achieved solely through accelerating the work pace. Knockdown part packing at the Takaoka plant needed sixty minutes for a set (which includes 20 cars) three years ago. Today it takes twelve minutes, and still the manpower has been reduced from 50 to 40. Before, workers stood in front of conveyors; now they rush around from one part to another, pushing mobile work desks with wheels.

At the assembly lines for passenger cars, parts have become larger and have increased in number, owing to exhaust-emission control. In addition, parts for various models come down the line all mixed together because of the simultaneous production of many models. Nevertheless, the speed of the conveyor belts only accelerates. The Tahara plant on the Chita Peninsula, which started its operation in January 1979, recently completed arrangements to produce 5,000 small trucks and 5,000 Corollas. To fill its manpower needs, many workers were taken from the other Toyota plants. Despite this loss, conveyor belts at each plant are running as if nothing had happened. Many workers have been moved onto the assembly line as "reinforcements." Workers are forced to work on Sundays and holidays. The reinforcement work and Sunday holiday work are a lubricant without which the conveyors could not run.

At the management–union convention mentioned above, Executive Director Yoshiaki Yamamoto said: "In this day and age of uncertainty and severe competition, we must and shall concentrate our production on popular models and adjust the imbalance of work loads among shops. So please be cooperative in establishing flexible shop arrangements that will be able to respond quickly to requests for help."

Reinforcement work is feared by workers who have had no work experience on conveyor lines. Most workers begin losing weight within a few days. Even without the everyday work they're expected to do, inexperienced reinforcement workers would be exhausted by such difficult labor in a totally unfamiliar environment. A directive to management ("On Accepting Reinforcement Workers: Daily Guidance and Management") from the Takaoka plant personnel division shows that reinforcement workers have many complaints and dissatisfactions, more than half of which pertain to safety issues. But the guidance policy goes no farther than the following:

> Management personnel and the long-time workers in the shop should "say hello and a few words" to reinforcement workers at least once a day, and unit members should make an effort to create a congenial atmosphere so that the management and senior workers can easily "say hello and a few words." . . . It is not easy for reinforcement workers to speak out.

One evening, I met with workers from various plants. I wanted to know the facts behind Toyota's remarkable production records. What the workers counted on their fingers was the number of suicides — more than twenty in the past year. These were only cases that they remembered at that moment. They told me that in June there were three suicides within a couple of days. There was a twenty-seven-year-old worker at the Takaoka plant who reported to work and then disappeared; he had thrown himself into the sea. A team leader at the same plant drove his car into a reservoir. These were the only cases reported in the newspapers. The other cases were all related by those who had been close to the suicides. There are no statistics.

The number, they said, is particularly high at the Takaoka plant, whose products are popular and whose production cannot keep pace with demand. On June 28, a forty-five-year-old worker at the Tsutsumi plant hanged himself in his company-rented apartment. Around the same time, a Takaoka plant reinforcement worker from the Tsutsumi plant committed suicide in his dormitory by taking sleeping pills. He was depressed after having been blamed by the team leader for his tardiness and forced to "apologize to his fellow workers for the inconvenience he caused." Also around the same time, a team leader of the Maintenance Department in the Head Office hanged himself. A body found at the Takaoka plant dormitory was taken away by a member of the Security Division staff. Afterwards he complained that while playing pinball, he imagined he saw the suicide's face in the glass of the pinball machine. The workers who met with me that evening talked endlessly of similar cases. I had heard rumors of mentally disturbed workers and suicides many times while I worked at Toyota. But the rapid increase in their numbers is frightening.

It is not uncommon these days for big industries to have many injuries and deaths, as well as occupational diseases which are dealt with as away-from-the job injuries and diseases. However, Toyota's methods of handling these cases are unique, perhaps because of the closed nature of the Toyota community or because the lower management has been so well indoctrinated in the ideology of "Production First." Cases of company-admitted occupational injury and death reached 267 between January and September 1979. Among them, 102 were workers with less than one year's experience, and 71 workers with less than three month's experience (*Safety and Health News*, December 24, 1979). These are the reinforcement workers in unfamiliar surroundings, the newly hired, the newly transferred, trainees, and the like. The work pace has been established, and newcomers who cannot adapt themselves to the speed are repeatedly injured. The foregoing figures bear this out. The acceleration of production also forces the workers to hold their bodies in unnatural postures for long periods of time and has produced many patients with back pains and "shoulder-arm-neck syndrome" (*keikenwan shokogun*). However, the company does not admit these as occupational diseases brought about by the work.

Mr. A entered Toyota as a "mid-career hiree" in September 1974 at thirty-six years of age. He had worked in the kitchen detail of the Maritime Self-Defense Force for five years and then at employee cafeterias and other places. He was assigned to the Takaoka plant, where he put shock absorbers on wheel axles for eight months. There he developed shoulder-arm-neck syndrome. A doctor in the city prescribed three weeks rest and treatment. The plant management forced him to continue working, however, and took him to the doctor by car after work. Finally, he was unable to move; the diagnosis was "acute sinal and nuchal muscle rigidity pain." He asked his boss to assign him lighter work, but the answer was: "There are no light jobs in Toyota. Come back after you have completely recovered, or go somewhere else where they have light work." With the doctor's intercession, he was finally assigned to "Goshiken" and given a job assisting in making fender covers. "Goshiken" was the workshop for the sickly and suffering workers. Officially it did not exist; when company executives made their visits, the workers had to hide themselves. There were no year-end or New Year parties in this workshop. No company newsletters were circulated. It was an island for exiles. Later, Mr. A was transferred to work installing air conditioners, and then to a fitting-out line. He now complains of "lower-back contusion," "hernia of the intervertebral disk," and "muscle-strain aggravation symptoms."

In October 1979, he was notified by the Head Office's Personnel Department that he would be discharged in a month owing to the expiration of his leave-of-absence period. (The discharge of occupational-disease patients is prohibited by law.) But whether out of ignorance of or indifference to the law, the company stated that it "hasn't admitted Mr. A.'s disease as an occupational disease even if the Labor Standards Inspection Office has." There have been plenty of similar episodes at Toyota. While warning against the rising number of accidents, a team leader is said to have told workers at a meeting in the Main Plant, "Your injuries won't trouble the company much. Only your family will be in difficulty." The labor union won't touch the work-injury and occupational disease issue. Gradually management has become more and more high-handed without being checked by the union. Thus, normal sensitivity becomes dulled at the workshops.

As regards Mr. A, the Takaoka plant personnel division eventually withdrew the discharge notice after receiving a decision from the Inspection Office to start the payment of Workmen's Compensation benefits. And this came only under pressure from a small workers' group and the Toyota District Labor Council.

While management journalism may applaud Toyota's high profit and the "kanban method" which they see as supporting it, the human costs of Toyota methods — suicides, injuries, job fatalities, and occupational disease — increase at a horrifying rate. The situation at Toyota is a sad but typical example of the victimization of workers in modern society. Workers suffer every day in front of conveyor belts. The panel in Toyota Hall increases every six seconds. Whenever I come to this city and talk with the workers, I feel as though I have strayed into some fantasy land. But this is a nightmare that I have lived, and the anger will not go away.

28. The Japanese Working Class
Rob Steven

The Japanese working class has the reputation, largely in the Western bourgeois press, of being notoriously hard-working, loyal to its employers, and lacking in class consciousness. Western managers envy their Japanese counterparts for the "harmony and cooperation" that is supposed to characterize industrial relations in Japan, but few of them have any idea why this supposed harmony exists. Even the Japanese bourgeoisie tends to attribute it to cultural values which are unique to Japan and which cannot be exported.

However, a truer explanation lies in the role that traditionally important attributes of persons — rankings by sex, age and education — play in channelling them into classes and into fractions within the working class. Because members of the bourgeoisie, the middle class, and the labor aristocracy are overwhelmingly middle-aged men from prestigious educational institutions, differences *between* classes take on the same form as differences *within* the working class. The power of the ruling class and the above-average conditions of the labor aristocracy seem to have the same origin: the sex, age, and education of the individuals themselves rather than the positions they occupy in the process of production. Differences between classes therefore become less visible, and Japan looks more like a stratified society than a class society.

The strong loyalty Japanese workers tend to show to their employers, as well as their overwhelming sense of rank, are direct results of the process by which people are channelled into classes. Because the same types of agents go into the same types of positions, the real determinants of class power lie concealed behind the visible attributes of persons. The dominance of the ideology of the traditional family and of one's rank in it therefore results from the fact that the personal attributes which accord rank in the traditional family are also the ones which grant access to ruling class positions. In more theoretical terms, it is only because traditional family relations function as production relations that the ideology of the traditional family can become dominant.[1] In other words, the dominance of "rank consciousness" is ensured by the ruling class positions occupied by persons of traditionally high rank. However, because such persons also occupy the upper fractions of the working class, differences between workers and managers come to look just like differences among workers and therefore lose their salience. To show why this is no more than the form assumed by class society in Japan requires examination of the real determinants of fractional divisions within the working class and of the reasons why agents are channelled into them according to age, sex, and education. I do so in some detail for each of the three main fractions: the labor aristocracy, the mass worker, and the reserve army.

Rob Steven: 'The Japanese Working Class' in *THE OTHER JAPAN: POSTWAR REALITIES*, edited by E.P. Tsurumi (M E Sharpe, Inc., 1988), pp. 91–111. Reproduced by permission of the Bulletin of Concerned Asian Scholars.

Theory of the structure and composition of the working class

From the outset it must be emphasized that all three fractions of the working class are in the same fundamental relationship to the capitalist class as a whole. Together they function to produce the social surplus and promote the circulation of the total social capital under the direct domination of the capitalist class. The distinctions between them are not based on different degrees of proximity to the ruling class or on different levels of income. Rather, their different levels of income result from the different roles *capital in general* requires the working class as a whole to play in order to assist the expanded reproduction of the capitalist relation. The fundamental law of capital accumulation — that within industries, between industries, and in the economy as a whole, development is uneven and is frequently interrupted by crises and dislocations — separates workers into three groups corresponding to the three main (contradictory) things the working class must be in order to prevent uneven development from destroying the capitalist relation. This relation could not survive uneven accumulation if exactly the same agents (persons) were required to fulfill all three functions simultaneously.

To identify these functions, I examine the three main effects on the working class of capital accumulation. The first is the development of the collective worker through the concentration and centralization of capital in large corporations, that is, the growth of monopolies through the reinvestment of profits and through mergers and takeovers. Since the division of labor is greatest in large enterprises, the function of producing the whole commodity belongs to the worker as a whole, or to the collective worker. Once this happens, the contradiction between social production (the fact of a cooperative labor process) and private appropriation of the product becomes sharper and can threaten the capitalist relation. Moreover, since workers are brought together in large numbers in giant corporations, they can be more threatening if they organize. To minimize the growing threat of revolutionary working class action, capital must at the very least stabilize their standard of living to ensure their loyalty to capital.

If the first thing the working class must be is willing to accept a relationship whose contradictions are becoming sharper, the second results from the effects of uneven accumulation *within* industries. Since this process is one of constant attempts by capitalists in each industry, either to gain a productivity advantage over rivals (by introducing more efficient techniques) or to catch up to a productivity disadvantage, more concentrated and centralized capitals will continually coexist with smaller less productive capitals. The survival of the latter depends on their paying lower wages than the former.[2] From the point of view of capital in general, this wage difference is essential, since the more threatening workers in monopoly firms are more likely to remain loyal if they have some material basis for seeing themselves as privileged. Uneven accumulation within industries, therefore, both creates some of the conditions for working class loyalty, by giving the most advanced workers the greatest material stake in capitalism, and it requires sizeable wage differentials among the working class as a whole, that is, a mass of low-paid workers in the large number of non-monopoly firms that necessarily exist side by side with the development of monopolies.

Finally, the working class must adapt to uneven accumulation of capital in general, that is, the periodic depressions in which the tendency for the rate of profit to fall manifests itself. At various times masses of workers must become unemployed for considerable periods, but they must remain available for re-employment when accumulation begins to pick up again. Marx referred to this as a reserve army role, and we discuss it in more detail when we examine the Japanese reserve army.

Clearly, it is impossible for the same persons to be all of these three things at the same time, and in Japan, as in other capitalist countries, the working class has been divided into three corresponding fractions. They are products of the dynamic laws of development of the fundamental relationship between the capitalist class and the working class. However, they can only be seen as traditional or natural divisions of rank to the extent that persons move into them according to the attributes which confer rank in the traditional family. Divisions within the working class appear to be no less natural than divisions between classes, because what are considered natural divisions within the traditional family — sex and age — allocate family members into different classes as well as into different fractions of the working class. To what extent and why has this happened?

The structure and composition of the Japanese working class

(a) The labor aristocracy

Rapid accumulation and the consolidation of Japanese monopoly capital around the time of the First World War was the most important development which produced a labor aristocracy in Japan and gave it its characteristic form. Productive forces were unleashed to an unprecedented extent and led to two forms of class struggle which stood in the way of further accumulation. The first was the opportunity seized by the limited supply of workers with the skills and experience required to operate the new technologies to bid up wages by frequently changing jobs. In some cases, capital had to face an annual rate of labor turnover of 100 percent and even used gangsters either to compel workers to return or to kidnap workers from rivals. Although the situation had been serious well before the war, it became intolerable afterwards. Carefully worked out agreements by employers to prevent "piracy" of one another's workers were not adhered to, and some permanent solution was desperately sought after. The second form of class struggle which intensified after the war was an escalation of strikes by the now unionized collective worker, strikes which reached tidal proportions in 1919.

It was as a result of the intensification of these forms of class struggle that capital consciously introduced an employment system to deal with the labor aristocracy. Rather than discuss the various components of this system historically, I only outline its central present-day features, many of which were consolidated during the post-World War II period of rapid accumulation.[3] The problem it was designed to solve was how to retain a stable supply of trained workers who would not resist accumulation in the monopoly sector. Workers in this sector had to be made loyal to capital and prevented from withdrawing their labor power through strike action or through switching employers. The solution to the problem was gradually worked out in class struggles after many years of trial and error. The reason for the present system's relative success, at least during boom periods, lies in how it combines a material basis for workers' loyalty with elements of the traditional superstructure which demand the loyalty of inferiors to superiors.

431

The major material components of the system are various methods of deferring wage payments for workers who are loyal to capital. The most effective of these methods is the system of payment by length of service, since few workers will risk the promise of a secure living wage after some fifteen years of service by engaging in industrial action that might result in a loss of their jobs and seniority. To make these deferred wages ideologically acceptable, capital confines new recruits to school-leavers and university graduates, so that payment for length of service takes the form of payment by age. The capitalist enterprise thereby takes the form of a traditional family which in return for loyal service also provides a secure position in the family hierarchy,

The function of the deferred wage is concealed not simply by the familial system of ranking by age, but also by the traditional roles assigned to the sexes. Since women who have children leave their jobs at least long enough to lose their seniority, most of them are separated from the labor aristocracy, and their "deferred" wages are seldom paid.

Table 1   Monthly payment, by age, sex, education and firm size (1976)

Sex and education	Age	Non-monopoly capital	Monopoly capital
	22	95,800	101,000
Male	25	116,400	133,300
University	35	174,500	220,800
Graduates	45	229,400	328,000
	55	275,600	406,700
	18	80,200	81,400
Male	25	116,100	126,500
High School	35	165,000	193,500
Graduates	45	209,900	262,800
	55	248,100	334,500
Female	18	77,200	79,000
High School	25	101,200	104,100
Graduates	30	115,900	120,900
	35	130,700	—
	15	69,000	70,000
Male	25	111,500	119,800
Middle School	35	151,100	166,000
Graduates	45	186,400	202,500
	55	231,100	233,300
Female	15	66,800	68,600
Middle School	25	96,400	99,000
Graduates	30	107,900	111,200

Monthly payments (¥)

Source: Chingin rōmu kanri kenkyūjo shochō [Head of the Wages and Personnel Management Research Institute], Furukawa Noboru ed., *Chingin kentō shiryō: 1977 nendokan* [1977 Research Materials on Wages] (Tokyo: Nihon Horei, 1976), p. 324.

What separates the labor aristocracy from the mass worker is the former's employment by monopoly capital, which, because of its more advanced productive forces, is both required to and can afford to provide a much more solid material basis for workers' loyalty than can non-monopoly capital. But because educational achievement (either the standing of the institution attended or the degree of success in a company entrance examination) allocates male workers into monopoly and non-monopoly firms, the different conditions of employment in the two sectors seem to result from the different educational qualifications of employees. Insofar as education also channels males into different classes, it makes divisions among workers look like divisions between workers and managers. Table 1 shows how far this is true of salary and wage differentials.

It is remarkable how divisions between classes and divisions within the working class take on the same form of strata bases on sex, age, and the "standing" of the firm employed in. For example, the salaries of middle-aged male university graduates, who by this time typically tend to enter the middle class or the bourgeoisie, are *lower* than the wages ultimately received (after many years of deferment) by elderly male workers. Both seem to be paid on the same basis of rank in the familial hierarchy, whereas in fact the former is increasingly paid out of surplus value for performing the function of capital. Also important to note is that, with the exception of women workers whose position in the reserve army makes the type of firm these are employed by irrelevant, deferred wages in monopoly firms are much greater than those in non-monopoly firms. Though men in both might have similar starting wages, the difference increases with length of employment and with education.

Education therefore serves, not merely to reproduce class agents and to legitimize class society, but to legitimize the allocation of workers into the labor aristocracy and the general mass. A worker in a non-monopoly firm is assumed to be less productive, not because he works with less advanced technology, but because he went to the wrong school or did not obtain the right grades. The educational background of a company's workers thereby seems to justify it as a first-, second-. or third-rate company, just as education seems to lie behind distinctions among members of a company. Moreover, because different levels of productive forces in monopoly and non-monopoly firms result in different pay scales between them for *all* employees, the fundamental basis of one's livelihood appears to be the type of company one works in rather than one's relationship to the means of production. Workers' loyalty to their employers therefore becomes not simply loyalty to their company, but a sense of rivalry with workers in other companies. Because of the reproduction of so many elements of the family ideology, the company assumes the form of a traditional family, and class conflict is smothered beneath the form of rivalry among companies.

The ideological effects of recruitment to the bourgeoisie, the middle class, and the labor aristocracy through competitive examination are fairly straightforward. However, it is not yet clear why, if ruling class power stems from the ownership and control of capital, and if the above-average conditions of the labor aristocracy stem from the above-average technologies of its employers, recruitment to these positions should be by educational achievement. The reason, it seems, lies in the dual function of education: to legitimize capitalist relations and to impart scientific knowledge, which is part and parcel of developing productive forces, to the only possible bearers of

433

that knowledge, namely, labor power. Monopoly firms therefore recruit by competitive examination because the above-average techniques they employ require above-average technical knowledge. But they also do so in order to legitimize the better conditions of their workers, the majority of whom in practice require no more skill than workers in non-monopoly firms. For most workers in the monopoly sector, more advanced productive forces mean a higher division of labor and therefore a reduction in the skills actually required on the job. For them, recruitment by competitive examination has much more to do with ideology and work discipline than with the skills displayed in the examination.

The deferment of wages by age is the single most important material condition which ties workers to their companies, but it is by no means the sole condition. Another form of deferred wages is the system of twice-yearly bonuses which represent the withholding of wages for periods of up to six months. However, because the amounts increase with each of the "familial" forms assumed by fractional divisions within the working class, bonuses serve three functions in addition to securing workers' loyalty. The most important is that they are a convenient means of cutting the value of labor power without reducing regular wages. Since in monopoly firms they comprise from 20–30 percent of workers' total annual income and are presented as a type of profit-sharing for high productivity, they offer considerable scope for manipulation by capital. For example, bonuses were cut by an average of 5 percent in 1976.[4] The second additional function of bonuses is that workers tend to save out of them for old age and for the education of their children, and they thereby release cheap money to capital through the banking system. Finally, since bonuses in non-monopoly firms comprise a smaller proportion of annual income than in monopoly firms, they allow pay differentials between the two to look narrower than they actually are, as revealed by Table 2.

Table 2   Bonuses and basic wages by firm size (1975, ¥000)

Firm Size (Operatives)	A Wages	B Bonuses	A+B	B A+B	Indices: largest firms = 100 A	B	A+B
Under 30	1,495.2	274.3	1,769.5	15.5	81	35	67
30–99	1,520.6	459.8	1,980.4	23.2	82	58	75
100–499	1,571.5	533.8	2,105.3	25.4	85	68	80
500–999	1,685.1	650.1	2,335.2	27.8	91	82	89
Over 1,000	1,864.4	788.8	2,635.2	29.9	100	100	100
Average	1,575.1	455.1	2,030.2	22.4	85	74	77

Source: Kokuzeichō chōkan kanbō sōmuka [Chief Secretary of the General Affairs Section of the National Taxation Agency], *Zeimu tōkei kara mita minkan kyūyo no jittai* [Private Incomes as Revealed in Taxation Statistics] (Tokyo: Okurashō insatsukyoku, 1976), p. 13.

Apart from deferring wages, capital employs one other main material incentive, namely, the system of company welfare, which is most highly developed in monopoly firms. The discrepancy between what they and what small firms can offer is particularly significant in the provision of cheap company housing and medical facilities, since housing and medicare are among the most costly as well as most essential wage goods workers require. The historical origins of company welfare and recreation facilities reveal unambiguously that their major purpose was to bind the worker to his/her company. Capital has consistently opposed state intervention in this area, and so long as state welfare continues to lag behind company welfare, a worker who chooses or who is compelled to leave a large company loses very much more than his/her seniority wages. A lifetime's savings for old age and emergencies can be ruined in a few years at current rates of inflation, and employment in a non-monopoly firm secures at most only about half the welfare s/he previously had: on average monopoly firms spent ¥367,846 per worker on welfare in 1975, while non-monopoly firms spent only ¥157,987.[5] Table 3 provides a general picture of the facilities that have been built up in the two sectors.

The material conditions which give the Japanese labor aristocracy its specific form do not, however, exclude certain contradictory elements. Although the employment system in monopoly firms is frequently seen as one of guaranteed lifelong employment and social welfare, even in boom periods the guarantees have definite limits. These derive from the fact that capital's total wage bill depends more on the average age of its total workforce than on the absolute number employed. For example, two workers under twenty-five cost less than one over fifty. This is why new recruits are almost entirely confined to young graduates and school leavers, and why total wage costs can actually fall in a boom where the workforce expands rapidly. However, the reproduction of this happy state of affairs has required placing a relatively low upper-limit on the age, soon after fifty-five, by which workers in the labor aristocracy have to retire. To continue the seniority payments and job security beyond that age would cause two main problems: a possibly rising average-age of the workforce and insufficient flexibility in being able to adjust its absolute numbers to any unevenness in the rate of accumulation.

Monopoly capital has therefore made a rigid distinction between so-called "regular employees" (unmarried females and males under the age of about fifty-five), and various types of "temporaries." But because workers move from one group to the other when they retire, the reproduction of a sizeable proportion of the reserve army is out of the labor aristocracy, and powerful forces are generated in opposition to those which secure the loyalty of the latter to capital. When the same working class agents are made to fulfill two contradictory functions required by capital accumulation, albeit at different times in their lives, the performance of both roles might be threatened. What has held the contradictory demands on the loyalty of the labor aristocracy in balance has been the postwar boom, which has allowed capital to provide job security until, and a living wage towards the time of, retirement, and that, after this, temporary jobs have been easy to get, even if at lower wages than before.

An analysis of the composition of the labor aristocracy requires identifying those working class members of public corporations, the civil service, and monopoly firms who receive the material benefits already outlined. This requires the exclusion of two main groups of workers: (1) all the different types of temporary, part-time, and day laborers who have no seniority and therefore no overriding reason to knuckle down in order one day to receive deferred wage payments: (2) almost all women workers, since most of those whom the company regards as "permanent" are under thirty-five and unmarried. They will "retire" when they marry and will never receive their deferred wages. Most married women are over thirty-five and are only hired on one or another temporary basis. The only women in the labor aristocracy are the small number in monopoly firms who never marry.

Table 3   Availability of company welfare by firm size

	Total of all firms	Large firms (over 5,000 employees)	Small firms (30–99 employees)
Housing			
Family	47.0%	93.9%	42.2%
Unmarried	34.9	89.9	28.8
House buying incentive	34.8	96.5	28.2
Homeowner layaway	4.5	74.9	1.0
Housing loan	18.8	93.9	10.8
Medical & health care			
Hospitals	3.2	31.3	2.2
Clinics	8.3	74.3	3.8
Medical offices	24.9	85.4	18.2
Preventive medicine	58.2	95.6	52.1
Family medical check-ups	2.4	37.4	1.1
Living support			
Barber shops, beauty salons	3.8	50.3	1.3
Purchasing facilities	9.6	70.2	4.1
Nurseries	1.8	12.0	0.8
Employee canteens	33.3	79.2	27.4
Food provision	27.7	62.2	22.9
Mutual-aid credit			
Marriage	94.7	98.0	93.2
Birth	87.4	90.6	85.2
Death	94.0	98.2	92.2
Disease	86.2	88.9	83.6
Accident	77.2	96.2	72.0
Private insurance system (premiums borne by employer)	46.6	48.8	48.2
Culture, sport, recreation			
Libraries	22.1	75.1	14.2
Gymnasiums	3.4	54.1	2.0
Athletic grounds	10.9	84.5	5.0
Seaside, mountain lodges & ski resorts	15.1	73.3	9.8
Rehabilitation facilities	16.0	95.6	9.4
Tennis courts	11.4	86.5	4.0
Swimming pools	2.8	48.8	1.3
Cultural clubs	31.5	94.7	19.5
Athletic clubs	56.5	95.3	46.5
Athletic meets	15.3	71.9	9.1
Pleasure trips	88.4	64.3	91.5
Others			
Employee shareholding	7.8	55.3	5.8
Supplemental labour compensation insurance	31.1	93.6	23.8
Supplemental health insurance	21.3	98.8	14.8
Extra payment above legal minimums)			

Source: Katsumi Yakabe, *Labour Relations in Japan: Fundamental Characteristics* (Tokyo: International Society for Educational Information, Inc. Japan, 1974), p.64.

Table 4   **Total economically active population* by age, education, and firm size, 1974 (1,000 persons)**

Firm size	Education	Age			
		15–34	35–55	over 55	Total
1–9	School	5,884	9,309	4,649	19,841
	University	639	645	277	1,562
10–99	School	4,087	3,923	1,238	9,245
	University	729	476	173	1,378
100–299	School	1,569	1,232	309	3,091
	University	405	207	46	659
Over 1,000	School	1,058	1,397	315	2,771
	University	740	790	96	1,626
Total	School	17,519	19,056	7,011	43,585
	University	3,839	2,881	725	7,445

Source: Shūgyō kōzō kihon chōsa hōkoku, p. 60.
* Persons who are also studying are excluded.

If we break down the total economically active population according to the main superstructural forms that channel the Japanese into classes and class fractions, we can get a general picture of the size of the labor aristocracy. Table 4 does this by firm size, age, and education (that is, the main elements apart from sex).

Although some firms with fewer than 1,000 operatives are in the monopoly sector, the clearest cut-off point for this sector is firms larger than this and government. Since almost all persons in these sectors are employees, to get a rough estimate of the labor aristocracy we must subtract the members of the bourgeoisie, the middle class, and the reserve army. If the first two largely coincide with university graduates, and the third with men over 55 and women (of whom there were about 2.7 million in 1974), the aristocracy would be about 5.6 million. But because these include some other types of temporary worker and the members of the repressive state apparatuses (in all about a million), the aristocracy is left with approximately 4.5 million persons.

Since a precise estimate of the size of the labor aristocracy is not possible until we have a clear idea of how many workers in the monopoly sector are in the reserve army, detailed estimates are made only after we have examined the conditions of the mass worker in the massive number of non-monopoly firms scattered throughout the country.

(b) The mass worker

If the labor aristocracy is a product of advanced productive forces, what determines and characterizes the mass worker is employment by less concentrated and centralized capitals. Though all workers are in identical relationships to capital in general, the fact of uneven development among the many capitals that constitute it requires a division of the working class according to the types of material conditions the different capitals are able to provide. Differences in these conditions — wages, bonuses, welfare, and so on — are not the *cause* of the divisions within the working class, but the *effects* of the fundamental cause: uneven accumulation and the continual coexistence of backward

437

with more advanced capitals. Wages and conditions are not determined independently of the rate of accumulation, but by that rate, and differences in wages and conditions are the effects of different levels of productive forces resulting from different rates of accumulation. The more backward capitals with below-average technology can only continue to exist so long as they provide below-average working conditions to compensate for their technical disadvantages. Although uneven rates of accumulation *among* industries have also required some compensating differences in working conditions, the major differences are between monopoly and non-monopoly capitals in all industries.

Tables 2 and 3 have already shown the extent of the variations in wages, bonuses, and welfare conditions. The differences do not, however, correspond to different needs to provide a material basis to secure workers' loyalty, since the deferment of wages is practiced by both monopoly and non-monopoly capital. Rather, the differences correspond to unequal abilities to withhold wages. In order to attract young workers in the first place, non-monopoly capital must offer starting wages which are comparable to starting wages in the monopoly sector. By doing so, the proportion of the total wage which it can defer is reduced, and with it the ability to use deferred wages as a means of securing workers' loyalty. The starting wages of all workers are not very different in large and small firms, but the differentials widen with length of service.

However, non-monopoly capital's reduced ability to secure workers' loyalty by means of material incentives does not mean that it has had significantly greater problems of industrial conflict. This is partly because in most cases the more backward productive forces in small firms have not yet created a division of labor and a collective worker with the power to make larger wage deferments necessary. The greatest problems of worker indiscipline have been in medium-sized firms, which cannot compete with monopoly capital's wages, but which have considerably socialized the labor process in factories that bring together fairly large numbers of workers.[6] Elsewhere, and increasingly as firms become smaller, the familial form assumed by class relations in Japan is reproduced as much by actual personal contact between workers and bosses as through the structure of material incentives.

What the employer in a small firm cannot provide in material conditions he provides in genuine personal concern. Although he* is typically more authoritarian and reactionary than the global capitalist (or the hierarchy which performs capital's function in the monopoly sector) he is also more respected, since the loyalty he cultivates is to himself personally. Since he is personally seen as the provider of his workers' livelihood, the familial form of the capitalist relation is reproduced more purely than in the monopoly sector. Even most incorporated non-monopoly firms are largely owned by single families, and the head of this household appears as the head of an extended family which includes all his workers. Class relations therefore more thoroughly assume the form of familial relations, particularly since some of the workers will be actual relatives, either younger sons and daughters, or more distant kin. The material basis of the employer's use of extra-economic coercion (the traditional ideology demanding loyalty and obedience to him personally) is therefore a much *closer* correspondence between family relations and production relations than exists in monopoly firms. The boss is both employer and head of the household which owns the firm.

The form of class action assumed by the mass workers' difficulty in reproducing his/her labor power on non-monopoly wages and conditions is not typically strike action, which is seen and treated as a mark of gross ingratitude to the employer, but a greater propensity to change jobs in search of better conditions. Rates of labor turnover in the non-monopoly sector vary widely and have been known to reach enormous proportions. A 1972 study of small firms in Tokyo revealed that almost 60 percent of employees in commerce and services, and 42 percent in manufacturing had changed jobs twice.[7] In the 35–45 age group, the annual rates of turnover are almost three times as high in the non-monopoly as in the monopoly sector, reflecting workers' reduced incentives to stay on in small firms even after acquiring some seniority (but well before retirement age when all workers have to leave anyway). The absolute rates of turnover are higher in both sectors for the under 35's, that is, before workers receive a stake in their seniority, but large differences between the sectors remain.

One form of deferred wages which has not been mentioned yet and which reinforces the pressure on the mass worker to "vote with his feet" is his retirement pay. Some firms provide only lump sums, while others separate the total amount into a lump sum and a division of the remainder into annual payments stretched over a number of years. In either case, monopoly firms can withhold large amounts from ordinary wages to pay for what appear to be very generous handouts.[8]

Apart from these and other types of withheld wages, which together result in much wider *real* differentials between the monopoly and non-monopoly sectors, workers in the latter must endure at least two additional disadvantages: longer working hours and higher risks of industrial accidents. Table 5 indicates the extent of the difference in hours as well as the difference in the number of working days per month.

Longer working hours in small firms form a major means by which non-monopoly capital compensates for its technical backwardness, almost the entire burden of which it places on the working class. Although functionaries must put up with lower salaries than their counterparts in the monopoly sector, they are nonetheless responsible for ensuring that workers accept the conditions capital can afford, not least exposure to industrial hazards. Table 6 shows how these hazards increase as firms become smaller. In a small firm with about 40 workers, one will have an accident every year, which means that at some stage during their working lives most workers will be affected. However, in firms with over 1,000 employees the rate is only about one worker every three or four years, and few will be affected.

Since in all respects the conditions of the mass worker are vastly inferior to those of the labor aristocracy, strategies for class struggle depend greatly on the relative size of each fraction. However, because there is some mobility between small and large firms as well as from regular to temporary jobs, these estimates must await analysis of the reserve army.

* Japanese employers are overwhelmingly male.

439

Table 5   Average number of working days and hours worked per month, by firm size, 1975

Firm size (operatives)	Days	Hours	
		Total	Of which fixed
Over 500	20.9	166.6	155.8
100–499	21.7	171.9	160.6
30–99	22.3	164.4	165.8
5–29	23.4	182.7	172.0

Source: Rōdō daijin kanbō tōkei jōhōbu [Statistical Information Bureau of the Secretary of the Ministry of Labour], *Maitsuki kinrō tōkei chōsa sōgō hōkokusho* [Composite Report on the Monthly Survey of Employment Statistics] (Tokyo: Rōdō daijin kanbō tōkei jōhōbu, 1976), pp. 75, 93.

Table 6   Rate of industrial accidents by firm size (manufacturing, 1975)

	Firm size					
	Over 1,000	500–999	300–499	100–299	50–99	30–49
Accident rate[a]	1.64	3.23	5.14	8.27	11.91	15.81
Rate of intensity[b]	0.29	0.34	0.43	0.48	0.74	0.91

Source: *1975 Rōdō hakusho*, p. 286.

a. Numbers of persons laid off more than one day per million working hours.
b. Number of days lost per thousand working hours.

(c) The reserve army

The function of the reserve army is to allow the usual forms of uneven development, which require reducing the value of the working class' labor power and shunting workers in and out of the labor process, to occur without threatening capitalist relations. In Japan, this role has been played more effectively than in most advanced capitalist societies and is a major reason for the relatively smooth reproduction of capitalist relations in that country. To clarify why this is so requires a detailed examination of what a reserve army is and how it works.

Since uneven development takes three main forms, the reserve army must play three corresponding roles. The first is related to the widespread increases in accumulation that (under appropriate conditions) can follow such cases of scientific or technical progress as the invention of the steam-engine or the motor car. Accumulation in a variety of industries can be favorably affected by such momentous advances in any one of them. However, a crucial condition on which this depends is whether capital has at its disposal sufficient workers to man the expansion. To avoid drawing them from other capitalist enterprises and either bidding up wages intolerably or provoking social unrest through the rapid destruction of backward firms, a large pool of *latent* workers must be available. So that the capitalist relation is not threatened at its existing and increasingly weakest point, the bulk of the workers needed for the new developments must come from outside capitalist production. Their *departure* from their previous productive activities can only avoid a serious threat to *capital in general* if these activities are under pre- or non-capitalist relations.

440

However, the coexistence of rapid accumulation in some industries, with modest and often declining accumulation in others, will sooner or later lead to a social crisis unless the difference is somehow gradually reduced. Industries, or capitals within industries, that remain backward in the long-term will need to disappear. To smooth over the transition, some workers will have to float to and fro for a while, though it might be possible for most to spend their working lives where they are. Since capital will not require their reproduction, the new generations of workers can move straight into the expanding sectors and help smooth over the transition.

Apart from these epochal stages in capitalist development, it is normal in any period for all capitals to make regular even if relatively small, adjustments to their work forces. Never sure of what lies ahead, no capital can be certain that the exact number of workers required one year will still be needed the next. For this reason as well, a pool of workers who are prepared to float from one employer to another, regardless of wages or working conditions, is necessary to the normal functioning of capitalist production.

In addition to *latent* and *floating* workers, about once each generation capital requires large numbers of workers to be shifted out of employment for extended periods corresponding to the length of these extended depressions. They will become *stagnant*, and because they have no form of subsistence, they can be the most dangerous from capital's point of view. Even outside conditions of general depression, some workers for whom no capital can find a use will be laid off and form a stagnant work force. Wherever possible, they must be somehow recycled into the latent pool, so that they have some form of subsistence to prevent their growth into a revolutionary force.

Each of the latent, floating, and stagnant groups of workers is both a product and a condition of the normal process of uneven development. Their main functions are to allow capital to adjust the *numbers* of workers needed at any time to the requirements of profitability, adjustments which involve continual movements of workers in and out of employment. However, profitability is also served by these shifts through their effects on the *value of the labor power* of the working class as a whole. The continual possibility of bringing in new workers enables capital to prevent existing ones from bidding up wages, and the reserve army as a whole ensures that the value of labor power does not rise above what profitability can tolerate.

As a cushion for uneven development in Japan, the reserve army has so far functioned close to the ideal. No large stagnant reserve has built up, and workers who are no longer needed have usually been convened into some or other latent reserve with a relatively independent subsistence. Floating workers have been available in sufficient numbers to permit fairly smooth adjustments to uneven development. Furthermore, the working class agents in the reserve army have on the whole been different from those in the other two fractions, and the danger of united working class action has been averted.

This last condition is important, because if all workers stand a more or less equal chance of sinking into the reserve, the danger that other fractions of the working class will make common cause with the reserve increases. Fortunately for the Japanese bourgeoisie, traditional familial relations have once again come to the rescue and channelled workers into the reserve army primarily according to age and sex. The

441

insecurity of these positions thereby takes the form of the insecurity of particular persons — women and the old — in the family hierarchy.

Although because of their relative predominance in certain jobs and industries (for example, typists and the service industry) women cannot fulfill all functions of the reserve army on their own, they do so to a degree far in excess of their sisters in other capitalist societies. They are particularly useful in the ease with which they can be converted from a stagnant to a latent reserve, since even when they are laid-off and cannot find jobs they secure through their husbands a subsistence independent of their own wages. Their role in the sexual division of labor in the family also predisposes them to accept the status of latent worker. A survey conducted in 1975 by the Office of the Prime Minister confirmed that they are both prepared and expected to sink into the latent reserve when they marry or have children. Table 7 presents their answers to the question, "What do you think of using marriage or having children as an opportunity [sic] to retire?"

Table 7   Strength of the ideology supporting the sexual division of labor (1975)

Should women retire on marriage or having children?

	Naturally	Inevitably	No	Don't Know
Men	22%	58%	12%	8%
Women	17%	61%	13%	9%

Source: Rōdōshō fujin-shōnen kyoku [Women and Youth Department of the Ministry of Labour]. *Fujin rōdō no jitsujō* [Conditions of Women Workers] (Tokyo: Ōkurashō insat-sukyoku, 1976), p. 75.

Far from being an opportunity for working women, early retirement allows capital to replace older and more highly-paid workers with cheap new recruits. The widespread practice of retiring women when they marry and have children therefore simultaneously reproduces the latent reserve and uses it to keep wage costs down. The young women who retire so willingly are never paid their deferred wages, since when capital draws on this latent reserve they re-enter the workforce without seniority. Neither do middle-aged mothers who have lost a few years' "experience" ever acquire any real seniority, since even if they work a full week, they receive the ambiguous status of "non-regulars" or "permanent temporaries." Table 8 shows that middle-aged men and women who enter new jobs are treated quite differently: some of the men's previous experience is recognized, but the women are treated like young girls.

Because men who switch jobs before they reach retirement age do not lose their seniority entirely, some can often get better wages by doing so, particularly when they move from smaller to larger firms. This type of labor turnover does not concern the floating reserve, because capital cannot with impunity take the initiative when it involves men under 55. What legitimizes capital's initiative in the case of the floating reserve is that the workers have all "retired." They can then be kept on or not, but only at *reduced wages* and with the ambiguous status of "non-regular employee." Since men and women "retire" at different ages, the ages at which they enter the floating reserve are correspondingly different. Only between the ages of 15 and 29 and again after 60, when both men and women are of pre- and post-retirement age respectively, is there any comparability in their membership of different fractions of the working class. Table 8 shows that wage differentials are narrowest during these years.[9]

Table 8 **Women's wages as a percentage of men's by age and length of service (1975)**

Age	Average	Length of service (years)								
		0	1	2	3–4	5–9	10–14	15–19	20–29	30–
– 17	92.7	92.6	91.9	91.7						
18–19	91.1	92.7	92.5	89.7	85.7					
20–24	85.3	84.1	85.8	86.5	87.4	83.6				
25–29	75.5	68.2	73.9	75.4	76.7	79.5	77.0			
30–34	63.9	55.1	58.2	60.0	62.9	67.1	76.5	72.1		
35–39	55.9	51.1	53.6	54.0	54.3	58.0	68.8	76.5	71.1	
40–44	54.1	50.3	52.3	53.9	53.1	55.6	62.6	69.3	81.9	85.2
45–49	56.1	52.4	54.2	55.0	55.2	57.7	62.9	66.4	82.1	96.2
50–54	53.5	50.8	62.8	55.8	53.9	57.6	63.7	64.3	73.5	90.4
55–59	58.2	60.1	58.1	56.2	57.3	59.2	66.9	67.9	71.4	85.4
60–	66.4	62.6	66.4	63.9	63.9	63.6	71.1	72.7	68.9	74.5
Average	61.4	86.6	70.7	69.7	68.3	67.0	68.1	69.4	73.8	84.5

Source: *Fujin rōdō no jitsujō.* p. 58.

However, since the overwhelming majority of women under 30 are never paid their deferred wages and can be retired as soon as they marry, women are almost entirely in the reserve army. Until retirement they form a reserve of cheap floating workers; they then sink into the latent reserve for varying lengths of time, and finally some re-enter the floating reserve. Out of a total of eleven and a half million women employees in 1974, only about a half a million were in the 30–55 age group and had never married. They were unambiguously outside the reserve army.

To estimate the size of the female latent reserve, we must first subtract from the total number of employees those who are in the bourgeoisie and the middle class. Since in 1974, only 5.36 percent of persons listed in the census as managers and officials were women,[10] there were approximately 308,830 women in the bourgeoisie (this number is 5.36 percent of the total bourgeois employees in the private and public sectors). If we add to them the 1,154,498 females in the middle class (mainly teachers and nurses) and ignore the 521,000 full-time women in the 30–55 age group who had never married (most were probably either bourgeois or middle class), the female floating reserve would comprise about 10 million persons. If all those in the favored age group who had never married were outside the working class, the number would have been 10,119,672 in 1974.

It is impossible to attempt a similarly precise estimate of the female latent and stagnant reserves, though some survey data can provide a general idea of the numbers of women capital can draw on. According to the government's 1974 employment status survey, a full 7.7 million women, of whom only 856,000 had never married, were "wishing to work."[11]

A rough division of these people into latent and stagnant reserves can be made according to the extent of their alternative sources of subsistence. We do so by examining the employment status and annual income of the heads of their households, though other sources of subsistence are possible. Table 9 suggests that most persons wishing to work are latent rather than stagnant workers.

Table 9   Persons wishing to work by sex and by employment status and income of household head 1974 (1,000 persons)

Employment status of household head	Total	Men	Women
Persons without a job	1,723	833	890
Persons with a job (annual income)	7,494	627	6,867
Under 0.4 ¥ million	158	23	135
0.4–1.0 ¥ million	1,023	121	902
Over 1.0 ¥ million	6,279	480	5,799
Not reported	35	3	32
Total Persons	9,217	1,459	7,757

Source: *Shūgyō kōcō kihon chōsa hōkoku.* pp. 236 and 240.

If under ¥0.4 million a year was too low for a family's subsistence and under ¥1 million was marginal, between one and two million women and just under one million men seem to have been in the stagnant rather than the latent reserve. Until recently, therefore, Japanese capitalism has been able to recycle unemployed married women through the sexual division of labor in the family into the less threatening of these two groups in the reserve army. We shall see below how the current crisis is beginning to interfere with this process and how the working class as a whole is affected by the changes.

Although women are overwhelmingly concentrated in and form the bulk of the reserve army, they are not the only members of it. They are joined by at least four categories of men: "non-regulars" (*shokutaku*), "part-timers" (*rinjikō*), and "day laborers" (*hiyatoi*) in the floating reserve, and the unemployed in the latent and stagnant reserves.

What distinguishes the rapid turnover of mass workers in the non-monopoly sector from the floating of reserve workers in and out of both sectors are the different reasons the two groups have for changing jobs. The former leave largely at their own initiative in search of improved conditions, while the latter typically move out of regular jobs to less secure and remunerative ones because they are of post-retirement age. This is confirmed by the reasons given by persons who changed jobs or gave up work in 1974. The overwhelming majority of the total over the age of 55 as well as women under 30 gave reasons which had little or nothing to do with any initiative of their own. In the case of men under 30, only 27.5 percent fell into this category. Table 10 reveals that, if we regard reasons for movements of workers as indicators of the class fraction to which they belong, there is a very clear distinction between the mass worker and the reserve army.

Table 10   **Movements of reserve army and mass workers by age and sex, 1974 (1,000 persons)**

	Nos.	%	Nos.	%	Nos.	%
			Age			
i) Persons who changed jobs*	1,102	100.0	852	100.0	169	100.0
Mass workers[a]	365	33.1	307	36.0	27	16.0
Floating workers[b]	359	32.6	316	37.1	116	68.6
Of which Men*	633	100.0	586	100.0	143	100.0
Mass workers	251	39.7	213	36.3	21	14.7
Floating workers	174	27.5	211	36.0	102	71.3
Of which Women*	469	100.0	266	100.0	26	100.0
Mass workers	114	24.3	94	35.3	6	23.1
Floating workers	185	39.4	105	39.5	14	53.8
ii) Persons who stopped work*	1,016	100.0	678	100.0	482	100.0
Mass workers	103	10.1	94	13.9	19	3.9
Latent/stagnant reserve[c]	720	70.9	429	63.3	415	86.1
Of which Men*	145	100.0	126	100.0	279	100.0
Mass workers	37	25.5	18	14.3	9	3.2
Latent/stagnant reserve	52	35.9	85	67.5	251	90.0
Of which Women*	871	100.0	552	100.0	203	100.0
Mass workers	66	7.6	76	13.7	10	4.9
Latent/stagnant reserve	668	76.7	344	62.3	164	80.8

*   Totals include persons who gave reasons other than the ones included in the classification.

a   Mass workers were regarded as those who either changed jobs or gave up work because of the wages or conditions in their former jobs.

b   Floating workers were seen as those who changed jobs for any of the following reasons: lay-offs, bankruptcies, the job was temporary, a family member was transferred, marriage or child care, retirement, illness and old age.

c   Stagnant or latent workers are those who gave up work for any of the reasons in b. They are not distinguished, because whether or not they have an alternative subsistence is not relevant here.

Source: *Shūgyō kōzō kihon chōsa hōkoku* pp. 258–261

Among men over the age of 55, 71 percent of those who changed jobs and 90 percent of those who gave up work seem to be in one or other group in the reserve army. Since the male members of this fraction of the working class are overwhelmingly elderly workers, we need to examine what happens to workers after retirement. In general, they must change their places of employment as well as the type of work they do, receive some form of temporary status, and accept large reductions in wages. According to a government survey of the persons (mainly men) who reached retirement age in 1967–1973, 63.3 percent had to move to jobs in different establishments, and they went overwhelmingly to smaller ones than they had been in before. Only 34.5 percent of these people did the same type of work they had done previously, revealing that they are used as mainly unskilled workers, and almost 76 percent of them received some or other form of temporary status: 66.7 percent became "non-regulars" and 9.2 percent "part-timers" or "day laborers." A full 33.7 percent had spent some time unemployed.[11] Although lower proportions of retired workers who remained on in the same establishments had to do different jobs and accept temporary status, this applied to only 36.7 percent of the people who retired during the period. Table 11 shows the average reduction in wages both groups had to accept as they changed jobs.

Table 11   Wage reductions of retired workers, by firm size 1967–1973 (% distribution of persons)

Firm size (Operatives)	% Wage reductions			
	Over 100%	25–100%	0–25%	No reduction
Over 5,000	18.9	43.4	21.3	16.4
1,000–4,999	14.1	42.1	24.2	19.6
500–999	16.1	34.3	22.5	27.1
300–499	12.8	31.2	22.9	33.1
100–299	20.6	24.1	14.9	40.4
Average	16.9	41.2	22.2	19.7

Source: *Teinen tōtatsusha chōsa no kekka*, p. 28.

Since the labor aristocracy which retires out of monopoly firms must tolerate massive wage reductions when it enters the reserve army, there is an important material basis for working class unity, which as we see below, is becoming firmer as the crisis of Japanese capitalism deepens.

So far most male members of the reserve army have managed to remain in the floating category, which in addition to "non-regulars," includes what are known as "part-timers" and "day laborers." These latter are closest to sinking into the latent (insofar as they have some form of subsistence), or worse still the stagnant reserves. Day laborers in particular are extremely insecure, since they must somehow find work each day. They tend to congregate in urban slums, such as the Sanya district in Tokyo or Kamagasaki in Osaka, and are herded onto buses employers send into the areas.

Day laborers come in all ages, though they are predominantly middle-aged men who dropped out of the normal process through which workers are fitted into the "familial" hierarchy. One study of day laborers in the Sanya district revealed that out of an average three day period, only 23.3 percent found work the full three days, 36.1 percent worked two days, and 13.4 percent remained on the streets.[12] Being used for mainly heavy work, such as concreting or miscellaneous factory jobs, they received about ¥2,900 a day in 1974,[13] which resulted in an annual income of less than half of what other workers receive.

The distinction between non-regulars, part-timers, and day laborers is primarily one of job security. A rough rule of thumb is the notice they receive should lay-offs be required: about a year for non-regulars, a month for part-timers, and of course no warning for day laborers. In the case of unmarried women under thirty, whom I have regarded as non-regulars even though they are accorded regular status so long as they remain single (or at least do not have children), this period is longer. The approximately four million women in this category are perhaps on the boundary between the reserve army and the other fractions of the working class.

It is not possible to make estimates of the numbers of persons in the Japanese reserve army, which turns out to be surprisingly large in view of that country's reputation for "lifelong employment." This is done in Table 12 on the basis of date previously provided and estimates explained in the Table.

Table 12 Estimated size of the Japanese reserve army by sex and sector of employment, 1974 (000 persons)

	Non-monopoly			Monopoly			Total		
	Men	Women	Total	Men	Women	Total	Men	Women	Total
A. Floating	2,150	7,114	9,264	983	3,005	3,994	3,139	10,100	13,258
Non-regulars[a]	1,231	5,911	7,142	615	3,303	1,846	1,846	8,601	10,447
Part-timers[b]	528	925	1,453	215	242	457	743	1,178	1,910
Day labourers	391	278	669	159	73	232	550	351	901
B. Latent							604	6,733	7,337
C. Stagnant							856	1,025	1,881
TOTAL RESERVE ARMY							4,559	17,877	22,476

a   The total number of women in this category is taken from the total number of women employees who are neither part-time nor day labourers (see *Shūgyō kōzō kihon chōsa hōkoku*, p. 62) and subtracting the bourgeois and middle class members. Their division into the two sectors is in the proportion in *Ibid.*, pp. 94, 100. To get the total number of male non-regulars, I have subtracted only corporation directors from the male employees over 55 who were neither part-time nor day labourers, since most capitalist functionaries are below the age of 55.

b   The totals for both sexes come from *Ibid.*, pp. 30 and 32 and they are divided into sectors according to the same proportions as are those persons who worked less than 35 hours a week in 1974, for which see *Ibid.*, pp. 94–100.

So long as the stagnant group remains such a small proportion of the total (8.4%), the potential vulnerability of capitalist relations in Japan will remain no more than that. Some 59 percent of the total are floating workers and have been able to find jobs, while the family has taken the place of the agricultural sector as a means of ensuring that otherwise stagnant workers are safely in the latent reserve.[14] However, the large proportion of women in the reserve army is a two-edged sword, since women cannot so overwhelmingly perform both of the two main functions required of a reserve army. Although they can carry the burden of working at high rates of exploitation through their low wages, they cannot on their own enable capital to regulate the numbers of workers to the required degree in time of crisis. This is because women do not do the whole range of jobs which are affected by the crisis to the same degree as men, but are concentrated in certain industries and occupations. Table 13 shows that these are largely clerical jobs in the service and retail sectors.

Table 13 Total employees, and sex, 1974 (000 persons)

Industry	Men	Women	Total	Women as % of Total
Primary	415	215	630	34.1
Mining	118	20	138	14.5
Construction	2,857	426	3,283	13.0
Manufacturing	7,449	3,681	11,180	32.9
Wholesale/Retail	3,408	2,618	6,026	43.4
Finance/Insurance/Real Estate	812	684	1,496	45.7
Transport/Communications	2,693	362	3,055	11.8
Electricity/Gas/Water	275	37	312	11.9
Services	3,110	2,897	6,007	48.2
TOTAL (excluding government)	21,187	10,940	32,127	34.0
Occupation				
Professional and Technical	1,919	1,252	3,171	39.5
Clerical	4,540	3,808	8,348	45.6
Sales	2,536	1,191	3,727	32.0
Farmers, Lumbermen, Fishermen	377	208	586	35.5
Miners	76	5	81	6.2
Transport/Communications	2,118	174	2,292	7.6
Craftsmen/Production Process	8,948	2,904	11,852	24.5
Labourers	894	461	1,355	34.0
Protective Service	564	14	578	2.4
Service	713	1,456	2,169	67.1
(Regrouped)	22,685	11,473	34,158	33.6
Construction Workers	509	113	622	18.2
Total (including government)	22,685	11,473	34,158	33.6

Source: *Shūgyō kōzō kihon chōsa hōkoku*, pp. 30–35, 44–45

Although the female reserve might be sufficient to allow capital in certain unproductive sectors[15] to tide over a prolonged crisis, other sectors will require more than women and the limited numbers of men in the floating reserve. Such a crisis would also make it extremely difficult even for this number to move from the floating to the latent (rather than to the stagnant) reserve, since the normal process through which this is done in Japan would break down in a prolonged crisis. Typically, retired male workers who cannot find temporary employment set up petty family enterprises, but these tend to yield an income per person engaged which is even less than what temporary workers receive. Even in boom times, therefore, the sinking of retired male workers into the petty bourgeoisie has been a less than ideal means of converting stagnant into latent workers.[16] In a prolonged crisis, the stagnant reserve is bound to build up, and if its sex, age, and educational composition changes significantly, it can become the focus of wider working class struggles. I pursue this question once I have examined the organisation and ideologies with which the Japanese working class must face the crisis, and conclude this section with a summary of its structure and composition.

As a means of ensuring the reproduction of capitalist relations, channelling the members of the working class into its three main fractions on the basis of sex and education is superior to doing so on the basis of age. This is because all workers eventually become old and will sooner or later be subjected to the demands placed on retired workers, while men who have once obtained a prestige education need not otherwise experience any of what being in the reserve army implies. The price capital must pay for its ability to make class society take the form of a familial-type stratified society is that the entire working class at some time or another gets a taste of being in the bottom "strata." So long as accumulation does not falter too greatly and male members of these "strata" can at least continue to find jobs, this disadvantage of relying on age to conceal class relations is more than outweighed by its advantages. Until recently capital has used age along with sex and education background to divide the working class into fractions, which take the form of divisions within the traditional family: an aristocracy comprising middle-aged men with the "best" education, a mass of less well-educated men, also in their prime, and a reserve of women and elderly men. The correspondence between the working class *positions* in each fraction and the superstructural attributes of the *agents* who occupy the positions, although never perfect, has been close enough to guarantee the appearance of divisions within the working class as resulting from personal merits or failures, rather than from capital's demands. Women and elderly men, for example, would blame their sex and age for the conditions under which they work (or fail or work).

On the basis of the estimates made so far, Table 14 presents an overall picture of the structure and composition of the working class. The key to the survival of Japanese capitalism therefore lies not in its alleged provision of life-long employment but in the fact that over half the economically active members of the working class have been conditioned to accept the antithesis of life-long employment.

Table 14   **Fractions of the Japanese working class**

		Total number
(A)	Economically active	25,749,083
	a) Labour aristocracy	4,626,850
	b) Mass workers	7,864,233
	c) Reserve army (floating)	13,258,000
(B)	Economically inactive	
	a) Latent reserve	7,337,000
	b) Stagnant reserve	1,881,000
TOTAL		34,967,083

Organization and ideology

Only when the phenomenal form assumed by class relations in fact becomes the capital-labor relation can the working class constitute itself into a revolutionary social force. This relation must not simply be determinant, it must also be *dominant*: classes must both exist and they must appear to exist. In other words, class society must take the form of class society, so that the most important *determining* influence on one's work, one's income, and one's consumption, as well as on the persons with whom one is brought together side by side in engaging in these activities, is at the same time the most *visible* influence. The essence of capitalist society, the creation and extraction of surplus value, must be laid bare so that it can dominate the minds, and not simply determine the lives, of the laboring masses.[17]

Bringing together the substance and the form of class relations is not, however, simply a matter of propaganda, but primarily of understanding the conditions on which their separation is based so as to hasten the conditions of their union. We have seen that the disjunction between the reality and the appearance of Japanese capitalism is based on the functioning of traditional familial relations as relations of production and as relations among the members of the working class. Through the traditional family's superimposition on the material forces which regulate capitalist development, the coincidence of material reality with familial relations determines the latter's dominance. It is to be expected, therefore, that the organization and ideology of the Japanese working class will reflect the familial form rather than the substance of class relations in that country.

Organization

The most striking and notorious feature of trade unions in Japan is their organization on the basis of enterprises rather than industries. Although the major enterprise unions[18] in any industry might form loose associations, the latter do little more than permit the exchange of information, while all negotiations take place between the employers of each particular company and its union, which is almost entirely autonomous in these matters. The sole external consideration is the tendency to confine what is negotiable to limits set by the top organizations of the bourgeoisie, such as *Keidanren*, in consultation with the state.

Since the *dominant* influences on union membership are identical to the *dominant* influences on class formation (the process by which classes assume their form), it is hardly surprising that unions function primarily to control workers and to contain class struggles rather than as vehicles of these struggles. The most important basis of union membership, which is also dominant in the formation of the labor aristocracy and the mass worker, is the status of regular employee. Union membership is limited, not simply to employees in a particular company but to its *regular* employees. Day laborers, part-timers, and persons hired temporarily after retirement — that is, the entire reserve army apart from young women (who are regulars in name only) — are excluded. Employees destined for managerial positions are included until they reach the rank of section manager, while the jobs of defeated or retired union officials are kept open at the level of seniority they would have attained had they not assumed this position. Unions are not therefore organizations of the working class, but of certain strata in the familial hierarchy, beneath which class relations are submerged in each company.

It is no accident, therefore, that organized workers are overwhelmingly in the labor aristocracy (the main exception being young women to whom we return below). Since these are potentially the most threatening workers and are in firms too large for employers to create loyalties to themselves as individuals, organizations are needed to personalize the family relations for which material incentives could only lay the foundation. The use of the company song is just one example of monopoly capital's quest for alternatives to non-monopoly capital's personal touch.

There is very little evidence that unions have had much influence on levels of wages, which vary instead with firm size and industry, that is, with variations in rates of accumulation. Rather, company unions have been essential to securing the labor aristocracy's compliance with such requirements of faltering accumulation as the recent cuts in real wages and in weekly working hours. Without company unions, wages in the monopoly sector could not be brought into line with the rate of accumulation as swiftly as they have been, particularly in the years 1972–1975. In the non-monopoly sector, this function is fulfiled by the close personal ties between workers and employers, and the former feel obliged to accept no more that what the latter can afford.

The enormous discrepancy between the degree of unionization in the monopoly and non-monopoly sectors therefore results from very much more than the greater ability of the collective worker in large factories to organize. It also has a lot to do with the fact that unions in the monopoly sector are tolerated by capital because they can be used to control workers. Monopoly capital's response to militant trade unions has rarely been an assault on unionism as such, but has almost always taken the form of encouraging the development of a rival company union, which can be used to bring workers into line. It is extremely difficult for militants to form an effective organization, because the company is the only realistic level at which this can be done, and since it will comprise only company employees, its members are always subject to the control of their employers. This means that the union can only exist on conditions which employers accept.[19] Table 15 shows that the labor aristocracy is almost completely organized in this way, since over 90% of all unions are enterprise unions, and the total employees column includes the bourgeois or middle class.

Only 3,445,776 of the total numbers of organized workers in 1975 were women, predominantly those in the monopoly sector who were of pre-retirement age.[20] Table 16 provides a breakdown of unionized workers by industry and sex.

The regular status awarded to young women, which allows them to become members of unions, does not in any way affect their position in the reserve army since unions have enforced the deferment of their wages and have excluded them when they re-enter the workforce as non-regulars. Far from assisting young female members, unions have subjected them to the political and ideological domination of the labor aristocracy, without allowing them the material advantages which this fraction of their class has been able to exact.

451

Table 15 Numbers of unionized workers and unions by firm size, 1975

Firm size (Operatives)	Number of unionists	Unionists as % of total employees	Number of unions	Average numbers of persons per union
Government	3,339,681	79.9	18,799	188.3
1,000 and over	5,226,963	67.6	13,960	374.4
300–999	1,365,469	44.1	6,750	202.3
100–299	1,023,031	27.2	10,110	101.2
30–99	454,009	8.4	11,645	39.0
Under 30	69,225	0.6	5,455	12.7
Other	912,022	—	2,614	348.9
TOTAL	12,590,400	34.9	69,333	181.6

Source: *Nihon rōdō nenkan*, 1977, p. 181; and *Chūshō kigyō to rōdō kumiai*, pp. 305 ff.

Table 16 Organized workers, by industry and sex, 1975

	Total numbers	Of which women (%)
Primary	114,431	11.6
Mining	65,517	7.0
Construction	676,366	15.4
Manufacturing	4,602,954	23.6
Wholesale/Retail	702,896	41.0
Finance/Insurance/Real Estate	961,382	55.2
Transportation/Communications	2,083,397	10.4
Electricity/Gas/Water	228,356	9.2
Service	1,545,389	42.2
Public Administration	1,420,047	32.8
Other	189,683	28.1
Total	12,590,400	27.6

Source: *Fujin rōdō no jittai*, p. 83

As will be shown below, not all unions, however, have been equally submissive to the requirements of their organizational form, although the differences must not be exaggerated. The unions affiliated with *Sōhyō* (*Nihon Rōdō Kumiai Sōhyōgikai*, or The General Council of Japanese Trade Unions), for example, have in general been more militant than those affiliated with *Dōmei* (*Zen Nihon Rōdō Sodomei Kumiai Kaigi*, or The Japan Confederation of Labour), the two major national federations which loosely bring together associations of mainly company unions in various industries.[21]

Ideology

There is little reason to doubt the general findings of a number of bourgeois studies that the Japanese working class sees the world primarily in terms of rank rather than class.[22] It is widely documented that sex, age, education, and the size of firm they are employed in are the uppermost considerations in workers' minds. However, since the most perceptive studies were based on in-depth interviews or participant observation, they do not tell us much about the relative dominance of the different forms which class relations assume. Neither do they examine variations in "rank consciousness" among different types of workers. Though these gaps result partly from the questions bourgeois scholars pose, they have as much to do with the limitations of in-depth studies of small groups of workers. While this method of probing ideas and feelings produces more accurate information, its advantage turns into a shortcoming when attempts are made to generalize about different types of workers and the dominant influences on them.

Recognizing that written questionnaires can end up with either incorrect or irrelevant information, I found that my survey (of 459 employees in 53 companies of varying sizes)[23] in the summer of 1976–77 did help fill in some gaps. The sample was, however, too small to allow firm conclusions, but the results suggest some interesting tendencies on questions not raised elsewhere and on which I have been unable to locate more reliable data. Three main aspects of class awareness were probed: how far the existence of classes was recognized, how far class interests were seen as contradictory, and the extent to which struggles between classes were perceived. In each case replies were grouped into two broad categories: minimal awareness and considerable awareness (None/Little and Fair/Great in the Tables). I did not contrast consciousness of rank and class, but examined the relationship between class consciousness and the various personal attributes associated with rank to see which of these attributes is most dominant in concealing class society and which can be employed in strategies to further an understanding of that society.

Table 17 provides a general picture of the degree to which class relations are concealed. It is interesting that all employees were more prepared to recognize the dynamics of these relations, the existence of class struggle, than to accept them as class relations or to see antagonistic interests as the cause of the struggles. In fact, the bourgeois members of the sample, perhaps not paradoxically, revealed the strongest tendency to deny that classes either exist or have conflicting interests and at the same time to realize that class struggles were a part of their lives. As far as the workers were concerned, only about a third to two-fifths could be described as having any understanding of the struggles which just under half of them acknowledged to exist.

Since about 90 percent of the female but only 40 percent of the male respondents were in the working class, one would expect the different general experiences of the two sexes even within this class to produce different degrees of class awareness. Since working men must see many of their own sex in the upper classes, they might be expected to be less class-conscious than women. However, Table 17 suggests that this has happened only to a limited degree, possibly because gender relations obscure class relations through men's ideological and political domination of women.

Only in their perceptions of contradictory interests do female workers seem to be more class conscious than male workers, while on the other two dimensions they appear to show less awareness. This might be because of the difficulties imposed on women to express their recognition of contradictions in actual struggles. The implications of these findings, to the extent that they are representative, are explored in the final section of the chapter on strategy.

The degree to which age (also a form of class relations and divisions within the working class) either conceals or can be used to heighten class awareness is not immediately clear, because age affects the sexes differently and together with education channels some men in to the upper classes but most women into the reserve army. Male workers are likely to exhibit diminished class consciousness as they approach the age of fifty-five, and women are considerably influenced by early retirement and non-regular employment after that. Should my small sample be representative, one could conclude that the ideological and political domination of male over female workers diminishes with age and experience, and that one way to fight sexism among workers is to emphasize the function of age in the reproduction of the reserve army. Even though they enter the reserve at different ages, the current crisis is bringing home to male and female workers that "lifelong employment" is a myth. To tackle capital on this question can provide both sexes with positive common ground from which to wage united struggles, although middle-aged male workers seem to exert a greater degree of ideological domination over young female than young male workers. This problem is also relevant to the discussion on strategy.[24]

The difficulty in trying to isolate the forms of class relations which can most effectively uncover their substance is that the processes through which class agents are produced are inseparably linked. I have shown elsewhere, on the basis of the same survey, that workers' class consciousness diminishes with education. Since education, like sex and age, channels agents into different classes as well as into different fractions within the working class, those with the highest education (or the favored age or sex qualification) are likely to have the greatest aspirations for class mobility, and they can exercise powerful ideological influences over less educated workers (as well as over younger ones, and females). Table 18 provides some confirmation that the less educated mass workers in small firms are more class-conscious than the aristocracy in the monopoly sector. The physical separation of these workers in different companies reduces the aristocracy's ideological dominance and seems to produce wide differences in class consciousness.

It is impossible to tell how far membership in a company union is an independent factor which suppresses class consciousness, since my sample included very few union members in small firms and very few non-members in large ones. Variations in class consciousness by union membership almost exactly coincided with variations by firm size. The unorganized mass workers in my sample showed a much greater recognition of the existence and antagonistic interests of classes than the labor aristocracy, though their perception of class struggles was more or less the same. Among the organized workers in the monopoly sector, about 20 percent of *Sōhyō* and *Chūritsurōren*[25] but only 10 percent of *Dōmei* affiliates revealed a strong class consciousness when an overall score was computed from all the relevant questions. This suggests that *Sōhyō* has perhaps played a less repressive role than *Dōmei* and *Chūritsurōren* but that it has not raised class awareness to levels which certain militant leaders might lead one to expect.

Table 17 Class consciousness, by class position and sex

	None/Little				Fair/Great				Subtotal		Total
	Men		Women		Men		Women		Men	Women	
	Nos.	%	Nos.	%	Nos.	%	Nos.	%			
i) Existence of classes											
Bourgeoisie	117	86.7	4	66.7	16	11.9	2	33.3	135	6	141
Middle class	47	73.4	3	50.0	15	23.4	3	50.0	64	6	70
Working class	86	64.2	65	65.0	46	34.3	30	30.0	134	100	234
ii) Antagonism of class interests											
Bourgeoisie	112	83.0	3	50.0	22	16.3	3	50.0	135	6	141
Middle class	40	62.5	1	16.7	21	32.8	4	66.7	64	6	70
Working class	82	61.2	42	31.3	44	32.9	48	48.0	134	100	234
iii) Existence of class struggles											
Bourgeoisie	48	43.0	2	33.3	72	53.3	2	33.3	135	6	141
Middle class	26	40.6	3	50.0	34	53.1	2	33.3	64	6	70
Working class	59	44.0	38	38.0	64	47.8	44	44.0	134	100	234

Table 18 Workers' class consciousness, by firm size

	None/Little		Fair/Great		Total
	Nos.	%	Nos.	%	Nos.
i) Existence of classes					
Under 100 workers	33	55.9	24	40.7	59
100–999	50	62.5	29	36.3	80
Over 1,000	68	71.5	23	24.2	95
ii) Antagonism of class interests					
Under 100	21	35.6	30	50.8	59
100–999	40	50.0	36	45.0	80
Over 1,000	63	66.3	26	27.4	95
iii) Existence of class struggles					
Under 100	18	30.5	28	47.5	59
100–999	35	43.8	40	50.0	80
Over 1,000	44	46.4	40	42.1	95

Table 19 Forms of redundancy, by firm size 1975 (% of firms)

	Firm size (operatives)		
	Under 21	21–300	Over 300
Refrain from recruiting	52%	77%	82%
Regulate overtime	36%	47%	73%
Increase holidays	35%	18%	18%
Lay off part-timers & temporaries	9%	34%	44%
Temporary layoffs of regulars	3%	33%	35%
Invite early retirement and lay off retired workers	18%	31%	17%

Source: Chūshō kigyō to rōdō kumiai, p. 122.

455

In conclusion, my survey suggests that class awareness among the Japanese working class, particularly mass workers and members of the reserve army, is greater than bourgeois studies (confined largely to the labor aristocracy) have found. Although each of the forms assumed by class relations — sex, age, education and firm size — to some extent conceals these relations by making differences between classes appear the same as differences within the working class, it also seems that, they can be used to heighten class awareness, particularly since the crisis is eroding their ability to conceal. We therefore need to examine how this is happening before some general points on strategy can be made.

The crisis and the Japanese working class

Although during the postwar boom the attributes of class agents (sex, age, etc.) seemed to determine life chances to a degree that left the real determinant, class position, in the background, the crisis has been bringing the latter to the fore through the growing inability of agents with the favored attributes to obtain what they had been promised. The immediate effects of the crisis on the working class have been fewer jobs and falling real wages, but these have so far overwhelmingly taken the form of a crisis of an aging society, a point which even a cursory glance at the press headlines cannot fail to bring out.[26]

The reason why the crisis takes this form is that its impact falls mainly on two groups of workers: school-leavers, who find that capital refrains from hiring its normal quota of new recruits (*shūshokusha*), and retired persons, who cannot always get second jobs (*saishūshokusha*). In order to prevent the numbers of unemployed older workers from growing, pressure has been mounting to postpone retirement, but to provide jobs for young people and to avoid rising wage bills, capital is under an equal pressure to encourage early retirement. So far, the burden has been falling mainly on school-leavers and college graduates, but the consequences of this are becoming intolerable. A propaganda campaign is being mounted to elicit public support for the state to resolve the contradiction, and capital is resorting to a combination of short-term expedients, some of which are affecting even so-called regular employees. Part of the propaganda campaign is somehow to sell the idea that "lifelong employment" is a premodern institution which must be rationalized. Table 19 shows the combinations of measures firms have been employing to deal with "over-employment."

Since large firms are resorting to measures which affect even the labor aristocracy, a material basis is being laid for working class unity. In 1974–1975 the employment of regulars fell by an average of 2.0 percent, though this concealed a fall of 7.5 percent in mining (a continuation of this industry's long–term decline), 5.7 percent in construction, and 5.4 percent in manufacturing. Among manufacturing industries, the reduction was 13.4 percent in textiles, 10.4 percent in lumber, 7.3 percent in each of furniture and rubber, 8.9 percent in metal goods, 0.2 percent in electrical appliances, and 7.5 percent in precision instruments.[27] In the same period, the proportion of total employees who worked less than 35 hours a week increased by 16.3 percent (from 8.6 percent to 10.0 percent).[28] Although it is difficult to show exactly to what extent the labor aristocracy is being reduced to mass workers and the latter to the reserve army, it appears that jobs have dried up in the monopoly sector and that only the smallest firms have been able to create new ones.

It seems that all workers are being affected in one way or another, though not entirely regardless of sex, age, and education, which cannot indefinitely obscure the determining role of class position. Increasingly, even university graduates are becoming sceptical about their chances of upward mobility. The very basis of the legitimacy of Japanese capitalism is being threatened, not simply because retired workers are finding it hard to get non-regular jobs, but because of the growing scarcity of regular jobs for young workers.

In 1976 Sony Corporation introduced a new scheme which might foreshadow a more general response by capital. It recruited for a new plant *only* older workers between 50 and 60, and offered them a basic salary which was only just over half that paid to its regular employees in other factories.[29] The reasons behind this decision seem to be closely related to an important change in the role of boom-time reserve army agents.

Since reserve workers are conditioned to accept low job security and below-average wages, one might expect them to carry the main burden of layoffs and wage reductions during a crisis. However, although they must accept more of both, the emphasis falls increasingly on the latter, while workers previously outside the reserve are more and more singled out for redundancy. The reasons why this change takes place are not hard to find, because while layoffs threaten only the legitimacy of capital in general, difficulty in cutting wages threatens the survival of particular capitals. Once the very existence of the latter is brought into question, members of the capitalist class find it harder to place their common interests above their individual interests, and they tend to rely on the state to ensure that this is done.

Sony Corporation's decision to keep on persons who might otherwise have moved from the floating to the stagnant reserve, and to allow persons who would have entered the labor aristocracy to become either mass or reserve workers, is quite consistent with capital's interests, at least in the short-term: declining profitability can be arrested by *bringing in* low-paid reserve workers, rather than by replacing them with young recruits whose deferred wages will have to be paid sooner or later. Since low wages are capital's most pressing need in times of crisis, traditionally low-paid workers are more likely to be the *last* to lose their jobs as a recession deepens.[30] Unless organized workers can prevent this through effective struggles, it will also help to bring about reductions in their wages and in the value of the labor power of the working class as a whole.

Although, because large proportions of earnings comprise deferred wages, it is difficult to calculate reductions in the value of labor power, in Table 20 we can get some idea of this from the annual increases in wages, bonuses, and consumer prices in 1970–1975.

The large annual increases in real wages to which workers had become accustomed since the mid-1960s were reduced to about 2 percent in 1974, and by 1975 they had ceased altogether. Annually since then, bonuses have risen by about 3 percent and wages by 8 percent, while inflation has remained in the region of 8 percent. The role of the reserve army in making possible these cuts in real wages is revealed by a survey conducted in 1978 by the Industrial Labor Research Institute. It noted that many firms were following Sony Corporation and hiring part-time employees as a "cheap and easily replaceable" labor force, and it pointed out that part-time wages had risen by only 10 percent a year since 1973, which was only about two-thirds of the increases regular workers had received.[31] Already in the years building up to the crisis, 1970–1973, the wages of day laborers as a proportion of those of regular workers fell from 43.7 to 38.6 percent.[32]

Table 20 Annual percentage increases in money wages, bonuses, and consumer prices, by firm size, 1971–1975

Year	Money wages		Summer bonuses		Winter bonuses		Consumer prices
	Large	Small	Large	Small	Large	Small	
1970	18.5	19.9	22.2	25.2	19.2	20.8	7.3
1971	16.9	18.3	13.7	14.2	5.2	7.6	5.7
1972	15.3	16.5	5.7	9.3	16.5	18.0	5.2
1973	20.1	21.1	23.9	30.9	42.4	45.0	16.1
1974	32.9	33.3	47.0	43.0	27.4	23.5	24.5
1975	13.1	14.4	7.4	0.4	–5.0	–2.4	11.8

Source: *Chingin kentō shiryō*, 1977, pp. 1, 4; *Chingin sōran, 1977*, p. 361

Another recent survey, by the Ministry of International Trade and Industry, showed that capital was preparing for a second round of employment retrenchment, because the cuts that began in 1974 had proved inadequate. These had reduced the numbers of employees in the 250 major firms surveyed by 7.5 percent in the period March 1974 to March 1978.[33] The expectation that further lay-offs will be required confirms that the Japanese bourgeoisie is shedding its illusions about a sudden end to the depression and is preparing for a new confrontation. It is gradually moving towards a strategy of keeping on traditional reserve army agents, in order to raise the rate of exploitation, and of allowing the labor aristocracy to bear more of the burden of unemployment than was ever practiced during the boom.

Working class strategy

Our analysis of the working class suggests a number of conclusions on possible strategies for revolutionary change in Japan which need to be considered in the light of the Japanese class structure as a whole.

Since the development of a revolutionary strategy is inseparable from the development of a movement to implement it, I concentrate here on the conditions that aid the growth of appropriate working class organization and ideology.

Although the relevant conditions can be divided into infrastructural and superstructural, these do not necessarily correspond to separate processes or institutions, but to different functions of what is often one and the same process or institution. The function of the economic base is to ensure the reproduction of the capitalist relation through the production, extraction, and realization of surplus value, while the function of the superstructure is the reproduction of class agents with the required skills and willingness to do all of these things. There is no reason why both functions should not be fulfilled simultaneously by a variety of institutions or activities. For example, in the production process, particularly through its allocation of agents into jobs according to their sex, age, and education, workers produce surplus value, they acquire relevant skills, and they are socialized into familial ideology and organizations. Similarly, in the circulation process, workers both imbibe ideas through their consumption activities and they ensure the realization of surplus value.

Since the ideas workers embrace and the organizations they form are inseparable from their day-to-day activities, revolutionary strategy requires identifying those activities, and the conditions of engaging in them, which can further revolutionary organizations and ideas. However, since the same activities perform infrastructural and superstructural functions, we must look to the economic base for the ultimate determinants of revolutionary action in order to help build a revolutionary movement.

We have seen that family ideology and company unions in Japan cannot be wished away, because both are rooted in the way the familial attributes of class agents function simultaneously as infrastructure and as superstructure. It is only because age, sex, and education slot workers into the positions created (and destroyed) by the process of capital accumulation that the ideas associated with them can serve to legitimize Japanese capitalism.

However, what our analysis of the working class has shown is that to forestall a prolonged interruption of the accumulation process, capital can no longer afford to allocate agents into the different positions in the way it did during the boom. Reserve army functions are now required of men and women of all ages, and positions in the aristocracy, not to mention mobility out of the working class, cannot be guaranteed for all agents with higher education, even when this is obtained in prestige universities.

Of the main attributes of class agents which conceal production relations, our analysis suggests that only age can be exploited to help uncover them. This is because once acquired, sex and education remain with one for life, and if they are emphasized in any way as legitimate bases for special treatment, they create contradictions among the masses which can divide them into antagonistic camps. It is therefore crucial to see in the growing insecurity of male workers with university education the emerging conditions on which these sources of division can be combated. Not until men and women with different levels of education are more equally affected by the crisis will the determining role of class assume dominance over sexism and educational elitism.

Of these two forms of working class disunity, gender is by far the less difficult to overcome, because the material factors that also make gender a form of class relations are not part and parcel of the capitalist mode of production, whereas the material factors that make education a form of class relations are much more intimately bound up with the functioning of capitalism itself. The questions raised here are important, because if essential conditions of the working class organization and unity needed for the revolutionary overthrow of capitalism include the elimination of sexism and elitism, and if both are inseparable consequences of capitalism itself, revolutionary change becomes impossible.

The reason why sexism is not peculiar to capitalism lies in certain material conditions which affect the reproduction of class agents but which are not essential to the general laws of capital accumulation, which concern the reproduction of class positions. The single most important of these conditions is women's *biological* function of *bearing* children, which so long as it is also associated with their *social* function of *rearing* children, predisposes women to serve as floating and latent agents. Since their role in the nuclear family requires them to move in and out of the workforce, they become unable to remain in the same job long enough for similar proportions as men to rise into the labor aristocracy or entirely out of the working class. The central material condition of male power in the family is therefore socially determined, because women's social role of rearing children makes them dependent on men for most of their subsistence requirements. Because most men do not leave their jobs to assume domestic responsibilities, they can remain outside the reserve army and have a more secure source of subsistence than women.

However, it is precisely because women can draw on part of their husbands' wages for their subsistence that capital is assured of women's reproduction and can pay them wages below the value of labor power. In times of crisis, therefore, other things being equal, capital will come to prefer lower-paid women to higher-paid men. Only when this happens on a wide scale, do conditions exist for child-rearing responsibilities to move either more into men's hands (if carried out privately), or (if two incomes are needed to support a family) to be socialized through the development of day nurseries as happens during wartime.

The biological function of bearing children might still, under certain conditions, place men and women in unequal social roles, but the equalization of child rearing and the associated domestic toil can reduce such inequalities to only minor questions. Making it possible for women to become regulars also makes it possible for some to enter the upper classes. Such a development, even though it is an essentially bourgeois reform, is essential if sexism among the working class is to be eliminated and class relations are to become more visible.

Unlike gender, however, technical skills are part of the forces of production which belong to labor power. To wait for a random distribution in each class of persons with different technical skills is to wait for the abolition of classes themselves. The same strategy cannot be adopted in dealing with educational divisions among workers as can be used in overcoming differences between the sexes, because the former requires a socialist revolution and not simply bourgeois democratic reforms.

Will divisions among the working class then inevitably assume the form of differences in technical skill? Not necessarily, because a period of prolonged capitalist crisis can homogenize the different working class *positions* and therefore undermine the material basis on which the dominance of educational differences rests. Once the large numbers of university-educated workers who do not move out of their class are subjected to the same job insecurities and wage reductions as other workers, the infrastructural cause of the divisions will disappear, leaving the superstructural form with nothing to ensure its reproduction. Even though the upper classes will never include anything like equal proportions of well-educated and less-educated persons, the important thing is that the Japanese working class is coming to do just that. Furthermore, the greater the proportion of workers with higher education the less will education appear as a form of class relations. The appropriate strategy is not, therefore, to support university graduates' demands for privileged jobs, but to emphasize how a sacrifice of one's youth to acquire a degree is irrelevant to the process by which classes are created. Since of all the personal attributes of workers I related to class consciousness, education emerged as the most significant, the task of uniting the labor aristocracy with the rest of the working class should not be underestimated.

The use of age in revolutionary strategy seems to be quite different, not simply because all workers sooner or later reach retirement age and are affected by capital's treatment of non–regulars, but because there are no material conditions which peculiarly suit agents of different ages to fill particular class positions. Established patterns, which were developed only in response to certain forms of class struggle, can quickly change when a crisis requires capital to adopt different solutions to problems which arose out of a solution to some earlier problem. That the current crisis so overwhelmingly takes the form of a crisis of an aging Japan only shows how easy it is for people to see divisions by age as based on "convention" rather than on "nature." The growing effects of the crisis on workers of all ages provides a unique opportunity to unite them, since all are or will be affected whichever age group capital singles out as special victims. Since even in the traditional ideology the parent-child relationship is stronger than the husband-wife relationship, there is a much firmer basis for common action between old and young in Japan than in other capitalist societies. Bringing age to the fore can therefore uncover class relations, rather than further their concealment.

Notes

1. See Maurice Godelier, "Infrastructures, Societies, and History," *Current Anthropology*, Vol. 19, No.4 (Dec. 1978).

2. Rob Steven, "The Japanese Bourgeoisie," *Bulletin of Concerned Asian Scholars*. Vol. 11, No. 2 (April–June, 1979) pp. 12 ff.

3. For detailed historical studies, see Koji Taira, *Economic Development and the Labour Market in Japan* (New York: Columbia University Press, 1970); Ronald Dore, *British Factory — Japanese Factory* (London: George Allen and Unwin, 1973); and Sydney Crawcour, "The Japanese Employment System," *Journal of Japanese Studies*, Vol. 4, No. 3 (Summer 1978).

4. Shūkan Tōyō Keizai, *Chingin sōran*, p. 89.

5. *Zaisei kin yū tōkei geppō*, No. 295, pp. 46–47.

6. For a discussion of industrial conflict in medium-sized firms, see Robert E. Cole, *Japanese Blue Collar: The Changing Tradition* (Berkeley: University of California Press, 1971).

7. Tokyo Metropolitan Government, *Minor Industries and Workers in Tokyo* (Tokyo Metropolitan Government, 1972), p. 30.

8. **Retirement pay and pensions, by firm size and education (1975, ¥ million)**

Education and firm size (Operatives)	Firms with only lump sum payments	Firms with pensions and lump sum payments	
		Lump sum	Present value of total pension
University			
over 1,000	13.0	10.5	4.4
300–999	9.1	8.2	4.7
100–299	7.6	7.4	4.3
30–99	7.4	7.1	3.2
High School			
over 1,000	12.2	10.1	4.3
300–999	8.6	8.5	4.6
100–299	7.6	6.9	4.2
30–99	7.0	7.5	3.4
Middle School			
over 1,000	10.0	8.2	3.4
300–999	7.8	6.8	3.7
100–299	6.6	6.3	3.9
30–99	6.2	5.6	3.4

Source: *Chingin kentō shiryō: 1977 nendokan*, p. 69.

9. **Average years of employment by age and sex, 1975**

Age	Men	Women
–17	1.2	1.4
18–19	1.4	1.4
20–24	3.3	3.1
25–29	5.8	5.0
30–34	9.2	6.2
35–39	11.7	6.4
40–44	14.1	7.7
45–49	17.4	8.8
50–54	18.6	9.6
55–59	13.7	9.3
60+	10.0	9.5
Average	10.0	5.4

Source: *Fujin rōdō no jitsujō*, p. 45.

10. *Shūgyō kōzō kihon chōsa hōkoku*, pp. 46 and 50.

11. *Teinen tōtatsusha chōsa no kekka*, pp. 5, 7, and 13.

    Persons wishing to work, by age and sex

Age	Sex		
	Male	Female	Total
15–24	696	1,218	1,914
25–34	147	2,998	3,144
35–39	49	1,074	1,123
40–54	150	1,702	1,852
55–64	205	534	738
65 and over	213	232	445
Total	1,459	7,757	9,217

Source: *Shūgyō kōzō kihon chōsa hōkoku*, pp. 229 and 233.

12. Nishioka Yukiyasu et al., "Hiyatoi rōdōsha: San'ya no seikatsu to rōdō" ["Day Labourers: Life and Work in Sanya"], *Shakai Kagaku Nenpō* [Social Science Yearbook], No 8 (1974), 36.

13. *Maitsuki kinrō tōkei chōsa sōgō hōkokusho*, 1975 p. 108.

14. During the prewar period of uneven accumulation, unwanted workers could eke out a subsistence by returning to agriculture. However, the decline of this sector in the postwar period has made such a solution impossible for large numbers of workers.

15. These are sectors in which capital is converted from one form to another, for example from commodity to money capital (that is, the retail sector).

16. See the chapter on the petty bourgeoisie in my forthcoming *Classes in Contemporary Japan*.

17. I am indebted to Maurice Godelier for this argument. See his "Infrastructures, Societies, and History."

18. Note that the US and Japanese usages of "enterprise union" differ. In the US, the enterprise union might lie somewhere between a company union and a business union.

19. The fact that company unions are used to control workers does not alter the fact that they remain the sole organizations workers have. Since no form of organization can transform workers into something different from what they are, it is to be expected that they will, from time to time, use even company unions to express their class interests. The occurrence of militant strikes by company unions does not therefore contradict the general point that company unions do more to suppress than to facilitate class struggles.

20. Women union members comprised 29.0 percent of the total number of women employees, while the corresponding proportion among men was 36.4 percent. See *Fujin rōdō no jittai* pp. 82–83.

21. **Affiliations of trade unionists, by industry and major national federations, 1975**

	Total	Sōhyō	Dōmei	Shinsanbetsu	Chūritsu Rōren	Other
Total Numbers (1,000)	12,590	4,573	2,266	70	1,369	4,705
Industry (%)						
Agriculture	100	21.0	19.5	—	7.4	52.2
Forestry, Hunting	100	78.6	13.6	—	—	7.8
Fisheries	100	0.3	12.9	—	17.4	69.4
Mining	100	55.4	16.9	0.1	2.6	25.0
Construction	100	19.1	4.6	—	35.1	42.0
Manufacturing	100	18.1	29.9	1.3	16.0	39.7
Wholesale/Retail	100	7.8	22.5	0.1	4.1	74.0
Finance/Ins.	100	2.3	1.1	—	32.0	65.2
Real Estate	100	26.5	6.7	0.0	0.2	87.4
Transport/Commun.	100	59.1	20.9	0.4	0.6	24.1
Elec./Gas/Water	100	26.1	62.4	—	10.1	2.7
Service	100	57.0	4.2	0.0	0.9	39.0
Public Admin.	100	89.3	1.5	—	—	9.3
Other	100	27.4	8.0	0.1	1.5	63.1

Source: *1977 Nihon rōdō nenkan*, pp. 185–186. The *Chūritsurōren*, or the National Council of Independent Unions, stands somewhere between the occasional militance of *Sōhyō* and the rabid anti-communism of *Dōmei*.

22. See, for example, the works by Ronald Dore, Robert Cole, and Thomas P. Rohlen, *For Harmony and Strength* (Berkeley: University of California Press, 1974).

23. Of the 69 companies initially approached, 53 agreed to cooperate, and of the 619 questionnaires distributed, 459 (74.2 percent) were returned.

24. **Workers' class consciousness, by age and sex**

		None/Little				Fair/Great				Total Nos.	
		Men		Women		Men		Women			
		Nos.	%	Nos.	%	Nos.	%	Nos.	%	Men	Women
i) Existence of classes											
Under 25		8	50.0	18	39.1	8	50.0	14	30.4	16	46
25–29		36	70.6	20	76.9	15	29.4	5	19.2	51	26
30–54		40	63.5	16	59.3	21	33.3	11	40.7	63	27
Over 54		2		1		2		0		4	1
ii) Antagonism of class interests											
Under 25		5	31.3	23	50.0	11	68.8	18	39.1	16	46
25–29		25	49.0	11	42.3	24	47.1	13	50.0	51	26
30–54		27	42.9	10	37.0	29	46.1	9	33.3	63	27
Over 54		1		1		2		0		4	1
iii) Existence of class struggles											
Under 25		6	37.5	16	34.8	9	56.3	22	47.8	16	46
25–29		25	49.0	11	42.3	24	47.1	13	50.0	51	26
30–54		27	42.9	10	37.0	29	46.1	9	33.3	63	27
Over 54		1		1		2		0		4	1

Above

To interpret these data requires knowing something about the women in the different age groups. Almost all of those under 25 were unmarried and anticipated leaving their jobs by the time they turned 30, while the same applied to about 60 percent of the 25–29 age group. Those older than this comprised almost equal proportions of unmarried, married and no-longer-married women, most of whom could either not say when they might leave (44 percent) or thought this would be between the ages of 50 and 60 (37 percent). Although the numbers of persons in the different categories are too small to generalize, a change seems to take place when women are transformed from nominally regular employees into non-regulars. They apparently become more inclined than men to recognize both the existence and the antagonistic interests of classes, but they seem to submit to their inability to engage in effective struggles and increasingly deny that class struggles take place.

25. The National Council of Independent Unions.

26. See, for example, the series of articles on "The Graying of Japan" in *Japan Times Weekly*, 13 January to 10 February, 1979.

27. *Maitsuki kinrō tōkei chōsa sōgō hōkokusho*, 1975, pp. 6–7.

28. *Fujin rōdō no jittai*, p. 51.

29. *Japan Times Weekly*, 19 June, 1976, p. 4.

30. A recent study of the reserve army in New Zealand, to which I am indebted for a number of insights on the subject, also found that the functioning of the reserve army changes in a recession. See R. M. Hill, "Women, Capitalist Crisis, and the Reserve Army of Labour" (Unpublished masters thesis, University of Canterbury, 1979).

31. *Japan Times Weekly*, 18 November, 1978, p. 10.

32. Nihon Kyōsantō chūō iinkai kikanshi keieikyoku [Bulletin Management Bureau of the Central Committee of the Japan Communist Party], *1974 Seiji Nenkan* [1974 Political Yearbook] (Tokyo, 1974), p. 264.

33. *Japan Times Weekly*, 2 December, 1978, p. 8.

29.   Men and Women
Janet Hunter

The disparity between the roles, activities and histories of men and women in Japan is as great as, if not greater than, that in any other society. Traditional historiography has concentrated on the activities of men, in Japan as elsewhere.[1] To redress the balance even partially it is necessary to acknowledge the part played by Japanese women in activities which are not the object of conventional historical record, to emphasize the fundamental role of women as the cornerstone of domestic life and to outline the changing status and role of women in modern Japan. Over the last century Japanese women have fulfilled an essential role both in the domestic sphere and in the economy, but a growing involvement in all aspects of national life has not always been reflected in a marked advance towards sexual equality as it is perceived in the West.

The image of Japanese women as exquisite but subservient adornments — an image still current in the West — was promoted by Westerners' experiences in the late nineteenth century. In as far as this stereotype was valid at all, it applied only to women from the middle and upper classes, or to entertainers; these were the only women encountered by Westerners on a social level. Women had not always been subordinate in Japan; some women enjoyed considerable power in ancient times, and the imperial line did not then exclude women. As late as the Kamakura period (twelfth to fourteenth centuries) women of the ruling class exercised a powerful political influence and enjoyed considerable legal and property rights. Much of Japan's great literature of the Heian period (784–1185) was written by women. However, the growing emphasis on military values helped to erode women's freedoms. In Japan, as elsewhere, the military role was considered unsuited to women, and from the Kamakura period the political, legal and economic power of women gradually declined in relation to that of men. By the mid-Tokugawa period the difference in role which formed the basis for subservience in the middle and upper classes had been rigidly defined within the Neo-Confucian-based official orthodoxy. During the course of the Edo period social values stressed by the ruling class filtered downwards through the other castes of society, and even among the peasantry the crucial importance of women's contribution to agricultural labour could not totally prevent the imposition of inferior status in a rigid family and community hierarchy. By the late Tokugawa period Japan was confirmed as a patriarchal society in which the stated functions of women were twofold: the perpetuation of the family line and the care and entertainment of men. Though mitigated by economic imperatives at the lower levels of the social structure, these two precepts were at least in part the ideal at all levels of society.

The position of samurai women in Edo Japan was based on a principle of respect for men and contempt for women (*danson johi*). At its root was a strict division between the functional roles of men and women, with the woman's place and role being exclusively within the household as wife and mother. Even within the domestic sphere,

Janet E. Hunter: 'Men and Women' in *THE EMERGENCE OF MODERN JAPAN: AN INTRODUCTORY HISTORY SINCE 1853* (Longman Group UK Ltd, 1989), pp. 137-157.

a woman was still subordinate to the dictates of men. A woman's supreme virtue was submissiveness, and her life was governed by what were known as the 'three obediences'. In childhood she obeyed her father or elder brother, after marriage her husband, and in widowhood her son. She received no legal protection against any abuses to which the male members of her family might subject her. Almost all women were expected to marry, and young brides were at the mercy of a strange household and the whims of an often domineering mother-in-law pleased to be replaced at the bottom of the hierarchy. Wives could be divorced without any substantive grounds and at any time by the husband and his family. No reciprocal right existed. Childbirth was a woman's main function, and any wife who failed to produce male heirs was likely to be returned to her own family; those children she did bear were part of her husband's family, and she had no claim to children or property in that family, remaining essentially an outsider. Only when a wife became a mother-in-law could she in her turn enjoy a brief heyday of influence. Women's education consisted of instruction in how to behave according to their low status, how best to fulfil their roles of childbirth and attendance to the needs of men, and, where the family's economic status allowed sufficient leisure, in gentle arts such as flower arrangement, poetry and the tea ceremony.

While the Western stereotype of the Japanese woman owed much to the ideal aspired to by the ruling élite, a further factor in its formation was the attributes expected of a different group of women — geisha, prostitutes and other women of entertainment. In Tokugawa society concubinage and prostitution were the norm and the number of women involved in male entertainment of some form was considerable. Those at the top of the entertainment hierarchy, for example, the geisha (lit. 'performer', 'artist'), were expected to possess a high degree of personal attractiveness, sophistication and cultural attainment which could be devoted to the diversion of the opposite sex. Necessary skills included musical performance (singing, dancing and playing of instruments), conversation, and often the art of sex. Such women as these existed solely for the diversion of men. Their growing contacts with Westerners arriving in the late nineteenth century enhanced the impression that Japan's women were fragile dolls supremely versed in the gentle arts. The greater degree of freedom and economic activity enjoyed by women in the non-samurai classes failed to shake this impression.

The ideal Western woman of the late nineteenth century, too, was *par excellence* mother and housewife, but even in propaganda the model was more complex. Women became missionaries, for example. They concerned themselves with moral issues and charitable purposes. The new exposure to Western civilization raised questions over the role and status of Japanese women. The years after the 1850s produced no immediate or dramatic change, but some women became active in spheres denied to them during the Tokugawa period and Western cultural influences began to stimulate a greater awareness of the position of women among the more educated. The first perceptible changes were essentially superficial. The initial craze for Western cultural habits was pursued by many female members of the ruling élite. Like men they adopted Western clothes and hairstyles; they were encouraged to participate in Western-style social gatherings to indicate to foreigners how Westernized Japan had become. The traditionally conceived role and position of women were seriously discussed by leading male intellectuals, and Mori Arinori, later Education Minister, went so far in 1875 as to engage in a contractual marriage, followed eleven years later by a contractual divorce. These discussions, however, rarely questioned the need for women to remain the repositories of the traditional attributes of obedience, chastity and gentleness. Their role was still to support their menfolk. Even the most progressive intellectuals desired an improvement in the status of and opportunities for women for the advancement that might ensue in the upbringing and development of Japan's ruling men, and hence in the welfare of the nation as a whole. There is little evidence of a desire to improve the status of women for its own sake or to encourage women to compete with men in areas traditionally reserved for men. Male and female roles remained strictly divided.

Yet any changes in the education of women and the opportunities open to them made more likely efforts to step beyond women's allotted role. Women from the better off sectors of society were the main beneficiaries of the first attempts to provide an alternative education for women spearheaded by Western missionaries such as Rev. J.C. Hepburn.[2] Tokugawa female education had been limited to moral training and the arts becoming to women. Women from the commercial classes had received some practical training, and instruction in reading and writing was spreading, but the literacy rate remained far lower than that of the male population, especially among lower social groups. The new Christian-influenced schools talked of equality and the dignity of the individual. Instruction began to include subjects such as languages, history, and even science and mathematics. The Meiji government increasingly subscribed to 'modern' education for women, although on the basis of the old Confucian perception of women's role. Among the first Japanese sent abroad to study by the Meiji government in 1871 were five girls. The most famous of these, Tsuda Umeko, studied for many years in the US and after returning to Japan became a pioneer in higher education for women and English language teaching. The government encouraged women to attend state elementary schools, which under the post-1880s system were coeducational. Normal schools trained female teachers, who in turn provided other girls with instruction. Private and state institutions for girls' education sprang up. Above the elementary level schools were strictly segregated and opportunities for women highly restricted, but by the turn of the century a small female élite was receiving higher education, and the vast majority of girls were attending elementary school, although the instruction they received there was often rudimentary and limited. The influence on women's attitudes of this change was most conspicuous among the highly educated élite, but there were some from outside this minority who sought a reappraisal of the status and role of women in the context of the radical social changes taking place. The Meiji period saw the emergence of an embryonic women's movement.

Some of the earliest female activists were those who were influenced by Christianity to campaign against concubinage and the existence of licensed prostitution in Japan. The Women's Temperance Association prominent in this activity was the Japanese counterpart of Western organizations such as the Women's Christian Temperance Union. The campaign was unsuccessful; both licensed and unlicensed prostitution continued to be legal under national law until after World War II. Nevertheless it signified a limited advance towards a concept of women's rights, albeit within the confines of home and motherhood.

More radical women campaigned as part of the popular rights movement during the 1880s. Two of the best known of these were Kishida Toshiko (1864–1901) and Fukuda Hideko (1865–1927). Kishida, a former lady-in-waiting at court, was a source of inspiration to many women through her fiery speeches in support of women being equal partners in the building of a new Japan. The outspokenness of her criticism of existing mores made her the subject of intimidation and harassment. Among those enthused by her oratory was Kageyama (later Fukuda) Hideko. Fukuda's association with the radical wing of the popular rights movement led to her imprisonment in 1885–9, but she remained a stalwart and vocal supporter of women's rights in the face of government suppression of the nascent socialist movement and acute poverty. She was dedicated to improving education opportunities and the chance of self-sufficiency for poorer women normally unable to afford them. Many of her later efforts were devoted to raising women's consciousness, particularly through journalistic activity. Though remaining doyenne of the women's movement until her death, Fukuda was an isolated figure. The decline of the popular rights movement put a severe damper on the women's rights' activity it had begun to stimulate. Kishida's activities became less public after her marriage in 1885, and with Fukuda in prison others, too, fell silent.

Notwithstanding the ferment of 1882–5, the mass of women remained relatively untouched by the campaigns of Christians and popular rights activists. Far more significant for them were the changes wrought by the economic transformation taking place in the country, which forced more and more women to adopt a lifestyle at odds with the role and status traditionally ascribed to them. As the number of women employed outside the home grew rapidly from the early Meiji period, the role and occupations of women in the labour force changed dramatically. Women from the artisan and commercial classes had long engaged in business; their numbers now increased, although some existing handicraft industries and commercial undertakings were displaced by newer rivals. Millions of women continued to engage in the arduous, exhausting manual labour of farmwork. The nature of agricultural work altered little all this time; substantial increases in output and productivity were secured by more, rather than less, labour. Many peasant women had traditionally carried on occupations such as weaving and spinning within the home, but the growth of factory-based industry also drove an increasing number to work as wage labour outside the home for extended periods. The textile industries, the cornerstone of early industrialization, had a largely female workforce; around 250,000 women worked in factories by the turn of the century. Most were under twenty; temporary migrants (*dekasegi*) from farming villages, they remitted much of their wages to their families and worked at the most for a few years before returning to their communities to marry. Other women became secretaries, telephonists, teachers, nurses, clerks — a few at first, but from the 1890s in rapidly growing numbers. As women were increasingly able to choose whether to sell their labour to the agricultural or industrial sectors, the prospects and expectations of those employed in the new growth areas had a growing effect on those working outside them.

Economic as well as social change was thus driving women away from the roles which they had traditionally occupied. Yet the essential nature of women's work did not lead to improvements in status or rights. From the 1890s the establishment increasingly sought to reimpose traditional virtues and status on women. Given the difficulty of

470

doing so in the face of dramatic economic and political changes, its success was substantial and long-lasting. Thirty to forty years after the Restoration the majority of Japanese, both men and women, still adhered closely to the Tokugawa ideal of a woman's role, and the new orthodoxy tried to build on and reinforce conservative attitudes of this kind.

The keystone of the political system, the Meiji Constitution of 1889, excluded women from any direct political participation, and other legislation prevented them from campaigning for change.[3] Women began to agitate for the vote in the years after World War I, but legal hindrances rendered their activity constantly vulnerable to official intervention. A more pervasive restriction was embodied in the 1898 civil code, which became the legal foundation of the patriarchal family (ie) system in the pre-1945 period, and placed a woman firmly within the locus of the family. Every clause of the civil code relating to women reinforced their subordinate, subservient position in Japanese society. A woman had no independent legal status, but was treated as a minor; all legal agreements on her behalf were concluded by the male to whom she was subordinate — father, husband or son.[4] She had no free choice of spouse or domicile. While women could, in theory, protest against this subordinate position in a non-political manner, to do so directly posed a challenge to the whole social orthodoxy on which the prewar Japanese state was founded. Women thus protested at their peril. Those who demonstrated their dissatisfaction by adopting non-conformist lifestyles or extra-marital sexual relationships could lay themselves open not merely to social opprobrium but to legal action.

Such women's organizations as existed in the late nineteenth century confined themselves to activities which met with official approval. The Christian Temperance movement concerned itself with temperance, prostitution and poverty. The Patriotic Women's Association of 1901 sought to provide physical and material comfort to soldiers and bereaved families in time of war. Upper class women were conspicuous in both these organizations, and although the Patriotic Women's Association, which had one million members by the end of World War I, could claim mass membership, activity at local level was minimal. Organizations such as the Patriotic Women's Association were essentially the creatures of the establishment.

Significantly, literature remained a vehicle for dissent for both sexes, and in the case of women served as the genesis of a renewed political movement for women's rights. Literary expressions of defiance from women unable to develop their creative abilities or express themselves to the full grew into a broader resentment against the subordinate status of women and their lowly position in the 'family state'. This new direction was marked by the formation of the famous Bluestocking Society (Seitōsha) of 1911 by a small number of women graduates led by Hiratsuka Raichō (1886–1971). Strongly influenced by the romantic literary movement and the pacifist poet Yosano Akiko and other women writers, the group determined to secure for itself personal liberation through expression in its own journal. Bluestocking (Seitō) was the first Japanese journal to be edited and written by women. Hiratsuka's declaration in the first issue was a harbinger of later developments. Entitled 'Originally woman was the sun', the statement called on women to regain their 'hidden sun' and reject their position of dependence, in which they could only shine in the reflected light of their men. The implied criticism of the whole family system and existing pattern of male–female relationships alienated many critics from the start.

In successive issues *Bluestocking* found itself moving away from an exclusive concern with individual liberation to the problems of women in society as a whole. Persecution of the group increased. Hiratsuka herself was propelled by her search for personal liberation toward more anti-establishment views, and the struggle to keep the journal going in the face of growing censorship gradually eroded support. The editorship was handed over to the politically radical Itō Noe early in 1915, but her advocacy of anarchism weakened support for the journal still further. It ceased publication in 1916. The membership of the group was never great, nor the circulation of the journal ever more than a few thousand, but its influence was out of all proportion to its size. Hiratsuka herself remained a leader of the women's movement until her death. Many other leaders of the interwar and post-1945 women's movement were readers of the journal or members of the group, and many more were caught up in the renewed concern for the position of women in Japanese society which the Bluestockings had initiated. They included Ichikawa Fusae (1893–1981), one of the founders of the New Women's Association (*Shinfujin kyōkai*) of 1919 which campaigned for greater legal rights for women, and better education and welfare facilities for them. This organization and its successor, the Women's Suffrage League of 1925, pressed for an end to the legal prohibition of political activity by women and female suffrage. In 1922 a partial amendment of the 1900 Peace Police Law allowed women to attend and hold political meetings, but the right to join parties and to vote was withheld until after 1945.

The Bluestockings and other intellectual groups searching for personal freedom were only one facet of women's rights activity after the Meiji period. Just as the 1880s popular rights movement had stimulated feminist ideas, so, too, did the emerging labour and socialist movements attract women who, despite their exclusion from political activity, sought to reassess the position of women in the light of socialist ideology and the growth of capitalist industry in Japan. The female industrial labour force grew rapidly after 1900, but although strikes by female workers in the 1880s had proved relatively successful, employers proved increasingly able to stifle sporadic communal expressions of protest. The majority of female workers endured appalling conditions or got out. The establishment of a women's section by the main labour organization, the Yūaikai, in 1916 acknowledged that women workers were a substantial element in the labour force, but for the most part little effort was made to organize female workers. The perspective that female workers were short term, uncommitted members of the workforce with little to gain from organization, in conjunction with the view that their sex rendered organization effectively impossible, made for a very low unionization rate.

The socialist political movement was no more successful in absorbing women into its ranks, although the legal ban on political activity did not prevent women from being informally involved with left-wing organizations. The Heiminsha of 1903–5 claimed an interest in women's rights, and socialist women's organizations often with proletarian party associations, existed during the 1920s. A series of women played a prominent part in the movement — Fukuda Hideko, Kanno Suga (executed with anarchist

Kōtoku Shūsui in 1911), Itō Noe, Yamakawa Kikue — but the disinterest of male socialist and labour leaders often drove them to sacrifice feminist concerns to what were considered the broader interests of the whole movement. As in other countries, male unionists feared women's advancement in the workplace; women encountered immense hostility to concepts such as equal work opportunities, equal wages and abolition of the patriarchal family system which threatened men's established hegemony. Socialist leaders continued to rely on the automatic liberation of women which they believed would accompany the advent of a socialist society. The activities of the few socialist women interested in women's rights and improving the lot of women workers were doomed to meet apathy, if not outright opposition, from male colleagues. Moreover, the socialist and non-socialist wings of the women's movement rarely came together in a united front.

Dynamic though many of these individuals were, the numbers interested in women's rights, labour and socialist activity paled into insignificance by comparison with the strength of the mass women's organizations, the first of which was the Patriotic Women's Association. These expanded rapidly in the 1920s and 1930s. The Patriotic Women's Association claimed three million members by the late 1930s, the army-sponsored National Defence Women's Association, formed in 1932, around eight million. Both had numerous local branches. These organizations were concerned not with women's rights, but with women's duties. Their task was the reinforcement of the patriarchal 'family state', and both became vehicles for the mobilization of the female population by the state for the purposes of war. They had a major impact on the lives of the majority, while agitation by the few non-establishment organizations and individuals seemed no more than peripheral to the concerns of most women.

Notwithstanding innate conservatism and the official reassertion of the traditional status of women, changing economic and labour market forces continued to exert a substantial influence on women's lives. Apart from their significance as wives, mothers and teachers, women continued to make up a large proportion of the workforce in the agricultural, industrial and commercial sectors. The agricultural smallholdings and tenancies which still sustained over 40 per cent of the population in the late 1930s became increasingly dependent on the labour contribution of the women of the family, both in the work of cultivation and in by-employment inside or outside the home. This process was accelerated by the absorption of men into the rapidly expanding industrial sector in the late 1930s, and into the armed forces. By 1940 women comprised over half the agricultural labour force (around seven million workers). This marked a reversal of the pattern earlier in the interwar years, when agricultural depression, climatic fluctuations and increasing population pressure on the land meant that poverty became increasingly severe in some villages. A woman's labour contribution was often considered less valuable to the farm, and the income she brought in had always been viewed as supplementary to the family budget. Thus in times of difficulty young women regarded as little more than extra mouths to feed tended to be among the first to be shed by the farm economy. More and more women and girls were forced to search for alternative sources of income at a time when industrial depression meant that employment opportunities outside the agricultural sector were declining. Male control over the female labour market weakened women's position still further. Since girls had no independent legal status, they had from the Meiji period been despatched to work in factories on the basis of contracts signed by their fathers or elder brothers, with or without the consent of the girl concerned. Although women became increasingly independent of their families in matters of employment in the 1920s and 1930s, they were still largely subject to legal and economic control by the males of the household. In the early 1930s girls from the depressed areas of the northeast were not infrequently sent into prostitution by their parents because no other employment was available. Brothel-keepers, like mill owners, paid a lump sum advance on wages to the head of the family — crucial to tide it over current difficulties — but the woman was in return committed to many years of service, if not life-long bondage. The effective 'sale' of female labour exacerbated by the depression demonstrated that under the law women were little higher than slaves and little more than chattels.

Their weak position at the bottom of the hierarchy made women particularly vulnerable to the impact of economic difficulties, but far from increasing the agitation for change by women, these harsh realities served to reinforce a broader sense of frustration and despair. While women's interests might have come to the fore in a time of prosperity they were now overtaken by the broader discontent among the working classes. Women's rights agitation was a luxury that could not be afforded; repression was certain and there were more immediate economic imperatives. In any case, for the mass of women local conservatism combined with efficient indoctrination and organization by the authorities to pre-empt any thought of feminist protest.

For some women the interwar years brought new opportunities. The number engaged in clerical and non-manual occupations grew apace. While the number of women employed in industry grew only marginally, those working in the tertiary sector expanded by over 70 per cent to nearly 3.4 million between 1920 and 1940. Around half of these were in the service industries. Women advanced further in the professions. The barriers to women's entering such careers as medicine and the law were slowly removed. Women teachers became increasingly responsible for the early education of children. Though poorly represented at higher educational levels, even in girls' schools, they accounted for nearly half of all elementary school teachers by the 1930s.

One of the most conspicuous areas of women's employment remained the entertainments industry. Licensed prostitution remained in operation throughout the prewar period and private prostitution also existed on a large scale. Girls driven into prostitution by destitution invariably found themselves at the bottom of the hierarchy, but the entertainments industry still embraced a range of occupations. All, from the highly sophisticated geisha with their long years of training, through bar girls, hostesses and nightclub entertainers, to a range of classes of prostitute, were dedicated to the entertainment of the male population. The size of this industry was the natural consequence of the position imposed upon the Japanese woman within the family, and a civil code which made adultery a crime for women and a permitted recreation for men. It is estimated that by the 1930s the number of girls involved ran to several hundred thousand.

In the interwar years a relative decline in the significance of female industrial labour was thus counterbalanced by a rise in other employments for women. By 1940 women constituted nearly 40 per cent of the economically active population of 32 million. In all sectors women were on lower grades or engaged in lower status work than their male colleagues, and received lower wages. The continuing predominance of unmarried women as employees and the tendency to leave on marriage produced a high turnover rate, reinforcing the allocation of females to lower status tasks. Married women worked in large numbers, but predominantly in agriculture or retailing. Women's economic activity continued to be regarded as subsidiary to their real role in the home as wife and mother.

The advance of women into the workforce was accelerated during the war years. The conscription of a large number of men into the armed forces meant the mobilization of the remainder of the population into essential occupations. While motherhood granted a privileged status, the unmarried female population was drafted on a vast scale into war-related production and other back-up services for the armed forces. In the face of growing labour shortages as the war progressed educational provision deteriorated and girls not yet in their teens were pressed into productive work.

While women were increasingly forced into the physical occupations and responsibilities formerly monopolized by men, they continued to carry out tasks assigned to them by the official mass organizations. A large proportion of women had already joined these by the late 1930s; in 1942 all were merged into a single body, the Greater Japan Women's Association. Membership for all women over twenty was compulsory; younger women joined youth organizations. Even before the start of the China War in 1937 these groups had coordinated women in specific back-up functions, such as savings campaigns, civil defence and care for the wounded and bereaved. Such functions were extended under the exigencies of war and the new political structure.

These official women's organizations were also a major element in the 'spiritual' mobilization of the female population, and under the influence of the miscellany of ideas they propagated the ideal of Japanese womanhood was built up into the 'mother of the nation'. A subordinate position in society had never concealed women's very real importance as wives and mothers as the organizers of domestic affairs and the foundation of family life. That these functions were essentially women's major role had long been assumed, but the highly charged militarist atmosphere of the 1930s overlaid this assumption with an idealized concept of the spiritual and emotional role of women in the Japanese state which, though building on this traditional role, yet remained distinct from it.

Military priorities meant that women were important as the bearers of sons who would fight Japan's wars. The sanctity of motherhood was enshrined in official statements and regulations as long as the war situation permitted the luxury of such favourable treatment. All women were depicted as mother-figures and consolers of men fighting overseas or serving on the home front. The ritual of girls seeing off men to the front was a highly charged emotional experience. Soldiers wore a belt or headband with a thousand stitches, each put in by a different woman; these *senninbari* were held to have talismanic qualities. Girls mobilized for overseas duties to cater to the sexual needs of the armed forces were euphemistically known as 'comfort girls' and said to be doing their part for the nation. Women found themselves bearing the burden of emotional support for the war effort which was such an important element in the spiritual mobilization programme.

475

The treatment to which women were subject was no more consistent with the idealized image than it had been in earlier years. Japanese employers, for example, had never resolved the contradictions over whether to treat their female employees as women or as a factor of production to be exploited to the full. Within the family, men glorified female attributes but expected women to fulfil the role of servants. This inconsistency of theory and reality was at its greatest during the early war years, when the physical and emotional burden on women became ever greater and the image they were expected to live up to increasingly lofty. As the pressures for survival at home increased, they fell to a growing extent on the shoulders of women. At the same time the ability of the official organizations to mobilize women in practical functions or spiritual campaigns was progressively impaired. The hothouse flower of the ideal Japanese woman of the war years was wilting long before the Occupation reforms attempted to kill it off completely. Economic imperatives, war weariness and the need for survival were key factors in its demise. The earlier ideal woman of which it had been an elaboration proved more hardy.

A change in the status and role of women was integral to the Occupation's 'democratization' programme. Even before the new constitution of 1947 guaranteed sexual equality, women were granted new legal and political rights. In the general election of Spring 1946, women were allowed to campaign, stand as candidates and vote. Against all expectations 67 per cent of women voted and 39 women — a figure never since exceeded — were elected to the lower house. Local politics also became open to them. Women became a significant force in the burgeoning labour movement; union membership peaked at 51 per cent of employed women in 1949, falling to 30 per cent by the following year. The revised civil code of 1948 removed women's subordination to the family head and the male. The abolition of the *ie* (family) and the end of primogeniture provided women with legal competence, equal rights regarding marriage, domicile, divorce and inheritance. The number of divorces initiated by women dramatically increased. However, the economic and social straits of the immediate post-defeat years were a limiting factor on women's availing themselves of their new rights. The immediate concern of most women was their own and their children's welfare, and 'freedom' was no substitute for income. The imposition of the reforms met with little outright opposition, but it was not to be expected that the old concepts of women's role and status could be abolished by the stroke of a pen. Even forty years on, social practice is far removed from legal possibilities and indirect discrimination is widespread. Although in the household sphere the woman's influence normally exceeds that of the man, in most other aspects of life traditionally the male preserve, for example employment, politics, even education, women remain acutely disadvantaged.

To be a 'good wife and wise mother' has continued to be what is expected of the majority of Japanese girls. If a woman is content to have her aspirations and ambitions lie within this traditional sphere society will delegate to her considerable power. In most Japanese households the woman has a large measure of autonomy over the family finances; the male breadwinner often hands over his income to his wife, who allots him a small amount for his personal expenses. The wife's disposition of the family budget can even extend to such major items as housing. The upbringing and education of children are also largely the responsibility of the wife. She not only cares for their physical wellbeing, but sees them through the competitive education system; postwar Japan has produced the notorious 'education mother' (kyōiku mama), who drives her children to study, and, she hopes, to succeed. Though home and children remain the wife's domain more families are consulting on these issues. For some this is a welcome step towards equal partnership. For other women — and there are many who are well-satisfied with the status quo — the increasing intervention by the husband in domestic affairs and the greater time he may spend at home as a result of changed working conditions and new attitudes among the younger generation is an unwelcome intrusion. In a society where social role is of such importance as it is in Japan, involvement by the male in domestic issues threatens the only social role which many women have. Moreover, women exercise this influence in the home merely because most men are content to let them do so.

Yet economic and social pressures and changes in their education and life cycle mean that more women than ever before find it impossible — and undesirable — to remain strictly within the domestic context for the greater part of their lives. Once a woman begins to harbour ambitions outside the household sphere she meets with social prejudice, economic disadvantage and, despite the constitution, legal obstacles.

The granting of voting rights to women after 1945 meant that politically they became a force to be reckoned with, but the momentum of the early years has not been sustained. Female membership of both houses of the Diet together has not exceeded thirty since 1947, and the appointment of a woman, Doi Takako, to leadership of the Japan Socialist Party in September 1986 was more an image-building exercise than a commitment to equal rights. Few women politicians have achieved the stature of Ichikawa Fusae, who was a member of the upper house almost continuously from 1953 to 1981. In the ruling Liberal Democratic Party, where connections are of continuing significance, women are particularly few, and female cabinet ministers since 1945 can be counted on the fingers of one hand. Women constitute a high political risk for all parties, and this limits necessary funding and encourages the appearance of well-known 'talent' candidates not chosen for their political ability. Conservatism at the local level has failed to allow women to build the local base often crucial in securing influence at national level, and it will be a long time before the national bureaucracy provides them with the stepping stone to national politics it grants to their male colleagues. Women have been unable to engineer dramatic changes in their position in society through direct political influence, and such laws as have been passed are weak. What appears a substantial advance, the Equal Employment Opportunity legislation of April 1986, is significantly weakened by lack of any legal penalty for contravention and the signs are that some employers are managing to circumvent it by indirect means of discrimination.

Lack of achievement in politics is paralleled by lack of success in other careers, for to attain the top a woman has to be of outstanding ability and determination. Parents and husbands are often unwilling or unable to provide the backing upon which most women are dependent if they are to have a successful career. Yet discrimination by men is far from being the only problem. Just as significant are the attitudes of women themselves. A recent survey suggested that no more than 15 per cent of all women wished to work on any long-term, let alone life-long, basis, and the basic assumption by the vast majority of women that careers are not for them reduces openings and saps the confidence of those who do have ambitions in this sector.

Women are also educationally less well qualified than men. Opportunities are fewer, and the persistence of the old hierarchy at higher educational institutions acts to exclude women. Lack of ambition on the part of girls and their families has inhibited active pressure for improvement. More girls than boys continue to high school after completing compulsory education (in 1984, 95 per cent of girls and 92.8 per cent of boys). Almost as many go on to some type of higher education (32.7 percent of women, compared to 38.3 per cent of men), but there is a substantial difference in the quality and type of higher education received by the sexes. The prestige national universities are dominated by men. The high-ranking private and prefectural/municipal colleges have many more men than women on four-year courses. A large proportion of female students in higher education take two-year courses at Junior colleges at the bottom of the institutional hierarchy, and many take such subjects as home economics, which are regarded as suitable preparation for marriage rather than a career. The proportion of well-qualified women is far lower than their representation in higher education would suggest, and the even greater scarcity of women in science and engineering subjects disqualifies them from many jobs in industry and technology.

The continuing assumption that women's main task is marriage and home is reflected both in marriage levels and in employment patterns. In 1985 nearly 93 per cent of women over twenty-five were married or had been married, and this reality dictates the structure of female employment. In 1985 women constituted around 40 per cent of the labour force and nearly a half of all women were in paid employment. The workforce participation rate for women peaks in the early twenties and among those aged thirty-five to fifty-five. Women are represented in all sectors of the economy, but are dominant in trade and retailing, and in the service industries, where they outnumber men. Light industry still employs many women, and as agricultural production becomes less labour intensive and employment opportunities for men elsewhere more attractive, it is the women who increasingly become the core of the productive unit in agriculture. Women are advancing into the professions, where barriers to equality are less conspicuous but they remain most numerous in the occupations traditionally conceived of as female, for example nursing and teaching.

The pattern of female employment in all sectors shows certain characteristics which largely result from a continuing reluctance to acknowledge the legitimacy of a woman's role outside the home. In the first place, the average duration of service for women is much shorter than that for men. Women work between finishing their formal education and the birth of their first child, and begin to re-enter the workforce after their youngest child starts school. This pattern excludes many women from the famed benefits of seniority wages and lifetime employment. Secondly, women are overwhelmingly concentrated in the lower grades of employment. Businesses such as banking and insurance have large numbers of female clerical and secretarial staff, many designated 'office lady', a term denoting an individual whose job is often little more than to make tea for her male colleagues and enhance general ambiance of the office. In government employment, regarded as relatively egalitarian, around 20 per cent of all employees are female, but women constitute only a minute percentage of management grade staff. Surveys show that in both national and local government, and in the judiciary, women lack the confidence and desire to fill higher positions and advance slower up the hierarchy. In teaching women predominate in elementary education, but are heavily outnumbered by men in high schools and further education, and almost all heads and administrators are male. Everywhere disproportionately few women reach the higher echelons and an almost exclusively male management structure persists. Thirdly, women's wages are lower than those of men. In 1985 average monthly earnings for women were little more than 50 per cent of those for men. The disparity was particularly great in manufacturing (42 per cent), trade (43 per cent) and finance and insurance (45 per cent). While starting salaries for entrants at all levels are relatively even, men soon move ahead. By the age of thirty, after equal years of service, men are already earning 20–30 per cent more than women.

An important factor in disparities is the recent expansion in the number of female part-time workers. Most women leave work either on marriage or when expecting a child. Where the aspirations of most lie within the domestic sphere the exercise of statutory maternity and other rights and a return to work while children are small can lead to accusations of neglecting family and domestic responsibilities. Childcare facilities are in any case totally inadequate. However, though a woman may remain the focus of home and family, these concerns are no longer the full-time, life-long concerns they used to be. Small families of closely spaced children mean that most women are freed of daily care for their youngest child by their mid-thirties. Fewer have parents-in-law for whom to care, husbands are usually out, and housework is much less time-consuming. While some women occupy this new-found leisure with education, social activities or voluntary work, many others seek to return to paid employment, even where the economic returns may be small. These women provide a pool of low-paid, part-time workers. They do not enjoy the benefits of a regular career structure and can be hired and fired almost at will. The number of female part-timers increased by more than four times between 1970 and 1984; a large proportion were in the late thirties to early forties age group, and they were concentrated in small operations where earnings are already lower than average. The growing prevalence of such workers perpetuates the assumption that a woman's income is supplementary to family needs normally provided for by the main, male breadwinner, and hence that conditions and continuity of employment are of less significance than for men. The reluctance of women to register as unemployed even where they may be entitled benefit suggests that they share this conservative view of their labour. The marginal nature of the jobs that women can secure reinforces their reluctance to compromise in any way their role in the household sphere.

Such restricted opportunities might be expected to provide fruitful soil for a women's movement in Japan. However, the postwar years have produced few campaigns capable of capturing the imagination and interest of a significant number of women. The Occupation reforms, by providing everything the prewar's women's movement had striven for, took the wind out of the sails of women's leaders. In the halcyon days after 1945 true legal equality and free participation in politics seemed to offer all that could be wished. To build on this basis, numerous women's groups did spring up. Many sought to raise political consciousness and achieve liberation from old social attitudes, and a vocal campaign for the abolition of licensed prostitution culminated in the passing of new legislation in 1956.

For the most part, though, women's organizations proved unable to work together. The gap between working women and housewives was rarely successfully bridged. The strong influence of the left made the movement vulnerable to the all too frequent application of political dogma and the adverse effects of official hostility. A long-standing role of women as mere adjuncts of reform and revolutionary movements, peripheral beings whose role was to give emotional and physical support to male leaders, seemed in danger of being perpetuated. For much of the fifties and sixties the movement was weak and divided. In the early 1970s the apparent impasse of the reform movements and the legacy of disunity stimulated the growth of a women's liberation movement. Strongly influenced by similar movements in other countries, members advocated individual liberation, sexual liberation and resistance to male rule. Apart from consciousness-raising, the movement conducted a vigorous opposition to proposed restrictions on the freedom of abortion.[5] Small though the number of feminists is, it has helped to stimulate a substantial interest in women's studies and feminist ideology, and some have hailed women's liberation as part of a rising tide of concern for sexual equality. In fact, much of its impact is restricted to intellectual women who might well have succeeded anyway in escaping the restrictions of the domestic sphere.

The failure of elements of the women's movement to appeal to large numbers of women has led many to divert their energies into other fields. Women are not unorganized. Millions of women belong to groups with nationwide affiliations, and these national organizations have proved powerful factors in national policy. Women's political and legal rights do not figure large among their concerns. Given the legal reforms of the Occupation and the persistent emphasis on women's domestic role it is not surprising that the most important manifestations of women's solidarity in the postwar years have been over problems of more immediate and obvious concern to the lives of the majority of women. Parent–teacher associations are run largely by women. Women are a crucial element in campaigns relating to civic concerns — for example, environmental issues. The prominent part played by women in the peace and anti-nuclear movements dates back to the Occupation years. The massive support given to the Japan Mother's Convention, which started in 1955, demonstrates clearly Japanese women's perceptions of their own role. Most significant, though, has been women's role in the consumer movement, since women are the major purchasers of consumer goods. Involvement in consumer issues dates back to immediate postwar economic dislocation and the founding in 1948 of the Housewives Federation (*Shufuren*), which is still a leading campaigner in this field. Consumer concerns have had a growing appeal as the Japanese economy has prospered, despite male politicians' initial distaste at having to consider such everyday problems.

In the final analysis the women's movement has been confined by having to rebel against social custom and attitudes rather than legal discrimination. A change in the law is just a single stage towards a real shift in the position of women. In the case of milestones such as the Anti-Prostitution Law and the Equal Employment Opportunities legislation it has proved only too easy to find legal methods of circumvention. The gulf between the *de jure* and *de facto* positions of Japanese women is immense; few women wish, or dare, to claim the equality that is their constitutional right since indirect discrimination is difficult to prove and social conservatism exists at every level of society. In a society where women enjoy a certain status as long as they do not try to step outside their traditionally prescribed roles, the attitude of many women is that rapid change is not only impossible but even undesirable. A very large number of women, even some who are highly educated, have little desire to seek a place in what has traditionally been a man's world and are content to find their metier as wife and mother. Japanese men essentially hold just as conservative a view of a woman's place as do women themselves. Most argue that the sexes are equal but different, and that in fact Japanese women are immensely powerful. On the left many advocates of true sexual equality concede that improvement or change in the position of women is desirable, but tend to argue that women will benefit more by broader reforms of society than through agitation by a specifically feminist lobby. The private lives even of these advocates all too often demonstrate an equally deep-rooted conservatism.

International and economic pressures make some modification in attitudes to women inevitable, but, without a major lead from the ruling élite of society, change will be slow and painful. Such a lead is unlikely. Few attempts have been made to encourage women to enter politics for example, or become business leaders, and the Women's and Minor's Bureau of the Ministry of Labour established in 1947 has hardly proved the hoped for spearhead of change. Anything resembling positive discrimination has been roundly denounced. Laudable bureaucratic intentions have had to contend with a weight of social conservatism and inertia. Consumer and environmental issues demonstrate that Japanese women acting together over common causes of dissatisfaction can be a powerful force, but while they continue satisfied with their role as good wives and wise mothers that potential will not be brought to bear on sexual inequalities and the gulf in status, role and influence between men and women will remain considerable.

Notes

1. Women's history is an even more recent development in Japan than in this country.

2. Hepburn worked in Japan for over thirty years to 1892, and produced the first English–Japanese, Japanese–English dictionaries.

3. The Peace Police Law of 1900, which prohibited political activity by women, was the major restriction.

4. There were some exceptions — for example, female household heads — but they were small in number.

5. Abortion was a major method of family planning since the pill was largely unavailable.

30.   The Company, Society and Change
Rodney Clark

The Japanese company system

The easiest way to perceive the logical consistency in the arrangements of the Japanese company is to set out its more obvious characteristics side by side with those of the generalized Western company, as in Table 1.

Table 1   The Japanese and Western company systems

Japan	*The West*
The industrial context	
Company part of one industry.	Company covers many industries.
Company not functional unit, depends on sub-contracting.	Company more nearly a functional unit, higher degree of self-sufficiency.
Shareholders principally associated companies, not primarily interested in profits and dividends.	Shareholders primarily interested in company as financial investment.
Financed by debt.	Financed by equity.
Relations with other companies hierarchical.	Relations with other companies more nearly egalitarian.
Market share a major measure of success.	Profit a major measure of success.
The labour market	
'Lifetime employment' an ideal.	No ideal of 'lifetime employment'.
Company recruits people of particular age and education to fill general vacancies.	Company recruits people with particular skills and types of experience to fill specified jobs.
Size of company correlated closely with employment practices.	No close correlation between size of company and employment practice.
Size of company correlated with quality of workforce.	Size of company less closely correlated with quality of work force. All companies contain representatives of all sections of the wider society.
Internal organization	
Company ideally a community.	Less emphasis on community ideal.
No major distinction between managers and workers.	Frequently sharp distinction between managers and workers.
Standard ranks, strong emphasis on hierarchy.	Management positions not standard, related to particular function, less emphatically hierarchical.
Age and length of service explicitly recognised as promotion criteria.	Age and length of service only marginally relevant to promotion.

Rodney Clark: 'The Company, Society and Change' from *THE JAPANESE COMPANY* (Yale University Press, 1979), pp. 223-261. © Yale University.

Table 1 (cont) The Japanese and Western company systems

Japan	*The West*
Authority and responsibility ostensibly diffuse.	Authority and responsibility ostensibly specific.
Attachment to company correlated with age and sex.	Attachment to company weaker, associated with skill as well as age and sex.
Enterprise unions.	Trade unions.
Managerial authority limited in practice by labour mobility.	Managerial authority challenged ideologically and practically by trade unions.

It hardly needs to be repeated at this stage that the comparison in Table 1 between the Japanese and the Western company is a very gross one. There are dozens of different types both of Japanese and Western companies, and not all of them have the characteristics attributed to them. Moreover, the characteristics themselves are more complicated than the brief descriptions of them suggest. The purpose of the table is not, however, to show how Japanese companies differ from Western ones in each particular respect, but to reveal how the characteristics on both sides can be resolved into a difference of systems.

If, instead of reading across the table, we read down the Japanese and Western columns, we see that any one attribute of each company is more or less closely related to many of the others. On the Japanese side, for example, the fact that firms are so often part of one industry makes market share a natural measure of success and an obvious management goal. To the extent that managers are not aiming primarily for profit, something that benefits only one group of people, but for growth of sales, which benefits everyone, management becomes not coercion but leadership. The distinction between managers and workers may be insignificant, especially when so many managers start out as workers and rise to management in the course of their 'lifetime' of service to their firms. The company can be a community in which everyone has interests in common, and work can be seen as at least partly a matter of self-interest. Similarly, there is an association between the firm's dependence on bank and trade credit, and the development of hierarchical relations between companies. A continuity exists between the ranking of companies in the society of industry and the ranking of company members within each company, because so many firms have standard ranks. Again, all these features are consistent with the predominance of enterprise unions. These obviously fit better into companies engaged in one industry than into companies involved in a number of different businesses. Enterprise unions help give rise to industrial gradation by encouraging their firms to pay higher wages than smaller enterprises can afford. The existence of an ideal of 'lifetime employment' is partly an historical result of the activities of enterprise unions. Within each company, the enterprise union contributes to the cohesion of the community by discouraging the differentiation of employees by skill or type of job; for the union itself depends on being able to represent the interests of workers doing every kind of work.

Reading down the right hand column of the table enables us to see the similarly consistent, but differently ordered, logic of the Western company. The firm, frequently involved in several industries, undertakes its business in the language of finance, which is common to all industries. Partly because of this, and partly because of the nature of its shareholders, it makes profit one of its most important goals. Within the company managers and workers alike fill more or less specialized positions relating to the function of the particular firm and, ultimately, to the achievement of financial success. The degree of interest managers and workers have in this success is different, and is widely assumed to be different. Managers are placed in a position of authority by the shareholders and they are expected to accept the goals of the company. Workers are to be cajoled and exhorted to contribute to those goals, which, it is implicitly admitted, are less directly beneficial to them. The involvement of the employee in the company is limited by the likelihood that he will change jobs, by his membership of a union, and by his participation in institutions outside the firm.

It is certainly remarkable that modern industrial countries can have developed apparently different ways of organizing industry; so remarkable that there is a temptation to suppose that the Japanese company, which appears, after all, to be the odd man out, will change so as to become more like the Western one. Later on I shall discuss 'convergence' hypotheses. I should like here, however, to examine the reasons why the Japanese company does *not* change, whether in a Western direction or otherwise.

The first reason, which scarcely needs labouring, is the success of the Japanese company. The resurgence of the Japanese economy after the Second World War was the result of many things, but one of them was surely the way Japanese industry was organized and the constitution of the company. One can see the progressive recognition of this in Western writings about Japan. Bemusement at the illogical nature of the Japanese company, with its disregard for universal principles of rationality and its precarious financial arrangements, has given way to respectful discernment of some of the Japanese advantages. Western businessmen are now aware, for example, that 'lifetime employment' and 'pay by age' make it easier to introduce new machinery without having to renegotiate wage rates or allay fears of dismissal. Industrialists everywhere are envious of the harmony which appears to be found in Japanese companies between management and labour. In countries like Britain, and in industries in which Japanese companies have become dominant, respect has been overtaken by fearful admiration. A converse process has occurred among the Japanese. In the 1950s the Japanese were modest about their own institutions and eager to learn. By the mid-1960s, when Japanese companies had become as productive as those in the West, their managements showed a new confidence in 'traditional' methods. By 1970 their pride in those methods was sufficiently well justified to permit them to deride the less efficient Western producers they were displacing for slapdash quality control, poor labour relations, or outdated technology.

Now it is true that not every Japanese company is a Matsushita, a Canon, or a Nippon Steel. It is also true that the formidable competitive power of such companies is partly derived from the sacrifices they can impose on smaller companies and, as I shall shortly explain, on the Japanese population as a whole. Even so, large Japanese companies, though they may be privileged, are also intrinsically efficient. They could hardly make

485

goods of such high quality and deliver them on time if they were not. No one, Westerner or Japanese, need be in any doubt that the Japanese system works; that it is able to coordinate and even inspire thousands of men and women to make and sell things; and the fact that it works is a powerful argument for not tampering with it.

Another reason for the stability of the company it systemic inertia. So many of the important characteristics of the company are logically interdependent, or at least closely adapted to one another, that it is difficult to change one without changing the others at the same time. The company cannot, for example, adopt profit as its supreme goal without adjustments to its relations with shareholders, a reconstitution of management ideals, and changes in the behaviour of its employees and in the attitude of the company union. Nor can a company suddenly introduce detailed job specifications without altering the relations between company and employee and modifying the nature of authority; with further implications for the strength of the distinction between managers and workers, and for the cohesion of the company union.

There is, however, an important corollary. It may be true that change is inhibited because it cannot occur in one respect alone. Yet if the company is forced to change merely in one respect, that apparently limited change may bring about many other alterations. We have already noted one instance of a seemingly minor change having very extensive consequences. The rapid ageing of the Japanese population makes it difficult for even the biggest firms to recruit employees straight from school, and allows younger people to change jobs easily. As a result, employers are having to modify pay by age systems, to extend the age of retirement, and to recruit from the labour market. It is not difficult to imagine how the need for better methods of recruiting mid-career entrants could lead to the growth of a job market based on skills rather than age, and how the new emphasis on skill within the firm could affect employees' attitudes to the company and to each other.

A third reason why the company remains as it is could be described as political, using that word in the widest sense. The company and Japanese industry as a whole confer their benefits on enough people for there to be considerable support for the status quo; while those who do not benefit from the company and from industry either do not realize it, or are unable to do anything about it.

To understand the nature of this political support, this implied bargain between the company and its beneficiaries, we shall have to consider at some length something that has only been mentioned in passing so far: the relations between the company system and society.

The company system and society

I intend to discipline the mass of questions that volunteer themselves for service in explaining the effect of the company on society by subordinating them to a naive preoccupation: who gains and who loses from the activities of companies and the way they are organized? We shall have to consider the matter in three stages. To begin with, how does industry as a whole impose itself on and contribute to the rest of society? Next, how are wealth and power distributed within industry, between different types of firm? Finally, how does the organization of the company affect the individuals concerned with it?

At the beginning of Japanese industrialization, as we saw, the prosperity of the peasantry was sacrificed for the development of industry. After the Second World War, too, Japan recovered from her devastation by placing all available resources at the disposal of industry. Even today, when Japan has a formidable industrial economy and many of her firms dominate world markets, business and industry continue to be favoured at the expense of the private citizen.

Consider, for example, the sources and uses of taxation, as set out in Table 2. Japanese companies (which are not, of course, the only source of business taxes) provide a surprisingly high proportion of all government income. But the proportion of national income taken in tax is low by international standards. In most of the major West European countries government revenues represent more than thirty per cent. of the Gross National Product, while in Japan they represent less than twenty-five per cent.[1] Moreover, in Japan a rather smaller share of government revenue is distributed to private households than in other industrial countries.

Another piece of evidence is the flow of funds between the main sectors of the economy: personal, business (Table 3 deals only with business corporations), and government. Each year the personal sector surplus, the bank deposits and savings accounts of private individuals, has gone to make up the business sector deficit. Industry has, in fact, borrowed on a vast scale from the private citizen, while the government until recently has been more or less self-sufficient. The scale of this transfer of funds is less significant than the terms on which the transfer has taken place. Most of it has been borrowed through the banking system, at interest rates which have been artificially set by the government at or below the inflation rate. Individual depositors have therefore received a negative real return on their bank deposits. Industry has been lent money at little or no real cost. The disadvantage of the depositor and the advantage of the industrial borrower have been compounded by tax, the depositor losing a percentage of the nominal interest due, and the borrower being able to charge the nominal interest expense against taxation. The cumulative effect of the movement of funds has been, therefore, a transfer of wealth from the individual to industry.

It is perhaps too early to say whether the increase in government debt in the years since the oil crisis, and the present reluctance of companies to borrow money, are indications of a permanent change in the direction in which funds flow. It is, however, possible that in the near future the government will benefit even more than industry and commerce from the willingness of the Japanese to save assiduously at low interest rates.

Another form of transfer has taken place in those industries where the government has used its influence to enable producers to take advantage of consumers by raising prices beyond those that would obtain on a free market. Government interference of this kind has perhaps been more conspicuous in agriculture rather than in industry. The Japanese consumer has to pay well above world market prices for rice and other crops in order to support the farming population. In a host of industries, however, the government has protected domestic manufacturers from cheap imports until

Table 2 General government income by source, and government disbursements to individuals, in relation to Gross National Product, 1955–74

(million million yen)

	1955		1960		1965		1970		1971		1972		1973		1974	
		%		%		%		%		%		%		%		%
Gross National Product	8.9	(100.0)	16.2	(100.0)	32.8	(100.0)	73.0	(100.0)	81.6	(100.0)	94.8	(100.0)	115.6	(100.0)	136.3	(100.0)
General government revenue	1.6	(18.0)	3.3	(20.3)	6.7	(20.4)	15.9	(21.8)	17.6	(21.6)	21.0	(22.2)	27.4	(23.7)	32.6	(23.9)
Government income from corporations	0.2	(2.2)	0.7	(4.3)	1.2	(3.7)	3.4	(4.7)	3.5	(4.3)	3.9	(4.1)	5.8	(5.0)	8.2	(6.0)
Government income from individuals	0.4	(4.5)	0.7	(4.3)	1.7	(5.2)	4.0	(5.5)	4.8	(5.9)	6.2	(6.5)	8.2	(7.1)	9.1	(6.7)
Government income jointly from corporations and individuals*	1.0	(11.2)	1.8	(11.1)	3.6	(11.0)	8.2	(11.2)	9.1	(11.2)	10.7	(11.3)	13.2	(11.4)	15.9	(11.7)
Government disbursements to individuals†	0.4	(4.5)	0.6	(3.7)	1.4	(4.3)	3.2	(4.4)	3.6	(4.4)	4.5	(4.7)	5.6	(4.8)	8.1	(5.9)

Source: Japan Statistical Yearbook, 1976: pp. 475-6: Table 329A, D.

*Indirect taxes + social insurance contributions.
† Includes social insurance benefits.

Table 3 Flow of funds between sectors, interest rates, and inflation, 1968–76

('000 million yen; fiscal years)

	1968	1969	1970	1971	1972	1973	1974	1975	1976
Net surplus funds of personal sector increase in personal bank deposits, etc.	4,475 (100)	5,355 (100)	5,767 (100)	7,877 (100)	10,936 (100)	9,393 (100)	13,750 (100)	17,138 (100)	18,006 (100)
Net deficit of government sector increase of borrowings by central and local governments, etc.	1,153 (26)	850 (16)	499 (9)	1,592 (20)	2,270 (21)	2,501 (27)	6,685 (49)	11,992 (70)	11,969 (66)
Net deficit (surplus) with rest of world funds passing out of (into) Japan from abroad in loans, investments, etc.	530 (12)	736 (14)	846 (15)	2,141 (27)	1,881 (17)	-1,127 (-12)*	-639 (-5)*	42 (0)	1,362 (8)
Net deficit of corporate sector increase of borrowings, etc. by companies	2,792 (62)	3,769 (70)	4,422 (77)	4,145 (53)	6,785 (62)	8,019 (85)	7,740 (56)	5,279 (31)	4,675 (26)

(percentages: calendar years)

	1968	1969	1970	1971	1972	1973	1974	1975	1976
	%	%	%	%	%	%	%	%	%
Increase in consumer price index	5.3	5.2	7.7	6.1	4.5	11.7	24.5	11.6	9.3
Maximum available interest rate on bank one year term deposit	5.5	5.5	5.75	5.75	6.25	6.25	7.24	6.75	6.75

Source: Bank of Japan, *Keizai Tōkei Geppō* (Economic Statistics Monthly): *316, 325, 340, 364* and other official sources.

* In 1973 and 1974 there was a net inflow of funds into Japan to finance industry and government.

489

'liberalization' was deemed possible. Some industries are still protected or strictly controlled by the government, and in certain of them, notably the food industry and finance, the consumer is clearly supporting the producer. The official price rigging in the meat industry has recently been explained to the public in a celebrated book.[2] In the world of finance (in which the manipulation of bank interest rates could be considered a form of price fixing), the customer gets poor value for his money from the insurance industry and, even more significantly for the future, from pension fund administrators. Government rules about the disposition of pension funds ensure that industry gains while the beneficiaries have little chance of receiving an adequate pension. No great effort is made to prevent trust banks, which share a monopoly of pension fund administration with life insurance companies, from generating profit for themselves from the funds they handle.[3]

The result of this transfer of wealth has been that those immediately engaged in industry can live comfortably, while those outside it are at a disadvantage. Factories and company apartments are grand and imposing, but private houses are cramped and very expensive. The restaurants of Japan are full of those conducting the world's business on tax-allowable expense accounts, while food prices in the shops are extremely high. In the hill resorts of Mount Fuji and the fashionable seaside towns the terraces and streets are crowded with lodges owned by large firms. For those not eligible to use them the cost of a holiday will be very considerable.

To recount these economic advantages of industry, and those within it, over the rest of society is to tell only part of the story. Ordinary people have given more than their wealth to industry. In some cases they have given their health and welfare and even their lives. For industrial pollution, for which Japan has become so notorious, is largely the cumulative effect of the priority accorded to the needs of industry over those of individuals, in a country where people have to live together in crowded conditions. Such an explanation seems bland and unsatisfactory when applied to the terrible tragedies which have now become so well known: the Minamata disease, caused by organic compounds of mercury contained in the waste products discharged from the chemical plants of two companies, Chisso and Shōwa Denkō, which has killed or paralysed hundreds of people; and the cadmium poisoning case involving Mitsui Mining & Smelting.[4] It would be hard indeed to excuse the heartless behaviour of some of the parties to these affairs. The Chisso management withheld its co-operation from the team of university medical researchers looking for the cause of the Minamata disease. It then tried, with the connivance of the Ministry of International Trade and Industry, to dissuade the victims from seeking legal redress, and finally employed 'general meeting men' gangsters to intimidate victims who came to a company meeting as shareholders.[5] Most pollution cases, however, are less apocalyptic and much easier to interpret as a mere misapplication (as it now appears) of policy.

Take, as a rather more typical example of a pollution problem than Chisso, the experience of the Osaka factory of Marumaru. The factory had been built in 1962 on an irregularly shaped plot of land surrounded by fields, within the jurisdiction of the suburban town of K———— . In the summer of 1968 a second corrugator was put into the factory to increase production. This was an event that would not have concerned outsiders, except that in the autumn of the same year a number of houses were built

490

in the vicinity of the factory. Almost immediately the town hall began to receive complaints about the intense and penetrating noise of the corrugators.

By rights, the neighbouring houses should never have been built, because their site was a piece of waste land between Marumaru's plot and a Hitachi factory, and was not officially recognized as suitable for housing. Some of the houses themselves contained factories, small workshops with one or two workers which were open to the street and no doubt caused as much nuisance to the other residents as Marumaru did, at least in the daytime. Unlike Marumaru, however, they did not work at night. The rest of the houses were shoddy blocks of flats, two stories high, with walls of grey corrugated iron. Between them ran unpaved roads.

In 1969 a second dispute arose. Until then the effluent from Marumaru's factory, which included waste corn starch and printing ink, had been drained away in an open unlined ditch. (Similar wastes from British corrugated board factories are collected in special containers and taken away by the local authorities.) The residents complained to the town hall of the smells carried past their windows, and the company built a new concrete ditch to drain both the factory and the houses. But nothing was done about the major problem of noise, even though the mayor of the town called several times at the factory to ask the manager to eliminate the nuisance. Nor did the company make any effort to discuss the matter directly with those who were being discomforted. Only in 1970, when the mayor sent official notice to Marumaru that the factory would be closed if the noise was not reduced, was action taken. The story of the mayor's threat was passed to the newspapers, and customers began to telephone Marumaru to find out whether their supply of boxes might be cut off. The company quickly enclosed the noisiest parts of the corrugators in sound-proofed boxes, and took certain other measures to bring the noise down to just above the official limit. The work was finished by February 1971, nearly two and a half years after the first complaints.

In this case, as in so many others, the pollution was not caused by a malevolent act on the part of a greedy company. Instead it was the consequence of the inadequacy of appropriate legislation, and the poverty of social services — both of which, however, reflected the priority historically given to industry. Marumaru's moral position was scarcely a strong one, but in a sense it too was a victim of the episode. The company had to pay for drains and for sound-proofing, so as not to inconvenience people who had illegally put up houses in an industrial zone. It was having to shoulder burdens for the whole community, even though, as a newcomer to the area, it had never benefited from the absence of restrictions and the low level of local taxation which had contributed so much to the cause of the problem.

The minor episode at Marumaru also illustrated how the isolation of a company from the local community and the strong collective sentiments within many firms can, in more serious cases, allow managements presumably composed of normal people to behave with such cruel indifference towards pollution victims. At the Marumaru Osaka factory there had never been much contact between anyone in the factory and those in the surrounding houses. The Marumaru employees lived in distant company apartments and did their shopping and found their entertainment near them. Since no one had had any cause to know the local people, when the problem arose it became all too easy to think of them as remote outsiders. Within Marumaru there was little or no controversy over the issue. Union leaders, workers and managers all took the same view. The situation was bad, but it was scarcely Marumaru's fault. The township could have prevented the problems arising but, inevitably, 'our company' would have to pay out of its own pocket. In cases like that of Chisso, too, where a company has stood accused of perpetrating acts with the most hideous consequences, remarkably few employees or groups of employees have chosen to criticize their firms, at least in public. Company members, particularly immobile ones, see their interests as lying with their companies and are at the same time emotionally committed to their firms and their fellow workers. Enterprise unions balk at jeopardizing their members' livelihoods.[6] It is significant that the few employees who have 'betrayed' their companies in the interests of the community have tended to be mobile employees, and particularly women, who have less commitment to their employers, less to gain from company careers, and greater attachment to local communities than other company members. In the second outbreak of Minamata disease, for example, it was women employees at Shōwa Denkō who made public certain of the company's activities which bore on the investigation into the disease.[7]

So far we have been discussing the distribution of wealth between industry and the rest of society. The next question, how wealth and influence are distributed within industry, is answered easily. Companies have the advantage of unincorporated businesses, and (which is partly the same thing) large firms dominate small ones.

The company has become pre-eminent in Japan for the same reason as elsewhere. Because it is a legal personality, the company is able to engage the co-operation of many people, shareholders, employees, lenders, suppliers and customers, in a way quite impossible for an individual entrepreneur; and because it is or can be of unlimited duration the company can plan and conduct business on a time scale beyond the range of any single human being. Companies also tend in most countries — and Japan is no exception — to be taxed much more lightly than individuals. Their marginal tax rates on income are lower, and they are allowed to charge expenses such as interest against tax; besides being immune, of course, from inheritance taxes.

The dominance of large firms over small ones is also seen to some extent in other industrial countries, but it is probably more marked in Japan than anywhere else. We have seen that the bigger a firm is, the more efficient it is (in certain respects at least), the better the equipment it possesses, the more satisfactory the sources of its finance, and the greater its ability to attract able employees. Just as nothing succeeds like success, so the superiority of large firms adds to their advantages. Their cheap finance allows them to undercut their small competitors and become bigger firms and safer borrowers still. Their able graduates run them ever more efficiently and make them yet stronger and more attractive to good recruits. As they turn in these virtuous circles, bigger firms can make use of another advantage. They can depend on small firms to keep them safe in adverse conditions. When a recession comes, Hitachi, Toyota, and Nippon Steel can keep their profit margins high by offering harsher terms to their suppliers and sub-contractors, and in extremities even deprive dependent smaller firms of their livelihood by making for themselves components they previously bought from outside. The primary suppliers and sub-contractors can in turn press hard upon their sub–contractors. The larger an enterprise is, therefore, the more economies of scale and market influence allow it to prevail over smaller rivals, and control and exploit subordinate firms.

The final consideration is how wealth and influence are distributed within the firm. If we take Marumaru as typical, it seems that women are paid lower wages than men, and are effectively excluded from authority in the firm. Among men pay and authority increase to a certain point simply with age, but beyond that they are conferred on those with ability, of which higher education is thought of as a precondition and an emblem.

What, then, is the combined effect of these three component influences? Who does gain and who loses as a result of the position of industry in society, the disposition of firms within industry, and the internal organization of the company? It is clear that the company system favours men over women, the educated over the less educated, and those of middle age over the very young and the old.

The difference between what men and women are offered by the company system is very marked. Women bear more than their share of the burden that industry imposes on the consumer and the citizen. Married women, it is true, need not be dismayed by high prices and low welfare benefits while their husbands are at work. Unmarried women, divorced women and (most significant for the future) widows do not always have male breadwinners to protect them. At the same time, within industry women are paid less than men for doing the same jobs, and have the poorest chances of ever achieving wealth or power. It is admittedly true that no industrial society gives women genuine parity with men in economic affairs, but Japanese women are more rigidly discriminated against than their Western counterparts. In addition, their position is made worse by the fact that skills are of such little account on the labour market, so that they cannot find better jobs by acquiring special expertise.

If the company system gives all men an advantage, it rewards more highly educated men far more generously than men of lower educational standards. Those who stay longest in school and college and go to the 'best' schools have the greatest chances of getting into the biggest and most influential companies, and then of rising within their chosen firms. The less educated a man is the more modest his prospects within industry. If he does enter a big company he will lose in the competition for promotion beyond a certain level. If he joins a smaller one he will be most unlikely to reach the very pinnacle of industrial success, though he may have the consolation of moderate achievement.

To be fair, a man's life-chances are not entirely determined by his education. There are several ways in which he can improve his lot even after he has left school and begun work. There will always be some possibility of a man's being promoted within his firm in spite of his poor academic record. He can go to night school to make good any educational deficiencies — many firms offer night school training to their less educated workers as a matter of course. He may change firms advantageously, a method of progression which has become more common with increasing labour shortage. He may also be lucky enough to be caught up in the success of a small firm, like Marumaru, that manages to become a big one. But all these paths to success are narrow, hard and, all too often, disappointingly short. The ten years of schooling between nine and nineteen provide far more opportunity for advancement than the thirty years of normal working life, from twenty-five onwards. It is incomparably easier for a schoolboy of eleven who is clearly on the way to Tokyo University eventually to become Chairman of Nippon Steel than for an eighteen year-old high school entrant to Marumaru, or even to Nippon Steel itself.

The degree to which industry rewards education and punishes the lack of it has had a formidable effect on the education system. When examinations mean so much, schools have to become crammers and their teachers coaches, while the curriculum reverts to its origin in a race track. It is now becoming essential for candidates for the 'best' universities to go to night schools or special tutors; for if they do not they will not be up to the standard. The physical strain on children of so much work is bad enough, but the moral one is worse. Children, who are anxious enough at the prospect of chancing their own futures on an exam, are often handicapped as much as encouraged by their parents' interest in their success, which will confirm that the whole family is rising in the world — and in their failure. Similar distortions of the education system have occurred in many countries, and for similar reasons. The well-educated people administering the powerful institutions of modern societies recruit to their ranks well-educated people like themselves, largely because well-educated people are genuinely necessary, but also out of self-esteem. Universal and compulsory education systems must select those to be given the highest training, and the selection process once established, selection for higher education becomes a crucial preliminary for selection into the powerful institutions. Because industry is of such moment in Japanese society, because of industrial gradation, and because of the Japanese preference for recruitment from school and college, the influence of industry on education is perhaps more marked in Japan than elsewhere. It should be added, however, that the influence is not entirely malign: the insistence of employers on high educational standards must surely be one reason why Japan does not have the problems of illiteracy that vex the United States or Britain.

It must not be forgotten that there are dangers to industry, too, in the fact that the education system has become its recruiting sergeant. When they commit themselves to taking only graduates and high school leavers from certain institutions, for example, companies put their trust in a process of selection they cannot easily check. If for any reason — and I shall offer one in a moment — the selection becomes biased, then the companies may be badly affected without even realizing it, or, if they do realize it, without being easily able to repair the damage.

The last of the three criteria by which industry chooses its favourites is age. Within most firms, but especially large ones, the older a man is the more his authority and dignity, and the better his pay. But to all except the handful of men who go on to become directors of their firms, retirement brings a decline in power and wealth. At eighteen a man has no authority and little pay. At forty he will be a sub-section head or a section head, with ten or twenty respectful subordinates and something on his name card to impress outsiders. At sixty, if he has a job at all[8], he will be a superannuated worker in the same firm, poorly paid and subordinate to his erstwhile juniors; or else a section or department head in a small subcontractor or associated firm, uncomfortably settled among the native employees. The arrangement of pay and retirement in this way is certainly beneficial to larger firms. They are able to promote younger, more able men in place of less able superannuated workers; and at the same time avoid having to pay higher salaries and to accumulate greater liabilities for separation allowances. Smaller firms gain people with first-class experience, but in taking on outsiders they risk lowering the morale of their younger existing employees. The disadvantage of early retirement on these terms for the superannuated employees is obvious: while they still consider themselves to be in good physical and mental condition they must lose both salary and position. Nor do they benefit in their declining years from the success of the large companies to which they gave the best part of their lives. Yet there are advantages as well. In some ways adjustment to inferior work at the age of fifty-five may be easier than adjustment to no work at all at the age of sixty-five. Moreover, if we allow that firms can only pay their middle-aged workers relatively well because they can superannuate their older ones, then the arrangement does not seem quite so unfair. Each man is borrowing from his old age, when expenses should be limited, to meet the greater expenses of his middle life. It is interesting to note how, in spite of the apparently illogical payment scheme within the individual firm, there is a close correlation between a man's contribution and his rewards over his entire working career. He receives most when he is at the height of his powers, and least when he is either too old or too young to give of his best.

Industry and class

This analysis of the differing effects of industry on people of different sex, education and age is hard to accommodate to the more usual interpretation of industrial society which relies on the concept of 'class'. Whatever the origins of the word 'class', its use today both by sociologists and by ordinary people has probably been most profoundly influenced by Karl Marx. The context for Marx's discussion of the subject was the passage of European societies from feudalism to capitalism, and the anticipated supersession of capitalism by socialism. He conceived of industry, the principal 'means of production' in the advanced capitalist countries, as the source of a distinction between antagonistic capitalist and working classes. The former owned property and thereby controlled the 'means of production'. The latter owned only their capacity to work, which they sold to capitalist employers on an impersonal labour market. Although the labour market appeared to be free and therefore fair, the wages received by the workers were always less than the value of the work they did. The capitalist class exploited the 'surplus value' of labour and used it to perpetuate the capitalist domination of society.

If this formulation was ever wholly applicable in Marx's time, events since then have made it less and less adequate as a guide to understanding even the Western industrial societies Marx himself was concerned with. Marx's general historical predictions have not been fulfilled, and his specific observations on the economy and society of capitalist countries now appear outdated. Within industry there has been, in Professor Dahrendorf's words[9], a 'decomposition' of both capital and labour. The individual capitalist entrepreneur has given place to the joint-stock company — an institution Marx himself recognized as weakening the control of the capitalist over industry, and considered to be a stage towards the capture of the 'means of production' by the proletariat.[10] Managements, too, have altered. Instead of a handful of stewards supervising each enterprise there are large and intricate bureaucracies, whose members comprise a burgeoning middle class. If the undifferentiated working masses ever existed, they have been transformed into a heterogeneous assortment of men and women engaged in different kinds of industry and possessed of different levels of skill; and in some countries workers have to be further distinguished by national origin and culture. There have been significant changes outside industry. Workers have won political and legal equality with their employers. They have used their votes to make governments responsive to their demands, and to institute tax and welfare systems to compensate those subordinate in industry for their inferiority. Partly as a result, the very nature of property, the institution on which the Marxian analysis relies so much, has changed. The rights of ownership over the older forms of property have become less absolute; and new forms of property like pension rights and insurance policies — conditional, social and not transferable — have come to comprise a large proportion of the national wealth.

Such developments have made it less plausible to talk about class in the sense in which Marx used the word. Those sociologists who feel they have to follow Marx at all costs have kept the word and the concept and reorganized reality to fit them. Sociologists who are not Marxists but who have been impressed by the facts that Marx drew attention to, that control over property and superordination and subordination in industry are of great importance in determining a person's position in society, have continued to use the word 'class', but with qualifications. They have cut its part and made it share a dressing-room with similar words such as 'status' or 'stratum'; or they have altered its definition, so that it no longer has exclusive reference to property or industry. In doing this they have risked making the word private, intelligible only to sociologists, or factions of sociologists.

Recently Anthony Giddens[11] has made a subtle and successful attempt to deal with modern European and American societies in terms of class; and to make use of Marx's insights without defending his misconceptions, or perpetuating those of his views that have become outmoded. For Giddens, as for Marx, there are classes because there are labour markets. People sell their labour or, more accurately, their skills on the market in return for wages and benefits. The differences between the market capacities of various types of people are, potentially, the origins of class differences. But every difference of market capacity does not constitute a difference of class. There are no separate classes of dustmen, machinists, farm workers and lawyers; for people can only be said to be aware of a limited number of classes.[12] The question is, therefore, how the differences in market capacity give rise to relatively simple class systems. They do so as a result of two sets of influences. The first set makes it easier or more difficult for people of one market capacity to adopt another. If dustmen and the sons of dustmen often become machinists but scarcely ever become lawyers, then dustmen and machinists may well belong to one class and lawyers to another. Normally there are three sorts of market capacity: ownership of property in the 'means of production', possession of educational qualifications, and ability to do manual labour. Mobility between those with each sort of market capacity tends to be limited: hence a common division into upper, middle and lower classes. The second set of influences on the class system of a given society consists of those arising from the organization of industry (and particularly the division of labour and the nature of authority within it), and from the way in which goods and property are distributed. All capitalist societies, however much they have changed since Marx's time, are 'intrinsically' class societies simply because they have highly developed labour markets; but in each of them classes differ in appearance and significance as a result of political and economic conditions.

The great advantage of Giddens' method of analysis lies in its flexibility. Classes no longer come in a standard, pre-conceived form. Instead they define themselves in each society, and differ from one society to the next. And Giddens', observations by induction from these differences are interesting and sometimes very plausible. He can, however, be criticized for making too rigid a distinction between capitalist societies, intrinsically divided by class, and state socialist ones, which he claims to be potentially and perhaps even actually classless.[13] His argument is also weakened by his failure to discuss the growth of institutional ownership, and the associated changes in the nature of property; so that his account of the upper class a capitalist societies is inadequate.

Now, the peculiarities of the Japanese case are two-fold. Industry remains more important in society than it does in other countries of comparable economic stature; and the decomposition of capital and labour, while in many ways more complete than in the West, has taken place in an unusual way. Industry has retained its influence because the state has done so little to qualify its effects. So uneven has been the distribution of wealth and power through the industrial labour market — consider the difference between the directors of Hitachi and the shop floor workers in a tiny sub-contractor — that one is immediately tempted to apply a Marxian analysis. The temptation is all the greater because it is clear that those at the top enjoy their wealth and power partly at the expense of those at the bottom. But Marx's original formulation is no longer useful. Capital has lost its integrity not by dilution among thousands of shareholders but by introversion: industry has come to own itself. In any case, the bulk of industry's capital comes not from shareholders but from banks; and these in Japan, perhaps more than in any other country, are under the control of professional managers. Labour has been dissociated not into categories of workers of different skills but, more conclusively, into groups of workers attached to different companies. Within each company labour and capital are hardly antithetical. The Hitachi directors are not the representatives of a class of capitalists so much as of the collective interests of the Hitachi employees from whose ranks they came. The shop floor workers in the sub–contractor are not Labour personified. Their position is weak because they belong to a powerless small company. If they were doing the same jobs in Hitachi itself they would be among the more privileged members of society.

It might be possible to preserve the Marxian scheme by assimilating the division between large and small firms to that between upper and lower classes[14], if it were not for two obstacles. In the first place there is a gradation of firms of all sizes, rather than a simple division between the large and the small. Secondly, people move between firms of different size. Most industrial employees who start in larger firms retire to smaller ones; and some employees of small firms join larger ones as mid–career entrants.

If Marx's original methods of diagnosis seem to bring indistinct results, does Giddens' more delicate technique work better? Is it more helpful to consider not class itself but the way in which classes form and the reasons why they persist? Japanese society proves almost as intractable to Giddens as to Marx, and for a simple reason. Marx and Giddens share one fundamental assumption, an assumption which is more justified in a European or American context than a Japanese one. Both of them derive class ultimately from the operation of the labour market. But the labour market they both have in mind is one where individualistic skills search for impersonal vacancies. The Japanese labour market, where employees of different ages and levels of education find employers, is of a different disposition.

There is no need to spoil a strong argument by over-emphasis. The word 'class' is not meaningless in Japan, and the concept is not without application. Within small-scale industry owner-entrepreneurs and those who work for them can easily be put into classes. In large-scale industry, too, the shop floor workers of Hitachi are not always closer to the directors of Hitachi than they are to the shop floor workers of a sub-contractor. In Japan, as elsewhere, the very fact that people can sometimes see society in terms of classes makes class important, whatever the justification for their perceptions.[15] The workers in large companies specifically attract attention to an identity of class interests with other workers when, during wage negotiations, they call themselves 'wage workers' and direct their imprecations against the capitalists who are keeping their wages low. Yet people often exercise an ability to think in circles and move in squares. After all, when the employees of a big company have been inspired by their slogans to win a wage claim which it is beyond their company's immediate ability to pay, the result of their action is to put two or three hundred of their fellow workers in sub-contracting companies out of a job.

There is also some possibility that in the future Japanese society may have more clearly defined classes than it does today. If mid-career job changing becomes more common, and if skills become more marketable — and there are signs that they may — Japan, too, may become 'intrinsically' a class society. If appropriate changes in the labour market were to occur, the extent to which classes did become distinctive and significant would depend largely on the ease with which individuals and families could change their labour market positions. In the past the impartial administration of the education system has made it relatively easy for the sons of the poorest and least educated people in Japan to rise in the world.[16] In the last ten years, however, it has become obvious that children with richer parents are rather more likely than children of poorer parents to go to university, and especially to a 'good' university.[17] The entrance examinations to high schools and universities are as fair as before; but it is easier for the children of the well-to-do to go to the cramming courses that are now necessary to meet the required standards, or to wait a year after failing the exams once in order to sit them again. Attempts to make the state school system more egalitarian, by preventing children applying directly to the famous public high schools which appeared to offer the best chance of entering Tokyo University, have had the perverse effect of encouraging the development of private high schools of excellent academic standard. The richer parents of gifted children, because they cannot be sure of having their children go to a good state school, now send them to these good private schools.

As a result, private schools are taking an increasing proportion of the places at Tokyo. We have seen how within industry education increases a man's chance of money. If money can in turn buy education there are prospects of a new class system, one based less on the labour market than on schools and universities. The immutability of such a system could even be enhanced by the workings of heredity. The educated class might become more intelligent than the uneducated class. There is, perhaps, a greater chance of an hereditary intelligentsia in Japan than elsewhere because of the Japanese practice of arranging marriages. Arrangements may facilitate more thoroughly than romantic chance the matching of rich, educated and intelligent men to the daughters of other rich, educated and intelligent men.[18]

Well within the period required to confirm or prove false these apocalyptic predictions, however, the way in which the education system is ceasing to be a mass transport to success, and is becoming instead a private vehicle of inheritance, may affect the workings of the Japanese company. At present the promotion of graduates to the higher ranks of firms is justified ideologically by the fact that graduates have been pre-selected for ability. The more entrance to higher education depends on being able to afford fees, and the expenses involved in sitting exams twice, the less justification there is for thinking that graduates are necessarily more able than others. At the worst, the rigidity which would result from an education system increasingly at the service of the rich, combined with a labour market which failed to allow employees to improve their positions by changing jobs, might lead to rather more uncomfortable social relations within companies, and encourage antagonism between those in the increasingly discrete categories of manager and worker.

But for the present, the question of who gains most from the organization of industry and of the company is best answered in terms not of class but of sex, age and education. The company system is to the advantage of men, the better educated, and the middle-aged. It is reasonable to suppose that people in these categories will want to conserve it. They will use their influence, which is considerable not least because of the power and wealth that flows to them from industry, to keep the company in its present state.

The forces for change

I have argued that three conditions have maintained the Japanese company as it is. Its organization has been validated by success. It has been protected from change by the logical consistency of its arrangements. It has been endorsed by those who benefit from it. This argument suggests an obvious inversion: that the company will change as a result of failure, or of events which confound the logic of the company system, or of a loss of political support.

Japan has achieved economic greatness so recently, and enjoys it with such confidence, that the possibility seems far-fetched of any universal failure: of her industries being outclassed or her manufacturers and merchants in wholesale disarray. But events during and since the oil crisis suggest that there may yet be failure of a comparative kind, failure to be quite as successful as before, with some effects at least on industry in general and on the company.

499

The recession which began after the major oil exporting countries raised petroleum prices in 1973 was more severe than any other within the last twenty years. Earlier business recessions in Japan tended to be like summer squalls. They were fierce and even dangerous for those not prepared for them, but they were soon over and quickly forgotten. As the demand for goods and services within the country fell, the position of companies became very uncomfortable. Most of them had borrowed from banks the greater part of the funds they needed to run their businesses — and to invest for an apparently rosy future. Unlike dividends to shareholders, which can be reduced in troubled times, bank borrowings are at fixed interest, which must be paid whether the borrower is doing well or badly. Companies were unable, therefore, to diminish the cost of their capital. They also found it difficult to lessen labour expenses. Firms could cut back on overtime and pay off temporary workers, but they could not easily dismiss their permanent employees. Company profits would fall very sharply and many firms would make considerable losses. Companies would adjust to the harsher conditions in two main ways. Firms of all sizes would increase exports, partly in order to keep production lines busy, and partly because exports were usually paid for more quickly than sales to domestic customers. At the same time, large firms would give less business, and on more rigorous terms, to smaller companies, with the result that hundreds of the smallest sub-contractors would go bankrupt. As exports rose, and as domestic interest rates fell because industry was borrowing less money, so the state of the economy would begin to improve. The recovery would be as rapid as the fall into recession had been. Firms would be able to do more business without borrowing more money or employing new workers; and because income would be rising faster than costs, profits would increase quickly. Soon regular employees would be earning overtime payments, and temporary workers would be back at their jobs. They would spend their increased earnings on the goods companies produced, and so encourage industrialists to invest in new factories and equipment and to recruit new staff.

The severity of the 1973–5 recession can be conveyed in a few simple figures. Between 1963 and 1973, a period which included the recessions of 1964–5 and 1970–1, the Gross National Product rose at an average annual rate of more than ten per cent. In 1974 the scale of the economy actually diminished, and even in 1975 the Gross National Product only grew by 2.4 per cent.[19] Equipment was made idle to an extent unparalleled in previous recessions. For most of 1973 firms were working at about ninety per cent. of capacity; by the winter months of 1974–5 they were working at only about seventy per cent.[20] Company profits were vastly reduced. In the first half of fiscal 1973 the profits of large firms represented 3.76 per cent. of their turnover. Two years later the ratio was 0.84 per cent.[21] In fiscal 1973, 9,349 firms went bankrupt. Two years later there were more than 13,000 bankruptcies, and the debts involved had doubled, to more than 2,000 billion yen.[22] Unemployment statistics are not very reliable in Japan, but according to official sources the average number of men without jobs rose from 440,000 during 1973 to 740,000 during 1976.[23]

The 1973–5 recession was more than simply harsh. Its origins in the rise in the price of oil made it qualitatively different from earlier depressions. Previously, when the economy was in difficulties prices fell, or at least ceased to rise quite so fast, in obedience to the laws of supply and demand. As goods and services became cheaper, firms and ordinary individuals would be tempted to spend more money on them, and so demand would be resuscitated. In 1974, however, prices were forced up very rapidly in spite of falling demand because of the new price of oil. People responded by spending less of their money and saving more. On this occasion, then, industry was not to be helped out of trouble by consumer buying.

Again, the increase in the price of oil affected certain types of industry far more profoundly than others. Some industries, such as man-made fibres, suffered badly because oil was their main raw material. Others, like shipbuilding — and most of the ships built in Japan have been oil tankers — had grown with the oil industry itself, and suddenly found their prospects altered for the worse. Clearly, for these industries the oil crisis brought not temporary discomfort but lasting agony. Their decline is likely to continue to have debilitating effects on the whole economy.

Another major difference between the 1973–5 recession and those before it lay in matters relating to foreign trade. As on previous occasions, Japanese companies turned to exports when domestic demand fell. Exports rose from 12,126 billion yen in 1973 to 23,838 billion yen in 1976,[24] this latter sum being enough to cover the greatly increased cost of oil and other imports. But this impressive achievement had — and continues to have — unfortunate consequences. Most of Japan's exports consist of a limited number of commodities, notably cars and transport equipment, electrical goods, steel and chemicals, and the successful Japanese penetration of foreign markets in these goods has caused resentment among Japan's trading partners, who are all too often her competitors. The resentment has been sharpened because Japanese imports of manufactured goods have not increased at a similar rate. To allay criticism and to forestall action against her, Japan has tried to reduce exports and encourage imports by the quickest possible means: the revaluation of the yen against other currencies. Since 1975 the yen has been allowed to appreciate against the United States dollar. The effect on trade has been disappointing, but within Japan large numbers of smaller companies have found themselves unable to compete on world markets and have gone bankrupt. The older and less educated people who worked in these smaller firms could be said to have contributed twice to the Japanese export effort: once in that the low wages they received when they were in employment enabled bigger firms to export fine goods at low prices; and once more in that by losing their jobs they have borne the brunt of the effects of the revaluation that the export drive made necessary. At all events, it has become clear that exports are not only diplomatically embarrassing, but are also the eventual cause of difficulties at home. The certain cure of previous recessions has come to have side effects which aggravate the disease.

In these circumstances, the recovery from the 1973–5 recession has been slow and uneven. While the economy as a whole grew at a respectable rate in 1976 and 1977, many industries were still in poor shape, and the unemployment rate and the number of bankruptcies continued to rise. It is very likely that from now on — and only partly because of the oil crisis[25] — Japan will grow more slowly. Certainly she will have great difficulty in achieving the very high growth rates of the 1960s, when she was able to buy superior foreign technology ready-made and, with her young and growing labour force, use it to make goods for sale on apparently limitless foreign markets. In the 1980s, having caught up with the most advanced nations, Japan will have to innovate

501

for herself. Her labour force will be older. Foreign markets will not be so open. Already, it seems, Japanese industry has begun to accommodate itself to a more sedate pace. Firms are borrowing less and spending less on new plant and equipment; and they are not making such intensive use of plant they already possess.

If there is no difficulty in predicting that the Japanese economy will grow more slowly from now on, it is very hard to say how slower growth will affect the organization of industry. It might have been thought, before the oil crisis, that the Japanese company system was predicated on success, and that it would be seriously disrupted by any lack of it. The precarious financial arrangements of so many Japanese companies and their extensive commitments to their employees, seemed sustainable only in a booming economy. Japan's was a bicycle trick, done at speed or not at all. The behaviour of the Japanese economy during and after the oil crisis has confounded such simple prophecies. If the company system has survived so fierce a jolt, it would be unwise to suppose that it will disintegrate merely because the going is harder and parts of the vehicle are in disrepair. It is more likely that slower growth will cause only gradual and superficial changes in the company system. If the recent fall in bank borrowing is indicative of permanent change, and Japanese companies do reduce their dependence on outside credit, then relations between companies may alter slightly. Bank groups may become even more fragile. Big firms may have slightly less control over small ones. If the economy as a whole is less active, then there will be less assurance that every type of business will do well, and more incentive, perhaps, for firms to diversify so as to be sure of representation in whatever industry is growing fastest. To the extent that in the past firms bought each others' shares in the knowledge that shares in no matter what industry would increase in value, then there may be one less justification for mutual shareholding in the future. But none of these changes is likely to occur precipitately or in revolutionary measure.

Nor is it probable that slower growth will of itself bring drastic alterations to the labour market. Larger Japanese employers responded to the 1973–5 recession, as to previous ones, by restricting overtime, cutting back on recruitment, and transferring workers to subsidiaries.[26] By these means they achieved as rapid a reduction of the actual number of working hours they paid for as American firms during the same period. But the Japanese firms, unlike the American ones, and in spite of the disheartening circumstances, still hesitated to dismiss regular employees. A survey of thirty-one large firms and seventy-four firms of intermediate size over 1974–6 showed that no large firm and only one or two smaller firms dismissed full employees in any year.[27] Even so, the number of regular employees in Japanese manufacturing industry did fall by about nine per cent. between September 1973, when the new oil prices were announced, and September 1976.[28] It is very possible that the proportion of workers enjoying some form of 'lifetime employment' will remain lower than it used to be. But there is no evidence that the employment system or the nature of the labour market has changed, or even that it is not entirely compatible with the new conditions.[29] It must not be forgotten that the slower growth predicted for Japan will not, after all, be very slow, either by comparison with the economic performances of other countries or in relation to the increase in the Japanese population. There is no reason why, simply because the company system worked impressively well when the growth rate was ten per cent. annually, it should not work at least moderately well when the growth rate is merely five or six per cent.

I have already discussed at some length the most important event that is causing the company to change by invalidating the logic of its arrangements. No other development poses as inexorable a threat to the company system as the ageing of the population. We have seen how it affected Marumaru, a company of modest size, in 1970–1. Today the shortage of young people and the growing number of old ones is a matter of the most serious concern to companies of far greater stature. I mentioned earlier that there are two obvious ways in which companies might adjust. They can abandon the 'traditional' Japanese system, by reducing the dependence of pay on age, and raising the age of retirement. The alternative is to preserve the 'traditional' system, by restricting the number of people who can benefit from it. The firm becomes, like construction companies in Japan and elsewhere, an organizing centre run by élite and privileged employees, co-ordinating the activities of dozens of associated companies and sub-contractors.

Either method of overcoming the demographic problem is likely to have important consequences for industry and society. If companies raise the age of retirement and keep their older workers, but at relatively lower salaries, then there may well be changes in the nature of authority within the firm and in the degree of labour mobility between companies. Within the firm, the association between age, status and authority will become weaker. Young managers will often have to command older workers who would previously have been superannuated, and, like the team leader at Marumaru with his older mid-career entrants, they may find it difficult to exercise their authority. The modification of the pay by age system is likely to lead to changes in the labour market. If employees cannot expect their earnings to rise more or less automatically with age and length of service, they will be encouraged to look for better terms with new employers. If mobility increases so, surely, will the significance of skill. Employers will recruit workers with particular skills on the labour market, and will assign them to specialized jobs. On the other hand, if companies adopt the alternative course, and restrict the number of people to whom they offer 'lifetime employment', the organization of industry will change rather less. The drawback of this solution, however, is that it will perpetuate the present distribution of wealth and power in society. The middle-aged and better educated will continue to benefit at the expense of the less educated and the old. I shall return to the question in a moment, but it seems unlikely that such a state of affairs will be politically acceptable to a rather older population.

It is as yet too early to do more than speculate upon which of the two modes of adjustment will become more common. Big companies appear, according to a recent survey[30], to be improvising various adaptations to the problem, without having devised a uniform solution. Some firms have resigned themselves to having to employ more older workers, and are making arrangements to use them more effectively. Nissan Motor, for example, is said to be spending between six and seven per cent. of its capital investment budget on equipment and reorganization aimed at improving the productivity of older workers. Companies like Hitachi and Ishikawajima-Harima have created project teams composed of older employees, and assigned them to tasks, such as design work or running sales campaigns, in which their age is no liability and their experience an asset. Other companies have created subsidiaries specifically to absorb older workers. Nippon Kōtsu Kōsha (the Japan Travel Bureau) encourages superannuated employees to join a subsidiary company which operates booths in department stores and hotels. Sony has a subsidiary called Max Seiki to which its employees over fifty may transfer. Chiyoda Chemical Engineering, Fujitsū, and Konishiroku Photo have all reduced the extent to which pay increases with age. At Chiyoda the salaries of those over the age of forty-two are now to be negotiated with the firm. Many companies, among them Mitsui & Co., Asahi Glass, and Sumitomo Metal Mining, tempt their employees to resign early by offering them larger separation allowances if they do.

Whether the average age of retirement rises or falls, there will still be an increasing proportion of the population beyond working age, or at least beyond the age when people can fully support themselves. Older men and women will have to rely on two sorts of income, state pensions and private annuities. The cost of increasing state pensions can be met simply by raising taxes, and there is no reason to think that a mere increase in taxation will upset the company system. In any case, personal and indirect taxes, which are at present low, will probably rise faster than taxes on industry. But people are unlikely to be content to depend entirely on the state. They will demand company pensions, and will contribute privately to endowment policies. The institutions which manage pension and insurance funds must surely, therefore, become larger and more powerful than they are now. Since their liabilities will be for the long term, they will have good reason to invest in the more durable assets, shares and land. In this they will behave quite differently from today's dominant financial institutions, the city banks, which borrow and lend for the short term. The demand for equities will rise, and there is every prospect, especially if a slower economic growth rate causes firms to borrow less money, of a change in the balance of debt and equity capital in industry. Companies will issue more shares, and, more important, they will have to pay more attention to their dividends; for the pension funds which will control much of their capital will have no other motive for holding shares than to secure income and capital gains. Management goals may therefore have to change. Profit and profitability, the rate of return on assets, may become much more significant; and if they do there will be some effect on social relations within the firm.

Another, rather less potent, threat to the logic of the company system comes from the new requirement that company accounts should be consolidated.[31] A company must incorporate the accounts of its subsidiaries (that is, companies in which it holds more than half the shares) with its own. Before this requirement passed into statute, a company could maintain high levels of profitability and productivity and so justify high wages by exploiting its subsidiaries, the accounts of which were quite separate. The parent company could buy in goods from its subsidiaries at artificially low prices, or require them to hold inordinately large amounts of stock on its behalf. The financial position of the parent company, which might be quoted on stock exchanges and so be bound to make its accounts public, would then appear rather better than it was. Now there is no advantage to a parent company in imposing on its subsidiary, for its subsidiaries' sales, stocks, profits and wages must be counted with its own. But big firms can still maintain themselves at the expense of smaller associated companies, in which they own less than half the shares, and of small sub-contractors which may be wholly dependent on them but in which they may have no stake at all. Moreover, a parent company can always sell some of its shares in a subsidiary to bring its shareholding down to less than fifty per cent. of the whole, and so avoid unpleasant revelations.[32] Consolidation can hardly be said, therefore, to sound the knell of industrial gradation; but it does reduce the value to larger companies of maintaining that gradation, and it may yet have a levelling effect.

Consolidation may also induce companies to place more emphasis on financial measurements and less on market shares. One of the principal methods by which Japanese companies have kept themselves homogeneous is by making their more successful specialized divisions into subsidiaries. An electrical company, for example, with a growing chemical division, may well establish that division as a separate chemical company. The management of the parent company can then continue to run an electrical company in the electrical industry, while the management of the subsidiary becomes the management of a chemical company in the chemical industry. The two companies will not, of course, be independent. Ultimate control over the subsidiary will rest with the parent company, and the subsidiary will be dependent upon its parent for much of its business, and especially, perhaps its credit. The subsidiary will also receive many of its staff from the parent. Nevertheless, the frame of reference of the two companies will be different in many important ways. The managers of each can pursue quite separate aims. The employees will compare their salaries with those offered by 'other firms in the same industry'. Outsiders will distinguish the reputations of the two firms. With consolidation, however, the frame of reference of two companies becomes more nearly the same. The managements both of the parent and the subsidiary now have to bear in mind that the subsidiary is contributing to (or detracting from) the financial standing of the whole group. It would only be a limited consolation, to take an extreme instance, that the subsidiary doubled its sales, if in doing so it halved the profit of the whole group. And just as financial measurements may become more important within the consolidated group, so there may be a tendency to use them to compare one consolidated group with another.

Other, slightly more remote eventualities may upset the system. In recent years, the federations of enterprise unions have joined together to conduct 'spring offensives' for higher wages and better conditions, as well as in support for demands for new government policies. These spring offensives' represent only a limited form of co-operation between unions; but if in the future unions were to draw closer together, and if at the same time the employees of smaller companies were to join unions in greater numbers, it might be more difficult for big companies to impose themselves on small ones, and easier for men to move between companies of all sizes.

There is potential for disruption, too, in the influence of foreigners. Foreign companies in Japan depend for their recruits on the secondary labour market, and they characteristically pay very much higher salaries than Japanese firms to men of given age and experience, and offer their employees greater responsibilities and more rapid promotion. So far, however, the influence of foreign-owned companies has been small. Only a tiny percentage of the working population has been in their employ. They have been unable to attract the kind of people they would have liked, in spite of their high salaries, because they were not well known. In addition, joining a foreign company, because it has meant working for foreigners, has been seen as something socially uncomfortable and mildly unpatriotic.

In the future, however, foreign companies may possibly employ a slightly higher proportion of the working population, though a lower one than in Britain or Germany. Foreign companies may also become better known. Even today IBM is as well known in Japan as its principal Japanese competitor, Fujitsū, and Japanese working for Nestlé or Shell need not fear obscurity. As more foreign-owned companies come to be staffed almost entirely by Japanese, and as the Japanese lose something of their commercial patriotism, the other objections to working for foreign companies may lessen. A time may come when major Japanese companies have to compete seriously with their Western rivals for recruits, and when the loss of middle managers and skilled workers to Western companies may be more than a minor irritant. If it does come, Japanese companies may have to make adjustments of considerable consequence. One of the first might be in the treatment of women. Even today foreign firms probably use their women employees more effectively and offer them better terms than Japanese companies do. Large numbers of well-educated and able Japanese girls already prefer to work for foreign companies. Although their loss to Japanese companies is presently accounted of no significance, an increase in the number and size of foreign firms, and a shortage of educated manpower in Japanese ones, might bring a change first of concern and then of policy.

There is the faint prospect of an even more rapid [change], because [of the] more direct effect of foreign companies on the Japanese company system. If foreigners were able to buy smaller and less efficient Japanese companies in order to improve them and make them better able to compete with their large rivals, then industrial gradation would rapidly become less marked and the privileges of big firms less assured. Foreigners have in the past bought small Japanese firms, but infrequently and with great difficulty, because the risks to the purchaser are considerable and the administrative barriers to the acquisition of Japanese companies hard to surmount. It is unlikely that the Japanese government will make things much easier for foreigners in the future, in spite of full capital 'liberalization'.

In any case, although it might be exciting, especially to Westerners, to picture a struggle on Japanese soil between the opposing company systems of West and East, it is best not to overestimate the extent to which foreign companies in Japan will cause Japanese arrangements to change. Foreign firms no longer have the authority of superior performance. They themselves have a greater respect than before for Japanese practices, and are as likely to allow their Japanese subsidiaries to 'go native' as their Dutch or Canadian ones. Above all, they are made aware by a suspicious government and a vaguely hostile press that they are in Japan on sufferance, and that they must be careful to avoid giving offence or causing an upset.

There is also the possibility that the Japanese company may be altered as a result of its own operations abroad. It might be thought, for example, that the *ringi* system of decision-making would have to be modified, because it would appear cumbersome and even unintelligible to senior foreign employees. This sort of hypothesis underestimates the ability of foreigners to adapt to practices which, though superficially different, are in many ways analogous to their own. It also underestimates the ability of Japanese to preserve their customs. After all, firms like the trading companies and the Bank of Tokyo, which must surely employ as many foreigners as Japanese if all their subsidiaries and affiliates are taken into account, conduct their Japanese operations, at least, in a quintessentially Japanese manner.

The third set of reasons why the company may change concerns its position in society, and the degree of support the industrial order can claim from the population as a whole. Industry has demanded considerable sacrifices of the Japanese people in the past. Two circumstances make it unlikely that it will be able to do so in the future. Industry has diminished its role in Japanese affairs by the very success with which it has played it. The country has become so rich that one need not be so sure that what is good for Mitsubishi is good for Japan. The clearest sign of a change in attitudes is the success of the consumer movements[33], which are frequently led, as one would expect, by women. The most effective of the many campaigns conducted by these movements is still, perhaps, that of Shufuren, the Housewives' Federation, against Matsushita Electric Industrial. When, in 1970–1, Matsushita, together with some of its chief rivals, appeared to be making inordinate profits on television sets in Japan, and to be selling them more cheaply in America than in the home market, Shufuren instituted a boycott of the company's products. After Matsushita's profits had fallen sharply, its management agreed to change its sales practices.[34] Similar campaigns have been directed against cosmetic manufacturers and banks; while property developers and construction companies have frequently been attacked for ignoring the rights and wishes of residents near the sites of their new buildings. The intense activity against pollution in recent years, too, is an indication of the ways attitudes to industry have been changing, as much as of the objective worsening of environmental conditions. Cases of pollution are not, after all, new to Japan. The first Minamata victims were struck down in the early 1950s. Then, however, pollution could be seen as an inevitable concomitant of economic growth, which was necessary for Japan's well-being; and industry could not be too severely censured for disturbing the environment when it was doing so much for the country. Today, however, the citizenry is, rightly, more concerned with the quality of life than with perennial industrial growth; and local communities are less likely to forgive a firm for the nuisances it commits simply because it is providing economic benefits.

The change in the relation between industry and society manifested in consumer movements and pollution campaigns may be accelerated because of a second circumstance. The ageing of the population, which is likely to have such profound consequences on the internal organization of industry, is also liable to affect industry's position in society. It will decrease the proportion of the population who benefit directly from the success and prosperity of industry, and increase the proportion who benefit only indirectly, if at all. The percentage of the population over sixty-five years of age is expected to move from 7.04% in 1970 to 9.52% in 1985 and 11.98% in 1995.[35] This will mean a vast rise in the number of adults (and therefore voters) who are not being looked after by employers, and who have no immediate incentive to allow

507

industry special privileges. Instead, the older people will probably demand better social services from the government, which will in turn no doubt look to industry for the money to provide them. The problem of looking after the older people will be acute, not only because so many of them will be growing old at the same time, but also because they will lack the independent financial resources they might have had, if the firms from which they retired had granted them better separation allowances and pensions. These new old, the burgeoning generations of an ageing Japan, are the very same people who gave their working lives to the economic rebirth of their nation. They will certainly be morally justified in calling for the repayment of the debt due to them. But that will not make it easier to pay, nor help industry to adjust to its new role as supporter of the community rather than its prodigal dependent, Japan's staff rather than her sword.

The political implications of the change in attitudes and in the composition of the electorate are already beginning to be apparent. The relations between government and industry, and between political parties and companies, have never been quite as close and harmonious as phrases like 'Japan, Inc.' imply. They have, however, been closer in the past than they are today. It is clear that the government, instead of closing its eyes to the peccadilloes of companies, is dissociating itself from them as quickly as possible. Cases of pollution, price fixing, or commercial conspiracy against the public interest, which ten years ago the government would have tut-tutted into oblivion, are now made the subject of dramatic enquiries. The most spectacular of these was the summoning to the Diet in 1974 of the presidents of the major trading companies, Mitsubishi, Mitsui, Marubeni, Sumitomo, C. Itoh, Nisshō-Iwai and Tōmen, and of three banks, the Bank of Tokyo, Dai-Ichi Kangyō, and Sumitomo Bank, to explain 'excess profits' and various irregularities, such as tax evasion.[36] There is little doubt that during the years of high inflation immediately after the oil crisis trading companies did increase their profit margins[37], and that companies had in the previous few years been partly responsible for pushing up the prices of a number of commodities, from wool and timber to land. Yet the companies were scarcely the prime cause of the inflation. The blame for that lay with the oil-producing countries and, to some extent, with the Japanese government itself. It was evident from the nature of the Diet proceedings, in which the presidents were not indicted on specific charges nor placed under oath, that the session was what one might call a 'blackwash'. The greatest businessmen of the land were being arraigned not so much for the particular acts their companies had done, as in the role of scapegoats for ills which it was not in the government's power to cure.

Eventually, no doubt, the decreasing importance of industry to society will be reflected in the decreasing importance of the company to the employee. Where he works and what he does at work may become merely an aspect of a man's existence — of more concern, certainly, than his golf club or where he lives — but part of the whole nevertheless. Opinion polls already suggest that people are slowly coming to take a more casual view of their employers, and are less willing to place work above their families and their personal interests.[38] Just as the change in social attitudes to industry as a whole is most easily observable in the activities of those who gain least from industry, particularly women; so within the firm the young men and women whom the company rewards least are the first to detach themselves from it. We saw in the case of Marumaru how young shop floor workers were most interested in affairs outside the firm, and most inclined to think of Marumaru as a means to their particular ends. Young women, from whom the same degree of commitment to work has never been expected, are probably readier than ever to think of their employment as merely a way of getting enough money to marry or to spend a year in Europe. There are signs that companies are having to compete with wives, families and hobbies for the time and energy even of their older workers. Senior managers are constantly inveighing against 'my home-ism', as the Japanese call 'private life', using that same derogatory half-English in which they term an ephemeral singing star a 'talento'. Perhaps in the future industry and the company will lose the friendship even of the highly educated, who, in great contrast to their European and American counterparts, have been industry's most loyal allies. The cleverest graduates of the finest universities will no longer fight to enter banks, and industry will receive as little intellectual honour as in Britain and, increasingly, in America.

Yet though work and the company will surely preoccupy employees less, the change will probably take place only slowly, and may not go as far as in the West. For some time to come the commitment to work and the company will remain strong. Working hours will be long and holidays short. Men will still spend as much time after work with their colleagues as with their wives. It will take the Japanese some time to learn the use of leisure, as opposed to the drinking parties and mah-jong sessions in which they pursue work by other means — though the large number of poetry circles, chess and *go* clubs and bookshops, the packed attendances at musical performances and baseball games, and the enormous if temporary enthusiasm for fads such as bowling, all suggest that they are learning hard. Until government welfare expenditure is greatly increased the Japanese will need to work more than Europeans and Americans do, for less will be provided for them if they do not. They will also continue to be bound by sentiments and ideals which made a virtue of work when work was more necessary to them than it is today: by the community spirit so carefully fostered by Japanese companies, which disengagement from the firm must betray; and by the sense of purpose, progress and service which comes from respect for science, nationalism, and Confucian theory.

Convergence and the search for efficient altruism

Will the result of all these changes be to bring the organization of the Japanese company closer to that of the Western one? Will the systems of West and East converge?

Indeed many considerations make it plausible that they will. The two systems are evidently coming to look alike in some respects. Japanese companies are recruiting from the labour market. Certain firms are making efforts to offer women careers more like those of men. Pay is gradually coming to depend less on age and more on skill and job content. Nor is it simply the Japanese who are changing, for Western companies are adopting Japanese arrangements. In Europe and America firms are offering more and more welfare benefits to their employees, partly because high marginal tax rates make salary rises pointless, and partly because state welfare schemes are proving to be of inadequate quality. Certain European countries have encouraged 'mensualization', the establishment of monthly pay and similar benefits on a uniform scale for employees of all types. Many companies in the West are ceasing to make the products they sell, and are relying on sub-contractors (often in Korea, Taiwan, or Japan itself) to manufacture goods for them to market under their own brand names. In the United States the recent decline in stock markets has caused companies to depend more on borrowed money and less on equity capital. The Joint Shop Stewards Committees in British factories have some of the characteristics of a Japanese enterprise union, in that they are confined to one firm, that their interests are opposed to those of the Committees of other firms, and that the shop stewards, like Japanese union leaders, hope for careers within the firm rather than within their unions, once their term of office is over.

In many cases the convergence of form is the result of the application of identical principles. Japanese companies are beginning to pay more attention to skill and job content partly because it is by reference to these attributes that it makes the best sense to employ mid-career entrants; and this is one of the chief reasons why Western firms rely so much on the idea of 'skill'. American companies have turned to sub-contracting for the same reasons as Japanese ones: to keep their market shares and pay high salaries at the same time. The British Joint Shop Stewards Committees are as much a recognition of the central importance of the corporation in fixing terms of employment as Japanese enterprise unions.

Yet there are many powerful reasons why a simple convergence seems most unlikely. It is not easy to find much justification in what has happened to Japanese industry in the past for a 'convergence hypothesis'. The organization of Japanese and Western industry was probably more similar in 1910 than in 1970. Many of the apparently exotic features of Japanese industry on that latter date — pay by age, 'lifetime employment', mutual shareholdings among companies, and so on — were not entirely or even largely historical residues which were slowly fading away. On the contrary, they were the results of relatively recent developments, which occurred when Japan had already had several decades of industrial experience and should, if convergence had been taking place, already have been half-way along the path to uniformity.

Next, in so far as there are Japanese and Western company systems (and the systems really exist as simplified extrapolations from an enormous variety of companies in different places and different industries, and of a multitude of sizes, qualities and shapes) the two are logically coherent and yet mutually incompatible. Similar forces acting on each of them do not have similar effects. Convergence between them, when it occurs, does not take the form of a steady progression. Instead it is discontinuous and desultory. Something may cause one aspect of the Japanese company to become more like an aspect of the Western company. As a result there may be further changes in the logically related aspects of the Japanese company. Some of these secondary changes, too, may be convergent, but others may be positively divergent because of the incompatibility of the two systems. It is possible to see this effect in the reactions of Japanese companies to the ageing of the working population. A firm can reduce the dependence of pay on age, and so bring its pay system closer to those in the West. Yet at the same time it can force its employees to transfer to subsidiaries at an early age, and so emphasize a Japanese organizational trait.

The third and perhaps most convincing argument against any idea of a general convergence in the future is that in Japan and in each of a dozen Western countries changes are taking place in quite separate directions. The British experiments with nationalization, and with the admission of trade unions to the councils of government, have not been repeated in the United States. The new rules for the administration and investment of American pension funds, which may in the long run have a considerable effect on the organization of industry, have no parallel in West Germany. The worker directors of that country do not have Japanese counterparts. Japanese statutory auditors, on whom great formal powers have been conferred by law, are not easily comparable with company officials anywhere else. It appears that developments in industry are no more conspicuously convergent than developments in politics, or broadcasting or literature. They have considerable relevance to what is going on in other societies, certainly, because of common preoccupations and much imitation; but they are at the same time conditioned by indigenous traditions, and prompted by forces and events different, and differently combined, from those in other nations.

Where does the future of the Japanese company lie, if not in simple convergence with the Western pattern? The forces for change are acting in two directions. Some are altering the nature of authority within the firm; others are affecting its position in society.

The Japanese company today represents an impressive solution to the problem of authority in industry. The employees, or more accurately male employees, of each company, matured by experience and chosen on merit, have exercised authority in a spirit of self-conscious harmony and public service. Their authority has been acceptable to those they commanded because their subordinates, given time and the acquisition of merit, could expect to have their own term in office; and because those in command used their authority in what was so obviously the best interests of those beneath them. In the future the ideological justification of authority may be less sure. There will be greater scope for debate about the nature of merit and the rightness of seniority. It will no longer be quite so plausible to talk of harmony or claim the privilege of public service. Some may even dispute the grounds on which men may rule women. The exercise of authority will also become more difficult, because it will no longer be so easy to arrange that everyone has a turn at the wheel, and because it will be harder to persuade subordinates that they are being disciplined for their own eventual benefit.

The position of the firm in society has been one of nearly unquestioned privilege. On the assumption that Japan must gain from it, the Japanese company has been allowed to pre-empt much of the wealth of the country and exert enormous influence; and it has been able to use that wealth and influence on behalf of its employees. From now on, the firm will surely have to give more to others and expect less for itself. It will have to pay pensions and support government programmes, and at the same time accept restrictions of law and public opinion.

The two sets of changes will be all the more disturbing because they call for almost irreconcilable adjustments. Firms have been well disciplined precisely because they have been selfish. The inner harmony of the company has depended on an opposition between each firm and others, and each firm and the rest of society. It will therefore be extremely difficult for the Japanese company to maintain its superb discipline, and at the same time learn to be charitable.

This difficulty is scarcely confined to Japan. No country has yet evolved what every advanced industrial society urgently needs: an association for production which is both efficient and altruistic. It must be efficient because it is only by the best possible use of materials and skills that rich nations can hope to stay rich. It must be altruistic because so many citizens cannot work for themselves. They are too old, too young, too preoccupied with education, or too weak to meet exacting standards, and they have therefore to be supported by others. Yet the common conditions of such societies make both efficiency and altruism hard to achieve. Educated workers, taught to think themselves every man's equal, will not have discipline thrust upon them. Money scarcely buys their acquiescence, certainly not their commitment. They must be persuaded or inspired into efficient order. At the same time, altruism is daunted by limitless needs and impersonal masses. People must give more and give willingly, but to an immensity of strangers. And everywhere efficiency and altruism seem to be counterpoised. One can only be had at the expense of the other. The conspiracies are well ordered, whether they are Japanese trading companies, American law firms, or British merchant banks. The instruments of service — schools, welfare bureaucracies, or nationalized industries — are poorly organized, confused in purpose, and often resented both by those who support them and those they are trying to aid.

By a happy set of circumstances, while the country was developing, and most of the population was young and at work, the Japanese company achieved a miracle of organizational alchemy. It was the efficient giver, the beneficial competitor, and the selfish philanthropist. It cannot be so in the future. To this extent there has been convergence, that Japan now shares the perplexity of other developed countries: how can wealth be created with energy and resolution, and yet distributed with compassion?

Starting from where they do, with their own talents and impediments, the Japanese are most unlikely to reproduce the particular compromises made in the West. We experiment with worker participation in the hope of achieving co-operative discipline, while trying to avoid licensing plots against the public interest. They have to organize kindness without copying our mistakes. They will strike their own balance, and we must hope that it will be successful. At any rate, they bring to the problem three great advantages. They have the opportunity and the ability to learn from others. They are ready to change, and yet have so far been able to resist utopian blandishments. They have, in the Japanese company, which has brought them so much so quickly, promising material to work upon.

Notes

1. For a comparison see Joseph A. Pechman and Keimei Kaizuka (1976) 'Taxation.' In Patrick, H. and Rosovsky, H. (eds) *Asia's New Giant*. Washington D.C., The Brookings Institute.

2. Yokota Tetsuji*, *Gyūniku wa naze takai ka* (Why is beef expensive?) Tokyo, Saimaru Shuppankai, 1977. For an account of the reaction to this publication see *Asahi Shinbun*, 13 July 1977, p. 3. 'Takai gyūniku: kaigai de mo akuhyō (Expensive beef: notorious even abroad).

3. By the rules of the Bank of Japan, a high proportion of pension fund money must be lent, rather than invested in land or shares, which have a better chance than loans of keeping their value. The rate of return on pension trust funds tends, therefore, to be below the rate of inflation. Trust banks systematically benefit by requiring companies to which they have lent money from their pension trusts at a low nominal rate of interest to deposit 'compensating balances' in the trust banks' banking accounts. This money can then be lent on to other borrowers, to the advantage of the banks.

4. For an account of these and similar cases see S. Prakash Sethi (1975: 77–93), *Japanese Business and Social Conflict*. Cambridge, Mass., Ballinger Publishing Co.

5. *Asahi Shinbun* (evening edition), 29 November 1971, p.9, 'Ichi-kabu kabunushi o katasukashi: Chisso Sōkai' (The Chisso general meeting: dodging the one-share shareholders).

6. For a lucid discussion of the Japanese labour unions and pollution see Shirai Taishirō* (1971).

7. Asahi Nenkan* (The Asahi Yearbook) *1972*: 236. This source also gives an account of a campaign by an enterprise union against pollution by a company. In the spring of 1970 the union of an oil refining company, General Sekiyū Seisei, incorporated demands that the company cease polluting the environment into the programme for its 'spring offensive'. In the course of the union's campaign nine workers were dismissed, and the company tried to found a rival, docile 'second union'.

8. Though most older workers do find jobs after retirement some cannot, especially during slumps. See *Nihon Keizai Shinbun*, 18 September 1976, p. 3, 'Kōreisha no Shitsugyō' (Rapid increase in unemployment of old). A Ministry of Labour survey conducted in 1974 showed that just over a third of a sample of more than 5,000 men who had retired had been out of work at some stage, usually immediately after retiring. Most of those who had been out of work had had no job for more than three months. *Rōdōshō: Rōdōkijunkkoku: Teinen Tōtatsusha Chōa no Kekka*. (1975): 12–14 (Ministry of Labour: Standards Bureau: Results of the survey of workers of retiring age).

9. Ralf Dahrendorf (1959: 36–71) *Class and Class Conflict in Industrial Society*. London, Routledge & Kegan Paul.

10. 'This result of the highest development of capitalist production is a necessary transition to the reconversion of capital into the property of individual producers, but as the common property of associates, as social property outright.' Karl Marx (1909: 517), *Capital* Vol III, Chicago, Charles H. Kerr & Co. Marx goes on to mention, however, that the mechanism of the joint-stock company emables individual entrepreneurs to raise outside funds, and so greatly increases their influence.

11. Anthony Giddens (1973: especially 100–12). *The Class Structure of Advanced Societies,* London, Hutchinson.

12. It is not entirely clear from Giddens' main discussion of the subject why there are only a limited number of classes (106). It is only later (134) that we learn that 'class structuration always presupposes at least class awareness'. I have therefore, perhaps unjustifiably, filled in the missing term of a syllogism.

13. Cf. W.G. Runciman (1974: 110–11). 'The Class Structure of the Advanced Societies', *British Journal of Sociology,* Vol. 25, pp. 108–11.

14. Cf. the attempt made by Ōhashi Ryūken* (1975: 105–13) to determine whether people in firms of different sizes belong to a ruling or a subordinate class, defined in Marxian terms.

15. A good explanation of how the Japanese themselves conceive of a class is to be found in Yasuda Saburō* (1973). Japanese tend to be less willing than people in many Western countries to think in terms of classes, or to divide society into 'them' and 'us'. Dr Yasuda's discussion of the increasing complexity of antagonistic relationships in Japanese society (206–8) parallels many of my arguments.

16. An account of the way in which education contributed to the careers of Japanese business leaders active in 1960 can be found in Hiroshi Mannari (1974: 64–82), *The Japanese Business Leaders,* Tokyo, University of Tokyo Press. A subsequent survey of business leaders in 1970 showed that though they were more highly educated than their 1960 counterparts, yet there was a smaller proportion among them of men of lowly origin. The sons of clerical and manual workers seemed to be finding it harder rather than easier to reach the top of industry. It should be noted, however, that if changes in educational selection are partly responsible for this tendency, they are changes which must have taken place thirty or forty years ago.

17. Much of this paragraph is based on Thomas P. Rohlen (1977), 'Japanese Education Becoming Less Egalitarian?' *Journal of Japanese Studies,* Vol. 3, No. 1, pp. 37–70.

18. Dore, R.P. (1975) 'The Future of Japan's Meritocracy'. In Fodella, G. (ed) *Social Structures and Economic Dynamics in Japan up to 1980.* Milan, Luigi Bocconi University.

19. OECD (1977: 6).

20. Calculated from the index of operating ratios published in *Keizai Tōkei Geppō* (Economic Statistics Monthly), on the assumption that the true operating ratio in the base year of 1970 was about ninety per cent. Cf. OECD (1977: 19 n).

21. *Keizai Tōkei Geppō* 356*: (November 1976): 131–4: Tables 90, 91V.

22. *Oriental Economist* 45: 806 (December 1977): 44.

23. *Nippon Tōkei Geppō* (Monthly Statistics of Japan) 198 (December 1977): 8: Table A–5.

24. OECD (1977: 53, Table A) *Economic Surveys: Japan.*

25. A good brief discussion is in OECD (1977: 26–7).

26. Details are given in Haruo Shimada (1977), from which much of the material in this paragraph is drawn. 'The Japanese Labour Market After the Oil Crisis', *Keio Economic Studies.* Vol. 14, No. 1, pp. 49–65.

27. Haruo Shimada (1977: 62, Table 9). A few firms did, however, solicit resignations. Cf. p. 183 above.

28. Calculated from figures given by Haruo Shimada (1977: 56–7, Table 5).

29. Cf. Haruo Shimada's own conclusion (1977: 64).

30. *Nikkei Business*, 23 May 1977, pp. 36–49, 'Kōreika shakai no kōzu' (Design for an ageing society: Japan).

31. For a discussion of consolidation see Robert J. Ballon *et al.* (1976: 243–52), *Financial Reporting in Japan.* Tokyo, Kodansha.

32. Kluge, H. (1977) *Financial Reporting in Japan.* Tokyo, Sophia Univ. Socio–Economic Research Institute Bulletin, No. 67.

33. A good case study in English of one of these is Savitri Vishwanathan (1977).

34. The chairman of Matsushita was later to remark that his company, too, had suffered from its own policy of 'dual pricing', and that he was glad that it had been forced to change its ways. *Asahi Shinbun*, 4 February 1971, p. 8. 'Zesei wa shōhisha no chikara'. (The correction was the power of the consumer).

35. Ōbuchi Hiroshi* (1975: 233) and Yamaguchi Kiichi* (1972: 43–6).

36. The proceedings took place from 25 February 1974, and accounts of them are to be found in all the major Japanese newspapers.

37. Return on equity of the three biggest trading companies (parent company figures only) between 1970–4 was:

Six months to	Sept 1970	March 1971	Sept 1971	March 1972	Sept 1972	March 1973	Sept 1973	March 1974
Mitsubishi	15.1%	15.3%	9.0%	14.3%	18.3%	18.5%	18.1%	17.4%
Mitsui	16.5%	15.8%	12.3%	14.5%	15.9%	14.1%	12.6%	15.2%
Marubeni	11.2%	11.7%	8.8%	10.2%	13.3%	16.2%	19.0%	17.9%

Source: Daiwa Securities Co., Ltd. *Analysts Guide, 1975.*

Note that Mitsui at least did not profit greatly from the oil crisis. It should also be recognized that much of the increase in profits came from 'stock profits', arising from the sale of stocks of goods bought at the lower prices prevailing before the oil crisis. 'Current cost' accounting methods would yield a much lower profit rate.

38. Sepp Linhart (1975: 204–8). 'The Use and Meaning of Leisure in Present Day Japan'. In Beasley, W.G. (ed) *Modern Japan: Aspects of History, Literature and Society*. London, George Allen & Unwin.

* For Japanese references refer to original text.

31. The Price of Affluence: The Political Economy of Japanese Leisure
Gavan McCormack

It is well known that Japan has in the past decade developed into an economic superpower — the world's greatest asset country, with the biggest per-capita GNP, the biggest aid budgets, home to all ten of the world's biggest banks and many of its biggest corporations, the base for 15 per cent of the world's economic activity, the centre of the most dynamic sector of the world trading system, whose land value is estimated at four times that of the United States, whose resource flows help keep the US dollar afloat, whose factories supply quality goods to the world, and whose construction companies are engaged in huge infrastructural projects across the globe.[1]

From this it is common to assume that Japan is resoundingly successful, the very model of success, and that its people are correspondingly wealthy and enjoying the fruits of that success. It is true that consumer income has risen to the point that sixty million cars clog the highways; one third of the world's tuna catch and two fifths of its shrimps pass through Japanese stomachs; one quarter of the world's tropical timber is imported.[2] But gourmet foods, overseas travel, cars and electronic gadgetry do not make up for housing inadequacy, lack of basic amenities such as sewerage, too few public parks and spaces, lack of time do one's own thing. High general levels of dissatisfaction with living conditions raise serious questions. On comparative tables Japan matches or surpasses the advanced capitalist countries of Europe and North America only in per-capita income, television sets and electronic equipment.[3] Nomura Research Institute reckons that even by 1995 Japan will still be well behind countries like the US and (West) Germany in terms of living standards.[4] In December 1990 it was reported that the average price of a 57-square-metre apartment in Tokyo was 80 million yen, or twelve times the average Tokyo resident's annual income, and that metropolitan housing was forty times oversubscribed.[5] Corporate prosperity has reached unparalleled heights while social poverty is real and widespread. Capitalism has always developed unevenly, but at a time when its productive capacity excites unalloyed admiration worldwide these contradictions deserve close attention.

Japan has steered its economic course with remarkable agility through the oil shocks and consequent economic restructuring of the past two decades. It has apparently led the way in the transition from a base in the 'modern' industries characterized by the 'heavy, thick, long and big' (ju-ko-cho-dai) industries of steel, ships, petrochemicals, and so forth, to the 'postmodern' or information-society industries characterized by the 'light, thin, short and small' (kei-haku-tan-sho) of the high technology and service sector. It is the particular recent shift into leisure industries, and its broader implications for economic and social policy, that are addressed in this paper. In short, is the massive effort to increase the range and qualities of recreational facilities

Gavan McCormack: 'The Price of Affluence: The Political Economy of Japanese Leisure', *NEW LEFT REVIEW* 188, (July-August 1991).

available in Japan a sign that the good life is beginning to dawn for citizens? Or is it merely an expression of that characteristically post-modern game, the casino, which is non-productive of social wealth, addictive, has many losers, and offers little solace even for its winners?

This article is based partly on an extensive study of regional development, planning, the impact of economic restructuring on remote local communities, and on the environment, undertaken between December 1989 and January 1990, which took me from sub-tropical Ishigaki island in the south to the farthest reaches of Hokkaido. I have also made use of the growing Japanese literature on these subjects, and some excellent documentary film material, virtually all in Japanese.[6]

The first paradox is that the massive increase in physical amenities is not accompanied by any increase in the time available for people to enjoy them. The leisure market was about 52 million million yen in 1985 and set to double by the turn of the century, but at the same time the average Japanese work year remains at 2,168 hours, virtually unchanged from the mid 1970s — between 200 and 500 hours more than elsewhere in the industrialized world and roughly on a par with Europe during the period of economic recovery in the early 1950s.[7] Fewer than 20 per cent of Japanese workers enjoy a two-day weekend; overtime, at an average of 190 hours per year, has increased since 1986 and annual paid leave in Japan amounts on average to 9 days, as against 19 in the US, 24 in the UK, 26 in France and 29 in (West) Germany.[8]

Although availability of leisure time seems scarcely to match that of facilities, the need for recreation seems clear, not only on the basis of reward for contribution to achievement but evidently also on the basis of physical need, since the Welfare Ministry figures show an eightfold increase in the general rate of ill health in the community between 1955 and 1985, with high blood pressure and nervous disorders marked by much greater increases.[9] Sudden death from overwork (*karoshi*) has become a widely noted social phenomenon.[10] It is perhaps not surprising that 58.5 per cent of people polled by the Economic Planning Agency in 1988 should say that their level of leisure, or time and space to do their own thing (*yutori*), was inadequate.[11]

Corporate Japan has recognized the existence of the problem and devised a battery of high-tech and ingenious solutions to stress, other, that is, than what might be thought the obvious — reduction in working hours, decentralization of population, and provision of facilities for cheap relaxation in natural surroundings. They include special kinds of chewing gum, meditation chambers (with one hundred 'PSY Brain Mind Gym Relaxation Salons' to open across the country in 1990), womb-like 'Refresh Capsules', equipped with tape facilities which allow one to be completely immersed in the environment of 'murmuring brooks, singing birds, and gently breaking waves' — the environment, in other words, that is rarely experienced in reality.[12]

The resort boom

One would like to think the Comprehensive Resort Region Provision Law, commonly known just as the 'Resort Law',[13] which passed the Diet in 1987, was part of a serious attempt to address the social need for rest, recuperation and return to nature, but the evidence suggests otherwise. The legislation specified reliance on 'utilizing the abilities of private entrepreneurs' to ensure the comprehensive provision of sporting, recreational, educational and cultural activities in 'areas possessing good natural conditions'. It had an immediate and remarkable effect. Towns, villages and prefectures throughout the country entered into such intense competition to be designated as 'resort' areas that as of December 1989 19.2 per cent of the entire land area of Japan was involved. 646 projects had reached the 'works' stage by then, with a further 205 at the planning level.[14] This means that much more of Japan's land area is to be devoted to 'resort' activities (7.25 million hectares) than to agriculture (5.5 million hectares).[15]

Ski resorts, golf courses and marinas sprout like autumn mushrooms. They rejoice in suggestive names such as Mie Sunbelt Zone, Aizu Fresh Resort, Snow and Green My Life Resort Niigata, Gunma Refresh My Life Resort, Chichibu Resort, 40° Longitude Seasonal Resort Akita, Nagasaki Exotic Resort, and so on. For the island of Kyushu, for example, 26.7 per cent of the land has been incorporated in plans for 135 resorts with an estimated investment of about 300 thousand million yen, including 100 golf courses and 10 Disneyland-type 'space-world' theme parks.[16] As for Okinawa, the poorest prefecture in Japan, all seventy of its islands have been declared a 'Tropical Resort'. Efforts are underway to increase the current 2.4 million annual tourist intake to 'Hawaiian' levels of about 6 million by the end of the century.[17]

Golf is a quintessential resort activity. The *Asahi* estimate in March 1990 was that Japan had 1,700 golf courses in existence, 325 under construction, 983 at the planning stage, and many more under consideration. The number planned or under construction had doubled during 1989. Japan, which had a mere 100 courses in 1955, will, when the 2,085 courses in existence or under construction are completed, have nearly 170,000 hectares, or 0.54 per cent of its narrow, mountainous lands devoted to golf.[18] This frenzied activity seems an ironic response to the need for relaxation and leisure. There is no real parallel for the phenomenon in other advanced industrial countries, although the forces driving it in Japan are now also expanding rapidly throughout the Pacific region. The economic, social and environmental implications are worthy of attention.

How do golf courses get built? Capital costs for an 18-hole course in the Osaka vicinity are estimated to be about 200 thousand million yen, so if one thousand members can be subscribed at an average of 40 million yen there is already a 100 per cent profit. Such profit is often realized before the course even opens. Club memberships are tradable commodities whose value has rocketed in recent years, appreciating by about 400 per cent between 1982 and 1989, and by an additional 190 per cent during 1989.[19] A course under construction in Chiba prefecture, just outside Tokyo in the so-called 'Golf Course Ginza' area, has a capital cost of 7 thousand million yen. The company concerned plans to put up 80 million yen of its own money and to enroll 1,400 members. This enrolment is done in several stages, membership being offered first to a limited group of several hundred at a special charter rate of about 3 million yen and gradually increasing through subsequent tranches to about 10 million yen. In this case, and if all goes well, the initial investment of 80 million yen yields a return of 3 thousand million yen. Since the average membership on the Osaka exchange is around 40 million yen, or four times what the last ones in this venture had to pay, no one is likely to complain. Nowadays million-dollar-membership country clubs (*okukan*) proliferate, and prices can range up to 400 million yen-plus for those who aspire to the exclusive.[20] One of the many attractive features of the golf-club corporate assets deriving from membership fees is that, technically, such monies are regarded as merely temporarily deposited funds, and are therefore not taxable.[21] A similar analysis can be made for ski-course developments. Currently there are between six and seven hundred of these, also expanding rapidly.[22]

The economic and social consequences of this type of development may be serious, particularly in terms of the in-built potential for corruption. The politicians, bureaucrats, and local or national men of power and influence who are enrolled as charter members of a country club at highly discounted rates have a vested interest in seeing that the permits for fast-track construction are secured and local opposition defeated. The proliferation of courses, with its attendant inflationary spiral, seems destined to continue. Politicians, who need a million dollars-odd a year to run their political machines, are enthusiastic about their new milch-cow, especially since the Supreme Court in 1982 held that club memberships were not valuable securities, so that there can be no issue of bribery involved.[23] The memberships are traded, and are used as collateral for bank loans, so the Supreme Court was taking a very narrow view. If the currently projected 1,500 courses were to go ahead, each with two to three hundred 'charter' members, the web of vested interest, whether or not technically one of corruption, is spun over an influential section of the population, perhaps 300,000 people.

In short, the golfing phenomenon is more supply-side driven than it is in response to increased demand (although that too has increased, and there were an estimated ten million players as of the end of 1988).[24] And it is from the castles of money built around the redoubts of golf in Japan than much of the expansion into the tourism and resort industries around the Pacific rim, especially Queensland, is financed. By the end of 1989 there were about one hundred overseas Japanese courses, as well as the many hotels and other resorts.[25] The Japanese offer, several years ago, to buy all the private courses in the Sydney area becomes understandable against this background.[26]

Environmental impact

In the long run, however, it is the environmental impact of the current golf boom that may be the most serious factor. Economic circumstances may cause many of the rash of resorts currently being built to collapse, sooner or later, but the swathes of the Japanese countryside now being cleared for development will not quickly recover. A golf-course development needs a site of about 100 hectares, preferably in undulating countryside with good access to major population centres. There are no such sites left free of housing or agricultural development in Japan. Consequently, as Kunihiro Yamada describes it, 'much golf course development has occurred in forested areas at the foot of mountains. Developers clear-cut the forests and use bulldozers to level off hilltops and fill in valleys. In this way, golf course construction is tantamount to the destruction of forests, pure and simple. Even though 67 per cent of Japan's total land area is covered by forests, its forest products self-sufficiency rate has fallen to only 30 per cent.'[27]

However, the passage of the 'Resort Law' was marked by a political and bureaucratic consensus at the highest level. In its wake, therefore, a series of administrative measures, and some other new laws, have been adopted to ease the restrictions on the use of agricultural or national-park, forest, water-catchment or other semi-public lands for resort purposes.[28] Tax breaks are generous, various financially attractive packages of incentives are offered, and administrative procedures are simplified. Not only is the area of land involved far greater than during the ill-famed 'Remodelling The Japanese Archipelago' years of the Tanaka government in the mid seventies, but legal and administrative measures then adopted to protect national parks and the mountain and coastal environment have been watered down or abandoned in the name of an officially promoted 'Human Green Plan'.

The 'green' quality of the mountain and coastal resorts promoted under this scheme is deceptive. In the case of each golf course, it is achieved by the application of three to four tons per year of herbicides, germicides, pesticides, colouring agents, organic chlorine and other fertilizers, including chemicals that are carcinogenic or cause various health abnormalities.[29] The Naoki Prize-winning author, Osamu Takahashi, describes the hills of Chiba prefecture over which one flies on approach to Narita Airport as resembling defoliated Vietnam, and likely to take as long to recover.[30] This rich brew, three times the intensity of what the most chemically minded farmer would apply to tomatoes, ultimately drains off into rivers, ponds, swamps, lakes or sea.[31] The Ministry of Health has found 950 places where the quality or quantity of water has been adversely affected by golf development.[32] Widespread damage to animal, bird, insect, marine and human life has been reported, and an environmental citizens' movement is being organized to oppose it. Though Okinawa was only returned to Japanese jurisdiction in 1972, already over 80 per cent of its coral is dead, its best beaches privatized, and its inshore fishermen reporting drastically reduced catches.[33] To meet the anticipated demand for water for tourist development to come, all the rivers of Okinawa must be dammed, which will wreak havoc on their upstream ecology and hasten the silting of their mouths.[34] The Japan Ecological Association has expressed profound concern at the damage being done to nature in the name of leisure, particularly at the encroachment on national parks. The denuding and remoulding of mountains for ski purposes also causes landslides, and the Association estimated that a single development might be responsible for the loss of the equivalent of between one and two hundred ten-ton dump-truck loads of soil into surrounding rivers in a year.[35] The case of a small island such as Awajishima, where developers plan to add ten new golf courses to the existing two, is indicative of the extraordinary dimensions of the problem.[36]

When one realizes that 'development' in Japan has — according to the Environment Agency — brought 628 of Japan's wildlife species and 899 of its wild plants to the brink of extinction, the potentially catastrophic consequences of current policies may be appreciated. Among the threatened fauna are the Satsuki trout of the Nagara River, the Iriomote wildcat of Okinawa, the crested ibis of Sado Island, the mudskipper (or *mutsugoro*) of Ariake Bay, the striped owl, the Japanese otter and the snow goose; among threatened flora are the fringed orchid and the primrose.[37]

521

Land price inflation

The process nevertheless proceeds with apparently inexorable force, driven by complex economic motivations. The problem of land-price inflation is central. Though Japan's commodity-price inflation level is among the lowest of industrial countries, the rate of land-price inflation has no contemporary (and perhaps no historical) precedent. It may be argued that Japan operates a dual currency system: the yen on the one hand, and 'land currency' (*doka*) which is linked to the real estate market and to political interests, the relationship between the two being articulated by bank credit issued against land or stock securities.[38] The scale of inflation of Japan's land and stock values over the past twenty years is remarkable.

Land-price inflation far exceeds growth rates in the 'real' economy, while at the same time driving it. Through the 1970s, Japan's GNP increased fivefold but its land assets tenfold, a disproportion that has continued to widen.[39] The real-estate industry, which employs about 790,000 people, generates an operating surplus almost on a par with manufacturing, which employs 14.68 million.[40] Its exponential growth has out-performed all other sectors of the economy. Needless to say, there is no net addition to real national wealth or welfare in this. The reverse may be true if one considers the burden for millions of ordinary people whose lives are outside the virtuous circles of speculation and for whom escalating land prices represent a nightmare. Land constitutes 65 per cent of Japan's national wealth, against comparable figures of 25 per cent for (West) Germany, 33 per cent for the US, and a mere 2.5 per cent for the UK.[41] On current prices a piece of land about 100 square metres in central Tokyo could be exchanged for a castle in Europe or a modest-sized island in Canada or Australia. The proportion in contemporary Japan appears to be without historical precedent, although England before the Glorious Revolution of 1688 went close.[42]

Let me turn back to the context within which the 'Resort State' of contemporary Japan evolved. Since the huge Japanese trade surpluses began to build up from the early 1980s, Japan has faced pressures arising from its trade 'wars' to prime its domestic pump and to promote imports. At the same time it has faced the growing discrepancy between life in Tokyo and the metropolitan megalopolis along its eastern seaboard and the rest of the country, particularly rural Japan. The attempts under the various 'Comprehensive National Development Plans', including the 'Technopolis' strategy, had achieved little, agriculture was in profound recession, with the rice support price being steadily reduced from 1986. Stockpiles of rice consumed huge subsidies, while perhaps only half the country's 200,000 hectares of rice fields would be enough to feed the people. Other agricultural and forest industries were also in crisis, especially from the consequences of trade liberalization. Japan's nationally owned forest enterprises were sunk in an apparently inescapable fiscal bog, with a cumulative deficit for the period 1975–88 of over 800 thousand million yen and a long-term debt of nearly 1.9 million million yen built up over the same period.[43] The insistence, under the 'administrative reform' principles of the 1980s, that they pay their way left no alternative to the removal of barriers to the 'development' of national lands and the active promotion of 'resort'.

Farm, fishing and mountain villages throughout the country were suffering from enormous debts, depopulation, ageing, isolation, and despair over the constant shifts and abandonment of one after another national policy for their recovery. With the massive appreciation of the yen following the 'Plaza' agreement of May 1985 these pressures became acute. The 'old style' export industries of steel and ships were shaken, manufacturing went offshore rather than to the regional bases designated under the various plans, and agriculture was again sacrificed to the imperative of expanded imports. The Maekawa Report of April 1986 enunciated these themes most clearly. Huge infrastructural, urban development and land-release programmes were undertaken. Reliance on the private sector (*minkatsu*) was the watchword throughout, and the domestic economy was both awash with the trade surplus and capital gains from the revalued yen, but stimulated by the low interest-rate policy. An urban land speculative boom gathered force during the so-called 'Urban Renaissance' of 1985–87 when Tokyo land prices rose by an average 300 per cent,[44] and was extended throughout the entire country from 1987 by the effects of the Fourth National Comprehensive Development Plan (*Yonzensō*) and the Resort Law. *Yonzensō* envisaged an investment of 1,000 million million yen between 1986 and the turn of the century in the provision of basic infrastructural amenity to the entire country. The public input was to come from the freeing of public assets, especially land, to be complemented by private investment in transport, housing, communications, information technology, and urban redevelopment. The Resort Law spelled out the detailed workings of the *Yonzensō* principles.

The 'Resort' and 'Leisure' strategy had the multiple merit of addressing the ends of domestic pump priming, responding to regional and agricultural sector crisis, reducing the public-sector debt at central and local levels, servicing the politically important construction and real-estate interests, and appearing to signify a slowing down in the expansionary thrust of Japanese capitalism, an intention to relax. Relaxation, along with freshness, greenness and 'my life' was to prove a hollow promise.

It is precisely 'relaxation' or 'slowing down' which is commonly interpreted among the bureaucratic and business elite as a symptom of the 'English disease' or the 'advanced country disease' and therefore to be avoided at all costs. The 'Resort Archipelago' formula devised by Prime Minister Nakasone was designed to reduce the surplus and placate trading partners without increasing demand; in short it created a huge new market and fed fierce expansionary pressures precisely by avoiding the sorts of structural reform that were needed. The wizards of financial magic (*zaiteku*) were invited to stretch their wands and practise their arcane arts of asset multiplying throughout the country. Instead of Japan's high growth flowing, it entered a more frenzied phase, involving not only the established real estate and development companies but also trading companies, hotel chains, railway companies, insurance companies, banks, shipbuilders and finance groups. In the 'Green Japan Plan Phase 2', published in July 1988, resorts were described for the first time as 'a new basic industry for Japan'.[45]

The circuits described in the earlier part of this paper are the functional equivalent of asset stripping, M. and A., and most recently of the savings and loan institutional phenomena in the Anglo-Saxon world, save that for Japan it is always land that is central to the patterns of accumulation. Land and stocks are collateral for borrowing and further investment in land and stocks. Taxation on profits is minimized by writing off interest payments on the portion of acquisition monies that is loan funded.[46] A well-known academic commentator suggested in his recent column in the Sunday edition of the *Nihon Keizai Shinbun* that the Seibu Group, with assets of about 12 million million yen, may have paid no taxes since the company was founded in 1920.[47]

As the Tokyo money spread over the countryside and began to replicate, it affected the whole country with a different 'advanced country' disease — speculation and inflation — which may in the end prove more debilitating than the one Japan struggles to avoid. The twin phenomena of *jiage* and *tochi korogashi*, loosely meaning 'deliberate inflation of land values' and 'quick turnover', exact as heavy a price on the social and moral values of local Japanese communities as do the resorts themselves of the physical environment.

The international dimension

Furthermore, as Japanese economic influence spreads, naturally the patterns of the Japanese domestic political economy are reproduced through a widening regional and global sphere of influence. Throughout the 1980s the level of capital flowing out of Japan into tourism and real-estate development around the region grew steadily, stimulated by the accumulation of trade surplus, the inflation of domestic land and stock assets, and the availability of cheap credit (commonly around 4 per cent) against the collateral of land. In 1990, Japan's outflow of direct foreign investment funds to the world ($44.1 thousand million) surpassed that of the US ($31.7 thousand million) and Britain ($31.8 thousand million),[48] while in Australia 1989–90 figures showed a negative net flow of funds from Australia to both the US ($A1.315 thousand million or approximately $1 thousand million) and Britain ($A2.018 thousand million or approximately $1.6 thousand million) but a continuing strong inflow of Japanese money ($A6.830 thousand million or approximately $5.5 thousand million).[49] In aggregate terms, too, Japan seems likely to become 'number one' in the near future. By the end of the 1980s, as a result, many of the first class hotels, golf courses, and luxury hotels and apartment buildings in places like the Australian Gold Coast, and in Hawaii, were in Japanese hands. Japanese funds flowed into the Gold Coast area at the rate of over $1 thousand million per year during the 1980s, rising in 1990 to $7.25 thousand million to Surfers Paradise alone,[50] where half the property in the Central Business District was by then reported to be under Japanese ownership.[51] Large projects for marinas, golf courses, luxury apartments and hotels were also under way in North Queensland, Western Australia and northern New South Wales.

There is a peculiar irony in this, succinctly expressed in a comment by Hiroshi Sakai, chief representative in Australia of Nomura Research Institute: 'Many Japanese businessmen work from eight o'clock in the morning to eleven o'clock at night and can't take long vacations. Strangely, this is done to invest in the US, Australia and other countries where people work nine to five and have four weeks vacation . . . [and] live in big houses with two-car garages and swimming pools.'[52] In such a 'conflict of cultures' it is hard to be sure of any outcome. Most Australians would probably hope that Japan's money and power could be absorbed while, Asterix-like, the values that helped create or inflate it were quietly subverted by a different vision of 'the good life'; many Japanese, too, incline spontaneously to understand and support an Australian value-orientation on work and leisure rather than their more familiar 'Japanese' models.

One index of the degree to which Japanese patterns are to be reproduced in Australia will be the fate of the 'Multifunction Polis' project.[53] Still little known outside Australia, this originated in a 1987 Japanese government proposal to Australia to construct a joint 'City of the Future' on Australian soil. The original design of the city, presented by the Japanese MITI, strongly suggested a fusion of the twin Japanese strategies of the 1980s: high-tech and high-touch, or technopolis and resort. Between the distinct Australian aspiration for the former and the Japanese focus on the peculiar version of the latter promoted by the resort boom, the issue is still to be settled. A straw in the wind was the appointment in August 1990 of Eishiro Saito as joint chairman of the International Advisory Committee to the MFP project. Saito, head of Keidanren in 1990, had been one of the central figures in the founding in 1979 of Japan Project Industrial Council (JAPIC), a group made up of 110 companies organized to fight the recession that then threatened basic industries such as steel and cement. JAPIC pressures succeeded in securing a series of measures of public sector subsidy and support for the expansion of private-sector role, first in the rebuilding of Japanese cities, then in the infrastructural development objectives of *Yonzensō*, and later still in the 'Green Japan' plans for resort development. How the advice he has to offer Australia will reflect the very mixed achievement of these various programmes remains to be seen, but there is no doubt that the expansive and reproductive energy of Japan's resort development will play a significant role in determining the meaning of 'development' in Australia's future, and in the future of many Pacific countries.

'Enrich the country, impoverish the people'

The phenomena that I describe are magnified in their import by the fact that Japanese money constitutes nearly 40 per cent of international bank assets,[54] or about the same proportion of total world capital and financial assets.[55] The core of this vast sum is money being used as stakes in, or deriving from winnings at, the land and money game in Tokyo. In addition a study of 839 top companies in the Tokyo Stock Exchange recently argued that land assets made up 44 per cent of their total assets, though nominally only 4 per cent.[56] Between January and October 1990 stock prices on the Japanese Nikkei index plunged 48 per cent, a loss equivalent to twice the Third World's outstanding debt, or 'more than four times the estimated 30 year $500 thousand million cost of bailing out America's savings and loan industry'.[57] Land prices, too, floating in a 'sea of debt', were reported to have begun to sink, by some 10 to 20 per cent from their peak. Credit was reported to be drying up, and financial and other institutions facing financial trauma from 'the bursting of the biggest speculative bubble seen this century'. Reflecting on the possible implications of all this, *The Economist* noted that 'It is therefore scary that such a large amount of the world's available credit has been extended to a market which is so inefficient and so illiquid.'[58]

That such phenomena will have large regional (and world) as well as domestic consequences cannot be doubted. Already, early in 1991, Australia's biggest foreign investor, the Japanese company EIE, was in the hands of its bankers, its sustaining mechanism of high leverage and low interest-capital availability having at least temporarily broken down. Other resort, real-estate and speculative companies were contracting, or were under investigation by police or tax authorities in Tokyo for share manipulation, insider trading, or tax evasion. Whether the great Japanese land bubble will eventually burst, or simply continue slowly deflating, remains to be seen. Whatever happens, the whole world will be affected.

Within Japan, the need for relaxation and leisure remains unfulfilled. If anything, the frenetic pace of life intensifies. The unspoiled natural environment that till recently made Japan one of the most attractive countries on earth is being progressively eroded by 'resort' development. The felling of 1 per cent of Japan's forests for golf course development[59] does complex damage to the environment: the diminishing of forest cover accelerates the 'Greenhouse' effect, but the reduction of Japan's domestic timber reserves also stimulates an increased reliance on imported timber, and therefore depredation of Third World forests, thus doubling the contribution to the 'Greenhouse' effect.

The human stock of both urban and rural Japan, the people, are disoriented and swept up in vast dislocating transformations occasioned by the inflation of the capital stock. These changes sow alienation and unrest, erode political and economic morality, and devastate the heritage of people received from their ancestors in trust. While the giant forest trees of Shiretoko in northern Japan are felled to try to achieve solvency for the Forest Agency,[60] one of the world's finest colonies of blue coral is threatened by planned resort development at Ishigaki island, far to the south.[61] Those who know Kawabata's classic novel *Snow Country*, with its opening lines 'The train came out of the long tunnel into the snow country. The earth lay white under the night sky', or who were ever able to go through that tunnel into the world of Kawabata, would be astounded today at the high-rise vistas that now confront one there.[62] The hot-spring village of Echigo Yuzawa received 7.2 million visitors in 1987, and its land price rose by a factor of ten in the three years to 1989; it was literally swallowed by Tokyo, though 167 kilometres distant.[63]

Rural Japan is gripped by quiet despair. In the towns the housing crisis worsens, with land inflation driving ordinary people to commute further and further to work — over 20 per cent of them in Tokyo commuting for more than three hours per day.[64] Symptomatic of the failure to solve this problem is the rise of what may be known as 'reverse' resort life style, where 'home village' or *furusato* is redefined as the place outside Tokyo where one leaves one's family during the week to live in a capsule hotel (or equivalent) in Tokyo, returning at weekends to the 'resort mansion'.[65] Resorts have little to do with leisure and recreation, much with the search for response to international pressures and the growing centrality within the domestic economy of construction and speculative capital. The resort strategy was designed to satisfy domestic pressure groups and mitigate foreign pressure by stimulating and expanding the domestic market (*naiju kakudai*), promoting foreign imports, especially of agricultural items, by further weakening domestic producers and liberalizing imports. These it can be said to have achieved. However, it was also presented as a strategy to invigorate declining local communities, relieve their isolation and chronic ageing profile, and to provide facilities to meet the need of the Japanese people as a whole for relaxation and recreation. These goals it has signally failed to achieve, and indeed they now look to have been essentially propaganda designed to facilitate promotion of the scheme.

In the long run it may turn out that even the macroeconomic gains were illusory or counter-productive and that the resort strategy has merely camouflaged a failure to resolve basic problems of urban and rural work, housing and food, while instead of alleviating trade pressures the growing wave of Japanese investment in the resort and tourist industries of the whole Pacific region may sharpen them.

In the Japanese islands homogeneous, vulgar and *nouveau riche* 'resorts' drawn to identical Tokyo design proliferate. Local interests or peculiarities are swallowed up and negated; the natural environment which originally justified the siting of the resort facilities is undermined; and environmental damage, whose ultimate costs — including economic costs — are incalculable, spreads; social morality is undermined and communities divided as speculative virus spreads and erodes the ethic of work and production that brought Japan 'success' in the first place.

Few were surprised in December 1990 when tax authorities began questioning Mr Toshiyuki Inamura, the man who, as director-general of the Environment Agency in 1986 and 1987, had presided over the first stages of the resort boom, for evading taxes on approximately 2.8 thousand million yen profit generated on stock dealings from companies actively involved in the 'development'.[66] The investigators were focusing on Inamura's connections with the well-known speculator, Mitsuhiro Kotani, who earlier had been indicted on charges of stock-price manipulation.

Resolution of these problems will not be easy. The tide of golf courses, ski resorts and marinas that now rises over the land is striking for its irrelevance to the needs and problems of local communities, many of whom now see the whole process as a contemporary form of enclosure movement, in which public land, forests, mountains and beaches are enclosed by private interests for corporate profit. While corporate Japan thrives, they say, the people suffer. Hence the recently coined slogan: *fukoku hinmin* (Enrich the country, impoverish the people). Such has been the cost of Japan's success in the quest for affluence.

Japanese commentators commonly agree on certain elements of an alternative prescription.[67] The regions will only be 'invigorated' by finding solutions to their problems which are locally driven, arising from and responding to local needs, and based upon strong institutions of local self-government that have the power and the will to control external interventions by big (Tokyo) corporations and bureaucrats. Small developments, rooted in agriculture, craft, or various low-cost, non-intrusive activities would be given precedence under such a prescription. The forests and mountains, home to the ancestors of local communities, would be protected, and the fields and seas which are the source of their basic livelihood respected. The speculative virus would be resisted like the plague, while the stressed workers and residents of the megalopolis could take rest and recuperation in close proximity to the natural world.

Ultimately, only a Japan which begins to overcome its frenetic restlessness and to deepen its democratic and ecological ethos along such lines will be able to resolve the stresses and frictions in its relationship with the outside world.

Notes

1. For other recent analyses of the significance of Japan's rise, see my 'Pacific Dream-time and Japan's New Millenialism', *Australian Outlook*, vol. 43, no. 2, August 1989, pp. 64–73; and 'Capitalism Triumphant?: The Evidence from "Number One"', *Kyoto Journal*, Spring 1990, pp. 4–10.

2. Muran Yoshinori, 'Hakyoku ni itaru kaihatsushugi to kajo shohi' (Developmentalism and overconsumption reach catastrophe proportions), *Keizai semina*, no. 422, 1990, pp. 12–16; and *Ebi to Nihonjin* (Shrimps and the Japanese), Iwanami 1988.

3. 'Nichubei kankei, 6', (Japan–US Relations, part 6), *Asabi shinbun*, 29 March 1990, p. 3.

4. Japan rates 58 to (West) Germany's 79, the USA's 80, the UK's 53; quoted in Takagake Yupu, 'En pawa no seijigaku' (The Politics of Yen Power), *Ajia Keizai*, September 1989, pp. 80–98, p. 94.

5. Paul Waley, 'Rabbit hutch life holds seeds of social fracture', *Japan Times*, 9 December 1990.

6. The following have been most helpful: *Gekkan Jichiken*, (Monthly local government), vol. 31, no. 361, October 1989, 'Kizutsuku nihon retto' (Wounded Japanese archipelago); Sato Makoto and NHK 'Ohayo janaru Shussaihan', *Dokyumento-rizoto* (Resorts-Documentation), Nihon hyoronsha 1989; Sato Makoto, *Rizoto retto* (Resort archipelago), Iwanami shinsho 1990; Yamada Kunihiro, *Gorufujo bokokuron* (Golf-Ruination of the Country), Shinhyoron 1989, and in English, 'The Triple Evil of Golf Courses', *Japan Quarterly*, July–September 1990, pp. 291–7; *Nogyo Kyodokumiai*, vol. 426, August 1990, special issue on 'Do suru- "Rizoto kaihatsu"' (What is to be done about resort development?). Also in audio-visual materials: NHK Kyushu supeshiaru, 'Kuzureyuku rakuen-Okinawa no shizen waima' (Paradise being destroyed — The present situation of nature in Okinawa), August 1989; and NHK Dokyumento supeshiaru, *Rizoto retto* (Resort archipelago), July 1990.

7. Sato, *Rizoto retto*, p. 156 (1989 figures).

8. Wataai Yumi, '90 nendai no yoka ichiba' (The Leisure Market of the 1990s), *Nibon Keizai shinbun*, 5 July 1990, p. 27.

9. From 37.9 per thousand in 1955 to 145.2 per thousand in 1985. Sato, *Rizoto Retto*, p. 157.

10. Teruoka Itsuko, *Yutakasa to ha nanika* (What is affluence?), Iwanami 1989, p. 142ff. (Teruoka also includes an excellent general discussion of the phenomenon of stress.)

11. Quoted in Sato, *Rizoto retto*, p. 157.

12. J. Walsh and Mizuho Toyoshima, 'All in Your Mind', *Look Japan*, April 1990, pp. 30–31.

13. 'Sogo hoyo chi-iki seibi ho' in Japanese Sogo.

14. Sato, *Rizoto retto*, p. 98 (slightly different figures in NHK Dokyumento supeshiaru).

15. Ibid., p. 98.

16. Ibid., pp. 3–4. For a recent table of projects, see also Honma Yoshito, 'Ima mata susumu retto kaizo' (Remodelling the Japanese archipelago under way again), *Sekai*, June 1990, pp. 118–30, p. 121.

17. *Sekai*, June 1990, p. 223 (quoting *Ryukyu shinpo*).

18. 'Gorufu retto — jichitai no shisei minaoshi' (Golf archipelago — Local Governments Reconsidering Position), *Asahi shinbun*, 24 March 1990.

19. Sato, *Rizoto retto*, p. 132; also NHK Dokyumento supeshiaru.

20. Sato, *Rizoto retto*, p. 131; also NHK Dokyumento supeshiaru. Both sources allude also to a development by Kumagai-gumi on the Boso peninsula (Chiba prefecture) where a clear profit of 17.3 thousand million yen is anticipated for a zero initial capital outlay.

21. Sato, *Rizoto retto*, p. 125.

22. 'Nihon seitai gakkai rizoto ni keisho' (Japan Ecological Association's warning on resorts), *Akahata*, 13 December 1989, p. 12; also various articles by Honda Katsuichi in *Asahi janaru*, April and May 1990.

23. Yamada, 'The Triple Evil of Golf Courses', p. 295.

24. 'Rizoto kaihatsu' (Resort development), *Nihon keizai shinbun*, 14 January 1990.

25. Sato, *Rizoto retto*, p. 132.

26. Abe David and Ted Wheelwright, *The Third Wave: Asian Capitalism and Australia*, Sydney 1989, p. 153 (quoting from the *Daily Mirror* of 13 January 1989).

27. Yamada, 'The Triple Evil of Golf Courses', p. 292.

28. Sato, *Rizoto retto*, pp. 163–4; NHK Dokymento supeshiaru; Fujiwara Makoto, 'Katsute naki shizen hakai e no michi' (The path to unprecedented destruction of nature), *Sekai*, June 1990, pp. 131–43.

29. Yamada, 'The Triple Evil of Golf Courses', p. 292; also *Gorufujo bokokuron*, passim.

30. See 'Rizoto tokushu' (Special issue on resorts), *Sekai*, June 1990, p. 60.

31. Tsukaisute okoku (6) noyaku o nagasu gorofujo' (Throwaway kingdom, part 6, golf courses emitting agricultural chemicals), *Asahi shinbun*, 20 December 1989, p. 10.

32. *Asahi shinbun*, 24 March 1990.

33. NHK Dokyumento supeshiaru.

34. Sato and NHK 'Ohayo janaru shusaihan', p. 30.

35. Sato, *Rizoto retto*.

36. See 'Rizoto tokushu', *Sekai*, June 1990, p. 60; also *Nogyo Kyodo Kumiai*, August 1990, p. 38.

37. 'Protection of Wildlife' (Editorial), *Mainichi Daily News*, 9 January 1990, p. 2.

38. Sato, *Rizoto retto*, p. 138.

39. Ibid., p. 136 (see tablets on pp. 136 and 137).

40. Ibid., p. 146.

41. Ibid., p. 138.

42. Ibid.

43. Fujiwara, 'Katsute naki shizen hakai e no michi', p. 140. On the general rural and fishing industry crisis the NHK film material is evocative.

44. Miyamoto Kenichi, 'Nihon kankyo hokoku — Rizoto ho o kangaeru' (Report on the Japanese Environment — Reflecting on the Resort Law), *Asahi janaru*, to November 1989, p. 53.

45. Sato, *Rizoto retto*, pp. 171–2.

46. Ibid., p. 144.

47. Nakati Gen, quoted in Tanaka Yasuo, ' Faddishu kogengaku' (Faddish phenomenology), *Asahi janaru*, 30 March 1990, p. 86.

48. 'Chokusetsu toshi — Nihon eibei nuki sekai ichi' (Japan surpasses Britain and America to become number one in foreign investment), *Asahi shinbun*, 21 December 1990.

49. Australian Bureau of Statistics figures.

50. Peter Wilmoth, *The Age*, 22 September 1990.

51. *The Australian*, 16–17 June 1990.

52. Quoted in Linda Korporaal, ' The bonsai effect shrinks Japan's global money tree', *The Age*, 1 February 1991.

53. On this project, see Gavan McCormack, ed., *Bonsai Australia Banzai: Multifunctionpolis and the Making of Special Relationship with Japan*, Sydney 1991.

54. Anthony Rowley, 'Feet of Clay', *Far Eastern Economic Review*, 25 October 1990, p. 44.

55. Economic Planning Agency, *Sekai Hakusho* (World whitepaper), 1989, quoted in Sato, *Rizoto retto*, p. 140.

56. Ibid., p. 144.

57. Christopher Wood, 'Japanese Finance', special supplement to *The Economist*, 8 December 1990, p. 3.

58. Ibid., p. 13.

59. Yamada, 'The Triple Evil of Golf Courses', p. 235.

60. Honda Katsuichi, *Asahi jamaru*, 15 December 1989.

61. Of many sources on this problem, most useful in English are the regular reports in *Japan Environment Monitor*.

62. See, for example, the photos in *Sekai*, June 1990, pp. 30–31, or in Sato and NHK 'Ohayo janaru shusaihan', pp. 27, 32.

63. Sato, *Rizoto retto*, p. 114.

64. Ibid., p. 20. Also NHK Dokymento supeshiaru.

65. A vision defined by then prime minister Takeshita in December 1987, quoted in Sato, *Rizoto retto*, p. 21.

66. Various Japanese media reports, 19 December 1990 and subsequent.

67. See, for example, Miyamoto Kenichi, Yokota Shigeru, and Nakamura Kojiro, *Chiiki keizaigaku* (Regional Economics), Yuhikaku bukkusu 1990, pp. 339ff; and, for a union response to the problem, Zen Nihon jichi dantai rodo kumiai (Union of All-Japan Local Government Workers), *Atarashii jidai no kuni-chiho kankei* (State-locality relations for a new era), October 1989, pp. 52–7.

32. The Japanese Polity
Bernard Eccleston

Continuous conservatism

The most significant feature of Japanese political life is that in contrast to all the other liberal democracies the Conservatives have exercised unbroken power for over 40 years. Since 1945 in only one short period of less than a year has an alternative party emerged with more Diet seats and even this victory did not produce a majority. Apart from this coalition led by Socialists in 1947–8, the subsequent fifteen post-war national elections have consistently resulted in Conservative majorities. Even after the two main Conservative groups were fused into a Liberal Democratic Party (LDP) in 1955 the prospects for such long-term dominance of national politics was not at all obvious. To this day the LDP has a very limited mass party membership, its structure is riddled with personality factions which appear to retain grievances with each other over long periods and its leadership has had a marked propensity for involvement in corruption scandals. Nevertheless the LDP even in its worst election year polled twice as many votes as the next largest party.

Cynics might suggest that the creation of an Asian bastion of conservatism was as significant to the reforming zealots of the US occupation as their desire to democratize Japan. It is clear that at least in their labour policies the US authorities were keen to support the anti-socialist stance of Japanese governments after 1948, but it is difficult to see how an externally imposed Constitution could have so successfully engineered such a prolonged era of LDP rule. As we have seen in earlier chapters even before the end of the occupation the spirit of the political reforms was already being reversed by the re-centralization of educational administration and the erosion of local government autonomy. Such informal amendments to democratic ideals should not however lead us to underestimate the significance of the changes to established political practices that were encapsulated in the 1947 Constitution.

The most fundamental political change was to shift the focus of sovereign power from the Emperor to a Diet in which both Chambers were to be elected for the first time by all adult men and women. An independent Judiciary was formally charged with the task of safeguarding the Constitution's commitment to 'eternal and inviolable human rights', but there was no formal separation of executive from legislative power as in the US presidential system. Instead executive power was vested in the Cabinet led by a Prime Minister elected from among Diet members. Of the two Diet Chambers the House of Representatives is the more important as its members have the final say in the event of any disagreement with the House of Councillors over the choice of Prime Minister. Democratizing Japanese politics also meant that the US occupation wanted increased popular participation through the tiers of local government, so elected assemblies and chief executives were to operate at regional, city, town and village

Bernard Eccleston: 'The Japanese Polity' from STATE AND SOCIETY IN POST-WAR JAPAN (Polity Press, 1989), pp. 123–139. Reproduced by permission of Basil Blackwell Limited.

levels. Hence the Local Autonomy Law of 1947 sought to prevent any return to the high degree of pre-war central government control and make local officials accountable to local electors.

In essence the US reforms were designed to uphold popular sovereignty against the exercise of arbitrary power by non-elected individuals or groups such as the military, the peerage, the bureaucracy or employers. In this vein the Land reform programme aimed to destroy the economic and political influence of landlords replacing the hierarchy of rural society based on tenancy with grassroots democracy based on small independent proprietors. The rights of labour to organize and bargain collectively and to expect equality of opportunity, were included in the Constitution as part of fundamental civil rights in contrast to the pre-war emphasis on duty to employers and thereby the state.

Although no significant changes have been made since 1947 to these formal provisions, we do need to ask how far they have been reflected in political practices. Has the Diet for example remained 'the highest organ of state power and the sole law-making organ of the state' (1947 Constitution Chapter IV Article 41)? As 'political principles differ widely from the conduct of practical affairs'[1] to what extent do elected members of the Diet control the legislative process? With such a long period of LDP rule and given the fusion of powers in Cabinets drawn overwhelmingly from LDP Diet members, many writers have argued that the Diet acts merely as a ratifier of legislation handed down by the government. It also is apparent that the majority of policy and legislative proposals are drafted by non-elected officials so is the power of the elected representatives being over-ridden by the entrenched influence of the bureaucracy? We have already seen how the US Occupation chose to administer Japan through the existing civilian administration and the purge of war-time political leaders served initially at least to confirm their dominance of the executive. The short tenure of both Prime Ministers and Cabinet Ministers over the past four decades has served to maintain the influence of bureaucrats whose lengthier years of continuous service in their ministries encourage incoming ministers to rely heavily on their expertise. In addition the fusion of executive and legislative power is sustained by the early retirement of bureaucrats into political life as Diet members, invariably with the LDP.

Just as the focus of the debate on the Japanese economy has tended to polarize the private market versus the state, so also have interpretations of political institutions crystallized around the disputed dominance of the bureaucracy over the elected representatives in the Diet. To an extent even the use of the term 'Diet' rather than 'Parliament' indicates a degree of uncertainty over the reality of the change from the pre-war consultative assembly to a truly independent and sovereign legislature. Equally the independent authority of the Judiciary especially in the Supreme Court has been used so sparingly as to raise doubts about its ability to challenge decisions of the executive. As we shall see this low-key approach has been most manifest in the Supreme Court's failure to oversee alterations to the gross inequalities in the size of electoral districts which has given the LDP a marked advantage in national elections.

Other elements of the political process throw up inconsistencies between the spirit and practice of the 1947 Constitution. Local autonomy was eroded especially in education and control of the police during the 1950s, but the election of non-LDP candidates as mayors and governors in many of the larger urban areas had by the 1970s brought the issue of central government encroachment firmly into the political arena. This tension was in itself part of a general trend which saw the establishment of a wide variety of citizens' groups which reflected a mood of dissatisfaction with the attitude of LDP governments towards environmental pollution and the provision of public goods. Refinements to the labour laws eroded the rights of public sector workers to strike and state support for non-political enterprise unions has had profound effects for the ability of opposition parties to coordinate support from the labour movement.

Against this background of refining or reversing the spirit of the Constitution the first part of this chapter will be concerned with explaining why and how the LDP has managed to retain power for so long. This discussion carries two dimensions; one concerning the attractiveness of the LDP itself and the other concerning the weaknesses and fragmentation of alternative parties who have been condemned to perpetual opposition. Matters of principle enshrined in the Constitution dealing with the supremacy of the Diet and the relative power of the bureaucracy or the Cabinet will be considered through the practices adopted by successive LDP governments. It is also necessary to examine other forms of citizen representation which continue to function between elections, that is interest group activity. In particular we need to ask about the equality of access to the state either through membership of public advisory bodies or through established pressure groups which focus on matters economic or social that cut across political divisions. In other words, to ask how far does the continuity of LDP governments reflect the legitimate outcome of the operation of representative political institutions?

The roots of conservative majorities

In the mid-1950s the prospect of one party enjoying continuous Diet majorities was hardly anticipated. Once the fusion of the socialist parties into the Japan Socialist Party (JSP) in October 1955 was followed within a month by the amalgamation of the two main Conservative parties into the LDP, alternating governments in a two-party system appeared to be the most realistic prospect. Even though the 1958 election gave the socialists only one-third of the seats in the Diet, the omens were promising for them to secure a majority in the next decade. Rapid urbanization was expected to produce solid support for the socialists among the more progressive groups of younger wage earners. An equivalent decline in the numerical predominance of Japan's rural areas foreshadowed a secular decline in the fortunes of the LDP. On particular issues too the socialist opposition seemed to be closer to public concern with the way the Conservatives had refined the spirit of constitutional safeguards for local control of education and the police, the labour rights of public sector workers and the demilitarization of Japan. Foreign policy was seen to be too closely dependent on the US with widespread demonstrations against the stationing of US forces with nuclear weapons on Japanese soil. Thus the JSP felt optimistic that it better represented the commitment of the Japanese people to neutrality and that by mobilizing a post-war generation of urban voters it could soon become the party of government.

Figure 1 indicates clearly that JSP optimism remains unfulfilled and that the expected decline of the LDP was not as dramatic as political forecasters had predicted. Though the JSP remains the largest single opposition party its share of the popular vote and seats won has halved and its 99 per cent dominance of the total opposition seats in 1958 had fallen to less than 40 per cent by 1986. LDP majorities were certainly cut, but even in the later 1970s when the party won only 49 per cent of seats in the House of Representatives, its position as the party of government was never seriously challenged. Technically the Diet votes of conservatively inclined unaffiliated members could usually be relied upon to secure the passage of important legislation, but of equal significance was the inability of the opposition to coordinate its numerical strength. As Figure 2 shows the opposition has become fragmented into four competing parties which offer little prospect of a consistently united front against the LDP. The expectation that the JSP could amass the votes of urban labour were undermined initially by the defection of centre-right socialists into the Democratic Socialist Party (DSP) in 1960 and then by the revival of the Japan Communist Party (JCP) in the later 1960s. If we add the other party *Komeito*, which is a quasi-religious populist organization, the picture of a fragmented multi-party opposition is confirmed.

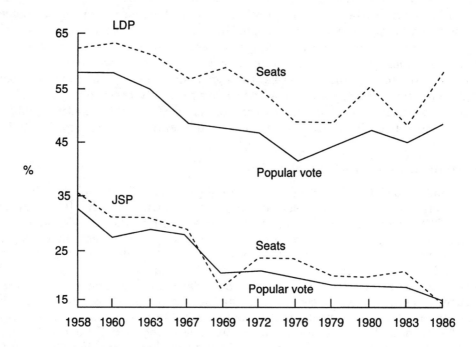

Figure 1   Shares of the popular vote and seats won by the JSP and LDP in House of Representative elections, 1958–86.

Source: Japan Statistical Yearbook.

Against this fragmentation of opposition parties the LDP itself has been beset with internal divisions but these have revolved around non-ideological disputes between rival factions which have not threatened its continuity in government. Even the defection of a group of conservatives to form the New Liberal Club (NLC) in 1976 resulted in a loss of only two or three members who in practice usually voted with the LDP and the new party was accommodated in a formal coalition from 1983. For the opposition not only are there real differences in ideology, but the example of the NLC coalition has encouraged members of the DSP and *Komeito* to see cooperation with the LDP rather than the JSP as their only route to government office.

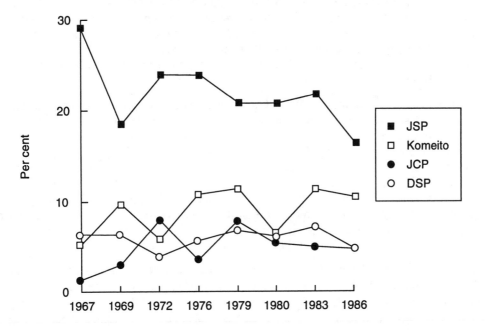

Figure 5   **A fragmented Opposition's share of seats won in the House of Representative elections, 1967–86.**

Source: Japan Statistical Yearbook.

If there was any consolation for the LDP in its decline during the 1970s it was based on the knowledge that unity among the opposition was very unlikely. There have been some attempts to operate electoral alliances in particular districts where the LDP support was thought to be fragile but there was little evidence that such cooperation would be sustained beyond the immediate ambition of winning particular seats. The bleak prospects for an alternative government formed by a coalition among the opposition has to be set against the consistency with which the LDP has won at least half of the seats in the House of Representatives even when its popular vote fell as low as 42 per cent in 1976. Figure 1 shows that the LDP has continuously managed to win a higher proportion of seats than its share of the popular vote would justify. In no small way this trend reflects the advantage the party derives from the uneven size of electoral districts.

As a much larger number of LDP members are elected from small districts, a lower proportion of the total votes cast produces more victorious candidates. Only painfully slow changes have been made to the spatial apportionment of seats since the organization of electoral districts was established on the basis of a population census taken immediately after the Pacific war. In the following four decades though there has been a significant change in residential patterns from one-third of the population living in urban areas to three-quarters in 1987; the urban voter is thus grossly under-represented and in rural areas over-represented. In practical terms this means that in some rural districts there is one seat of 115,000 electors whereas some urban seats represent 500,000. Inequalities of the order of 4:1 are not uncommon which means that some candidates can win with 40,000 votes while others lose despite polling 120,000. The principal beneficiary of this degree of maldistribution is the LDP whose main strength lies in the rural districts which regularly yield 60 per cent of their Diet representation.[2]

The worst cases of inequality in district size do occur at the extremes of population density and sparsity. None the less the overall impact is significant in at least three other senses. First, the turn-out of voters in rural areas tends to be much higher at around 80 per cent making it easier for LDP candidates to gather even the small numbers required to win seats in rural districts. Secondly, even semi-urban areas contain sufficiently high numbers of rural voters to swing results towards the LDP. Finally, eligible urban voters knowing that their vote is grossly under-represented in national elections tend to turn out in smaller numbers. So unequal electoral districts trigger a process which magnifies the advantages of the LDP by encouraging most abstentions where their own support is weakest.

Electoral gerrymandering has, as might be expected, been a longstanding source of dissatisfaction but there is no independent body to impose a redistribution of seats on an unwilling Diet, which means on an uncooperative LDP majority. The Supreme Court has ruled explicitly that three out of the last five elections were unfair and actually labelled the 1983 election as unconstitutional because of the disproportionate allocation of seats. Only one out of fourteen Justices though, was prepared to nullify the result; of the rest only five warned that if no changes were made they might nullify the outcome of the next election. Despite the evidence of the 1985 census which shows that the differential value of votes between some urban and rural districts had widened to nearly 5:1, the Supreme Court as on other issues appears reluctant to use its Constitutional right to check the abuse of power by the Diet. Instead 'it prefers to see popular sovereignty as resting on the legislative branch . . . and wishes to avoid any repetition of pre-war executive encroachment on legal terrain'.[3] The relatively short tradition of a truly independent judiciary, assisted so the opposition argues by the preferential appointment of conservative judges, makes the Supreme Court more acquiescent than its US counterpart which was the exemplar in the 1947 Constitution.

It would be wrong to suggest that no changes at all have been made to the distribution of seats but re-allocation has been limited to the addition of a few extra seats to urban districts. Even this limited change allows the LDP to claim that it is not impervious to public concern or to the rulings of the Supreme Court. Recent proposals by the Government could certainly be designated as 'limited' as their best offer promises to reduce the inequity in representation to not more than 3:1! The unwillingness of the Supreme Court to become embroiled in a constitutional conflict leaves the opposition little choice but to accept the few conciliatory crumbs offered by the self-styled 'natural' party of government. In itself the hesitancy of the Supreme Court sheds some light on the reality of constitutional checks and balances especially when this involves leaving the LDP with 'a built-in advantage which it will jealously preserve at all costs'.[4]

Election results in the 1980s tend to show that the LDP is not entirely a party representing rural districts and it has gained more support at the expense of socialists in urban Japan. But the rural vote is still strongly conservative enough to tolerate its more tenuous position in densely populated urban areas and makes the LDP reluctant to alter the imbalance in voter representation. How then have conservatives managed to retain such a secure foothold in rural districts?

Despite the fierce suppression of rural socialism under the guise of ultranationalism in the 1930s, the socialist parties did have the opportunity immediately after the war to establish their presence in farmers' unions that opposed the domination of landlords. But by choosing to uphold the principles of dispersed ownership for most small farmers and security of tenure for the remainder, the conservatives effectively undermined the ability of socialist parties to exploit the divisive issues of landownership. Indeed by denying dispossessed landlords the opportunity to recover some of their lost authority in the 1950s, conservative governments thereby made 'Japanese villages safe for conservatism'.[5] This pattern has continued and in one sense reflects a distrust of socialist parties that attach priority to propertyless workers rather than owners and proprietors. But other political processes serve to maintain high levels of support for the LDP not least those characteristically conservative policies which protect domestic agriculture as the main prop of the rural economy.

The right of small Japanese farmers to own land was one thing but their ability to earn a reasonable income from their land was quite another. Severe economic difficulties beset the new class of farm-owners because the average size of their holding at two or three hectares was too small to offer much prospect of any substantial reductions in cost through improvements in productivity. As a result if a free market was to rule for rice then imports at a third of Japanese prices would totally undermine the viability of domestic farming. To safeguard the position of indigenous agriculture and its own rural support base, LDP Governments have restricted food imports and used subsidies to mitigate the full impact of higher Japanese production costs. As the main vehicle through which agricultural producers are represented in national negotiations over the level of state intervention, the agricultural cooperatives exercise political functions as an interest group but they also have crucial economic and political roles at local level. Over 90 per cent of farmers belong to cooperatives which organize the provision of credit, the sharing of capital equipment and joint purchasing schemes for inputs like fertilisers as well as coordinating the sale of output to the government

Elected officials of the cooperatives inevitably become closely involved with LDP members because of the party's dominance in government and its attachment to agricultural protection. Diet members from rural districts are expected to maintain the level of support programmes, oppose moves to dismantle market controls or the perennial proposals from the Ministry of Finance to reduce the level of public subsidies. For rural areas where the politics of agriculture is paramount, cooperative officials also provide the leadership of elected local or regional assemblies. Where landowning notables previously exercised power and influence, land reform saw this role pass to owners of larger more prosperous farms or to owners of small firms. As elected political leaders and in many cases as key officials of the cooperative, the fusion of political and economic power continues to cement village solidarity through the administration of agricultural support programmes.

Protection for agriculture as a whole is only one link in the chain that connects rural districts to the LDP. The particular needs of local constituencies are expected to be satisfied through the personal intercession of Diet representatives whose own standing is judged, for example, by their ability to secure a share of centrally financed public investment. Most farms are too small to generate an adequate income from farming if this is the only occupation, and this is clearly one reason for the migration of local people to the towns. To slow down the rate of depopulation, public investment in roads and railways is required to foster the growth of non-agricultural employment and so diversify the rural economy. In addition despite their falling population, rural residents demand improvements in the provision of schools and hospitals to prevent further decay to the vitality of their communities. As we saw in [Chapter 4] the scale of Japanese public investment is extensive, and higher levels of support for LDP candidates is expected to yield direct tangible rewards through the allocation of resources from central government.

Beneath the general commitment to agriculture that is expected from the LDP, another dimension of a 'patron–client democracy has taken root in agricultural communities, the bastion of LDP strength, under the banner of public investment in rural areas'.[6] Continued loyalty to particular candidates then is based not so much on their party label but to a representative with 'a pipeline to the central sources of government largesse'.[7] One of the outstanding examples of patron–client practices can be seen in the ability of ex-Prime Minister Tanaka to influence the allocation of public investment to his home district of Niigata, a remote area of western Japan. From 1947 onwards he promised roads, tunnels, railroads, reclamation projects, schools and snow clearing services in return for local votes and throughout his climb through the hierarchy of the LDP he certainly delivered what he promised. Despite his fall from power in 1974 which was precipitated by charges of corrupt dealings with the Lockheed Corporation, and his resignation from official membership of the LDP, Niigata citizens continue to benefit from his patronage. In 1982 for example public investment *per capita* was six times as great as the amount people in Niigata paid in taxes. Tokyo residents in the same year paid twice as much per head in taxes as they received in spending on public works.[8]

Mutual relations of loyalty to Diet members who deliver tangible rewards to their constituency are crucial to the higher rate of voter mobilization which is a feature of rural districts. In addition agricultural cooperatives act as both an administrative vehicle and a political machine to maintain support for the LDP. But the 80–90 per cent support for the LDP recorded in many rural districts also requires careful nurturing between elections. Many small farmers, for instance, produce so little rice beyond their own subsistence needs, that they gain few direct benefits from government subsidies. The importance of the cooperatives is that they give local political leaders the authority to maintain village solidarity to particular candidates by acting as the organizer of a Diet member's support group. Such personal support networks are not simply vehicles for electioneering but they serve to maintain a continuous local presence for elected representatives. The key intermediary — the local political boss — acts as an agent organizing support group meetings, making sure the candidate subscribes to local societies, sending presents on his behalf to local notables or delivering wreaths to the funeral of important residents. As Diet members rely on local politicians to nurse their districts, they provide in return assistance to the political career of their disciples in local assemblies or public institutions. This may mean providing financial assistance in elections to the cooperative and local council or exerting pressure on regional government to make sure that the appropriate villages receive grants that reflect favourably on the work of village leaders. 'By these means Diet members and local officials mutually strengthen each others position'.[9] The personal support groups then serve as the mechanism for voter mobilization and also bridge the gap between the members presence at the centre in Tokyo and their constituents in the periphery.

In the initial selection of candidates, area loyalties and personal ties are particularly important in order to portray potential members as people who will know how best to look after 'our' interests because they are 'one of us'. But in maintaining what may be only distant blood or land ties, personal support networks are as vital as affiliation to the LDP. As we shall see, the Japanese electoral system which uses large districts each with between three and five seats, means that members of the same party compete for the single non-transferable vote of each elector. Hence even in rural districts candidates need the security of safe havens in particular villages and towns and it is exactly this solidarity that local support groups can deliver.

It is not at all unusual for conservatives to regard rural areas as their own preserve. But what makes the Japanese political process somewhat different is the way unequal representation magnifies the effect of a solid rural base for the LDP. The intimate connections between agricultural cooperatives, local conservative leaders and sitting members makes it virtually impossible for opposition candidates to break through this web of influence. Having neither a power base in the cooperatives nor any favoured access to central government favours, the opposition can offer little prospect of matching the LDP's 'calculating contractual relations'.[10] Political practices which involve the exchange of personal loyalties to particular candidates in return for direct local benefits is not, though, peculiar to rural Japan. Multi-member constituencies mean that individual candidates need support groups to press their personal cause even against candidates from the same party. The ensuing degree of intra-party competition is also one reason why the LDP continues to be organized around competing factions.

The LDP and factional politics

Once the principle of universal suffrage was enshrined in a reformed structure of political institutions by the US occupation, the choice of electoral system was left to the Japanese themselves. After a brief experiment with a limited version of proportional representation, elections to the more influential House of Representatives reverted to the system used before the war: multiple-member constituencies with single votes. By

1986 there were 130 large districts divided nearly equally into three-, four- and five-member constituencies and with 512 seats to be contested, a majority for one party requires the election of on average two candidates per district. Inevitably a degree of rivalry thus prevails among members representing the LDP as well as against opposition candidates because they are all competing for a single non-transferable vote. So in contrast to single member systems the contest can be 'chaotic as candidates (particularly from the ruling party) attack one another regardless of their affiliation'.[11]

This type of electoral system was established in the 1890s as a mechanism through which non-elected elites might limit the cohesion of political parties and so retain their power. Until 1945 military personnel and members of the Emperor's circle of advisors shared office with elected politicians in what were usually non-party governments. Since then although Cabinet government through elected representatives is now the rule, political parties have inherited an electoral system which still encourages an unusual amount of intra-party competition. With several seats available, the key problem for the parties is to estimate accurately their likely total vote in order to endorse just the appropriate number of candidates. Too many candidates from the LDP for example may split their total vote to the detriment of them all; too few candidates may produce enough votes to have won extra seats. The delicate act of balancing the number of officially endorsed candidates with estimates of their expected total vote in particular districts is therefore crucial.

In 1986, for example, when the LDP gained a 20 per cent increase in its Lower House majority, Prime Minister Nakasone interpreted the result as 'The voice of god speaking from heaven.' More circumspect political commentators pointed out that this 'landslide' reflected only an 8 per cent increase in the popular vote. One explanation of the discrepancy attributed the extra seats gained to a much more accurate prediction of how many candidates to endorse in contrast to 1983 when too many LDP candidates produced a large number of narrow defeats. What remains a problem for the LDP is the unpredictable impact of the weight electors attach to the performance of their member in delivering local benefits since the last election. Even an official endorsement cannot always counteract the impression that an elected member has neglected local interests either in pursuing their own career in government or following the dictates of national LDP policies.

To increase their chances of election, candidates need local connections which allow them to establish a support network strong enough for them to be considered worthy of endorsement. In the national allocation of official party candidates, sponsorship from one of the main factions is imperative because the whole process of endorsement is the outcome of informal bargaining between faction leaders. Generally factions aim to secure the endorsement of just one representative per district in order to avoid dissipating their financial resources and to prevent intra-factional rivalry. In return for the initial patronage needed simply to become endorsed, those so selected pledge their commitment to the leadership ambitions of one or sometimes two faction leaders. These reciprocal obligations are then maintained by the efforts of faction leaders to secure party or government posts for their followers in return for providing faction members with the finance needed to continue winning elections.

The ability of faction leaders to provide for the political expenses of their followers is one reason why the Japanese political process continues to function with factions as an integral institution. Although the precise figures are shrouded in mystery, newspaper estimates suggest that the average cost of winning a Diet seat in 1986 was over one billion yen ($7 million or £5 million). A large proportion of this is spent lubricating local constituents with food, drink or presents as well as the more usual expenses of producing leaflets or posters and organizing meetings. To meet these costs the LDP candidate can expect only limited support from central party funds because the party is relatively weak in terms of a mass membership contributing regular subscriptions. Political donations from business are extensive but they are made directly to faction leaders who then distribute the funds to finance the election of their followers. Up to 70 per cent of election expenses are estimated to be met from within the faction's own resources which thus heightens the dependence of faction members on the continued patronage of their leader. Financial backing is also crucial between elections as Diet members need a flow of funds to maintain their local support groups and pay the local election expenses of their district representatives. As a channel of political funds an LDP faction thus extends the network of reciprocal obligations from national to local level and thereby ensures the continuity of its own strength in the Diet.

The existence of sub-groups within political parties which coalesce around the personality of ambitious individuals is a perennial feature in the struggle for power. Where party factions act as a vehicle to challenge entrenched orthodoxies or where they offer alternative policies it could be argued that they offer the electorate the opportunity to influence changes in political goals. Factions rooted in competing ideologies are common among Japanese socialists and have been one reason why parties which claim to represent labour have split into three or four rival parties. Some political scientists have argued that in the absence of any realistic alternative government from among the opposition parties, factions within the LDP serve the function of presenting the electorate with a choice of policies. In other words intra-party competition within an amorphous group of conservatives is a healthy sign that guarantees constructive argument and debate even within a party as dominant as the LDP. Superficially this assessment is appealing yet what appears to be most important in maintaining divisions between the factions are personal disputes between their leaders. These personal differences are usually based on the failure of the faction leader to obtain the senior post they covet or that their followers have not been treated fairly in the allocation of cabinet offices. One such conflict between the Fukuda and Tanaka factions has been a continuous source of division within the LDP ever since 1972 when Tanaka broke the convention that a member of the retiring Prime Minister's faction should not be his successor. Fifteen years later when the two principals had stepped aside as leaders, the acrimonious dispute was still evident among their successors in the battle to replace Nakasone.

It is of course possible to detect that some factions espouse greater or lesser degrees of explicit support for reviving Japan's own defence forces or to see more fervent nationalism in the new right policies of Nakasone. But other factions contain members who would support this platform while at the same time denying the prerogatives of an opposing faction leader. Although factions do have separately organized offices and institutions they tend not to produce distinctively different political manifestos. Hence interfactional bitterness which may last over lengthy periods is perpetuated by personality conflicts with 'barely a hint of any factor even remotely linked to an issue of public policy'.[12]

The very origins of the LDP in the fusion of two separate parties which had competed for the limited number of government posts in pre-war Japan, would inevitably have produced competition for the leadership of the newly integrated LDP. But even within these two parties there were divisions. One problem in the 1950s concerned the need to accommodate those politicians who had been purged for their wartime activities and some factions favoured their preferential inclusion. Other factions were dominated by a new generation of Diet members who not only resented the way pre-war leaders had returned to senior positions, but also rejected the right of retiring bureaucrats to take *amakudari* into Cabinet office. Yet other factions developed under the leadership of charismatic figures especially where they were able to deliver their supporters with large amounts of election finance from large Japanese companies. Some factions disintegrated when their leader retired or died without an obvious heir-apparent with reasonably secure prospects for high office. Hence some re-alignment takes place when a faction disappears but otherwise movement between factions is unusual. Faction numbers can be reinforced from the ranks of newly elected Diet members which reinforces the desire of each faction leader to influence the selection of endorsed candidates. 'Small wonder it is then that come election time the Presidential faction gets as a rule the lion's share of newly elected members'.[13]

There is a parallel here between continuity in faction membership and the prospect of lifetime employment offered to certain workers in large Japanese companies. Just as secure tenure is seen as the reward for company loyalty, so also will a faction leader offer to reward personal loyalty from a follower with the prospect of promotions on the ladder of their political career. Just as movements between large companies are effectively precluded by the accompanying loss of seniority, so also are movements between political factions constrained by lost status and rank. 'Soiling one's *curriculum vitae*' for a disloyal faction member means starting again at the bottom of the promotion ladder in their new faction. Factions therefore developed as 'devices by means of which a member of the party in the Diet hoped to acquire either a government post, a party post, political funds or all of these'.[14] As an integral feature of the Japanese political scene, factions are officially registered organizations with offices, procedures and meetings that are separate from the central administration of the LDP. Their focus is primarily based on the preoccupation of the leader or his nominee in securing election to the party presidency — hence in the case of the LDP becoming Prime Minister. The numerical strength of a faction allows the leader to participate in the negotiated distribution of party and government posts which preserves a leader's role as a dispenser of patronage.

When several factions compete over the right to dispense a limited number of appointments there has to be some way of sharing patronage between them. It is unusual for the allocation of senior government and LDP offices to be conducted in public view but the process seems to involve job rotation among the bigger factions. Cabinet appointments apart from the Ministries of Finance, Foreign Affairs or Trade and Industry, appear to be re-shuffled annually to ensure a degree of power sharing between the rival factions. Sato who was Prime Minister from 1964–72 gave Cabinet posts to over 100 LDP members — 'a notable feat in view of the fact that he had only 20 Cabinet-rank jobs at his disposal'.[15] As for the most senior Cabinet offices it is almost a requirement for any party leader to have been Minister of Finance or Trade and Industry which therefore makes these jobs the subject of the most intense horse-trading. In essence support for a rival faction leader in the election to the LDP Presidency usually results in other faction heads being rewarded with senior Cabinet posts or top party jobs.

The Secretary-Generalship of the LDP is one of the key prizes partly because this position offers the opportunity to influence the endorsement of new candidates and so build up the strength of his faction in the Diet. In addition, since 1978 LDP members outside the Diet have been consulted in the process of choosing a new leader through a party primary election which gives the Secretary-General a power base outside the Diet. Thus a faction that is dissatisfied with the current leadership can mobilize opposition to the Prime Minister within the party at large. Such a dispersal of factional power centres within the LDP has not only led to 'The absurd frequency with which cabinets are made and then re-constructed'[16] but has also shortened the tenure of Prime Ministers. In the eight years after the fall of Tanaka in 1974 there were five different Prime Ministers whose tenure was fraught with inter-party squabbles over the allocation of senior posts. Faction rivalries continue to make 'considerations of coalition maintenance and personal power maximization often take precedence over those of government performance'.[17] Not only do these endless struggles undermine public confidence in their elected representatives but they also tend to diminish the power of the Prime Minister.

Elections for the leadership of the LDP are the occasion of quite vitriolic disputes between the factions and the extent of their disagreement has resulted on several occasions in the election of the least offensive candidate from a minority faction. Prime Ministers such as Miki, Ohira or Suzuki presided over their Cabinets in the manner of acting executive chairmen subsequently evoking little respect or loyalty from their ministers. Even a more forceful leader experiences recurring problems as recalcitrant colleagues in Cabinet produce uncertainty which weakens his authority as Prime Minister and encourages rivals to oppose his re-election as party leader. Even though Nakasone lasted as Prime Minister for six years from 1982 his period in office saw a continued process of post rotation as competing factions manoeuvred their followers into positions which would pave the way for a successor.

Frequent changes of ministerial personnel and the apparently endless leadership struggles helps to explain why many writers stress the role of the non-elected officials in governing Japan. In the absence of a settled pattern to cabinet government the bureaucracy participates more extensively in the initiation and formulation of policy as well as overseeing its implementation. Non-elected officials with long tenure and experience in their respective ministries draft legislative proposals and supervise consultation with interest groups outside the Diet even before such proposals are submitted for cabinet approval. Bureaucrats also guide what may be a very inexperienced minister through the Diet Committee hearings by drafting both the questions and answers that LDP Diet members ask. Continuity of service gives bureaucrats a source of expertise which although it does not go completely unchallenged, remains significant so long as factional rivalries diminish the tenure of LDP cabinet appointments.

Highlighting the implications of sharing government posts between competing factions does not necessarily imply that the bureaucracy dominates either the cabinet, the LDP or the legislature. But the rotation of ministers does allow bureaucrats to take more responsibility for policy initiation. Conventional models of decision-making in liberal democracies tend to assign to non-elected officials the role of implementing policies which are formulated by elected representatives. In practice it is not always easy to distinguish the two when limited ministerial tenure makes politicians reliant on the experience and expertise of the bureaucracy. What is even more significant in the Japanese case is that one party has dominated government for so long which serves to institutionalize the close relationship between the LDP and non-elected officials.

In some ways these close connections are the product of a homogeneous social background for elites within the bureaucracy and the leadership of the LDP not least in their common educational careers at Japan's prestigious universities. There is also a tradition of movement by senior bureaucrats into the LDP so that over the past three decades they have made up roughly 30 per cent of Diet members and taken up to 50 per cent of cabinet posts. But in addition to personnel transfers, the general commitment of the LDP to conservative values stressing above all national cohesion and consensus, coincides with the bureaucracy's own brief to preserve social harmony against divisive social forces. Although the LDP likes to make a virtue of not 'having anything so concrete or clear cut as an ideology'[18] it does claim to be the custodian of the mystical essence of Japanese values for an exposed and vulnerable island race. By tapping the inheritance of the enveloping idea of a total society from the pre-war Emperor system, the LDP portrays the opposition especially those that can be labelled 'socialist', as divisive because they place the protection of class interests before that of the 'nation'.

It is revealing to note how the words 'divisive' and 'class' are associated with representing labour but not in connection with the LDP's own financial backers from business. But whether or not the image of the LDP as a party representing the whole nation is real or imaginary it is clear that each of the opposition parties draws its support from distinct social groups. None of these groups is big enough by itself to produce a majority and it is doubtful if any could do so even with a radical re-apportionment of electoral districts. So in practical terms the bureaucracy can expect to continue working with the same party in government and in such circumstances their relationships with the LDP inevitably become more accommodating.

Secure in the knowledge that disunity among the opposition is endemic the LDP can afford to tolerate the luxury of intraiparty strife. The apparent obsession of each faction in taking their turn to provide a Prime Minister, a senior cabinet minister or a high-ranking party official reflects the certainty that their years in government will be prolonged. Factional disputes are certainly intense but they have not thus far been pressed to the point where one large faction deserts the LDP. There are few real differences in ideology to separate the faction leaders and if sooner or later they can expect high office why jeopardize their chances in an alliance with one of the opposition parties? Ultimately what has held the LDP together is not so much a coherent philosophy of conservatism but the unequalled opportunity the party offers for government office.

The public response to the venality and self-seeking opportunism of LDP leaders is reflected in 'astounding levels of political dissatisfaction'.[19] As the party in government the reliance of the LDP on election finance from business has seen the fine line between political donations and bribery transgressed by several of its leaders. Their subsequent trial and conviction has in the process fuelled the alienation of large numbers of electors. Yet amidst the public disenchantment with the LDP, the opposition has singularly failed to capitalize on scandals which in most circumstances would have led a disillusioned electorate to throw the party out of office.

Notes

1. Baerwald, H.M. (1986) *Party Politics in Japan*. London, Allen & Unwin, p. 155.

2. Ike, N. (1978) *A Theory of Japanese Democracy*. Colorado, Westview Press, ch. 5.

3. Buckley, R. (1985) *Japan Today*. Cambridge, C.U.P., p. 40.

4. *ibid.*, p. 40.

5. Dore, R.P. (1958), p. 88.

6. Sasaki, T. (1987) Review of *The Liberal Democratic Party in Power. Japan Foundation Newsletter*. Vol. 14, No. 5, p. 15.

7. Flannagan, S.C.L. (1980) 'National and Local Voting Trends'. In Steiner, K. *et al.* (eds) *Political Opposition and Local Politics in Japan*. Princeton, Princeton U.P. p. 166.

8. Johnson, C. (1986) 'Tanaka Kakuei, Structural Corruption and the Advent of Machine Politics in Japan'. *Journal of Japanese Studies*. Vol. 12, No. 1, p. 8.

9. Dore, R.P. (1959) *Land Reform in Japan*. Oxford, O.U.P., p. 149.

10. *ibid*

11. Steven, R. (1983) 'The High Yen Crisis in Japan'. *Capital and Class*, No. 34, Spring, p. 303.

12. Baerwald, H.M. (1986) *Party Politics in Japan*. London, Allen & Unwin, p. 170.

13. Fukui, H. (1984) Book Review of 'Japan's Electoral Process' in *Journal of Japanese Studies*, Vol. II, No. 2, p. 402.

14. Fukui, H. (1970) p. 128.

15. Christopher, R.C. (1984) *The Japanese Mind*. London, Pan Books, p. 199.

16. Buckley, R. (1085) *Japan Today*. Cambridge, C.U.P, p. 27.

17. White, J.W. (1974) 'Tradition and Politics in Studies of Contemporary Japan'. *World Politics*. Vol. 26, No. 3, p. 424.

18. Christopher, R.C. (1984) *The Japanese Mind*. London, Pan Books, p. 198

19. Flannagan, S.C.L. (1980) 'The Partisan Politicization of Local Government'. In Steiner, K. *et al.* (eds) *Political Opposition and Local Politics in Japan*. Princeton, Princeton U.P. p. 458.

33. Minorities
[from Chapter 4 — Japan's Pseudo-Democracy]
Peter Herzog

Ainu

Japan has the reputation of being a homogeneous country and Japanese often emphasise the ethnic, linguistic and cultural unity of their country. In its 1980 report to the Commission on Human Rights, the Japanese government stated that there were no ethnic minorities in Japan. This view was immediately attacked by the Ainu and termed erroneous by Japanese anthropologists and sociologists. Nevertheless, while trying to explain his racist remarks on minorities in the United States, the then Prime Minister Yasuhiro Nakasone told a Diet committee in October 1986 that Japan was an ethnically homogeneous country and declared before the House of Representatives that there was no member of an ethnic minority group with Japanese nationality in Japan that was subject to discrimination.

Actually, there are minorities in Japan and their existence involves numerous difficult problems. The Ainu, who are basically different from the Japanese, are often referred to as the original inhabitants of Japan. They were called *ebisu* (barbarians) until the Meiji era and may once have occupied the largest part of Japan but had been pushed back to the northern part of Honshu, Hokkaido, Sakhalin, the Kuriles and Kamchatka by the close of the seventh century. They are of paleoasiatic origin and differ from today's Japanese particularly by their heavy beards and hairy chests. They may have numbered about 50,000 at the beginning of the seventeenth century, but their number has steadily declined.

During the Edo era the Ainu were decimated by internal struggles as well as by the oppressive rule of the Matsumae clan and were exploited by unscrupulous Japanese merchants. The Ainu complain that from 1868 the government secluded them in deserted areas and forced them to work as slaves for colonists who came from the mainland. Under the policy of assimilation, Ainu children were prohibited from using their language in school and were taught to become subjects of the Emperor like other Japanese. Before the war, children had to learn by heart the names of Japan's 124 Emperors.

In 1899 the government enacted a protection law which attempted to transform the Ainu, who were hunters and fishermen, into farmers and forced them to adopt a completely alien life-style. The law, called Hokkaido Ex-Natives Protection Law (the Japanese title, *Hokkaido Kyū Dojin Hogo-hō*, is derogatory), is still on the books. Ninety years later in December 1989 the government, recognising that the law was discriminatory, organised a committee made up of officials of the Hokkaido Development Agency and three ministries involved in the issue, to prepare a new law

Herzog, P.J: 'Minorities' from *JAPAN'S PSEUDO-DEMOCRACY* (Japan Library: Curzon Press Ltd, 1993), pp. 70-98.

for the Ainu. At present, the Ainu need the approval of the Hokkaido government to sell or purchase land. Under the assimilation policy, the Ainu were forced to abandon their culture, religion and language. The government treated Hokkaido as no-man's land and distributed most of the habitable areas to aristocrats, bureaucrats, settlers from the mainland and soldiers called *tondenhei* (soldier-colonists).

A survey carried out by the prefectural government in 1986 put the Ainu population at 24,331, living in 70 towns and cities. Of the Ainu in Hokkaido, 42.3 per cent are engaged in farming and fishing, compared with 8.6 per cent of the non-Ainu population of the island. A survey undertaken by Professor Jiro Suzuki in 1988–9 found that 35.6 per cent of Ainu households in Tokyo have annual incomes of between ¥ 2 to 3 million while over 40 per cent of Tokyo households have annual incomes of ¥ 5 million. Most of the Ainu men living in Tokyo are blue-collar workers while many women are bar hostesses. Since Ainu face discrimination in employment, their average income is only about half of the national average and nearly 60 out of 1,000 receive welfare assistance. Recipients of welfare assistance account for 2.3 per cent of Tokyo Ainu residents while the percentage is 1.8 per cent for all Tokyo households. The ratio of unmarried people between the ages of 35 and 40 is 26.9 per cent among Ainu but only 15.9 per cent for the general population.

Serious discrimination also exists in education. Ainu children are often teased on account of their physical appearance (e.g., they are called 'gorilla' because of their thick hair on arms and legs). While most Ainu now in their 50s and 60s taught their children to hide their ethnic identity, today's Ainu are more aware of their roots, and associations such as the Hokkaido Utari (Ainu for 'fellow men') Society fight against discrimination. Roughly 70 per cent of the Ainu covered in a 1986 survey had experienced some kind of discrimination, 43 per cent in the form of opposition to marriage and about the same percentage had suffered insults in society. At the seventh UN Human Rights Commission working session for minorities in August 1989, the Ainu Association of Hokkaido criticised the Japanese government's unwillingness to adopt the UN human rights declaration for aborigines and to preserve indigenous Ainu culture.

Okinawa

Another ethnic minority almost completely assimilated into the predominant Japanese mainland culture is the indigenous population of Okinawa. In the fifteenth century, the rulers of Shuri claimed authority over the Ryukyu islands and in 1451 the first embassy came to Kyoto and was received by the Shogun Yoshimasa. From that time on, embassies were sent periodically to Japan but at the same time, the Ryukyuans paid tribute to China which asserted suzerainty over the islands. In 1609 Iehisa Shimazu, daimyō of Satsuma, sent a force to the island which took the king's son and 100 of his nobles as prisoners to Kagoshima. The Ryukyuans had to pay a yearly tribute to Satsuma; moreover, a merciless exploitation impoverished the islands. In 1873 the king of the Ryukyus came to Tokyo and received the investiture of his domains but in 1879 the islands were annexed and made into a prefecture. In spite of China's protests, ex-President Ulysses S. Grant, who acted as arbitrator, ruled in favour of Japan.

Okinawa is the only part of Japan which directly experienced the horrors of war. Many Okinawans committed suicide when the island became a battlefield, others were executed as spies by the Japanese Army. The islands remained under American control until 15 May 1972, but even thereafter, the American bases continued to play an important role in the life of Okinawa. While the American presence has made a considerable contribution to the island's economy, problems such as the lease of land for the American bases, the environmental impact of the airfields and military exercises, and the unanswered question of the presence of nuclear weapons have caused the Okinawans to complain that they are being victimised for objectives unrelated to their own lives. Although there is no discrimination in the usual sense of the word, Okinawa is the poorest of all prefectures and has been left behind in the country's economic development.

The Ryukyuan language is different from Japanese. It comprises several different dialects: spoken on Amami Oshima, the northern part of Okinawa, the southern part of this island, on Miyakojima and on the Yaeyama islands. At school, however, children learn only standard Japanese. Ryukyuan is widely considered a Japanese dialect, not an independent language.

Burakumin

Numerous problems are presented by a minority usually referred to as *burakumin*, (literally 'village people'). They are the descendants of people outside the four classes of the Tokugawa society (warriors, farmers, artisans and merchants) called *hinin* (non-men) or *eta* (outcast, pariah) engaged in occupations deemed unclean (by Shinto standards) such as flayers, tanners and curriers. In August 1871 a decree of the *Dajōkan* (*mibun kaihō-rei* — social position emancipation order) abolished the designation *hinin* or *eta* and prescribed that they were to be considered equal to commoners (*heimin*). But the decree could not abolish the social discrimination. The new commoners, (*shin-heimin*), as they were sometimes called, continued to live in separate communities (hence the designation *burakumin*; '*buraku*' were the traditional villages whereas '*mura*' were the villages set up as administrative units by the government). Some of the *buraku* were Japan's worst slums, with narrow, unpaved roads, and substandard housing without sewers.

A survey of the Management and Coordination Agency carried out in 1985 counted 4,603 *buraku* communities with a population of 1.7 million but *buraku* activists claim that there are 5,365 communities with 3 million people. About 80 per cent of the *burakumin* live in agricultural communities but only a few can engage in farming; most men work as day labourers. Those living in fishing villages are usually excluded from fishing grounds and do not own large boats or advanced equipment.

In the cities, *burakumin* often depend on piecework, simple manufacturing or assembling for cottage industries and other intermediates. Leatherwork and braiding used to be the main types of work. They are deprived of job opportunities and form the lowest rank of labour, working on construction sites or hired as auxiliary labour and for odd jobs. Other typical occupations are the reclamation of waste material or peddling. The unemployment rate among *buraku* people is high, sometimes over 20 per cent. The number of people living on welfare is 6 or 8 times the national average.

549

Discrimination is rampant in education, employment and marriage. According to a survey by a *burakumin* organisation, 60 per cent of all *buraku* marriages are with other *burakumin*; even then the families often oppose the marriage. The custom of engaging enquiry or detective agencies to check the families of prospective marriage partners is mainly to prevent marriage with somebody of *buraku* background. Discrimination followed the *burakamin* even beyond death. Some old graves in northern Kanto bear derogatory posthumous names (*kaimy-o*) and temple registers contain the remark 'eta'.

Some years ago the number of publications listing *buraku* communities (e.g. *Buraku Chimei Sōkan*, Register of Buraku Place Names) increased. They are bought by enquiry agencies and large enterprises. Usually, a copy of the family register must be attached to a job application; if the applicant comes from a *buraku* community, his job application will not be considered. In March 1985 Osaka Prefecture passed an ordinance for private enquiry or detective agencies. They were required to notify the prefecture of their business and prohibited to carry out discriminatory investigations and prepare reports related to marriage and employment in *buraku* districts. Osaka has the largest concentration of *buraku* people.

In education, *buraku* children are handicapped by their living conditions and are often victims of harassment. The percentage of *buraku* children advancing to high school or university is below the national average. Graffiti such as '*buraku* people are not human beings' are scribbled on school walls. Crimes such as robbery or murder are blamed on *buraku* people without any proof. On the other hand, the Japanese try to conceal the existence of *buraku* not only from the outside world but also from the general public. The Japanese translation of Professor Reischauer's book *The Japanese* omitted all passages referring to *buraku*. James Clavel's novel *Shogun* contained some derogatory remarks on *eta* and the Japanese translation prepared by TBS Britannica had to be withdrawn.

According to a 1984 survey of the Buraku Research Institute, 16 per cent of the *burakumin* covered by the survey were 'completely illiterate' or 'hardly literate', and 30 per cent were 'slightly illiterate'. Women constituted the largest part of the illiterate. Of the 6 per cent of the respondents who did not attend or finish elementary school and were deemed 'completely illiterate', 68 per cent were women. Of the respondents, 66 per cent finished elementary school only, while of Japan's entire population, only 0.3 per cent did not attend or finish elementary school and 39 per cent did not advance beyond elementary school.

The first organised attempt of the *burakumin* to fight discrimination and attain equality was the Suihei Undō (Horizontal Movement) starting with the foundation of the Suiheisha (Horizontal Society) in Kyoto in 1922. The movement was reconstituted in 1946 with the establishment of the Buraku Kaihō Zenkoku Iinkai (National Buraku Emancipation Committee) which was transformed in 1955 into the Buraku Kaihō Dōmei (Buraku Emancipation League). Since this organisation was closely linked to the Socialist Party, the Liberal-Democratic Party started a rival organisation Zen-Nippon Dōwa-kai (All Japan Dōwa Association; *dōwa* [integration] is a euphemism now used for *buraku*) in 1960. The Communist Party launched a third organisation in

1970: Buraku Kaihō Dōmei Seijōka Zenkoku Renraku Kaigi (Buraku Emancipation League Normalisation National Liaison Conference).

In 1984 the Buraku Kaihō Dōmei had about 170,000 registered members, the Communist-affiliated organisation 80,000 and Dōwa-kai 35,000. The combined membership accounted for about 30 to 40 per cent of the *burakumin*. The activities of these organisations have been hurt by poor leadership and internal squabbles. Dōwa-kai was dissolved in 1986 because of internal dissensions. Members accused the leaders of bureaucratic and overbearing behaviour, misuse of their positions for personal gain and disregard of the members' interests. Basically, all three groups professed to work for the same goals: the guarantee of occupational and educational equality, equality in agricultural communities, social security and the improvement of the environment.

For a long time the government ignored the problems of the *burakumin* but in 1969 a law (*Dōwa Taisaku Jigyō Tokubetsu Sochi-hō* Law for Special Measures for Dōwa Countermeasure Activities) aimed at improving the social and environmental conditions of the *buraku*. The law was first limited to a period of ten years but was subsequently extended several times. Since money was made available for the improvement of roads, housing and other facilities, educational grants and support of cultural activities, to secure money became the main purpose of the *buraku* organisations. Some of these organisations resorted to strong-arm tactics to obtain what they wanted and soon the name *dōwa* became associated with intimidation and violence.

This gave rise to a special type of Japanese gangster organisation called '*ese dōwa*' (pseudo-*dōwa*) which used the name of *dōwa* for a large variety of money-making schemes. They secured licences for land use which they sold for large sums to real-estate companies. They acted as mediators for obtaining loans from financial institutions, secured government funds for *buraku* projects and demanded rebates or commissions from the enterprises executing the projects. They sought orders from government agencies or enterprises, e.g., for studies on *dōwa* problems, for which they pocketed exorbitant 'research' fees. They squeezed money out of individuals and corporations by ferreting out mistakes or scandals, collected contributions to fictitious social causes, had people buy a variety of goods, subscribe to publications or buy advertising space. They even used the courts to make money by obtaining preliminary injunctions (such as *tachi-iri kinshi*, prohibition to enter, or *shōmu bōgai kinshi*, prohibition to obstruct business) which they only withdrew against outrageous payments.

They helped tax frauds by arranging fictitious debts which could be deducted from the inheritance, they took charge of negotiations for compensation in traffic accidents, bribed officials in charge of public works or of *buraku* projects. Two officials involved in such briberies committed suicide. Some years ago, about 270 sham *dōwa* groups were active. A survey of the Ministry of Justice covering 5,700 enterprises found that one in three firms had been victimised by sham *dōwa* groups. Insurance, finance and construction companies suffered most damage. The situation was worst in Osaka, but conditions were also bad in Tokyo, Fukuoka, Nagoya, Sendai, Takamatsu and Sapporo.

551

The most notorious case of discrimination in which, according to *buraku* organisations, one of their people became the victim of police prejudice involved the rape-murder of a 16-year-old senior high school student, Yoshie Nakada, of Sayama (Saitama Prefecture). A note demanded a ransom of ¥200,000 but the police failed to apprehend the criminal who came to collect the ransom. Since the case occurred shortly after the abduction of a boy in Tokyo, there was considerable pressure to solve the case. The police botched the investigation and in a fishing expedition, 23-year-old Kazuo Ishikawa was arrested on a charge of violence and theft.

The case had been settled by the parties involved and Ishikawa was released, but he was rearrested as a suspect in the Nakada case. Ishikawa's education had ended with the second grade at elementary school; he could hardly write and had no knowledge whatever of the law. He had been taught to see in his lawyer his enemy and declined to talk to him. While in police custody he confessed to the murder and repeated his confession in the trial by the Urawa District Court.

The defence pointed out numerous discrepancies between the confession and the material evidence in the case. Ishikawa could not have written the threatening letter demanding ransom, and the belongings of the murdered girl discovered on the basis of the confession (bag, wrist watch and fountain pen) had been arranged in a completely unnatural way. The court acknowledged that there were inconsistencies but attributed them to the shortcomings of the investigation. The confession was a mixture of truth and falsehood.

Ishikawa was found guilty and condemned to death in March 1964. The Buraku Emancipation League called the verdict an expression of discrimination and the defence appealed. The proceedings lasted ten years; the Tokyo High Court held 80 sessions and the presiding judge changed five times during the trial. Ishikawa pleaded innocent and claimed that he had been deceived by the police. If he confessed, he had been told, he would be set free in ten years; if he did not, he would be hanged. The High Court ruled that the confession was essentially true but reduced the punishment to life imprisonment. The defence contended that the sentence was based on prejudice and appealed to the Supreme Court. In August 1977 the court rejected the appeal and upheld the life sentence. Although some details of the evidence remained doubtful, Ishikawa was the murderer, the court said.

The verdict provoked violent protests by *burakumin*, involving attacks on police boxes with Molotov cocktails. The lawyers appealed to the Tokyo High Court asking the court to reopen the case because they could prove that the confession was a put-up job. The court denied the petition in February 1980. The lawyers then protested to the Supreme Court demanding to be allowed to submit new evidence and asking the court to examine the facts (which the Supreme Court usually does not do). In May 1985 the court rejected the petition stating that there was no clear evidence necessitating a not guilty verdict. The lawyers called the court's ruling an unjust, highly political sentence.

Koreans

According to the Ministry of Justice, officially registered foreigners living in Japan at the end of 1990 numbered 1.07 million, accounting for 0.87 per cent of the country's total population (123.6 million). Koreans represented the largest group with 687,940, of whom 610,924 were officially recognised as first generation, i.e., Koreans having lived in Japan before the end of the Second World War and their children. Most of the genealogically second and third generation Koreans, born and raised in Japan, speak Japanese as their first and often their only language. Osaka has the largest concentration of Koreans; of the 200,000 inhabitants of Ikuno Ward, 40,000 are Koreans. Chinese constituted the second largest group with 150,339, followed by Brazilians with 56,429.

The Russo–Japanese War led to a growing infiltration of Japan into Korea and the Treaty of Portsmouth, which ended the war, formally recognised Korea as a Japanese sphere of influence. The forced abdication of the Korean Emperor in favour of his son in 1907 brought a renewal of the armed uprisings against the Japanese occupation which were brutally suppressed. The assassination of Prince Ito by a Korean in 1909 led to the annexation of Korea in 1910.

Through the annexation, Korea became an integral part of the Japanese Empire. The name of Seoul was changed to Keijō, and Pyongyan became Heijō. Japanese was made the official language. All important administrative posts were filled by Japanese; in some cities the elected mayors were dismissed and Japanese mayors were installed. All judges were Japanese and Japanese police were not only very numerous but also entrusted with broad powers: they could make arrests without a warrant, detain suspects for an unlimited period and frequently used torture. Schools had to have Japanese principals and at least three Japanese teachers. Korean history books were destroyed and new textbooks introduced. Instruction was in Japanese in all schools and Korean teachers were sometimes even stricter than Japanese teachers in enforcing the ban on Korean. Pupils using Korean were punished.

According to a 1988 survey covering 1,106 first-generation Koreans who came to Japan between 1910 and the end of the war, Koreans were forced to change both their given and family names and three-quarters complied. Japanese *bonzes* and *kannushi* were sent to Korea to offset the influence of the Christian missionaries. The government commanded worship at Shinto shrines although 70 per cent of the interviewees said that they did not comply. When boarding the ship to Japan, people were made to sing '*Kimi ga yo*', the Japanese national anthem, and those who did not know the song were forced to board the ship on hands and knees.

On of the most traumatic events in the experience of Koreans in Japan was the massacre of Koreans at the time of the Great Kanto Earthquake in 1929. Rumours spread by the government blamed the Koreans for fictitious atrocities. Vigilante groups slaughtered about 6,000 Koreans in the days following the earthquake.

Of the two million young Korean men brought to Japan between 1938 and 1945, 60,000 were sent to Sakhalin, then Japanese territory named Karafuto. Shortly before the end of the war, 20,000 men were moved to Hokkaido, but 43,000 remained on Sakhalin. Some later became Soviet citizens but others became stateless. Their wives, who had remained in Japan, were left without support because neither the Japanese nor the Korean government cared for them. About 35,000 Koreans are still living on Sakhalin (47,000 Japanese were repatriated after the end of the war).

Since South Korea had no diplomatic relations with the Soviet Union, the Koreans were left without protection or support. Japan declared that the Koreans were no longer Japanese subjects, did nothing to help these people and failed to pay any compensation for their treatment. Instead of wasting billions of yen on prestige projects in far-away developing countries, the Japanese government should have honoured its moral obligation to people deported from their home country by Japan. In 1963 a 'Russianisation' programme enforced under Nikita Kruschev closed all Korean schools and theatres. Since *perestroika*, however, Korean language classes have been provided in high schools and the local university at Yuzhno Sakhalinsk.

Taking advantage of the Occupation's repatriation programme, over one million Koreans returned to their homeland after the war. Many chose to stay in Japan and others, disillusioned with conditions in Korea, tried to return to Japan illegally. When the San Francisco Peace Treaty came into effect, the Koreans who had remained in Japan, together with Taiwanese, were automatically deprived of their Japanese citizenship by an administrative notice issued on 19 April 1952, in the name of the chief of the Civil Affairs Bureau of the Ministry of Justice. They were henceforth treated as foreigners. The measure was particularly arbitrary since these people had declined repatriation and opted to stay in Japan. The change was made without any kind of hearing and without giving the people involved any opportunity of contesting the order.

Under an agreement between the Japanese government and the Republic of Korea which went into effect in January 1966, Koreans could apply for permanent residence status. The agreement applied to first- and second-generation Koreans (legally, first generation are those who came to Japan before the end of the Second World War and their offspring born prior to 16 January 1971; second generation are those born after that date).

Under a Japan–South Korea Treaty signed in 1965, neither government is liable to compensate Koreans who were forced to fight for Japan in the Second World War. In October 1990, 22 Koreans living in South Korea filed suit in the Tokyo District Court demanding compensation from the Japanese government. In January 1991 Chong Sang Gun, a Korean living in Japan, who had served in the Japanese navy and lost his right arm while fighting in the Marshall Islands sued the government for ¥ 10 million in compensation for his injury and mental suffering. Chong had applied for compensation after the war but his claim was rejected. The law limits compensation for injuries and allowances to surviving families to Japanese nationals.

Six Koreans who had been drafted into the Japanese Imperial Army and convicted of war crimes by the Allies and the family of another conscript executed for war crimes filed suit demanding ¥ 130 million in compensation and a formal apology by the Prime Minister. A total of 148 Korean conscripts were tried after the war for Class B and C war crimes. Of these, 23 were executed and 125 sentenced to prison. They were accused of having violated the Geneva Convention by forcing prisoners of war to work, abusing prisoners and mistreating them by failing to provide food and medicine. The Japanese government has maintained that it has no obligation to compensate the former soldiers whom it deprived of their Japanese citizenship.

'Comfort' girls

During the war about 870,000 Koreans were brought to Japan where they were mainly used for heavy work — Koreans constituted 32 per cent of the workforce in the coal mines. In the course of the war 142,000 Koreans were drafted into the Japanese army and 101,000 into the navy. 22,000 Korean conscripts were killed in action. Between 80,000 and 200,000 Korean women were conscripted by the Japanese army to serve as 'comfort women' (*ianfu*) for the troops (the officers were furnished with Japanese prostitutes). A large number of these women were teenagers who did not know what they would be forced to do until they arrived at their destination. Sometimes they had to serve 70 to 80 soldiers a day each. Many of them were killed at the end of the war because the Japanese army sought to destroy the evidence of the infamous treatment of these women. Those who survived were reluctant to return to their homeland because they were ashamed to meet relatives and friends.

Among the many claims for compensation by Koreans, Taiwanese, Indonesians and Chinese against the Japanese government for backpay, mistreatment, injuries and other wrongs was also a demand that Japan pay damages and issue an apology to the women forced into prostitution. In addition to women from Asian countries, the military also forced at least 35 Dutch women living in the former Dutch East Indies to serve as prostitutes in military brothels. In June 1990 the Japanese government denied any responsibility asserting that the women were recruited by private brokers and not conscripted under the National Mobilization Law of 1938. In November 1990 the Korean Council for Women Drafted Under Japanese Rule issued an open letter to the Japanese government seeking compensation and an apology but the government again denied its responsibility.

Strict military rules regulated all aspects of what the army called 'houses of relaxation', including hours of operation, prices and hygienic conditions. The regulations for a facility in Manila stipulated that the 'geisha and hostesses' had to turn over half of their income to the Japanese manager of the brothel. In the period from August to October 1944, the cost of a 40-minute session was set at ¥ 1.50 for enlisted men, ¥ 2.50 for non-commissioned officers and ¥ 4 for civilian employees. In the Shanghai area prices varied according to the nationality of the prostitutes. Officers and warrant officers paid ¥ 3 for a one-hour session with a Japanese or Korean prostitute and ¥ 2.50 for a Chinese. Regulations provided that association with hostesses was forbidden to those who refused to use condoms and that the women were not to be kissed. An army document dated 1938 called for the speedy installation of brothels in order to stop the widespread rape of local women in China by Japanese soldiers. Korea was divided into a number of districts which each had to furnish a fixed number of women .

When a volunteer group set up a telephone hotline in Tokyo in February 1992, veterans, doctors and nurses called in to confirm Japan's official involvement in the operation. According to a Japanese who was involved in the procurement of 'comfort girls', the government's contention that these women were recruited by private brokers is a shameless lie. Sometimes an entire village was surrounded by troops or police, all women were herded together and the young women put on a truck and carried away.

Wartime documents found in January 1992 confirmed that the Imperial Japanese Army had been involved in the kidnapping and forced prostitution of women from Korea and other Asian countries. A confidential war-time directive of the Ministry of the Army stated that the military should control the recruitment process and ensure that no mistakes were committed so as not to cause social repercussions and protect the reputation of the army. Foreign Minister Michio Watanabe's acknowledgement of the participation of the army in the forced prostitution of foreign women was the first time that the Japanese government recognised the country's responsibility for the misdeeds and brought official apologies — half a century after the atrocities — but left the issue of compensation unsettled.

Further investigations revealed that primary schoolgirls aged 11 or 12 years were drafted into a corps that included prostitutes for Japanese troops. During his visit to Seoul in January 1992 Prime Minister Kiichi Miyazawa expressed regret at Japan's actions while occupying Korea but failed to make any commitment on the question of compensation. The chairman of the Social Democratic Party urged the government to stop its insistence that legal claims had been met and to recognise its moral obligations to the victims of Japan's aggression by paying compensation to individual claimants.

In December 1991 35 Koreans filed a lawsuit in the Tokyo District Court demanding ¥ 700 million (¥ 20 million per person) in wartime damages from the Japanese government. The plaintiffs included former soldiers who served in the Japanese army, three 'comfort girls' and the families of soldiers killed in action. The plaintiffs based their claims on the assertion that they were victims of crimes against humanity which, they contended, had been established as justifiable by the war-crime trials.

One of the 'comfort girls', Kim Huk Sun, was 17 when the Japanese came along in a truck, beat a number of women and dragged them into the truck. She was raped the first day, sent to China and attached to a military brothel. For the next three months, she had to accommodate dozens of soldiers every single day. Kim tried to escape three times; twice she was caught and severely beaten; she succeeded on her third try with the help of a Korean man whom she later married. Her experience left an emotional trauma. 'I feel sick when I am close to a man', she said, and even her husband, now dead, made her feel that way .

There were, however, Japanese who opposed the payment of compensation to former 'comfort girls' on the ground that the 1965 normalisation treaty with South Korea settled all claims. The understanding of human rights prior to the Second World War was very different from today's recognition of human rights. The opponents also contend that at the time of the war, Korea formed part of Japan so that there was no question of national discrimination.

Discrimination

During Japan's occupation of what was then the Dutch East Indies, the army and navy employed about 45,000 Indonesians. Of the 23,000 who served as *heiho* (auxiliary soldiers), about 3,000 were killed and some 7,000 have died since the end of the war. An organisation of former Indonesian soldiers and survivors claim that Japan owes them about $ 650 million because the soldiers were forced to deposit one-third of their salaries at military posts and were not paid their outstanding stipends when the war ended. The organisation used the visit of the Imperial couple to Indonesia in 1991 to press their claim against Japan. Unlike Japan, the Netherlands still pays military pensions to the Indonesians who served with the Dutch forces.

Koreans are plagued by numerous social antagonisms. First, there is the animosity of the Japanese against Koreans. Secondly, the Koreans are divided between those adhering to the Republic of Korea (organised in the Korean Residents Union in Japan — Mindan) and those supporting the North (who belong to the General Association of Korean Residents in Japan — Chongryon). Thirdly, relations between Koreans living in Japan and in the peninsula are not always harmonious. Lastly, the regional antagonisms of the homeland also affect Koreans living abroad (e.g., the discord between the provinces of Kyeongsando and Cheollada, the native provinces respectively of President Roh Tae Woo and opposition leader Kim Dae Jung).

Koreans in Japan experience some of the worst forms of discrimination and harassment. Education and employment are the areas in which Koreans encounter the most unfair treatment but they are also disadvantaged in marriage, social security, housing and generally in daily life. Schools established by Korean organisations for Korean children were not recognised by the Ministry of Education as ordinary schools but were classified as 'special schools' (*tokushu gakkō*), a category which applies to vocational schools. Students of Korean high schools were not allowed to participate in prefectural or national sports events; only recently have some prefectures allowed Korean high school students to take part in prefectural athletic meets.

In a show of solidarity, the student council of Hiroshima's Nishi High School sent a petition with 9,253 signatures of students from 62 high schools to the Hiroshima High School Athletic Association asking to grant membership to Hiroshima Senior High School for Children of Korean Descent. The school, which has ties to North Korea, is not recognised as a regular high school by the Ministry of Education and the students are barred from taking part in prefectural sports events organised by the association. The students' at Nishi High School have held cultural and sports exchanges with the students at the Korean school for eight gears . They called on other high schools in the prefecture to join in the efforts to overturn the 'unfair and discriminatory' policy against schools for foreign residents. The Japan High School Baseball Federation allowed high schools affiliated with North Korea in Kanagawa and Hiroshima prefectures and Kobe to participate in regional competitions for the August national championship games and later extended this permission to high schools in Tokyo, Aichi and Ibaraki Prefectures.

Of about 430,000 students graduating from Japanese universities each year, around 15,000 are ethnic Koreans. They seldom succeed in finding employment in large corporations but due to the labour shortage which developed in the latter part of the 1980s even large companies began to take on non-Japanese employees. Some of the worst cases of discrimination occur in public employment. Japanese nationality is considered a requirement for teaching in public schools. On principle, no legal restrictions prevent employment of non-Japanese by local governments but, based on the theory that administration is an exercise of sovereignty, the Cabinet Legislative

Bureau and the Home Ministry maintain that posts executing public authority must be held by Japanese and that this rule applies to teaching. In June 1983 the Home Ministry notified local governments that the restriction no longer applied to nurses. As of November 1986 22 prefectures had foreigners on their payrolls; most were doctors and nurses serving in remote areas. Many prefectural and municipal governments retain restrictions on administrative positions when they open jobs to foreign nationals. As a result, 30 prefectures had regulations containing the nationality clause and 25 prefectures did not employ any foreigners.

Some Korean residents have demanded to be given the right to vote in local elections. In a lawsuit filed with the Fukui District Court in May 1991 by four Koreans who have lived in Japan for over 40 years, the plaintiffs contended that the provisions in the Public Office Election Law and the Local Government Law concerning the qualification to vote were unconstitutional. They asserted that the constitution gives the right to elect the members of local assemblies to all residents (*jūmin*) whereas the Public Office Election Law restricts the right to Japanese nationals.

In Article 93 (paragraph 2) the constitution regulates the election of the chief executive officers of all local public bodies, the members of their assemblies and other local officials. The English text says that these persons shall be elected by direct popular vote but the Japanese text stipulates that the *residents* of these local public bodies shall directly elect them (*sono chihō kōkyō dantai no jūmin ga chokusetsu kore wo senkyo suru*). The same difference between the English and Japanese texts is found in Article 95 which concerns special laws applicable to only one public entity. According to the English text, such laws need the consent of the 'majority of the voters of the local public entity concerned'. The Japanese text says that the Diet cannot make such laws 'unless it obtains the consent of the majority in the voting of the residents of this public body' (*sono chihō kōkyō dantai no jūmin no tōhyō ni oite kahansū no dōi wo enakereba*).

The Public Office Election Law (*Kōshoku Senkyo-hō*) provides that the right to vote in local elections is given to persons who are Japanese nationals (*Nihon kokumin-taru mono*) of at least 20 years of age who have possessed a residence (*jūsho*) in the local public body uninterruptedly for at least three months (Art. 9, par. 2). The plaintiffs claimed that this legal requirement was contrary to the provision that the *residents* of the local public body were entitled to vote.

Prime Minister Masayoshi Ohira was of the opinion that local governments should be allowed to devise means of creating employment opportunities for non-Japanese residents in their regions. The Osaka municipal government had considered a plan which was to open more jobs to Koreans and other foreigners who had lived a long time in Japan. But due to pressure from the Home Ministry, which is opposed to foreigners serving as public employees, the municipal government dropped its plan of removing the restrictions barring foreigners from municipal employment. When the city abandoned its plan, it counted, besides school teachers and nurses, 54 foreigners among its 46,000 employees.

The Kawasaki Local Administration Research Centre drafted a report calling for corrective measures in municipal employment. Discriminatory practices against foreigners, notably Koreans, without legal grounds should be abolished, notwithstanding the central government's uniform policy of not allowing non-

Japanese employment in public posts. The report supported the system adopted by Machida (a Tokyo suburban city) under which non-Japanese were hired but not promoted to section chiefs exercising public authority.

In May 1991 an association of 70 municipal governments in Hyogo Prefecture decided to abolish the regulation barring foreign nationals from taking examinations for public jobs. A third-generation Korean whose application for taking the examination required for teaching at public schools had been rejected by the Fukuoka Prefectural Board of Education three times was finally allowed to take the test. But in accordance with the instruction of the Ministry of Education, he will only be hired as a 'full-time lecturer'.

Teachers at Korean schools asked Transport Minister Kanezo Muraoka to have commuter tickets for Korean students priced the same as those for Japanese students. Private railroad companies apply the same rate to Japanese and Korean students but the JR companies continued the practice of the Japan National Railways and priced commuter tickets for Korean students 43 per cent higher than those for Japanese students. The reason is that the Ministry of Education classifies Korean schools as special schools to which the student discount for ordinary schools does not apply.

A Korean paid the contributions for the national insurance (old age pension) system and applied for a pension when he reached the age of 65. But he was told that he was ineligible because the system applied only to Japanese and he should not have been admitted in the first place. The man sued but lost in the District Court. The Tokyo High Court, however, reversed the decision explaining that the expectation and reliance on the receipt of a pension should be given legal protection. The law has been amended and the requirement of Japanese nationality for the national pension system and child allowances abolished.

Another Korean, a victim of the atomic bomb, secretly returned to Japan for treatment. He applied for a certificate entitling him to treatment but the Fukuoka prefectural government refused to give him the document. The Fukuoka District Court rejected his demand to quash the refusal of the prefecture but the Fukuoka High Court ordered the district court to nullify the prefecture's rejection and the Supreme Court upheld the decision of the High Court. Being a victim of the bomb, the court declared, is the result of the war which was an action of the state. The Law for the Medical Treatment of the Atomic Bomb Victims was partly enacted for the humanitarian purpose of helping the victims because the state itself was responsible. The law should apply without distinction to all living victims of the bomb.

Koreans experience difficulty in taking out loans from Japanese banks or obtaining credit cards. In localities with a large Korean population, apartment owners mean Koreans when they put up signs reading 'No foreigners allowed'. The most serious difficulty facing Koreans in Japan is the traditional Japanese dislike of foreigners. In June 1981 seven Koreans applied for positions at public schools in Aichi Prefecture and four in Nagoya city but all applicants were turned down because they did not possess Japanese citizenship. One of each group filed suit in Nagoya District Court asking for cancellation of the rejection but the suits were dismissed on a technicality without discussing the merits of the case. The Nagoya High Court upheld the ruling of the District Court.

A Korean high school student was recommended by her school for employment by the Kawasaki Agricultural Credit Cooperative and in August 1989 went to the cooperative's office for an interview. She had been asked to bring a copy of the family register to the interview and in the afternoon the cooperative contacted the school's placement officer and explained that they would not let the girl take the employment test because of her nationality. It would be better for the girl to look for a job with a different enterprise than to be failed in the examination. The school replied that the refusal obviously constituted discrimination on account of nationality which was contrary to the Labour Ministry's guidelines. The cooperative, however, refused to reconsider its decision saying that it was the policy of the cooperative not to employ non-Japanese. The prefecture's Labour Bureau declared that the cooperative's action was regrettable but it could do nothing more than demand a change in policy.

The harassment of Koreans became worse after the bombing of a Korean airliner. Particularly girls wearing the *chima chogori* became victims of verbal and physical abuse. In Hamamatsu (Shizuoka Prefecture), about ten Japanese high school students surrounded a Korean girl riding a bicycle and wearing a Korean dress, poked at her and shouted 'What did you come to Japan for? Go to your own country!' A middle-aged man on a bus hurled obscenities at six elementary school children returning home from school. Another man grabbed a female student by the neck and threw her on the ground on a station platform. Koreans have been spat at and schools run by Chongryon have received threatening telephone calls. The Pachinko scandal had a similar effect. Korean residents received anonymous phone calls and Korean schools were threatened with arson.

In a sharply-worded statement distributed to reporters at the Foreign Correspondents Club, Pak Jae Ro, vice-chairman of Chongryon's Central Committee, accused the Liberal-Democratic Party of racial harassment of Koreans. He rejected the allegations by LDP politicians that the Korean Pachinko operators had made donations to members of the Socialist Party to gain political favours as groundless and slanderous and denied that Chongryon had been involved in attempts to interfere in Japan's internal affairs. He said that he had documented 50 cases of violence against Korean residents, including children.

A glaring example of the arrogance and stupidity of Japanese politicians and bureaucrats in handling Koreans was the treatment of a North Korean table-tennis team taking part in the Asian Table Tennis Championship games held at Niigata in May 1988. The Japanese government had imposed so-called sanctions on North Korea for the destruction of a South Korean aircraft allegedly by North Korean agents. Under these sanctions, North Korean officials were not allowed to enter Japan and no North Korean could come to Japan for political activities. The table-tennis team was allowed to participate in the game on condition that no government official would accompany the players and that the team would not attend meetings of a political nature.

While the championship games were still going on, the 18 players and officials were invited to a reception at the Okura Hotel, Niigata, sponsored by the General Association of Korean residents in Japan (Chongryon) and a Japanese group. About 150 people, including the mayor of Niigata, Genki Wakasugi, and Chongryon chairman

Han Dok Su attended the reception. At 1 p.m., while dinner was being served, the Ministry of Justice telephoned the organisers of the reception and informed them of the decision of the Entry Division of the Immigration Bureau that the North Koreans were not permitted to attend the function. Complying with the government's instructions, the organisers made the North Koreans leave the hotel without finishing dinner.

Li Jong Ho, the leader of the team, told a press conference that they had withdrawn from the competition, were going home immediately and would never again take part in any event held in Japan. A spokesman for the Physical Education Association of Korean Residents in Japan expressed the common sentiment of the North Koreans shared by many Japanese: 'We can't understand why eating dinner with the North Korean delegates and Japanese constitutes a political activity.' Minister of Justice Yukio Hayashida, trying to justify the action of his bureaucrats, remarked that although the reception itself may not have been a political activity, it was undesirable that the North Korean team had contacts with members of Chongryon. An official of the Foreign Ministry defended the action of the Immigration Bureau stating that the North Koreans should have observed the conditions of their entry into Japan. This is difficult if the conditions are interpreted by an arrogant bureaucracy to mean whatever they want them to mean.

Korean names & 'nationality'

Prior to the war Koreans were often forced to assume Japanese names and even today, many Koreans use Japanese names in elementary, junior and senior high school which is what the prefectural Boards of Education want. A growing number of students change to their Korean name when they go to college. Many Koreans, however, keep their Japanese name for business use.

The pronunciation of Korean names has been a source of irritation. Since the names are written in Chinese characters (ideographs), the Japanese usually pronounce them according to the *on* reading of the characters (i.e., a pronunciation derived from the Chinese reading) which is quite different from the Korean pronunciation (e.g., Roh Tae Woo becomes Ro Tai Gu; Chinese names are pronounced in the same way, e.g., Den Xiaoping becomes Tō Shō Hei). In a broadcast, NHK, the public broadcasting system, pronounced the name of a Korean clergyman living in Japan in the Japanese way. The clergyman complained that he had been treated as a colonial and demanded an apology. Since NHK demurred, the clergyman sued demanding ¥ 1 and an apology.

The Fukuoka District Court turned down his demand in 1977 and when the Fukuoka High Court rejected his appeal, he took the case to the Supreme Court. (The clergyman's name is Chci Chan Hwa; NHK pronounced it Sai Shō Ka. The pronunciation based on the Japanese *on* reading was the rule when Korea was a Japanese colony, hence the clergyman's complaint.) In 1983 the Japanese government changed its regulation and decreed that names written in Chinese characters had to be pronounced in accordance with their reading in the original language.

A 34-year-old teacher born of a Japanese mother and a Korean father asked the Family Court to be permitted to use her Korean name (Yun Cho Ja) instead of her Japanese name (Oshima Teruko). When she was born her mother had had to register her as an illegitimate child so that she could obtain Japanese nationality. The court denied her request. Devotion to her father's place of origin, the judge said, was no reason for changing the name in the family register. But three years later, the Kawasaki branch of the Yokohama Family Court allowed her to change her Japanese name for the Korean name she had been using for over a decade. She wanted the change, she told the court, because her volunteer work for Korean children in Kawasaki and Osaka had made her aware of the discrimination suffered by Korean residents in Japan.

When she submitted her application for registration to the ward office, she wrote her name in Chinese characters with the phonetic transcription in *kana* at the side of the characters. The ward office delayed accepting her application until it had consulted the Ministry of Justice, stating the most peremptory reason of the bureaucracy for refusing to act: 'It has never been done before. There are no precedents for putting a pronunciation beside a surname in the register.'

Under the 1985 revision of the Nationality Law, children with one Japanese parent born after 1 January 1985 can have dual nationality until the age of 22 (the usual age when young people graduate from university). A second-generation Korean, Pak Yong Bok, married to a Japanese, Akiko Takahashi, wanted his daughter, born 7 March 1989, to have Japanese nationality but a Korean name, Pak Sa Lee. The Shibuya Ward Office officials refused to accept the registration. Under a notice issued by the Ministry of Justice, they said, those who want Japanese nationality must register under a Japanese name. Pak did not fill out the registration form but when he visited the office again in May, he discovered that his daughter had been registered under the name of Sara Takahashi.

Pak pointed out that the Nationality Law did not stipulate that a child must have a Japanese name in order to get Japanese nationality and that the local or national government did not have the right to determine the name of his child. Minoru Tagawa, head of the Family Registration Section, apologised, admitting that he had ordered the registration but insisted that he could not disregard the Ministry of Justice's directive. The notice of the ministry again shows its authoritarian attitude and its tendency to claim legal validity for its usurpation of authority.

For many years the Ministry of Justice required applicants for naturalisation to adopt a Japanese name. This requirement had no basis in law; it was enforced, the ministry said, to facilitate the assimilation into Japanese society. This policy was the direct outcome of the pre-war efforts to amalgamate the colonies and it was continued after the war because the administration found it convenient. With the growing national consciousness of the Koreans living in Japan, the practical necessity of retaining or adopting a Japanese name kept many Koreans from applying for naturalisation despite the obvious benefits they would gain from such a step.

A second-generation Korean, Cho Geon Chi, filed suit with the Shimonoseki branch of the Yamaguchi District Court demanding restoration of his Japanese nationality, a solatium of ¥ 300 million and an apology by the Prime Minister for the discriminatory treatment of Koreans. Cho was born in February 1944 in Yukahashi (Fukuoka Prefecture) and automatically became a Japanese citizen. But, as mentioned above, with the conclusion of the San Francisco Peace Treaty in September 1951, people from

Japan's former colonies residing in Japan were deprived of their Japanese nationality by an administrative decision. Cho contended that under the Japanese Nationality Law, Japanese nationality is only lost when a person voluntarily acquires another nationality.

The Yamaguchi District Court rejected Cho's claim, siding with the government's contention that, when Japan gave up sovereignty over Korea as a result of the peace treaty, it also gave up sovereignty over the people. The flaw in this argument is that the Koreans living in Japan at that time were not Korean but Japanese nationals and that the renunciation of sovereignty over Korea did not affect the Koreans living in Japan. There have been many cases of general deprivation of citizenship after the First World War but Paragraph 2 of Article 15 of the Declaration of Human Rights states: 'No one shall be arbitrarily deprived of his nationality.' According to international law, a state can determine by *legislation* who are its nationals but no state can determine how a foreign nationality can be acquired or lost (The Hague Convention on the Conflict of Nationality Laws). Koreans born after the annexation of Korea by Japan and particularly second-generation Koreans born in Japan never possessed Korean nationality.

In January 1989 the Fukuoka High Court rejected an appeal by Kim Chon Kap and upheld a District Court decision denying Kim's demand to have his Japanese nationality restored and to be paid ¥ 30 million for having been forcibly brought to Japan during the war. The court relied on a 1961 decision of the Supreme Court holding that the Peace Treaty of San Francisco resulted in the loss of Japanese nationality by Koreans living in Japan. Under the Peace Treaty, the High Court said, Japan gave up its sovereignty over Korean territory and thereby also over the Korean people. Moreover, the court said, even if the deprivation of Japanese nationality had involved an unlawful act, the statute of limitation applied.

The plaintiff had argued that the Peace Treaty concerned territorial matters and did not affect the nationality of Koreans residing in Japan. The Japanese government violated international law because it did not allow Korean residents to choose either Japanese or Korean nationality. While the statute of limitations may apply to the claim for damages, it is irrelevant to the question of nationality. The court's reasoning that people who ought to belong to Korea lost their Japanese nationality when Japan renounced sovereignty over Korea is wrong. When North and South Korea became sovereign states, ethnic Koreans did not become *ipso facto* Korean nationals. That Koreans living in Japan 'ought to belong to Korea' is an assumption of the Japanese bureaucracy and judiciary without foundation in law and is only an attempt to mask an arbitrary and illegal measure.

Japan has no official relations with North Korea and the antipathy has been mutual. The North Korean government jailed the captain of a Japanese boat and his mate because Japan refused to extradite a Korean soldier who had smuggled himself to Japan on this boat. In the latter half of 1990, however, both sides probed the possibility of finding a less antagonistic *modus vivendi*.

Fingerprinting & the Alien Registration Law

A major confrontation between foreigners living in Japan and the Japanese bureaucracy arose from the fingerprinting regulations in the Alien Registration Law. Prior to the revision of the law in 1985, foreigners over the age of 14 intending to stay in Japan for a period of one year or longer had to register at the city office and obtain a registration certificate which they had to carry with them at all times and produce whenever requested by the police. At registration, they had to be fingerprinted, and this was repeated whenever they had to renew their registration (which depended on their residence status and varied from one to five years). At the time of the initial registration, foreigners had to put their fingerprints on three official documents: the original register for storage with the local authorities, the registration certificate for personal use, and the fingerprint register for storage by the central government. In a notice issued in April 1974 the Ministry of Justice permitted the local authorities to dispense with the fingerprinting for the original fingerprint register at the renewal of registration but this simplification was cancelled in August 1982. On account of the protests against the fingerprinting, black ink for fingerprinting was replaced by a colourless fluid and the left forefinger need no longer be rolled in the ink but only pressed.

Originally, the Alien Registration Ordinance contained no provision for fingerprinting but in 1952 fingerprinting was made obligatory in the Alien Registration Law. The authorities considered it necessary for dealing with the practice of some Koreans to obtain several registration certificates and sell the surplus certificates to Koreans who smuggled themselves into Japan. The Ministry of Justice maintains that the system remains necessary because there are about 500 illegal entrants annually from the Korean peninsula. It is also true that in the immediate post-war period, many Koreans engaged in black-marketeering but so did many Japanese; often Koreans worked for Japanese bosses.

A further revision of the Alien Registration Law which took effect on 1 June 1988 provided that fingerprinting would only be required once, at the time of the first registration. A laminated card replaced the registration certificate to which the fingerprint taken at the initial registration is transferred. The fingerprints are now translated into computer signals which means that they can be reproduced many times without the slightest deterioration and that the police can have immediate access to the prints. Local government employees do not use the fingerprints for identification but usually rely on the photos on the registration certificates. The Ministry of Justice wants to keep the fingerprinting system because it is the most efficient way of identifying criminals. Because 99 per cent of the foreign residents are not criminals it means that the system is enforced for the one per cent who might be. Critics of the fingerprinting system did not fail to point out the government's inconsistency. Until the 1988 revision, the government had maintained that fingerprinting at each renewal was necessary for identification; in June 1988 this was no longer the case.

The enforcement of the Immigration Law required an ever-growing number of staff. In 1987 about 600,000 visa renewals were processed, more than half of which were handled by the Tokyo Immigration Bureau. In the first half of 1988, the Tokyo bureau examined over 180,000 applications for renewal. Since the bureau is chronically short of manpower and office space, foreign residents often have to wait several hours; on some days, it can he as long as seven hours. The number of officials has been increased every year, from 61 in 1984 to 79 in 1988, and though they sometimes put in four to five hours overtime, they cannot cope with the growing amount of work.

Since local governments are charged with the administration of the registration procedure, they also have to deal with the opposition to the fingerprinting requirement. Some municipalities issued registration certificates to foreigners who refused to be fingerprinted or failed to notify the police of the refusal. At one time in 1985 only three of the 23 Tokyo wards followed the instructions of the Ministry of Justice on the handling of refusers. Mayor Saburo Ito of Kawasaki announced that he would not ask the police to investigate foreigners who refused to be fingerprinted. The municipality, Ito said, arrived at this decision for humanitarian reasons. Japanese, as members of the world community, should respect the human rights of other people. Ito's decision infuriated the Ministry of Justice and Justice Minister Hitoshi Shimasaki made the Kanagawa Prefectural Office warn the mayor and admonish him to obey the law.

Resolutions calling for a revision of the Alien Registration Law were adopted by 702 municipal assemblies and in 1983 the National Council of Mayors asked the government to discontinue fingerprinting and abolish the requirement to carry the certificate at all times. The Ministry of Justice exerted great pressure on the municipalities to execute the law, and the revisions in the registration procedures were mainly intended to alleviate the burden on the municipalities. The demand to abolish the system was reiterated by individual local governments such as the mayors of Kyoto's 11 wards. The mayors supported the refusers' argument that they were treated as criminals and that the compulsory fingerprinting violated their human rights.

While in the past the number of refusers has risen to several thousands (1985: 14,000), there have been relatively few arrests. Arrests and criminal prosecutions have occurred in Okayama, Kobe, Tokyo, Yokohama, Nagoya and Fukuoka. One of the first to be arrested was Kim Myong Kwan, a lecturer at Seika Junior College in Kyoto. He had refused to be fingerprinted in 1981 and was taken into custody when he failed to comply with several summonses to appear voluntarily for questioning by the police. The Korean government expressed concern because the arrest came at a time when negotiations on reforming the fingerprinting system were pending. In May 1985 Lee Sang Ho, a leader of the Kawasaki Korean community, was arrested for having refused to be fingerprinted since May 1983. His arrest drew violent protests.

Arrests have not been confined to Koreans. The first American to be arrested was Robert Ricketts, a freelance translator. He stated in court that his refusal was a form of civil disobedience to protest the 'institutionalised racial discrimination' in Japan's immigration system. Ricketts complained that his arm was injured when five police officers at the Shibuya Police Station forcibly took his fingerprints. In December 1988 the Tokyo District Court imposed a fine of ¥ 10,000 on Ricketts who said that the court should consider the origin of the fingerprinting. He said that it was introduced after the war with the collaboration of the Occupation authorities for the surveillance of Korean and Chinese residents whom the authorities suspected of being Communists. At present, Ricketts asserted, the system is irrational.

Judge Yoshifusa Nakayama repeated the government's old assertion that the system was rational and a necessary method of confirming the identity of foreigners. To treat foreigners differently from Japanese, the judge said, was natural since they had no inherent right to stay in Japan. The attitude of the bureaucracy may have been influenced by the inclination to consider the admission of foreigners into the country as granting a privilege and to expect them to behave like guests. Although every state can regulate the entry and sojourn of foreigners, the UN Convention on Human Rights guarantees these rights also for persons living abroad or travelling in foreign countries.

Actually, Japan's use of fingerprinting as a control mechanism for people other than criminals goes back to pre-war times. The South Manchurian Railway Co. used to fingerprint Chinese labourers forced by the Kwangtun Army to work in the company's coal mines. After Japan's occupation of Manchuria in 1931 Koreans settled in the so-called 'strategic hamlets' were fingerprinted and had to present an identification card when entering or leaving the camps. Controls by fingerprinting and identification documents were extended after the outbreak of the war with China in 1937. From 1939 Koreans living in Japan had to register with an organisation called Kyōwakai and carry a Kyōwakai passbook. The organisation was under direct police control.

In the post-war era the Occupation initiated a registration and passbook system for the Koreans who had refused repatriation by having the Japanese government issue an Alien Registration Ordinance in 1947. To prevent the entry of Communist agents, a revision of the ordinance in 1949 required Koreans to have a Korean registration certificate which was to be renewed periodically. Criminal sanctions were imposed for failure to carry the certificate on one's person. The Korean War prompted the Occupation authorities to insist that the Japanese government take further measures, including fingerprinting, based on the US Alien Registration Act of 1940 and the Internal Security Act of 1950. The purpose of the legislation was strictly political, the prevention and suppression of subversion and espionage, and had nothing to do with ordinary administrative regulations. The Alien Registration Law which came into effect with the Peace Treaty is tainted by this pedigree.

Because fingerprinting affects mainly Koreans, the Korean government has repeatedly expressed its concern over the situation and requested that Koreans should be treated like Japanese by upgrading their legal status and promoting welfare and education. When Prime Minister Nakasone visited Seoul, he promised to work for an improvement of the registration system. The improvement was a farce. At the same time as changing the method of fingerprinting (billed as an improvement) the government strengthened the enforcement of the fingerprinting. In October 1982 the Ministry of Justice adopted the policy of disqualifying refusers from living in Japan and denying re-entry permits. The ministry issued an order to all mayors instructing them not to issue registration certificates to foreigners refusing to be fingerprinted. Local governments should try to persuade the refusers to comply with the law during a three-month grace period but after the expiration of that time, the local authorities should inform the police for further legal action.

The Seoul government also wanted the Japanese to abolish the deportation system for Korean residents convicted of crimes. This system was instituted in 1965 on the basis of a Japan–South Korea agreement but for a number of years, Seoul refused to accept deportees.

The South Korean government had often urged the Japanese authorities to abolish fingerprinting for first- and second-generation Koreans but the Japanese government maintained that the system could not be scrapped until a suitable substitute for fingerprinting was found. In November 1990, however, Japan promised the South Korean government that fingerprinting would be discontinued for Koreans residing in Japan. The Ministry of Justice was preparing a revision of the Immigration Law which would give the same legal status to South and North Koreans and Taiwanese who were deprived of their Japanese nationality in 1952, and their descendants, regarding deportation and re-entry.

Concerning the government's revision of the Alien Registration Law, Koreans pointed out that the law treats foreigners in Japan basically as a law-and-order problem. It takes the view that they are all potential criminals and the purpose of registration is to control them. The revision which replaces fingerprinting by registration of signature, photograph and family records and retains the obligation to carry the alien registration card at all times remains a system of control.

The fingerprinting controversy

Basically, Japanese legal thinking and political practice lack a philosophical foundation and the idea of justice, in particular, has been replaced by ingeniousness in interpreting legal norms to reach a desired conclusion. The government is just as much bound to the common good as the people. The arbitrary exercise of authority not respecting the common good cannot impose moral obligations. The reason why the government does not discontinue the fingerprinting requirement for the registration of foreigners was stated clearly by Shunji Kobayashi, former Director-General of the Immigration Bureau of the Ministry of Justice, 'There is no example in the world', he said, 'where a law was changed because a movement violated the law.'

The crusade against fingerprinting has been supported by foreign missionaries, both Catholic and Protestant. A Protestant missionary, Ronald Susumu Fujiyoshi, first refused to be fingerprinted in 1981. He was prosecuted and found guilty by the Kobe District Court in 1986 and fined ¥ 10,000. Although his registration certificate was without a fingerprint, he was given a three-year extension in 1984 but was refused an extension in 1987. Jesse Jackson, a friend of Fujiyoshi's since his days at a theological college in Chicago, interceded for him with the Japanese Embassy in Washington, but he was ordered to leave Japan and went to Hawaii in February 1988.

Etienne de Guchteneere, who came to Japan as a Catholic missionary in 1956 and also taught French at the Miyagi University of Education in Sendai, refused to be fingerprinted in 1984. He was given a three-month extension in 1985 but told he would be deported at the end of this period if he did not comply with the fingerprinting requirement. The Catholic Bishops' Conference asked the government for an explanation of the threatened deportation order but in the end, Father de Guchteneere agreed to be fingerprinted. However, he was given only a one-year extension instead of the usual three years.

Another missionary, Father Jules Rand, who had lived in Japan for 29 years, refused to be fingerprinted because he considered the system a symbol of the discrimination against Koreans. The Shiraishi Ward Office (Sapporo) renewed his certificate without the three-month delay. It would be useless, an official of the ward of office said, to try to persuade Father Rand to change his mind. Another French missionary, Father Edward Brgostowski, who had refused to be fingerprinted in order to protest the arrest of Lee Sang Ho, agreed to the procedure in order to obtain a re-entry permit so he could go home to attend the funeral of his father. But Father Constantin Louis who had been working in Tokyo since 1956 gave up his plan to go home for the funeral of his mother rather than comply with the fingerprinting law to get a re-entry permit. He commented that one-third of the residents in his neighbourhood were Koreans and he refused to be fingerprinted to protest against the racial discrimination from which they suffered.

Minister of Justice Yukio Hayashida announced a more flexible policy regarding re-entry permits for fingerprint refusers in March 1988. The first person to receive a re-entry permit under the new policy was Pak Hong Kyu, a teacher at a junior high school in Higashi, Osaka. She had applied for a re-entry permit in order to take the ashes of her deceased father to Cheju Island. In October 1988 the Ministry of Justice, in a noteworthy departure from past practice, granted re-entry permits to senior members of Chongryon, the association supporting North Korea, for attending an international conference. Until then, the ministry had refused the issue of re-entry permits to Chongryon members for trips with political implications.

Confirming an earlier decision of the Japanese government to abolish the fingerprinting system for foreigners, the foreign ministers of Japan and the Republic of Korea signed a memorandum on the occasion of Prime Minister Kaifu's visit to Seoul in January 1991 in which the Japanese government pledged to end fingerprinting and to open jobs in local governments to Koreans and allow teaching in public schools. The government planned to introduce a system similar to the Japanese family register consisting of photos, signatures and the names of parents and grandparents. Japan also promised to reduce the crimes for which Koreans can be deported.

The government prepared a revision of the Alien Registration Law to exempt Koreans and Taiwanese who had been deprived of their Japanese citizenship in 1952 from the obligation to submit to fingerprinting. The exemption was to be extended to their descendants and to other foreign nationals with permanent residence status. The Foreign Office and the Ministry of Justice intended to abolish fingerprinting for all foreign residents but the National Police Agency opposed this measure claiming that the increase in the number of foreigners involved in crimes or working without proper visas required the continuation of fingerprinting.

In the same way as the Koreans, the Taiwanese residing in Japan were deprived of Japanese nationality when the San Francisco Peace Treaty came into effect; they were considered as Chinese nationals. An estimated 210,000 Taiwanese who had served in the Japanese army thereby were stripped of their right to pensions. It was only in 1988 that the Diet passed a law stipulating payment of ¥ 2 million to Taiwanese who were wounded in the Second World War or to the surviving relatives of those who were killed. Compounding the injustice of the long delay, the ungenerous terms of the payments was a further blow. Payments were to be made in bonds redeemable at the end of March 1993. Actually, payments were made earlier and by the middle of 1991, the equivalent of $ 389 million had been paid to 27,491 of the roughly 28,000 former soldiers or their families who had applied for compensation. At about the same time, the government decided to pay ¥ 100,000 to each of the 260,000 Japanese soldiers detained in Siberia after the war or to the families of those who had died.

The Liberal-Democratic Party and the government used the demise of Emperor Hirohito to declare a general amnesty. About 10,000 foreigners, most of them Koreans, were pardoned. But some violators of the Alien Registration Law claimed to reject the amnesty. All 34 fingerprint refusers on trial at the beginning of February 1989 released a statement expressing their intention to reject the pardon. The government, they claimed, was going to use the amnesty to avoid the issue of the violation of human rights raised by the lawsuits. Cho Geon Chi, a resident of Shimonoseki, who was being prosecuted on charges of refusing to be fingerprinted, destroyed the registration certificate given to him when the Hiroshima High Court dismissed the charges against him. The amnesty, he said, had deprived him of an opportunity to challenge the government's unjust attitude towards Korean residents. He hoped he would again be put on trial.

In June 1989, 13 Chinese, Korean and American fingerprint refusers filed a lawsuit against the state and seven prefectural and municipal governments complaining that the amnesty had deprived them of their right to a trial in which they could have attacked the constitutionality of the fingerprinting regulations. They demanded ¥ 13 million in compensation for the mental distress caused by the amnesty.

In order to stem the influx of foreigners seeking work in Japan without proper visas, the Immigration Bureau initiated a revision of the Immigration Control Law making it illegal for employers to hire foreigners without working status certificates. There are about 50,000 to 100,000 South Koreans in Japan who were repatriated after the war but drifted back to Japan before the normalisation of relations between Japan and the Republic of Korea in 1965. Moreover, there is a large number of Koreans who came recently to Japan attracted by better living conditions. Under the revised law, legal Korean residents will have to apply for the new certificate in addition to their alien registration certificate.

Under the new law passed by the Diet in November 1989, certificates are issued to legitimate workers whose visa status entitles them to work in Japan. Employers who hire workers without proper working status can be fined ¥ 2 million; in case of repeated infractions, employers can be imprisoned for up to three years. Employment agencies must obey the same regulations and violations of the law entail the same penalties. The authorities claim that the law does not impose new burdens but only clarifies the working status of the foreigner. Actually, in its tenacity to drive all 'illegal' aliens out of Japan, the government resorted to a new form of harassment.

The law is a new demonstration of the xenophobia of the bureaucracy and its efforts to make Japan a closed society. The trend towards an open society which started in the Meiji era and was furthered by such different individuals as Yukichi Fukuzawa, Eiichi Shibuzawa and Shigenobu Okuma was stopped by the nationalism of the Taisho era because the liberalism of the monied classes was not channelled into organisational forms capable of gaining the support of the masses.

In April 1988 a private US human rights fact-finding mission organised by the US National Council of the Churches of Christ called Japan's Alien Registration Law an 'instrument of institutionalised racism' giving legal sanction to political, economic and social discrimination against Koreans in Japan.

A meeting of the UN Commission on Human Rights in July 1988 discussed Japan's Alien Registration Law and particularly the fingerprinting requirement. The Japanese officials attending the meeting explained that fingerprinting had been useful in preventing false registrations, the forging of passports and other crimes, but their answers were evasive and even discriminatory.

A revision of the Immigration Control and Refugee Recognition Law in June 1990 aimed at encouraging the entry of foreign nationals with special skills while shutting out unskilled workers. At a time when many Japanese enterprises, especially small outfits, go bankrupt on account of the labour shortage, the Justice and Labour Ministries devote their main efforts to finding and deporting every one of the estimated 100,000 so-called illegal workers staying in the country. Because they have no proper visas, many of these workers are in desperate circumstances, without any guaranteed rights to life, employment, welfare and educational benefits which affects not only the workers themselves but also their families.

Illegal workers have to pay their medical bills in full because they are not covered by health insurance and the Health and Welfare Ministry has instructed local governments not to pay for medical expenses out of welfare funds. Foreign workers, therefore, hesitate to go to a hospital when they become sick and hospitals sometimes refuse to handle emergency cases because of the uncertainty of payment. If foreigners without proper visas are involved in labour accidents, they are allowed to stay in the country until the investigation and procedures for accident insurance are completed but they are not allowed to stay for the purpose of recovering their outstanding wages. There are no provisions for amnesty or relief measures to protect the basic human rights of illegal workers. A group calling itself Lawyers for Foreign Labourers' Rights demanded an amnesty for foreigners working without proper visas as a way of protecting their basic human rights. The 1965 International Convention on the Elimination of All Forms of Racial Discrimination is one of about a dozen international treaties, conventions or protocols signed by Japan but not ratified because the bureaucracy does not want to change relevant laws (which would limit their arbitrariness).

In December 1990 the UN General Assembly adopted a 93-article treaty called the International Convention on the Protection of the Rights of All Migrant Workers and Members of Their Families. The convention guarantees human and labour rights, whether workers are legally documented or not, including basic human rights such as freedom of thought, expression and religion and the right to form labour unions. It also protects the right to receive the same medical services, social welfare and unemployment insurance as the citizens of the host country and stipulates that free language assistance is to be given if migrant workers become involved in legal procedures.

The treaty requires the signatory governments to institute appropriate court procedures in case of forced deportation. Other provisions concern invitations to visit or live with resident families, to change jobs or make temporary home visits. Documented workers are entitled to placement services and job training. Workers are guaranteed the use of their mother tongue and their children have the right to educational services and to acquire the nationality of the parents' country of employment (in states where nationality is determined by the place of birth).

The convention was backed by developing countries but opposed by industrialised nations such as Germany, Britain and Japan, who did not sign the convention. An official of Japan's Foreign Ministry said: 'The convention was written by labour-exporting countries in line with their own interests. Many of the articles of the convention do not suit Japan.'

There are no laws prohibiting discrimination in housing. Real estate companies and individuals can get long-term, low-interest loans from the government's Housing Loan Corporation or buy apartments under very favourable conditions from the Housing and Urban Development Corporation. The contract with the HUDC prohibits selling during a certain period of time and the exaction of 'key money' (usually two months rent, not refundable) from tenants. Otherwise, the owners are free to choose their tenants and they do not let their apartments to foreigners, not even foreigners married to Japanese. The usual reason given for this sort of discrimination is that foreigners do not take good care of the apartments or that they may leave without paying the rent.

Koreans and other Asians are not the only foreigners experiencing racial discrimination in Japan. Blacks have been the victims of racial prejudice in various ways. In localities where American servicemen are stationed, restaurants and bars have sometimes shut out all foreigners because they wanted to keep out blacks. Landlords have often refused to accept them as tenants. Japanese firms have frequently used caricatures of black people in their advertising and 'Little Black Sambo' featured on toys and in books has drawn sharp criticism from the US.

Blacks have encountered racial prejudice in employment. Under the government-sponsored Japan Exchange Teaching Programme, Americans come to Japan to serve as Assistant English Teachers (AET). Although Japanese racism is different from the discrimination practised in the US, it is just as cruel. An American accepted as an AET by a high school in Hamamatsu was refused a renewal of her one-year contract although there never had been any questions regarding her academic credentials or her teaching performance. The teacher had a master's degree in English literature, had studied French at the Sorbonne and had grown up speaking Spanish with her Latin-American-born mother.

At her first visit to the school, the head of the high school's English department greeted her with the exclamation 'Hey, are you big' and then asked her whether she would teach the 'black dialect'. Later, she would regularly hear 'Can you speak standard English?' A group of male colleagues asked 'At what age do women begin to have sex in your country?' followed by 'What about blacks? Do they usually get married first?' After having been told that the high school did not want her to stay on, she tried to find employment at other schools but the colour of her skin proved to be an insurmountable obstacle.

She related an episode exemplifying the prejudice against blacks. A friend of hers, a third-generation American of Japanese descent, applied for a credit card at a department store and was issued one immediately, no questions asked. She found the card convenient and suggested to her black friend that she should get one. To her amazement, the black woman was told that she needed a sponsor and documents proving her solvency.

The popular Japanese stereotype that Americans are white, blond, with blue eyes is reinforced by the selection of AETs. Apart from Japanese-Americans, a disproportionally large number are middle-class Caucasians which perpetuates the biased picture of foreigners held by the Japanese.

34. The Japanese Peasantry and Economic Growth Since the Land Reform of 1946–47

Bernard Bernier

The Land Reform of 1946–47 marks a definite break in the history of Japanese rural society. It thoroughly eradicated the landlord-tenant class relation which had been a dominant feature of the Japanese countryside since the late Edo period (1600–1868). The Reform was imposed on the Japanese government by the Supreme Command of Allied Powers (SCAP). One of its basic tenets was that landlordism had been a major cause of the jingoistic and militaristic tendencies which characterized Japanese society in the 1930s and 1940s. It thus had to be eliminated. But a more important goal of the Reform was to stamp out rural radicalism which had been an important aspect of agrarian Japan in the 1920s and 1930s. Rural intransigence, prompted by the misery of the peasants under the landlord system, was a major potential source of social unrest, and it was feared that the peasantry might support left-wing parties. In order to eliminate all dangerous socialist tendencies in the countryside, it was necessary to return the land to the tillers, that is to transform the majority of agriculturalists into small property owners. This rural 'middle-class' would hopefully become a conservative political force, thus insuring that Japan remained in the anti-communist camp.

The Land Reform has in fact been successful, at least until recently, in transforming the peasantry into a conservative bloc[1]. Since 1948 the countryside has voted overwhelmingly for right-of-center parties, despite mounting difficulties for peasants and growing protests against various aspects of the State's agricultural policy. But the Reform never achieved its goal of creating a "middle class" of farmers. In the first place, the Reform did not equalize land holdings. For example, in 1950, 73 percent of all farm households owned less than one hectare of arable land (see Table 1). Secondly, since about 1955, Japanese agriculture has had to bear up under the pressures of rapid economic growth whose prime moving force has been the heavy and chemical industries dominated by monopoly capitalism. Thus it will be necessary both to assess the various forces at work within the agricultural sector itself and to examine the national context in which these tendencies occur, taking into account the effects of Japan's "economic miracle" and the State's agrarian policy. Perforce it will be useful to examine, albeit briefly, Japan's place in the international farm market.

Bernard Bernier: 'The Japanese Peasantry and Economic Growth Since the Land Reform of 1946–47 from *THE OTHER JAPAN: POSTWAR REALITIES*, edited by E.P. Tsurumi (M E Sharpe, Inc., 1988), pp. 78-90. Reproduced by permission of the Bulletin of Concerned Asian Scholars.

The agricultural sector since the land reform

Demographic aspects

Throughout the twentieth century, the rural population has been decreasing in proportion to the total Japanese population. From a level of about 60 percent around 1900, it fell to 48 percent in 1950, 31 percent in 1965, and 19.9 percent in 1977 (see Table 2). In absolute terms, the rural population had grown between 1900 and 1950 (from 26 to 37 millions, with various ups and downs), but thereafter, a sharp decline has occurred, dropping to 22.5 million in 1977. Of course, the 1950 figure is inflated because of the influx of population to the rural areas after the war, due to the destruction of homes and industrial installations in the cities and the repatriation of Japanese soldiers and former colonists. But this decline was still noticeable even after industrial production had attained its prewar level in 1953. In fact, the average annual decrease in the 22 year period between 1955 and 1977 was about 2 percent, and nearly 8 percent since 1968.

The evolution of the population actively engaged in agriculture has followed a different course. The 1955 proportion was nearly equal to that of 1920: 15 million or 45 percent of the total active population in 1955: 14 million, or 52 percent in 1920 (see Table 2). However the farm population fell to about 12 million (30 percent) in 1960, and 6.2 million (11.5 percent) in 1977. The annual rate of decrease stands at about 3 percent for the period from 1955 to 1977. This downward trend in the active farming population can be seen partly as a continuation of a trend — already present in the late Edo period — which intensified with industrial development in the Meiji (1868–1912) and Taisho (1912–1926) periods. This is the increase in the proportion of non-agricultural to farm labor, at least part of which is due to the exodus from overpopulated rural areas. However, this postwar trend, as I will show, did not remove only *excess* farm population. It has increasingly taken *needed* labor from the farms, transforming cultivators into low-paid workers employed in factories, the construction industry and the services. Thus, the incorporation of agriculture into the capitalist economy has now entered a new phase in Japan, a process which calls for further analysis.

This fact is borne out by the decrease in the number of farm households after 1960. From 1950 to 1960, the number of farm units remained relatively stable at the unprecedented high level of about 6 million. Only between 1965 and 1970 was the prewar level reached — a level that had been maintained from the late Edo period until 1945 at between 5.3 and 5.5 million families. Thereafter a sharp decrease occurred, and in 1977 the number of farm households was 4.8 million. The decline between 1960 and 1970 can be viewed as a process of elimination of the excess farm households created by the unusual conditions of the immediate postwar period, but the downward trend that has prevailed since 1970 cannot be explained in this way. In fact, in 1975, for the first time in two centuries, the number of farm families fell below 5 million. This trend has continued. According to most observers, the quasi-mystical attachment to the land is now breaking down among many Japanese peasants. An important feature of the feudal period when land was for many the only means of survival, this attachment has persisted because, until now, farming has been the only way for most rural inhabitants to earn a living. Now survival can be secured by non-agricultural work, and the sale of land, which until recently was thought of as disrespectful toward the family ancestors

Table 1   Number of farm households by size, 1940–1977 (in thousands)

Acreage Categories	1940	1950	1960	1965	1970	1972	1973	1976	1977
0.0–0.3 ha*	1796	2531	1283	1142	1100	1922	1922	1920	1911
0.3–0.5			992	954	899				
0.5–0.7	1768	1973	866	808	747	733	727	695	682
0.7–1.0			1041	954	857	820	805	741	734
1.0–1.5	1322	1339	1002	945	868	832	805	727	710
1.5–2.0			404	407	404	393	383	347	342
2.0–2.5	309	208	157	156	170	174	167	164	161
2.5–3.0			54	59	71	74	73	78	80
3.0 et plus	195	125	36	41	61	68	72	88	88

Source: Yujiro Hayami. *A Century of Agricultural Growth in Japan* (Tokyo, Tokyo University Press, 1975). p. 9;
Nihon Nōgyō Nenkan, (Tokyo, Ie no Hikari, 1974). p. 156.
Nihon Nōgyō Nenkan, (Tokyo, Ie no Hikari, 1978). p. 158.

Table 2   Number of farm households, agricultural population and population active in agriculture, 1945–1977

Year	Number of farm households (1000)	Agricultural population (1000)	Percentage of total population	Population active in agriculture (1000)	Percentage of total active population
1945	5.698			13.934	
1950	6.176	37.760	48.3	15.886	45.2
1955	6.043	36.347	40.8	15.172	37.9
1960	6.057	34.411	36.5	11.960	30.0
1965	5.655	30.083	31.0	9.810	22.8
1970	5.342	36.595	25.3	8.110	17.8
1973	5.098	24.380	22.0	6.820	13.1
1975	4.953	23.195	21.3	6.500	12.5
1976	4.891	22.900	20.5	6.429	12.1
1977	4.835	22.650	19.9	6.201	11.6

Source: Bureau of Statistics. *Statistical Handbook of Japan*, 1974, p. 29:
Oriental Economist. Nov. 1975, p.25:
Nihon Nōgyō Nenkan, (Tokyo, Ie no Hikari, 1978). p. 155–159.
Statistical Yearbook of Ministry of Agriculture and Forestry. 1976–77. pp. 22–23.

* ha. or hectare is equal to 10,000m² or 2.47 acres [Editor]

who bequeathed the land,[2] is now based on cold economic calculations. This is the case in peri-urban areas but is also true of outlying regions.

Agricultural production

Agricultural production has accounted for an increasingly low percentage of the Gross National Product (see Table 3). From a level of 16.5 percent in 1934–1936, it reached 31 percent in 1946, but settled back to its prewar level in 1954. Thereafter, it has decreased constantly, falling from 13 percent in 1960, to a mere 2.5 percent in 1977. The major reason for this decline is the fantastic development of the industrial and service sectors. Overall agricultural production has increased however, at least until 1968. In fact, from 1960 to 1968, the average annual rate of increase of agricultural production in current prices has been near 4 percent[3]. But since 1969, there has been a slow decline every year, except 1972 and 1975 (good harvests, higher rice prices; see Table 4).

Table 3   Agricultural production as a percentage of GNP, 1936–7 to 1977

Year	Percentage
1934–36	16.6
1946	31.1
1950	21.3
1954	16.7
1958	13.5
1960	10.8
1970	5.5
1972	4.0
1975	3.0
1977	2.5

Source: Ogura, Ed., op cit., p. 69. Danno, op cit., p. 295

Table 4   Rice price index, 1960–1978 (1965=100)

Year	Index
1960	63.8
1966	109.2
1968	126.1
1970	126.0
1972	137.0
1974	196.0
1976	248.0
1977	264.0
1978	274.5

Source: OCDE. op ch., p. 27. *Japan Times*, July 7, 1976. p. 1.
Oriental Economist. *Japan Economic Yearbook*. 1976. p. 50.
Oriental Economist. *Japan Economic Yearbook*. 1977–78. p. 48.

A main reason for the decrease in farm production is, first, a reduction in the total area of land under cultivation. For example, between 1969 and 1976, an annual average of 50,000 hectares were transferred out of cultivation. While much of this is the result of urban and industrial development, it is also due to the abandonment of agriculture by many peasants, partly because of the government's policy of encouraging the curtailment of rice production. Secondly, rice yields per hectare have decreased. For example, between 1967 and 1971, the yield per hectare on large farms fell from 45.4 qt. to 41 qt. Finally, many farmers have abandoned winter crops, and consequently, the rate of land use has declined from 134 percent in 1960 to 100 percent in 1973. Since then, it has risen somewhat to 103 percent in 1976.

The increase in production which occurred before 1969 is the result of two trends. The first is an increase in the yield per hectare which took place chiefly before 1955. This increase was prompted by the generalization of many technical innovations previously used only sporadically or regionally such as chemical fertilizers, herbicides, insecticides, high-yield varieties, etc. In this period, the emphasis was on a more intensive use of the land, and not on an increase in the productivity of labor. Labor was abundant in the countryside; there was no need to "save" it. In fact, there was a 10 percent increase in the ratio of labor per hectare between 1934–36 and 1953.

The second trend, which gathered momentum after 1955, is the increase in labor productivity. This increase became necessary in order to offset the heavy drain on rural labor caused by the demand for cheap labor power in the industrial and service sectors. Relieved of their surplus workers, and even, later, of their required labor power, farm families have had to look for ways to save labor. Indeed, from 1955 to 1970, labor productivity in agriculture increased an average of 6.4 percent annually. Between 1970 and 1976, the increase of labor productivity in agriculture has outstripped that in industry (44.2 percent compared to 30.8 percent).

This second trend is the result of the massive use of small-scale agricultural machinery. In fact, peasants have tried to replace labor, which could be more gainfully employed outside agriculture, by machinery and also by the more intensive use of chemical products. To a certain extent, this shift was successful but it has not been without its cost. Once given the possibility of buying machines, many full-time farmers have also discovered the possibility of taking occasional outside jobs in order to increase family revenues, and even, in some cases, of financing the purchase of farm machinery. Thus off-farm wage labor entails the closer subordination of farm households to the capitalist economy not only as a source of wage labor, but also as a profitable market for industrial farm goods. There have also been ecological effects; the use of fertilizers, herbicides and machinery cannot regenerate the soil the way hard work does. For example, the hand tractor which is widely used now does not plow the land as deeply as the old ox-drawn plows; furthermore, chemicals have changed the soil into a sticky matter that bears no resemblance to the rich organic soil which was the hallmark of Japanese wet rice agriculture. The major result of this labor saving agriculture has been a decrease in yield which I mentioned earlier. A second consequence is the weakened resistance of plants to cold temperature.

Another danger is chemical poisoning. Together with industrial pollution, pollution by agricultural chemicals has hit all Japanese but especially peasants. Matsushima states that 25 percent of all peasants are affected one way or another by such chemical intoxication and 4 percent are seriously poisoned. Most chemicals used in agriculture have not been tested previously (a consequence of very lax rules regarding the testing of industrial products in Japan), and their side effects are not known.

Agricultural products

Japanese agriculture is still strongly centered on cereals, particularly rice. However, since 1950 specialization in other crops has been gaining ground. In 1950 cereals accounted for more than 70 percent of total farm production. This is only slightly lower than comparable figures for the early 20th century. But since 1950 the importance of cereals has decreased. In 1960 they accounted for 55 percent of total agricultural production but this percentage had fallen to 36 percent by 1973 and to about 33 percent in 1977. The decline has been much more dramatic for cereals other than rice (wheat, barley, buckwheat, corn). In 1950 these other cereals accounted for more than 10 percent of the total farm output, but less than 1 percent in 1976. The major reason for this rapid drop in production lies in the fact that cereals cultivated in Japan are expensive. In 1969, Japanese wheat sold at more than double the international price. However, this in itself is not a sufficient condition, for in the same year the price of Japanese rice was about three times that of American rice. A second important factor is U.S. pressure on the Japanese government to import large quantities of American farm goods. This pressure has been applied more or less consistently since 1945. Just after the war, the Japanese government had little power to resist. The U.S. was producing large surpluses, especially of wheat and soy beans, and Japan proved to be an ideal market both because of the immediate food shortage and because of low farm productivity. Agreements were even signed in 1954 to insure the flow of certain American agricultural products into Japan. The net result was a slackening off in production of many Japanese crops, including wheat, barley and soy beans.

Conversely, the production of livestock, dairy goods, fruits, and vegetables has increased tremendously. From 35 percent of total production in 1960, these products have grown to 57 percent in 1972 and almost 60 percent in 1975. The increase in the production of fruits, vegetables, meat, milk and eggs, together with the decline of cereal production, is a sign of a more diversified diet, a consequence of the higher standard of living brought about by the economic growth of the 1960s. However, the sustained growth of non-cereal production has been possible only through heavy tariff protection. Since 1971 international pressure has been applied, especially by the United States, to force the easing of Japanese trade barriers on many agricultural goods. These pressures, which are analyzed in more detail below, have strained the growth of many types of products, including beef, dairy products, and citrus fruits. To offset the effects of liberalization on the peasants, the Japanese government has had to ease up on its policy of rice production control, thus putting an end to its 10-year-old farm diversification program. This policy change has led to new rice surpluses. However, by 1973, the policy of restricting rice production was again revived, resulting in a drop in Japan's overall agricultural output.

Categories of farms

Farm households in Japan, as was mentioned earlier, did not receive equal amounts of land during the Land Reform. This inequality of households based on land holdings has been a constant feature of Japanese agriculture up to the present (see Table 1). In the decade from 1940 to 1950, there was an increase in the number of farms in the small holder categories (less than 2 hectares), but a decline in relative and absolute terms of large farms. This is due in large part to the unusual conditions that prevailed in the immediate postwar period. After 1950 these tendencies were reversed. From 1950 to 1960, there was an increase in the number of farms in all acreage categories except for small farms of less than one hectare. From 1960 to 1965, the decline affected the 1 to 1½ hectare category, and the 0.7 to 1 hectare group decreased at a faster rate (see Table 5). From 1965 to 1970, the decline reached the 1½ to 2 hectares category and quickened for farms with 1 to 1½ hectare of land. But there was a slowdown in the rate of decline of the smallest farms. From 1970 to 1975, all small holder categories, that is farms with less than 2½ hectares, showed a decline. This process was particularly clear in the 0.7 to 2 hectare categories. Conversely the largest farms, i.e. more than 3 hectares, showed a 10 percent increase. In '76–'77, the rate of decline slackened off for the 0.7 to 2 hectare categories, but it increased for the smaller farms and for the 2 to 2½ hectare category.

Table 5   **Annual rate of increase or decrease in the number of farm households by acreage categories, 1960–1977 (in percentage)**

Acreage categories	1960–65	1965–70	1970–75	1976–77
0.0–0.3 ha	−2.2	−0.8		
0.3–0.5	−0.8	−1.2	−0.3	−0.5
0.5–0.7	−1.3	−1.6	−1.7	−1.9
0.7–1.0	−1.7	−2.1	−2.9	−1.0
1.0–1.5	−1.1	−1.7	−3.6	−2.3
1.5–2.0	0.2	−0.2	−3.0	−1.7
2.0–2.5	1.1	1.8	−1.2	−1.8
2.5–3.0	1.9	3.8	0.6	2.1
3.0 plus	2.7	8.2	10.0	0.3

Source: Nihon Nōgyō Nenkan, 1974, p. 156; Nihon Nōgyō Nenkan, 1978, p. 158.

In fact, what we see here is a sort of stabilization of the number of smaller farms accompanied by a rather rapid decrease in the number of larger farms, a decrease which is even more rapid now for these farms than it was for smaller ones in earlier years. Thus the downward drift which used to characterize small farms is now spreading to medium-size operations. According to Ouchi, this means that the lower stratum of the peasantry, i.e. farm households with insufficient land to live independently (that is, without regular off-farm work), now includes families which used to be in the middle stratum (1 to 2 hectares). The middle stratum is now confined to the 2 to 3 hectare categories, and even these seem to be dwindling at present. Only the larger farms are thriving, and they are in a small minority. According to Ouchi and others, this is the increasingly polarized form the "decomposition of the peasantry" assumes, a form, it should be noted, that is normally found in all capitalist societies.

The determination of peasant strata, however, cannot be made solely on the basis of farm size, as the above definition of the lower stratum makes clear. It is necessary to take into account the importance of full-time or part-time farming in the different farm households. Table 6 traces the evolution of full-time and part-time farm families from 1947 to 1977. What this table shows is that the proportion of full-time or specialized farms to total farm households has dropped from 55.4 percent in 1947 to 12.4 percent in 1975. But this percentage has gone up to 13.3 percent in 1977. The fastest rate of decline was between 1960 and 1965 when the number of full-time operations decreased from 2.1 millions to 1.2 million for an average annual decline of more than 10 percent.

Table 6   Number and percentage of farm households by source of income, 1947–1977 (in 1000 and percentage)

Year	Full-time agricultural households	Percentage of total member of farm households	Part-time farm households category I	Percentage of total member of farm households	Part-time farm households category II	Percentage of total member of farm households
1947	3.270	55.4	1.680	28.5	0.951	16.1
1950	2.770	45.2	1.950	31.8	1.410	23.0
1955	2.020	34.7	2.210	37.9	1.590	24.4
1960	2.100	34.3	2.030	35.0	1.940	30.0
1965	1.200	21.5	2.080	35.5	2.360	43.0
1970	0.832	16.0	1.800	32.0	2.710	52.0
1973	0.675	12.0	1.300	23.0	3.120	65.0
1975	0.616	12.4	1.259	25.4	3.080	62.1
1976	0.659	13.5	1.002	20.5	3.231	66.1
1977	0.643	13.3	0.927	19.2	3.265	67.5

Source: Hayami. op. cit.: Bureau of Statistics, op. cit., p. 29; *Japan Times*, July 7, 1976, p. 1; *Nihon Nōgyō Nenkan*, 1974, p. 156; *Nihon Nōgyō Nenkan*, 1978, p. 155

Part-time farms in category I (i.e. farm households whose income derives partly from non-agricultural work but which receive more than half their total income from agriculture) grew in absolute and relative number from 1947 to 1955, levelled off in the decade 1955–1965, then decreased slowly until 1970, and since then have declined rapidly. The number of part-time farm households in category II (i.e. farm households who earn less than 50 percent of their income from agriculture) has increased constantly, both in real numbers and as a percentage of total households, from 1947 to the present. From just below 1 million (16%) in 1947, these households jumped to 2.3 million (43%) in 1965, and to 3.2 million (67.5%) in 1977. It is clear from these figures that agriculture has become a secondary occupation for about two-thirds of all farming families. The net result has been a decrease in the portion of the total income all farm households derive from agriculture. This has fallen from 50 percent in 1961 to 36 percent in 1972 and finally to 31.6 percent in 1976.

Table 7 Percentage of households by source of income according to acreage categories, 1960 to 1973

Acreage categories	Full-time farm households				Part-time, category I				Part-time, category II			
	1960	1965	1972	1973	1960	1965	1972	1973	1960	1965	1972	1973
Total	33.7	20.5	13.5	12.3	34.1	37.2	27.1	25.3	39.3	42.3	59.4	62.4
0.0–0.3	12.5	8.8	8.1	7.9	10.3	5.9	3.9	3.1	79.2	85.5	88.0	89.0
0.3–0.5	18.6	10.5			30.9	19.7			50.5	69.8		
0.5–0.7	27.9	14.7	9.4	8.9	45.7	39.6	16.2	13.5	26.5	45.7	74.4	77.6
0.7–1.0	39.9	21.8	12.6	11.3	48.9	55.2	33.2	29.8	11.2	23.0	54.3	58.9
1.0–1.5	64.6	31.7	18.6	17.1	42.9	60.5	52.8	49.8	3.6	7.8	28.6	33.0
1.5–2.0	63.3	40.5	25.2	22.7	35.3	56.8	63.4	63.4	1.4	2.7	11.7	13.8
2.0–2.5	68.4	45.9	28.7	24.6	30.7	52.5	64.9	67.7	1.0	1.6	6.3	8.4
2.5–3.0	71.3	50.1	29.7	26.0	27.8	48.6	66.2	68.5	0.9	1.3	4.1	4.1
3.0 plus	73.0	54.6	35.3	30.6	26.0	43.6	61.8	65.3	1.0	1.8	2.9	4.2

Source: Nihon Nōgyō Nenkan, 1974. p. 157.

Table 7 gives the breakdown of full-time and part-time farm households by acreage categories between 1960 and 1973. The clearest trend is the constant decrease of full-time operations in all farm-management categories during this period. Larger farms have always fared better, starting at a much higher level of full-time farms (about 72 percent for categories over 2½ hectares, compared to less than 20 percent for small farms of less than ½ hectare), and declining less rapidly (to about 28 percent and 3.1 percent respectively for the same categories in 1973). In fact, the proportion of full-time farms increases at a constant rate as we move up in size. Conversely, the proportion of type II part-time farms has increased in all categories, especially among small holders: 89 percent of farm families owning less than ½ hectare belong to this category. And the percentage of this type of farm operation decreases constantly as we move into the larger farm categories.

The category I part-time group, which is devoted primarily to agriculture, has undergone a special evolution. In 1960, these holdings were concentrated in the medium-sized categories (½ to 1½ hectare). Smaller farms had the smallest representation and larger ones occupied an intermediate position. But from 1960 to 1973, fewer smaller farms were included in the category I group while the proportion of medium-sized farms increased until 1965, but decreased afterward. The percentage of farms in the 1½ to 2 hectare category increased from 1960 to 1972, but this trend seems to be reversing itself at the present time since, in 1973, it remained stable at the same levels as in 1972. Finally, all categories above 2 hectares have shown a constant increase.

It is thus clear that part-time and full-time farm operations are very closely related to farm size. The link is not absolute, and we will see why below. But what is clear for the moment is that large farms tend to specialize in agriculture, although a growing proportion of even the very largest have non-agricultural sources of income.

The reasons for these trends are complex. One is that farm owners are hesitant to sell their land even when they engage in farming only as a secondary activity. As I mentioned previously, the ideological restraints on selling farm land have been weakened and peasants actually sell more than they did previously. For example, in one year, in 1971–1972, 3.5% of all cultivated land in Nagano, 4.4% in Gumma, 2.9% in Chiba and Saitama, 2.7% in Ibaragi, and 2% in Hiroshima was sold for non-agricultural purposes. But despite this increase in land sales, the general tendency remains for farmers to hold on to the soil. The reasons for this "attachment" to the land are usually very concrete. Many cultivators own land whose price is rising faster than the interest they could obtain on the amount of money they would receive for their land, so, if the price is not high enough or if they do not really need to sell, they prefer to keep their land. Moreover, many farm owners prefer converting their land partly to other uses, such as apartment building, near the cities. Still others, and they are in the majority, want to keep the land as an insurance against hard times. Many farmers still remember the famine of the middle '40s and they want to be protected should the same difficulties arise again. Besides, given the inadequacy of social security programs in Japan, old people generally have a hard time of it particularly when they own nothing, and this encourages peasants to cling to their land as a form of old-age insurance. Finally, prices for land or houses are so high that even should a farm owner sell at a good price, he/she is likely to spend most of it on the purchase of a new house.

Small holders thus prefer to keep their land: some cultivate it, part-time or full-time; others rent it, even if rents are very low; and still others simply allow it to lie fallow. A second reason for the trend toward part-time farming is the income differential that exists between agriculture and wage-labor. The higher wage level in non-agricultural employment lures farmers, especially those with smaller farms, into outside employment. However, two facts must be noted in this regard. In the first place, given the low general wage level obtaining in Japan until 1973, non-farm income was not high enough to entice farmers entirely away from agriculture. Secondly, most non-agricultural jobs for farmers are still low-paid and non-permanent and are found primarily in the construction industry. Farmers thus represent an important source of cheap labor. This is particularly true of seasonal workers (*dekasegi*), although their working and living conditions have improved somewhat in the last few years.

What is interesting, though, is that type II part-time households tend to engage in more lucrative non-agricultural pursuits, that is they are more often permanently or self-employed. Thus many smaller farms, which constitute the majority of part-time category II operations, have managed to obtain a household and even *per capita* income higher than that of medium-size farms whose land is too small for full-time farming but too large to depend primarily on non-agricultural sources of income. It is also interesting to note that the average family revenues and, since 1972, even the *per capita* revenues for farm households, have surpassed those of working-class families. However, this is true only of type II households and has been achieved by putting to work outside of agriculture a larger number of family members whose jobs are not always stable. Furthermore, until recently, the average *per capita* income for workers in Japan was quite low; it was just a little under $1,000 a year in 1972, at the then-prevailing exchange rate. With the later wage increases as well as the increase in the value of the yen, this average has gone up to $4,000 in 1978.

The consequences of these trends are complex and far-reaching. In the first place, the refusal of small holders to sell their land, coupled with high land prices resulting from urban development, have retarded farm consolidation. Thus the constitution of a substantial group of prosperous family farms has been thwarted. Secondly, the possibility of keeping the land while working outside of agriculture has led to an increase in the number of farms short of even one full-time worker (man or woman). In 1973, as well as in 1977, 50 percent of farm households were of this type. Another 15 percent had only one woman as a full-time worker. In this case, it is considered "normal" for women to keep on doing household chores, a fact that cannot but diminish their effectiveness as farm workers. Moreover, if we take into account the fact that a sizeable proportion of farms with full-time employees are geared to subsistence farming and worked by old people, the percentage of farm operations run on a less than adequate basis is very high, probable near 75 percent. This leads to the type of farm management that has become the trade mark of Japanese agriculture. Farming is done part-time either in the evenings or on weekends by women and old people.

A third consequence is that part-time cultivators tend to withdraw from cooperative ventures and deal with their problems individually. The net result is the breakdown of village cooperation and the purchase of agricultural machinery at a pace much faster than is really needed. Each household requires its own machinery in order to complete the farmwork in the short periods when manpower is available.

Fourthly, as has been mentioned earlier, there has been a reduction in the yield per hectare for many types of crops despite an increase in farm productivity. The replacement of labor by industrial goods does not result in as productive a use of the land. Besides, it increases the danger of toxic poisoning.

A fifth consequence is the growing strain on village and family life. Although conditions for seasonal workers have improved, it remains that, with the departure of so many villagers for the cities, the families left behind encounter serious problems and many villages have become deserted, with schools closed, etc. The devastation of the countryside and urban over-population are really two sides of the same coin: the uneven regional development which characterizes all capitalist societies — Japan being, however, in this instance, an extreme case.

Finally, the preservation of so many part-time farms has encouraged rice cultivation even in the period of surplus production, which began in 1966. In the last decade or so, wet rice cultivation has become highly mechanized and heavily dependent on chemicals, thus making it a very suitable activity for small-scale part-time operations. In fact, in 1971, only 9 percent of full-time farms were dependent on rice production. The main reason that producers keep growing rice at high levels remains the State's policy of maintaining high rice prices, as we will see below. Farmers' cooperatives, which operate as business concerns and whose profits rely heavily on the government-controlled rice market also encourage rice production. But necessities of part-time farming, which has as a corollary a high degree of mechanization, and the increase in subsistence farming[4] have strengthened the tendency to support rice cultivation.

The national context

The state's agricultural policy

An analysis of agricultural programs in Japan since the Land Reform is not easy because the policy-making process has many contradictory aspects which have forced the government to change course at different times or even devise and implement contradictory measures. One important aspect is the fact that, since the end of World War II, the Japanese government has been structured to accommodate even more closely than before the war the interest of giant business concerns. Since the economic strength of dominant *zaikai* interests is based on the export of manufactured goods, and since it is necessary to compensate for these exports by importing foreign products, the *zaikai* and its related organizations (*Keidanren*, etc.) have, since 1955, applied pressure on the government to liberalize agricultural imports, terminate government control of the rice market and consolidate farms and encourage their mechanization.

A second aspect is the dependence of the ruling Liberal Democratic Party, whose relations to the *zaikai* are well known, on the rural vote. In order to get the agricultural producers to vote conservative, the government has had to make concessions to them, mainly by maintaining rice prices at a high level. This points to another important aspect of agricultural policy: it must take into account the fact that agriculture is at one and the same time an economic sector and the means of livelihood for several million people.

A final aspect is the pressure exerted by foreign countries, especially the United States, to liberalize the Japanese farm market. The policy on rice prices has had the greatest importance for the peasantry since 1945. At first, the rice-price policy was geared to the regulation of foodstuffs needed for the war effort. The first government controls on the rice market were imposed in 1939, but only in 1942 were these controls explicitly applied to prices. The price of rice at that time was calculated on the costs of agricultural means of production and the price of consumer goods needed by the peasants. This policy had a double goal: to insure that agricultural production would be sufficient for the war effort, and that foodstuffs would be priced low enough to depress wages in the industrial sector. This policy lasted until 1946.

In 1946, due to new economic and political circumstances, the method of determining rice prices was modified. Instead of taking as a base the cost of agricultural means of production, the price of rice was tied to a basic price-index for all products purchased by agricultural producers. This policy was devised at a time when these producers were prospering because of the food shortage and was meant to curb the inflation of food prices.

Peasant affluence was short-lived. In 1949, the "Dodge plan," a package of anti-inflationary measures, was implemented, cutting deeply into peasants' gains. Rural income fell rapidly in comparison to urban working-class earnings, and in 1951 peasant unrest forced the government to change its agricultural policy. The price of rice was now calculated on the basis of income parity between the country-side and the city. This new method of calculation was based not only on a comparison of prices between agricultural products and all items deemed essential to farm families, but also on a comparison of consumption levels between peasants and urban workers. The main objective of this new formula was to raise the peasants' standard of living.

However, even with this type of computation, farm household revenues were deteriorating in comparison to working-class incomes. The primary cause was wage increases linked to the heavy labor demand brought about by rapid economic growth. Under rural pressure, the government, with the implementation of the Fundamental Law on Agriculture in 1961, adopted a new way to determine rice prices by adding to the production costs of the least productive farms an amount of money intended to raise the standard of living of farm families. This method of calculating rice prices has in fact led to an increase in rural incomes, but it also resulted in a doubling of the price of rice paid to producers between 1960 and 1968 (see Table 8). It is during this period that the price of Japanese rice rose far above international prices. Moreover, so as not to accelerate inflation, and to keep wages at a fairly low level while avoiding public outcry, the government has not allowed the sales price of rice to rise at the same pace as the purchase price at the farm.

One of the most visible results of the 1961 policy was the rapid accumulation of a vast rice surplus which has been very difficult to sell. In fact, in 1970, this surplus was equivalent to the total national consumption for about one year. Secondly, by encouraging rice production, this policy has gone contrary to the government's effort to diversify agricultural production. Thirdly, the Ministry of Agriculture has had to shoulder increasing deficits.

Table 8   Income of farm households by size, 1976 (1000 yen and percentage)

Acreage categories	Income of farm household	Agricultural income	Non-agricultural income	Rate of dependance on agriculture
0.1–0.5 ha	3506.1	284.9	3221.2	8.1
0.5–1.0	3563.7	922.8	2640.9	25.9
1.0–1.5	3718.1	1662.1	2056.0	44.7
1.5–2.0	3847.0	2226.0	1621.0	57.9
2.0–2.5	3929.3	2717.4	1211.9	69.2
2.5–3.0	4524.1	3084.7	1439.4	68.2
3.0 plus	4781.0	3812.7	968.3	79.7

Source: *Nihon Nōgyō Nenkan*, 1974. p. 294; *Nihon Nōgyō Nenkan*, 1978, p. 312.

What prompted this curiously contradictory policy is, first of all, the necessity for the LDP to please its rural constituency. The party is elected by the rural vote. With the defection of the urban working class, the LDP has had to make some concessions to the peasants to acquire their votes. Furthermore, with a higher standard of living, rice has lost its importance as the main food item in workers' diets, and its price has been able to rise. Before 1955, it was necessary to guard against increases in the price of rice in order to keep wages low: rice was the major food item and low wages were a must for small enterprises. However, it is important to note that, even though it became possible to let rice prices climb after 1960, the rate of increase was not high enough to prevent the spread of part-time farming. In fact, with the rapid progress of mechanization, the new rice policy encouraged this development by allowing small holders who normally would have been evicted from agriculture to maintain a certain level of rice production while working only part-time in agriculture, thus obtaining good secondary incomes. However, given price levels, social needs, the size of farm plots, and agricultural productivity, it was impossible for the majority of rice producers to depend mainly on agriculture for their income. Most of them have had to rely increasingly on wage labor, usually in low-paying industrial jobs. Actually, the rice policy has had to accommodate the need of many industrial sectors for a steady supply of low-paid rural labor, and the price of rice has had to satisfy rural voters while insuring a constant outflow of cheap labor to factories, shops and construction sites.

There is no doubt that the maintenance of this labor force on the land has allowed for lower real wages. On the one hand most part-time farmers are considered seasonal or temporary workers. They thus earn much less than the permanent work-force even though they work at least as much. Furthermore since they derive an income from agriculture and can live partly off of their own farms, they're prepared to accept lower wages. On the other hand, their continuing presence on the land allows their employers and the government to duck social security measures since part-time farmers are expected to live solely or mainly off the land when they are unemployed. Besides, given the fact they consider themselves peasants rather than workers even though the majority earn most of their income from wage labor, part-time farmers are often opposed to working-class organizations and labor movement activities.

The government's farm policy is not limited to the price of rice. Since 1956, when the first hints of trouble in agriculture appeared, the government has tried to encourage the specialization of farms in one crop and, on a national level, the diversification of farm production. The Fundamental Law of 1961 was a major plank in the government's new farm policy. Its main goal was to create through specialization and diversification independent farms, large enough to survive without off-farm wage employment and without government subsidies. However, this goal was not achieved, as the increase in part-time farms between 1961 and 1977 amply demonstrates.

All through the '60s, the government attempted in various ways to speed up farm consolidation, mechanization and diversification — in short, the establishment of viable family farms. However, these efforts went contrary to the necessity, for electoral reasons, to maintain the majority of peasant families on the land. Furthermore, since diversification has to be backed up by high tariff barriers, this policy drew fire from the *zaikai* whose interests required a more open internal market for agricultural imports. Criticism also came from the U.S. government which was pushing for trade liberalization. Nevertheless, the Japanese government succeeded temporarily in its efforts to protect local producers in key sectors of livestock, dairy, fruit and vegetable production. But this was done at the expense of cereal production (except rice), raw materials for fodder, and soybeans.

The entire farm program had to be changed between 1968 and 1971. In the first place, pressures from the *zaikai* and the urban working class forced the government to halt rice-price inflation for three years beginning in 1968. In fact, the new policy was only carried out for two years (1969 and 1970), for in 1971, the price of rice was hiked 3 percent, then 6.1 percent in 1972, 32.2 percent in 1974, 14.4 percent in 1975, 10.2 percent in 1976, and 4 percent in 1977. Moreover, in order to reduce rice surpluses, the government initiated its policy of subsidies for the curtailed rice production. These subsidies were supposed to encourage diversification, but, in fact, as we saw, they very often resulted in the non-utilization of agricultural land. The net result, however, was to lessen the rice surplus to about 20 percent of annual consumption in 1977.

The "Nixon shock" of 1971 was the main blow to the government's diversification program. As a result of U.S. pressures, the Japanese government had to lower or abolish trade barriers on agricultural products. This led to difficulties for many agricultural producers. To compensate, the government decided to raise the price of rice, which encouraged many producers to revert to rice production. However, international pressures were not limited to the Nixon shock alone. The year 1972 saw the disappearance of the world's agricultural surpluses which had been maintained for the previous 25 years, and world food production became insufficient. Japan, whose degree of self-sufficiency in food[5] had plummeted from about 80 percent in 1960 to less than 50 percent in 1973, thus faced severe problems in obtaining badly needed farm goods on the international market. The most acute problem centered on soybeans. In 1971, Japan imported 96 percent of its soybeans, 97 percent of which came from the U.S. In 1972, the U.S., for various reasons, put an embargo on soybean exports to Japan. Because of such difficulties in the international market, many groups in Japan have proposed a return to food self-sufficiency partly for security reasons. But still, in 1975, Japan depended for 97 percent on imports of soybeans, 92 percent of which came from the United States.

Confronted with these many-sided problems, the government has remained indecisive since 1971. There have been tentative plans to reduce the number of farm families and industrialize the countryside, etc. But most of these have been as severely criticized by the representatives of Japanese capital as by peasants and workers. However, the vacillation of the government has not prevented the uncontrolled implantation of industries in the countryside. The city continues to encroach on rural areas, and pollution is increasingly hazardous to farm villages. Rural unrest has been increasing and the rural vote no longer goes automatically to the LDP. In these circumstances, it is possible that the LDP will sacrifice its rural constituency to the interest of the *zaikai*. But what would become then of this stablizing force that is the peasantry?

Big business and agriculture

A good share of the Japanese farm market is controlled by giant monopolies. And if we include among these the farmers' cooperatives which are very often more concerned with capitalistic pursuits than with family farmers, monopoly capital's control of the farm market is almost complete. The case of the milk industry, which is controlled by three companies, is probably the clearest case in point. All sectors of the market for agricultural means of production are also dominated by giant companies (machinery, fertilizers, feeds, herbicides, insecticides, etc.). The cooperatives are in this instance often reduced to the role of middle men: one exception is Zenkōren, associated with the co-operative movement, which is a producer of concentrated feeds, but on a much smaller scale than either Nihon Haigo Shiryō (Mitsui group) or Nihon Nōsan. Furthermore, most agricultural imports are controlled by giant trading companies (Mitsui Bussan, Mitsubishi Shōji, etc.). These companies are also attempting to take over various supermarket chains.

Vertical integration, a characteristic feature of agriculture in all advanced capitalist countries, has progressed very rapidly in Japan in the last decade. Vertical integration actually reduces the producer to the status of a wage laborer who works at home and is paid on a piecemeal basis. It has been gaining ground chiefly in livestock and dairy production (pigs, chickens, eggs, milk), but also in fruit and vegetable production. Even some rice producers have entered into this type of arrangement with *sake* brewers and candy manufacturers.

However, vertical integration is only one step in the control of agriculture by monopoly capitalism. Since 1970, giant food combines (*Kombinats*) have been set up, especially by trading companies such as Mitsubishi Shōji, Mitsui Bussan, Itoh and Marubeni.

These *Kombinats* are sometimes limited to processing only foodstuffs or feeds using local or imported products. But the trading companies have also taken over a good share of the actual production of chickens, eggs, and pigs. The four trading companies mentioned above controlled up to 71.4 percent of the total production of chicken in 1970. These companies have organized production on an industrialized scale, making use of automated plants with a capacity of several million chickens a year — a far cry from small-scale farming. It must be noted that most of these plants have been established in rural areas and employ local part-time farmers. They require very little land and are thus exceptions among smaller farms. They engage in agricultural production on a full-time basis.

Finally, these trading companies have established plantation-type ventures in countries such as Indonesia and the Philippines where they produce cheap agricultural products which are then shipped to Japan for processing. The effects of the increasing control of monopoly capital over agricultural production have been deeply felt by small-scale family farms. In the first place, many small cultivators have had to become vertically integrated to giant companies. Secondly, many others have decreased farm production to become workers in giant food factories. Thirdly, direct monopoly control over certain types of production, either in Japan or abroad, has weakened the position of small holders, thus forcing more family members to seek wage-employment. Fourthly, as mentioned above, this has led to a decrease in self-sufficiency in food production. Finally, the use of chemical feeds for animals in giant plants has increased the chances of poisoning consumers.

Conclusion

Since 1950, the Japanese peasantry has had to adjust to the encroachment of monopoly capitalism on the countryside[6]. This had not been a smooth process as many peasant protest movements have clearly shown. But in the long run, the peasants have obviously not had the strength to resist these pressures. Indeed, the cooperatives, which represent the strongest farmers' organization to appear in the postwar period, have been one of the agents of capitalist extension in the countryside, mainly through the sale of various means of agricultural production.

In search of profit[7], giant companies have gained an increasingly tighter control over the entire agricultural scene: production, markets, imports, etc. Their interest is to obtain cheap agricultural products for processing and to tear various sectors of production away from small-scale farmers. They also require labor. A good portion of the cheap, young, docile and partially qualified labor force which is needed by the giant companies comes from the countryside. These are farmers' sons and daughters who, since early Meiji and up until now, have left the farm permanently to become workers. But companies also need "coolie" labor, and a good portion of this is furnished by part-time farmers.

In fact, the development of postwar capitalism in Japan has had a curious impact on the rural areas. One consequence, "normal" in capitalist societies, has been the expropriation of more than 1 million farms between 1960 and 1977. Another has been the maintenance of a majority of farm owners on the land. This, as we saw, results from the dependence of the conservative parties, who represent business interests, on the rural vote. The continuing presence of so many small holders on the land is a feature unique to Japan. It is found in no other capitalist society.

Another consequence of capitalist encroachment on the countryside has been the proletarianization of many farmers, even though these have managed to keep their land. Part-time "farm-owners" who do very little farming, sometimes only for home consumption and always on a small-scale, can hardly be considered "peasants" any longer. They are really workers. To be sure, keeping the land has a certain importance. The land can be sold or used as a hedge against hard times. But for most cultivators, as long as they work for wages, it is their job which most effects and defines their life: agriculture is only a secondary occupation, a source of subsidiary income. The land actually serves to devalue the labor force. Because part of their subsistence comes from their own farms, these cultivators accept low wages. Moreover, below a certain size (2½ hectares in 1972; see Table 8) the more land a farm household has, the lower its *per capita* income. Land is thus, paradoxically, a strain on income. Farm families with smaller holdings enjoy higher incomes than larger farms, but only where their members work outside agriculture.

With agricultural income so low (despite high prices), the trends toward the proletarianization of farmers and a decrease in agricultural output are bound to continue. The first trend is apparent in the inclusion of farms with relatively more land into the lower stratum of the "peasantry." In fact the majority of peasants owning less than 2 hectares of land are increasingly caught up in the transition to part-time farming. Not all are really workers: many still depend heavily on agriculture for a living and see farming as their primary occupation. But even here the trend toward part-time agriculture is in evidence and in fact now appears irreversible.

We arrive at the paradoxical conclusion that today more than half of all Japanese "peasants" are in reality workers. The rest can be classified into four categories: those who are vertically integrated to big companies and who are therefore in the process of becoming workers; the truly independent family farmers who live exclusively or primarily from their own production but still depend entirely on farm labor; the prosperous specialized farmers who employ a quasi-permanent labor force; and finally, capitalist agricultural entrepreneurs. The last have nothing to do with the peasantry as they are part of the monopoly capital entering agriculture from the outside. Prosperous farmers, whose numbers probably do not exceed half a million, are those who have established themselves in specialized areas of production and who have gained control of most specialized cooperatives. These also cannot be classified as peasants. As for the independent family farms, their number has decreased markedly with the inclusion of medium size farms in the part-time II category, and the tendency seems to be for a greater number of formerly independent farms to go this same route.

If the trends described above continue, and there is no indication that they will not, it is to be expected (1) that up to 90 percent of Japanese "farmers" will become workers owning a small plot of land; (2) that agricultural production will continue to decrease; (3) that, consequently, agricultural imports will increase; and finally (4) that big business will consolidate its grip on the entire food production process. What will be left of Japanese agriculture then?

Notes

1. I use the term peasant not only to refer to so-called "peasant societies" but to all types of small-holding family farming undertaken in a class society. The majority of Japanese farmers, up to the present, fit such a definition. The term has, of course, no derogatory meaning. In fact, it is intended to render the Japanese word *hyakusho*.

2. All through the late Edo, Meiji, Taisho and early Showa periods, some peasants were forced to part with their land, very often in order to repay debts. This kind of land loss was seen as shameful, but it was inevitable. Now many farmers sell their land for cash without a thought for the ancestors.

3. This increase in current prices does not mean an equivalent rise in production in tonnage: a comparatively high price for agricultural products would mean an artificially high share for agriculture in the GNP.

4. Non-commercial farms, which accounted for 14.5 percent of all farms in 1970, increased to 18.2 percent in 1973 and to 23 percent in 1977. These are prevalent mainly among small holders. In fact non-commercial farms account for 43 percent of the nearly 2 million farms owning less than half a hectare.

5. The figures given here are calculated on the basis of calorie equivalence, i.e. they include not only foodstuffs *per se* but animal feed as well. In terms of foodstuffs only, the rate of self-sufficiency was 72 percent in 1971.

6. The penetration of the market economy actually dates back to the feudal period. But the encroachment of monopoly capitalism began sometime in the Meiji period. However, its expansion since the end of World War II has been much more rapid because of the elimination of landlordism and because of the high rate of economic growth which has benefitted chiefly the big companies.

7. Christian Sautter in his book *Japon: le prix de la puissance* (Paris: Seuil, 1973, pp. 141 ff.) has shown that, contrary to a widespread conception, profit *is* the prime motive of Japanese capitalists: indeed it would be surprising were it otherwise. Sautter has also shown that, not only do Japanese capitalists seek profits like any other, but they also enjoy a higher rate of profit and of capital accumulation than capitalists in other countries. This high rate of accumulation is, to some, the utmost progress and growth. What is certain, however, is that it represents the utmost in unequal income division. See Martin Schnitzer, *Income Distribution: A Comparative Study* (New York: Praeger, 1974).